GLENCOE

LITERATURE

The Reader's Choice

GLENCOE LITERATURE

The Reader's Choice

Program Consultants

Beverly Ann Chin
Denny Wolfe
Jeffrey Copeland
Mary Ann Dudzinski
William Ray
Jacqueline Jones Royster
Jeffrey Wilhelm

Course 1

Glencoe McGraw-Hill

New York, New York   Columbus, Ohio   Woodland Hills, California   Peoria, Illinois

Acknowledgments

Grateful acknowledgment is given authors, publishers, photographers, museums, and agents for permission to reprint the following copyrighted material. Every effort has been made to determine copyright owners. In case of any omissions, the Publisher will be pleased to make suitable acknowledgments in future editions.

Acknowledgments continued on page R122.

The Standardized Test Practice pages in this book were written by The Princeton Review, the nation's leader in test preparation. Through its association with McGraw-Hill, The Princeton Review offers the best way to help students excel on standardized assessments.

The Princeton Review is not affiliated with Princeton University or Educational Testing Service.

Glencoe/McGraw-Hill

A Division of The McGraw·Hill Companies

Copyright © 2000 by The McGraw-Hill Companies, Inc. All rights reserved. Except as permitted under the United States Copyright Act of 1976, no part of this publication may be reproduced or distributed in any form or means, or stored in a database or retrieval system, without the prior written permission of the publisher.

Printed in the United States of America

Send all inquiries to:
Glencoe/McGraw-Hill
8787 Orion Place
Columbus, OH 43240

ISBN 0-02-635367-9
(Student Edition)

ISBN 0-02-635368-7
(Teacher's Wraparound Edition)

1 2 3 4 5 6 7 8 9 10 003/043 04 03 02 01 00 99

Senior Program Consultants

Beverly Ann Chin is Professor of English, Co-Director of the English Teaching Program, former Director of the Montana Writing Project, and former Director of Composition at the University of Montana in Missoula. In 1995–1996, Dr. Chin served as President of the National Council of Teachers of English. She currently serves as a Member of the Board of Directors of the National Board for Professional Teaching Standards. Dr. Chin is a nationally recognized leader in English language arts standards, curriculum, and assessment. Formerly a high school English teacher and adult education reading teacher, Dr. Chin has taught in English language arts education at several universities and has received awards for her teaching and service.

Denny Wolfe, a former high school English teacher and department chair, is Professor of English Education, Director of the Tidewater Virginia Writing Project, and Director of the Center for Urban Education at Old Dominion University in Norfolk, Virginia. For the National Council of Teachers of English, he has served as Chairperson of the Standing Committee on Teacher Preparation, President of the International Assembly, member of the Executive Committee of the Council on English Education, and editor of the SLATE Newsletter. Author of more than seventy-five articles and books on teaching English, Dr. Wolfe is a frequent consultant to schools and colleges on the teaching of English language arts.

Program Consultants

Jeffrey S. Copeland is Professor and Head of the Department of English Language and Literature at the University of Northern Iowa, where he teaches children's and young adult literature courses and a variety of courses in English education. A former public school teacher, he has published many articles in the professional journals in the language arts. The twelve books he has written or edited include *Speaking of Poets: Interviews with Poets Who Write for Children and Young Adults* and *Young Adult Literature: A Contemporary Reader.*

Mary Ann Dudzinski is a former high school English teacher and recipient of the Ross Perot Award for Teaching Excellence. She also has served as a member of the core faculty for the National Endowment for the Humanities Summer Institute for Teachers of Secondary School English and History at the University of North Texas. After fifteen years of classroom experience in grades 9–12, she currently is a language arts consultant.

William Ray has taught English in the Boston Public Schools; at Lowell University; University of Wroclaw, Poland; and, for the last fourteen years, at Lincoln-Sudbury Regional High School in Sudbury, Massachusetts. He specializes in world literature. He has worked on a variety of educational texts, as editor, consultant, and contributing writer.

Jacqueline Jones Royster is Associate Professor of English at The Ohio State University. She is also on the faculty of the Bread Loaf School of English at Middlebury College in Middlebury, Vermont. In addition to the teaching of writing, Dr. Royster's professional interests include the rhetorical history of African American women and the social and cultural implications of literate practices.

Jeffrey Wilhelm, a former English and reading teacher, is currently an assistant professor at the University of Maine where he teaches courses in middle and secondary level literacy. Author of several books and articles on the teaching of reading and the use of technology, he also works with local schools as part of the fledgling Adolescent Literacy Project and is the director of two annual summer institutes: the Maine Writing Project and Technology as a Learning Tool.

Teacher Reviewers

Bill Beyer
General Wayne Middle School
Malvern, Pennsylvania

Sister Marian Christi
St. Matthew School
Philadelphia, Pennsylvania

Christine Ferguson
North Buncombe Middle School
Asheville, North Carolina

Elizabeth Fischer
Tower Heights Middle School
Centerville, Ohio

Diane Gerrety
Bridgetown Junior High
Cincinnati, Ohio

Susan Giddings
Marble Falls Middle School
Marble Falls, Texas

Denise Goeckel
Magsig Middle School
Centerville, Ohio

Debbie Hampton
Central Davidson Middle School
Lexington, North Carolina

Tammy Harris
Walnut Springs Middle School
Columbus, Ohio

Marlene Henry
Northwood Elementary
Troy, Ohio

Brian Hinders
Tower Heights Middle School
Centerville, Ohio

Cheryl Keffer
Fayette County Schools Gifted
Program
Oak Hill, West Virginia

Sheryl Kelso
Oldtown School
Oldtown, Maryland

Gail Kidd
Center Middle School
Azusa, California

Karen Mantia
Northmont City Schools
Clayton, Ohio

Nancy Mast
Hobart Middle School
Hobart, Indiana

Chiyo Masuda
Albany Middle School
Albany, California

Kim Mistler
Delhi Junior High School
Cincinnati, Ohio

Wilma Jean Nix
Baldwin Junior High School
Montgomery, Alabama

Joe Olague
Alder Junior High
Fontana, California

Bonita Rephann
Musselman Middle School
Bunker Hill, West Virginia

Marie Rinaudo
St. John Berchman's Cathedral
School
Shreveport, Louisiana

Carol Schowalter
El Roble Intermediate School
Claremont, California

Joan Slater
Strack Intermediate
Klein, Texas

Joyce Stakem
St. Catherine of Siena School
Wilmington, Delaware

Elizabeth Struckman
Bridgetown Junior High School
Centerville, Ohio

Debbie Trepanier
Jenkins Middle School
Chewelah, Washington

Sarah Vick
Central Davidson Middle School
Lexington, North Carolina

Erin Watts
Albright Middle School
Houston, Texas

Anne Welch
Huntsville Middle School
Huntsville, Alabama

James Zartler
Centennial Middle School
Portland, Oregon

Book Overview

Contents

THEME ❧ ONE

Where I Belong

🌐🌐 *indicates world literature*

THEME ✿ TWO

Through Other Eyes

CONTENTS

THEME ❧ THREE

Growing Times

CONTENTS

THEME ❧ FOUR

What's Most Important

CONTENTS

THEME ❧ FIVE

The Will to Win

CONTENTS

THEME ❧ SIX

Getting Through Hard Times.......490

THEME ✿ SEVEN

Old Tales, New Twists

CONTENTS

THEME ❀ EIGHT

To Strange Places 688

CONTENTS

Reference Section

Features

MEDIA Connection

COMPARING SELECTIONS

GENRE FOCUS

Active Reading Strategies

Interdisciplinary Connection

Writing WORKSHOP

Skills

Grammar Link

Listening, Speaking, and Viewing

Reading and Thinking Skills

Technology Skills

Vocabulary Skills

Writing Skills

FEATURES

Skill Minilessons

VOCABULARY

Selections by Genre

Drama

Myths, Legends, Folktales

Electronic Media

Song

Comic Strip

Advertisement

Where I Belong

66 America is . . . like a quilt—many patches, many pieces, many colors, many sizes, all woven and held together by a common thread. 99

–Jesse Jackson

THEME 1

THEME CONTENTS

GENRE FOCUS *AUTOBIOGRAPHY*

Exploring the Theme

Where I Belong

In this theme, you will meet people who face new situations. They struggle to find places for themselves. Reading about them may help you to handle new situations in your own life. Try one of the options below to begin thinking about how people find where they belong.

Starting Points

WHEN YOU'RE "THE NEW GUY"
Certain cartoons are funny because people recognize their own thoughts and feelings in them.

- Draw an outline of a fishbowl. Write your name in the middle. Imagine that this sketch represents you in some situation in your life. How do you feel about the others in the bowl? How do you imagine others see you? How do you see yourself? Jot down words and phrases that describe your feelings.

THE PLACE YOU BELONG
Think about a place or a situation where you feel "at home." What makes you feel you belong? Certain objects in that place? Certain people?

- With a small group, share a photograph or a drawing that represents this place. Point out important things or people.

" WATCH THE NEW GUY. I DON'T TRUST HIM. "

Theme Projects

As you read the selections in this theme, try your hand at one of the projects below. Work on your own, with a partner, or with a group.

MULTIMEDIA PROJECT
Local Access
With a partner, plan the first episode of a local cable program about your community.

1. Decide what pictures or visuals you can use to represent your community.
2. Choose a guest or guests who can help highlight important things about the community.
3. Write up your program plan and share it with the class.

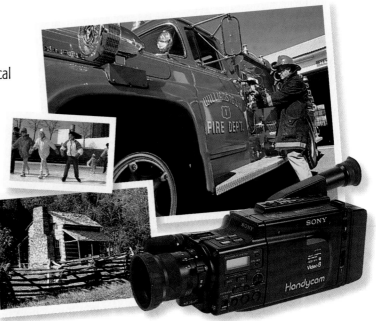

LEARNING FOR LIFE
School Brochure
Design a brochure to advertise your school. Include information on school rules, subjects offered, school teams, and the school building and facilities. If your school already has a brochure, propose changes to it and explain why you want to make them. Illustrate your brochure with photographs or drawings.

INTERDISCIPLINARY ACTIVITY
Geography
Keep a map of the world handy as you read through the selections in this theme.

1. Find the countries, cities, or states that are important to each selection.
2. Attach a label to the map, listing the name of the selection.
3. After reading all the selections, take turns telling a partner about how each location was important to the story.

interNET CONNECTION

Check out the Web for more project ideas. Find out more about the selections in this theme. Here's the address: lit.glencoe.com

Before You Read
The Circuit

MEET
FRANCISCO JIMÉNEZ

S ince Spanish was the dominant language during my childhood, I generally write about those experiences in Spanish," says Francisco Jiménez (frän sēs′ kō   hē men′ ez). Now a professor of literature at Santa Clara University in California, Jiménez once worked as a migrant laborer.

"The Circuit" is based on journal notes that Jiménez wrote while in college. He says, ". . . I wrote [the notes] because I wanted to keep in touch with my family roots."

Francisco Jiménez was born in Mexico in 1943. This story was first published in 1973.

FOCUS ACTIVITY

What is the hardest physical work you have ever done? What made it hard? How did you feel about it?

QuickWrite
Write some details about the work, what was hard about it, and how you felt about it.

Setting a Purpose
Read "The Circuit" to find out how work affects a boy and his family.

BACKGROUND

The Time and Place
The story takes place during the 1950s in California.

Did You Know?   Migrant workers travel from farm to farm to pick vegetables and fruit by hand. They follow the harvest, moving to another farm after each type of crop is harvested. Often they live in houses provided by the farm owners.

VOCABULARY PREVIEW

sharecropper (shār′ krop′ ər) *n.* a farmer who farms land owned by someone else and shares the crop or the proceeds from its sale with the landowner; p. 5

acquire (ə kwīr′) *v.* to get or have as one's own; p. 8

drone (drōn) *n.* a steady, low, humming sound; p. 9

instinctively (in stingk′ tiv lē) *adv.* in a way that comes naturally; p. 9

savor (sā′ vər) *v.* to take great delight in; p. 10

hesitantly (hez′ ət ənt lē) *adv.* in a way that shows one is undecided or fearful; p. 11

The Circuit

Francisco Jiménez ~

It was that time of year again. Ito,[1] the strawberry <u>sharecropper</u>, did not smile. It was natural. The peak of the strawberry season was over and the last few days the workers, most of them *braceros*,[2] were not picking as many boxes as they had during the months of June and July.

---

1. *Ito* (ē′ tō)
2. *Braceros* (brä sä′ rōs) are Mexican farm laborers.

Vocabulary

sharecropper (shār′ krop′ ər) *n.* a farmer who farms land owned by someone else and shares the crop or the proceeds from its sale with the landowner

The Circuit

As the last days of August disappeared, so did the number of *braceros*. Sunday, only one—the best picker—came to work. I liked him. Sometimes we talked during our half-hour lunch break. That is how I found out he was from Jalisco,[3] the same state in Mexico my family was from. That Sunday was the last time I saw him.

When the sun had tired and sunk behind the mountains, Ito signaled us that it was time to go home. "*Ya esora*,"[4] he yelled in his broken Spanish. Those were the words I waited for twelve hours a day, every day, seven days a week, week after week. And the thought of not hearing them again saddened me.

As we drove home Papa did not say a word. With both hands on the wheel, he stared at the dirt road. My older brother, Roberto, was also silent. He leaned his head back and closed his eyes. Once in a while he cleared from his throat the dust that blew in from outside.

Yes, it was that time of year. When I opened the front door to the shack, I stopped. Everything we owned was neatly packed in cardboard boxes. Suddenly I felt even more the weight of hours, days, weeks, and months of work. I sat down on a box. The thought of having to move to Fresno[5] and knowing what was in store for me there brought tears to my eyes.

That night I could not sleep. I lay in bed thinking about how much I hated this move.

A little before five o'clock in the morning, Papa woke everyone up. A few minutes later, the yelling and screaming of my little brothers and sisters, for whom the move was a great adventure, broke the silence of dawn. Shortly, the barking of the dogs accompanied them.

While we packed the breakfast dishes, Papa went outside to start the "Carcanchita."[6] That was the name Papa gave his old '38 black Plymouth. He bought it in a used-car lot in Santa Rosa in the winter of 1949. Papa was very proud of his little jalopy. He had a right to be proud of it. He spent a lot of time looking at other cars before buying this one. When he finally chose the "Carcanchita," he checked it thoroughly before driving it out of the car lot. He examined every inch of the car. He listened to the motor, tilting his head from side to side like a parrot, trying to detect any noises that spelled car trouble. After being satisfied with the looks and sounds of the car, Papa then insisted on knowing who the original owner was. He never did find out from the car salesman, but he bought the car anyway. Papa figured the original owner must have been an important man because behind the rear seat of the car he found a blue necktie.

Papa parked the car out in front and left the motor running. "*Listo*,"[7] he yelled. Without saying a word, Roberto and I began to carry the boxes out to the car. Roberto carried the two big boxes and I carried the two smaller ones. Papa then threw the mattress on top of the car roof and tied it with ropes to the front and rear bumpers.

---

3. *Jalisco* (hə lēs′ kō)
4. *[Ya esora]* Ito is trying to say "Ya es hora" (yä es   ō′ rə), which means "It is time."
5. *Fresno* is a city in one of California's main farming regions.

---

6. *Carcanchita* (kär′ kən chē′ tə)
7. *Listo* (lēs′ tō) means "Ready."

Trabajadores, 1950. Castera Bazile. Oil on canvas, 27 x 19½ in. Private collection.

Viewing the painting: *Trabajadores* (tra bä ha dō′ rāz) means "workers" in Spanish. Do you think it is the beginning or the end of the workers' day?

The Circuit

Everything was packed except Mama's pot. It was an old large galvanized pot she had picked up at an army surplus store in Santa María the year I was born. The pot had many dents and nicks, and the more dents and nicks it acquired the more Mama liked it. "Mi olla,"[8] she used to say proudly.

I held the front door open as Mama carefully carried out her pot by both handles, making sure not to spill the cooked beans. When she got to the car, Papa reached out to help her with it. Roberto opened the rear car door and Papa gently placed it on the floor behind the front seat. All of us then climbed in. Papa sighed, wiped the sweat off his forehead with his sleeve, and said wearily: "Es todo."[9]

As we drove away, I felt a lump in my throat. I turned around and looked at our little shack for the last time.

At sunset we drove into a labor camp near Fresno. Since Papa did not speak English, Mama asked the camp foreman if he needed any more workers. "We don't need no more," said the foreman, scratching his head. "Check with Sullivan down the road. Can't miss him. He lives in a big white house with a fence around it."

When we got there, Mama walked up to the house. She went through a white gate, past a row of rose bushes, up the stairs to the front door. She rang the doorbell. The porch light went on and a tall husky man came out. They exchanged a few words. After the man went in, Mama clasped her hands and hurried back to the car. "We have work! Mr. Sullivan said we can stay there the whole season," she said, gasping and pointing to an old garage near the stables.

The garage was worn out by the years. It had no windows. The walls, eaten by termites, strained to support the roof full of holes. The dirt floor, populated by earth worms, looked like a gray road map.

That night, by the light of a kerosene lamp, we unpacked and cleaned our new home. Roberto swept away the loose dirt, leaving the hard ground. Papa plugged the holes in the walls with old newspapers and tin can tops. Mama fed my little brothers and sisters. Papa and Roberto then brought in the mattress and placed it on the far corner of the garage. "Mama, you and the little ones sleep on the mattress. Roberto, Panchito, and I will sleep outside under the trees," Papa said.

Early next morning Mr. Sullivan showed us where his crop was, and after breakfast, Papa, Roberto, and I headed for the vineyard to pick.

Around nine o'clock the temperature had risen to almost one hundred degrees.

Did You Know?
This lamp can burn *kerosene,* a liquid fuel made from petroleum.

---

8. Mama's favorite olla (ō´ yä) is a *galvanized pot,* an iron pot with a thin coat of zinc. She got it at an *army surplus store,* which sells goods not needed by the U.S. military.

9. *Es todo* (es   tō´ dō) means "That's everything."

Vocabulary
acquire (ə kwīr´) *v.* to get or have as one's own

I was completely soaked in sweat and my mouth felt as if I had been chewing on a handkerchief. I walked over to the end of the row, picked up the jug of water we had brought, and began drinking. "Don't drink too much; you'll get sick," Roberto shouted. No sooner had he said that than I felt sick to my stomach. I dropped to my knees and let the jug roll off my hands. I remained motionless with my eyes glued on the hot sandy ground. All I could hear was the drone of insects. Slowly I began to recover. I poured water over my face and neck and watched the dirty water run down my arms to the ground.

I still felt a little dizzy when we took a break to eat lunch. It was past two o'clock and we sat underneath a large walnut tree that was on the side of the road. While we ate, Papa jotted down the number of boxes we had picked. Roberto drew designs on the ground with a stick. Suddenly I noticed Papa's face turn pale as he looked down the road. "Here comes the school bus," he whispered loudly in alarm. Instinctively, Roberto and I ran and hid in the vineyards. We did not want to get in trouble for not going to school. The neatly dressed boys about my age got off. They carried books under their arms. After they crossed the street, the bus drove away. Roberto and I came out from hiding and joined Papa. "*Tienen que tener cuidado,*"[10] he warned us.

After lunch we went back to work. The sun kept beating down. The buzzing insects, the wet sweat, and the hot dry dust made the afternoon seem to last forever. Finally the mountains around the valley reached out and swallowed the sun. Within an hour it was too dark to continue picking. The vines blanketed the grapes, making it difficult to see the bunches. "*Vámonos,*"[11] said Papa, signaling to us that it was time to quit work. Papa then took out a pencil and began to figure out how much we had earned our first day. He wrote down numbers, crossed some out, wrote down some more. "*Quince,*"[12] he murmured.

When we arrived home, we took a cold shower underneath a water-hose. We then sat down to eat dinner around some wooden crates that served as a table. Mama had cooked a special meal for us. We had rice and tortillas with *carne con chile,*[13] my favorite dish.

The next morning I could hardly move. My body ached all over. I felt little control over my arms and legs. This feeling went on every morning for days until my muscles finally got used to the work.

It was Monday, the first week of November. The grape season was over and I could now go to school. I woke up early that morning and lay in bed, looking at the stars

---

10. *Tienen que tener cuidado* (tye′ nen kā tā nār′ kwē dä′ dō) means "You have to be careful."

11. *Vámonos* (vä′ mə nōs) means "Let's go."

12. *Quince* (kēn′ sā) is the number 15.

13. A *tortilla* (tôr tē′ yə) is made from corn or wheat meal and baked on a griddle so that it resembles a very flat pancake. *Carne con chile* (kär′ nā kōn chē′ lā) is meat cooked with red peppers and beans.

Vocabulary
drone (drōn) *n.* a steady, low, humming sound
instinctively (in stingk′ tiv lē) *adv.* in a way that comes naturally

and savoring the thought of not going to work and of starting sixth grade for the first time that year. Since I could not sleep, I decided to get up and join Papa and Roberto at breakfast. I sat at the table across from Roberto, but I kept my head down. I did not want to look up and face him. I knew he was sad. He was not going to school today. He was not going tomorrow, or next week, or next month. He would not go until the cotton season was over, and that was sometime in February. I rubbed my hands together and watched the dry, acid stained[14] skin fall to the floor in little rolls.

When Papa and Roberto left for work, I felt relief. I walked to the top of a small grade next to the shack and watched the "Carcanchita" disappear in the distance in a cloud of dust.

Two hours later, around eight o'clock, I stood by the side of the road waiting for school bus number twenty. When it arrived I climbed in. Everyone was busy either talking or yelling. I sat in an empty seat in the back.

Despedida, 1941. Hector Poleo. Oil on linen, 60 x 50 cm. Private collection.

Viewing the painting: _Despedida_ (des pǝ dē′ dǝ) means "departure" in Spanish. Does the mood of the painting remind you of anything in the story? Explain.

When the bus stopped in front of the school, I felt very nervous. I looked out the bus window and saw boys and girls carrying books under their arms. I put my hands in my pant pockets and walked to the principal's office. When I entered I heard a woman's voice say: "May I help you?" I was startled. I had not heard English for months. For a few seconds I remained speechless. I looked at the lady who waited for an answer. My first instinct was to

---

14. The narrator's hands were _acid stained_ by grapes.

Vocabulary
savor (sā′ vǝr) _v._ to take great delight in

answer her in Spanish, but I held back. Finally, after struggling for English words, I managed to tell her that I wanted to enroll in the sixth grade. After answering many questions, I was led to the classroom.

Mr. Lema, the sixth grade teacher, greeted me and assigned me a desk. He then introduced me to the class. I was so nervous and scared at that moment when everyone's eyes were on me that I wished I were with Papa and Roberto picking cotton. After taking roll, Mr. Lema gave the class the assignment for the first hour. "The first thing we have to do this morning is finish reading the story we began yesterday," he said enthusiastically. He walked up to me, handed me an English book, and asked me to read. "We are on page 125," he said politely. When I heard this, I felt my blood rush to my head; I felt dizzy. "Would you like to read?" he asked hesitantly. I opened the book to page 125. My mouth was dry. My eyes began to water. I could not begin. "You can read later," Mr. Lema said understandingly.

For the rest of the reading period I kept getting angrier and angrier with myself. I should have read, I thought to myself.

During recess I went into the restroom and opened my English book to page 125. I began to read in a low voice, pretending I was in class. There were many words I did not know. I closed the book and headed back to the classroom.

Mr. Lema was sitting at his desk correcting papers. When I entered he looked up at me and smiled. I felt better. I walked up to him and asked if he could help me with the new words. "Gladly," he said.

The rest of the month I spent my lunch hours working on English with Mr. Lema, my best friend at school.

One Friday during lunch hour Mr. Lema asked me to take a walk with him to the music room. "Do you like music?" he asked me as we entered the building.

"Yes, I like *corridos*,"[15] I answered. He then picked up a trumpet, blew on it, and handed it to me. The sound gave me goose bumps. I knew that sound. I had heard it in many *corridos*. "How would you like to learn how to play it?" he asked. He must have read my face because before I could answer, he added: "I'll teach you how to play it during our lunch hours."

That day I could hardly wait to get home to tell Papa and Mama the great news. As I got off the bus, my little brothers and sisters ran up to meet me. They were yelling and screaming. I thought they were happy to see me, but when I opened the door to our shack, I saw that everything we owned was neatly packed in cardboard boxes.

---

15. *Corridos* (kōr rē′ dōs) are songs, especially slow, romantic ones.

Vocabulary
hesitantly (hez′ ə ənt lē) *adv.* in a way that shows one is undecided or fearful

Responding to Literature

PERSONAL RESPONSE

How do you feel about what happens at the end of the story?

Analyzing Literature

RECALL

1. Name three things you learn about the narrator.
2. What is a day's work like on Mr. Sullivan's farm?
3. Who is Mr. Lema?
4. What happens at the end of the story?

INTERPRET

5. What are three feelings that Panchito has at different points in the story? How and why do his feelings change?
6. How does the author make you feel about a day of work on the farm? Review your QuickWrite from the **Focus Activity** on page 4 to compare your physical work experiences with Panchito's.
7. Why do you think Mr. Lema takes a special interest in Panchito?
8. How does the ending relate to the title?

EVALUATE AND CONNECT

9. The original **title** of this story was "Cajas de cartón" (Cardboard Boxes). Do you prefer "The Circuit" to this title? Explain.
10. Theme Connection   If Panchito was in your class, how could you help him to feel comfortable?

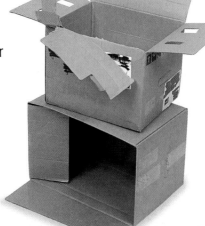

LITERARY ELEMENTS

Fiction

"The Circuit" is based on Francisco Jiménez's experiences as a migrant worker. The narrator of the story, however, is not named Francisco Jiménez, and the family may or may not be similar to Jiménez's family. "The Circuit" is **fiction**. Jiménez is making up a story about problems and events in a character's life, not describing his own family and experiences.

1. What is the main difference between fiction and nonfiction?

2. What fictional books or stories have you read that are based on authors' experiences?

● See **Literary Terms Handbook,** p. R3.

Extending Your Response

Writing About Literature

Details   Look at the notes you wrote for the **Focus Activity.** Then think about Panchito's work. What details does Jiménez provide about the work? What makes it hard? How does Panchito feel while he's doing it? How does he feel the next morning? Write a paragraph about Panchito's work.

Interdisciplinary Activity

Social Studies   How many kinds of fruits and veg-etables are grown in California during a year? Which ones do you think require hand picking? What fruits and vegetables are grown in Florida? In Texas?

Literature Groups

Which Moment?   Decide which moment in the story is

- the saddest
- the happiest
- the most surprising
- the most difficult
- the most loving
- the most embarrassing

Justify your choices and share your group's ideas with the class.

Creative Writing

We're Moving Again . . .   Write a journal entry as if you were Panchito on the afternoon at the end of the story. Remember that journals often contain both "what happened" and "how I felt about it." Tell what happened at school and what you felt about learning to play the trumpet. Tell what you saw and how you felt when you came home.

Reading Further

If you would like to read more about migrant fami-lies, try these books:

The Circuit: Stories from the Life of a Migrant Child by Francisco Jiménez

Children of the Dust Bowl by Jerry Stanley

📖 **Save your work for your portfolio.**

Skill Minilesson

VOCABULARY   • BORROWED WORDS

The name for Panchito's favorite food, *carne con chile,* is a combination of the Native American word *chilli,* "red pepper," and the Spanish word *carne,* "meat." Many English words are borrowed from Spanish. Some of these Spanish words were bor-rowed earlier from Native American languages. Other English words are borrowed from French or other languages.

PRACTICE Match each word with its history.

1. savor
2. mosquito
3. cafeteria
4. tomato
5. chocolate

a. Spanish *café,* "coffee"
b. Native American *chocolatl,* "food from cocoa seeds"
c. Native American *tomatl*
d. a form of Spanish *mosca,* "fly"
e. French *savour,* "flavor, seasoning"

NEWSPAPER ARTICLE

Some schools are trying to make things better for students like Panchito.

A Better Way

by Mike Clary—*Los Angeles Times*, November 27, 1997

Homestead, Fla.— Twelve-year-old Jaime Bautista, Jr., was a sixth grader when his school year began in rural Echols County, Georgia. After he and his family returned here for the winter vegetable season two weeks ago, he was suddenly a fifth grader again.

"This is the way it happens," explained Jaime's older sister, Maria, 21, as she sat in the family's home in a migrant campground, her brother bent over his homework at a kitchen table. "The school systems are different, credits don't transfer, and then he falls further behind."

By the time the child of a migrant farm worker turns 14—the legal age for full-time field work—the need for another income and the toll of travel often mean an end to formal education. The average migrant will attend 24 schools by the time he or she reaches fifth grade, according to recent studies. The probability of a migrant student earning a high school diploma is about 50-50.

In a state that ranks just behind California and Texas in migrant population, the Dade County schools Migrant Education Program has come up with a plan to provide more continuity. With a $600,000 annual grant, about 500 migrant families with school-age children will be given portable computer hookups and toll-free telephone numbers so they can stay in touch with home-based teachers while traveling.

By the time south Florida tomatoes and beans have been harvested, and Jaime Bautista and his family leave here for the squash fields of Georgia next spring, he and other students like him should be well-acquainted with one of five bilingual teachers who will track their academic progress through video-conferences and frequent e-mail contact over the web.

The teachers are to develop a learning plan for each student, go over lessons with students online when possible, and encourage parents to participate by learning to use the computer. The Dade teachers will also keep in touch with the teachers in Georgia, the Carolinas, Virginia, and Pennsylvania, when Jaime and the others show up there.

Respond

1. Would you like to attend school this way?

2. What would you miss about your school?

Cesar Chavez

Cesar Chavez moved from Arizona to California with his family when he was ten years old. He and his family worked as migrant farm laborers. Chavez attended more than thirty-eight schools during his childhood. After eighth grade, he worked full-time to help his family until he left home to fight in World War II.

When he returned home after the war, Chavez learned all he could about labor law and worked at organizing protest marches for the rights of farm laborers. In 1962 he organized the National Farm Workers Association, called *La Causa,* in Fresno, California. *La Causa* wanted farm owners to pay better wages and to stop using dangerous chemicals in the fields. "Our belief is to help everybody, not just one race," Chavez said.

Most farm owners refused to negotiate with *La Causa.* Some reacted with violence, and local police usually supported the owners. Chavez urged protesting workers to leave their guns and knives at home. "If we used violence, we would have won contracts long ago," he said, "but they wouldn't be lasting because we wouldn't have won respect."

La Causa called for Americans to boycott, or refuse to buy, lettuce and grapes to show their sympathies for the workers. The boycotts were so successful that owners agreed to contracts with the workers.

By the time Chavez died in 1993 he had helped create better lives for thousands of people. Senator Robert F. Kennedy called Chavez "one of the heroic figures of our time."

ACTIVITY

In 1966 Cesar Chavez walked three hundred miles with supporters to attract publicity for the migrant workers' cause. He began walking with only sixty-seven people, but ten thousand people had joined him by the time the march had ended. What cause is so important to you that you would walk three hundred miles to support it?

Make a poster representing your cause. Use images you have drawn or cut from a magazine to make a poster that communicates your feelings and ideas about your cause.

Before You Read

from *Little by Little*

MEET JEAN LITTLE

J ean Little had very poor vision as a child. She says, "I was very fortunate . . . in having two doctors for parents and two brothers and a sister. I was never 'the handicapped child'— only the second oldest of four children."

As an adult, Little became a teacher of disabled children and eventually a writer of award-winning books for young people. In the second part of her life story, *Stars Come Out Within*, Little tells about losing her sight altogether.

Jean Little was born in 1932. Her autobiography, Little by Little: A Writer's Education, *was published in 1987.*

FOCUS ACTIVITY

How do you feel when a person in your class or in another group is picked on by others in the group? What can you do? What can you do if this happens to you?

Think/Pair/Share

Jot down your responses to these questions. Discuss your answers with a partner. Then share ideas with the class.

Setting a Purpose

Read this selection to learn about Little's problem and how she handles it.

BACKGROUND

The Time and Place This selection takes place in Guelph, a town in Ontario, Canada, in the 1940s. The Little family had recently moved to Guelph from Toronto, where Jean Little had attended a special school for children with vision problems.

Did You Know? Today, schools often provide ways to help students who have limited vision. Students can use magnifying devices, books with large print, and adjustable bookstands to help them read. Some students use tape-recorded books or computers that display text in large letters or that "read" aloud.

VOCABULARY PREVIEW

hostile (host′ əl) *adj.* feeling or showing strong dislike; p. 20
pang (pang) *n.* a sudden sharp feeling of pain or distress; p. 21
taunt (tônt) *n.* an insulting remark; p. 21
menacing (men′ əs ing) *adj.* threatening; dangerous; p. 22
emphatically (em fat′ i kəl ē) *adv.* forcefully; p. 24
mishap (mis′ hap′) *n.* an unfortunate accident; p. 24
reverently (rev′ ər ənt lē) *adv.* in a way that shows deep honor; respectfully; p. 24

from
Little
by
Little

Jean Little ⁓

I followed Mother through the girls' door of St. John's School. It was nine o'clock and the hall was empty. I stared at all the coats hanging on hooks outside the grade four classroom door. There were so many of them! I swallowed and hung back.

Mother, feeling my hand tug at hers, turned and saw the panic in my eyes. She smiled at me and paused long enough to murmur words meant to be comforting.

"Your teacher's name is Mr. Johnston. He knows we're coming. I'm sure you'll like him."

What she did not seem to understand was that it was not the thought of Mr. Johnston that was frightening me. I had no doubt that my teacher and I would like each other. I had not yet met a teacher who had not liked me.

School's Out, 1936. Allan R. Crite. Oil on canvas, 20¼ x 36⅛ in. National Museum of American Art, Washington, DC.

Viewing the painting: What do you think the group of girls in front are saying to each other?

The sound of children's voices came from behind the closed door. It was those children who worried me. How would they feel about a cross-eyed girl joining their class at the end of November?

Mother knocked once, opened the door and propelled[1] me gently but inexorably into the classroom. The buzz of conversation stopped instantly. I knew, without turning my head, that every child in the room was staring at me. Out of the

corner of my eye I glimpsed what seemed like hundreds of boys and girls seated in long straight rows. I later learned that there were only forty-one students in Mr. Johnston's room. But compared to the twelve students in Miss Bogart's class, forty-one seemed like a multitude.

Mr. Johnston came to meet us, smiling a welcome.

"You must be Jean," he said, speaking directly to me. "We have a place ready and waiting for you. Boys and girls, this is Jean Little, the newest member of our class."

---

1. The author was moved forward steadily.

There was silence. As he escorted me to an empty desk in the front row, our footsteps seemed to make a deafening clatter on the wooden floor. I slid into the seat, my head down, my cheeks flaming.

"See you at noon, Jean," Mother said, her tone casual.

I held onto the word "noon" the way a drowning man would clutch at a rope. Noon was only three hours away.

The teacher and my mother walked together to just outside the classroom door and stood talking in voices too low for anyone inside the room to hear.

From across the aisle, I heard a sharp whisper.

"She's cross-eyed."

I did not look to see who had said it. I was struggling to control the tears that were threatening to well up and spill over. Even though this was my first day in a regular classroom in Canada, I knew that crying right then would be a fatal mistake. I did not dare blink. I gazed straight ahead.

Mr. Johnston came back and the whispers stopped. He smiled down at me. The warmth of that smile dried up the betraying tears. I smiled tremulously[2] back.

I did not know yet that being Teacher's Pet was almost worse than being a cross-eyed crybaby.

"Jean will have lots of interesting things to share with us," Mr. Johnston told the class. "She was born in Formosa. Who knows where Formosa is?"

Nobody knew. Nobody liked not knowing. The teacher went to the board, reached

up, and somehow released a map of the world so that it unrolled and hung down over the blackboard. He got a pointer and indicated the faraway island that the Chinese called Taiwan, where I had lived for the first six years of my life. As he did so, I saw that there was something wrong with his left arm and hand. He held it awkwardly and did everything with his right hand.

My new teacher was handicapped like me. But there was no time to think about this now.

"Here it is," he said, "right off the coast of China. Jean has also lived in Hong Kong."

His pointer moved to another invisible speck.

"Can you speak Chinese?" he asked me.

I was feeling happier. I nodded proudly. It did not cross my mind that with this introduction, Mr. Johnston was giving the bullies in the class added ammunition.

"Could you say Hello?" he asked.

I hesitated. When Christians greeted each other in Taiwan, they used the word for Peace. I knew that non-Christians used a different salutation. I decided to use the word my family used. These Canadians would not know the difference.

"Peng-an," I said.

A muffled titter sounded all around me. Too late, I realized that I should have kept quiet. Mr. Johnston frowned at the noise and the class hushed. I heard him sigh. He would keep trying to help. But nobody, least of all the teacher, could make them like me.

"Well, we are very glad you have joined us, Jean," he said to me. Looking at the

---

2. *Tremulously* is the adverb form of *tremulous* and, here, means "timidly."

from **Little by Little**

others, he added, "I know you will all do your best to make Jean feel welcome here in Guelph."

I stood up with the rest to sing "God Save the King"[3] and mumbled the Lord's Prayer. When I slid out of the desk, however, the hinged seat flipped up. I had never sat at that kind of desk before. It took me a second to find out how to make it drop down again. In my hurry, I let it go down with a resounding bang. There were more muffled giggles.

When the teacher gave me my reader, I opened it eagerly. I had to hold it up close, as usual, to see the words. I had no idea how odd I looked when I read, since I had never seen myself doing it. My nose touched the page, as always, and I moved both the book and my head back and forth as I followed the line of print along. I caught more smothered laughter, but I was too pleased with the new book to pay attention.

As the others took turns reading aloud, I realized with relief that I read as well as any of them, better than most. It was my turn. I would show them.

"Good, Jean. You read with expression," Mr. Johnston said as I came to the end of the page.

I glowed.

Then it was time for the writing lesson. Printing was easier for a visually impaired[4] child to read than cursive writing which was taught in grade four. Because of this, I was not supposed to learn to write with all the letters joined together, but to go on printing. When Mr. Johnston's class got out the lined notebooks in which they practiced rows of loops and squiggles, I had to be given a different activity.

That morning Mr. Johnston should have had me do extra arithmetic problems. Since I had skipped grade three, I was extremely shaky when it came to knowing my times tables. But Mr. Johnston gave me a box of colored chalk instead and sent me to the board to draw a picture.

I loved doing it, of course. I drew a huge castle with a flag flying from its tallest tower. I put in trees. I felt I drew trees especially well. I used all the colors in the box. I did not feel the hostile glances aimed at my back. I was having fun while they worked.

No wonder, before the first recess bell had rung, I had forty enemies.

They never knew that I practiced "real writing" like theirs at home and envied them their chance to use those specially lined writing books.

When we went out for recess, nobody spoke to me. It was as though I had suddenly become invisible. Everyone else knew what to do, where to go. I stayed close to the door, shivering in the November wind and wishing recess would end.

At noon, Hugh[5] told us all about some boys he had met. I listened to stories about

---

3. In the 1940s, Canada was part of the British Empire; Canadians sang "God Save the King," the British national anthem.
4. Someone who is *visually impaired* has a vision problem, which might be anything from crossed eyes to blindness.

---

5. *Hugh* is the author's brother.

Vocabulary
hostile (host′ əl) *adj.* feeling or showing strong dislike

Dick and Bill Weber with a <u>pang</u>. Never mind. Perhaps I would make a friend that afternoon.

But nobody except Mr. Johnston spoke to me when I got back to school. We had a spelling bee. I was one of the best spellers in the class. I was slowest at arithmetic, though, and I could not see where the Eskimos lived on the big map. When four o'clock came, I was very glad it was time to go home.

The name-calling began the instant I left the shelter of the playground. Boys going in my direction started up the chant as soon as they knew Mr. Johnston could not see or hear them.

"Cross-eyed! Cross-eyed!"
"Chinky-chinky Chinaman!"
"Teacher's Pet!"

"Knock, knock.
Who goes there?
Little Jean Little
In her underwear!"

I began to run, but they swarmed after me, screaming <u>taunts</u>. I ran faster, my heart thudding, my eyes blurring with tears.

"Crybaby, cry! Crybaby cry!
Stick your finger in your eye
And tell your mother it wasn't I.
Crybaby, cry!"

As I fled, each pounding step jarred my whole body. What would they do to me if they caught me? Home was only five short blocks away, but even though I positively flew along the sidewalk, it seemed to take hours to get there.

Author Jean Little enjoys a book with one of her readers.

Vocabulary
pang (pang) *n.* a sudden sharp feeling of pain or distress
taunt (tônt) *n.* an insulting remark

from Little by Little

In my breathless dash, I slipped on a patch of ice and went crashing down on one knee. There were shrieks of delight. They sounded so <u>menacing</u> that I did not take time to inspect my wounds but was up and running on like a fox with a pack of hounds after it.

I had not realized before how fast I could run. I also had not realized before how much I had depended on my two brothers for protection when we lived in Toronto. St. John's was a two-room school, with only third- and fourth-grade classes. Hugh, in grade one, and Jamie, in grade six, went to Victory School, several blocks away. No longer were the boys there to help fight my battles. No longer could I threaten bullies with what my big brother would do to them.

Sobbing with relief, I reached our house at last. The cat calls died away as I pulled open the big front door and stumbled inside. Then I stood still and wailed, "Mother!"

She came running and gathered me into her arms.

"What happened?" she demanded, holding me close.

I displayed my torn stocking and scraped knee. She led me into the office examining room.[6] Gently she peeled off my stocking and cleaned up the smear of blood.

As she tended my hurt knee, Mother listened to the story of the bullies chasing me home and calling me names. She did not gasp or shudder. Her calm helped to quiet my storm of tears.

"I want you to walk there with me," I finished up. "They'd leave me alone if you were there."

She did not answer at once. When she had helped me change into other stockings, she sat down in the rocking chair and took me on her lap. I was a bit big, but neither of us noticed.

"I'm so sorry you had such a bad time," she said. As she rocked the chair slowly back and forth, her cheek rested against my hair. Little by little, peace filled me. In drowsy content I listened as she went on, "But you'll have to learn to laugh at teasing, Jean. If I walked you to school each day, you would never make friends. Remember that rhyme . . ."

I remembered it. I did not like it. It was not true. I gave a wriggle of protest but she repeated it anyway.

> The cat calls died away as I pulled open the big front door and stumbled inside.

---

6. Little's house has an *office examining room* because her parents are doctors.

Vocabulary
menacing (men′ əs ing) *adj.* threatening; dangerous

"Sticks and stones
May break my bones,
But names will never hurt me."

"But names *do* hurt me!" I growled. "And I want you to walk with me. I don't want them for friends. I hate them."

"It is hard not to hate people when they've made you so miserable," she agreed. "But you'll just have to laugh it off. They won't tease you when they see that you don't mind."

"But I *do* mind!"

She laughed softly, gave me a last hug, and tipped me back onto my own two feet. Didn't she care? I knew the answer. Her calm, steady words did not fool me. She hated anyone being cruel. She loved me very much. If she could fix things, she would.

But this was something even my mother could not fix. I would have to work it out for myself.

And I didn't know how.

Then why wouldn't she come and tell the teacher? Why wouldn't she fight my battles for me?

Because they were my battles. Because she could not win them for me any more than Mr. Johnston had helped when he had told the others to make me welcome.

The doorbell rang.

"Maybe it's for you," Mother said. "Run and answer it."

She was trying to distract me, I knew, but I went.

Mary Weber stood on the step and smiled at me. She lived across the street, and she was almost as old as Jamie. I waited politely to see who she wanted to see.

"Hi, Jean," she said. "Your mum says you like to read. I wondered if you'd like to come to the library with me and get some books?"

I stared at her blankly for a long moment. Then I totally forgot the name-calling and my sore knee.

"I'd love to," I said. "I'll tell Mother."

As we walked side by side down the snowy sidewalk, I felt too shy to start a conversation with such a big girl. I hoped somebody from my class would see us. If they found out Mary Weber was my friend, it might make a difference.

"Starting school in a new town can be pretty rough at first," Mary said gently.

I shot a startled look up at her. Did she know or was she guessing? She knew. Living right across the street, she traveled the same route as I did. She must have seen me fleeing from those boys.

"Yes," I said, comforted.

We went on in a friendly silence. Then she took my arm and steered me to the right.

"We're here," she said. "The Children's Library is downstairs. The door is at the back."

Once we were inside, we went down a flight of stairs and entered a large room filled with books. Shelves ran around three walls and there were extra bookcases in front of them. In the center of the room were some low tables with big picture books spread out on them. Windows at ground level let the last light of afternoon pour in. Right inside the door was a corner walled off by an L-shaped counter. Behind it, a woman was repairing books. Another lady stood at the long desk checking out books for a couple of boys. When they left, she smiled at Mary.

from Little by Little

"Miss Metcalf, this is Jean Little," Mary said to her. "She wants to join the library."

"How old are you, dear?" the lady asked.

"Nearly nine."

"Can you write your name?"

I felt indignant.[7] Of course I knew how to write my name! Then I realized she might mean "write" with the letters all joined together the way the others were learning to do at school. I thought fast. There were several letters I did not know how to make yet—*z* and *k* and *y* and a small *j*. But none of those were in my name. "Jean" was easy, but "Little" was trickier with that capital *L*. I tried picturing it. It went up and around in a loop, swept down and looped again in the opposite direction, didn't it? I could do it.

I nodded.

I had hesitated a little too long. Miss Metcalf studied me. I nodded again, <u>emphatically</u> this time.

"Come over here," she said.

She led us over to a smaller table with a huge book on it. Beside it was a big ink bottle and a straight pen, the kind you had to keep dipping. I had never used one of those before. It was not till grade five that you had an inkwell in your desk and learned to use a straight pen. Mr. Johnston's class were doing their writing lessons with a pencil. I had written with my parents' fountain pens, though. I knew you had to be careful not to press down on it. You weren't supposed to grip the pen too tightly, either. It was complicated.

Breathing hard and biting my tongue in order to concentrate, I picked up the long pen, dipped the nib into the ink bottle and began to write.

I had not known enough to let the excess ink drain back into the ink bottle. The first thing I did, on that tidy page, was make a black blot. The librarian tut-tutted. My face burned. I stared down at the stain. It looked gigantic.

"Never mind, dear," Miss Metcalf said in a kindly but faintly disapproving voice. "Go ahead."

My hand shook. I wrote "Jean" and paused for breath. Then I did the "L" carefully. I started at the bottom and drew it rather than wrote it, but when it was done, it looked all right. I sighed with relief and finished signing the register without any further <u>mishaps</u>.

My name was in the book.

A few minutes later, Miss Metcalf handed me my first library card. I took it <u>reverently</u>.

"You can take out four books a day," she rhymed off. "Two white card books and

Did You Know?

A *straight pen* does not have ink inside it, so a writer has to dip the point (called a *nib*) into ink. A *fountain pen* contains an ink-filled tube that must be refilled.

---

7. Feeling *indignant* is being quietly angry because of an insult or unfairness.

Vocabulary

emphatically (em fat′ i kəl ē) *adv.* forcefully

mishap (mis′ hap′) *n.* an unfortunate accident

reverently (rev′ ər ənt lē) *adv.* in a way that shows deep honor; respectfully

La Lectura. Arturo Gordon Vargas (1883–1944). Private collection.

Viewing the painting: *La lectura* (lek tur′ a) means "the reader." How does this girl feel about reading?

two blue. Or, if you like, four blue. Never more than two white cards in one day, though. You must take good care of them. If you keep them out longer than two weeks, there's a fine of two cents per book per day. Remember to be quiet, because other children are reading."

I liked the way she made reading sound important. I understood, from the way the librarian spoke, that the library was a place sacred to books and the people who read them. Readers mattered here.

And I was a reader.

I followed Mary to the nearest set of shelves. They had the *W*s on them. I ran my glance over the backs of the books. They did not have bright paper covers. Most of them had been rebound in dark wine or brown or

from Little by Little

blue. Their names, and the names of the people who had written them, were printed in gold on the spines.

Jean Webster, Kate Douglas Wiggin, Nelia Gardner White, T. H. White. I stared at them greedily. So many!

"Which are white card ones?" I whispered to Mary. It sounded mysterious, a secret language only taught to children possessing library cards.

Mary explained, also in a whisper, what the difference was. White cards were in the back of story books. *Heidi*, *The Secret Garden*, all the Oz books, and the Anne books had white cards. The nonfiction ones, filled with facts every child should know, had blue cards tucked into the cardboard pocket inside the back cover.

I had not heard of the Oz books or the Anne books. But I knew right away that white card books were what I wanted.

Mary did not think to tell me that books of poetry also had blue cards in the back, and so did biographies. There really were some good books in the shelves of nonfiction. In time, I found them.

I wandered up and down, staring at the hundreds of books I could choose from. Mary went off to get books for herself. I took volumes down and flipped through the pages, looking for books with lots of conversation in them. With my impaired vision, it was easier for me to read short paragraphs than long, solid ones. I also liked books with people in them, and people tended to talk.

I left clutching *The Dutch Twins* and *Anne of Green Gables*.

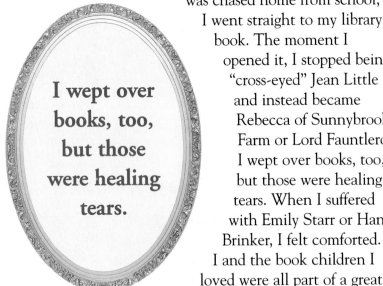

I wept over books, too, but those were healing tears.

From that day on, when I was chased home from school, I went straight to my library book. The moment I opened it, I stopped being "cross-eyed" Jean Little and instead became Rebecca of Sunnybrook Farm or Lord Fauntleroy. I wept over books, too, but those were healing tears. When I suffered with Emily Starr or Hans Brinker, I felt comforted. I and the book children I loved were all part of a great fellowship. I was not alone any longer.

The name calling did not stop. I did my best to laugh off the teasing, to ignore it, to believe that names could never hurt me, but I was not a brave child. I was a coward and, what was worse, a crybaby. I knew that if I could manage to look as though I did not care, my tormentors would find another victim. But I could not manage to appear other than terrified and humiliated. I always cried, however hard I tried not to, and I always ran.

Responding to Literature

PERSONAL RESPONSE

◆ Which incidents from the selection stay in your mind?
◆ Look back at the notes you made in the **Focus Activity** on page 16. Have any of your ideas about being picked on changed?

Analyzing Literature

RECALL

1. What does Jean Little fear the most about her new school? How does she show her discomfort?
2. How does her mother react to the hard time that Little is having?
3. What does Mary Weber do that helps Little?
4. How do things change for Little after the afternoon at the library? How do they stay the same?

INTERPRET

5. Why do you think that Little has so much trouble adjusting to her new school?
6. In your opinion, does Little's mother help her? Explain your answer.
7. Why is visiting the library a good idea for Little?
8. Is Little a happy child? Use examples to support your answer.

EVALUATE AND CONNECT

9. **Conflict** is the struggle between two opposing forces in a plot. What is the conflict in the selection? Is the conflict resolved? Explain.
10. What advice would you give to a younger brother or sister who had problems getting along at school like Little?

LITERARY ELEMENTS

Theme

A story usually includes a **theme**, a general statement about life that is the main idea of the story. In an autobiography, which is a life story, there may be several themes. They are general ideas the author has about the meaning of his or her life. The author usually doesn't state the theme but develops it gradually through the events and characters of the story and through telling his or her thoughts and feelings about these events and people.

1. What is an important theme of this selection?
2. How does Little communicate this theme to her readers?

● See **Literary Terms Handbook,** p. R9.

Literature and Writing

Writing About Literature

Writing a Description   A new world opens for Jean Little when she walks into the library. Reread Little's description of that important place beginning on page 23. Can you imagine yourself in the room she describes? Write a description in your own words, telling how you picture the Children's Library.

Creative Writing

"Dear Jean, . . ."   Do you have any advice for young Jean Little as she begins class in a new school? Perhaps you would like to sympathize with her troubles or compliment her on her behavior. Write a letter to the young Jean. Tell her what you would do in her situation, or let her know your feelings about the way she handled her situation.

Extending Your Response

Literature Groups

Debate   Do you agree with Little's opinion of herself and her actions? What is your opinion of her strengths and weaknesses? What is your opinion of the children who teased her? Find examples in the story that back up your opinion. Be prepared to share your group's opinions with the class.

Listening and Speaking

You're on the Air!   Make a tape recording of a favorite story or a part of a favorite book. Pretend that you are on the radio, and people can hear but not see you. Use your voice to bring out the feelings and drama in the story. Then play your tape for the class.

Learning for Life

Books and Booklets   With a partner, write a brochure to promote your library. You may want to describe the types of books found there, mention library services, or give information about programs that people might enjoy. Does your library have special services, such as video check-outs? Does it have summer reading programs, puppet shows, story hours, guest speakers, or book discussion groups? An effective brochure should provide information, but it should also be colorful and fun to read. Include illustrations or diagrams. Distribute copies of your brochure to classmates.

Reading Further

If you'd like to read more by Jean Little, you might enjoy these books:
Mine for Keeps
Mama's Going to Buy You a Mockingbird

📖 **Save your work for your portfolio.**

Skill Minilessons

GRAMMAR AND LANGUAGE • PREPOSITIONAL PHRASES

A **preposition** is a word that relates a noun to another word in a sentence. A **prepositional phrase** begins with a preposition and ends with a noun or pronoun called the object of the preposition. Jean Little uses prepositional phrases to help readers visualize the setting of the story. Coats were hanging "on hooks" "outside the grade four classroom door." Children's voices come from "behind the closed door." Little's desk was "in the front row."

PRACTICE Copy these sentences from the selection. Underline the prepositional phrases.

1. I slid into the seat, my head down, my cheeks flaming.
2. I drew a huge castle with a flag flying from its tallest tower.
3. In my breathless dash, I slipped on a patch of ice and went crashing down on one knee.
4. She lived across the street, and she was almost as old as Jamie.
5. She must have seen me fleeing from those boys.

● For more about prepositions, see **Language Handbook,** p. R26.

READING AND THINKING • CAUSE AND EFFECT

If a person bumps a table and a book falls off, there is a cause-and-effect relationship between these two events. Bumping the table *causes* the book to fall off. The book would not have fallen if the table had not been bumped. In this case, bumping the table is called a **cause;** the book falling off is called an **effect.**

In *Little by Little,* Jean Little writes that because she was allowed to draw at the board during writing practice, the other students resented her. Getting special treatment was a cause; students' resenting her was an effect.

PRACTICE Find other causes and their effects in the story. List at least four causes followed by their effects.

● For more about cause and effect, see **Reading Handbook,** p. R78.

VOCABULARY • SYNONYMS

Synonyms are words with similar meanings. The words *taunt* and *insult* are synonyms, but their meanings are different in an important way. A taunt is a particular kind of insult. It's deliberately mean in a way that makes fun of someone. The words *menacing* and *warning* are synonyms also, but they also have somewhat different meanings. A traffic guard can hold up a hand as a warning sign without being menacing at all.

It is rare for synonyms to mean exactly the same thing. There are almost always small but important differences between their meanings.

PRACTICE Answer each question by thinking about the meanings of the underlined synonyms.
1. Which word is better for describing a time you scraped your knee—mishap or tragedy?
2. Which word better describes a person who ignores you—hostile or unfriendly?
3. How do you say no if you *really* don't want to be asked again—seriously or emphatically?
4. How would you compliment a friend's new outfit—admiringly or reverently?
5. Which word better describes the feeling of a sore muscle that hurts for days—ache or pang?

GRAMMAR LINK

Avoiding Sentence Fragments

Do you remember Jean Little's awe as she looked at the books in the library? She was thrilled to see the titles and authors' names on the spines. She writes,

"Jean Webster, Kate Douglas Wiggin, Nelia Gardner White, T. H. White. I stared at them greedily. So many!"

A sentence fragment is a group of words that does not express a complete thought. When writers answer questions or write a person's thoughts or speech, they sometimes use sentence fragments. In the passage above, Little uses two fragments.

A complete sentence has both a subject and a predicate and expresses a complete thought. "I stared at them greedily" is a complete sentence. Its subject ("I") tells whom the sentence is about. Its predicate ("stared at them greedily") tells what the subject does. Notice how these fragments can be made into complete sentences.

Fragment	Problem	Sentence
Jean Little.	The fragment lacks a predicate. What does Jean Little do?	Jean Little writes about her school years.
Moved from Toronto.	The fragment lacks a subject. Who moved from Toronto?	Little's family moved from Toronto.
In 1987.	The fragment lacks both a subject and a predicate.	Little's autobiography was published in 1987.

● For more about sentence fragments, see **Language Handbook,** p. R10.

EXERCISE

Write each sentence. Underline the subject once and the predicate twice. Rewrite fragments into complete sentences.

1. Jean forgot the name-calling and teasing.
2. Children who like to read.
3. Into the doors of the library.
4. Hurrying up and down the rows of beautiful books.
5. Jean loved books.

Vo•cab•u•lar•y *Skills*

Using Word Webs

A **word web** is a kind of chart. It's a quick way to put down your thoughts without worrying about grammar and punctuation. Just let your mind make connections and jot them down. Draw lines between words and ideas to show connections.

A word web can be very simple. The synonym web shown here is one word with synonyms clustered around it.

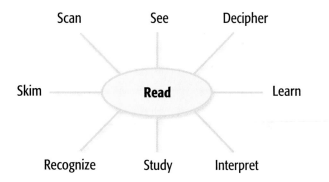

A word web can be very complicated. The word-association web shown here includes words for people, services, things, and other words associated with libraries.

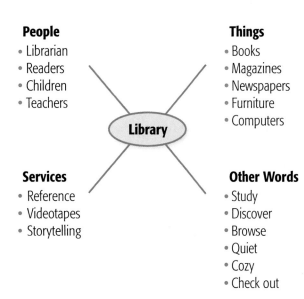

Work with a small group to make a word-association web for *school.* Be sure to include important people, places, feelings, and other words that come to mind as you think of *school.*

Before You Read

To Young Readers and Arithmetic

MEET GWENDOLYN BROOKS

"I loved poetry very early and began to put rhymes together at about seven," Gwendolyn Brooks says. At thirty-three Brooks became the first African American to win the Pulitzer Prize in poetry.

Gwendolyn Brooks was born in 1917. "To Young Readers" was first published in 1983.

MEET CARL SANDBURG

Carl Sandburg left school at fourteen and worked as a truck driver, firefighter, house painter, traveling salesman, and newspaper writer. In his later years, he was able to devote himself to his prizewinning poetry and biographies.

Carl Sandburg was born in 1878 and died in 1967. "Arithmetic" was first published in 1950.

FOCUS ACTIVITY

What is your favorite school subject? Why? Which subject do you like least?

Web It!

Make a word-association web about a school subject. Write the subject name. Then attach related ideas using specific words to describe the subject and your feelings about it. Share your ideas.

Setting a Purpose

Read the poems to see what these poets have to say about two school subjects.

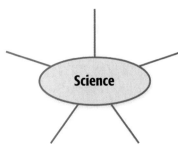

Science

BACKGROUND

Both Gwendolyn Brooks and Carl Sandburg are associated with Chicago and Illinois. Gwendolyn Brooks has lived most of her life in Chicago and is Poet Laureate of Illinois. "To Young Readers" was written for the Chicago Public Library. Sandburg was born in Galesburg, Illinois. *Chicago Poems* was his first book, and "Chicago" is one of his most famous poems.

The Harold Washington Library Center in Chicago.

The Library, 1960. Jacob Lawrence. Tempera, 60.9 x 75.8 cm. National Museum of American Art, Washington, DC.

To Young Readers

Gwendolyn Brooks ∿

Good books are
bandages
and voyages
and linkages° to Light;

5   are keys and hammers,
ripe redeemers,°
dials and bells and
healing hallelujah.

Good books are good nutrition.
10   A reader is a Guest
nourished, by riches of the Feast,
to lift, to launch, and to applaud
the world.

---

4 *Linkages* is another way of saying *links,* or connections.
6 *Redeemers* are rescuers or saviors.

Arithmetic

Carl Sandburg

Arithmetic is where numbers fly like pigeons in and out of your head.
Arithmetic tells you how many you lose or win if you know how many you
    had before you lost or won.
Arithmetic is seven eleven all good children go to heaven—or five six
5   bundle of sticks.°
Arithmetic is numbers you squeeze from your head to your hand to your
    pencil to your paper till you get the answer.
Arithmetic is where the answer is right and everything is nice and you can
    look out of the window and see the blue sky—or the answer is wrong
10   and you have to start all over and try again and see how it comes out
    this time.
If you take a number and double it and double it again and then double
    it a few more times, the number gets bigger and bigger and goes
    higher and higher and only arithmetic can tell you what the number
15   is when you decide to quit doubling.
Arithmetic is where you have to multiply—and you carry the
    multiplication table in your head and hope you won't lose it.
If you have two animal crackers, one good and one bad, and you eat one
    and a striped zebra with streaks all over him eats the other, how many
20   animal crackers will you have if somebody offers you five six seven
    and you say No no no and you say Nay nay nay and you say Nix
    nix nix?
If you ask your mother for one fried egg for breakfast and she gives you
    two fried eggs and you eat both of them, who is better in arithmetic,
25   you or your mother?

4–5 *[seven eleven . . . sticks]* These are lines from a children's counting rhyme.

0 Through 9, 1961. Jasper Johns. Oil on canvas, 1.372 x 1.048 m. Tate Gallery, London.

Viewing the painting: How many numbers can you find?

Responding to Literature

To Young Readers and *Arithmetic*

PERSONAL RESPONSE

Do these poems describe how you feel about reading books and about arithmetic? Explain your answer.

Analyzing Literature

RECALL

1. In "To Young Readers," Gwendolyn Brooks compares books to many things. What are five of them?
2. According to "Arithmetic," what are some of the things arithmetic can do?

INTERPRET

3. How could books be "good nutrition," as the speaker says in "To Young Readers"?
4. How do you think the speaker of "Arithmetic" feels about arithmetic?

EVALUATE AND CONNECT

5. Do you agree with Brooks that books can heal and redeem?
6. How has a book ever become a "voyage," a "key," or a "hammer" for you?
7. What is the effect of Sandburg's mixing nonsense with realistic statements about arithmetic?
8. What are two additional "uses" for arithmetic that you could add to Sandburg's poem?
9. An **image** is a picture a writer creates with words. What images are created in these poems?
10. Does either of the poems leave out anything important about reading or arithmetic? What?

LITERARY ELEMENTS

Metaphor

A **metaphor** compares two things in a fresh, sometimes surprising way—without the use of the word *like* or *as.* Poets often use metaphors because they can say a lot in just a few words. For example, Gwendolyn Brooks begins "To Young Readers" with this metaphor: "Good books are / bandages." In just four words, she is saying that books can help to heal a broken heart, for example, or help to cure loneliness or sadness.

1. Reread "To Young Readers" and find three more metaphors.

2. Reread "Arithmetic" and find at least one metaphor.

● See **Literary Terms Handbook**, p. R5.

Extending Your Response

Writing About Literature

Speaker   The **speaker** is the voice a poet uses when writing a poem. Speakers are like characters in plays or short stories; they are not necessarily the poets themselves. Write two paragraphs telling about the speaker of each of these poems. How old is each speaker? Why do you think so?

Literature Groups

Poetry   **Rhyme** is the repetition of sounds at the end of words. Rhyme is the first thing most people think of when they think of poetry. Does one of these poems contain rhyme? Discuss what you notice about these poems. What makes them poems rather than prose? Share your group's conclusion with the class.

Art Activity

Posters   Work with a partner to make a poster that will advertise the benefits of reading discussed in "To Young Readers." Your school librarian may want to display your poster in the library.

Personal Writing

List Poem   "Arithmetic" could be called a list poem. It describes a subject by listing its qualities and giving examples. Use the word-association web you made for the **Focus Activity** on page 32 to write a list of several sentences about a school subject. Use specific words and examples to make your list interesting.

Reading Further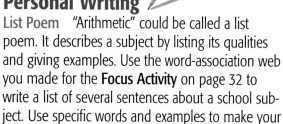

If you would like to read more poetry by these poets, you might enjoy these books:
Poetry for Young People by Carl Sandburg
Bronzeville Boys and Girls by Gwendolyn Brooks
Very Young Poets by Gwendolyn Brooks

Save your work for your portfolio.

Skill Minilesson

READING AND THINKING • PARAPHRASING

Paraphrasing means restating someone else's ideas in your own words. Paraphrasing something you have read often helps you to understand it better and to remember it. To write a paraphrase of a poem, first read it carefully. Look up any words you do not understand in a dictionary. Then, sentence by sentence, write the poet's ideas in your own words.

PRACTICE Paraphrase "To Young Readers." First, reread the poem. Look for the points Brooks makes about good books. Write these ideas in your own words. You do not need to use images or metaphors. Read over your sentences to be sure your ideas are the same as those in the poem.

● For more about comprehension strategies, see **Reading Handbook,** p. R81.

MEDIA Connection

WEB SITE

People from different cultures use different table manners.

Chopsticks

Address: ▼ **www.cuisinenet.com**

It is not known when chopsticks first began to be used, although it is fairly certain that they were invented in China, where they have been traced back at least as far as the third century B.C. The philosopher Confucius, who lived over 200 years earlier, may have influenced the development of chopsticks with his nonviolent teachings. Thus, knives, with all their associations with war and death, were not brought to the dinner table, as they were in the West.

Chopsticks in China

In China, chopsticks are usually made of bamboo or other wood. They are called *k'uai-tzu* (kwī tzoo), meaning "something fast." The word *chopsticks* came into use during the 1800s, when Chinese was translated by traders into Pidgin English. The word *chop* means fast—as in the phrase "chop chop!"

Chopsticks in Japan

The Japanese word for chopsticks, *hashi,* means "bridge." Unlike Chinese chopsticks, which are squared-off and blunt at the end, the Japanese utensils are rounded and tapered to a point. This shape makes it easier for the user to remove bones from fish, which makes up a great part of the Japanese diet.

Taboos

There are several taboos in Japan regarding the handling of chopsticks at the table, mostly derived from associations with the use of chopsticks in Buddhist funeral rites. Passing food to another person using your chopsticks resembles a ritual in which bone fragments from the cremated body are removed from the pyre and passed among the mourners. It is also important not to leave the chopsticks sticking upright in the rice bowl. A dead family member's personal pair is often positioned this way in an offering bowl of uncooked rice placed at the family altar.

Respond

1. What kinds of difficulties might newcomers to Japan or China have with table manners?

2. What kinds of difficulties might newcomers to the United States have with U.S. table manners?

Before You Read

The All-American Slurp

MEET
LENSEY NAMIOKA

Lensey Namioka (len' sē nä mē' ō kä) and her family moved several times within China before coming to the United States. Because they moved so often, Namioka and her sisters had few toys. "To amuse ourselves, my sisters and I made up stories," she says. Namioka became quite a story-teller. Many of her books are adventure stories that take place in Japan and China hundreds of years ago. Namioka, a mathematician and math instructor for several years, says, "My long years of training in mathematics had little influence on my writing. . . ."

Lensey Namioka was born in 1929. This story was published in 1987.

FOCUS ACTIVITY

Have you ever moved to a new city or a new school? What things surprised or confused you? What things did you especially like?

Sharing Ideas

Jot down your answers to these questions. If you've never experienced such changes, write what you think you might notice. Share responses in a small group.

Setting a Purpose

Read "The All-American Slurp" to find out how a family learns new table manners.

BACKGROUND

Did You Know?

Many thousands of people immigrate to the United States every year. During one year in the 1990s, about 54,000 people moved from

China to the United States. More than 111,400 people came from Mexico; 14,700 from Cuba; and 41,300 from Vietnam.

VOCABULARY PREVIEW

lavishly (lav' ish lē) *adv.* abundantly; generously; p. 42
mortified (môr' tə fīd') *adj.* greatly embarrassed; p. 43
smugly (smug' lē) *adv.* in a self-satisfied way; p. 43
systematic (sis' tə mat' ik) *adj.* well-organized; following a certain way of doing things; p. 45
consumption (kən sump' shən) *n.* the act of eating, drinking, or using up; p. 46
cope (kōp) *v.* to deal with something successfully; p. 48

The All-American SLURP

Lensey Namioka

The first time our family was invited out to dinner in America, we disgraced ourselves while eating celery. We had emigrated to this country from China, and during our early days here we had a hard time with American table manners.

In China we never ate celery raw, or any other kind of vegetable raw. We always had to disinfect the vegetables in boiling water first. When we were presented with our first relish tray, the raw celery caught us unprepared.

We had been invited to dinner by our neighbors, the Gleasons. After arriving at the house, we shook hands with our hosts and packed ourselves into a sofa. As our family of four sat stiffly in a row, my younger brother and I stole glances at our parents for a clue as to what to do next.

Mrs. Gleason offered the relish tray to Mother. The tray looked pretty, with its tiny red radishes, curly sticks of carrots, and long, slender stalks of pale green celery. "Do try some of the celery, Mrs. Lin," she said. "It's from a local farmer, and it's sweet."

Mother picked up one of the green stalks, and Father followed suit. Then I picked up a stalk, and my brother did too. So there we sat, each with a stalk of celery in our right hand.

Mrs. Gleason kept smiling. "Would you like to try some of the dip, Mrs. Lin? It's my own recipe: sour cream and onion flakes, with a dash of Tabasco sauce."

The All-American Slurp

Most Chinese don't care for dairy products, and in those days I wasn't even ready to drink fresh milk. Sour cream sounded perfectly revolting. Our family shook our heads in unison.

Mrs. Gleason went off with the relish tray to the other guests, and we carefully watched to see what they did. Everyone seemed to eat the raw vegetables quite happily.

Mother took a bite of her celery. *Crunch.* "It's not bad!" she whispered.

Father took a bite of his celery. *Crunch.* "Yes, it *is* good," he said, looking surprised.

I took a bite, and then my brother. *Crunch, crunch.* It was more than good; it was delicious. Raw celery has a slight sparkle, a zingy taste that you don't get in cooked celery. When Mrs. Gleason came around with the relish tray, we each took another stalk of celery, except my brother. He took two.

There was only one problem: long strings ran through the length of the stalk, and they got caught in my teeth. When I help my mother in the kitchen, I always pull the strings out before slicing celery.

I pulled the strings out of my stalk. *Z-z-zip, z-z-zip.* My brother followed suit. *Z-z-zip, z-z-zip, z-z-zip.* To my left, my parents were taking care of their own stalks. *Z-z-zip, z-z-zip, z-z-zip.*

Suddenly I realized that there was dead silence except for our zipping. Looking up, I saw that the eyes of everyone in the room were on our family. Mr. and Mrs. Gleason, their daughter Meg, who was my friend, and their neighbors the Badels—they were all staring at us as we busily pulled the strings of our celery.

That wasn't the end of it. Mrs. Gleason announced that dinner was served and invited us to the dining table. It was <u>lavishly</u> covered with platters of food, but we couldn't see any chairs around the table. So we helpfully carried over some dining chairs and sat down. All the other guests just stood there.

Mrs. Gleason bent down and whispered to us, "This is a buffet dinner. You help yourselves to some food and eat it in the living room."

Vocabulary
lavishly (lav´ ish lē) *adv.* abundantly; generously

Our family beat a retreat back to the sofa as if chased by enemy soldiers. For the rest of the evening, too mortified to go back to the dining table, I nursed[1] a bit of potato salad on my plate.

Next day Meg and I got on the school bus together. I wasn't sure how she would feel about me after the spectacle our family made at the party. But she was just the same as usual, and the only reference she made to the party was, "Hope you and your folks got enough to eat last night. You certainly didn't take very much. Mom never tries to figure out how much food to prepare. She just puts everything on the table and hopes for the best."

I began to relax. The Gleasons' dinner party wasn't so different from a Chinese meal after all. My mother also puts everything on the table and hopes for the best.

Meg was the first friend I had made after we came to America. I eventually got acquainted with a few other kids in school, but Meg was still the only real friend I had.

My brother didn't have any problems making friends. He spent all his time with some boys who were teaching him baseball, and in no time he could speak English much faster than I could—not better, but faster.

I worried more about making mistakes, and I spoke carefully, making sure I could say everything right before opening my mouth.

> ## Meg was the first friend I had made after we came to America.

At least I had a better accent than my parents, who never really got rid of their Chinese accent, even years later. My parents had both studied English in school before coming to America, but what they had studied was mostly written English, not spoken.

Father's approach to English was a scientific one. Since Chinese verbs have no tense, he was fascinated by the way English verbs changed form according to whether they were in the present, past imperfect, perfect, pluperfect, future, or future perfect tense. He was always making diagrams of verbs and their inflections,[2] and he looked for opportunities to show off his mastery of the pluperfect and future perfect tenses, his two favorites. "I shall have finished my project by Monday," he would say smugly.

Mother's approach was to memorize lists of polite phrases that would cover all possible social situations. She was constantly muttering things like "I'm fine, thank you. And you?" Once she accidentally stepped on someone's foot, and hurriedly blurted, "Oh, that's quite all right!" Embarrassed by her slip, she resolved to do better next time. So when someone

1. To *nurse* food or a drink is to eat or drink it slowly so it will last longer.

2. An *inflection* is the form a verb takes in each tense—*go, went,* and *gone,* for example.

Vocabulary
mortified (môr′ tə fīd′) *adj.* greatly embarrassed
smugly (smug′ lē) *adv.* in a self-satisfied way

stepped on *her* foot, she cried, "You're welcome!"

In our own different ways, we made progress in learning English. But I had another worry, and that was my appearance. My brother didn't have to worry, since Mother bought him blue jeans for school, and he dressed like all the other boys. But she insisted that girls had to wear skirts. By the time she saw that Meg and the other girls were wearing jeans, it was too late. My school clothes were bought already, and we didn't have money left to buy new outfits for me. We had too many other things to buy first, like furniture, pots, and pans.

The first time I visited Meg's house, she took me upstairs to her room, and I wound up trying on her clothes. We were pretty much the same size, since Meg was shorter and thinner than average. Maybe that's how we became friends in the first place. Wearing Meg's jeans and T-shirt, I looked at myself in the mirror. I could almost pass for an American—from the back, anyway. At least the kids in school wouldn't stop and stare at me in the hallways, which was what they did when they saw me in my white blouse and navy blue skirt that went a couple of inches below the knees.

When Meg came to my house, I invited her to try on my Chinese dresses, the ones with a high collar and slits up the sides. Meg's eyes were bright as she looked at herself in the mirror. She struck several sultry poses,[3] and we nearly fell over laughing.

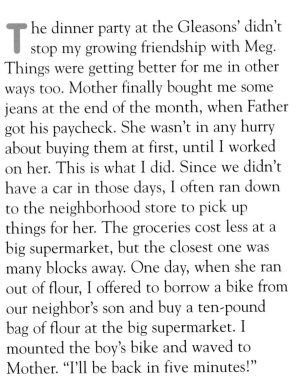

The dinner party at the Gleasons' didn't stop my growing friendship with Meg. Things were getting better for me in other ways too. Mother finally bought me some jeans at the end of the month, when Father got his paycheck. She wasn't in any hurry about buying them at first, until I worked on her. This is what I did. Since we didn't have a car in those days, I often ran down to the neighborhood store to pick up things for her. The groceries cost less at a big supermarket, but the closest one was many blocks away. One day, when she ran out of flour, I offered to borrow a bike from our neighbor's son and buy a ten-pound bag of flour at the big supermarket. I mounted the boy's bike and waved to Mother. "I'll be back in five minutes!"

Before I started pedaling, I heard her voice behind me. "You can't go out in public like that! People can see all the way up to your thighs!"

"I'm sorry," I said innocently. "I thought you were in a hurry to get the flour." For dinner we were going to have pot-stickers (fried Chinese dumplings), and we needed a lot of flour.

---

3. When Meg strikes *sultry poses,* she is trying out different looks that she thinks are seductive or flirty.

"Couldn't you borrow a girl's bicycle?" complained Mother. "That way your skirt won't be pushed up."

"There aren't too many of those around," I said. "Almost all the girls wear jeans while riding a bike, so they don't see any point buying a girl's bike."

We didn't eat pot-stickers that evening, and Mother was thoughtful. Next day we took the bus downtown and she bought me a pair of jeans. In the same week, my brother made the baseball team of his junior high school, Father started taking driving lessons, and Mother discovered rummage sales. We soon got all the furniture we needed, plus a dart board and a 1,000-piece jigsaw puzzle (fourteen hours later, we discovered that it was a 999-piece jigsaw puzzle). There was hope that the Lins might become a normal American family after all.

Then came our dinner at the Lakeview restaurant.

The Lakeview was an expensive restaurant, one of those places where a head-waiter dressed in tails conducted you to your seat, and the only light came from candles and flaming desserts. In one corner of the room a lady harpist played tinkling melodies.

Father wanted to celebrate, because he had just been

Did You Know?
The headwaiter is wearing a formal suit with a jacket that has long panels in the back. This kind of suit is called *tails* because the panels look like the tail of a bird.

promoted. He worked for an electronics company, and after his English started improving, his superiors[4] decided to appoint him to a position more suited to his training. The promotion not only brought a higher salary but was also a tremendous boost to his pride.

Up to then we had eaten only in Chinese restaurants. Although my brother and I were becoming fond of hamburgers, my parents didn't care much for western food, other than chow mein.

But this was a special occasion, and Father asked his coworkers to recommend a really elegant restaurant. So there we were at the Lakeview, stumbling after the head-waiter in the murky dining room.

At our table we were handed our menus, and they were so big that to read mine I almost had to stand up again. But why bother? It was mostly in French, anyway.

Father, being an engineer, was always systematic. He took out a pocket French dictionary. "They told me that most of the items would be in French, so I came prepared." He even had a pocket flashlight, the size of a marking pen. While Mother held the flashlight over the menu, he looked up the items that were in French.

"*Pâté en croûte*,"[5] he muttered. "Let's see . . . *pâté* is paste . . . *croûte* is crust . . . hmm . . . a paste in crust."

The waiter stood looking patient. I squirmed and died at least fifty times.

---

4. At work, Father's *superiors* are his managers or bosses.
5. Father is partly right. *Pâté en croûte* (pätā̇ ən krōōt) is finely ground meat baked in a small pie shell.

Vocabulary
systematic (sis′ tə mat′ ik) *adj.* well-organized; following a certain way of doing things

The soup arrived in a plate. How do you get soup up from a plate?

At long last Father gave up. "Why don't we just order four complete dinners at random?"[6] he suggested.

"Isn't that risky?" asked Mother. "The French eat some rather peculiar things, I've heard."

"A Chinese can eat anything a Frenchman can eat," Father declared.

The soup arrived in a plate. How do you get soup up from a plate? I glanced at the other diners, but the ones at the nearby tables were not on their soup course, while the more distant ones were invisible in the darkness.

Fortunately my parents had studied books on western etiquette[7] before they came to America. "Tilt your plate," whispered my mother. "It's easier to spoon the soup up that way."

She was right. Tilting the plate did the trick. But the etiquette book didn't say anything about what you did after the soup reached your lips. As any respectable Chinese knows, the correct way to eat your soup is to slurp. This helps to cool the liquid and prevent you from burning your lips. It also shows your appreciation.

We showed our appreciation. *Shloop*, went my father. *Shloop*, went my mother. *Shloop, shloop*, went my brother, who was the hungriest.

The lady harpist stopped playing to take a rest. And in the silence, our family's consumption of soup suddenly seemed unnaturally loud. You know how it sounds on a rocky beach when the tide goes out and the water drains from all those little pools? They go *shloop, shloop, shloop*. That was the Lin family, eating soup.

At the next table a waiter was pouring wine. When a large *shloop* reached him, he froze. The bottle continued to pour, and red wine flooded the tabletop and into the lap of a customer. Even the customer didn't notice anything at first, being also hypnotized by the *shloop, shloop, shloop*.

It was too much. "I need to go to the toilet," I mumbled, jumping to my feet. A waiter, sensing my urgency, quickly directed me to the ladies' room.

I splashed cold water on my burning face, and as I dried myself with a paper towel, I stared into the mirror. In this perfumed ladies' room, with its pink-and-silver wallpaper and marbled sinks, I looked completely out of place. What was I doing here? What was our family doing in the Lakeview restaurant? In America?

The door to the ladies' room opened. A woman came in and glanced curiously at me. I retreated into one of the toilet cubicles and latched the door.

---

6. If you do something *at random,* you don't have a plan.
7. Books on *etiquette* discuss manners and polite behavior.

Vocabulary

consumption (kən sump′ shən) *n.* the act of eating, drinking, or using up

Time passed—maybe half an hour, maybe an hour. Then I heard the door open again, and my mother's voice. "Are you in there? You're not sick, are you?"

There was real concern in her voice. A girl can't leave her family just because they slurp their soup. Besides, the toilet cubicle had a few drawbacks as a permanent residence. "I'm all right," I said, undoing the latch.

Mother didn't tell me how the rest of the dinner went, and I didn't want to know. In the weeks following, I managed to push the whole thing into the back of my mind, where it jumped out at me only a few times a day. Even now, I turn hot all over when I think of the Lakeview restaurant.

But by the time we had been in this country for three months, our family was definitely making progress toward becoming Americanized. I remember my parents' first PTA[8] meeting. Father wore a neat suit and tie, and Mother put on her first pair of high heels. She stumbled only once. They met my homeroom teacher and beamed as she told them that I would make honor roll soon at the rate I was going. Of course Chinese etiquette forced Father to say that I was a very stupid girl and Mother to protest that the teacher was showing favoritism toward me. But I could tell they were both very proud.

The day came when my parents announced that they wanted to give a dinner party. We had invited Chinese friends to eat with us before, but this dinner was going to be different. In addition to a Chinese-American family, we were going to invite the Gleasons.

"Gee, I can hardly wait to have dinner at your house," Meg said to me. "I just *love* Chinese food."

That was a relief. Mother was a good cook, but I wasn't sure if people who ate sour cream would also eat chicken gizzards stewed in soy sauce.

Mother decided not to take a chance with chicken gizzards. Since we had western guests, she set the table with large dinner plates, which we never used in Chinese meals. In fact we didn't use individual plates at all, but picked up food from the platters in the middle of the table and brought it directly to our rice bowls. Following the practice of Chinese-American restaurants, Mother also placed large serving spoons on the platters.

The dinner started well. Mrs. Gleason exclaimed at the beautifully arranged dishes of food: the colorful candied fruit in the sweet-and-sour pork dish, the noodle-thin shreds of chicken meat stir-fried with tiny peas, and the glistening pink prawns in a ginger sauce.

At first I was too busy enjoying my food to notice how the guests were doing. But soon I remembered my

Did You Know?
Prawns are large shrimp.

duties. Sometimes guests were too polite to help themselves and you had to serve them with more food.

---

8. *PTA* stands for Parent-Teacher Association.

I glanced at Meg, to see if she needed more food, and my eyes nearly popped out at the sight of her plate. It was piled with food: the sweet-and-sour meat pushed right against the chicken shreds, and the chicken sauce ran into the prawns. She had been taking food from a second dish before she finished eating her helping from the first!

Horrified, I turned to look at Mrs. Gleason. She was dumping rice out of her bowl and putting it on her dinner plate. Then she ladled prawns and gravy on top of the rice and mixed everything together, the way you mix sand, gravel, and cement to make concrete.

I couldn't bear to look any longer, and I turned to Mr. Gleason. He was chasing a pea around his plate. Several times he got it to the edge, but when he tried to pick it up with his chopsticks, it rolled back toward the center of the plate again. Finally he put down his chopsticks and picked up the pea with his fingers. He really did! A grown man!

All of us, our family and the Chinese guests, stopped eating to watch the activities of the Gleasons. I wanted to giggle. Then I caught my mother's eyes on me. She frowned and shook her head slightly, and I understood the message: the Gleasons were not used to Chinese ways, and they were just coping the best they could. For some reason I thought of celery strings.

When the main courses were finished, Mother brought out a platter of fruit. "I hope you weren't expecting a sweet dessert," she said. "Since the Chinese don't eat dessert, I didn't think to prepare any."

"Oh, I couldn't possibly eat dessert!" cried Mrs. Gleason. "I'm simply stuffed!"

Meg had different ideas. When the table was cleared, she announced that she and I were going for a walk. "I don't know about you, but I feel like dessert," she told me, when we were outside. "Come on, there's a Dairy Queen down the street. I could use a big chocolate milkshake!"

Although I didn't really want anything more to eat, I insisted on paying for the milkshakes. After all, I was still hostess.

Meg got her large chocolate milkshake and I had a small one. Even so, she was finishing hers while I was only half done. Toward the end she pulled hard on her straws and went *shloop, shloop*.

"Do you always slurp when you eat a milkshake?" I asked, before I could stop myself.

Meg grinned. "Sure. All Americans slurp."

Vocabulary
cope (kōp) *v.* to deal with something successfully

Responding to Literature

PERSONAL RESPONSE

- ◆ Does the ending of the story surprise you? How does it make you feel?
- ◆ Look at your notes from the **Focus Activity** on page 39. Did the characters in the story have any of the same feelings that you describe? Explain.

Analyzing Literature

RECALL

1. What "mistakes" does the Lin family make at the Gleasons' dinner party?
2. How does the narrator persuade her mother to buy her a pair of jeans?
3. What happens to embarrass the narrator at the restaurant?
4. What does the narrator notice about the Gleasons at the Lins' dinner party?

INTERPRET

5. Why is the narrator so uncomfortable whenever her family makes a "mistake"?
6. Why is it important for the narrator to get a pair of jeans?
7. Why does the narrator behave as she does at the restaurant?
8. What do you think the narrator learns from watching the Gleasons' table manners?

EVALUATE AND CONNECT

9. The author uses **humor** to make her points about not fitting in. Find at least three events in the story, and tell how the author uses humor in presenting each one.
10. The narrator constantly tries to fit into U.S. society. Do you think fitting in is important? Why or why not?

LITERARY ELEMENTS

Point of View

When a story is told by a character who is referred to as "I," that story is told from the **first-person point of view.** "I" is the narrator, or storyteller. The reader sees everything that happens through the narrator's eyes. When Namioka writes, "I took a bite," she is saying that the narrator took a bite. When she uses the plural "we," she is speaking of the narrator and one or more other characters.

1. In the very first sentence, which character's feelings are revealed? Find three other places where her feelings are shown.

2. Why is the first-person point of view especially effective for this story?

● See **Literary Terms Handbook,** p. R6.

Literature and Writing

Writing About Literature

Point of View   Rewrite an episode from "The All-American Slurp" from the point of view of another character. Choose a story event. Which other characters were present when this event happened? Select a character, and try to imagine the scene from his or her point of view. Then tell that person's version of the event.

Creative Writing

"If you want my advice . . ."   Imagine that the narrator is a new student in your class. You have been made responsible for showing her around and helping her. What advice would you give her to help her fit in? What ways would you recommend for making friends? What are some ways of acting that she should avoid? Write a paragraph of advice.

Extending Your Response

Literature Groups

Crying on the Inside?   Often your outlook determines whether something is funny or sad. In "The All-American Slurp," the author has written about serious feelings, but she has used humor to describe them. Can you find the serious ideas behind the comedy? Are all of the anecdotes in the story funny? Which parts are serious? Discuss your opinions in the group. Then share your conclusions in class.

Art Activity

Dinner Time   Work with a partner to show the settings at a typical Chinese dinner table. On a large sheet of paper, draw a life-size dinner table. What kinds of foods are served? What kinds of plates, bowls, and utensils are used? Label each item and add descriptions.

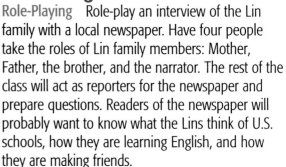

Performing

Role-Playing   Role-play an interview of the Lin family with a local newspaper. Have four people take the roles of Lin family members: Mother, Father, the brother, and the narrator. The rest of the class will act as reporters for the newspaper and prepare questions. Readers of the newspaper will probably want to know what the Lins think of U.S. schools, how they are learning English, and how they are making friends.

Reading Further

If you'd like to read more by Lensey Namioka, you might try these books:
Yang the Youngest and His Terrible Ear
Yang the Third and Her Impossible Family

 Save your work for your portfolio.

Skill Minilessons

GRAMMAR AND LANGUAGE • PAST TENSE

Mr. Lin is fascinated by the way English verbs change form, or show **tense.** These changes show the time at which the verb's action takes place. The present tense names an action that is happening now. The past tense names an action that already happened. You form the past tense of most verbs by adding -ed to the present tense form. Some past tenses are irregular, such as *teach/taught.*

PRACTICE Copy each sentence below, using the past tense of the verb in parentheses.

1. Last year, I always (wear) dresses to school.
2. Mother (give) me money for jeans.
3. I (ride) my bike to the store.
4. I tried on different jeans and (buy) two pairs.
5. The next day, I (feel) so much better at school.

● For more about verb tense, see **Language Handbook,** p. R13.

READING AND THINKING • PREDICTING

Readers often make **predictions** as they read. They use clues in the story to guess what will happen next. The narrator of "The All-American Slurp" says that the family "disgraced" themselves the first time they went to a dinner party. She also says they were having difficulties with U.S. table manners. Readers can predict that the family will make a mistake involving table manners.

PRACTICE Find another place where readers can make a prediction about what will happen next. Write a paragraph describing the situation. Include your prediction of what you would expect to happen next. Give the clues from the story that helped you make your prediction.

● For more about making predictions, see **Reading Handbook,** p. R76.

VOCABULARY • UNLOCKING MEANING

If you had to learn words one at a time, developing a good vocabulary would take a long time. Luckily, you don't. Once you have learned *depend,* you probably understand *dependable* and *independent.* Using what you already know can sometimes help you figure out something you don't know.

PRACTICE Use what you know about the words on the left to finish the sentences.

1. **lavishly** A mother who lavishes attention on her son gives him
   a. little of it.   c. a lot of it.
   b. just enough of it.

2. **consumption** The consumer of a product
   a. makes it.   b. uses it.   c. sells it.
3. **smugly** People who show smugness act
   a. superior.   b. frightened.   c. silly.
4. **resolve** When you make a New Year's resolution, you are making a
   a. threat.   b. firm plan.   c. bad mistake.
5. **mortified** A feeling of mortification would most likely make you
   a. blush.   b. grin.   c. shiver.

Technology Skills

Word Processing: Using Word Processing Software

A word processor lets you move your words and ideas around until you find the best way to present them. That way, you don't have to write them again in pen or type them a second or a third time. Each type of word processing software is a bit different, but they all share common characteristics. They all help you plan, draft, revise, edit, and present neat and attractive documents.

Menus, Toolbars, and Rulers

Open a word processing document. Copy a few paragraphs into it so that you can explore some important word processing features. At the top of your monitor screen, locate the menu bar, one or more toolbars, and a ruler. (If you don't see a toolbar or ruler, pull down the **View** menu and select the missing item.)

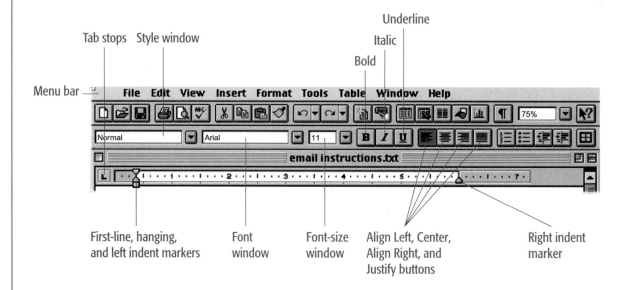

Menu Bar Menus help you perform important processes. The File menu, for example, allows you to open, close, save, and print documents. Take the time to become familiar with each menu by clicking on it and holding down the mouse button to examine its list of items. The little pointer at the right side of the menu for some items shows that there is a submenu with still more choices for that item. Other menu items will bring up a dialogue box when you select them. A dialogue box asks you to make choices by clicking on a button or typing something into a box. Select a few of these to see what you find. (Click on the **Cancel** button in a dialogue box to close it without changing your document.)

Toolbars Your word processing program will have one or more toolbars containing icons you can click on. There are two basic types of tools. **Function tools** perform some kind of computer function, like checking a document's spelling or printing a document. **Formatting tools** are used to change the way a document looks—for example, changing its font (typeface) or style. Use **Help** to find out what each toolbar item will do. (Help has its own menu and may be on a toolbar as well.)

The ▼ Icon Notice the ▼ icons next to the style, font, and font-size windows. Wherever you see this icon, you can click on it and hold down the mouse button to display a pull-down menu of choices. The font window, for example, will open to show the names of all of the fonts available to you. Select a portion of text on your document, and use the font menu to change the typeface. Click and hold on the other ▼ icons on your toolbar to see what is revealed.

Ruler The ruler looks like a measuring stick with little markers at each end. These markers control the margins of your document. Try changing the margins on your document. You can also put tabs on the ruler so that you can use the tab key on your keyboard to send your cursor to those positions. Click on the tab-stops button to see the different types of tabs you can use in a document.

Choosing Your Way to Work

There is almost always more than one way to perform a basic word processing action. You can choose the method that works best for you. To open a new document, for example, you can pull down the File menu and select New, or you can click on the new-document icon on the toolbar. There's even a third way. Pull down the File menu. To the right of New, you'll see "Ctrl + N." This **keyboard shortcut** stands for "Control plus N." To open a new document without using your mouse, hold down the Control key (the apple key on a Mac), and then press the N key.

ACTIVITIES

1. Find the keyboard shortcut for each of these functions.

   a. cut   **c.** paste   **e.** print

   b. copy   **d.** save   **f.** undo

2. In your journal or learning log, keep a list of the word processing skills you want to acquire. Check them off as you master them.

3. Use what you've learned about word processing to complete the Writing Workshop at the end of this theme.

Before You Read

The Land of Red Apples

MEET ZITKALA-ŠA

"As free as the wind that blew my hair, and no less spirited than a bounding deer." Zitkala-Ša (zēt kä′ lä shä), or Gertrude Bonnin, used these words to describe herself as a young child on a Sioux reservation in South Dakota. At age eight, she was sent east to a boarding school for Native American children in Indiana. She returned four years later but left to attend college.

Later in life, Bonnin took the name Zitkala-Ša—Red Bird—and became a writer and an activist for Indian rights.

Zitkala-Ša was born in 1876 and died in 1938. This selection was published in 1900.

FOCUS ACTIVITY

Imagine that you are being sent far away from your family for several years. You are going somewhere where people speak another language and wear unfamiliar clothing.

Journal
How would you feel? Jot down your responses in your journal.

Setting a Purpose
Read "The Land of Red Apples" to discover what happens when a girl's life changes suddenly and completely.

BACKGROUND

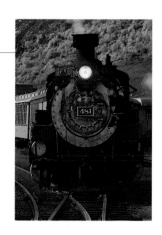

Did You Know?   During the late 1800s and early 1900s, U.S. government policy demanded that Native American children be sent to boarding schools far from their reservations. At these schools, teachers did not allow children to speak their own languages or wear traditional clothing. Children wore uniforms and were taught in English. Because the schools were so far from their homes, the children were away from their families for years at a time. The purpose of this policy was to "Americanize" the children, but for most children and their families it seemed a harsh punishment.

VOCABULARY PREVIEW

anticipate (an tis′ ə pāt′) *v.* to look forward to; expect; p. 55
resent (ri zent′) *v.* to feel anger toward a person or thing; p. 56
reprove (ri proōv′) *v.* to scold; p. 56
verge (vurj) *n.* the point just before something occurs or begins; the edge; p. 56
trifling (trī′ fling) *n.* the act of treating or handling something as if it had little value or importance; p. 56
bewildering (bi wil′ dər ing) *adj.* very confusing; p. 57

The Land of Red Apples

Zitkala-Ša

There were eight in our party of bronzed children who were going East with the missionaries. Among us were three young braves, two tall girls, and we three little ones, Judéwin, Thowin, and I.

We had been very impatient to start on our journey to the Red Apple Country, which, we were told, lay a little beyond the great circular horizon of the Western prairie. Under a sky of rosy apples we dreamt of roaming as freely and happily as we had chased the cloud shadows on the Dakota plains. We had <u>anticipated</u> much pleasure from a ride on the iron horse, but the throngs[1] of staring palefaces disturbed and troubled us.

On the train, fair women, with tottering babies on each arm, stopped their haste and scrutinized[2] the children of absent mothers. Large men, with heavy bundles in their hands, halted nearby, and riveted their glassy blue eyes upon us.

---

1. *Throngs* are great crowds.
2. If you *scrutinize* something, you look at it closely.

Vocabulary
anticipate (an tis′ ə pāt′) *v.* to look forward to; expect

The Land of Red Apples

I sank deep into the corner of my seat, for I resented being watched. Directly in front of me, children who were no larger than I hung themselves upon the backs of their seats, with their bold white faces toward me. Sometimes they took their forefingers out of their mouths and pointed at my moccasined feet. Their mothers, instead of reproving such rude curiosity, looked closely at me, and attracted their children's further notice to my blanket. This embarrassed me, and kept me constantly on the verge of tears.

I sat perfectly still, with my eyes downcast, daring only now and then to shoot long glances around me. Chancing to turn to the window at my side, I was quite breathless upon seeing one familiar object. It was the telegraph pole which strode[3] by at short paces. Very near my mother's dwelling, along the edge of a road thickly bordered with wild sunflowers, some poles like these had been planted by white men. Often I had stopped, on my way down the road, to hold my ear against the pole, and, hearing its low moaning, I used to wonder what the paleface had done to hurt it. Now I sat watching for each pole that glided by to be the last one. . . .

It was night when we reached the school grounds. The lights from the windows of the large buildings fell upon some of the icicled trees that stood beneath them. We were led toward an open door, where the brightness of the lights within flooded out over the heads of the excited palefaces who blocked the way. My body trembled more from fear than from the snow I trod[4] upon.

Entering the house, I stood close against the wall. The strong glaring light in the large whitewashed room dazzled my eyes. The noisy hurrying of hard shoes upon a bare wooden floor increased the whirring in my ears. My only safety seemed to be in keeping next to the wall. As I was wondering in which direction to escape from all this confusion, two warm hands grasped me firmly, and in the same moment I was tossed high in midair. A rosy-cheeked paleface woman caught me in her arms. I was both frightened and insulted by such trifling. I stared into her eyes, wishing her to let me stand on my own feet, but she jumped me up and down with increasing enthusiasm. My mother had never made a plaything of her wee daughter. Remembering this I began to cry aloud.

They misunderstood the cause of my tears, and placed me at a white table loaded with food. There our party were united again. As I did not hush my crying, one of the older ones whispered to me, "Wait until you are alone in the night."

---

3. *Strode* is the past tense of *stride,* to walk with long steps that are bold or lively.

4. *Trod* is the past tense of *tread,* to step on or walk across.

Vocabulary

resent (ri zent′) *v.* to feel anger toward a person or thing

reprove (ri proov′) *v.* to scold

verge (vurj) *n.* the point just before something occurs or begins; the edge

trifling (trī′ fling) *n.* the act of treating or handling something as if it had little value or importance

It was very little I could swallow besides my sobs that evening.

"Oh, I want my mother and my brother Dawee! I want to go to my aunt!" I pleaded; but the ears of the palefaces could not hear me.

From the table we were taken along an upward incline[5] of wooden boxes, which I learned afterward to call a stairway. At the top was a quiet hall, dimly lighted. Many narrow beds were in one straight line down the entire length of the wall. In them lay sleeping brown faces, which peeped just out of the coverings. I was tucked into bed with one of the tall girls, because she talked to me in my mother tongue[6] and seemed to soothe me.

I had arrived in the wonderful land of rosy skies, but I was not happy, as I had thought I should be. My long

These three Native American girls were students at the Carlisle Indian School in Pennsylvania prior to 1900. They are also pictured on page 55.
Viewing the photograph: How have they changed?

___

5. An *incline* is a surface that goes up at an angle, such as a ramp.
6. Your *mother tongue* is your first language, the one you learned while growing up.

travel and the <u>bewildering</u> sights had exhausted me. I fell asleep, heaving deep, tired sobs. My tears were left to dry themselves in streaks, because neither my aunt nor my mother was near to wipe them away.

___

Vocabulary
bewildering (bi wil′ dər ing) *adj.* very confusing

Responding to Literature

PERSONAL RESPONSE

How do you feel about the way Zitkala-Ša was treated? Are you affected by how she felt? Explain.

Analyzing Literature

RECALL

1. Where are the children on the train going, and with whom?
2. What do the people on the train do that frightens or upsets Zitkala-Ša?
3. What do the children expect life in the "red apple country" to be like?
4. How is Zitkala-Ša treated when she reaches her destination?

INTERPRET

5. How do the children feel before their journey? How, do you think, do they feel after their journey ends? Explain.
6. Do you think that the people on the train are usually as rude as they behave toward Zitkala-Ša? Explain.
7. What do you think the Native American children were told about their destination before their journey?
8. Does the school seem to be a pleasant place? Explain.

EVALUATE AND CONNECT

9. Zitkala-Ša describes the telegraph poles from the **point of view** (see page R6) of a small child. What is another object or event in the selection that is described from this point of view?
10. Have you ever become used to a situation that was, at first, very upsetting? How do you think Zitkala-Ša felt after a week at school? Why?

LITERARY ELEMENTS

Description

Description includes details that help a reader imagine people, places, things, and events. These details often appeal to the reader's senses of sight, hearing, touch, taste, and smell. Zitkala-Ša describes details that a small child would notice. The white people on the train stare at her with "glassy blue eyes." The trees at the school are "icicled," and the noise of shoes on wooden floors increases the "whirring" in her ears.

1. Think about other descriptive details in "The Land of Red Apples." Which details are things a young child might notice?

2. To which senses do the details appeal?

● See **Literary Terms Handbook,** p. R2.

Plains Indian moccasins.

Extending Your Response

Writing About Literature

Summarizing Information Look back at the journal entry you wrote for the **Focus Activity** on page 54. Then look for places in the selection where Zitkala-Ša talks about how she felt. Write a paragraph summarizing her feelings and the reasons for them. Use information from the selection.

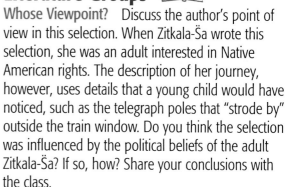

Find out more about Native American history. Browse the Web under *Native Americans—Sioux* and *Heard Museum,* a museum of Native American cultures and art. Share your research with the class.

Creative Writing

Details Zitkala-Ša describes the passengers on the "iron horse." What if you were writing a **fictional** story about children being sent away on a long journey? What details would be interesting in such a story? Write a paragraph telling what details you would invent.

Literature Groups

Whose Viewpoint? Discuss the author's point of view in this selection. When Zitkala-Ša wrote this selection, she was an adult interested in Native American rights. The description of her journey, however, uses details that a young child would have noticed, such as the telegraph poles that "strode by" outside the train window. Do you think the selection was influenced by the political beliefs of the adult Zitkala-Ša? If so, how? Share your conclusions with the class.

Save your work for your portfolio.

Skill Minilesson

VOCABULARY • ANTONYMS

Antonyms are words that mean the opposite of each other. *Big* and *small* are antonyms. Some words have many antonyms. *Happy* has *unhappy.* It also has *sad, miserable, discontented, gloomy,* and many more. Some words, such as *rabbit* or *wooden,* don't have any antonyms at all.

PRACTICE Think about each word on the left. Then choose the letter of the best antonym.

1. **anticipate**
   a. choose   b. wonder   c. dread
2. **resent**
   a. fear   b. approve   c. dislike
3. **trifling**
   a. valuing   b. wasting   c. teasing
4. **bewildering**
   a. strange   b. simple   c. puzzling
5. **reprove**
   a. guess   b. praise   c. ignore

AUTOBIOGRAPHY

"The Land of Red Apples" tells of one event in the life of its author, Zitkala-Ša. It is taken from her autobiography, *The School Days of an Indian Girl*. An autobiography is the story of someone's life written by the person who lived it. An autobiography is one kind of nonfiction. It's about people who really lived and events that really happened rather than people and events the writer makes up.

● For more about nonfiction, see **Literary Terms Handbook,** p. R6.

A Lakota girl.

When you read an autobiography, look for the following elements:

POINT OF VIEW Autobiographies are written from the first-person point of view. The writer is the "I" of the story, and any thoughts or feelings described are those of the writer. It is this point of view that helps us to feel involved in the writer's life.

A STORY An autobiography isn't *just* facts. The facts alone would be about as interesting to read as a phone book. The writer of an autobiography shapes the raw material of facts into a story with a beginning, a middle, and an end. This means you can read autobiographies just the way you read other stories.

CHRONOLOGICAL ORDER Chronological order means that the events are told in the order in which they happened. This is how most autobiographies are organized. A writer may begin with his or her childhood or family background and continue forward in time.

AUTHOR'S PURPOSE Unlike a diary, an autobiography is written to be shared. Writers may want to communicate important ideas about their lives or to explain why they made certain decisions.

You can see many elements of an autobiography in just a paragraph of "The Land of Red Apples."

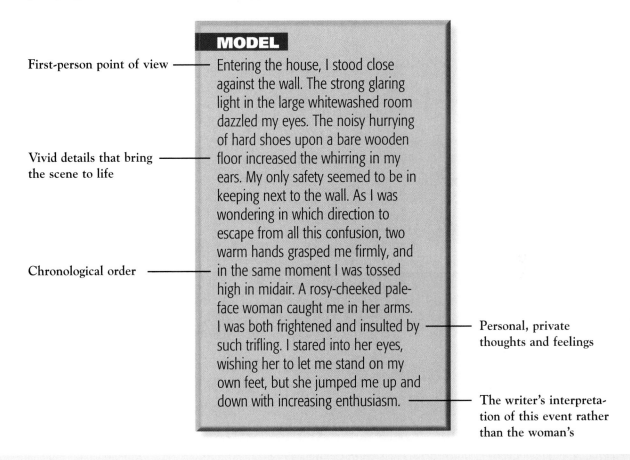

First-person point of view ——————

Vivid details that bring the scene to life ——————

Chronological order ——————

MODEL

Entering the house, I stood close against the wall. The strong glaring light in the large whitewashed room dazzled my eyes. The noisy hurrying of hard shoes upon a bare wooden floor increased the whirring in my ears. My only safety seemed to be in keeping next to the wall. As I was wondering in which direction to escape from all this confusion, two warm hands grasped me firmly, and in the same moment I was tossed high in midair. A rosy-cheeked pale-face woman caught me in her arms. I was both frightened and insulted by such trifling. I stared into her eyes, wishing her to let me stand on my own feet, but she jumped me up and down with increasing enthusiasm.

—————— Personal, private thoughts and feelings

—————— The writer's interpretation of this event rather than the woman's

DETAILS Writers make their autobiographies interesting by providing different kinds of details.
- facts about the writer's life
- descriptions of people and places
- feelings and opinions
- important anecdotes about the writer's life

ONE INTERPRETATION The writer of an autobiography offers just one interpretation of events. Events can always be interpreted in more than one way. Think about the different views on your school that you, a first-grade student, and your teacher would have.

THE PERSONAL MADE PUBLIC Autobiographies are personal stories. When you are reading one, you may feel like the writer's friend—someone trusted with the writer's private thoughts and feelings. You may feel a bond with the writer, even if the writer's life is very different from your own. You may recognize some of your own thoughts, feelings, and conflicts in the writer's life story.

Active Reading Strategies

Tips for Reading Autobiographies

Active readers react and respond to the text as they read. Use the suggestions below to actively read autobiographies and other nonfiction narratives.

● For more about these and other reading strategies, see **Reading Handbook,** pp. R63–R94.

CONNECT

The selection may remind you of thoughts, feelings, or experiences you have had. You may feel connected to the feelings or ideas the author is expressing.

Ask Yourself . . .

● Does this remind me of something I have experienced?

● Have I ever felt this way, too?

● Have I ever handled a problem like this?

QUESTION

Check that you understand what you have read. Go back and reread sentences if their meaning is unclear. Make sure that new information fits with what you have already read.

Ask Yourself . . .

● Do I understand what is happening?

● Have I read this correctly?

● Why is this happening?

● Does this make sense based on what I have already read?

● What might happen next?

EVALUATE

Follow the writer's thoughts throughout the selection. Ask yourself why the writer interacts with other people and responds to events as he or she does. Think about how the writer's feelings and opinions influence the selection.

Ask Yourself . . .

- Do I see the writer's feelings in the comments he or she makes?

- Why does the writer have this opinion?

- Do I agree with the opinions voiced here?

RESPOND

Think about your reactions as you read and after you finish reading the selection.

Ask Yourself . . .

- How am I reacting to what I have read?

- What surprises me about the selection?

- To whom would I recommend this autobiography? Why?

APPLYING THE STRATEGIES

Read "Primary Lessons" from Judith Ortiz Cofer's autobiography *Silent Dancing.* Use the Active Reading notes in the margins as you read. Write your responses on a separate piece of paper to look over when you have finished reading.

Before You Read
Primary Lessons

MEET
JUDITH ORTIZ COFER

Judith Ortiz Cofer says that as a child she lived in "a bubble created by my Puerto Rican parents in a home where two cultures and languages became one. I learned to listen to the English from the television with one ear while I heard my mother and father speaking in Spanish with the other." When her father was at sea serving in the U.S. Navy, her family lived in Puerto Rico. At other times, they lived in Paterson, New Jersey.

Judith Ortiz Cofer was born in 1952. This selection is from Silent Dancing: A Partial Remembrance of a Puerto Rican Childhood, *which was published in 1990.*

FOCUS ACTIVITY

Do you remember your first day of school? How old were you? How was it like or unlike what you expected?

Make a Web
In the center, write the words *First Day of School.* In outer circles, write details you remember about what happened on this day and how you felt about it.

Setting a Purpose
Read "Primary Lessons" to find out about the author's first school experiences.

BACKGROUND

The Time and Place
"Primary Lessons" takes place in Puerto Rico in the late 1950s. Puerto Rico is a commonwealth of the United States. It is a tropical island in the Caribbean Sea about one thousand miles southeast of Florida.

VOCABULARY PREVIEW

emerge (i murj′) *v.* to come out; p. 66
chaos (kā′ os) *n.* complete confusion and disorder; p. 66
defiance (di fī′ əns) *n.* bold resistance to authority; p. 66
indifference (in dif′ ər əns) *n.* a lack of feeling or concern; p. 67
yearning (yur′ ning) *n.* a strong feeling of longing: p. 68
unique (ū nēk′) *adj.* having no like or equal; p. 70
unmindful (un mīnd′ fəl) *adj.* not aware; p. 71
relish (rel′ ish) *v.* to take pleasure in; enjoy; p. 71
mimicry (mim′ ik rē) *n.* the act of copying closely; imitation; p. 71

El Sol Asombre, 1989. Rafael Ferrer. Oil on canvas, 60 x 72 in. The Butler Institute of American Art, Youngstown, OH.

Primary Lessons

Judith Ortiz Cofer ∼

My mother walked me to my first day at school at La Escuela
Segundo Ruiz Belvis,[1] named after the Puerto Rican patriot
born in our town. I remember yellow cement with green trim.
All the classrooms had been painted these colors to identify
them as government property. This was true all over the Island.

---

1. *La Escuela Segundo* (lä   es kwä′ lə   sä goon′ dō) *Ruiz Belvis* (rōō′ ēz   bel′ vēs)

Primary Lessons

ACTIVE READING MODEL

QUESTION

Where is Judith Ortiz Cofer staying?

QUESTION

Why does Cofer say she had a "gypsy lifestyle"?

EVALUATE

Is Cofer's argument for staying home a good one? Why or why not?

Everything was color-coded, including the children, who wore uniforms from first through twelfth grade. We were a midget army in white and brown, led by the hand to our battleground. From practically every house in our barrio[2] emerged a crisply ironed uniform inhabited by the wild creatures we had become over a summer of running wild in the sun.

At my grandmother's house where we were staying until my father returned to Brooklyn Yard in New York and sent for us, it had been complete chaos, with several children to get ready for school. My mother had pulled my hair harder than usual while braiding it, and I had dissolved into a pool of total self-pity. I wanted to stay home with her and *Mamá,* to continue listening to stories in the late afternoon, to drink *café con leche*[3] with them, and to play rough games with my many cousins. I wanted to continue living the dream of summer afternoons in Puerto Rico, and if I could not have that, then I wanted to go back to Paterson, New Jersey, back to where I imagined our apartment waited, peaceful and cool for the three of us to return to our former lives. Our gypsy lifestyle had convinced me, at age six, that one part of life stops and waits for you while you live another for a while—and if you don't like the present, you can always return to the past. Buttoning me into my stiff blouse while I tried to squirm away from her, my mother tried to explain to me that I was a big girl now and should try to understand that, like all the other children my age, I had to go to school.

"What about him?" I yelled pointing at my brother who was lounging on the tile floor of our bedroom in his pajamas, playing quietly with a toy car.

"He's too young to go to school, you know that. Now stay still." My mother pinned me between her thighs to button my skirt, as she had learned to do from *Mamá,* from whose grip it was impossible to escape.

"It's not fair, it's not fair. I can't go to school here. I don't speak Spanish." It was my final argument, and it failed miserably because I was shouting my defiance in the language I claimed not to speak. Only I knew what I meant by saying in Spanish that I did not speak Spanish. I had spent my early childhood in the U.S. where I lived in a bubble

---

2. *Barrio* (bä′ rē ō) refers to a Hispanic neighborhood.
3. *Café con leche* (kä fā′ kōn lä′ chā) is coffee with milk.

Vocabulary

emerge (i murj′) *v.* to come out
chaos (kā′ os) *n.* complete confusion and disorder
defiance (di fī′ əns) *n.* bold resistance to authority

ACTIVE READING MODEL

created by my Puerto Rican parents in a home where two cultures and languages became one. I learned to listen to the English from the television with one ear while I heard my mother and father speaking in Spanish with the other. I thought I was an ordinary American kid—like the children on the shows I watched—and that everyone's parents spoke a secret second language at home. When we came to Puerto Rico right before I started first grade, I switched easily to Spanish. It was the language of fun, of summertime games. But school—that was a different matter.

I made one last desperate attempt to make my mother see reason: "Father will be very angry. You know that he wants us to speak good English." My mother, of course, ignored me as she dressed my little brother in his playclothes. I could not believe her <u>indifference</u> to my father's wishes. She was usually so careful about our safety and the many other areas that he was forever reminding her about in his letters. But I was right, and she knew it. Our father spoke to us in English as much as possible, and he corrected my pronunciation constantly—not "jes" but

QUESTION

What do readers learn about Cofer's father?

Library on Wheels. Puerto Rico, 1953.

Vocabulary
indifference (in dif′ ər əns) *n.* a lack of feeling or concern

Primary Lessons

ACTIVE READING MODEL

QUESTION

What are some of Cofer's fears?

CONNECT

Have you ever felt comforted by seeing others with the same problem you have?

QUESTION

What does Cofer mean by the term *child-proof?*

QUESTION

What does the teacher want the student to do?

EVALUATE

How does Cofer feel about the slipper procedure?

"y-es." Y-es, sir. How could she send me to school to learn Spanish when we would be returning to Paterson in just a few months?

But, of course, what I feared was not language, but loss of freedom. At school there would be no playing, no stories, only lessons. It would not matter if I did not understand a word, and I would not be allowed to make up my own definitions. I would have to learn silence. I would have to keep my wild imagination in check. Feeling locked into my stiffly starched uniform, I only sensed all this. I guess most children can intuit their loss of childhood's freedom on that first day of school. It is separation anxiety[4] too, but mother is just the guardian of the "play-ground" of our early childhood.

The sight of my cousins in similar straits[5] comforted me. We were marched down the hill of our barrio where *Mamá's* robin-egg-blue house stood at the top. I must have glanced back at it with yearning. *Mamá's* house—a place built for children—where anything that could be broken had already been broken by my grandmother's early batch of off-spring (they ranged in age from my mother's oldest sisters to my uncle who was six months older than me). Her house had long since been made child-proof. It had been a perfect summer place. And now it was September—the cruelest month for a child.

La Mrs., as all the teachers were called, waited for her class of first-graders at the door of the yellow and green classroom. She too wore a uniform: it was a blue skirt and a white blouse. This teacher wore black high heels with her "standard issue." I remember this detail because when we were all seated in rows she called on one little girl and pointed to the back of the room where there were shelves. She told the girl to bring her a shoebox from the bottom shelf. Then, when the box had been placed in her hands, she did something unusual. She had the lit-tle girl kneel at her feet and take the pointy high heels off her feet and replace them with a pair of satin slippers from the shoebox. She told the group that every one of us would have a chance to do this if we behaved in her class. Though confused about the prize, I soon felt caught up in the competition to bring *La Mrs.* her slippers in the morning. Children fought over the privilege.

---

4. When you *intuit* (in tōo′ it) something, no one teaches or explains it to you; you just know it. *Separation anxiety* is the fear and worry that some people feel when they are separated from their loved ones.
5. Here, *straits* means "a troublesome or difficult situation."

Vocabulary
yearning (yur′ ning) *n.* a strong feeling of longing

Judith Ortiz Cofer ∿

Our first lesson was English. In Puerto Rico, every child has to take twelve years of English to graduate from school. It is the law. In my parents' schooldays, all subjects were taught in English. The U.S. Department of Education had specified that as U.S. territory, the Island had to be "Americanized," and to accomplish this task, it was necessary for the Spanish language to be replaced in one generation through the teaching of English in all schools. My father began his school day by saluting the flag of the United States and singing "America" and "The Star-Spangled Banner" by rote, without understanding a word of what he was saying. The logic[6] behind this system was that, though the children did not understand the English words, they would remember the rhythms. Even the games the teacher's manuals required them to play became absurd adaptations.[7] "Here We Go Round the Mulberry Bush" became "Here We Go Round the Mango Tree." I have heard about the confusion caused by the use of a primer[8] in which the sounds of animals were featured. The children were forced to accept that a rooster says *cockadoodledoo*, when they knew perfectly well from hearing their own roosters each morning that in Puerto Rico a rooster says *cocorocó*.[9] Even the vocabulary of their pets was changed; there are still family stories circulating about the bewilderment of a first-grader coming home to try to teach his dog to speak in English. The policy of assimilation by immersion failed on the Island. Teachers adhered to it on paper, substituting their own materials for the texts, and no one took their English home. In due time, the program was minimized[10] to the one class in English per day that I encountered when I took my seat in *La Mrs.*'s first-grade class.

Catching us all by surprise, she stood very straight and tall in front of us and began to sing in English: "Pollito—Chicken, Gallina—Hen, Lápiz—Pencil, Y Pluma—Pen."

"Repeat after me, children: Pollito—Chicken," she commanded in her heavily accented English that only I understood, being the only child in the room who had ever been exposed to the language. But I too remained silent. No use making waves, or showing off. Patiently *La Mrs.* sang her song and gestured for us to join in. At some point it must

QUESTION

Does the teaching method described here seem like a good one? Why or why not?

---

6. If you do a thing *by rote,* you do it without thinking about it, as if you were a machine. *Logic* involves a lot of thought to make sense of something.
7. *Absurd* means "ridiculous." An *adaptation* is something that is changed to meet the needs of a certain situation.
8. A *primer* (prim′ ər) is a book for teaching children to read.
9. *cocorocó* (kō kō rō kō′)
10. This *policy* is the method of teaching English by conducting all school work in English. After a while, the program was cut back, or *minimized,* until only one class each day was all-English.

Judith Ortiz Cofer as a child.

EVALUATE

What does Cofer mean when she says that "everyone is a second-class citizen"?

have dawned on the class that this silly routine was likely to go on all day if we did not "repeat after her." It was not her fault that she had to follow the rule in her teacher's manual stating that she must teach English *in* English, and that she must not translate, but must repeat her lesson in English until the children "begin to respond" more or less "unconsciously." This was one of the vestiges of the regimen followed by her predecessors[11] in the last generation. To this day I can recite "Pollito—Chicken" mindlessly, never once pausing to visualize chicks, hens, pencils, or pens.

I soon found myself crowned "teacher's pet" without much effort on my part. I was a privileged child in her eyes simply because I lived in "Nueva York," and because my father was in the Navy. His name was an old one in our pueblo, associated with once-upon-a-time landed people and long-gone money. Status is judged by <u>unique</u> standards in a culture where, by definition, everyone is a second-class citizen. Remembrance of past glory is as good as titles and money. Old families living in decrepit old houses rank over factory workers living in modern comfort in cement boxes—all the same. The professions raise a person out of the dreaded "sameness" into a niche of status, so that teachers, nurses, and everyone who went to school for a job were given the honorifics of *El Míster* or *La Mrs.*[12] by the common folks, people who were likely to be making more money in American factories than the poorly paid educators and government workers.

My first impression of the hierarchy[13] began with my teacher's shoe-changing ceremony and the exaggerated respect she received from our

---

11. *[vestiges . . . predecessors]* In other words, this repetition was one of the last remains of the old "all-English" system that earlier teachers had used.
12. The *professions* are occupations that require special training, such as law, medicine, and education. In Spanish, adding *el* or *la* (which mean "the") to *Mr.* or *Mrs.* is a sign of respect.
13. A *hierarchy* (hī ər är′ kē) is a ranking of people or things based on certain standards.

Vocabulary
unique (ū nēk′) *adj.* having no like or equal

parents. *La Mrs.* was always right, and adults scrambled to meet her requirements. She wanted all our schoolbooks covered in the brown paper now used for paperbags (used at that time by the grocer to wrap meats and other foods). That first week of school the grocer was swamped with requests for paper which he gave away to the women. That week and the next, he wrapped produce in newspapers. All school projects became family projects. It was considered disrespectful at *Mamá's* house to do homework in privacy. Between the hours when we came home from school and dinner time, the table was shared by all of us working together with the women hovering in the background. The teachers communicated directly with the mothers, and it was a matri-archy[14] of far-reaching power and influence.

There was a black boy in my first-grade classroom who was also the teacher's pet but for a different reason than I: I did not have to do any-thing to win her favor; he would do anything to win a smile. He was as black as the cauldron that *Mamá* used for cooking stew and his hair was curled into tight little balls on his head—*pasitas*,[15] like little raisins glued to his skull, my mother had said. There had been some talk at *Mamá's* house about this boy; Lorenzo was his name. I later gathered that he was the grandson of my father's nanny. Lorenzo lived with Teresa, his grandmother, having been left in her care when his mother took off for "Los Nueva Yores" shortly after his birth. And they were poor. Everyone could see that his pants were too big for him—hand-me-downs—and his shoe soles were as thin as paper. Lorenzo seemed unmindful of the giggles he caused when he jumped up to erase the board for *La Mrs.* and his baggy pants rode down to his thin hips as he strained up to get every stray mark. He seemed to relish playing the lit-tle clown when she asked him to come to the front of the room and sing his phonetic version of "o-bootifool, forpashios-keeis" leading the class in our incomprehensible[16] tribute to the American flag. He was a bright, loving child, with a talent for song and mimicry that everyone com-mented on. He should have been chosen to host the PTA show that year instead of me.

ACTIVE READING MODEL

CONNECT

Have you ever made covers for books? What did you use?

CONNECT

Is this how you do your homework?

QUESTION

Why does the class giggle when Lorenzo jumps up to erase the board?

CONNECT

Have you ever sung something when you didn't understand the words?

QUESTION

Why does Cofer think Lorenzo should have been chosen for the PTA show?

---

14. In a *matriarchy* women have the greatest authority.
15. *Pasitas* (pə sē′ təs) means "raisins."
16. *Phonetic* (fə net′ ik) means "having to do with speech sounds." *Incomprehensible* means "difficult or impossible to understand."

Vocabulary
unmindful (un mīnd′ fəl) *adj.* not aware
relish (rel′ ish) *v.* to take pleasure in; enjoy
mimicry (mim′ ik rē) *n.* the act of copying closely; imitation

Primary Lessons

At recess one day, I came back to the empty classroom to get something, my cup? My nickel for a drink from the kioskman? I don't remember. But I remember the conversation my teacher was having with another teacher. I remember because it concerned me, and because I memorized it so that I could ask my mother to explain what it meant.

"He is a funny *negrito*, and, like a parrot, he can repeat anything you teach him. But his *mamá* must not have the money to buy him a suit."

"I kept Rafaelito's First Communion suit; I bet Lorenzo could fit in it. It's white with a bow-tie," the other teacher said.

"But, Marisa," laughed my teacher, "in that suit, Lorenzo would look like a fly drowned in a glass of milk."

Both women laughed. They had not seen me crouched at the back of the room, digging into my schoolbag. My name came up then.

"What about the Ortiz girl? They have money."

"I'll talk to her mother today. The superintendent, *El Americano* from San Juan, is coming down for the show. How about if we have her say her lines in both Spanish and English."

The conversation ends there for me. My mother took me to Mayagüez[17] and bought me a frilly pink dress and two crinoline petticoats[18] to wear underneath so that I looked like a pink and white parachute with toothpick legs sticking out. I learned my lines, "Padres, maestros, Mr. Leonard, bienvenidos[19]/ Parents, teachers, Mr. Leonard, welcome . . ." My first public appearance. I took no pleasure in it. The words were formal and empty. I had simply memorized them. My dress pinched me at the neck and arms, and made me itch all over.

I had asked my mother what it meant to be a "mosca en un vaso de leche,"[20] a fly in a glass of milk. She had laughed at the image, explaining that it meant being "different," but it wasn't something I needed to worry about.

Did You Know?
A *kiosk* is a small structure with one or more open sides, such as a newsstand or bus shelter.

CONNECT

How would you feel if you overheard teachers discussing your family?

CONNECT

Do you understand what Cofer feels?

RESPOND

Do you agree with Cofer's mother?

---

17. *Mayagüez* (mī′ ə gwez′) is a city in western Puerto Rico.
18. *Crinoline petticoats* are half-slips made of stiff fabric that give a skirt or dress more fullness.
19. *Padres* (pä′ drās), *maestros* (mīs′ trōs), *bienvenidos* (byen′ ve nē′ dōs)
20. *Mosca en un vaso de leche* (mäs′ kə en ōōn vä′ sō dā lā′ chä)

Responding to Literature

PERSONAL RESPONSE

- ◆ What feelings did you have as you finished the story?
- ◆ Was Judith Ortiz Cofer's first day of school like yours? In what ways? Use your web from the **Focus Activity** on page 64.

Active Reading Response

Look back at the strategies described in the **Active Reading Model** notes. Which strategy helped you most? How did it help you?

Analyzing Literature

RECALL

1. What reasons does Cofer give for not wanting to go to school in Puerto Rico? What are her real reasons?
2. What do the children take turns doing for their teacher? Why does Cofer want to do it?
3. What is the native language of Puerto Rico? What other language did every child have to learn in school? Why?
4. How does Cofer become "teacher's pet"?

INTERPRET

5. How do you think Cofer feels about her life back in the United States?
6. Why do both students and parents do anything that the teacher asks?
7. Does Cofer seem to agree or disagree with the school's policy on English? Why?
8. How do you think Cofer feels about the "privileged" classes in Puerto Rico? What story events explain her feelings?

EVALUATE AND CONNECT

9. What **details** does Cofer provide that help readers understand the teacher in the story? Explain.
10. Would you have felt comfortable in Cofer's school? Why or why not?

LITERARY ELEMENTS

Characters

Characters are the people in stories. In fictional stories, the characters are made up. In autobiographies, the characters are real people. Just as in fictional stories, they are revealed to readers by how they act, think, talk, and feel. As we read, we may ask ourselves, what kind of person is this? Why does this character act as he or she does? What personality traits does this character have?

1. Name three important traits of the main character. Support your answer by referring to the selection.
2. Describe one adult character in the story. What do we learn from the character's words and actions?

● See **Literary Terms Handbook,** p. R2.

Literature and Writing

Writing About Literature

Viewpoint What details does Judith Ortiz Cofer provide about her first day of school? Does she describe the day as a child would experience it? What does she tell us about that day that she did not understand until she was an adult? Write a paragraph telling about Cofer's first day of school.

Personal Writing

Welcome to Our School! Think about your first day of school. What was the best and the hardest part of the day? What were you thinking and feeling? What did you notice in the classroom? Would you want to go through that day again? Why or why not? Write a paragraph about your first day of school.

Extending Your Response

Literature Groups

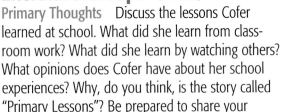

Primary Thoughts Discuss the lessons Cofer learned at school. What did she learn from classroom work? What did she learn by watching others? What opinions does Cofer have about her school experiences? Why, do you think, is the story called "Primary Lessons"? Be prepared to share your group's ideas with the class.

Performing

Rockin' to Learn With a partner, make up a song that teaches something to younger children, such as how to add, how to identify colors, or how to remember the names of the planets. You can make up your own melody or sing the song to a favorite tune. Practice the song with your partner. Then present it to a group of younger students.

Learning for Life

Hierarchies In "Primary Lessons," Cofer describes a hierarchy of authority. In the classroom, teachers have the highest authority, and mothers support the teachers' work. Ask the leader of a club or school group, such as student council, about the organization of the group. Who has the highest authority? Who works at the next level? Who is served by the organization? Take notes, and share what you learn with the class.

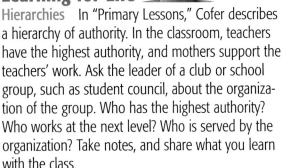

Reading Further

If you would like to read more autobiographies, try these:

Bill Peet: An Autobiography by Bill Peet
The Moon and I by Betsy Byars

💼 **Save your work for your portfolio.**

Skill Minilessons

GRAMMAR AND LANGUAGE • COMMON AND PROPER NOUNS

Remember that **proper nouns** name specific persons, places, or things. They begin with capital letters. **Common nouns** are general names of classes of persons, places, or things. They are not capitalized. Here are some examples of both.

	COMMON NOUNS	PROPER NOUNS
Person	pupil	*Lorenzo*
Places	island	Puerto Rico
	city, state	Paterson, New Jersey
Thing	language	Spanish

PRACTICE Practice showing the difference between proper and common nouns. Copy the words on this list, and capitalize the proper nouns.

1. school
2. mango tree
3. day
4. united states
5. english
6. new york
7. teacher
8. friday
9. july
10. grandmother

● For more about nouns, see **Language Handbook,** p. R26.

READING AND THINKING • AUTHOR'S PURPOSE

A writer usually has a **purpose** or goal for a piece of writing. Most writing has one of these purposes:

- to entertain readers
- to inform readers about something
- to persuade readers of something

What do you think Judith Ortiz Cofer is trying to achieve in "Primary Lessons"? Reread the selection. Use these questions to help you think about her purpose.

1. What kind of writing is this? What is the usual purpose of this kind of writing?

2. What do you learn? Is information the most important part of the selection?
3. Is the author presenting an issue that affects a lot of people? Do you think it is important to the author that you share her views?

PRACTICE Write a paragraph telling the author's purpose for "Primary Lessons." Use ideas and quotations from the selection to explain your answer.

● For more about author's purpose, see **Reading Handbook,** p. R87.

VOCABULARY • SPECIFIC WORDS

Some words, such as *disaster,* are strong words. *Furious* is a stronger word than *angry. Terrified* is a stronger word than *afraid.* If you feel *frantic,* you're not just *worried.* If we didn't have such strong words, we would have to use *very* a lot more than we do. "Primary Lessons" contains several strong words.

PRACTICE Write the vocabulary word from the story that belongs in each blank.

1. Three-year-old triplets don't just cause untidiness and noise; they create _____ .
2. There is no other necklace like that one. It's not just unusual; it's _____ .
3. After a week away, I wanted to go home. After six weeks, the feeling had become a _____ .
4. Her behavior was more than just disobedience. It was _____ .
5. He won't just enjoy the performance; he will _____ it.

Before You Read

from *The Lost Garden*

MEET LAURENCE YEP

Laurence Yep explains why teenagers enjoy his books: ". . . I'm always pursuing the theme of being an outsider— an alien—and many teenagers feel they're aliens." Yep's first book, *Sweetwater*, is a science fiction story about a young alien. Yep continued to explore this theme in books such as *Dragonwings* and *Child of the Owl*. Yep did years of research about Chinese-American history before writing *Dragonwings*. *Child of the Owl* is based on Yep's own experience of getting to know his Chinatown grandmother.

Laurence Yep was born in 1948. His autobiography, The Lost Garden, *was published in 1991.*

FOCUS ACTIVITY

Do you have a favorite grandparent or older family member? Why is this person interesting?

QuickWrite

How would you describe this person to others? Jot down some words and phrases that tell about this person.

Setting a Purpose

Read this selection to share the writer's memories of a special person.

BACKGROUND

The Time and Place   Laurence Yep attended school in San Francisco's Chinatown in the 1950s. You can find other "Chinatowns" in New York, Boston, and many other cities. People from China created these communities when they came to the United States. Filled with shops, restaurants, and uniquely styled buildings, the neighborhoods provided the things from "home" that the residents missed.

VOCABULARY PREVIEW

maneuver (mə noo′ vər) *v.* to move or handle skillfully; p. 79

incompetent (in kom′ pət ənt) *adj.* not having enough ability; not capable; p. 79

periodically (pēr′ ē od′ i kəl ē) *adv.* once in a while; p. 79

replenish (ri plen′ ish) *v.* to provide a new supply for; restock; p. 79

acute (ə kūt′) *adj.* sharp and strong or intense; p. 80

extravagantly (iks trav′ ə gənt lē) *adv.* going beyond reasonable limits; p. 81

irony (ī′ rə nē) *n.* an event or result that is the opposite of what was expected; p. 82

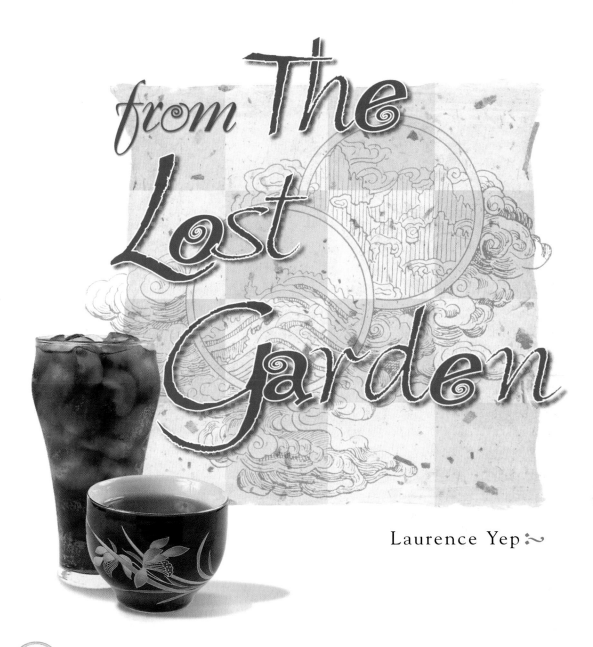

from The Lost Garden

Laurence Yep

My mother tells me that my grandmother dressed stylishly in the twenties; but by the time I knew her, she dressed "sensibly," usually wearing several sweaters and vests over a blouse or pajama top to be covered—when we went out—by a heavy cloth coat. As a result, when I hugged her, it was difficult to tell how much was her and how much was her wardrobe.

She lived in a studio apartment in an alley called Brooklyn Place. At one end of the studio apartment was a tiny shower and toilet; and at the other was a kitchenette into which my grandmother could barely squeeze. Every inch of space in the studio was accounted for.

Chinatown, San Francisco, mid-1900s.

times cookies, sometimes comic books.

Her "Chineseness" began with the smell of her studio apartment—a smell that clung even to her clothes when we went outside; and that I noticed on the clothes of some of the older Chinese. It was a mixture of tiger balm, a kind of cure-all salve,[2] and the incense sticks she would burn for the gods and goddesses on top of her bureau.

The incense sticks caused my mother no end of trouble when she tried to buy them for my grandmother. If the company changed the label, my grandmother would suspect that they were a different—and probably inferior—brand.

Between the door and the bathroom sat her phonograph player and Chinese records as well as her radio within reach of the bed. On the opposite wall was a cabinet and boxes neatly stacked with most of her possessions. Next to them was a small table with two chairs. On the table itself was a checkerboard cloth and a restaurant napkin dispenser.[1] Finally, on the other side of the kitchen doorway was her bureau with her statues and her gifts for any of her nine grandchildren who might visit—sometimes four silver quarters or other change, some-

Since she didn't have enough English and I didn't have enough Chinese, we couldn't talk about such things as the statues on her bureau. On the other hand, the plastic Jesus on our car dashboard was the "pretty lady with the beard." She could no more discuss America with me than I could discuss China with her.

Instead, what I learned, I picked up in a subtle fashion, soaking up things like a sponge so that years later I was able to use it in a book. It happened during those weekly walks with her, down the thirteen

---

1. *Dispense* means "to give out in portions." In restaurants, the napkin boxes are called *dispensers*.

2. *Balms* and *salves* are oils and ointments that heal or relieve pain. *Tiger balm* is used to relieve temporary muscle aches.

steps from her studio to the apartment porch and down the four steps to the sidewalk. She moved slowly but determinedly like the little engine that could, down Brooklyn Place, across busy Sacramento Street and down another alley that now has a sign calling it Hang Ah Alley but that was nameless then as far as I know.

I became fairly good at <u>maneuvering</u> to give her maximum support as she held onto my arm. Often, we would chat about the obstacles on the way—the bumps and cracks becoming almost like old friends in their familiarity.

We would head down Sacramento Street to Waverly Place and down a steeply slanting sidewalk to Uncle's. It was a typical old-timers' place with Formica[3] tables and elderly men in suits almost as old. Sometimes the suits would bag on the wearers as if their bodies had once been bigger—as if the wearer were shrinking with age. Food there was good if simple, plentiful, and cheap. (If you want to pay for food rather than for decor, throw away the tour books and gourmet guides[4] and look in Chinatown for the restaurants where the old-timers and families are eating.)

The waiter in a short-sleeve white shirt and bow tie would bring my grandmother a huge, steaming plate of rice heaped with freshly cooked *bok choy*—a kind of green vegetable that can come in a variety of sizes. My grandmother could be quite fussy about even that simple vegetable, preferring it when it was picked young with little yellow flowers still on the small stalks because it was most tender and juiciest then. At the restaurant, my grandmother would even send it back if she thought the chef had used too much oil. Oil, she liked to sniff, was what sloppy and <u>incompetent</u> cooks used to hide their mistakes.

My mother and I would get our orders, usually a veal cutlet dinner with mashed potatoes. Though my grandmother took Chinese food quite seriously—almost religiously, she had the opposite opinion of American food. One time when my second niece, Lisa, was having lunch with my grandmother, she was delighted to hear that Lisa's two favorite foods were catsup and mashed potatoes. She got a catsup bottle from the waiter and urged Lisa to mix the two together, creating a pink mess that Lisa dutifully ate.

We always topped off the meal with slices of orange custard pie. As if my mother were a little girl again, my grandmother would take a fork and scrape off the whipped cream from her pie and add it to my mother's portion. My mother never protested.

<u>Periodically</u> when we ate at Uncle's, my grandmother would <u>replenish</u> her napkin supply. Waiting until the waiter was

---

3. *Formica* (fôr mī′ kə) is a heat- and water-resistant plastic material that was commonly used in the 1950s and 1960s.
4. *Decor* is the way a place looks, including its design, colors, and style of furniture. *Gourmet guides* are books that tell you the best places to eat.

Vocabulary

maneuver (mə noo̅′ vər) *v.* to move or handle skillfully
incompetent (in kom′ pət ənt) *adj.* not having enough ability; not capable
periodically (pēr′ ē od′ i kəl ē) *adv.* once in a while
replenish (ri plen′ ish) *v.* to provide a new supply for; restock

out of sight, my grandmother would squeeze her fingers into the napkin dispenser so she could take out napkins by the handful. Treating the napkins as if they were sheaves of government secrets, my grandmother would slip them to my mother underneath the table so my mother could hide them in her large purse.

If she was feeling up to it, we might then make an expedition down to Grant Avenue—which could prove complicated because of the hoards of tourists. My grandmother, however, didn't mind them. In fact, it was as if they had spent all their money and traveled all the way across America simply to entertain her. It would have been better at those times if she could have spoken in Chinese; but for my sake, she would use English. Much to my acute embarrassment, she would point at a passing tourist only a yard away and announce in a loud voice to me, "Look at that funny red hair. Is it real?"

She treated the expensive art stores with the same enthusiasm. She would walk into a store that sold expensive jade or ivory carvings and act as if it were a museum, ignoring the frowns from owners and clerks until we had made a

Did You Know?
Jade is a green stone, and *ivory* comes from the tusks of elephants. Both have been used to make jewelry and carved ornaments.

complete circuit of their establishment. Eventually, though, we would reach her real goal and make her purchases—sometimes it was the store that sold Chinese sausage, *lop cheong*. Then we would retrace the route back to her apartment, observing more tourists on the way.

Occasionally we might also stop at her social club, where she would show off her family to the other club members. At the club, though, she liked to light an incense stick at the altar and say a silent prayer—something that I, a Catholic in those days, felt uncomfortable about.

As a result, I did my best to show that I was different, becoming one of those obnoxious[5] children who had to have a fork instead of chopsticks at a banquet in Chinatown—I didn't learn how to use chopsticks until I was twelve. I also insisted on having Coca-Cola instead of tea.

There are so many things that I did as a child that I regret now. My father gave me the wooden box with the cunning lock[6] that he used when he came to America. On the bottom were the original customs stickers;[7] but I managed to scrape most of them off.

Before my parents bought the store, they had lived near Chinatown, as did most Chinese Americans. As a result, my brother had gone to St. Mary's Grammar School. Technically, the school was a Catholic mission to convert Chinese Americans into Catholics. Uncle Francis's

---

5. *Obnoxious* means "very annoying and disagreeable."
6. Here, *cunning* means "sly and tricky."
7. U.S. officials put the *customs stickers* on the box to show that the father had paid the required duty taxes.

Vocabulary
acute (ə kūt′) *adj.* sharp and strong or intense

children had also gone there, so when it came to start kindergarten, my parents decided to enroll me there.

It wasn't always easy adjusting to Chinatown. Around the fourth grade, the nuns decided to imitate another school that their order[8] ran. During the daytime, that other school offered an hour of French instruction. Now in the late afternoon, after regular classes, our school building went from a Catholic school to a Chinese one. Chinese teachers moved into the classrooms and taught there. However, the nuns decided to institute an hour of Chinese during the regular school day.

The result was a disaster for me. I was placed in the dummies' class where simple Chinese words were taught with even simpler ones. However, we spoke no Chinese at home so I didn't even know the teacher's basic commands. As a result, I had to watch the other students and take out a book when they did or put it away.

The simplest thing, of course, would have been to learn those basic words. However, having been an A-student in the American part of the curriculum,[9] I resented being put into the dummies' class and forced to learn a foreign language.

Moreover, I hated the teacher who seemed to be this shrill witch who liked to beat children. To this day, I can't think

of calligraphy lessons without wincing. In calligraphy, which is the art of Chinese writing, we would practice the strokes of a character, trying to make it look as pretty as possible.

Did You Know?
The simplest meaning of *calligraphy* is "handwriting; penmanship," and it doesn't apply to Chinese writing only. People can do calligraphy in any language.

For those lessons, we bought special books of rice paper. Special inserts were placed behind them and then we got out our ink.

Now Chinese ink is as rich and black as poster paint. Scholars and true calligraphers have ink sticks which they mix themselves with water. They have a little ink stand with a well into which they put water and then rub the stick on the side until they have the ink blended the way they want. Most of the ink sticks also have a slight perfume smell.

However, schoolchildren simply buy their ink premixed in a bottle. You then bought a little container called a *mok-op* which was about the size of a woman's compact and came in various shapes and sizes. Some might be as simple as a plastic jar with a screw-on lid. Others might be made out of metal with a design on the top, some of them square, others circular. Inside was a wad of cotton that was soaked in ink that was so thick that you could keep adding water without diluting it noticeably. Into this you would dip your brush and trace the strokes of the characters.

One classmate extravagantly used a bottle of ink. Unfortunately, as the

---

8. An *order* is a religious group. Nuns from the same order have the same purpose, follow the same rules, and, sometimes, live together.

9. A *curriculum* includes all of the subjects taught at a school. When the narrator says "the American part," he means everything except foreign language studies.

Vocabulary
extravagantly (iks trav′ ə gənt lē) *adv.* going beyond reasonable limits

teacher passed by one day, my classmate or my teacher knocked it over, ruining the Chinese silk dress the teacher was wearing.

She lectured us angrily in broken English. I gather that she had little use for American-born Chinese who were all lazy and disrespectful. And I suppose by the standards back in China we probably were.

Resenting both the teacher and the situation, I went out of my way to pass the course but not learn Chinese. Each week, we had a new lesson in the reader that we were expected to memorize, recite aloud, and then write out. So each week, I memorized a new pattern of sounds like a song and a new pattern of pictures like a cartoon. I wound up doing more work than anyone else in that class but I achieved my purpose: I passed without learning Chinese. The irony, of course, is that even if I had learned Chinese in that class, I wouldn't necessarily have been able to hold a conversation with my grandmother. She spoke the *Say-yup*, or four districts, dialect—actually a subdialect from the Yan-ping district—while we were learning the *Sam-yup*, or three districts, dialect from Canton.

Chinese American students, San Francisco, mid-1900s.

Vocabulary

irony (ī′ rə nē) *n.* an event or result that is the opposite of what was expected

Responding to Literature

PERSONAL RESPONSE

Does this selection remind you of any of your own experiences? What memories of your own do you associate with feelings like those the author describes? Use your notes from the **Focus Activity** on page 76.

Analyzing Literature

RECALL AND INTERPRET

1. What were some of the things about Laurence Yep's grandmother that contributed to her "Chineseness"?

2. Although Yep and his grandmother could not speak each other's languages, he has strong memories of her. How did he and his grandmother come to know each other?

3. What things does the author wish he had done differently?

EVALUATE AND CONNECT

4. Do you think that the way Yep's school taught Chinese was effective? Why?

5. Yep refused to learn Chinese. Have you ever felt this way about something? Explain.

6. How important is it for people to learn about their origins and heritage? Is it important to learn the language of their parents or grandparents? Why?

LITERARY ELEMENTS

Sequence in Narration

In **narration,** events are usually described in **sequence,** the order in which they occur. In the selection from *The Lost Garden,* Yep tells about a typical walk with his grandmother. He describes their route through the neighborhood, their lunch, and their stroll afterwards. He uses words and phrases like *then, afterwards, on the way,* and *eventually* to indicate when things happen.

1. Give the sequence of events of a stroll by Yep and his grandmother down Grant Avenue (page 80).

2. Which words are clues that indicate sequence?

● See **Literary Terms Handbook,** p. R5.

Extending Your Response

Literature Groups

Learning Chinese   Laurence Yep says that even if he had learned Chinese in school, he probably would not have been able to talk to his grandmother in her dialect of that language. He seems, however, to regret the attitude he had then toward Chinese. What other things does he regret? Discuss why he feels this way. Share your conclusions.

Writing About Literature

Writing Questions for an Interview   If he had been able to hold a conversation with his grandmother, what are some questions Yep might have asked in order to learn more about her and her attitudes toward life? With a partner, make a list of questions you think are important.

COMPARING SELECTIONS

Primary Lessons and *from The Lost Garden*

COMPARE **CHARACTERS**

Which autobiography's main character reminds you most of yourself? Which feelings about school do you share? Consider your feelings and experiences and those of the author of one of these autobiographies. How are they alike? How are they different?

COMPARE **CONFLICTS**

The main characters deal with learning a second language in school in different ways. One cooperates and the other resists.

1. Discuss the conflicts in each story and each character's responses.
2. Which response do you think worked better? Why?

COMPARE **FAMILIES**

Imagine that you are the main character in either "Primary Lessons" or the selection from *The Lost Garden*.

- Plan a letter to a parent or grandparent of that character. You may make it a letter of complaint, thanks, appreciation, or apology.
- Think about the feelings that the author of each selection had toward the parent or grandparent.
- Then write the letter and share it with the class.

Reading and Thinking Skills

Cause-and-Effect Relationships

Imagine you are telling some friends about a movie you really liked. Your friends keep asking, "And then what happened?" as they try to follow the connections between the events in the story.

Stories are filled with cause-and-effect relationships. They tie together what happens. They explain the *reason* things are as they are or turn out as they do. A **cause** is something that happens that sets something else in motion. **Effects** are the results or outcomes.

To find out if there is a cause-and-effect relationship between two events, ask yourself: Did this happen because of something else? Sometimes clue words, such as *because, as a result, therefore, since, thus,* and *so,* let you know of a cause-and-effect relationship. Notice the cause-and-effect relationship in the following example from page 81 by Laurence Yep.

Cause ... the nuns decided to institute an hour of Chinese during the regular school day.	→	**Effect** The result was a disaster for me.

Readers know that the nuns' decision causes a "disaster" for the author. Notice the clue word "result," which indicates that the disaster is an outcome, or effect.

● For more about cause and effect, see **Reading Handbook,** p. R78.

ACTIVITY

Look for cause-and-effect relationships in this excerpt from the selection.

... we spoke no Chinese at home so I didn't even know the teacher's basic commands. As a result, I had to watch the other students and take out a book when they did or put it away.

1. According to this quotation, what causes Yep to have a problem at school?

2. What is the effect of this situation? How does he handle it?

Before You Read

from *Homesick*

MEET JEAN FRITZ

N o one is more patriotic than the one separated from his country," Jean Fritz once said. She knows what it's like. Her parents were missionaries in China, where she was born and spent her first thirteen years.

Often lonely as a child, Fritz enjoyed writing about children doing the things she dreamed of doing in the United States. Fritz's interest in writing continues. She has written more than forty-five books—most of them biographies of figures from American history and historical fiction.

Jean Fritz was born in 1915. This story, the first chapter in her autobiography, was published in 1982.

FOCUS ACTIVITY

Imagine that you and your family had to move to a foreign country. Think about what you would miss most about your life in the United States.

List Ideas
Jot down five things you would miss. Then circle the two most important ones. Discuss them with a partner.

Setting a Purpose
Read this selection to find out who is homesick and where he or she wishes to be.

BACKGROUND

The Time and Place
The story takes place in 1925 in Hankow, China. Hankow is now part of the city of Wuhan. People from many countries lived in Hankow at that time, and each foreign country had its own district within the city.

China in 1925.

VOCABULARY PREVIEW

sideline (sīd′ līn′) *n.* the side boundary line of a playing field; p. 89

flustered (flus′ tərd) *adj.* embarrassed, nervous, or confused; p. 91

unsanitary (un san′ ə ter′ ē) *adj.* dirty in a way that could cause disease; unclean; p. 92

solemn (sol′ əm) *adj.* serious; p. 93

jaunty (jôn′ tē) *adj.* lively and carefree; p. 94

gravely (grāv′ lē) *adv.* very seriously; p. 97

saunter (sôn′ tər) *v.* to walk in a leisurely way; stroll; p. 99

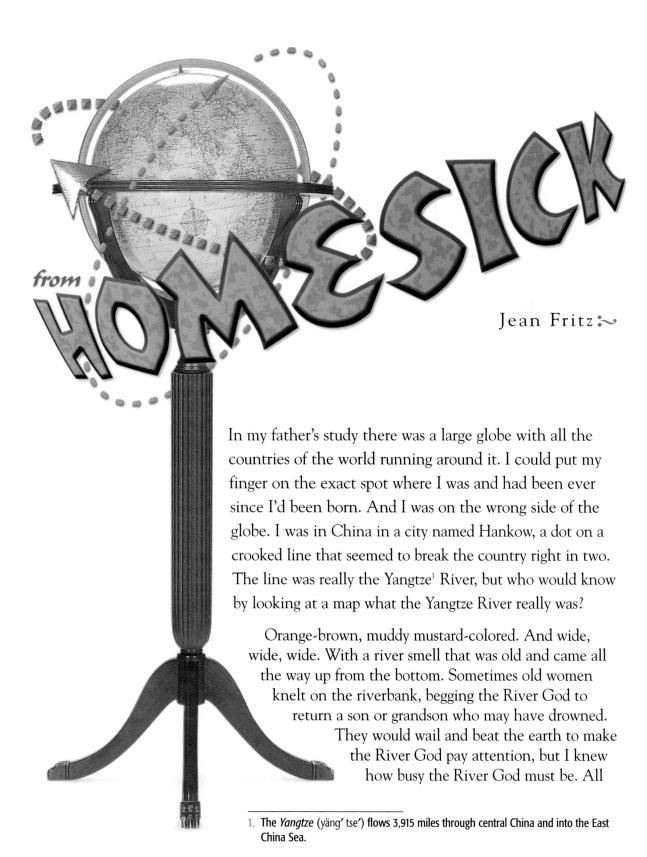

from HOMESICK

Jean Fritz

In my father's study there was a large globe with all the countries of the world running around it. I could put my finger on the exact spot where I was and had been ever since I'd been born. And I was on the wrong side of the globe. I was in China in a city named Hankow, a dot on a crooked line that seemed to break the country right in two. The line was really the Yangtze[1] River, but who would know by looking at a map what the Yangtze River really was?

Orange-brown, muddy mustard-colored. And wide, wide, wide. With a river smell that was old and came all the way up from the bottom. Sometimes old women knelt on the riverbank, begging the River God to return a son or grandson who may have drowned. They would wail and beat the earth to make the River God pay attention, but I knew how busy the River God must be. All

---

1. The *Yangtze* (yäng′ tse′) flows 3,915 miles through central China and into the East China Sea.

from HOMESICK

Did You Know?

A *junk* is a large, flat-bottomed ship that has four-sided sails. The *prow,* or front of the ship, is square, not pointed.

those people on the Yangtze River! Coolies[2] hauling water. Women washing clothes. Houseboats swarming with old people and young, chickens and pigs. Big crooked-sailed junks with eyes painted on their prows so they could see where they were going. I loved the Yangtze River, but, of course, I belonged on the other side of the world. In America with my grandmother.

Twenty-five fluffy little yellow chicks hatched from our eggs today, my grandmother wrote.

I wrote my grandmother that I had watched a Chinese magician swallow three yards of fire.

The trouble with living on the wrong side of the world was that I didn't feel like a *real* American.

For instance. I could never be president of the United States. I didn't want to be president; I wanted to be a writer. Still, why should there be a *law* saying that only a person born in the United States could be president? It was as if I wouldn't be American enough.

Actually, I was American every minute of the day, especially during school hours. I went to a British school and every morning we sang "God Save the King." Of course the British children loved singing about their gracious king. Ian Forbes stuck

out his chest and sang as if he were saving the king all by himself. Everyone sang. Even Gina Boss who was Italian. And Vera Sebastian who was so Russian she dressed the way Russian girls did long ago before the Revolution[3] when her family had to run away to keep from being killed.

But I wasn't Vera Sebastian. I asked my mother to write an excuse so I wouldn't have to sing, but she wouldn't do it. "When in Rome," she said, "do as the Romans do." What she meant was, "Don't make trouble. Just sing." So for a long time I did. I sang with my fingers crossed but still I felt like a traitor.

Then one day I thought: If my mother and father were really and truly in Rome, they wouldn't do what the Romans did at all. They'd probably try to get the Romans to do what *they* did, just as they were trying to teach the Chinese to do what Americans did. (My mother even gave classes in American manners.)

So that day I quit singing. I kept my mouth locked tight against the king of England. Our teacher, Miss Williams, didn't notice at first. She stood in front of the room, using a ruler for a baton, striking each syllable so hard it was as if she were making up for the times she had nothing to strike.

(Miss Williams was pinch-faced and bossy. Sometimes I wondered what had ever made her come to China. "Maybe to try and catch a husband," my mother said.

A husband! Miss Williams!)

"Make him vic-tor-i-ous," the class sang. It was on the strike of "vic" that Miss Williams noticed. Her eyes lighted

---

2. *Coolies* are unskilled, poorly paid laborers who often do hard work that no one else is willing to do.

3. The *Revolution* in Russia took place in 1917, when the czar was overthrown.

on my mouth and when we sat down, she pointed her ruler at me.

"Is there something wrong with your voice today, Jean?" she asked.

"No, Miss Williams."

"You weren't singing."

"No, Miss Williams. It is not my national anthem."

"It is the national anthem we sing here," she snapped. "You have always sung. Even Vera sings it."

I looked at Vera with the big blue bow tied on the top of her head. Usually I felt sorry for her but not today. At recess I might even untie that bow, I thought. Just give it a yank. But if I'd been smart, I wouldn't have been looking at Vera. I would have been looking at Ian Forbes and I would have known that, no matter what Miss Williams said, I wasn't through with the king of England.

Recess at the British School was nothing I looked forward to. Every day we played a game called prisoner's base, which was all running and shouting and shoving and catching. I hated the game, yet everyone played except Vera Sebastian. She sat on the sidelines under her blue bow like someone who had been dropped out of a history book. By recess I had forgotten my plans for that bow. While everyone was getting ready for the game, I was as usual trying to look as if I didn't care if I was the last one picked for a team or not. I was leaning against the high stone wall that ran around the schoolyard. I was looking up at a little white cloud skittering across the sky when all at once someone tramped

down hard on my right foot. Ian Forbes. Snarling bulldog face. Heel grinding down on my toes. Head thrust forward the way an animal might before it strikes.

"You wouldn't sing it. So say it," he ordered. "Let me hear you say it."

I tried to pull my foot away but he only ground down harder.

"Say what?" I was telling my face please not to show what my foot felt.

"*God save the king.* Say it. Those four words. I want to hear you say it."

Although Ian Forbes was short, he was solid and tough and built for fighting. What was more, he always won. You had only to look at his bare knees between the top of his socks and his short pants to know that he would win. His knees were square. Bony and unbeatable. So of course it was crazy for me to argue with him.

"Why should I?" I asked. "Americans haven't said that since George the Third."

He grabbed my right arm and twisted it behind my back.

"Say it," he hissed.

I felt the tears come to my eyes and I hated myself for the tears. I hated myself for not staying in Rome the way my mother had told me.

"I'll never say it," I whispered.

They were choosing sides now in the schoolyard and Ian's name was being called—among the first as always.

He gave my arm another twist. "You'll sing tomorrow," he snarled, "or you'll be bloody sorry."

As he ran off, I slid to the ground, my head between my knees.

Vocabulary

sideline (sīd′ līn′) *n.* the side boundary line of a playing field

from HOMESICK

Oh, Grandma, I thought, why can't I be there with you? I'd feed the chickens for you. I'd pump water from the well, the way my father used to do.

It would be almost two years before we'd go to America. I was ten years old now; I'd be twelve then. But how could I think about *years*? I didn't even dare to think about the next day. After school I ran all the way home, fast so I couldn't think at all.

Our house stood behind a high stone wall which had chips of broken glass sticking up from the top to keep thieves away. I flung open the iron gate and threw myself through the front door.

"I'm home!" I yelled.

Then I remembered that it was Tuesday, the day my mother taught an English class at the Y.M.C.A.[4] where my father was the director.

I stood in the hall, trying to catch my breath, and as always I began to feel small. It was a huge hall with ceilings so high it was as if they would have nothing to do with people. Certainly not with a mere child, not with me—the only child in the house. Once I asked my best friend, Andrea, if the hall made her feel little too. She said no. She was going to be a dancer and she loved space. She did a high kick to show how grand it was to have room.

Andrea Hull was a year older than I was and knew about everything sooner. She told me about commas, for instance, long before I took punctuation seriously. How could I write letters without commas? she asked. She made me so ashamed that for months I hung little wagging comma-tails all over the letters to my grandmother. She told me things that sounded so crazy I had to ask my mother if they were true. Like where babies came from. And that someday the whole world would end. My mother would frown when I asked her, but she always agreed that Andrea was right. It made me furious. How could she know such things and not tell me? What was the matter with grown-ups anyway?

I wished that Andrea were with me now, but she lived out in the country and I didn't see her often. Lin Nai-Nai, my amah,[5] was the only one around, and of course I knew she'd be there. It was her job to stay with me when my parents were out. As soon as she heard me come in, she'd called, "Tsai loushang," which meant that she was upstairs. She might be mending or ironing but most likely she'd be sitting by the window embroidering. And she was.

---

5. In some parts of Asia, *amah* means "nanny," a female servant who takes care of a family's children.

---

4. *Y.M.C.A.* stands for Young Men's Christian Association.   The Yangtze River.

90   THEME 1

She even had my embroidery laid out, for we had made a bargain. She would teach me to embroider if I would teach her English. I liked embroidering: the cloth stretched tight within my embroidery hoop while I filled in the stamped pattern with cross-stitches and lazy daisy flowers. The trouble was that lazy daisies needed French knots for their centers and I hated making French knots. Mine always fell apart, so I left them to the end. Today I had twenty lazy daisies waiting for their knots.

Lin Nai-Nai had already threaded my needle with embroidery floss.

"Black centers," she said, "for the yellow flowers."

I felt myself glowering.[6] "American flowers don't have centers," I said and gave her back the needle.

Lin Nai-Nai looked at me, puzzled, but she did not argue. She was different from other amahs. She did not even come from the servant class, although this was a secret we had to keep from the other servants who would have made her life miserable, had they known. She had run away from her husband when he had taken a second wife. She would always have been Wife Number One and the Boss no matter how many wives he had, but she would rather be no wife than head of a string of wives. She was modern. She might look old-fashioned, for her feet had been bound up[7] tight when she

was a little girl so that they would stay small, and now, like many Chinese women, she walked around on little stumps stuffed into tiny cloth shoes. Lin Nai-Nai's were embroidered with butterflies. Still, she believed in true love and one wife for one husband. We were good friends, Lin Nai-Nai and I, so I didn't know why I felt so mean.

She shrugged. "English lesson?" she asked, smiling.

I tested my arm to see if it still hurt from the twisting. It did. My foot too. "What do you want to know?" I asked.

We had been through the polite phrases—Please, Thank you, I beg your pardon, Excuse me, You're welcome, Merry Christmas (which she had practiced but hadn't had a chance to use since this was only October).

"If I meet an American on the street," she asked, "how do I greet him?"

I looked her straight in the eye and nodded my head in a greeting. "Sewing machine," I said. "You say, 'Sew-ing ma-chine.'"

She repeated after me, making the four syllables into four separate words. She got up and walked across the room, bowing and smiling. "Sew Ing Ma Shing."

Part of me wanted to laugh at the thought of Lin Nai-Nai maybe meeting Dr. Carhart, our minister, whose face would surely puff up, the way it always did when he was flustered. But part of me didn't want to laugh at all. I didn't like it when my feelings got tangled, so I ran downstairs and played chopsticks on the

---

6. *Glowering* means "scowling."
7. The Chinese once believed that it was beautiful for a woman to have tiny feet. The feet of many Chinese girls were tightly wrapped to limit their growth. This painful process resulted in very small but very badly deformed feet.

Vocabulary
flustered (flus′ tərd) *adj.* embarrassed, nervous, or confused

from HOMESICK

piano. Loud and fast. When my sore arm hurt, I just beat on the keys harder.

Then I went out to the kitchen to see if Yang Sze-Fu, the cook, would give me something to eat. I found him reading a Chinese newspaper, his eyes going up and down with the characters.[8] (Chinese words don't march across flat surfaces the way ours do; they drop down cliffs, one cliff after another from right to left across a page.)

"Can I have a piece of cinnamon toast?" I asked. "And a cup of cocoa?"

Yang Sze-Fu grunted. He was smoking a cigarette, which he wasn't supposed to do in the kitchen, but Yang Sze-Fu mostly did what he wanted. He considered himself superior to common workers. You could tell because of the fingernails on his pinkies. They were at least two inches long, which was his way of showing that he didn't have to use his hands for rough or dirty work. He didn't seem to care that his fingernails were dirty, but maybe he couldn't keep such long nails clean.

He made my toast while his cigarette dangled out of the corner of his mouth, collecting a long ash that finally fell on the floor. He wouldn't have kept smoking if my mother had been there, although he didn't always pay attention to my mother. Never about butter pagodas, for instance. No matter how many times my mother told him before a dinner party, "No butter pagoda," it made no difference. As soon as everyone was seated, the serving boy, Wong Sze-Fu,

would bring in a pagoda and set it on the table. The guests would "oh" and "ah," for it was a masterpiece: a pagoda molded out of butter, curved roofs rising tier upon tier, but my mother could only think how <u>unsanitary</u> it was. For, of course, Yang Sze-Fu had molded the butter with his hands and carved the decorations with one of his long fingernails. Still, we always used the butter, for if my mother sent it back to the kitchen, Yang Sze-Fu would lose face and quit.

Did You Know?
A *pagoda* is a temple two or more stories high. Each level, or *tier,* is a little smaller than the one below it, and each has its own partial roof.

When my toast and cocoa were ready, I took them upstairs to my room (the blue room) and while I ate, I began *Sara Crewe* again. Now there was a girl, I thought, who was worth crying over. I wasn't going to think about myself. Or Ian Forbes. Or the next day. I wasn't. I wasn't.

And I didn't. Not all afternoon. Not all evening. Still, I must have decided what I was going to do because the next morning when I started for school and came to the corner where the man sold hot chestnuts, the corner where I always turned to go to school, I didn't turn. I walked straight ahead. I wasn't going to school that day.

I walked toward the Yangtze River. Past the store that sold paper pellets that opened up into flowers when you dropped

---

8. Chinese languages use *characters* to represent ideas and objects.

Vocabulary
unsanitary (un san′ ə ter′ ē) *adj.* dirty in a way that could cause disease; unclean

them in a glass of water. Then up the block where the beggars sat. I never saw anyone give money to a beggar. You couldn't, my father explained, or you'd be mobbed by beggars. They'd follow you everyplace; they'd never leave you alone. I had learned not to look at them when I passed and yet I saw. The running sores, the twisted legs, the mangled faces. What I couldn't get over was that, like me, each one of those beggars had only one life to live. It just happened that they had drawn rotten ones.

Oh, Grandma, I thought, we may be far apart but we're lucky, you and I. Do you even know how lucky? In America do you know?

This part of the city didn't actually belong to the Chinese, even though the beggars sat there, even though upper-class Chinese lived there. A long time ago other countries had just walked into China and divided up part of Hankow (and other cities) into sections, or concessions, which they called their own and used their own rules for governing. We lived in the French concession on Rue de Paris.[9] Then there was the British concession and the Japanese. The Russian and German concessions had been offically returned to China, but the people still called them concessions. The Americans didn't

How would I spend my day?

have one, although, like some of the other countries, they had gunboats on the river. In case, my father said. In case what? Just in case. That's all he'd say.

The concessions didn't look like the rest of China. The buildings were solemn and orderly with little plots of grass around them. Not like those in the Chinese part of the city: a jumble of rickety shops with people, vegetables, crates of quacking ducks, yard goods, bamboo baskets, and mangy dogs spilling onto a street so narrow it was hardly there.

The grandest street in Hankow was the Bund, which ran along beside the Yangtze River. When I came to it after passing the beggars, I looked to my left and saw the American flag flying over the American consulate[10] building. I was proud of the flag and I thought maybe today it was proud of me. It flapped in the breeze as if it were saying ha-ha to the king of England.

Then I looked to the right at the Customs House,[11] which stood at the other end of the Bund. The clock on top of the tower said nine-thirty. How would I spend the day?

I crossed the street to the promenade[12] part of the Bund. When people walked

9. The foreign countries used their *concessions* to manufacture, import, and export goods for their own profit. *Rue de Paris* (rōō də pä rē) is French for "Street of Paris," or Paris Street.

10. A *consul* is a government's official representative in a foreign city, and the *consulate* is his or her home and office.
11. The *Customs House* is the office building where officials inspect imported goods and collect any taxes that are required.
12. A *promenade* is a public walkway where people can take long strolls.

Vocabulary
solemn (sol′ əm) *adj.* serious

A Chinese junk.

here, they weren't usually going anyplace; they were just out for the air. My mother would wear her broad-brimmed beaver hat when we came and my father would swing his cane in that <u>jaunty</u> way that showed how glad he was to be a man. I thought I would just sit on a bench for the morning. I would watch the Customs House clock, and when it was time, I would eat the lunch I had brought along in my schoolbag.

I was the only one sitting on a bench. People did not generally "take the air" on a Wednesday morning and besides, not everyone was allowed here. The British had put a sign on the Bund, NO DOGS, NO CHINESE. This meant that I could never bring Lin Nai-Nai with me. My father couldn't even bring his best friend, Mr. T. K. Hu. Maybe the British wanted a place where they could pretend they weren't in China, I thought. Still, there were always Chinese coolies around. In order to load and unload boats in the river, coolies had to cross the Bund. All day they went back and forth, bent double under their loads, sweating and chanting in a tired, singsong way that seemed to get them from one step to the next.

To pass the time, I decided to recite poetry. The one good thing about Miss Williams was that she made us learn poems by heart and I liked that. There was one particular poem I didn't want to forget.

Vocabulary
jaunty (jôn′ tē) *adj.* lively and carefree

I looked at the Yangtze River and pretended that all the busy people in the boats were my audience.

"'Breathes there the man, with soul so dead,'" I cried, "'Who never to himself hath said, This is my own, my native land!'"[13]

I was so carried away by my performance that I didn't notice the policeman until he was right in front of me. Like all policemen in the British concession, he was a bushy-bearded Indian[14] with a red turban wrapped around his head.

Did You Know?
A *turban* is a long scarf wound around the head.

He pointed to my schoolbag. "Little miss," he said, "why aren't you in school?"

He was tall and mysterious-looking, more like a character in my Arabian Nights book than a man you expected to talk to. I fumbled for an answer. "I'm going on an errand," I said finally. "I just sat down for a rest." I picked up my schoolbag and walked quickly away. When I looked around, he was back on his corner, directing traffic.

So now they were chasing children away too, I thought angrily. Well, I'd like to show them. Someday I'd like to walk a dog down the whole length of the Bund. A Great Dane. I'd have him on a leash— like this—(I put out my hand as if I were holding a leash right then) and he'd be so big and strong I'd have to strain to hold him back (I strained). Then of course sometimes he'd have to do his business and I'd stop (like this) right in the middle of the sidewalk and let him go to it. I was so busy with my Great Dane I was at the end of the Bund before I knew it. I let go of the leash, clapped my hands, and told my dog to go home. Then I left the Bund and the concessions and walked into the Chinese world.

My mother and father and I had walked here but not for many months. This part near the river was called the Mud Flats. Sometimes it was muddier than others, and when the river flooded, the flats disappeared underwater. Sometimes even the fishermen's huts were washed away, knocked right off their long-legged stilts and swept down the river. But today the river was fairly low and the mud had dried so that it was cracked and cakey. Most of the men who lived here were out fishing, some not far from the shore, poling their sampans[15] through the shallow water. Only a few people were on the flats: a man cleaning fish on a flat rock at the water's edge, a woman spreading clothes on the dirt to dry, a few small children. But behind the huts was something I had never seen before. Even before I came close, I guessed what it was. Even then, I was excited by the strangeness of it.

It was the beginning of a boat. The skeleton of a large junk, its ribs lying bare, its backbone running straight and true down the bottom. The outline of the

---

13. [*Breathes . . . native land.*] These are lines from a poem by Sir Walter Scott, a nineteenth-century British writer.
14. This *Indian* is from India, which was then a British colony.

15. A *sampan* is a small, flat-bottomed boat used in Asia. It can be propelled by a single sail, by a long oar at the back, or, in shallow water, by a pole. Often, a sampan has a rounded shelter made of mats.

prow was already in place, turning up wide and snubnosed, the way all junks did. I had never thought of boats starting from nothing, of taking on bones under their bodies. The eyes, I supposed, would be the last thing added. Then the junk would have life.

The builders were not there and I was behind the huts where no one could see me as I walked around and around, marveling. Then I climbed inside and as I did, I knew that something wonderful was happening to me. I was a-tingle, the way a magician must feel when he swallows fire, because suddenly I knew that the boat was mine. No matter who really owned it, it was mine. Even if I never saw it again, it would be my junk sailing up and down the Yangtze River. My junk seeing the river sights with its two eyes, seeing them for me whether I was there or not. Often I had tried to put the Yangtze River into a poem so I could keep it. Sometimes I had tried to draw it, but nothing I did ever came close. But now, *now* I had my junk and somehow that gave me the river too.

I thought I should put my mark on the boat. Perhaps on the side of the spine. Very small. A secret between the boat and me. I opened my schoolbag and took out my folding penknife that I used for sharpening pencils. Very carefully I carved the Chinese character that was our name. Gau. (In China my father was Mr. Gau, my mother was Mrs. Gau, and I was Little

Then the junk would have life.

Miss Gau.) The builders would paint right over the character, I thought, and never notice. But I would know. Always and forever I would know.

For a long time I dreamed about the boat, imagining it finished, its sails up, its eyes wide. Someday it might sail all the way down the Yangtze to Shanghai, so I told the boat what it would see along the way because I had been there and the boat hadn't. After a while I got hungry and I ate my egg sandwich. I was in the midst of peeling an orange when all at once I had company.

A small boy, not more than four years old, wandered around to the back of the huts, saw me, and stopped still. He was wearing a ragged blue cotton jacket with a red cloth, pincushion-like charm around his neck which was supposed to keep him from getting smallpox.[16] Sticking up straight from the middle of his head was a small pigtail which I knew was to fool the gods and make them think he was a girl. (Gods didn't bother much with girls; it was boys that were important in China.) The weather was still warm so he wore no pants, nothing below the waist. Most small boys went around like this so that when they had to go, they could just let loose and go. He walked slowly up to the boat, stared at me, and then nodded as if he'd already guessed what I was.

---

16. *Smallpox* is a highly contagious disease that once killed thousands of people every year.

"Foreign devil," he announced gravely.

I shook my head. "No," I said in Chinese. "American friend." Through the ribs of the boat, I handed him a segment of orange. He ate it slowly, his eyes on the rest of the orange. Segment by segment, I gave it all to him. Then he wiped his hands down the front of his jacket.

"Foreign devil," he repeated.

"American friend," I corrected. Then I asked him about the boat. Who was building it? Where were the builders?

He pointed with his chin upriver. "Not here today. Back tomorrow."

I knew it would only be a question of time before the boy would run off to alert the people in the huts. "Foreign devil, foreign devil," he would cry. So I put my hand on the prow of the boat, wished it luck, and climbing out, I started back toward the Bund. To my surprise the boy walked beside me. When we came to the edge of the Bund, I squatted down so we would be on the same eye level.

"Good-bye," I said. "May the River God protect you."

For a moment the boy stared. When he spoke, it was as if he were trying out a new sound. "American friend," he said slowly.

Interior of Chinese city, artist unknown, c. 1910–1930.
Viewing the painting: How is this scene like the "Chinese world" Fritz describes?

When I looked back, he was still there, looking soberly toward the foreign world to which I had gone.

The time, according to the Customs House clock, was five after two, which meant that I couldn't go home for two hours. School was dismissed at three-thirty and I was home by three-forty-five unless I had to stay in for talking in class. It took me about fifteen minutes to write "I will not talk in class" fifty times, and so I often came home at four o'clock. (I wrote up and down like the Chinese: fifty "I's," fifty "wills," and right through the sentence so I never had to think what I was writing. It wasn't as if I were making a promise.) Today I planned to arrive home at four, my "staying in" time, in the hope that I wouldn't meet classmates on the way.

Meanwhile I wandered up and down the streets, in and out of stores. I weighed

---

Vocabulary
gravely (grāv′ lē) *adv.* very seriously

myself on the big scale in the Hankow Dispensary[17] and found that I was as skinny as ever. I went to the Terminus Hotel and tried out the chairs in the lounge. At first I didn't mind wandering about like this. Half of my mind was still on the river with my junk, but as time went on, my junk began slipping away until I was alone with nothing but questions. Would my mother find out about today? How could I skip school tomorrow? And the next day and the next? Could I get sick? Was there a kind of long lie-abed sickness that didn't hurt?

I arrived home at four, just as I had planned, opened the door, and called out, "I'm home!" Cheery-like and normal. But I was scarcely in the house before Lin Nai-Nai ran to me from one side of the hall and my mother from the other.

"Are you all right? Are you all right?" Lin Nai-Nai felt my arms as if she expected them to be broken. My mother's face was white. "What happened?" she asked.

Then I looked through the open door into the living room and saw Miss Williams sitting there. She had beaten me home and asked about my absence, which of course had scared everyone. But now my mother could see that I was in one piece and for some reason this seemed to make her mad. She took me by the hand and led me into the living room. "Miss Williams said you weren't in school," she said. "Why was that?"

I hung my head, just the way cowards do in books.

---

17. A *dispensary* is a place where medicines and medical treatment are given.

My mother dropped my hand. "Jean will be in school tomorrow," she said firmly. She walked Miss Williams to the door. "Thank you for stopping by."

Miss Williams looked satisfied in her mean, pinched way. "Well," she said, "ta-ta." (She always said "ta-ta" instead of "good-bye." Chicken language, it sounded like.)

As soon as Miss Williams was gone and my mother was sitting down again, I burst into tears. Kneeling on the floor, I buried my head in her lap and poured out the whole miserable story. My mother could see that I really wasn't in one piece after all, so she listened quietly, stroking my hair as I talked, but gradually I could feel her stiffen. I knew she was remembering that she was a Mother.

"You better go up to your room," she said, "and think things over. We'll talk about it after supper."

I flung myself on my bed. What was there to think? Either I went to school and got beaten up. Or I quit.

After supper I explained to my mother and father how simple it was. I could stay at home and my mother could teach me, the way Andrea's mother taught her. Maybe I could even go to Andrea's house and study with her.

My mother shook her head. Yes, it was simple, she agreed. I could go back to the British School, be sensible, and start singing about the king again.

I clutched the edge of the table. Couldn't she understand? I couldn't turn back now. It was too late.

So far my father had not said a word. He was leaning back, teetering on the two hind legs of his chair, the way he always did after a meal, the way that drove my mother crazy. But he was not the kind of person to keep all four legs of a chair on the floor just because someone wanted him to. He wasn't a turning-back person so I hoped maybe he would understand. As I watched him, I saw a twinkle start in his eyes and suddenly he brought his chair down slam-bang flat on the floor. He got up and motioned for us to follow him into the living room. He sat down at the piano and began to pick out the tune for "God Save the King."

A big help, I thought. Was he going to make me practice?

Then he began to sing:

"My country 'tis of thee,
Sweet land of liberty, . . ."

Of course! It was the same tune. Why hadn't I thought of that? Who would know what I was singing as long as I moved my lips? I joined in now, loud and strong.

"Of thee I sing."

My mother laughed in spite of herself. "If you sing that loud," she said, "you'll start a revolution."

"Tomorrow I'll sing softly," I promised. "No one will know." But for now I really let freedom ring.

Then all at once I wanted to see Lin Nai-Nai. I ran out back, through the courtyard that separated the house from the servants' quarters, and upstairs to her room.

"It's me," I called through the door and when she opened up, I threw my arms around her. "Oh, Lin Nai-Nai, I love you," I said. "You haven't said it yet, have you?"

"Said what?"

"Sewing machine. You haven't said it?"

"No," she said, "not yet. I'm still practicing."

"Don't say it, Lin Nai-Nai. Say 'Good day.' It's shorter and easier. Besides, it's more polite."

"Good day?" she repeated.

"Yes, that's right. Good day." I hugged her and ran back to the house.

The next day at school when we rose to sing the British national anthem, everyone stared at me, but as soon as I opened my mouth, the class lost interest. All but Ian Forbes. His eyes never left my face, but I sang softly, carefully, proudly. At recess he sauntered over to where I stood against the wall.

He spat on the ground. "You can be bloody glad you sang today," he said. Then he strutted off as if he and those square knees of his had won again.

And, of course, I was bloody glad.

Vocabulary
saunter (sôn′ tər) *v.* to walk in a leisurely way; stroll

Responding to Literature

PERSONAL RESPONSE

- ◆ What feelings or thoughts did you have while reading?
- ◆ Look back at your notes from the **Focus Activity** on page 86. Did Jean Fritz miss any of the same things about living in the United States that you would miss?

Analyzing Literature

RECALL

1. What happens in school that makes Fritz never want to go back?
2. What is Fritz's bargain with her amah?
3. What is the most exciting thing Fritz sees on the Wednesday she skips school?
4. What solutions do the author's mother and father have for her problem at school?

INTERPRET

5. Why does Ian Forbes try to force Fritz to say, "God save the king"?
6. Why, do you think, does Fritz tell her amah the wrong words for a greeting?
7. Why does Fritz give her orange to the small boy?
8. Which parent offers the better solution for Fritz's problem at school? Explain your answer.

EVALUATE AND CONNECT

9. What does Fritz seem to like about living in China?
10. What appeals to you about China as it is presented in this selection? Why?

Literature and Writing

Writing About Literature

Writing Interview Questions If you could interview Jean Fritz, what else would you want to know about her life in China? Write a list of questions you would ask. Use information in the story to help you write good questions. You might begin with questions like these:

- When did you leave China?
- Did you go to live with your grandmother?
- Did your parents take you to live in any other countries?

Creative Writing

A Poem to Hold Onto Jean Fritz said, "Often I had tried to put the Yangtze River into a poem so I could keep it." Choose something in nature from the area where you live—animal, plant, flower, tree, or favorite outdoor spot—and write a short poem about it. For example, you might write a poem describing dandelions on your lawn:

> New dandelions
> Yellow as the bright sunlight
> Brightening our grass.

Extending Your Response

Performing

News Analysis: Today's China How much has life in China changed since Jean Fritz lived there in 1925? Find newspaper and magazine articles in the library about modern life in China. Then prepare and present a feature for the evening news that tells what life is like in China today.

Art Activity

Create a Chinese Junk Make or design a Chinese junk that will represent you. Make the boat your own by including your name or initials and the eyes that will help your boat "see" as it travels down an imaginary river.

Reading Further

If you'd like to read more by Jean Fritz, you might enjoy these books:
China Homecoming
Make Way for Sam Houston!
The Double Life of Pocahontas

Literature Groups

Completing a Time Line Discuss with your group the most important events in this selection. Why are some events more important than others? How is Fritz affected by these events? As a group, arrange the events you discussed on a time line like the one shown. Share the time line with the class.

📖 **Save your work for your portfolio.**

Tuesday A.M.		Wednesday A.M.	
Jean doesn't sing	P.M.		P.M.

Skill Minilessons

GRAMMAR AND LANGUAGE • COMMAS

Before she understood punctuation, Jean Fritz "hung little wagging comma-tails all over" her letters. One important use of **commas** is to set off words that interrupt the flow of a sentence. Notice how Fritz uses commas in this sentence: *Our teacher, Miss Williams, didn't notice at first.*

Because the words *Miss Williams* interrupt the sentence *Our teacher didn't notice at first,* they are set off with commas.

● For more about commas, see **Language Handbook,** p. R33.

PRACTICE Add two commas to separate an interrupting element in each of these sentences.

1. Jean Fritz you may remember was born in China.
2. She could never she feared be American enough.
3. Tuesday the day Fritz's mother taught an English class was when the trouble began.
4. Yang Sze-Fu the cook was in the kitchen.
5. Fritz was glad of course that she could sing.

READING AND THINKING • COMPARE AND CONTRAST

In the selection from *Homesick,* the author uses many **comparisons.** Some are presented as young Jean Fritz compares life in China with life as she imagines it in the United States. *Comparing* means telling how things are alike. *Contrasting* is telling how things are different.

● For more about comparing and contrasting, see **Reading Handbook,** p. R82.

PRACTICE Write how the following are alike and different. Find the information you need in the story. Compare and contrast these items:

1. the appearance of the Yangtze River on the globe and in real life
2. the topics of the two letters exchanged between Jean and her grandmother
3. Chinese and American flowers, according to Jean
4. Chinese and American writing
5. the concessions and the Chinese section of Hankow

VOCABULARY • COMPOUND WORDS

A **compound word** is made up of two or more words. Often you can figure out the meaning of a compound word by thinking about the meanings of the words that make it up. For example, *schoolyard* is a compound word made up of *school* and *yard.* It means "the yard of a school"–the outdoor area next to a school.

● For more about compound words, see **Language Handbook,** Spelling, p. R42.

PRACTICE Write the following words on a separate piece of paper. Underline the individual words that make up each compound word. Then write a definition for each compound word.

1. sideline
2. houseboat
3. riverbank
4. earthquake
5. homesick
6. fingernail
7. pincushion
8. courtyard
9. schoolbag
10. backbone

Writing Skills

Writing an Opening

Look back at the opening of the selection from *Homesick*. Jean Fritz talks about examining a globe. She makes a surprising statement, "And I was on the wrong side of the globe." Then she traces the Yangtze River with her finger and goes on to re-create the real river in her mind—and in her readers' minds.

> Orange-brown, muddy mustard-colored. And wide, wide, wide. With a river smell that was old and came all the way up from the bottom.

An opening paragraph is like an open door: It leads your readers into your writing. You can choose from several strategies to make your openings inviting. Look at each of the strategies below.

Surprising Statement Jean Fritz begins by saying that she is on the wrong side of the globe. A statement that raises questions in your readers' minds can make them read on to find the answers.

Striking Scene Fritz describes the Yangtze River. "Primary Lessons" begins with what the author saw as her mother walked her to her first day of school. Details of sight, sound, smell, touch, and taste can pull readers into the narrative.

Quotation or Conversation People's exact words can catch your readers' interest. For example, a story can begin with a conversation among family members.

Action An exciting scene of conflict or action can get your readers' attention. For example, readers can begin a story in the middle of an argument between a boy and a girl about sports.

ACTIVITIES

1. Write an opening for a narrative about one of your earliest memories of school. Use either action or a surprising statement.

2. Write an opening for a narrative about a good time you had with friends or family. Use either a striking scene or a quotation.

Writing WORKSHOP

Narrative Writing: Personal Narrative

Do you remember a time when something really funny happened to you? Did you laugh out loud? Were you by yourself, or with friends or family? Do you remember something sad or bittersweet that happened to you? An event that meant a lot to you can make an interesting nonfiction story.

Assignment: Write a personal narrative about an event that happened to you. This workshop will help you tell your story in a way that will make real life as colorful as fiction.

● As you write your personal narrative, refer to the **Writing Handbook,** pp. R43–R47.

The Writing Process

PREWRITING

PREWRITING TIP
Close your eyes to recall your event. Picture details of the place and the people. Notice what you see, hear, and feel. Make notes of the details you want to remember.

● Recall Events

Think of events, large or small, that mean something to you. Some may be from when you were a very young child. Others may be from just last week. You might fill in clusters like those below.

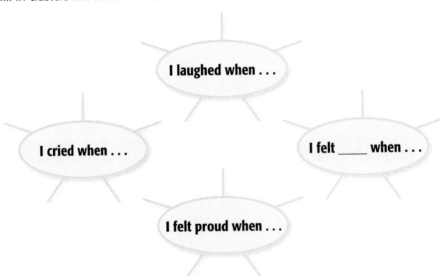

Choose an event that you would like to write about, one that you remember well. Think about what led up to your event and what happened afterward. Freewrite what you remember.

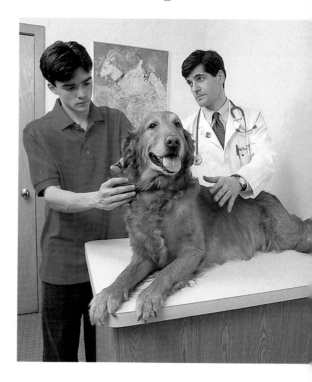

● Think About Your Audience

Imagine sharing your narrative with others. Who will read it? Your teacher? Your classmates? Should you submit it to a school newspaper or magazine?

● Decide on a Purpose

Which selection from this theme do you remember best? Why do you remember it? Did the author make you laugh, cry, or sympathize?

As an author you need to decide, before you begin writing, how you want your readers to feel when they finish your narrative. Your decision will help you choose what to put in and what to leave out.

● Plan Your Narrative

Plan to start by setting the stage for your readers. When did events take place? Where were you? What other people were there? Then think about what happened first, next, and last. Finally, decide how to show at the end of the narrative what you learned or how you felt. A story plan like the one below can help you organize your narrative.

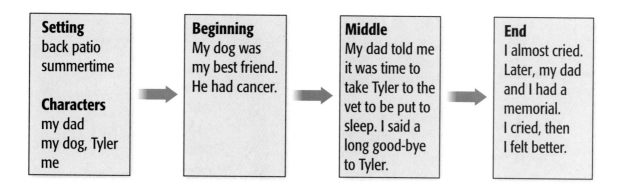

| **Setting**
back patio
summertime

Characters
my dad
my dog, Tyler
me | **Beginning**
My dog was
my best friend.
He had cancer. | **Middle**
My dad told me
it was time to
take Tyler to the
vet to be put to
sleep. I said a
long good-bye
to Tyler. | **End**
I almost cried.
Later, my dad
and I had a
memorial.
I cried, then
I felt better. |

DRAFTING

DRAFTING TIP

Use **sensory details**—details of color, texture, sound, scent, and taste—from your prewriting notes.

● Capture Your Readers

A good writer pulls readers in at the beginning. Experiment with different ways to open your narrative, as in the **Writing Skills** activities on page 103. Remember that even your first sentence can capture your readers. Consider *I went out to the back patio* versus *The back patio was cool and moist when I stepped out.* Which sentence interests you more?

● Go into Detail

Use your story plan to guide you as you draft. As you write, choose details that will create pictures in a reader's mind.

MODEL · DRAFTING

The patio was cool and moist when I stepped out. Tyler lay there, thumping his stubby tail weakly. I knelt and scratched his shaggy ears. Tears welled up in my eyes. I knew this would be the day I had dreaded.

REVISING

REVISING TIP

After you and a friend revise, read your draft one more time. Make sure it expresses exactly what you want it to.

● Evaluate Your Work

Revising is a key step for authors. Reread your draft after letting it sit for a day. Use the **Questions for Revising** to help you improve it. Be honest with yourself. Decide where the narrative could be better.

Now have a friend listen to your story. Ask your friend to use the questions as a guide to help you revise.

QUESTIONS FOR REVISING

☑ Does the opening paragraph capture the reader's interest?

☑ Does the story have a clear beginning, middle, and end?

☑ Is there enough information about the time, place, and people involved?

☑ Are there enough sensory details for the reader to picture what is happening?

☑ Do you show the reader clearly how you felt or what you learned?

EDITING/PROOFREADING

Using the **Proofreading Checklist,** go over your narrative for mistakes in grammar, mechanics, and spelling. The **Grammar Link** on page 30 reminds you about the parts of a sentence. It can help you eliminate sentence fragments from your story.

Grammar Hint

Check your narrative for mistakes in verb forms. Past tense forms of most verbs end in -ed. Past tense forms of irregular verbs vary. You may need to look up some of these irregular forms.

PROOFREADING CHECKLIST

☑ Each sentence has a complete subject and predicate.

☑ Present and past tense forms of verbs are correct.

☑ Quotation marks, commas, and other punctuation marks are used correctly.

☑ Capitalization is correct.

☑ Words are spelled correctly. (On a computer, use the spell-check function.)

MODEL · EDITING/PROOFREADING

I knelt ~~and scratched~~ *to scratch* his ears, and his tail *wagging* thumped ~~and wagged~~.

PUBLISHING/PRESENTING

Consider publishing your personal narrative as an illustrated story. You might use drawings or clip art for your illustrations. Plan how the pictures will go with the text. You might have one per paragraph, or one each for the beginning, the middle, and the end. Copy your narrative neatly and read it aloud to your classmates, showing your illustrations at the appropriate points.

PRESENTING TIP

Read at a relaxed pace. When you show your pictures, be sure to give your listeners time to enjoy them.

Reflecting

How did this writing experience affect your views about the event you chose? Use your journal to reflect on any new insights you have about your event. What other real-life events might you write about in the future?

📖 **Save your work for your portfolio.**

Theme Wrap-Up

Responding to the Theme

1. Which selection in this theme helped you understand how people find their place? Explain your answer.

2. What new ideas do you have about the following as a result of reading this theme?
   - the need to belong or to fit in
   - how people can be comfortable in new situations

3. Present your theme project to the class.

Analyzing Literature

CHOOSE A FAVORITE SELECTION
Think about the autobiographical selections that you read in this theme. Which autobiographies would you like to read in full? Why did you like these selections? Choose one autobiographical selection from this theme, and tell why you like it. Discuss characters, setting, and theme in the selection.

Evaluate and Set Goals

1. Which of the following was most enjoyable to you? Which was most difficult?
   - reading and thinking about the selections
   - doing independent writing
   - analyzing the selections in discussions
   - making presentations
   - doing research

2. How would you assess your work in this theme, using the following scale? Give at least two reasons for your assessment.
   4 = outstanding   2 = fair
   3 = good   1 = weak

3. Based on what you found difficult in this theme, choose a goal to work toward in the next theme.
   - Write down your goal and three steps you will take to reach it.
   - Meet with your teacher to review your goal and your plan for achieving it.

Build Your Portfolio

SELECT
Choose two pieces of work you did in this theme to include in your portfolio. Use these questions to help you choose.

- Which do you consider your best work?
- Which challenged you the most?
- Which did you learn the most from?
- Which did you enjoy the most?

REFLECT
Write some notes to accompany the pieces you selected. Use these questions to guide you.

- What do you like best about the piece?
- What did you learn from creating it?
- What might you do differently if you were beginning this piece again?

Reading on Your Own

If you have enjoyed the literature in this theme, you might also be interested in the following books.

Boy: Tales of Childhood
by Roald Dahl The popular novelist tells funny and sometimes sad stories about his school years.

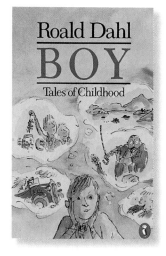

The Endless Steppe: Growing Up in Siberia
by Esther Hautzig This autobiography tells of how the author and her family make a new life in difficult conditions.

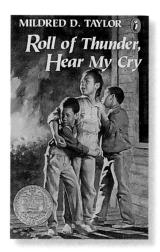

Roll of Thunder, Hear My Cry
by Mildred D. Taylor This story of an African American family is set in rural Mississippi during the 1930s. Cassie and her family are determined to hang on to their land and remain where they belong.

Letters from Rifka
by Karen Hesse Letters tell the story of a Russian girl's journey to the United States in 1919.

Standardized Test Practice

Read the following passage. Then read each question on page 111. Decide which is the best answer to each question. Mark the letter for that answer on your paper.

A Great Grain

Rice serves as an essential grain in the diets of about half the people in the world. Rice is produced all around the globe, from the high rice lands of Nepal to the productive rice fields of Australia. Americans frequently have rice with their meals, but rice is not <u>consumed</u> in the U.S. to the extent that it is consumed in Asia. Many people in Asia eat rice every day. In poorer countries, rice may be the only food people can depend on having each day. In the U.S., each person eats an average of six pounds of rice each year. In Japan, however, each person eats about a third of a pound of rice each day. That's more than six pounds every three weeks!

The Plant   Rice plants grow best in warm and wet weather, and they take three to six months to fully mature. Some rice plants can grow up to five meters tall. Once mature, the rice grain has two main parts, the hull and the kernel. The hull is the outer shell that surrounds the edible fruit, or kernel, and it is removed in a process called "milling." Then the rice can be boiled or steamed to eat.

Uses   Rice can be eaten many different ways. People consume rice by itself, mixed into soups, baked into puddings, and served with meat, beans, or vegetables. However, people also use the rice plant for purposes besides nutrition. The dried stalks can be burned as fuel, used as straw to help make thatched roofs, or made into products such as ropes, sandals, hats, bags, baskets, and brooms. There are many uses for rice, no matter where in the world it is grown.

Customs   There are also many customs associated with rice. In Asia, ceremonies are held at the beginning of the rice-growing season or at harvest time. Traditionally, many Asian cultures associate rice with happiness and long life. In India, rice is considered a gift from the gods, and in Western cultures, people throw rice at brides and grooms as a way to wish them well as they start their lives together.

Rice is a grain that the world cannot do without. Its many uses make it popular throughout the world. Besides providing necessary nutrients, rice enriches our lives with products that have nothing to do with food. Rice is a grain worth growing and cultivating.

1   You can tell from the article that the word <u>consumed</u> in the first paragraph means —

   A   spread

   B   eaten

   C   grown

   D   thrown away

2   The comparison between the amounts of rice eaten in the United States and Japan show that —

   F   Americans eat more rice than the Japanese do

   G   the Japanese eat more rice than Americans do

   H   both countries eat about the same amount of rice

   J   no comparison can be made

3   Milling is the process in which —

   A   rice is boiled

   B   rice is eaten

   C   the hull is grown

   D   the hull is removed

4   The main idea of the third paragraph is that —

   F   rice is a very common food

   G   rice can only be eaten

   H   rice has many purposes

   J   rice is hard to grow

5   You can conclude from the passage that rice —

   A   is slowly becoming less popular

   B   is a grain many people in the world rely on

   C   tastes really good

   D   is not grown all year round

6   Which is a FACT in this passage?

   F   Rice plants are all five meters tall.

   G   Everyone in Asia eats rice every day.

   H   In India, rice is considered a gift from the gods.

   J   Rice is grown in every country around the world.

Through Other Eyes

66 *Look into the eyes of a wolf. In its yellow stare you will see, among other things, great intelligence.* 99

—Jim Brandenburg, *Brother Wolf*

THEME 2

THEME CONTENTS

GENRE FOCUS *POETRY*

Exploring the Theme

Through Other Eyes

How might the world look through the eyes of other creatures who share the planet with us? What kind of connections do people have with animals? In the selections in this theme, you will find a variety of answers to these questions— some serious and some fanciful. Try one of the options below to begin thinking about the theme.

Starting Points

THE VIEW FROM THE FAR SIDE

Cartoonist Gary Larson says the question he's asked most is, "Where do you get your ideas?" followed by, "Why do you get your ideas?"

- What ideas do you have about how animals experience the world?
- Draw your own cartoon showing animals involved in a familiar human activity.

HOW WE LOOK TO THEM

Think about a funny, surprising, or maybe even a frightening experience you've had with an animal.

- Put yourself in the animal's place and write a few notes describing the experience from the animal's point of view.

THE FAR SIDE   By GARY LARSON

"These little ones are mice . . . These over here are hamsters . . . Ooh! This must be a gerbil!"

Theme Projects

As you read the selections in this theme, try your hand at one of the projects below. Work on your own, with a partner, or with a group.

CRITICAL VIEWING
Animals in Art

1. Collect a dozen expressive photos and illustrations of animals. Look in magazines, catalogs, and old calendars for a variety of creatures.
2. Study the images. What does each animal's expression tell you? Write a caption to describe what is happening from the animal's point of view.

LEARNING FOR LIFE
Policy Statement

1. Develop a policy for the ethical treatment of animals in science classrooms. Start with your own ideas.
2. Gather input from your science teacher, other students, and the local humane society.
3. Draft your policy statement. Share it with your class.

*inter*NET
CONNECTION

Check out the Web for more project ideas. Try exploring with a search engine under the topic *Animal Rights.* Find out more about the selections in this theme at this address: lit.glencoe.com

MULTIMEDIA PROJECT
Animal News
Plan a news feature about animal care in your community.

1. Schedule interviews with workers at a wildlife refuge, a veterinarian's office, a zoo, or an animal shelter.
2. Ask questions about the workers' jobs and the animals in their care.
3. Record the interviews and present them in class.

Before You Read

from *Brother Wolf and Why Dogs Are Tame*

MEET JIM BRANDENBURG

In 1986 Jim Brandenburg photographed wolves for *National Geographic* magazine. He camped in the territory of a wolf pack and photographed their activities. The wolves accepted him completely. He has been fascinated with wolves ever since and has written several books about them.

Jim Brandenburg was born in 1945. Brother Wolf was published in 1993.

MEET JULIUS LESTER

Julius Lester, an award-winning writer of folktales, has hosted his own TV and radio shows, directed a folk festival, and performed with other folk singers. He is a teacher at the University of Massachusetts.

Julius Lester was born in 1939. This story, from The Last Tales of Uncle Remus, *was published in 1994.*

FOCUS ACTIVITY

Picture a wolf running through the woods and a dog running in a backyard. What do you know about each kind of animal? How are they alike? How are they different?

Partners

Share your responses with a partner. Then discuss your ideas with the class.

Setting a Purpose

Read the selections to learn about how dogs and wolves are alike and different.

BACKGROUND

Did You Know?
Dogs became domesticated thousands of years ago. No one really knows whether people "tamed" dogs, or whether dogs adopted people. Because dogs are good scavengers, they may have decided to live near people to eat their scraps and cast-off food. All dogs are descended from wolves.

VOCABULARY PREVIEW

gait (gāt) *n.* a particular manner of moving on foot; p. 119
meander (mē an′ dər) *v.* to wander aimlessly; p. 119
commiserate (kə miz′ ə rāt) *v.* to express sympathy; p. 120
proposition (prop′ ə zish′ ən) *n.* something offered for consideration; suggestion; p. 120
lurk (lurk) *v.* to stay hidden, ready to attack; p. 122

from Brother Wolf

Jim Brandenburg ❧

Since only the sun
and moon made light,
I have known you. I
watched you from the
once vast, impenetrable
forest. I was witness as you
discovered fire and strange
tools. From ridges, I watched
you hunt, and envied your
kills. I have eaten your scraps.
You have eaten mine.

I have heard your songs and watched your dancing shadows around bright fires. In a time so distant that I can barely remember, some of us joined you to sit near those fires. We became part of your packs, joined in your hunts, protected your pups, helped you, feared you, loved you.

We have existed together a long time. We were much alike. It is why the tame ones adopted you. Some of you, I know, respected me, the wild one. I am a good hunter. I respected you, too. You were a good hunter. I would see you hunt in a pack with the tame ones and catch meat.

Then there was always plenty. Then there were few of you. Then the woods was big. We howled to the tame ones in the night. Some came back to hunt with us. Some we ate, for they had become very strange. It was this way for a long long time. It was a good way.

Sometimes I would steal from you, as you did from me. Do you remember when you were starving and the snow was deep and you ate the meat we killed? It was a game. It was a debt. Some might call it a promise.

Like many of the tame ones, most of you have become very strange. Now I do

We wild ones are now very few.

not recognize some of the tame ones. Now I do not recognize some of you. We were once so much alike. You made the meat tame, too. When I began to hunt your tame meat (they are foolish creatures and do not honor death, but the wild meat was gone), you hunted me. I do not understand. When your packs grew larger and fought among themselves, I saw. I watched your great battles. I feasted on those you left behind. Then you hunted me more. I do not understand. They were meat. You killed them.

We wild ones are now very few. You made the woods small. You have killed many of us. But I still hunt, and I feed our hidden pups. I always will. I wonder if the tame ones who live with you made a good choice. They have lost the spirit to live in the wild. They are many, but they are strange. We are few. I still watch you, too, so I can avoid you.

I do not think I know you any longer.

Canis Lupus[1]

---

1. *Canis lupus* is the scientific name of the wolf species.

Why Dogs Are Tame

Julius Lester ∼

Back in the days when people and animals lived on the earth like kinfolk, Brer[1] Dog ran with the other animals. He galloped with Brer Fox and loped with Brer Wolf, and cantered with Brer Coon. He went through all the <u>gaits</u> and had as good a time as the other animals and as bad a time too.

It was after one of them bad times that Brer Dog started thinking. Somewhere between Monday morning and Saturday night Brer Dog was sitting in the shade, scratching and thinking about the winter that had just ended. The wind had carried knives and cut through everything standing in its path. Hungriness built a sky-scraper in Brer Dog's stomach and moved in with all his kin. Brer Dog was so thin he would've counted his ribs if he had known his numbers. He didn't want to go through another winter like that.

That's what Brer Dog was thinking when Brer Wolf came <u>meandering</u> along.

---

1. *Brer* is a shortened way to say "Brother."

Vocabulary
gait (gāt) *n.* a particular manner of moving on foot
meander (mē an′ dər) *v.* to wander aimlessly

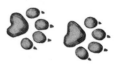

"Howdy, Brer Dog!"

"Howdy back, Brer Wolf!"

"Brer Dog, you look like you and food are angry at each other. Not that I'm on the friendliest of terms with food myself."

"I hear you," Brer Dog responded.

They commiserated with one another for a while and then Brer Wolf asked, "So what are you up to today?"

"It don't make no difference what I'm up to if I don't find dinner."

"You can't have dinner if you don't have a fire."

"Where am I going to get fire?"

Brer Wolf thought for a minute. "Well, the quickest way I know is to borrow some from Mr. Man and Miz Woman."

"That's a risky proposition."

"I know it."

Mr. Man had a walking cane that he could point at you and blow your lights out.

Brer Dog was desperate, though. "I'll go for the fire," he told Brer Wolf, and off he went.

Before long he was sitting by the gate outside Mr. Man's house. If the gate had been closed, Brer Dog would've gone back from where he came. But some of the children had been playing and left the gate open. Brer Dog didn't want to go through the gate 'cause he didn't want to get his lights blown out. On the other hand, his lights were getting dim because he was so hungry. He walked through the gate as scared as scared can be.

He heard hogs grunting and pigs squealing and hens cackling and roosters crowing, but he didn't turn his head toward grunt or squeal, cackle or crow. He started toward the front door, but it looked too big and white. He went to the back door, and from inside he heard children laughing and playing. For the first time in his life, Brer Dog felt lonely.

He sat down by the back door, afraid to knock. He waited. After a while somebody opened the door and then shut it real quick. Brer Dog didn't see who it was because his eyes were on the ground.

A few minutes later Mr. Man came to the door. In his hand was the stick that would put your lights out. "What you want?" he asked Brer Dog.

Brer Dog was too scared to say anything, so he just wagged his tail.

"As far as I know, you ain't got no business here, so be on your way," Mr. Man said.

Brer Dog crouched down close to the ground and wagged his tail some more. Mr. Man looked at him real hard, trying to decide whether or not to shoot him.

Miz Woman wondered who her husband was talking to. She came to the door and saw Brer Dog crouching on the ground, wagging his tail, his tongue hanging out of the side of his mouth, his eyes so big and wet that he looked like he was going to cry at any minute.

"Poor fella," Miz Woman said. "You not going to hurt anybody, are you?"

"No, ma'am," Brer Dog responded. "I just come to ask if I could borrow a chunk of fire."

Vocabulary

commiserate (kə miz′ ə rāt′) v. to express sympathy

proposition (prop′ ə zish′ ən) n. something offered for consideration; suggestion

"My goodness! What you need a chunk of fire for?" she wanted to know.

"He wants to burn us out of house and home," Mr. Man put in.

"I wouldn't do that," Brer Dog said. "I need the fire so that if I get something to eat, I can cook it. And if I don't get nothing to eat, at least I'll be able to keep warm on these chilly nights."

"You poor thing. Why don't you come in here to the kitchen and get as warm as you want."

"I don't want that animal in my house," Mr. Man protested.

"He's so cuuuuute," Miz Woman said.

Brer Dog didn't say anything. He just tried to look cute as he trotted in the house.

There was a big fireplace in the kitchen, and he sat down on the hearth.[2] The children were sitting around the table eating their supper. After a while, Brer Dog was feeling right splimmy-splammy.

But he was still very hungry. He looked up with his big eyes and saw the children eating corn bread and collard greens and ham hocks. His eyes followed the children's hands from plate to mouth, mouth to plate, plate to mouth, mouth to plate.

Miz Woman saw Brer Dog watching the children. She went to the cabinet and got a plate and put some ham, corn bread, and juice from the greens on it and set it down in front of Brer Dog.

Brer Dog gobbled it up with one gulp. It wasn't enough to satisfy his hunger, but he was afraid that if they saw how hungry he really was, they wouldn't let him stay.

So he stretched out in front of the fire, yawned loudly, and put his head across his paws and pretended he had fallen asleep.

Hound Dog (II), 1992. Christian Pierre. Acrylic on canvas, 30 x 20 in. Collection of the artist.
Viewing the painting: How can you tell this dog is tame?

---

2. The *hearth* is the floor of a fireplace. It often extends out into the room.

Why Dogs Are Tame

Wasn't long before he smelled a familiar smell. He smelled the familiar smell of Brer Wolf. He raised his head and looked toward the door.

Mr. Man noticed the dog looking toward the door. "Is there something sneaking around out there?"

Brer Dog got up, trotted to the door, and growled a low growl.

"There's a varmint[3] out there, ain't it?" Mr. Man said, getting his rifle from over the fireplace. He opened the door, and what should he see but Brer Wolf running out the gate. Mr. Man raised the rifle and—*kerblam!* Brer Wolf howled. The shot missed Brer Wolf, but the scare was a bull's-eye.

After that Mr. Man had a new appreciation for Brer Dog. Brer Dog showed he could be useful in many ways. He headed the cows off when they made a break to go into the woods. He took care of the sheep. Late up in the night, he warned Mr. Man if any varmints were <u>lurking</u> around. When Mr. Man went hunting, Brer Dog was there to keep him company. And he played with Mr. Man's and Miz Woman's children as if he was one of them. And for all that, Brer Dog didn't want anything more than food to eat and a place in front of the fire.

Before long Brer Dog was fat and sleek. One day he was out by himself in the woods when he met up with Brer Wolf.

"Howdy, Brer Wolf."

Brer Wolf don't say nothing for a while. Finally, "So why didn't you come back with the fire that day?"

Brer Dog pointed to the collar around his neck. "See this? I belong to Mr. Man and Miz Woman now."

"You look like you haven't missed a meal in a long time. How come I can't come there and have them own me?"

"Come on!"

The next morning Brer Wolf knocked on Mr. Man's door. Mr. Man looked out to see who it was. When he saw Brer Wolf, Mr. Man got his rifle and went to the door.

Brer Wolf tried to be as polite as he could. He smiled. I don't know if you've ever seen a wolf smile. It is not a pleasant sight. Mr. Man saw a mouth full of teeth as sharp as grief. Mr. Man raised his rifle and—*kerblam!*—took a shot at Brer Wolf.

Some folks say he missed. Others say he gave him natural air-conditioning. I don't know how that part turned out. What I do know is that Brer Dog has been living in people's houses ever since.

---

3. Here, *varmint* means "a pesky animal." It's an informal way of saying *vermin*, insects or animals that are harmful or destructive.

Vocabulary
lurk (lurk) *v.* to stay hidden, ready to attack

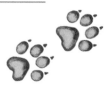

Responding to Literature

PERSONAL RESPONSE

- ◆ How do you feel after reading the selection from *Brother Wolf*?
- ◆ How does the ending of "Why Dogs Are Tame" affect you? How do you feel about Brer Dog? Do you feel sorry for Brer Wolf?

Analyzing Literature

RECALL

1. What is the subject of the letter *Canis Lupus* writes?
2. Who are the "tame ones," according to *Canis Lupus*? What do wolves think of them?
3. Where does Brer Dog live at the beginning of "Why Dogs Are Tame"? How well is he surviving?
4. Who tries to help Brer Dog? What advice does he give?

INTERPRET

5. *Canis Lupus* says of human hunters, "We were much alike." How do you think people and wolves were alike?
6. According to *Canis Lupus,* how have people changed? Why do you think this change has happened?
7. How does Lester show that his story takes place "back in the days when people and animals lived on the earth like kinfolk"?
8. Why do you think Brer Dog is accepted by Mr. Man and Miz Woman, but Brer Wolf is not? Support your answer with examples from the selection.

EVALUATE AND CONNECT

9. **Theme Connection** In what ways does *Canis Lupus* help you see the world "through other eyes"?
10. Which selection, in your opinion, presents a more appealing image of the wolf? Explain your answer.

LITERARY ELEMENTS

Tone

Tone is the attitude an author has toward a subject or toward his or her audience. From listening to a person's tone of voice, a listener can tell whether the speaker is sad or happy, angry or amused. By noting the details an author uses to describe a setting, reveal a character, or narrate an event, a reader can "pick up" the author's tone. When Julius Lester has the wolf say, "Brer Dog, you look like you and food are angry at each other," he is using a light, humorous tone.

1. What is Lester's overall tone in "Why Dogs Are Tame"? How does he set the tone? Use examples from the story.

2. What is Brandenburg's tone in the selection from *Brother Wolf*? How does he set the tone?

3. Why do you think each author uses the tone he does?

● See **Literary Terms Handbook,** p. R9.

Literature and Writing

Writing About Literature

Origin Tales   An **origin tale** is a story that tells how something in the natural world came to be as it is. Write a paragraph explaining what situation "Why Dogs Are Tame" tells about and what the letter from *Brother Wolf* has to say about that same situation.

Personal Writing

My View   Think back to your discussion in the **Focus Activity** on page 116. Do the selections present the dog and the wolf the way you pictured them? Write a few paragraphs telling whether you agree with the way the dog or the wolf is presented in one of these selections.

Extending Your Response

Literature Groups

Man's Best Pal   Imagine that a wolf and a dog are both candidates for becoming "man's best friend." What differences exist in their temperaments and personalities? What assets and problems would each bring to the position? Stage a debate between Dog and Wolf. Candidates can use incidents or ideas from the selections to argue their points of view.

Interdisciplinary Activity

Science   *Canis Lupus* says, "Then there were few of you [humans]. Then the woods was big." Find out about the shrinking habitat of wolves. What kind of habitat do wolves need? How much land do they require to hunt? What kind of game do they eat? You might use the Internet as a source. Share your findings with the class.

Performing

Readers Theater   "Why Dogs Are Tame" is a good tale for telling aloud, especially to a group of younger children. Enjoy the story's dialogue as different speakers read the parts of Brer Dog, Brer Wolf, Mr. Man, and Miz Woman, with a narrator reading the connecting text.

Reading Further

You might enjoy these books by Julius Lester:

How Many Spots Does a Leopard Have?

The Tales of Uncle Remus: The Adventures of Brer Rabbit

Save your work for your portfolio.

Skill Minilessons

GRAMMAR AND LANGUAGE • DOUBLE NEGATIVES

The word *not* is a negative word, expressing the idea of "no" in a sentence. It often appears at the end of words in its shortened form, the contraction *n't*. Other words that express the idea of "no" are *nobody, nothing, none, never, nowhere,* and *hardly.* When two negative words are used together to express the same idea, the result is called a **double negative.** Try to avoid double negatives in your writing.

Incorrect: He can't say nothing for a while.

Correct: He can't say anything for a while.

Correct: He says nothing for a while.

PRACTICE Correct sentences with double negatives. If the sentence is correct, write *C.*

1. It won't make no difference where I'm going if I don't find dinner.
2. You can't have a party if you don't have music.
3. She hadn't never heard anything quite like it.
4. As far as I know, you never had no reason to be here.
5. If I don't find nothing better, I can still use my brother's CD player.

● For more on correct usage, see **Language Handbook,** pp. R10–R23.

READING AND THINKING • AUTHOR'S PURPOSE

What was Brandenburg's purpose for writing–to entertain, to inform, or to persuade? Ask yourself:
• How does he show how he feels about wolves?
• How does he try to make me feel?
• How does my point of view change after reading?

PRACTICE Think of a wild animal you particularly like. Using the letter from *Brother Wolf* as a model, take the viewpoint of the animal and write a letter to humans, explaining an ecological problem.

● For more on author's purpose, see **Literary Terms Handbook,** p. R1.

VOCABULARY • HOMOPHONES

Homophones are words that sound the same but have different meanings and, usually, different spellings. The words *to, too,* and *two* are homophones. So are *gait* and *gate.* Brer Dog's *gaits* have nothing to do with *gates,* but the words have the same pronunciation. Substituting one homophone for another is often a problem of hurrying or carelessness.

PRACTICE If the underlined word is correct, write *C.* If it is a homophone for the correct word, write the word that should be used.

When Brer Dog was <u>threw</u> eating, he <u>past</u>
        1   2
time keeping warm by the fire. He <u>new</u> he
                            3
wanted to stay. Within a few <u>daze</u>, he had
                        4
made himself useful, and it was <u>plane</u> to the
    5   6
people that he was a <u>grate</u> help. For <u>one</u>
            7   8
thing, <u>no one</u> <u>wood</u> <u>steal</u> <u>there</u> chickens with
      9   10   11   12
Brer Dog around.

Gorilla Saves Tot in Brookfield Zoo Ape Pit

by Jeffrey Bils and Stacey Singer—*Chicago Tribune*, August 17, 1996

A crowd of visitors at Brookfield Zoo looked on in horror Friday afternoon as they watched a toddler tumble more than 15 feet into a pit, landing near seven gorillas.

But as zoo patrons cried out for help, expecting the worst for the 3-year-old boy lying battered on the concrete below, an unlikely hero emerged.

A female ape, with her own baby clinging to her back, lumbered over to the boy, cradled him in her arms, carried him to a doorway and laid him gingerly at the feet of waiting paramedics.

Zoo spokesperson Sondra Catzen said Binti Jua, a rare western lowland gorilla who has received training on how to be a good mother, appeared to act "out of purely maternalistic compassion for the human child.

"She picked up the boy, kind of cradling him, and walked him around," said Catzen.

Binti Jua and her baby.

"Another gorilla walked toward the boy, and she kind of turned around and walked away from the other gorillas and tried to be protective," said Carrie Stewart, a zoo visitor who witnessed the incident.

At first it appeared the boy had been knocked unconscious by the fall, witnesses told zoo officials. But "he was alert and crying when the paramedics came and got him," Catzen said.

Respond

1. Why do you think Binti Jua acted as she did?

2. Do you know stories about animals who have protected human children?

Before You Read

Mowgli's Brothers

MEET RUDYARD KIPLING

R udyard Kipling was born in India and spent his first five years there. He never forgot the folktales he was told by his Indian nurse. When his parents sent him to school in England, Kipling was miserable. He was treated badly by the family with whom he lived and bullied at school. His health was poor, and he began to go blind. When he was seventeen, he rejoined his parents in India and began writing stories set in the country he had always considered his home.

Rudyard Kipling was born in 1865 and died in 1936. This story, which is part of The Jungle Book, *was published in 1894.*

FOCUS ACTIVITY

What are some words and ideas that come to your mind when you try to imagine living in a jungle?

Three-Step Interview
In a group of three, interview each other about the above topic and take notes. Then share your ideas with the class.

Setting a Purpose
Read "Mowgli's Brothers" to find out how a boy learns to live in a rain forest.

BACKGROUND

The Time and Place
The story takes place in a rain forest in India. At the time the story was written, India had dense rain forests (called "jungle" in the story). Now, many of these rain forests have been cleared.

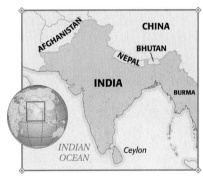

India about 1890.

VOCABULARY PREVIEW

spitefully (spīt′ fəl lē) *adv.* in a way that shows bad feelings toward another; hatefully; p. 130

scour (skour) *v.* to make a thorough search of; p. 130

quarry (kwôr′ ē) *n.* anything that is hunted or pursued, especially an animal; p. 132

lair (lār) *n.* a home or resting place, especially of a wild animal; p. 133

cunning (kun′ ing) *n.* craftiness; intelligence; p. 134

clamor (klam′ ər) *n.* a loud, noisy outcry; p. 135

sullenly (sul′ ən lē) *adv.* in a sulky or gloomy way due to feeling angry or hurt; p. 140

maim (mām) *v.* to injure so that a part of the body is lost or unusable; p. 142

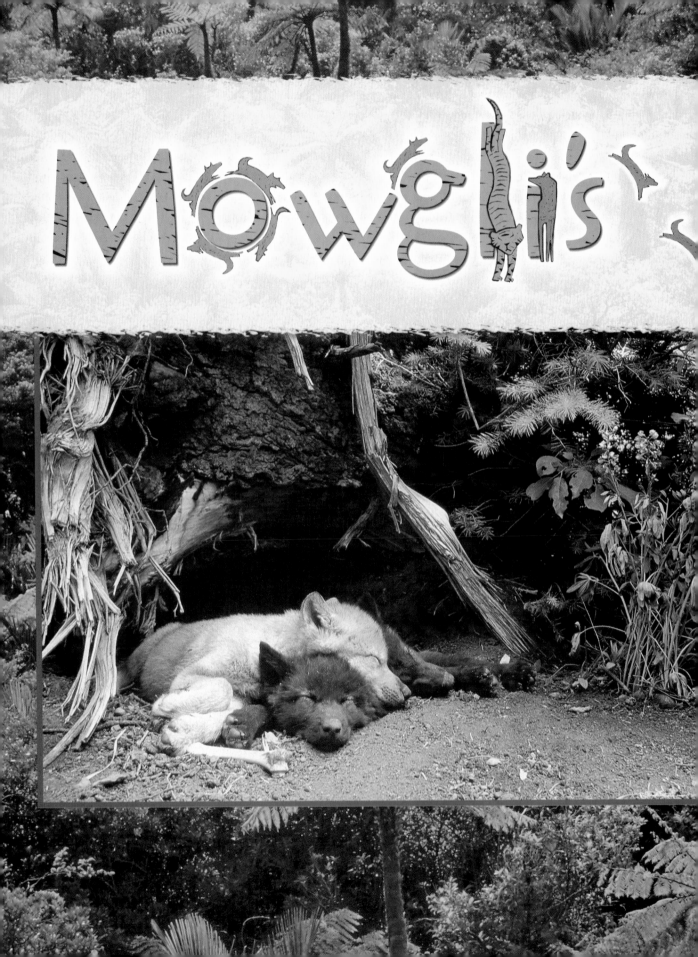

Mowgli's

Brothers

Rudyard Kipling

IT WAS SEVEN O'CLOCK OF A VERY WARM EVENING in the Seeonee hills when Father Wolf woke up from his day's rest, scratched himself, yawned, and spread out his paws one after the other to get rid of the sleepy feeling in their tips. Mother Wolf lay with her big gray nose dropped across her four tumbling, squealing cubs, and the moon shone into the mouth of the cave where they all lived. "Augrh!" said Father Wolf, "it is time to hunt again"; and he was going to spring down hill when a little shadow with a bushy tail crossed the threshold and whined: "Good luck go with you, O Chief of the Wolves; and good luck and strong white teeth go with the noble children, that they may never forget the hungry in this world."

It was the jackal—Tabaqui,[1] the Dish-licker—and the wolves of India despise Tabaqui because he runs about making mischief, and telling tales, and eating rags and pieces of leather from the village rubbish-heaps. But they are afraid of him too, because Tabaqui, more than anyone else in the jungle, is apt to go mad, and then he forgets that he was ever afraid of anyone, and runs through the forest biting everything in his way. Even the tiger runs and hides when little Tabaqui goes mad, for madness is the most disgraceful thing that can overtake a wild creature. We call it hydrophobia, but they call it *dewanee*[2]— the madness—and run.

"Enter, then, and look," said Father Wolf, stiffly; "but there is no food here."

"For a wolf, no," said Tabaqui; "but for so mean[3] a person as myself a dry bone is a good feast. Who are we, the Gidur-log [the jackal people], to pick and choose?" He scuttled to the back of the cave, where he found the bone of a buck with some meat on it, and sat cracking the end merrily.

"All thanks for this good meal," he said, licking his lips. "How beautiful are the noble children! How large are their eyes! And so young too! Indeed, indeed, I might have remembered that the children of kings are men from the beginning."

---

1. *Tabaqui* (tə bä′ kē)
2. *Hydrophobia* (hī′ drə fō′ bē ə) and *dewanee* (də wä′ nē) are other names for *rabies,* an infectious disease that destroys brain cells and can be fatal unless treated immediately.
3. The word *mean* here means "humble and poor in quality."

Now, Tabaqui knew as well as anyone else that there is nothing so unlucky as to compliment children to their faces; and it pleased him to see Mother and Father Wolf look uncomfortable.

Tabaqui sat still, rejoicing in the mischief that he had made, and then he said spitefully:

"Shere Khan, the Big One, has shifted his hunting-grounds. He will hunt among these hills for the next moon, so he has told me."

Shere Khan was the tiger who lived near the Waingunga River, twenty miles away.

"He has no right!" Father Wolf began angrily—"By the Law of the Jungle he has no right to change his quarters without due warning. He will frighten every head of game within ten miles, and I—I have to kill for two, these days."

"His mother did not call him Lungri [the Lame One] for nothing," said Mother Wolf, quietly. "He has been lame in one foot from his birth. That is why he has only killed cattle. Now the villagers of the Waingunga are angry with him, and he has come here to make *our* villagers angry. They will scour the jungle for him when he is far away, and we and our children must run when the grass is set alight. Indeed, we are very grateful to Shere Khan!"

"Shall I tell him of your gratitude?" said Tabaqui.

"Out!" snapped Father Wolf. "Out and hunt with thy master. Thou hast done harm enough for one night."

Vocabulary

spitefully (spīt′ fəl lē) *adv.* in a way that shows bad feelings toward another; hatefully
scour (skour) *v.* to make a thorough search of

"I go," said Tabaqui, quietly. "Ye can hear Shere Khan below in the thickets. I might have saved myself the message."

Father Wolf listened, and below in the valley that ran down to a little river, he heard the dry, angry, snarly, singsong whine of a tiger who has caught nothing and does not care if all the jungle knows it.

"The fool!" said Father Wolf. "To begin a night's work with that noise! Does he think that our buck are like his fat Waingunga bullocks?"

"H'sh. It is neither bullock nor buck he hunts tonight," said Mother Wolf. "It is Man." The whine had changed to a sort of humming purr that seemed to come from every quarter of the compass. It was the noise that bewilders woodcutters and gypsies sleeping in the open, and makes them run sometimes into the very mouth of the tiger.

"Man!" said Father Wolf, showing all his white teeth. "Faugh! Are there not enough beetles and frogs in the tanks that he must eat Man, and on our ground too!"

The Law of the Jungle, which never orders anything without a reason, forbids every beast to eat Man except when he is killing to show his children how to kill, and then he must hunt outside the hunting-grounds of his pack or tribe. The real reason for this is that man-killing means, sooner or later, the arrival of white men on elephants, with guns, and hundreds of brown men with gongs and rockets and torches. Then everybody in the jungle suffers. The reason the beasts give among themselves is that Man is the weakest and most defenseless of all living things, and it is unsportsmanlike to touch him. They say

too—and it is true—that man-eaters become mangy,[4] and lose their teeth.

The purr grew louder, and ended in the full-throated "Aaarh!" of the tiger's charge.

Then there was a howl—an untigerish howl—from Shere Khan. "He has missed," said Mother Wolf. "What is it?"

Father Wolf ran out a few paces and heard Shere Khan muttering and mumbling savagely, as he tumbled about in the scrub.

"The fool has had no more sense than to jump at a woodcutters' camp-fire, and has burned his feet," said Father Wolf, with a grunt. "Tabaqui is with him."

"Something is coming uphill," said Mother Wolf, twitching one ear. "Get ready."

The bushes rustled a little in the thicket, and Father Wolf dropped with his haunches under him, ready for his leap. Then, if you had been watching, you would have seen the most wonderful thing in the world—the wolf checked in mid-spring. He made his bound before he saw what it was he was jumping at, and then he tried to stop himself. The result was that he shot up straight into the air for four or five feet, landing almost where he left ground.

"Man!" he snapped. "A man's cub. Look!"

Directly in front of him, holding on by a low branch, stood a naked brown baby who could just walk—as soft and as dimpled a little atom as ever came to a wolf's cave at night. He looked up into Father Wolf's face, and laughed.

"Is that a man's cub?" said Mother Wolf. "I have never seen one. Bring it here."

---

4. Here, *mangy* (mān′ jē) means "worn, dirty, and shabby in appearance." It can also refer to a skin disease that produces scaly pimples and loss of hair in certain animals. However, this disease is caused by tiny insects, not by eating humans.

A wolf accustomed to moving his own cubs can, if necessary, mouth an egg without breaking it, and though Father Wolf's jaws closed right on the child's back not a tooth even scratched the skin, as he laid it down among the cubs.

"How little! How naked, and—how bold!" said Mother Wolf, softly. The baby was pushing his way between the cubs to get close to the warm hide. "Ahai! He is taking his meal with the others. And so this is a man's cub. Now, was there ever a wolf that could boast of a man's cub among her children?"

"I have heard now and again of such a thing, but never in our Pack or in my time," said Father Wolf. "He is altogether without hair, and I could kill him with a touch of my foot. But see, he looks up and is not afraid."

The moonlight was blocked out of the mouth of the cave, for Shere Khan's great square head and shoulders were thrust into the entrance. Tabaqui, behind him, was squeaking: "My lord, my lord, it went in here!"

"Shere Khan does us great honor," said Father Wolf, but his eyes were very angry. "What does Shere Khan need?"

"My quarry. A man's cub went this way," said Shere Khan. "Its parents have run off. Give it to me."

Shere Khan had jumped at a woodcutters' camp-fire, as Father Wolf had said, and was furious from the pain of his burned feet. But Father Wolf knew that the mouth of the cave was too narrow for a tiger to come in by. Even where he was, Shere Khan's shoulders and fore paws were cramped for want of room, as a man's would be if he tried to fight in a barrel.

"The Wolves are a free people," said Father Wolf. "They take orders from the Head of the Pack, and not from any striped cattle-killer. The man's cub is ours—to kill if we choose."

"Ye choose and ye do not choose! What talk is this of choosing? By the bull that I killed, am I to stand nosing into your dog's den for my fair dues? It is I, Shere Khan, who speak!"

Vocabulary

quarry (kwôr′ ē) *n.* anything that is hunted or pursued, especially an animal

The tiger's roar filled the cave with thunder. Mother Wolf shook herself clear of the cubs and sprang forward, her eyes, like two green moons in the darkness, facing the blazing eyes of Shere Khan.

"And it is I, Raksha [The Demon], who answer. The man's cub is mine, Lungri—mine to me! He shall not be killed. He shall live to run with the Pack and to hunt with the Pack; and in the end, look you, hunter of little naked cubs—frog-eater—fish-killer—he shall hunt *thee*! Now get hence, or by the Sambhur that I killed (*I* eat no starved cattle), back thou goest to thy mother, burned beast of the jungle, lamer than ever thou camest into the world! Go!"

Did You Know?
The sambar, or *Sambhur,* (säm′ bər) is a large deer of southern Asia that has antlers and a reddish-brown coat.

Father Wolf looked on amazed. He had almost forgotten the days when he won Mother Wolf in fair fight from five other wolves, when she ran in the Pack and was not called The Demon for compliment's sake. Shere Khan might have faced Father Wolf, but he could not stand up against Mother Wolf, for he knew that where he was she had all the advantage of the ground, and would fight to the death. So he backed out of the cave-mouth growling, and when he was clear he shouted:

"Each dog barks in his own yard! We will see what the Pack will say to this fostering of man-cubs. The cub is mine, and to my teeth he will come in the end, O bush-tailed thieves!"

Mother Wolf threw herself down panting among the cubs, and Father Wolf said to her gravely:

"Shere Khan speaks this much truth. The cub must be shown to the Pack. Wilt thou still keep him, Mother?"

"Keep him!" she gasped. "He came naked, by night, alone and very hungry; yet he was not afraid! Look, he has pushed one of my babes to one side already. And that lame butcher would have killed him and would have run off to the Waingunga while the villagers here hunted through all our lairs in revenge! Keep him? Assuredly I will keep him. Lie still, little frog. O thou Mowgli—for Mowgli the Frog I will call thee—the time will come when thou wilt hunt Shere Khan as he has hunted thee."

"But what will our Pack say?" said Father Wolf.

The Law of the Jungle lays down very clearly that any wolf may, when he marries, withdraw from the Pack he belongs to; but as soon as his cubs are old enough to stand on their feet he must bring them to the Pack Council, which is generally held once a month at full moon, in order that the other wolves may identify them. After that inspection the cubs are free to run where they please, and until they have killed their first buck no excuse is accepted if a grown wolf of the Pack kills one of them. The punishment is death where the murderer can be found; and if you think for a minute you will see that this must be so.

Vocabulary
lair (lār) *n.* a home or resting place, especially of a wild animal

Father Wolf waited till his cubs could run a little, and then on the night of the Pack Meeting took them and Mowgli and Mother Wolf to the Council Rock—a hill-top covered with stones and boulders where a hundred wolves could hide. Akela, the great gray Lone Wolf, who led all the Pack by strength and <u>cunning</u>, lay out at full length on his rock, and below him sat forty or more wolves of every size and color, from badger-colored veterans[5] who could handle a buck alone, to young black three-year-olds who thought they could. The Lone Wolf had led them for a year now. He had fallen twice into a wolf-trap in his youth, and once he had been beaten and left for dead; so he knew the manners and customs of men. There was very little talking at the rock. The cubs tumbled over each other in the center of the circle where their mothers and fathers sat, and now and again a senior wolf would go quietly up to a cub, look at him carefully, and return to his place on noiseless feet. Sometimes a mother would push her cub far out into

"Look—look well, O Wolves!"

the moonlight, to be sure that he had not been overlooked. Akela from his rock would cry: "Ye know the Law—ye know the Law. Look well, O Wolves!" and the anxious mothers would take up the call: "Look—look well, O Wolves!"

At last—and Mother Wolf's neck-bristles lifted as the time came—Father Wolf pushed "Mowgli the Frog," as they called him, into the center, where he sat laughing and playing with some pebbles that glistened in the moon-light.

Akela never raised his head from his paws, but went on with the monoto-nous cry: "Look well!" A muffled roar came up from behind the rocks—the voice of Shere Khan crying: "The cub is mine. Give him to me. What have the Free People to do with a man's cub?" Akela never even twitched his ears: all he said was: "Look well, O Wolves! What have the Free People to do with the orders of any save the Free People? Look well!"

There was a chorus of deep growls, and a young wolf in his fourth year flung back Shere Khan's question to Akela: "What have the Free People to do with a man's

5. Here, *veterans* means "those who have had much experience."

Vocabulary
cunning (kun′ ing) *n.* craftiness; intelligence

cub?" Now the Law of the Jungle lays down that if there is any dispute as to the right of a cub to be accepted by the Pack, he must be spoken for by at least two members of the Pack who are not his father and mother.

"Who speaks for this cub?" said Akela. "Among the Free People who speaks?" There was no answer, and Mother Wolf got ready for what she knew would be her last fight, if things came to fighting.

Then the only other creature who is allowed at the Pack Council—Baloo, the sleepy brown bear who teaches the wolf cubs the Law of the Jungle: old Baloo, who can come and go where he pleases because he eats only nuts and roots and honey— rose up on his hind quarters and grunted.

"The man's cub—the man's cub?" he said. "*I* speak for the man's cub. There is no harm in a man's cub. I have no gift of words, but I speak the truth. Let him run with the Pack, and be entered with the others. I myself will teach him."

"We need yet another," said Akela. "Baloo has spoken, and he is our teacher for the young cubs. Who speaks beside Baloo?"

A black shadow dropped down into the circle. It was Bagheera the Black Panther, inky black all over, but with the panther markings showing up in certain lights like the pattern of watered silk. Everybody knew Bagheera, and nobody cared to cross his path; for he was as cunning as Tabaqui, as bold as the wild buffalo, and as reckless as the wounded elephant. But he had a voice as soft as wild honey dripping from a tree, and a skin softer than down.

"O Akela, and ye the Free People," he purred, "I have no right in your assembly; but the Law of the Jungle says that if there is a doubt which is not a killing matter in regard to a new cub, the life of that cub may be bought at a price. And the Law does not say who may or may not pay that price. Am I right?"

"Good! good!" said the young wolves, who are always hungry. "Listen to Bagheera. The cub can be bought for a price. It is the Law."

"Knowing that I have no right to speak here, I ask your leave."

"Speak then," cried twenty voices.

"To kill a naked cub is shame. Besides, he may make better sport for you when he is grown. Baloo has spoken in his behalf. Now to Baloo's word I will add one bull, and a fat one, newly killed, not half a mile from here, if ye will accept the man's cub according to the Law. Is it difficult?"

There was a clamor of scores of voices, saying: "What matter? He will die in the winter rains. He will scorch in the sun. What harm can a naked frog do us? Let him run with the Pack. Where is the bull, Bagheera? Let him be accepted." And then came Akela's deep bay,[6] crying: "Look well—look well, O Wolves!"

Mowgli was still deeply interested in the pebbles, and he did not notice when

---

6. *Bay* can mean "the barking of a dog or wolf." Here, it refers to Akela's speaking voice.

Vocabulary
clamor (klam′ ər) *n.* a loud, noisy outcry

the wolves came and looked at him one by one. At last they all went down the hill for the dead bull, and only Akela, Bagheera, Baloo, and Mowgli's own wolves were left. Shere Khan roared still in the night, for he was very angry that Mowgli had not been handed over to him.

"Ay, roar well," said Bagheera, under his whiskers, "for the time comes when this naked thing will make thee roar to another tune, or I know nothing of man."

"It was well done," said Akela. "Men and their cubs are very wise. He may be a help in time."

"Truly, a help in time of need; for none can hope to lead the Pack for ever," said Bagheera.

Akela said nothing. He was thinking of the time that comes to every leader of every pack when his strength goes from him and he gets feebler and feebler, till at last he is killed by the wolves and a new leader comes up—to be killed in his turn.

"Take him away," he said to Father Wolf, "and train him as befits one of the Free People."

And that is how Mowgli was entered into the Seeonee wolf-pack for the price of a bull and on Baloo's good word.

Now you must be content to skip ten or eleven whole years, and only guess at all the wonderful life that Mowgli led among the wolves, because if it were written out it would fill ever so many books. He grew up with the cubs, though they, of course, were grown wolves almost before he was a child, and Father Wolf taught him his business, and the meaning of things in the jungle, till every rustle in the grass, every breath of the warm night air, every note of the owls above his head, every scratch of a bat's claws as it roosted for a while in a tree, and every splash of every little fish jumping in a pool, meant just as much to him as the work of his office means to a business man. When he was not learning he sat out in the sun and slept, and ate and went to sleep again; when he felt dirty or hot he swam in the forest pools; and when he wanted honey (Baloo told him that honey and nuts were just as pleasant to eat as raw meat) he climbed up for it, and that Bagheera showed him how to do. Bagheera would lie out on a branch and call, "Come along, Little Brother," and at first Mowgli would cling like the sloth, but afterward he would fling himself through the branches almost as boldly as the gray ape. He took his place at the Council Rock, too, when the Pack met, and there he discovered that if he stared hard at any

Did You Know?
The *sloth* is a shaggy-haired, tree-dwelling animal native to the tropical forests of Central and South America. It has long arms and legs with curved claws that help it hold onto branches.

wolf, the wolf would be forced to drop his eyes, and so he used to stare for fun. At other times he would pick the long thorns out of the pads of his friends, for wolves suffer terribly from thorns and burs in their coats. He would go down the hillside into the cultivated lands by night, and look very curiously at the villagers in their huts, but he had a mistrust of men because Bagheera

showed him a square box with a drop-gate so cunningly hidden in the jungle that he nearly walked into it, and told him that it was a trap. He loved better than anything else to go with Bagheera into the dark warm heart of the forest, to sleep all through the drowsy day, and at night see how Bagheera did his killing. Bagheera killed right and left as he felt hungry, and so did Mowgli— with one exception. As soon as he was old enough to understand things, Bagheera told him that he must never touch cattle because he had been bought into the Pack at the price of a bull's life. "All the jungle is thine," said Bagheera, "and thou canst kill everything that thou art strong enough to kill; but for the sake of the bull that bought thee thou must never kill or eat any cattle young or old. That is the Law of the Jungle." Mowgli obeyed faithfully.

And he grew and grew strong as a boy must grow who does not know that he is learning any lessons, and who has nothing in the world to think of except things to eat.

Mother Wolf told him once or twice that Shere Khan was not a creature to be trusted, and that some day he must kill Shere Khan; but though a young wolf would have remembered that advice every hour, Mowgli forgot it because he was only a boy—though he would have called himself a wolf if he had been able to speak in any human tongue.

Shere Khan was always crossing his path in the jungle, for as Akela grew older and feebler the lame tiger had come to be great friends with the younger wolves of the Pack, who followed him for scraps, a thing Akela would never have allowed if he had dared to push his authority to the proper bounds. Then Shere Khan would flatter them and wonder that such fine young hunters were content to be led by a dying wolf and a man's cub. "They tell me," Shere Khan would say, "that at Council ye dare not look him between the eyes"; and the young wolves would growl and bristle.

Bagheera, who had eyes and ears everywhere, knew something of this, and once or twice he told Mowgli in so many words that Shere Khan would kill him some day; and Mowgli would laugh and answer: "I have the Pack and I have thee; and Baloo, though he is so lazy, might strike a blow or two for my sake. Why should I be afraid?"

It was one very warm day that a new notion came to Bagheera—born of something that he had heard. Perhaps Sahi the Porcupine had told him; but he said to Mowgli when they were deep in the jungle, as the boy lay with his head on Bagheera's beautiful black skin: "Little Brother, how often have I told thee that Shere Khan is thy enemy?"

"As many times as there are nuts on that palm," said Mowgli, who, naturally, could not count. "What of it? I am sleepy, Bagheera, and Shere Khan is all long tail and loud talk—like Mor the Peacock."

"But this is no time for sleeping. Baloo knows it; I know it; the Pack know it; and even the foolish, foolish deer know. Tabaqui had told thee, too."

"Ho! ho!" said Mowgli. "Tabaqui came to me not long ago with some rude talk that I was a naked man's cub and not fit to dig pig-nuts; but I caught Tabaqui by the tail and swung him twice against a palm-tree to teach him better manners."

"That was foolishness; for though Tabaqui is a mischief-maker, he would have told thee of something that concerned thee closely. Open those eyes, Little Brother. Shere Khan dare not kill thee in the jungle; but remember, Akela is very old, and soon the day comes when he cannot kill his buck, and then he will be leader no more. Many of the wolves that looked thee over when thou wast brought to the Council first are old too, and the young wolves believe, as Shere Khan has taught them, that a man-cub

"Open those eyes, Little Brother."

has no place with the Pack. In a little time thou wilt be a man."

"And what is a man that he should not run with his brothers?" said Mowgli. "I was born in the jungle. I have obeyed the Law of the Jungle, and there is no wolf of ours from whose paws I have not pulled a thorn. Surely they are my brothers!"

Bagheera stretched himself at full length and half shut his eyes. "Little Brother," said he, "feel under my jaw."

Mowgli put up his strong brown hand, and just under Bagheera's silky chin, where the giant rolling muscles were all hid by the glossy hair, he came upon a little bald spot.

"There is no one in the jungle that knows that I, Bagheera, carry that mark—the mark of the collar; and yet, Little Brother, I was born among men, and it was among men that my mother died—in the cages of the King's Palace at Oodeypore. It was because of this that I paid the price for thee at the Council when thou wast a little naked cub. Yes, I too was born among men. I had never seen the jungle. They fed me behind bars from an iron pan till one night I felt that I was Bagheera—the Panther—and no man's plaything, and I broke the silly lock with one blow of my paw and came away; and because I had learned the ways of men, I became more terrible in the jungle than Shere Khan. Is it not so?"

"Yes," said Mowgli; "all the jungle fear Bagheera—all except Mowgli."

"Oh, *thou* art a man's cub," said the Black Panther, very tenderly; "and even as I returned to my jungle, so thou must go back to men at last—to the men who are thy brothers—if thou art not killed in the Council."

"But why—but why should any wish to kill me?" said Mowgli.

"Look at me," said Bagheera; and Mowgli looked at him steadily between the eyes. The big panther turned his head away in half a minute.

"*That* is why," he said, shifting his paw on the leaves. "Not even I can look thee between the eyes, and I was born among men, and I love thee, Little Brother. The others they hate thee because their eyes cannot meet thine; because thou art wise; because thou hast pulled out thorns from their feet—because thou art a man."

"I did not know these things," said Mowgli, sullenly; and he frowned under his heavy black eyebrows.

"What is the Law of the Jungle? Strike first and then give tongue. By thy very carelessness they know that thou art a man. But be wise. It is in my heart that when Akela misses his next kill—and at each hunt it costs him more to pin the buck— the Pack will turn against him and against thee. They will hold a jungle Council at the Rock, and then—and then—I have it!" said Bagheera, leaping up. "Go thou down quickly to the men's huts in the valley, and take some of the Red Flower which they grow there, so that when the time comes thou mayest have even a stronger friend than I or Baloo or those of the Pack that love thee. Get the Red Flower."

By Red Flower Bagheera meant fire, only no creature in the jungle will call fire by its proper name. Every beast lives in deadly fear of it, and invents a hundred ways of describing it.

"The Red Flower?" said Mowgli. "That grows outside their huts in the twilight. I will get some."

"There speaks the man's cub," said Bagheera, proudly. "Remember that it grows in little pots. Get one swiftly, and keep it by thee for time of need."

"Good!" said Mowgli. "I go. But art thou sure, O my Bagheera"—he slipped his arm round the splendid neck, and looked deep into the big eyes—"art thou sure that all this is Shere Khan's doing?"

"By the Broken Lock that freed me, I am sure, Little Brother."

"Then, by the Bull that bought me, I will pay Shere Khan full tale[7] for this, and it may be a little over," said Mowgli; and he bounded away.

"That is a man. That is all a man," said Bagheera to himself, lying down again. "Oh, Shere Khan, never was a blacker hunting than that frog-hunt of thine ten years ago!"

Mowgli was far and far through the forest, running hard, and his heart was hot in him. He came to the cave as the evening mist rose, and drew breath, and looked down the valley. The cubs were out, but

---

7. Here, *tale* has a meaning that's rarely used now: "a numbering or counting of things." Mowgli is saying that he'll get even.

Vocabulary
sullenly (sul′ ən lē) *adv.* in a sulky or gloomy way due to feeling angry or hurt

Mother Wolf, at the back of the cave, knew by his breathing that something was troubling her frog.

"What is it, Son?" she said.

"Some bat's chatter of Shere Khan," he called back. "I hunt among the plowed fields tonight"; and he plunged downward through the bushes, to the stream at the bottom of the valley. There he checked, for he heard the yell of the Pack hunting, heard the bellow of a hunted Sambhur, and the snort as the buck turned at bay.[8] Then there were wicked, bitter howls from the young wolves: "Akela! Akela! Let the Lone Wolf show his strength. Room for the leader of the Pack! Spring, Akela!"

The Lone Wolf must have sprung and missed his hold, for Mowgli heard the snap of his teeth and then a yelp as the Sambhur knocked him over with his fore foot.

He did not wait for anything more, but dashed on; and the yells grew fainter behind him as he ran into the crop-lands where the villagers lived.

"Bagheera spoke truth," he panted, as he nestled down in some cattle-fodder[9] by the window of a hut. "Tomorrow is one day both for Akela and for me."

Then he pressed his face close to the window and watched the fire on the hearth. He saw the husbandman's wife get up and feed it in the night with black lumps; and when the morning came and mists were all white and cold, he saw the man's child pick up a wicker pot plastered inside with earth, fill it with lumps of red-hot charcoal, put it under his blanket, and go out to tend the cows in the byre.[10]

"Is that all?" said Mowgli. "If a cub can do it, there is nothing to fear"; so he strode round the corner and met the boy, took the pot from his hand, and disappeared into the mist while the boy howled with fear.

"They are very like me," said Mowgli, blowing into the pot, as he had seen the woman do. "This thing will die if I do not give it things to eat"; and he dropped twigs and dried bark on the red stuff. Half-way up the hill he met Bagheera with the morning dew shining like moonstones on his coat.

"Akela has missed," said the Panther. "They would have killed him last night, but they needed thee also. They were looking for thee on the hill."

"I was among the plowed lands. I am ready. See!" Mowgli held up the fire-pot.

"Good! Now, I have seen men thrust a dry branch into that stuff, and presently

---

8. Here, *bay* refers to the position of a cornered animal that is forced to turn and face its pursuers.

9. *Fodder* is hay, alfalfa, or grass that has been cut and dried to feed cattle.

10. A *byre* is a cow barn.

the Red Flower blossomed at the end of it. Art thou not afraid?"

"No. Why should I fear? I remember now—if it is not a dream—how, before I was a Wolf, I lay beside the Red Flower, and it was warm and pleasant."

All that day Mowgli sat in the cave tending his fire-pot and dipping dry branches into it to see how they looked. He found a branch that satisfied him, and in the evening when Tabaqui came to the cave and told him rudely enough that he was wanted at the Council Rock, he laughed till Tabaqui ran away. Then Mowgli went to the Council, still laughing.

Akela the Lone Wolf lay by the side of his rock as a sign that the leadership of the Pack was open, and Shere Khan with his following of scrap-fed wolves walked to and fro openly being flattered. Bagheera lay close to Mowgli, and the fire-pot was between Mowgli's knees. When they were all gathered together, Shere Khan began to speak—a thing he would never have dared to do when Akela was in his prime.

"He has no right," whispered Bagheera. "Say so. He is a dog's son.[11] He will be frightened."

Mowgli sprang to his feet. "Free People," he cried, "does Shere Khan lead the Pack? What has a tiger to do with our leadership?"

"Seeing that the leadership is yet open, and being asked to speak—" Shere Khan began.

"By whom?" said Mowgli. "Are we *all* jackals, to fawn on this cattle-butcher? The leadership of the Pack is with the Pack alone."

There were yells of "Silence, thou man's cub!" "Let him speak. He has kept our Law"; and at last the seniors of the Pack thundered: "Let the Dead Wolf speak." When a leader of the Pack has missed his kill, he is called the Dead Wolf as long as he lives, which is not long.

Akela raised his old head wearily:

"Free People, and ye too, jackals of Shere Khan, for twelve seasons I have led ye to and from the kill, and in all that time not one has been trapped or maimed. Now I have missed my kill. Ye know how that plot was made. Ye know how ye brought me up to an untried buck to make my weakness known. It was cleverly done. Your right is to kill me here on the Council Rock, now. Therefore, I ask, who comes to make an end of the Lone Wolf? For it is my right, by the Law of the Jungle, that ye come one by one."

There was a long hush, for no single wolf cared to fight Akela to the death. Then Shere Khan roared: "Bah! what have we to do with this toothless fool? He is doomed to

---

11. In this story, wolves are "a free people," whereas dogs are owned by humans. Calling someone a dog or a *dog's son* is an insult.

Vocabulary

maim (mām) *v.* to injure so that a part of the body is lost or unusable

die! It is the man-cub who has lived too long. Free People, he was my meat from the first. Give him to me. I am weary of this man-wolf folly. He has troubled the jungle for ten seasons. Give me the man-cub, or I will hunt here always, and not give you one bone. He is a man, a man's child, and from the marrow[12] of my bones I hate him!"

Then more than half the Pack yelled: "A man! a man! What has a man to do with us? Let him go to his own place."

"And turn all the people of the villages against us?" clamored Shere Khan. "No; give him to me. He is a man, and none of us can look him between the eyes."

Akela lifted his head again, and said: "He has eaten our food. He has slept with us. He has driven game for us. He has broken no word of the Law of the Jungle."

"Also, I paid for him with a bull when he was accepted. The worth of a bull is little, but Bagheera's honor is something that he will perhaps fight for," said Bagheera, in his gentlest voice.

"A bull paid ten years ago!" the Pack snarled. "What do we care for bones ten years old?"

"Or for a pledge?" said Bagheera, his white teeth bared under his lip. "Well are ye called the Free People!"

"No man's cub can run with the people of the jungle," howled Shere Khan. "Give him to me!"

---

12. *Marrow* is the soft tissue inside bones or the essence of something. Shere Khan means that his hatred for Mowgli comes from the deepest part of himself.

"He is our brother in all but blood," Akela went on; "and ye would kill him here! In truth, I have lived too long. Some of ye are eaters of cattle, and of others I have heard that, under Shere Khan's teaching, ye go by dark night and snatch children from the villager's door-step. Therefore I know ye to be cowards, and it is to cowards I speak. It is certain that I must die, and my life is of no worth, or I would offer that in the man-cub's place. But for the sake of the Honor of the Pack—a little matter that by being without a leader ye have forgotten—I promise that if ye let the man-cub go to his own place, I will not, when my time comes to die, bare one tooth against ye. I will die without fighting. That will at least save the Pack three lives. More I cannot do; but if ye will, I can save ye the shame that comes of killing a brother against whom there is no fault—a brother spoken for and bought into the Pack according to the Law of the Jungle."

"He is a man—a man—a man!" snarled the Pack; and most of the wolves began to gather round Shere Khan, whose tail was beginning to switch.

"Now the business is in thy hands," said Bagheera to Mowgli. "*We* can do no more except fight."

Mowgli stood upright—the fire-pot in his hands. Then he stretched out his arms, and yawned in the face of the Council; but he was furious with rage and sorrow, for, wolf-like, the wolves had never told him how they hated him. "Listen you!" he cried. "There is no need for this dog's jabber. Ye have told me so often tonight that I am a man (and indeed I would have been a wolf with you to my life's end), that I feel your words are true. So I do not call ye my brothers any more, but *sag* [dogs], as a man should. What ye will do, and what ye will not do, is not yours to say. That matter is with *me*; and that we may see the matter more plainly, I, the man, have brought here a little of the Red Flower which ye, dogs, fear."

He flung the fire-pot on the ground, and some of the red coals lit a tuft of dried moss that flared up, as all the Council drew back in terror before the leaping flames.

Mowgli thrust his dead branch into the fire till the twigs lit and crackled, and whirled it above his head among the cowering[13] wolves.

"Thou art the master," said Bagheera, in an undertone. "Save Akela from the death. He was ever thy friend."

Akela, the grim old wolf who had never asked for mercy in his life, gave one piteous[14] look at Mowgli as the boy stood all naked, his long black hair tossing over his shoulders in the light of the blazing branch that made the shadows jump and quiver.

"Good!" said Mowgli, staring round slowly. "I see that ye are dogs. I go from you to my own people—if they be my own people. The Jungle is shut to me, and I must forget your talk and your companionship; but I will be more merciful than ye are. Because I was all but your brother in blood, I promise that when I am a man among men I will not betray ye to men as ye have betrayed me." He kicked the fire with his foot, and the sparks flew up. "There shall be no war between any of us in the Pack. But here is a debt to pay before I go." He strode forward to where Shere Khan sat blinking stupidly at the flames, and caught him by the tuft on his chin. Bagheera followed in case of accidents. "Up, dog!" Mowgli cried. "Up, when a man speaks, or I will set that coat ablaze!"

---

13. To *cower* is to crouch down, as in fear or shame.
14. *Piteous* means "deserving or arousing pity," or "sad and pitiful."

Shere Khan's ears lay flat back on his head, and he shut his eyes, for the blazing branch was very near.

"This cattle-killer said he would kill me in the Council because he had not killed me when I was a cub. Thus and thus, then, do we beat dogs when we are men. Stir a whisker, Lungri, and I ram the Red Flower down thy gullet!"[15] He beat Shere Khan over the head with the branch, and the tiger whimpered and whined in an agony of fear.

"Pah! Singed jungle-cat—go now! But remember when next I come to the Council Rock, as a man should come, it will be with Shere Khan's hide on my head. For the rest, Akela goes free to live as he pleases. Ye will *not* kill him, because that is not my will. Nor do I think that ye will sit here any longer, lolling out your tongues as though ye were somebodies, instead of dogs whom I drive out—thus! Go!" The fire was burning furiously at the end of the branch, and Mowgli struck right and left round the circle, and the wolves ran howling with the sparks burning their fur. At last there were only Akela, Bagheera, and perhaps ten wolves that had taken Mowgli's part. Then something began to hurt Mowgli inside him, as he had never been hurt in his life before, and he caught his breath and sobbed, and the tears ran down his face.

"What is it? What is it?" he said. "I do not wish to leave the jungle, and I do not know what this is. Am I dying, Bagheera?"

---

15. *Gullet* is another name for the throat.

"No, Little Brother. That is only tears such as men use," said Bagheera. "Now I know thou art a man, and a man's cub no longer. The Jungle is shut indeed to thee henceforward. Let them fall, Mowgli. They are only tears." So Mowgli sat and cried as though his heart would break; and he had never cried in all his life before.

"Now," he said, "I will go to men. But first I must say farewell to my mother"; and he went to the cave where she lived with Father Wolf, and he cried on her coat, while the four cubs howled miserably.

"Ye will not forget me?" said Mowgli.

"Never while we can follow a trail," said the cubs. "Come to the foot of the hill when thou art a man, and we will talk to thee; and we will come into the crop-lands to play with thee by night."

"Come soon!" said Father Wolf. "Oh, wise little frog, come again soon; for we be old, thy mother and I."

"Come soon," said Mother Wolf, "little naked son of mine; for, listen, child of man, I loved thee more than ever I loved my cubs."

"I will surely come," said Mowgli; "and when I come it will be to lay out Shere Khan's hide upon the Council Rock. Do not forget me! Tell them in the jungle never to forget me!"

The dawn was beginning to break when Mowgli went down the hillside alone, to meet those mysterious things that are called men.

Responding to Literature

PERSONAL RESPONSE

◆ Do the wolves in the story act the way you expect wolves to act? If not, how are they different?

◆ Think back to the notes you made in the **Focus Activity** on page 127. Have your ideas about life in the jungle changed?

Analyzing Literature

RECALL

1. How does Mowgli come to live with Mother and Father Wolf?
2. Who speaks against Mowgli at the Council meeting? Why?
3. Later, why does Akela have to step down as leader?
4. Why does Mowgli go to the village and get fire?

INTERPRET

5. Why, do you think, does the story start with the wolves in their family group?
6. Why does the pack accept the man's cub?
7. How is Mowgli's last Council meeting different from his first?
8. After Mowgli has defeated his enemies, why does he hurt "as he had never been hurt in his life before"?

EVALUATE AND CONNECT

9. Do the rules that the wolves live by remind you of human rules and laws? If so, in what ways?
10. If you were present at the Council meeting, would you accept Mowgli as part of the pack? Why or why not?

Extending Your Response

Writing About Literature

Characters   Kipling lets readers know something about his characters by the names he gives them. Choose a character in the story. Write a paragraph explaining how the name fits the character.

*inter*NET CONNECTION

Do wolves really live in families? Do they live in packs? Who is the "top dog" of a wolf grouping? Use a search engine to find out about how wolves behave toward each other. One place to find information might be *The National Wildlife Foundation.*

Creative Writing

Jungle Law Book   Gather some of the "Laws of the Jungle" from "Mowgli's Brothers" and rewrite them in your own words. Write a brief reason, based on information in the story and common sense, for each law you gather. Then add other laws you think would have helped this animal community.

Literature Groups

Talking Animals   Folktales like "Why Dogs Are Tame" often feature animal characters that talk and act like people. Kipling's stories in *The Jungle Books* also include talking animals. What human qualities do the characters in "Mowgli's Brothers" have? Discuss character traits shown in Tabaqui, Shere Khan, Akela, Baloo, Bagheera, and other characters. Share your conclusions with the class.

📖 **Save your work for your portfolio.**

Skill Minilesson

VOCABULARY • SYNONYMS

Synonyms are words that mean the same or nearly the same thing. *Search* and *hunt* are both synonyms for *scour,* but neither is an exact synonym. When you scour your house searching for something, you look high and low; you turn the place inside out. To communicate the same idea of carefully looking everywhere, a better synonym is *comb.*

PRACTICE   Choose the best synonym for each word.

1. **quarry**
   a. victim   b. goal   c. prey
2. **maim**
   a. cripple   b. hurt   c. damage
3. **cunning**
   a. wise   b. clever   c. smart
4. **lair**
   a. den   b. bed   c. house
5. **clamor**
   a. noise   b. sound   c. uproar

Before You Read

The Boy Who Lived with the Bears

MEET JOSEPH BRUCHAC

J oseph Bruchac (brōō'shak) is a storyteller in the tradition of his Native American ancestors. Of his stories, he says, "For more than thirty years I have listened to Iroquois elders tell these stories—though the stories might be told more often today in a living room while the television is still playing. . . ." For Bruchac, the stories are always current. They "teach important lessons about caring and responsibility and the dangers of selfishness and pride. . . ."

Joseph Bruchac was born in 1942. This story is from The Boy Who Lived with the Bears and Other Iroquois Stories, *which was published in 1995.*

FOCUS ACTIVITY

What are some rules that communities live by? If you were writing some rules for living in a community, what would they be?

Think/Pair/Share
Write your answers to these questions. Then compare and discuss ideas with a partner. Share your responses with the class.

Setting a Purpose
Read "The Boy Who Lived with the Bears" to find out what rules the Haudenosaunee, an Iroquois people, lived by.

BACKGROUND

The Time and Place   The story takes place in and around an Iroquois village. The Iroquois are a Native American people from the area of present day New York state and the Lake Ontario region of Canada.

Did You Know?   Oral storytelling has always been important to Native American cultures. Stories are told and retold, not just to children but to everyone in the community. The storyteller uses hands, body language, sound effects, and even singing, to bring a story to life. Stories are used to tell young people about their history and about legends and myths that are important to their group. Stories let young people see what is important in their society and what will be expected of them as they grow older.

VOCABULARY PREVIEW

troublesome (trub' əl səm) *adj.* causing trouble, p. 150
shuffle (shuf' əl) *v.* to walk by dragging the feet; p. 151
burrow (bur' ō) *n.* a hole dug in the ground, as by a rabbit, for shelter; p. 151

Long ago, in a small village of the Haudenosaunee people, there lived a little boy whose parents had died. This boy was living with his uncle, as was the custom in those days, for it was said that no child would ever be without parents.

But this boy's uncle did not have a straight mind. Although it was his duty to take care of his nephew, he resented the fact that he had this boy to care for.

THE BOY WHO LIVED WITH THE BEARS

Joseph Bruchac

Instead of taking care of him, he treated him badly. He dressed him in ragged clothes; he gave him only scraps of food to eat; he never even called the boy by his name. He just would say, "Hey, you, get out of my way!"

Now, this boy had always been taught by his parents to treat elders with respect. So he tried to do everything he could to please his uncle. His uncle was very respected in the village because he was a great hunter. When he and his dog went out, they always brought back game. One day, the uncle woke up with an idea in his mind. It was a twisted-mind idea, for what the uncle thought was this: "Too long have I been bothered with this <u>troublesome</u> boy. Today, I will get rid of him."

And so he called, "You, come here!" The boy quickly came, because he wanted to please his uncle. The uncle said, "You and I, we're going to go hunting together."

They left the lodge and started for the woods, and that was when the boy noticed something strange. He said, "Uncle, aren't you going to take your dog?" The uncle looked at the boy and said, "Today, you will be my dog."

Then the boy noticed another thing that was strange—they were going toward the north. In the village, when people went hunting, they would go to the east, or the south, or the west, but they would never go to the north, because there, it was said, strange things happened in the forest. Farther and farther the boy and his uncle went, away from any of the trails that people would follow, farther and farther to the north. The boy stayed close behind his uncle.

Finally, they came to a small clearing in the deep forest. On the other side, in the hillside, there was a small cave. The uncle said, "There are animals in there. You are my dog. Crawl in and chase them out." The boy was frightened, but then he thought back to what his parents had always told him: "Do what your elders say. Trust your elders."

So he crawled into the cave, but there was nothing there, no animal at all. As he turned around and began to crawl out, the circle of light that was the mouth of the cave suddenly vanished—the cave mouth had been blocked by a big stone. That was when the boy realized that his uncle meant to leave him there, and he began to cry.

But as his tears came, he remembered the song his mother had taught him to sing when he needed a friend. Softly, he began to sing:

> "Weyanna, weyanna, weyanna, hey.
> Weyanna, weyanna, weyanna, hey.
> Weyanna, weyanna, weyanna, hey.
> Wey, hey yo-o-o, wey hey yo."

Then he stopped, because it seemed as if he could hear soft singing answering him on the other side of that rock. So he sang a little louder:

Vocabulary
troublesome (trub′ əl səm) *adj.* causing trouble

"*Weyanna, weyanna, weyanna, hey.*
Weyanna, weyanna, weyanna, hey.
Weyanna, weyanna, weyanna, hey.
Wey, hey yo-o-o, wey hey yo."

And from the other side of that rock came back:

"*Wey, hey yo-o-o, wey hey yo.*"

The boy knew now that someone was out there, singing back to him, so he sang louder again. From the other side of the rock the song came back, strongly now. Then, together, the song was sung from both sides of the stone, and it ended together very loudly:

"*Wey, hey yo-o-o, wey hey yo.*"

As the song ended, the rock was rolled away, and the boy crawled out into the bright sunlight, blinking his eyes. All around him in the clearing many people were gathered: big people, small people, tall people, skinny people, fat people, people of all shapes and sizes. He blinked his eyes again, and he saw they were not people at all. They were animals, all the animals of the forest: bears, deer, foxes, wolves, beavers, muskrats, and even the small animals—squirrels, woodchucks, chipmunks, moles. All of them were gathered there and all were looking straight at him. He stood up,

and all of those animals took one step toward him! The boy did not know what would happen next. And that was when an old grandmother woodchuck shuffled up to him, poked him in the leg, and said, "Grandson, we heard your song. Do you need a friend?"

"Yes," said the boy. "I do need a friend. You've come to help me?"

"Yes," said the old grandmother woodchuck, "but where is your family? Why are you here, trapped in this cave?" The boy shook his head sadly. "My parents died, and only my uncle was left to care for me. But he did not want me. He put me in this cave and left me here to die, so I have no family anywhere in the world."

The old grandmother woodchuck said, "Grandson, we will be your family! Pick any of us, and we will adopt you!" The boy looked around. All the animals were looking at him, but how could he decide?

"My friends," he said, "tell me what your lives are like. Then I can decide which one I will come and live with."

So the animals began to tell him about their lives: The mole told him how he lived in a warm burrow and dug in the earth and ate delicious worms; the beaver described how he swam underwater and lived in a warm lodge and ate

Vocabulary
shuffle (shuf′ əl) *v.* to walk by dragging the feet
burrow (bur′ ō) *n.* a hole dug in the ground, as by a rabbit, for shelter

tree bark. The boy thanked each animal politely, but said that he did not have the claws to dig like the mole, and that he could not hold his breath and swim underwater like the beaver.

Then the old mother bear came up. "My boy, you would like to be a bear. We take our time going through the forest. We eat the most delicious honey and berries. We sleep in our warm cave. And my two children here will play with you as much as you want." The boy quickly said, "I will be a bear."

And indeed, it was as the old mother bear said. Their lives were very good together. They took their time going through the forest. They ate delicious berries and honey, and the boy grew fat and happy. The bear cubs would wrestle and play with him as much as he wanted. In fact, he began to look like a bear himself, because when they wrestled and played, if their claws scratched him, hair would grow there, so that after some time had passed, that boy looked just like a bear, covered with black hair himself.

For two seasons, they lived this way. But then one day, as they were walking through the forest, the old mother bear stopped suddenly and said, "Listen! . . . Listen!"

Well, the boy listened. And before long, he heard the sound of feet walking through the forest, stepping on twigs and brushing past the leaves. The old mother bear began to laugh. "That is the sound of a hunter trying to hunt the bear. But he makes so much noise going through the forest, we call him Heavy Foot. He will never catch a bear!" And so they continued on their way.

Another day came, and again as they walked through the forest, the old mother bear stopped and said, "Listen!" The boy could hear the sound of someone talking to himself, saying, "Ahhh, it is a very good day for hunting. Ah-ha, today I will surely catch a bear! Uh, yes, uh, I will probably catch more than one bear, for I am a great hunter!"

Old mother bear began to laugh. "That's the one who talks to himself while he hunts. We call him Flapping Jaws. He will never catch a bear!"

And so it went on. Each day they listened. They heard the hunter called Bumps into Trees, and the one called Falls in the Lake. None of these hunters was good enough to catch a bear.

But then one day, as they walked along, the old mother bear said, "Stop. Listen!" For a long time, the boy could hear nothing. Then, very, very faintly, he could hear the sound of soft feet, moving through the forest. But it did not sound like two feet. It did not sound like four feet. It sounded like two feet and four feet.

The old mother bear quickly nodded. She said, "This is the one we fear. It is Two Legs and Four Legs. We must RUN!" And she began to run. The boy and the two cubs ran behind her through the forest, but Two Legs and Four Legs were behind them. They ran through the swamps, but Two Legs and Four Legs were getting closer. They ran up the hills, but still Two Legs and Four Legs followed, and now the boy could hear behind them a sound growing louder: "*Wuf, wuf, wuf, wuf, wuf!*" And the boy knew that Two Legs and Four Legs were very close behind.

They came to a clearing where an old tree had fallen. It was hollow. The boy and the two cubs and the old mother bear went into that hollow log to hide.

The boy listened. He heard Two Legs and Four Legs come into the clearing and right up to the log. And then everything became quiet.

"Perhaps they've gone away," the boy thought. But then he began to smell smoke. Smoke was coming into the log! Two Legs had made a fire and was blowing the smoke into the log to make them come out.

It was just at that moment that the boy remembered that he, too, was a Two Legs. He was a person, a human being, and that was a hunter and a dog out there. The boy shouted, "Stop! Don't hurt my family!" And upon these words, the smoke stopped coming into the log.

The boy crawled out, blinking his eyes against the light. There in front of him stood the hunter, and the hunter was his uncle! The uncle stared at the boy. The boy stood up and came closer. The uncle reached out and touched him, and all the hair fell off the boy's body, and he looked like a person again.

"My nephew!" said the uncle. "Is it truly you? Are you alive?"

"Yes, I am, Uncle," said the boy.

"How could this be?" said the uncle. "I went back to the cave, because I realized I had done a twisted-mind thing. But when I got there, the stone had been rolled away. There were the tracks of many animals. I thought they had eaten you."

"No," said the boy. "The bears adopted me. They are my family now, Uncle. You must treat them well."

The uncle nodded. He said, "My nephew, your words are true. Call your family out. I will greet them and I will be their friend." So the boy called, and the old mother bear and the two cubs came out from the log; they came out and sniffed the hunter. He stood there patiently, letting them approach him.

From that day on, the hunter and his nephew were a family, and the bears were part of their family. And ever since then, this story has been told to remind parents and elders always to treat their children well and to show as much love in their hearts as a bear holds in its heart for its children.

That is how the story goes. *Ho? Hey.*

Responding to Literature

PERSONAL RESPONSE

- ◆ What feelings did you have while reading about the boy in the cave? What feelings did you have at the end of the story?
- ◆ Refer to your notes from the **Focus Activity** on page 148. Are any rules that you suggested found in the story?

Analyzing Literature

RECALL AND INTERPRET

1. At the beginning of the story, how does the uncle treat the boy? Why does the boy respond as he does?
2. How do the animals treat the boy? How do they show that the teaching of the boy's parents was right?
3. How does the boy meet again with his uncle? What happens to the boy? Why, do you think, does this happen?

EVALUATE AND CONNECT

4. How do you respond to the animal characters?
5. Which characters change the most and why?
6. Do you think telling a story like this is a good way to teach values? Explain.

LITERARY ELEMENTS

Folktale

A **folktale** is an old story that originally was passed down orally, or by word of mouth. "The Boy Who Lived with the Bears" was originally told among the Iroquois. Folktales were told for entertainment, but many also teach lessons about proper behavior and show what values are important to the community. Folktales are usually short and may feature animals who behave like humans.

1. What does the story say about proper behavior?
2. What values seem to be important to the Iroquois?

● See **Literary Terms Handbook**, p. R3.

Extending Your Response

Literature Groups

Story Themes   What are some stories you know that show proper behavior? Which behaviors are encouraged or discouraged? How can you tell? Discuss how these stories are similar to or different from "The Boy Who Lived with the Bears."

Writing About Literature

Bear's-Eye View   Tell the story from the point of view of one of the bear cubs. How does the cub's life change after the boy joins the family? What does the cub notice about the boy? How does the boy change?

COMPARING SELECTIONS

Mowgli's Brothers and THE BOY WHO LIVED WITH THE BEARS

COMPARE **SETTINGS**

"Mowgli's Brothers" and "The Boy Who Lived with the Bears" each takes place in a kind of forest. Find places in each story where the forest is described. Analyze the words and sentences. Do they give you a warm, safe feeling or a more uneasy feeling? What kind of a place is each forest?

COMPARE **CHARACTERS**

In both stories, many characters have interesting, descriptive names. Kipling's story uses names like "Dishlicker" and "the Big One," while Bruchac's bears call people "Heavy Foot," "Flapping Jaws," and "Bumps into Trees."

1. Compare the authors' use of names. What do these names show about the characters?

2. What names would you give the characters in the stories? Compare your choices with a partner's and discuss the names each of you chose.

COMPARE **EXPERIENCES**

Many years after leaving the forest, when they were adults, what would Mowgli and the boy who lived with the bears each say that he missed most about the forest?

- Think about what you know about these characters and write a brief response.
- Share your response with a partner or a small group.

Vo•cab•u•lar•y Skills

Using Context Clues

Context is the sentence or passage in which a word appears. It often provides clues to what an unfamiliar word means. Some kinds of **context clues** are:

Definition: "I felt ravenous—absolutely greedy for food."

- ◆ In this kind of context clue, the writer provides almost exactly what would appear in a dictionary. *Ravenous* means "greedily hungry."

Example: "The bear was as ravenous as a victim of starvation."

- ◆ Here, an example is provided. A victim of starvation would be extremely hungry.

Restatement: "Feeling ravenous made me grouchy. The gnawing hunger got on my nerves."

- ◆ The writer has restated the idea. Clearly, *ravenous* means a gnawing feeling of hunger.

Contrast: "It's hard to teach when students are either ravenous or the opposite—too full."

- ◆ Here, a contrast is provided. The reverse of *ravenous* is said to be "too full," so *ravenous* must mean something like "too hungry."

- ● For more on context clues, see **Reading Handbook,** p. R64.

EXERCISE

Use context clues to figure out what each underlined word means. Write a synonym or short definition for the word.

1. The bears arrived at a clearing. Where could they hide with no trees nearby?

2. The boy stood up straight and said with dignity, "This is my family."

3. Mother Wolf shows valor when she stands up to Shere Khan in order to protect the naked man's cub from him.

4. Bagheera teaches Mowgli how to scale a tree to reach the high branches where honey might be found.

5. Mowgli says that he will show fidelity to the wolves, not the disloyalty that they have shown to him.

Reading and Thinking Skills

Varying Reading Rate

Read the following passage from "Mowgli's Brothers," by Rudyard Kipling, paying attention to how quickly you move from one detail or phrase to the next.

The sentences are long and complex— the entire passage is only two sentences.

> It was the jackal—Tabaqui, the Dishlicker— and the wolves of India despise Tabaqui because he runs about making mischief, and telling tales, and eating rags and pieces of leather from the village rubbish-heaps. But they are afraid of him too, because Tabaqui, more than anyone else in the jungle, is apt to go mad, and then he forgets that he was ever afraid of anyone, and runs through the forest biting everything in his way.

Readers have to remember unusual character names.

Readers must figure out the meaning of words that are not in common use today.

Kipling's formal writing style and choice of words are pleasing to the ear, but reading his stories requires concentration. You probably read these sentences at a slower rate than you would read sentences in many other stories.

These tips can help you as you read:

- ◆ Slow down for a difficult passage.
- ◆ Reread sentences that don't seem to make sense.
- ◆ Remember characters' names. Then as the names reappear, you will recognize them and quickly move on.

● For more on reading strategies, see **Reading Handbook,** p. R67.

ACTIVITY

1. Choose two passages of equal length, one from "Mowgli's Brothers" and one from "The Boy Who Lived with the Bears" or another story. Record the time it takes you to read each passage. Which passage took longer to read? Why?

2. Record details you remember from each passage. Then reread the passages and add information you missed. Did you recall one better than the other? Why?

Before You Read

Koko: Smart Signing Gorilla

MEET JEAN CRAIGHEAD GEORGE

When she was young, Jean Craighead George spent her summers on her family's farm in southern Pennsylvania. Tagging along with her older brothers, she fished, swam, caught frogs, studied falcons, and developed a genuine love of nature and its creatures. In her autobiography, George says, "With two such brothers, a younger sister *had* to be a writer to find her niche and survive." As a writer, George has combined her loves of nature and literature to create many popular books.

Jean Craighead George was born in 1919. "Koko" was published in 1994.

FOCUS ACTIVITY

People talk to their pets all the time. What would you do if your pet talked back?

Whole-Class Discussion

What experiences have you had communicating with animals? How much do you think an animal understands of what you say? How does an animal communicate with you?

Setting a Purpose

Read "Koko: Smart Signing Gorilla" to find out how Koko communicates.

BACKGROUND

In the 1960s, researchers taught American Sign Language to a chimpanzee named Washoe. Around the same time, researchers taught a chimpanzee named Lana to communicate by using a computer console. Scientists at Stanford University believed that gorillas could also learn human language.

VOCABULARY PREVIEW

frustrating (frus′ trāt ing) *adj.* disappointing or irritating; p. 159

touching (tuch′ ing) *adj.* affecting or appealing to the emotions; heartwarming; p. 161

fulfill (fool fil′) *v.* to carry out or bring to completion; cause to happen; p. 161

endearing (en dēr′ ing) *adj.* arousing affection or warm feelings; lovable; p. 161

resort (ri zôrt′) *v.* to make use of something for support or relief; p. 161

inspire (in spīr′) *v.* to be the cause or source of something; p. 162

Koko:
Smart Signing Gorilla

Jean Craighead George

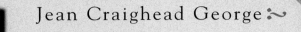

"Fine animal gorilla," said a young gorilla, Koko, in American Sign Language. A door to the silent world of the animals had been opened.

Using sign language and eventually a talking computer, Koko—under the devoted tutelage[1] of her "mother," Francine (Penny) Patterson—has told us what it is like to be a gorilla. It is just as frustrating and pleasant as being a human being.

---

1. Here, *tutelage* (tōot′ əl ij) means "instruction; act of teaching."

Vocabulary
frustrating (frus′ trāt ing) *adj.* disappointing or irritating

Koko

Koko was born July 4, 1971, in the San Francisco Zoo. Penny saw the infant three months later and knew what she wanted to do for a graduate study: She would teach Koko to speak in sign language. After another month the zoo and Stanford University[2] agreed to let her try, and a most remarkable experiment began. It demonstrated that gorillas, which have no vocal cords, can nevertheless use language. With sign language Koko expressed her inner emotions. "This gentle animal," Penny wrote, "feels all the emotions you and I experience; grief, hope, greed, generosity, shame, love and hate."

Koko's first word was "drink," the hand made into a fist with the thumb up, then put to the mouth. When that got her a bottle of milk, she quickly learned more signs. One lesson later, she signed "food" and Penny fed her. Koko was so pleased that she put a bucket over her head and ran around wildly. Two months later, when her vocabulary had expanded to eight words and combinations of those words, Penny wrote that Koko did "something

---

2. *Graduate study* is research done by an advanced student under the supervision of a professor. *Stanford University* is in Stanford, California.

simple but somehow very touching." She took Penny gently by the hand and led her around her room, pausing frequently to adjust the position of their hands.

Gorillas have long been known to be moody and Koko was no exception. She was a very stubborn youngster. It took her two long months to learn the word for "egg," which she disliked, and one minute to learn "berry." She loved to eat berries.

A sense of humor often rose out of her stubbornness. When asked the color of her white towel for a boring umpteenth[3] time, she signed "red." When asked twice again, she replied "red," then carefully picked a tiny speck of red lint off her towel. She chuckled, and again said "red."

Koko turned the pages of picture books and named the animals, recognized herself in photographs and in the mirror, carefully cleaned her room, and played with her pets. So deeply did she grieve when her cat died that she was allowed to choose a new kitten from a litter. She took care of it with gentleness and love.

Eventually Penny purchased Koko from the zoo and moved her and her trailer to the Stanford campus. At the end of moving day, Koko signed, "Go home." When this request was not fulfilled, she sobbed the tearless cry of the gorilla.

As Koko learned more words, she was able to express not only her likes, but her dislikes. She hated the noisy blue jays at the zoo, so she called people who annoyed her "bird." One day when Kate, an assistant, would not open the refrigerator, Koko signed, "Kate bird rotten." When truly angry she had a humdinger[4] of an insult, "rotten toilet," which she invented herself. Mike, her young gorilla friend, was "Mike nut" when she felt jealous of him. Ron Cohn, Penny's coworker and the person who disciplined Koko, came in for the worst abuses. "Stupid devil devilhead" was an expletive[5] for him. One day when a teacher asked Koko to tell her something funny, she did. "Koko love Ron," she signed, and kissed him on the cheek—then she chuckled. She liked the irony of her own jokes.

Koko could be moody, but she could also be endearing. When Mike was having his picture taken, she told him, "Smile."

Koko liked words. She caught on to pig Latin when workers resorted to it to disguise words like "candy." She also rhymed words. Part of her training consisted of hearing the spoken word when her teachers signed. Asked one day if she could sign a rhyme, she replied, "hair bear" and "all ball."

She was a wizard at inventing new words. After drinking her juice through a long rubber tube one day, she called herself an "elephant gorilla." A cigarette lighter

3. *Umpteenth* refers to any large but unnamed number.

4. Anyone or anything that's unusual, remarkable, or excellent is a *humdinger*.

5. An *expletive* (eks′ plə tiv) is a word or phrase that is rude or indecent.

Vocabulary

touching (tuch′ ing) *adj.* affecting or appealing to the emotions; heartwarming
fulfill (fool fil′) *v.* to carry out or bring to completion; cause to happen
endearing (en dēr′ ing) *adj.* arousing affection or warm feelings; lovable
resort (ri zôrt′) *v.* to make use of something for support or relief

Koko

was a "bottle match," and a mask was an "eye hat." A ring was a "finger bracelet."

Several years ago Koko, Mike, Ron, and Penny moved to the country, where the gorillas could behave like gorillas. Today Koko and Mike climb fruit trees and eat the pears, plums, apples, and apricots. Each has a modular[6] building, an outdoor play yard, and a computer that speaks. Here is a sign conversation between Penny and Koko after Koko had asked for more words on her computer:

Koko: Do bean.

Penny: Oh, she wants bean.

Koko: Bad fake bird fake bird bird. Apple. (Koko uses the sign "bird" for word.)

At this point Penny realized Koko didn't want a bean but a being, a human being. She asked Koko if that was what she wanted.

Koko: (excitedly) Do bean, do bean.

She was quite satisfied when the icon for human being appeared.

Koko is one of an endangered species. The foundation she <u>inspired</u>, The Gorilla Foundation, is dedicated to breeding gorillas in captivity. If all goes as planned, Koko will teach her own baby to sign, use a computer, and tell the "beans" more about themselves and gorillas.

---

6. Here, *modular* (moj′ ə lər) means that each building is made of standardized parts that can be put together in different ways.

Vocabulary

inspire (in spīr′) *v.* to be the cause or source of something

Responding to Literature

PERSONAL RESPONSE

- ◆ Would you like to talk to Koko? What would you want to ask her or say to her?
- ◆ Think back to the **Focus Activity** on page 158. Do you think other animals are able to understand as much as Koko does?

Analyzing Literature

RECALL

1. What emotions is Koko able to express through sign language?
2. What are two incidents that caused Koko great sadness?
3. Why does Koko call people who annoyed her "bird"?
4. What is the purpose of The Gorilla Foundation?

INTERPRET

5. Were you surprised that Koko has the same emotions as humans? If so, why?
6. Do you think Koko and Mike are happy in their present home? Why?
7. In addition to learning words, what else does Koko do that shows her intelligence?
8. Do you think Koko will be able to teach her baby to use language? Explain your answer.

EVALUATE AND CONNECT

9. Theme Connection   If all animals could communicate with language, do you think people would be more sensitive to their problems as endangered species? Explain.
10. Do you think animals like Koko should be used in research like that described in this selection? Explain.

LITERARY ELEMENTS

Exposition

"Koko: Smart Signing Gorilla" is **expository text**—writing in which something is explained. As writers of expository text explain important points, they illustrate them with examples and other kinds of details that reinforce these ideas. For example, George begins a paragraph, "A sense of humor often rose out of [Koko's] stubbornness." Then George tells about the time when Koko identified the color of a speck of lint on a towel, rather than the color of the towel, to get back at Penny for asking her a boring question. George's example supports her point about Koko's stubbornness.

1. Name the most important idea and list the supporting examples in the paragraph beginning "As Koko learned more words. . . ."

2. What do supporting examples add to a piece of expository writing?

● See **Literary Terms Handbook,** p. R3.

Extending Your Response

Writing About Literature

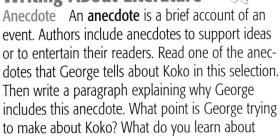

Anecdote   An **anecdote** is a brief account of an event. Authors include anecdotes to support ideas or to entertain their readers. Read one of the anecdotes that George tells about Koko in this selection. Then write a paragraph explaining why George includes this anecdote. What point is George trying to make about Koko? What do you learn about Koko from the anecdote?

Creative Writing

Late-Night Talking   Try to imagine what Koko and Mike might talk about once Penny and all the workers have gone home for the night. Jot down some topics they might discuss. Then write an imaginary conversation between Koko and Mike.

Literature Groups

Through Koko's Eyes   George says that Koko has "told us what it is like to be a gorilla." Discuss what specific information about gorillas' thoughts and feelings Koko has communicated and *how* she has communicated this information.

Listening and Speaking

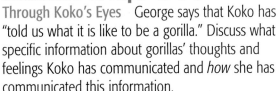

What's Up, Koko?   Write interview questions for Koko as if she were going to appear with you on a show called "Animals Talk Back." Include questions for Penny as well. You may want an update on Penny's research or an overview on other research involving gorilla or chimpanzee use of language. Then read your questions to the class.

Reading Further

If you'd like to read more by Jean Craighead George, you might enjoy these books:
Fiction: *My Side of the Mountain*
The Cry of the Crow
Nonfiction: *Animals Who Have Won Our Hearts*
The Moon of the Gray Wolves

📔 **Save your work for your portfolio.**

Skill Minilesson

VOCABULARY • CONTEXT CLUES

You can often guess the meaning of a word from **context clues.** The context of a word is the sentence or passage in which it appears. What do context clues tell you about *resort?*

Workers resorted to pig Latin to disguise words like "candy."

You might have guessed that *resorted* means "used."

PRACTICE Find the following words in the selection, and use context clues to guess their meanings. Then check your meanings with the dictionary meanings.

1. expanded (page 160)
2. moody (page 161)
3. sobbed (page 161)
4. irony (page 161)
5. captivity (page 162)

Dian Fossey and Her Gorillas

In 1966 Dian Fossey left her home in California for the rain forest in Rwanda, Africa. There she spent the next thirteen years living with and studying mountain gorillas. Her careful research dispelled common myths about the supposedly violent and aggressive nature of gorillas.

Fossey tracked gorillas through the rain forest for several months before she could get near enough to observe them. Then she discovered the secret to getting close to one gorilla group:

> "To be perfectly frank, I think they are quite confused as to my species! I've gotten them accustomed to me by aping them, and they are fascinated by my facial grimaces and other actions that I wouldn't be caught dead doing in front of anyone. I feel like a complete fool, but this technique seems to be working."

From her careful and detailed written records, Fossey was able to document many details of gorilla behavior, including at least nine types of vocal communication. Dian Fossey's life and work ended tragically when she was murdered in her rain forest camp in 1985. The mystery of her murder has never been solved, but her accomplishments live on. Her remarkable patience, curiosity, and courage greatly increased our knowledge of gorillas and helped ensure a future for the few hundred gorillas that remain in the wild.

ACTIVITY

Observe an animal in sessions of at least fifteen minutes each. The animal may be a household pet, a neighborhood or farm animal, or a zoo animal. Vary the time of your observations to include many different activities. Use your senses, recording what you see, hear, and smell during each session. Share the results of your research and your conclusions about it with the class.

Before You Read

Zlateh the Goat

MEET ISAAC BASHEVIS SINGER

Of life in his boyhood village in Poland, Isaac Bashevis Singer once wrote, ". . . many of the people that I describe no longer exist, but to me they remain alive." He believed that "to the storyteller yesterday is still here."

Singer grew up in a house of stories and books. His father was a rabbi, a Jewish religious leader. In 1935 Singer came to the United States and became an American citizen. In 1978 he was awarded the Nobel Prize for Literature.

Isaac Bashevis Singer was born in 1904 and died in 1991. This story was published in 1966.

FOCUS ACTIVITY

How might a person feel if caught outside in very bad weather? How might you react if this happened to you?

QuickWrite
Briefly write down your responses to these questions. Then share your answers with a small group.

Setting a Purpose
Read "Zlateh the Goat" to experience a bad storm with a boy and his goat.

BACKGROUND

Did You Know? The story takes place around the time of Hanukkah, an eight-day Jewish holiday in early winter. Hanukkah celebrates a miraculous event that took place during the rededication of the Jewish Temple in Jerusalem more than two thousand years ago. The Temple had been in the hands of the Jews' enemies and had been used for worshipping Greek gods and goddesses. When the Temple was rededicated it is said that only one small container of oil kept the Eternal Flame burning for eight days. Hanukkah is celebrated by exchanging small gifts and lighting candles each of the eight nights.

VOCABULARY PREVIEW

dense (dens) *adj.* thick; difficult to get through; p. 168
penetrate (pen' ə trāt') *v.* to pass into or through; p. 168
astray (ə strā') *adv.* off the right path; p. 169
eddy (ed' ē) *n.* small whirlwind or whirlpool; p. 169
glazed (glāzd) *adj.* covered with a smooth, shiny coating; p. 169
splendor (splen' dər) *n.* a great display, as of riches or beautiful objects; p. 171

Zlateh the Goat

Isaac Bashevis Singer

Translated by the author and Elizabeth Shub

At Hanukkah time the road from the village to the town is usually covered with snow, but this year the winter had been a mild one. Hanukkah had almost come, yet little snow had fallen. The sun shone most of the time. The peasants complained that because of the dry weather there would be a poor harvest of winter grain. New grass sprouted, and the peasants sent their cattle out to pasture.

For Reuven the furrier[1] it was a bad year, and after long hesitation he decided to sell Zlateh the goat. She was old and gave little milk. Feivel the town butcher had offered eight gulden[2] for her. Such a sum would buy Hanukkah candles, potatoes and oil for pancakes, gifts for the children, and other holiday necessaries for the house. Reuven told his oldest boy Aaron to take the goat to town.

Aaron understood what taking the goat to Feivel meant, but had to obey his father. Leah, his mother, wiped the tears from her eyes when she heard the news. Aaron's younger sisters, Anna and Miriam, cried loudly. Aaron put on his quilted jacket and a cap with earmuffs, bound a rope around Zlateh's neck, and took along two slices of bread with cheese to eat on the road. Aaron was supposed to deliver the goat by evening, spend the night at the butcher's, and return the next day with the money.

While the family said goodbye to the goat, and Aaron placed the rope around her neck, Zlateh stood as patiently and good-naturedly as ever. She licked Reuven's hand. She shook her small white beard.

---

1. A *furrier* is one who sells furs or makes and sells clothing made of fur.
2. *Gulden* (gōōl′ dən) is the name of a gold or silver coin once used in several European countries.

Zlateh trusted human beings. She knew that they always fed her and never did her any harm.

When Aaron brought her out on the road to town, she seemed somewhat astonished. She'd never been led in that direction before. She looked back at him questioningly, as if to say, "Where are you taking me?" But after a while she seemed to come to the conclusion that a goat shouldn't ask questions. Still, the road was different. They passed new fields, pastures, and huts with thatched roofs. Here and there a dog barked and came running after them, but Aaron chased it away with his stick.

The sun was shining when Aaron left the village. Suddenly the weather changed. A large black cloud with a bluish center appeared in the east and spread itself rapidly over the sky. A cold wind blew in with it. The crows flew low, croaking. At first it looked as if it would rain, but instead it began to hail as in summer. It was early in the day, but it became dark as dusk. After a while the hail turned to snow.

In his twelve years Aaron had seen all kinds of weather, but he had never experienced a snow like this one. It was so <u>dense</u> it shut out the light of the day. In a short time their path was completely covered. The wind became as cold as ice. The road to town was narrow and winding. Aaron no longer knew where he was. He could not see through the snow. The cold soon <u>penetrated</u> his quilted jacket.

At first Zlateh didn't seem to mind the change in weather. She, too, was twelve years old and knew what winter meant. But when her legs sank deeper

Vocabulary
dense (dens) *adj.* thick; difficult to get through
penetrate (pen′ ə trāt′) *v.* to pass into or through

and deeper into the snow, she began to turn her head and look at Aaron in wonderment. Her mild eyes seemed to ask, "Why are we out in such a storm?" Aaron hoped that a peasant would come along with his cart, but no one passed by.

The snow grew thicker, falling to the ground in large, whirling flakes. Beneath it Aaron's boots touched the softness of a plowed field. He realized that he was no longer on the road. He had gone astray. He could no longer figure out which was east or west, which way was the village, the town. The wind whistled, howled, whirled the snow about in eddies. It looked as if white imps[3] were playing tag on the fields. A white dust rose above the ground. Zlateh stopped. She could walk no longer. Stubbornly she anchored her cleft hooves[4] in the earth and bleated as if pleading to be taken home. Icicles hung from her white beard, and her horns were glazed with frost.

Aaron did not want to admit the danger, but he knew just the same that if they did not find shelter they would freeze to death. This was no ordinary storm. It was a mighty blizzard. The snowfall had reached his knees. His hands were numb, and he could no longer feel his toes. He choked when he breathed. His nose felt like wood, and he rubbed it with snow. Zlateh's bleating began to sound like crying. Those humans in whom she had so much confidence had dragged her into a trap. Aaron began to pray to God for himself and for the innocent animal.

Suddenly he made out the shape of a hill. He wondered what it could be. Who had piled snow into such a huge heap? He moved toward it, dragging Zlateh after him. When he came near it, he realized that it was a large haystack which the snow had blanketed.

Aaron realized immediately that they were saved. With great effort he dug his way through the snow. He was a village boy and knew what to do. When he reached the hay, he hollowed out a nest for himself and the goat. No matter how cold it may be outside, in the hay it is always warm. And hay was food for Zlateh. The moment she smelled it she became contented and began to eat. Outside, the snow continued to fall. It quickly covered the passageway Aaron had dug. But a boy and an animal need to breathe, and there was hardly any air in their hideout. Aaron bored a kind of a window through the hay and snow and carefully kept the passage clear.

Zlateh, having eaten her fill, sat down on her hind legs and seemed to have regained her confidence in man. Aaron ate his two slices of bread and cheese, but after the difficult journey he was still hungry. He looked at Zlateh and noticed her udders were full. He lay down next to her, placing himself so that when he milked her he could squirt the milk into his mouth. It was rich and sweet. Zlateh was not accustomed to being milked

---

3. Here, the *imps* are playful, fairylike spirits.
4. A *cleft* is a space, opening, or crack. Goats, sheep, cattle, and pigs all have *cleft hooves.*

Vocabulary
astray (ə strā′) *adv.* off the right path
eddy (ed′ ē) *n.* small whirlwind or whirlpool
glazed (glāzd) *adj.* covered with a smooth, shiny coating

Zlateh the Goat

that way, but she did not resist. On the contrary, she seemed eager to reward Aaron for bringing her to a shelter whose very walls, floor, and ceiling were made of food.

Through the window Aaron could catch a glimpse of the chaos outside. The wind carried before it whole drifts of snow. It was completely dark, and he did not know whether night had already come or whether it was the darkness of the storm. Thank God that in the hay it was not cold. The dried hay, grass, and field flowers exuded[5] the warmth of the summer sun. Zlateh ate frequently; she nibbled from above, below, from the left and right. Her body gave forth an animal warmth, and Aaron cuddled up to her. He had always loved Zlateh, but now she was like a sister. He was alone, cut off from his family, and wanted to talk. He began to talk to Zlateh. "Zlateh, what do you think about what has happened to us?" he asked.

"Maaaa," Zlateh answered.

"If we hadn't found this stack of hay, we would both be frozen stiff by now," Aaron said.

"Maaaa," was the goat's reply.

"If the snow keeps on falling like this, we may have to stay here for days," Aaron explained.

"Maaaa," Zlateh bleated.

"What does 'maaaa' mean?" Aaron asked. "You'd better speak up clearly."

"Maaaa, maaaa," Zlateh tried.

"Well, let it be 'maaaa' then," Aaron said patiently. "You can't speak, but I know you understand. I need you and you need me. Isn't that right?"

"Maaaa."

Aaron became sleepy. He made a pillow out of some hay, leaned his head on it, and dozed off. Zlateh, too, fell asleep.

When Aaron opened his eyes, he didn't know whether it was morning or night. The snow had blocked up his window. He tried to clear it, but when he had bored through to the length of his arm, he still hadn't reached the outside. Luckily he had his stick with him and was able to break through to the open air. It was still dark outside. The snow continued to fall and the wind wailed, first with one voice and then with many. Sometimes it had the sound of devilish laughter. Zlateh, too, awoke, and when Aaron greeted her, she answered, "Maaaa." Yes, Zlateh's language consisted of only one word, but it meant many things. Now she was saying, "We must accept all that God gives us— heat, cold, hunger, satisfaction, light, and darkness."

Aaron had awakened hungry. He had eaten up his food, but Zlateh had plenty of milk.

For three days Aaron and Zlateh stayed in the haystack. Aaron had always loved Zlateh, but in these three days he loved her more and more. She fed him with her milk and helped him keep warm. She comforted him with her patience. He told her many stories, and she always cocked her ears and listened. When he patted her, she licked his hand and his face. Then she said, "Maaaa," and he knew it meant, I love you, too.

The snow fell for three days, though after the first day it was not as thick and the wind quieted down. Sometimes Aaron

---

5. To *exude* (ig zōōd′) is to give off or ooze forth.

felt that there could never have been a summer, that the snow had always fallen, ever since he could remember. He, Aaron, never had a father or mother or sisters. He was a snow child, born of the snow, and so was Zlateh. It was so quiet in the hay that his ears rang in the stillness. Aaron and Zlateh slept all night and a good part of the day. As for Aaron's dreams, they were all about warm weather. He dreamed of green fields, trees covered with blossoms, clear brooks, and singing birds. By the third night the snow had stopped, but Aaron did not dare to find his way home in the darkness. The sky became clear and the moon shone, casting silvery nets on the snow. Aaron dug his way out and looked at the world. It was all white, quiet, dreaming dreams of heavenly <u>splendor</u>. The stars were large and close. The moon swam in the sky as in a sea.

On the morning of the fourth day Aaron heard the ringing of sleigh bells. The haystack was not far from the road. The peasant who drove the sleigh pointed out the way to him—not to the town and Feivel the butcher, but home to the village. Aaron had decided in the haystack that he would never part with Zlateh.

Aaron's family and their neighbors had searched for the boy and the goat but had found no trace of them during the storm. They feared they were lost. Aaron's mother and sisters cried for him; his father remained silent and gloomy. Suddenly one of the neighbors came running to their house with the news that Aaron and Zlateh were coming up the road.

Vocabulary

splendor (splen′ dər) *n.* a great display, as of riches or beautiful objects

There was great joy in the family. Aaron told them how he had found the stack of hay and how Zlateh had fed him with her milk. Aaron's sisters kissed and hugged Zlateh and gave her a special treat of chopped carrots and potato peels, which Zlateh gobbled up hungrily.

Nobody ever again thought of selling Zlateh, and now that the cold weather had finally set in, the villagers needed the services of Reuven the furrier once more. When Hanukkah came, Aaron's mother was able to fry pancakes every evening, and Zlateh got her portion, too. Even though Zlateh had her own pen, she often came to the kitchen, knocking on the door with her horns to indicate that she was ready to visit, and she was always admitted. In the evening Aaron, Miriam, and Anna played dreidel. Zlateh sat near the stove watching the children and the flickering of the Hanukkah candles.

Once in a while Aaron would ask her, "Zlateh, do you remember the three days we spent together?"

And Zlateh would scratch her neck with a horn, shake her white bearded head, and come out with the single sound which expressed all her thoughts, and all her love.

Did You Know?
Similar to a spinning top, the *dreidel* (drād′ əl) is a toy used in a game played during Hanukkah.

Responding to Literature

PERSONAL RESPONSE

- ◆ How did you feel as you read about the snowstorm?
- ◆ Look back at your notes from the **Focus Activity** on page 166. Do the characters in the story have the feelings that you would expect them to have?

Analyzing Literature

RECALL

1. Where is Aaron supposed to take Zlateh? Why?
2. Why doesn't the goat resist?
3. How does Zlateh save Aaron during the snowstorm?
4. How do Aaron and the family repay Zlateh?

INTERPRET

5. How do Aaron and his family feel about Zlateh? How can you tell?
6. How does Singer let you know what the goat is thinking? Is this technique effective? Give an example.
7. What emotions or characteristics does Singer give to Zlateh? How does the goat express these qualities?
8. *Hanukkah* means "dedication" and is a holiday about saving something important. In what ways does the conclusion of the story reflect the meaning of Hanukkah?

EVALUATE AND CONNECT

9. Singer uses **description** to help readers visualize where the characters are and what they are doing. How effective is this description? Find two examples of description that helps you picture a scene.
10. What other story do you know in which a person and an animal depend on and love each other? How is that story like "Zlateh the Goat"?

LITERARY ELEMENTS

Characterization

Singer develops the **characters** in "Zlateh the Goat" by showing what each character does and says and what others say and think about the character. For example, Singer tells us that Aaron's mother wipes the tears from her eyes when she learns that Zlateh is to be sold. Instead of directly telling us that Zlateh is a sweet and loving animal, Singer tells about Zlateh indirectly by showing how Aaron's mother feels about the goat.

1. What do the actions of others let us know about Zlateh? Give examples.

2. What do we learn about Zlateh by her own actions?

3. What does Zlateh say and what does it mean?

● See **Literary Terms Handbook,** p. R2.

Literature and Writing

Writing About Literature

Analyzing Aaron's Decision   Do you agree with the decision Aaron makes about Zlateh? Why? What is Aaron's situation as he makes his decision? How does Aaron's family react to his decision? Write a paragraph explaining what decision Aaron makes at the end of the story and why he makes it.

Personal Writing

In Trouble!   Write a journal entry—or several entries—telling of a harrowing experience. Maybe you were caught in a lightning storm or got lost in a strange place. Tell how you felt and what gave you the strength to get out of the situation. If you had a companion, describe how you helped or hindered each other during the crisis.

Extending Your Response

Literature Groups

The Wisdom of Zlateh   To Aaron, one meaning of Zlateh's bleats is, "We must accept all that God gives us—heat, cold, hunger, satisfaction, light, and darkness." Find places in the story where Aaron experiences each of these things. Discuss how he shows that he learns Zlateh's lesson.

Interdisciplinary Activity

Math   Jewish families light candles on a special candle holder called a Hanukkah *menorah* every night during Hanukkah. On the first night, one candle is lit; on the second night, two candles; and so on for eight nights. The candles are lit each night by a special "extra" candle separated from the others on the candle holder. If new candles, including a new "extra" candle, are used each night, how many candles are burned altogether during Hanukkah?

Listening and Speaking
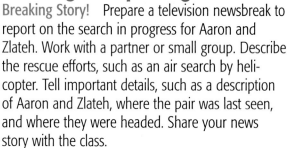

Breaking Story!   Prepare a television newsbreak to report on the search in progress for Aaron and Zlateh. Work with a partner or small group. Describe the rescue efforts, such as an air search by helicopter. Tell important details, such as a description of Aaron and Zlateh, where the pair was last seen, and where they were headed. Share your news story with the class.

Reading Further
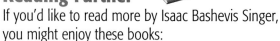

If you'd like to read more by Isaac Bashevis Singer, you might enjoy these books:

Fiction: *When Shlemiel Went to Warsaw and Other Stories*

The Fools of Chelm and Their History

Autobiography: *A Day of Pleasure: Stories of a Boy Growing Up in Warsaw*

📖 **Save your work for your portfolio.**

Skill Minilessons

GRAMMAR AND LANGUAGE • ADVERBS

Adverbs modify verbs and tell how, when, or where things are done. Many adverbs end in *-ly.*

Zlateh stood *patiently* and *good-naturedly.*

The adverbs in italics describe **how** Zlateh acts.

PRACTICE Look through the story, find five adverbs ending in *-ly,* and list them. Next to each adverb, write another adverb that would make sense in the sentence.

● For more on adverbs, see **Language Handbook,** p. R24.

READING AND THINKING • VISUALIZING

Visualizing means picturing a scene that is described in words in a story. In the **Analyzing Literature** activity, you found two examples of description that helped you visualize a scene.

PRACTICE Find another scene in the story you can visualize. Draw a detailed picture and write a description of the scene. Read your description to a partner and then share your picture. Discuss whether it shows the scene as your partner visualized it.

● For more on reading strategies, see **Reading Handbook,** p. R77.

A Goat and Pigeons in a Farmyard. Edgar Hunt (1876–1953). Private collection.

VOCABULARY • RELATED MEANINGS

Both a forest and a person can be *dense.* If you know one meaning of *dense,* you can figure out the other, related, meaning. With a dense forest, it's trees that are thick. With a dense person, it's the skull that is thick (although not literally, of course). You can't "get through" to a dense person. The meanings of *glazed* are also closely related. People whose eyes are *glazed* don't actually have a shiny coating on their eyes. Their eyes look glassy, probably from fear, shock, boredom, or illness.

PRACTICE Use the familiar meaning of each underlined word to answer each question.

1. If a certain kind of toy floods the market, is that toy rare, expensive, or plentiful?
2. If you mirror someone's behavior, do you imitate it, laugh at it, or ignore it?
3. If someone's speech is fluff, is it serious, unimportant, or upsetting?
4. If you can't phrase something well, do you have trouble saying it, understanding it, or hearing it?
5. If you breeze down the street, do you move slowly, clumsily, or easily?

POETRY

Poetry generally is the shortest form of writing, but it can be the hardest to read. A writer of prose develops ideas or relationships between characters over several pages. A poet might use only a few words. Poets choose their words carefully, and not just for their meaning. Poets find words that will appeal to readers' emotions, senses, and imaginations, and use these words to create effects of **sound** and **imagery.**

● For more on poetry, see **Literary Terms Handbook,** p. R6.

SOUND

POETRY is usually arranged in lines. Poetry often has a regular **rhythm,** or pattern of beats, and sometimes has a regular **rhyme,** or repetition of similar sounds at the end of words. Listen to the regular, predictable rhythm and rhyme in "The Hippopotamus" by Ogden Nash.

"The Hippopotamus"

Behold the hippopotamus!
We laugh at how he looks to us,
And yet in moments dank and grim
I wonder how we look to him.

ONOMATOPOEIA is the use of words that imitate or suggest the sound of what they describe. For example, *roar* suggests a lion's roaring, and *purr* imitates the sound of a contented cat. Notice Jack Prelutsky's use of onomatopoeia when you read "Ankylosaurus" on page 185.

from "To Young Readers"

Good **b**ooks are
bandages
and voyages
and **l**inkages to **L**ight . . .

REPETITION of certain lines, phrases, or words helps to emphasize an idea or create a feeling. Poets also repeat sounds within words to create a mood. **Alliteration** is the repetition of sound at the beginning of words, as in these lines from Gwendolyn Brooks's poem "To Young Readers" on page 33.

FORMS OF POETRY

Narrative poems tell stories. They can be serious stories of life and death, or they can be light and humorous. "The Pied Piper of Hamelin" on page 693 is a narrative poem.

Lyric poems express personal thoughts and feelings. They are short and present vivid images of a particular thing. "A Minor Bird" on page 200 is a lyric poem.

Free verse is poetry that has the irregular rhythms of ordinary speech. "Arithmetic" on page 34 is written in free verse.

IMAGERY

POETS use **imagery,** or "word pictures" that appeal to readers' senses and help them visualize what they are reading about. Some images can almost make readers see, hear, smell, taste, or feel the thing described in the poem.

from "The Armadillo," by Ogden Nash

> For housewives use an armadillo
> To scour their pots, instead of Brillo.

FIGURES OF SPEECH can be used to compare ordinary things in unexpected ways. Showing an unexpected similarity between things helps readers see them in a new way and is another way of making "word pictures." A **simile** compares unlike things using the words *like* or *as.* A **metaphor** is a comparison that does not use *like* or *as.*

from "Whatif"

> Some Whatifs crawled inside my ear
> And pranced and partied all night long
> And sang their same old Whatif song . . .

PERSONIFICATION, another kind of figure of speech, is talking about an animal, object, or idea as though it were human. Shel Silverstein uses personification to illustrate anxiety in "Whatif" on page 495.

Active Reading Strategies

Tips for Reading Poetry

Poetry can be difficult to read, but many readers find that it's worth the effort. Use the suggestions below to help you get the most out of a poem.

● For more on reading strategies, see **Reading Handbook,** pp. R63–R94.

QUESTION

Ask questions of yourself about the poem's title, form, shape on the page, and length. Look for end punctuation. Listen for rhymes and rhythm and repetition of sounds in words. Allow yourself to wonder about words and phrases that seem important.

Ask Yourself . . .

● Do these lines rhyme?

● Is this the end of a sentence?

● What is the poem about?

● Is the poet implying something?

VISUALIZE

Most poems use surprising comparisons and words and phrases that appeal to your senses. Try to picture these things or imagine how you might experience them.

Ask Yourself . . .

● How does this look? sound? feel? smell? taste?

● What words help me picture this?

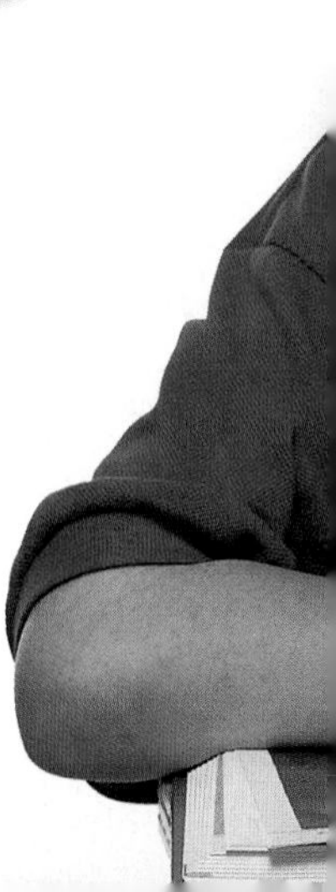

EVALUATE

Look at the poet's methods of communicating with the reader. Notice how well the poet communicates a feeling, an observation, or a message. Think about the poet's goals as well as his or her techniques. Think about why the poet chose particular words. Do the poet's thoughts make sense to you?

Ask Yourself . . .

- What kind of person seems to be speaking in this poem?

- Why did the poet choose this voice for the poem?

- What feelings does the poet want me to have about this?

- Would I like to share this poem with a friend? Why?

CONNECT

Poems invite readers to share feelings and experiences. As you reread a poem, it may come to mean even more to you. It can tie into your own thoughts and experiences on deeper and deeper levels.

Ask Yourself . . .

- Have I ever seen this?

- What does this remind me of?

- Have I ever felt this way?

- What would I have done?

APPLYING THE STRATEGIES

Read "The Naming of Cats" by T. S. Eliot. Use the Active Reading Model notes in the margins as you read. Write your responses on a separate piece of paper or use stick-on notes. Look them over when you have finished reading.

Before You Read
The Naming of Cats

MEET
T. S. ELIOT

Poet T. S. Eliot loved cats and owned several. His poems about cats show both his sense of humor and his love for the animals. Three of his cats were named Pettipaws, Wiscus, and George Pushdragon. "Old Possum" was Eliot's nickname among close friends.

Born in St. Louis and educated at Harvard, Eliot left the United States and eventually became a British subject. He is considered a British poet. In 1948, Eliot was awarded the Nobel Prize for Literature.

T. S. Eliot was born in 1888 and died in 1965. This poem was published in 1939.

FOCUS ACTIVITY

Have you ever tried to name a pet? What helped you decide on a name?

Brainstorm

In a small group, list and compare names of pets you know. Discuss possible reasons why pet owners chose these names.

Setting a Purpose

Read "The Naming of Cats" to find out what names are given to cats in the poem.

BACKGROUND

Imagine the curtain rising on a darkened theater stage. Slowly, dramatically colored lighting reveals the actors on stage. They are all dressed as cats, all kinds of cats. Some are wearing elegant, long-haired outfits, and some are wearing tattered, scruffy fur. The cat-actors are lounging around on fence tops and garbage cans. A single cat begins to sing—slowly, sadly—about memories.

This is a scene from the famous Broadway musical play *Cats. Cats* has been produced in major cities across the country. The play is based on T. S. Eliot's *Old Possum's Book of Practical Cats,* which begins with "The Naming of Cats."

CATS

NOW AND FOREVER.

A MUSICAL BY ANDREW LLOYD WEBBER
BASED ON OLD POSSUM'S BOOK OF PRACTICAL CATS BY T.S. ELIOT

♦ WINTER GARDEN THEATRE
50TH STREET AND BROADWAY

The Naming of Cats

T. S. Eliot ᔰ

Night Garden Kitty, 1992. Christian Pierre. Acrylic on canvas, 14 x 11 in. Private collection.

The Naming of Cats is a difficult matter,
　It isn't just one of your holiday games;
You may think at first I'm as mad as a hatter°
When I tell you, a cat must have THREE DIFFERENT NAMES.
5　First of all, there's the name that the family use daily,
　Such as Peter, Augustus, Alonzo or James,
Such as Victor or Jonathan, George or Bill Bailey—
　All of them sensible everyday names.

---

3 In this expression, *mad* means "crazy." In the 1800s, poisonous chemicals used in hat manufacturing made workers behave so oddly that people began to call them "mad hatters."

The Naming of Cats

CONNECT

What "particular" and
"peculiar" names for
pets do you know?

10 There are fancier names if you think they sound sweeter,
    Some for the gentlemen, some for the dames:
Such as Plato, Admetus, Electra, Demeter—
    But all of them sensible everyday names.
But I tell you, a cat needs a name that's particular,
    A name that's peculiar,° and more dignified,
15 Else how can he keep up his tail perpendicular,°
    Or spread out his whiskers, or cherish his pride?
Of names of this kind, I can give you a quorum,°
    Such as Munkustrap, Quaxo, or Coricopat,
Such as Bombalurina, or else Jellylorum—
20   Names that never belong to more than one cat.
But above and beyond there's still one name left over,
    And that is the name that you never will guess;
The name that no human research can discover—
    But THE CAT HIMSELF KNOWS, and will never confess.
25 When you notice a cat in profound meditation,°
    The reason, I tell you, is always the same:
His mind is engaged in a rapt contemplation°
    Of the thought, of the thought, of the thought of his name:
      His ineffable° effable°
30   Effanineffable
Deep and inscrutable° singular° Name.

QUESTION

What is the cat think-
ing about?

---

14 Here, *peculiar* means "special; different from any other."

15 If the cat's tail is *perpendicular* (pur′ pən dik′ yə lər), it's standing straight up.

17 A *quorum* (kwôr′ əm) is the minimum number of members required for a committee or legislature to have a meeting. In this case, the speaker uses the word to
mean "enough."

25 A cat in *profound meditation* appears to be deep in thought.

27 A cat in *rapt contemplation* is completely absorbed in its thoughts.

29 *Effable* means "capable of being spoken." If a thing is *ineffable,* it can't be said aloud
because no words can capture how special it really is.

31 Here, *inscrutable* (in skrōō′ tə bəl) means "mysterious," and *singular* means
"extraordinary" and "one-of-a-kind."

Responding to Literature

PERSONAL RESPONSE

Are the names of the cats in the poem like names you know?

Active Reading Response
Choose one of the **Active Reading Strategies** on pages 178–179 and find another place in the poem where you could apply it.

Analyzing Literature

RECALL AND INTERPRET

1. What does a cat think about in "profound mediation"?
2. Why does the speaker say that a cat needs "a name that's particular"?
3. Why do you think the speaker says that the cat "will never confess" his name?

EVALUATE AND CONNECT

4. A poem's **meter** is the pattern of stressed and unstressed syllables. What kind of mood does the meter in "The Naming of Cats" help to create?
5. How does the poet show his sense of humor in "The Naming of Cats"? Give examples.
6. Following the rules in the poem, if you had three names, what would they be?

LITERARY ELEMENTS

Repetition

Notice how Eliot uses the word *name* over and over throughout the poem. This **repetition** contributes to the overall rhythm, reminds the listener of the subject, and adds to the humor of the poem.

1. Why, do you think, does Eliot repeat "Of the thought, of the thought, of the thought of his name" in line 28?

2. Read lines 29 and 30 again. Why do you think Eliot expresses his idea this way?

● See **Literary Terms Handbook,** p. R7.

Extending Your Response

Personal Writing

Your Own Name   Do people call you by more than one name? How well do your names describe you? Write your legal name, as well as any nicknames. Tell how you received each name and whether you think it suits you.

Literature Groups

Naming and Renaming   Look at the names you listed in the **Focus Activity** on page 180. Discuss what T. S. Eliot would think about these names. Which of these names would Eliot like? What kinds of names would Eliot suggest for these pets?

Before You Read

Ankylosaurus and *The Shark*

MEET JACK PRELUTSKY

Jack Prelutsky (prə lut′ skē) tried many occupations— singer, actor, photographer, carpenter, cab driver, artist. He wrote his first poems to go with some paintings he had done. A friend encouraged him to send them to a publisher. Since then he has published several books of poetry for young people.

Jack Prelutsky was born in 1940. "Ankylosaurus" was first published in 1988 in Tyrannosaurus Was a Beast: Dinosaur Poems.

MEET JOHN CIARDI

A professor, poet, writer, translator, and editor, John Ciardi (chär′ dē) once said, "My work for children is based on the premise that poetry and learning are both fun."

John Ciardi was born in 1916 and died in 1986.

FOCUS ACTIVITY

Have you ever seen a movie about dinosaurs or sharks? Why do you think movies about these animals are popular?

Whole-Class Discussion
Discuss why people like to watch movies about dinosaurs or sharks.

Setting a Purpose
Read the poems to decide which of these two creatures is more frightening.

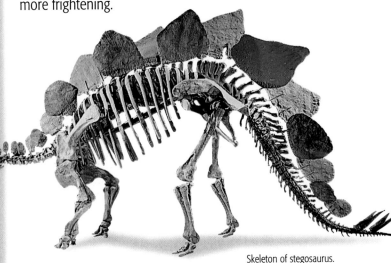

Skeleton of stegosaurus.

BACKGROUND

Dinosaurs first appeared in the Triassic period, about 225 million years ago. Many more dinosaurs, including stegosaurus (shown above), appeared during the Jurassic period, about 190 million years ago.

The ankylosaurus (ang′ kə lō sôr′ əs) was a dinosaur that lived during the Cretaceous Period, from roughly 140 million to 65 million years ago. This dinosaur's 15- to 30-foot body was covered in thick, bony armor, right up to its eyelids. Spines protected its head, and a mass of bone formed a club on its tail. Other dinosaurs could not easily pierce the ankylosaurus's armor, and its tail was like a war club, swinging through the air. Of course, there was a price to pay for such heavy armor. The ankylosaurus moved very slowly!

Ankylosaurus

Jack Prelutsky

Clankity Clankity Clankity Clank!
Ankylosaurus° was built like a tank,
its hide was a fortress as sturdy as steel,
it tended to be an inedible° meal.

5   It was armored in front, it was armored behind,
there wasn't a thing on its minuscule° mind,
it waddled about on its four stubby legs,
nibbling on plants with a mouthful of pegs.

Ankylosaurus was best left alone,
10   its tail was a cudgel° of gristle° and bone,
Clankity Clankity Clankity Clank!
Ankylosaurus was built like a tank.

---

2 *Ankylosaurus* (ang′ kə lō sôr′ əs)
4 *Inedible* means "not suitable to be eaten."
6 Something that's *minuscule* is very, very small.
10 A *cudgel* is a short, thick club used as a weapon; *gristle* is the tough, bendable
tissue that connects muscles to bones.

Model of ankylosaurus.

the Shark

John Ciardi

My dear, let me tell you about the shark.
Though his eyes are bright, his thought is dark.
He's quiet—that speaks well of him.
So does the fact that he can swim.
5   But though he swims without a sound,
Wherever he swims he looks around
With those two bright eyes and that one dark thought.
He has only one but he thinks it a lot.
And the thought he thinks but can never complete
10   Is his long dark thought of something to eat.
Most anything does. And I have to add
That when he eats his manners are bad.
He's a gulper, a ripper, a snatcher, a grabber.
Yes, his manners are drab. But his thought is drabber.°
15   That one dark thought he can never complete
Of something—anything—somehow to eat.

Be careful where you swim, my sweet.

---

14 Here, *drab* means "untidy; messy."

Responding to Literature

PERSONAL RESPONSE

What images from the poems linger in your mind? Which animal seems more scary? Why?

Analyzing Literature

RECALL

1. Prelutsky compares the ankylosaurus to a tank. How are they alike?
2. What qualities of the shark does Ciardi praise?

INTERPRET

3. Why was the ankylosaurus "best left alone"?
4. What is the shark's "one dark thought"? Why is it never satisfied?

EVALUATE AND CONNECT

5. **Onomatopoeia** is the use of a word, such as *buzz,* or a phrase, such as *tick-tock,* that imitates or suggests the sound of what it describes. What is an example of onomatopoeia in one of the poems? What sound is the word imitating?
6. What words or phrases in "Ankylosaurus" and "The Shark" add to the humorous tone of the poems?
7. In your opinion, why does Ciardi end "The Shark" with a line of advice separated from the rest of the poem? What effect does this have on you?
8. Prelutsky compares the ankylosaurus to a tank, a fortress, armor, and a cudgel. What is the effect of these comparisons?
9. Theme Connection   Why, do you think, did both poets write humorous poems about strong and powerful animals?
10. Do these poems remind you of any others you have read? Which ones? In what ways?

LITERARY ELEMENTS

Rhyme Scheme

The rhyme scheme is the pattern of rhyme in a poem. It is based on **end rhyme,** the rhyme of the last word in a line with the last word in another line. Letters are used to describe the pattern. See how it works in one verse of "Ankylosaurus."

Clankity Clankity Clankity Clank!	*a*
Ankylosaurus was built like a tank,	*a*
its hide was a fortress as sturdy as steel,	*b*
it tended to be an inedible meal.	*b*

Clank rhymes with *tank,* so lines 1 and 2 are given letter *a. Steel* rhymes with *meal;* those lines are given letter *b.* The rhyme scheme of the whole poem is this: *aabbccddeeaa.*

1. What is the rhyme scheme of "The Shark"?

2. The very last line in "The Shark" breaks the pattern of the rhyme scheme. Why does the poet do this?

● See **Literary Terms Handbook,** p. R7.

Extending Your Response

Writing About Literature

Thinking Aloud   Both Prelutsky and Ciardi suggest the thoughts–or lack of thoughts–in the minds of the creatures they write about. Imagine that the shark and the ankylosaurus are talking to themselves. What would each of them say? Write some thoughts each might have. Use the poems for ideas.

Personal Writing

Creature Features
Think of a time you saw a shark or dinosaur in a movie. What impression did the creature make on you? Is it like the feeling you get from reading these poems? Use ideas explored during the **Focus Activity** on page 184. Write a paragraph sharing your impressions.

Literature Groups

Discussing Metaphor   In "Ankylosaurus," Prelutsky says that the ankylosaurus's hide was a "fortress." This is a metaphor–it suggests a comparison between two things that are not usually considered alike and helps you picture the ankylosaurus. Discuss other metaphors in "Ankylosaurus." Then brainstorm to find good metaphors to describe the shark.

Performing

Singing a Poem   Jack Prelutsky says he often performs "Ankylosaurus" as a song. He sings the words to the tune of "Sweet Betsy from Pike," and adds a "clankity-clankity-clankity-clank" chorus. Try it yourself, using the same music or another song that fits the rhythm of the poem. You will probably find the tune Prelutsky uses in a book about, or on a recording of, American folk music. Perform the song for the class.

📖 **Save your work for your portfolio.**

Skill Minilesson

GRAMMAR AND LANGUAGE   • SPECIFIC NOUNS

In "The Shark," John Ciardi says that the shark is "a gulper, a ripper, a snatcher, a grabber." These nouns make clear for the reader the shark's "manners" and its fierceness. Using specific nouns always makes writing more interesting and enjoyable.

PRACTICE   Finish each sentence with a specific noun. (A thesaurus can help.)

1. A dinosaur is a/an . . .
2. A cat is a/an . . .
3. A bird is a/an . . .
4. A dog is a/an . . .
5. A pig is a/an . . .

● For more on nouns, see **Language Handbook**, p. R26.

Subject-Verb Agreement

A **subject** tells who or what is doing something. A **verb** tells what the subject is doing. These two parts of a sentence must agree. With a singular subject, use the singular form of a verb. With a plural subject, use the plural form of a verb.

Singular
A shark eats almost anything.
His one thought is about eating.

Plural
Sharks eat greedily.
Their manners are bad.

Problem	Solution
The wolves with the leader agrees to accept Mowgli.	If a verb is separated from its subject, make sure that it agrees with its subject, not with the noun closest to it. The wolves with the leader agree to accept Mowgli.
There is many dangers in the jungle.	If a sentence begins with *here* or *there,* the subject of the sentence will come after the verb, but the verb must still agree with the subject. There are many dangers in the jungle.
Ron and Penny works with Koko.	A sentence may have a *compound subject*—two or more subjects that have the same verb. When the subjects are joined by *and,* the verb must be in its plural form. Ron and Penny work with Koko.
Neither the bears nor the boy are harmed by the hunters.	In a sentence with a compound subject, when the subjects are joined by *or* or *nor,* the verb agrees with the subject closer to it. Neither the bears nor the boy is harmed by the hunters.

● For more on subject-verb agreement, see **Language Handbook,** p. R12–R13.

EXERCISE

For each sentence, write the correct form of the verb in parentheses.

1. People of every nation (likes, like) stories about animals.
2. Dogs or gorillas or a goat (holds, hold) our attention.
3. There (is, are) lessons in the stories.
4. A story about animals (teaches, teach) us things about ourselves.
5. Zlateh and Aaron (helps, help) each other, just as true friends would.

Technology Skills

E-Mail: Internet Etiquette

When you're riding along a highway, you expect other drivers to stop at red lights. You also expect them to signal before they turn and slow down when they approach yield signs. When you're cruising on the information superhighway, you should expect those who share the road with you to uphold similar rules. These Internet "rules of the road" are called Netiquette.

Netiquette

Just twenty years ago, no one dreamed that middle-school students would be concerned with Internet etiquette, but here you are, forging your way into a new frontier. In a small group, brainstorm some rules of etiquette one might be expected to uphold on the Internet. Then compare them with the following rules.

1. Use the subject line wisely. Be as brief as you can, but let your recipient know what your E-mail is about.

2. Use appropriate capitalization. If you type your messages in all capital letters, it is considered the same as SHOUTING. If you want to emphasize something, use an underline character before and after it, _like this_ . Using asterisks before and after is also *acceptable.*

3. Avoid "flaming" and "flame wars." Flaming involves sending a hostile E-mail message. To repeatedly send and receive such messages is to engage in a flame war. Sending an E-mail response is quick and easy, but don't toss off a comment or a response on the spur of the moment, particularly if your feelings are running strong. With reflection, you may decide that you're not as angry or disappointed or passionate as you thought you were about something. Don't flame someone because you acted too hastily.

4. Spelling is important. The E-mail you send tells people something about you. You don't want it to tell them that you can't spell—or that you don't consider them important enough to take the time to spell correctly. At least use the spell-check feature of your E-mail software before you send a message. While you're at it, and for the same reasons, check your grammar, too.

5. Always include your E-mail address at the bottom of any electronic message.

6. Never forward chain mail. It eats up server space and annoys recipients.

7. Be careful when using humor or sarcasm. Emotions are difficult to convey in text. If possible, use "emoticons" to indicate when you're joking. An emoticon (a word made by putting together *emotion* and *icon*) is a combination of keystrokes that expresses an emotion through the use of a typographical icon. Following are some sample emoticons. To see them best, turn your book sideways.

:-)   A smiley face can show that you are happy or joking.

:-(A sad face shows sadness or disappointment.

8-)   You might use this smiley if you wear glasses.

;-)   This emoticon can stand for a wink.

8. Keep E-mail messages concise and relevant. To abbreviate your messages, use commonly accepted acronyms. Acronyms are combinations of initials that stand for words or phrases. Here are a few commonly used Net acronyms.

BFN	Bye for now	FYI	For your information
BTW	By the way	IMHO	In my humble opinion
BRB	Be right back	OTOH	On the other hand
FAQ	Frequently asked questions	TYVM	Thank you very much

You'll discover more as you become an experienced Net surfer. Don't overdo them, however; and be sure the person you're writing to understands the acronyms you use. An E-mail filled with acronyms you can't figure out can be unreadable.

9. Don't include someone's entire message when you reply to an E-mail. All unnecessary words contribute to slowing down Net traffic. If necessary, and especially if the original message includes several topics, you can always include a brief reminder in your message:

You asked about my brother Raul. He's feeling much better now that the cast is off. The doctor says he'll be pitching again in four to six weeks.

10. Finally, remember that good behavior on the Internet is no different from good behavior in face-to-face situations. The golden rule works on the Net, too. Treat others as you'd like them to treat you.

ACTIVITIES

1. Log on to the World Wide Web, and use a search engine to find Netiquette sites. Look for sources of additional emoticons and Net acronyms as well. Share any useful tips and suggestions you find with your class.

2. Choose a partner and exchange E-mail messages. Discuss each other's messages. Did you both follow the rules of Netiquette and still communicate effectively?

Before You Read

Dinner Together and *How soft a Caterpillar steps—*

FOCUS ACTIVITY

Have you ever stopped to watch an insect scurry along or a spider create a web?

QuickWrite

In a few sentences, explain how you feel about insects or spiders. Do they scare you? Are they a nuisance? Do you like or admire something about them?

Setting a Purpose

Read to find out how each poet describes an encounter with a tiny animal.

BACKGROUND

A woman of Emily Dickinson's time was expected to stay quietly at home until she married. Dickinson remained at home until she died at fifty-five. As she grew older, she became more and more reluctant to meet strangers or to leave her home or garden.

She busied herself with housework, cooking, and gardening. In moments of leisure, she scribbled lines of poetry on scraps of paper. In her room, she would make clean copies of her poems, sew several poems together into a booklet, and lock the booklet in a box that she kept hidden in a drawer.

She insisted that she did not want to publish her poems. She called them "snow" because she wanted them to remain pure. "How can you print a piece of your own soul?" she once asked.

After her death, her sister discovered Dickinson's booklets of poetry and worked to have them published. Soon Dickinson's unconventional rhythms and surprising ways of expressing herself made her poetry famous. Today, Dickinson is considered one of America's greatest poets.

Dinner Together

Diana Rivera

Sitting by the barbecue
waiting for sausages and hot dogs
blue-gray smoke the same color
of the sky
5 I see a tiny spider
walking down from the sky with tiny six-
footed steps
down
down
10 in a perfectly straight
line
all the way
down
to the floor
15 then back up
the same line
rising from one cloud
up to another,
a silver speck
20 glistening
at its mouth,
climbing the invisible ladder.

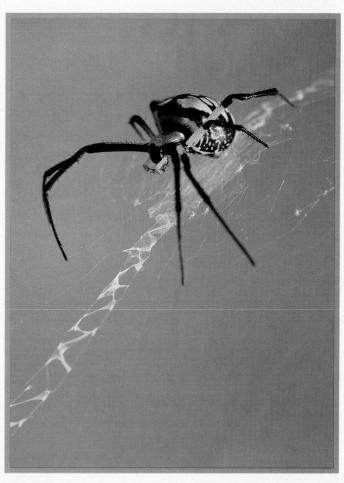

How soft a Caterpillar steps

Emily Dickinson

How soft a Caterpillar steps—
I find one on my Hand
From such a velvet world it comes
Such plushes° at command
Its soundless travels just arrest
My slow—terrestrial° eye
Intent° upon its own career
What use has it for me—

4 *Plushes* are velvety soft fabrics or other things
that are very soft.
6 Here, *terrestrial* (tə res′ trē əl) means "ordinary;
common."
7 To be *intent* is to be firmly fixed, or focused, on
something.

Responding to Literature

PERSONAL RESPONSE

Do spiders and caterpillars make good subjects for poems? Explain why or why not.

Analyzing Literature

RECALL

1. In "Dinner Together," how does the speaker happen to see the spider?
2. Where is the caterpillar in Dickinson's poem?

INTERPRET

3. Rivera writes that the spider was "walking down from the sky." What do you think she means?
4. How do you think the speaker in Dickinson's poem feels about the caterpillar? Explain your answer.

EVALUATE AND CONNECT

5. Why, do you think, does the speaker in Rivera's poem watch the spider?
6. Why, do you think, did Rivera choose "Dinner Together" for the title of her poem?
7. Dickinson ends her poem with this line: "What use has it for me." How would you answer her question?
8. Look at the shape of the poem "Dinner Together." How is this shape related to the poem's subject?
9. Poets use **description** to help readers visualize their subjects. What are some words in each poem that help you visualize?
10. Theme Connection   Does either poem change your thinking about insects or spiders? In what ways?

LITERARY ELEMENTS

Lyric Poetry

Lyric poems express personal thoughts and feelings. The poems are usually short, and they often describe a quick observation or experience. Because of their rhythm and rhyme, they are songlike and almost musical when read aloud. In fact, lyric poems got their name from the lyre, a harp-like musical instrument. Its music was used to accompany the reading of poems in ancient Greece.

1. Reread "How soft a Caterpillar steps—" and then explain why it is or is not a lyric poem.

2. Why, do you think, is lyric poetry such a popular form of poetry?

● See **Literary Terms Handbook,** p. R5.

Extending Your Response

Writing About Literature

Viewpoint   How different would the poems be if the speaker in Rivera's or Dickinson's poem was afraid of spiders or disgusted by caterpillars? In a paragraph or a short poem, describe the same encounter with the spider or the caterpillar from the point of view of a speaker who dislikes the creature.

Personal Writing

Remembering   Think of things in nature that have interested you or caught your imagination. Were you ever awed by thunder and lightning, or did you ever wonder how lightning bugs glow? Jot down any observations you recall that might be good subjects for your own lyric poems.

Literature Groups

Understanding Feelings   In the **Focus Activity** on page 192, you wrote about your feelings about spiders and insects. Look back over what you wrote and compare it with the feelings and observations in the poems. Discuss any new ideas you have about spiders and insects as a result of reading the poems.

Interdisciplinary Activity

Science   Use library or Internet resources to learn more about spiders or caterpillars. Two topics you might research are spiders' webs or the life cycles of butterflies. Share what you learn with the class.

Listening and Speaking

Reading Poems   Practice reading each of these poems aloud to a partner. Think about the meaning of the words as well as rhythm and rhyme. Try to express in your reading the feelings of each speaker.

Reading Further

If you'd like to know more about Emily Dickinson, you might enjoy these books:

Poetry: *Poems for Youth* by Emily Dickinson, edited by Alfred Leete Hampson

Biography: *Emily Dickinson* by S. L. Berry

📖 **Save your work for your portfolio.**

Skill Minilesson

GRAMMAR AND LANGUAGE • SENSORY WORDS

Even in such a short poem as "How soft a Caterpillar steps–," Emily Dickinson refers to all of the following senses:

- **sight:** the movement of the caterpillar
- **touch:** a "velvet" world, suggesting great softness
- **sound:** "soundless" movements

These sensory words help readers feel that they are right next to Dickinson, watching the caterpillar.

PRACTICE Write a paragraph or short poem describing something you like. Include as many sensory words as you can.

COMIC STRIP

The characters in the strip *Mutts* try looking at the world from the point of view of a bat.

by Patrick McDowell

Mutts

Respond

1. What does the dog mean when he says, ". . . their eyes are weak, so they don't 'look' good"?

2. What does Mooch mean when she says, "I can see that"?

Before You Read

The Bat and A Minor Bird

MEET
THEODORE ROETHKE

Many of Theodore Roethke's (ret′ kē) poems show his close observation of nature. His habit of observing things closely was developed, he said, through working with plants in his father's greenhouses.

Theodore Roethke was born in 1908 and died in 1963. "The Bat" was first published in 1938.

MEET
ROBERT FROST

Robert Frost once said that his life's ambition was to write "a few poems it will be hard to get rid of." By the end of his life, Frost had won the Pulitzer Prize four times—more than any other poet. Most of his poetry is about his life in New England.

Robert Frost was born in 1874 and died in 1963. "A Minor Bird" was first published in 1928.

FOCUS ACTIVITY

What do you think about when you think of a bat? How about a bird?

Make Two Webs

Write *bat* in the center of one web and *bird* in the center of the other. In a small group, brainstorm and list ideas you associate with each creature.

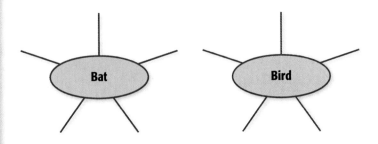

Setting a Purpose

Read the poems to find out whether the associations you have listed are mentioned in the poems.

BACKGROUND

Robert Frost lived on a farm in New England. Frost's poems use the natural rhythms of speech, and many of them are about the things he noticed as he did his farm work.

On close reading, however, his poems are not ordinary speech, but very carefully put together combinations of words and sounds. Usually the poems rhyme. Frost once said that he would "as soon play tennis without a net as write free verse."

The Bat

By day the bat is cousin to the mouse.
He likes the attic of an aging house.

His fingers make a hat about his head.
His pulse beat is so slow we think him dead.

5   He loops in crazy figures half the night
Among the trees that face the corner light.

But when he brushes up against a screen,
We are afraid of what our eyes have seen:

For something is amiss or out of place
10   When mice with wings can wear a human face.

Theodore Roethke

A Minor Bird

Robert Frost

I have wished a bird would fly away,
And not sing by my house all day;

Have clapped my hands at him from the door
When it seemed as if I could bear no more.

The fault must partly have been in me.
The bird was not to blame for his key.

And of course there must be something wrong
In wanting to silence any song.

Responding to Literature

PERSONAL RESPONSE

Are the poems' comments on the bat and the bird what you would expect? Compare these comments with the words you listed in the **Focus Activity** on page 198.

Analyzing Literature

RECALL

1. According to "The Bat," what do bats do during the day and at night?

2. In "A Minor Bird," what is it about the bird that the speaker doesn't like?

INTERPRET

3. How do people sometimes see bats at night, according to Roethke?

4. How does the speaker in "A Minor Bird" feel about himself or herself? Why does the speaker feel that way?

EVALUATE AND CONNECT

5. Who is the speaker in each poem? How can you tell?

6. What feelings do the bat and the bird stir in the speakers of these poems?

7. In what ways is the bat described like a human? Why do you think the poet did this?

8. Why is the bird called a "minor" bird? What does *minor* usually mean?

9. Do you think animals in flight could trigger fear or discomfort in some people? Explain.

10. Have any creatures ever irritated or bothered you? What did they do? How did you feel?

LITERARY ELEMENTS

Mood

Mood is the emotional quality or atmosphere of a poem or story. The mood of a poem affects how the reader feels as he or she reads the poem. Writers create mood with the details they give and the words they choose. For example, in "The Bat," Roethke says the bat "brushes up against a screen." Roethke uses this description to make his readers uneasy.

1. What is the mood of each of these poems?

2. What details from each poem help create the mood?

● See **Literary Terms Handbook,** p. R5.

Extending Your Response

Writing About Literature

Paraphrase **Paraphrasing** is putting something you have read or heard into your own words. You can do this with a poem to help yourself understand it and to look at it as a whole. Try paraphrasing "A Minor Bird" or "The Bat."

inter**NET**
CONNECTION

Use a search engine to scan information about *bats* on the Internet. You might narrow your search by using these keywords: *science–biology–wildlife.* Share the results of your research with the class.

Personal Writing

Bird and Bat Lessons The speaker in "A Minor Bird" learns something about himself or herself. What do you learn about yourself from reading either of these poems?

Literature Groups

Silencing Songs In "A Minor Bird" the speaker says ". . . there must be something wrong / In wanting to silence any song." Discuss what the speaker means by this. Then discuss situations in which people might want to silence others. Do you agree that this always "must be" wrong?

Reading Further

If you liked these poems, you might enjoy these books of poetry:

Party at the Zoo by Theodore Roethke

You Come, Too: Poetry for Young People by Robert Frost

📖 **Save your work for your portfolio.**

Skill Minilesson

GRAMMAR AND LANGUAGE • CONNOTATION

Connotation is the unspoken or unwritten meanings associated with a word that go beyond the word's dictionary meaning. For example, in "A Minor Bird," Frost talks about the bird's song. The general connotation of *song* is happy and joyous, but in this poem the bird's song is annoying.

● For more on connotation, see **Reading Handbook,** p. R74.

PRACTICE Indicate whether each of the following words generally has a positive or negative connotation. Then tell whether the word is used with the usual connotation in the poems.

1. bats
2. aging
3. minor
4. human face
5. birds

LISTENING, SPEAKING, and VIEWING

Sharing Poetry

There are several ways you can make sure that a poem you share with others is understood and appreciated by your audience.

Tips for Reading Poetry Aloud

- Choose a poem that you like.
- Become familiar with the poem. More than one reading may be necessary.
- Look up any unfamiliar words.
- Restate the poem's meaning in prose form. This will help clarify its meaning.
- Read the poem aloud, listening to the sounds of the words. A poem's meaning is often conveyed through sound as well as through word meaning.
- Experiment with reading rate, being careful not to read too quickly. Remember, poems are generally written in sentences. Be sure to use punctuation as a cue for short and long pauses.

- Read so that the rhythmical pattern is felt but not overemphasized. Do not distort the natural pronunciation of words to fit a rhythmical pattern or rhyme pattern.
- Mark up a copy of the poem to remind yourself of where you want to pause, read faster or slower, or raise or lower your voice.
- Think about reading with musical accompaniment. What kind of music would go with your poem?
- Think about reading with another person or with a group. Different voices could read certain lines, or a chorus of voices could read important lines.

ACTIVITIES

1. Listen to recordings of poets reading their work. Your librarian or your teacher can help you to find recordings. If possible, read along in your own copy of a poem. Would you read the poem the same way as it is read on the recording?

2. Organize a class poetry reading. Take turns sharing poetry from this book or from other sources. Rehearse your reading with a partner, giving each other suggestions about speaking loud enough and making eye contact with the audience.

Writing WORKSHOP

Descriptive Writing: Character Sketch

Who meant a lot to you when you were younger? Who means a lot to you now—perhaps a person or a pet? To capture a memory of someone special, you might take a photo or make a drawing. You might also create a **character sketch**—a portrait in words. This workshop will help you create a portrait with words, so that others can see this special person or animal as you do.

Assignment: Write a character sketch of someone important in your life.

● As you write your character sketch, refer to the **Writing Handbook,** pp. R43–R47.

The Writing Process

PREWRITING

PREWRITING TIP
To get more ideas, talk with friends or family members about people or animals you remember.

● **Choose a Character**

The subject of your sketch might be a family member, a friend, or even an animal. Try the following strategies to decide on a subject.

● Look through a photo album or watch home videos. Think about those pictured. Who has had an impact on your life?

● List events when you felt a strong emotion, such as happiness or sadness. Who else was involved?

● Fill in a questionnaire like the one below.

Who has . . .
made me happy? _____
needed me? _____
helped me? _____
earned my respect? _____
taught me something? _____

● Think About Audience and Purpose

Your subject might greatly enjoy reading your sketch. Your teacher and classmates will probably also be part of your audience. Your purpose is to describe your subject so clearly that even strangers will feel they know him or her.

● Gather Details

You need plenty of good, specific, descriptive words to create your character sketch. A brainstorm board like the following one can help. Think about what makes your subject special—physical traits, inner qualities, interests you share. Then brainstorm words or phrases to fill each space.

Physical Traits

- tall, lean, bent
- gravelly voice
- deeply lined face
- smelled like aftershave

Character's Name
Grandpa Cliff

Inner Qualities

- gruff manner
- dry humor
- open-minded
- loved the outdoors

Shared Interests

- his fossil collection
- his workshop
- camping in desert

● Focus and Organize

What impression of this character do you want to create? Do you want readers to smile with you at someone who makes you happy or to share your admiration of someone you respect? Plan to focus on one main impression. Then decide how you want to organize the details. Will you describe physical traits in one section and inner qualities in another? Will you weave the two together?

Writing WORKSHOP

DRAFTING

DRAFTING TIP

Quote conversation to let readers "hear" as well as "see" your subject. Try to catch your subject's unique way of talking.

TECHNOLOGY TIP

On a computer, save a copy of your draft. Then use the "cut" and "paste" functions to try out different ways to organize it.

● Start Anywhere

You don't have to write your introduction first. Some authors write introductions last–when they know exactly what they're introducing. Start your draft with what most interests you. Later, you can rearrange the parts of your draft as needed.

● Paint with Words

Good authors do more than explain. They "paint" with precise words. Your brainstorm board should provide a rich palette of words. Choose the most precise words to show your subject's traits. Make it clear why he or she is important to you.

MODEL · DRAFTING

Grandpa Cliff helped set my love of nature firmly in place. I remember visiting him one summer. "You want to see a dinosaur bone?" he growled.

"Y-y-yes," I replied in a shaky voice. I followed his tall, bent form downstairs.

REVISING

REVISING TIP

To make the verb *said* more precise, add an adverb or an adverb phrase: "I found this fossil in the desert," Grandpa said in his gravelly voice.

● Evaluate Your Work

Come back to your draft after a day, and read it aloud twice. The first time, use the **Questions for Revising.** You might have a friend listen and respond with you. Make notes about changes. The second time, listen for the effects of your changes. Keep adjusting your sketch until it sounds right to you.

QUESTIONS FOR REVISING

☑ Where do I show my subject's inner qualities, as well as physical traits?

☑ What main impression of my subject do my details support?

☑ Which part makes it clear what my subject means to me?

☑ Where might more precise words help readers imagine my subject?

☑ Which parts might I rearrange to make my sketch clearer?

EDITING/PROOFREADING

Find and correct errors in grammar, mechanics, or spelling so that readers can easily understand your character sketch. Use the **Proofreading Checklist** as a guide. The **Grammar Link** on page 189 can help you make sure all your verbs agree with their subjects.

PROOFREADING CHECKLIST
☑ Subjects and verbs agree.
☑ There are no fragments or run-on sentences.
☑ End marks, commas, and other punctuation marks are used correctly.
☑ Quotation marks set off each speaker's words.
☑ Capitalization and spelling are correct.

Grammar Hint

When checking subject-verb agreement, don't be fooled by other nouns between the subject and verb.

(singular subject)   (singular verb)

One of the puppies **was** jet black.

MODEL · EDITING/PROOFREADING

One of the fossils ~~were~~ was shiny as a jewel.

PUBLISHING/PRESENTING

If possible, share your character sketch with your subject, or with others who know or knew him or her. You might bind it in a cover illustrated with things that you associate with your subject.

PRESENTING TIP
If your subject lives far away, mail or E-mail your sketch. Include a note explaining why and how you wrote it.

Reflecting

Write a response to each question. Then share your responses in a small group.

● Which part of your character sketch was easiest to write, and which was hardest? Why?

● What new insights did you gain about your subject?

📖 **Save your work for your portfolio.**

Theme Wrap-Up

Responding to the Theme

1. Which selection in this theme helped you understand how animals experience the world? Explain your answer.

2. What new ideas do you have about the following as a result of your reading in this theme?
   - relationships between people and animals
   - how to understand an animal's point of view

3. Present your theme project to the class.

Analyzing Literature

COMPARE POEMS

Choose two poems from this theme to compare. First, compare rhyme and rhythm in each poem. Then, compare the use of imagery and metaphor. Finally, tell the meaning of each poem and what you think about it.

Evaluate and Set Goals

1. Which of the following was most enjoyable to you? Which was most difficult?
   - reading and thinking about the selections
   - doing independent writing
   - analyzing the selections in discussions
   - making presentations
   - doing research

2. How would you assess your work in this theme, using the following scale? Give at least two reasons for your assessment.

   | 4 = outstanding | 2 = fair |
   | 3 = good | 1 = weak |

3. Based on what you found difficult in this theme, choose a goal to work toward in the next theme.
   - Write down your goal and three steps you will take to try to reach it.
   - Meet with your teacher to review your goal and your plan for achieving it.

Build Your Portfolio

SELECT

Choose two pieces of work you did in this theme to include in your portfolio. Use these questions to help you choose.

- ✦ Which do you consider your best work?
- ✦ Which challenged you the most?
- ✦ Which did you learn the most from?
- ✦ Which did you enjoy the most?

REFLECT

Write some notes to accompany the pieces you selected. Use these questions to guide you.

- ✦ What do you like best about the piece?
- ✦ What did you learn from creating it?
- ✦ What might you do differently if you were beginning this piece again?

Reading on Your Own

If you have enjoyed the literature in this theme, you might also be interested in the following books.

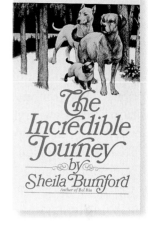

Julie of the Wolves
by Jean Craighead George
In this dramatic survival story, a girl is befriended by a pack of wolves.

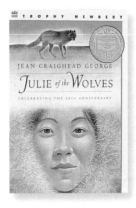

The Incredible Journey
by Sheila Burnford Two dogs and a cat set out on a 250-mile journey through the Canadian wilderness.

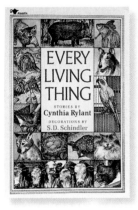

Every Living Thing
by Cynthia Rylant Each of the short stories in this collection tells how a character's life was made better by an animal.

Joyful Noise: Poems for Two Voices
by Paul Fleischman These poems about insects are intended for two readers to read aloud together.

Standardized Test Practice

Read the following passage. Then read each question on page 211. Decide which is the best answer to each question. Mark the letter for that answer on your paper.

Baked Apples for Grandma

Becky wanted to help her parents cook dinner for her grandmother's birthday celebration. She went to the library and checked out *Cooking for Youngsters*. She found a recipe that she could follow without too much help from her mother or father.

On the day of the birthday party, she made sure she had all the ingredients, and then she followed the recipe. The dessert came out of the oven smelling wonderful. Becky's father scooped the Baked Apples over vanilla ice cream and put a candle in Grandma's. Grandma loved the Baked Apples, and so did the rest of the family!

Baked Apples

Baked Apples are a delicious snack or dessert that is also good for you. You should have an adult help you since you will be using an oven to bake. The preparation time for this recipe is 15 minutes, and the cooking time is 15–20 minutes. Make sure you have all of the ingredients before you begin.

Ingredients:	Cooking Utensils:	
12 apples	knife	baking dish
3 Tablespoons sugar*	vegetable peeler	timer
3 Tablespoons cinnamon	mixing bowl	wooden spoon

* for <u>diabetics</u>: 1 Tablespoon of a sugar substitute can be used instead of 3 Tablespoons of sugar

Directions: First, mix the sugar and cinnamon together in the mixing bowl. Set the bowl aside. Next, peel the apples using the peeler. Cut off the ends of the apples and remove the stems and seeds. Cut the apples into bite-size pieces. Put the pieces into the baking dish. Then, sprinkle the sugar and cinnamon mix over the apples. Bake the apples at 350 degrees for 15 minutes or until brown and soft. (You may need an extra 5 minutes of baking time.)

Remove the pan from the oven. Let cool for 10 minutes. Finally, serve and enjoy!

---

1   How much time should be allowed altogether to prepare, cook, and cool the dessert?

A   approximately 15 minutes

B   approximately 20 minutes

C   approximately 35 minutes

D   approximately 50 minutes

2   What should you do after you peel the apples?

F   set the bowl aside

G   mix the ingredients

H   cut them into pieces

J   measure the sugar

3   According to the list of ingredients, you can conclude that <u>diabetic</u> can mean someone who —

A   likes sugar

B   likes apples

C   shouldn't have sugar

D   shouldn't have a sugar substitute

4   How can you tell when the apples are ready?

F   by their color

G   by their smell

H   by their taste

J   by their temperature

5   Which of the following statements is an OPINION the writer of the recipe holds about Baked Apples?

A   They are baked at 350 degrees.

B   They have cinnamon on top.

C   They are delicious.

D   They can be served as a dessert.

6   Becky's family will probably —

F   not let her cook anything until she is much older

G   ask her to make the Baked Apples again soon

H   begin serving more than one dessert after dinner

J   write to the cookbook's author, explaining that the recipe is flawed

7   Which is the best summary of this passage?

A   Becky learns that not all recipes work well.

B   Becky helps make her Grandma's birthday great by making a delicious dessert.

C   Becky needs to ask for help with the oven while making a dessert.

D   Becky takes a book out of the library.

Growing Times

66 It doesn't happen all
at once. You become.
It takes a long time. 99

—Margery Williams

THEME CONTENTS

GENRE FOCUS *BIOGRAPHY*

Exploring the Theme

Growing Times

What does it mean to be growing up? Do the changes that happen during your "growing times" take place overnight or a little at a time? In this theme, you will read about people near your own age who are dealing with the ups and downs of growing times.

Starting Points

BRAINSTORMING

Most stories include problems characters must solve. With a partner, list some television shows or movies with characters who are growing up. What problems do these characters face? What if one of these characters asked for your advice? Share what you would say to this person.

DRAWING ON EXPERIENCE

Draw a cartoon that shows one of the most difficult things about being your age. Draw another showing one of the best things about this age. Write dialogue or captions for the cartoons.

Theme Projects

Choose one of the projects below to complete as you read the selections in this theme. Work on your own, with a partner, or with a group.

LEARNING FOR LIFE
People Watching

Remember how you had to learn to print before you could write? How do people change as they grow?

1. Observe a group of younger children at recess or in the classroom. Take notes about their activities. What can kids that age do?

2. Find information in the library about children in the age group you observed. What do they like? What games do they play? What is important to them? A librarian can help.

3. Create a booklet of information about this age group.

4. Write an introduction for your booklet. Address it to the children you have observed. Tell them what they can look forward to as they grow to your age. The selections in this theme can help you think of ideas to write about.

interNET
CONNECTION

Check out the Web for more project ideas. Contact the Glencoe Web site to find out more about the selections in this theme. Here's the address: lit.glencoe.com

INTERDISCIPLINARY ACTIVITY
Music

Imagine that you are putting together an album of songs about growing up.

- Design the front and back of the album cover. List song titles and recording artists. Include on the back of the cover a paragraph explaining why you chose the songs you did.

MULTIMEDIA PROJECT
Collective Narrative

1. As you read through the selections, write down ideas about growing up.

2. Interview adult relatives or neighbors to discover what each person remembers about being your age. Use questions based on your notes.

3. Cut out magazine pictures and words to represent things you have in common with these adults.

4. Make a collage with cut-out pictures and words.

5. Write a story, a report, an essay, or a poem about what you learned from this project.

Before You Read

La Bamba

"Writing is my one talent," says Gary Soto. "There are a lot of people who never discover what their talent is. . . . I am very lucky to have found mine." Soto published several books of poetry and a book of autobiographical stories before he tried writing fiction. In his stories, Soto says, he tries to recreate the friends and Mexican-American neighborhood of his early years. "I wrote, rewrote, and rewrote the rewrite, so that my friends would jump up and down on the page."

Gary Soto was born in 1952. This story was first published in 1990.

FOCUS ACTIVITY

Have you ever performed in public? How did you feel while you were performing? How did you feel afterward?

Journal
Write your responses to these questions in your journal. Then share your feelings with a small group.

Setting a Purpose
Read "La Bamba" to find out how the main character handles an exciting experience.

BACKGROUND

Did You Know? Ritchie Valens was a teenage idol in the 1950s, one of the first Mexican American rock-and-roll stars. "La Bamba" was one of his biggest hits. Valens died in an airplane crash when he was only seventeen years old.

VOCABULARY PREVIEW

limelight (līm′ līt) *n.* the center of interest or attention; p. 218
flail (flāl) *v.* to wave or swing, especially swiftly or violently; p. 219
debut (dā bū′) *n.* a beginning, as of a career or course of action; first public appearance; p. 219
coordinator (kō ôr′ də nā′ tər) *n.* one who brings people or events into proper order; p. 219
hygiene (hī′ jēn) *n.* practices that support good health; p. 219
classic (klas′ ik) *adj.* serving as a standard, model, or guide, because of excellence or lasting appeal; p. 222
intently (in tent′ lē) *adv.* in a focused way; with attention; p. 222
mingle (ming′ gəl) *v.* to join together; mix; p. 224
jargon (jär′ gən) *n.* terms used in certain art, science, or other field that may not be understood by outsiders; p. 224

La Bamba

Gary Soto ⁓

Manuel was the fourth

of seven children and looked like a lot of kids in his neighborhood: black hair, brown face, and skinny legs scuffed from summer play. But summer was giving way to fall: the trees were turning red, the lawns brown, and the pomegranate[1] trees were heavy with fruit. Manuel walked to school in the frosty morning, kicking leaves and thinking of tomorrow's talent show. He was still amazed that he had volunteered. He was going to pretend to sing Ritchie Valens's "La Bamba" before the entire school.

---

1. A *pomegranate* (pom′ gran′ it) is a thick-skinned fruit filled with seeds covered by crimson, tart-tasting pulp.

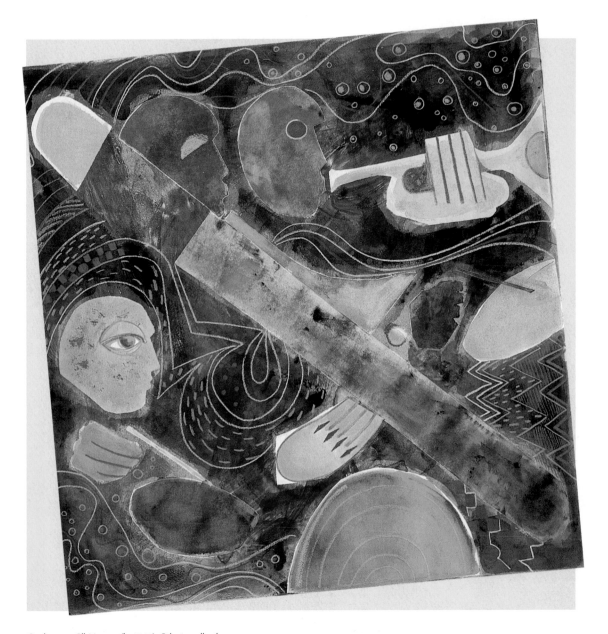

Seabreeze. Gil Mayers (b. 1947). Private collection.

Viewing the painting: How does the mood of this painting compare to Manuel's mood at the beginning of the story?

Why did I raise my hand? he asked himself, but in his heart he knew the answer. He yearned for the limelight. He wanted applause as loud as a thunderstorm, and to hear his friends say, "Man, that was bad!" And he wanted to impress the girls, especially Petra Lopez, the second-prettiest girl in his class. The prettiest was already taken by his friend Ernie. Manuel knew he should be reasonable, since he himself was not great-looking, just average.

Vocabulary

limelight (līm′ līt) *n.* the center of interest or attention

Manuel kicked through the fresh-fallen leaves. When he got to school he realized he had forgotten his math workbook. If his teacher found out, he would have to stay after school and miss practice for the talent show. But fortunately for him, they did drills that morning.

During lunch Manuel hung around with Benny, who was also in the talent show. Benny was going to play the trumpet in spite of the fat lip he had gotten playing football.

"How do I look?" Manuel asked. He cleared his throat and started moving his lips in pantomime. No words came out, just a hiss that sounded like a snake. Manuel tried to look emotional, flailing his arms on the high notes and opening his eyes and mouth as wide as he could when he came to *"Para bailar[2] la baaaaammmba."*

After Manuel finished, Benny said it looked all right, but suggested Manuel dance while he sang. Manuel thought for a moment and decided it was a good idea.

"Yeah, just think you're like Michael Jackson[3] or someone like that," Benny suggested. "But don't get carried away."

During rehearsal, Mr. Roybal, nervous about his debut as the school's talent coordinator, cursed under his breath when the lever that controlled the speed of the record player jammed.

"Darn," he growled, trying to force the lever. "What's wrong with you?"

"Is it broken?" Manuel asked, bending over for a closer look. It looked all right to him.

Mr. Roybal assured Manuel that he would have a good record player at the talent show, even if it meant bringing his own stereo from home.

Manuel sat in a folding chair, twirling his record on his thumb. He watched a skit about personal hygiene, a mother-and-daughter violin duo, five first-grade girls jumping rope, a karate kid breaking boards, three girls singing "Like a Virgin," and a skit about the pilgrims. If the record player hadn't been broken, he would have gone after the karate kid, an easy act to follow, he told himself.

As he twirled his forty-five record, Manuel thought they had a great talent show. The entire school would be amazed. His mother and father would be proud, and his brother and sisters would be jealous and pout. It would be a night to remember.

Benny walked onto the stage, raised his trumpet to his mouth, and waited for his cue. Mr. Roybal raised

Did You Know?
Phonograph records turn at different rates of speed. A *forty-five record* makes 45 complete turns each minute. Other common speeds are 78 and 33⅓.

---

2. This phrase is repeated often throughout the song. *Para bailar* (pär′ə bī′ lär) means "to dance." According to the song, dancing the bamba requires "a little bit of grace."
3. During the 1980s and 1990s, *Michael Jackson* was famous for his music videos and his original style of dancing.

Vocabulary
flail (flāl) *v.* to wave or swing, especially swiftly or violently
debut (dā bū′) *n.* a beginning, as of a career or course of action; first public appearance
coordinator (kō ôr′ də nā′ tər) *n.* one who brings people or events into proper order
hygiene (hī′ jēn) *n.* practices that support good health

his hand like a symphony conductor and let it fall dramatically. Benny inhaled and blew so loud that Manuel dropped his record, which rolled across the cafeteria floor until it hit a wall. Manuel raced after it, picked it up, and wiped it clean.

"Boy, I'm glad it didn't break," he said with a sigh.

That night Manuel had to do the dishes and a lot of homework, so he could only practice in the shower. In bed he prayed that he wouldn't mess up. He prayed that it wouldn't be like when he was a first-grader. For Science Week he had wired together a C battery and a bulb, and told everyone he had discovered how a flashlight worked. He was so pleased with himself that he practiced for hours pressing the wire to the battery, making the bulb wink a dim, orangish light. He showed it to so many kids in his neighborhood that when it was time to show his class how a flashlight worked, the battery was dead. He pressed the wire to the battery, but the bulb didn't respond. He pressed until his thumb hurt and some kids in the back started snickering.

But Manuel fell asleep confident that nothing would go wrong this time.

The next morning his father and mother beamed at him. They were proud that he was going to be in the talent show.

"I wish you would tell us what you're doing," his mother said. His father, a pharmacist who wore a blue smock with his name on a plastic rectangle, looked up from the newspaper and sided with his wife. "Yes, what are you doing in the talent show?"

"You'll see," Manuel said with his mouth full of Cheerios.

The day whizzed by, and so did his afternoon chores and dinner. Suddenly he was dressed in his best clothes and standing next to Benny backstage, listening to the commotion as the cafeteria filled with

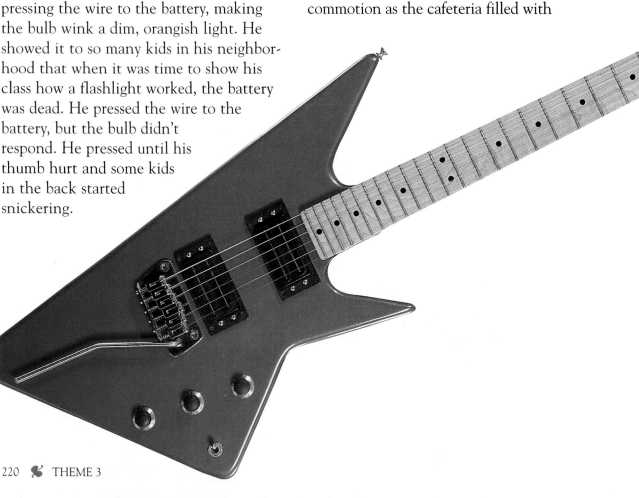

school kids and parents. The lights dimmed, and Mr. Roybal, sweaty in a tight suit and a necktie with a large knot, wet his lips and parted the stage curtains.

"Good evening, everyone," the kids behind the curtain heard him say. "Good evening to you," some of the smart-alecky kids said back to him.

"Tonight we bring you the best John Burroughs Elementary has to offer, and I'm sure that you'll be both pleased and amazed that our little school houses so much talent. And now, without further ado,[4] let's get on with the show." He turned and, with a swish of his hand, commanded, "Part the curtain." The curtains parted in jerks. A girl dressed as a toothbrush and a boy dressed as a dirty gray tooth walked onto the stage and sang:

Brush, brush, brush
Floss, floss, floss
Gargle the germs away—
hey! hey! hey!

After they finished singing, they turned to Mr. Roybal, who dropped his hand. The toothbrush dashed around the stage after the dirty tooth, which was laughing and having a great time until it slipped and nearly rolled off the stage.

Mr. Roybal jumped out and caught it just in time. "Are you OK?"

The dirty tooth answered, "Ask my dentist," which drew laughter and applause from the audience.

The violin duo played next, and except for one time when the girl got lost, they sounded fine. People applauded, and some even stood up. Then the first-grade girls maneuvered onto the stage while jumping rope. They were all smiles and bouncing ponytails as a hundred cameras flashed at once. Mothers "aahed" and fathers sat up proudly.

The karate kid was next. He did a few kicks, yells, and chops, and finally, when his father held up a board, punched it in two. The audience clapped and looked at each other, wide-eyed with respect. The boy bowed to the audience, and father and son ran off the stage.

Manuel remained behind the stage shivering with fear. He mouthed the words to "La Bamba" and swayed from left to right. Why did he raise his hand and volunteer? Why couldn't he have just sat there like the rest of the kids and not said anything? While the karate kid was on stage, Mr. Roybal, more sweaty than before, took Manuel's forty-five record and placed it on the new record player.

"You ready?" Mr. Roybal asked.

"Yeah . . ."

Mr. Roybal walked back on stage and announced that Manuel Gomez, a

Why did he raise his hand and volunteer?

---

4. *Ado* (ə dōō′) means "fuss; difficulty."

La Bamba

fifth-grader in Mrs. Knight's class, was going to pantomime Ritchie Valens's classic hit "La Bamba."

The cafeteria roared with applause. Manuel was nervous but loved the noisy crowd. He pictured his mother and father applauding loudly and his brother and sisters also clapping, though not as energetically.

Manuel walked on stage and the song started immediately. Glassy-eyed from the shock of being in front of so many people, Manuel moved his lips and swayed in a made-up dance step. He couldn't see his parents, but he could see his brother Mario, who was a year younger, thumb-wrestling with a friend. Mario was wearing Manuel's favorite shirt; he would deal with Mario later. He saw some other kids get up and head for the drinking fountain, and a baby sitting in the middle of an aisle sucking her thumb and watching him intently.

What am I doing here? thought Manuel. This is no fun at all. Everyone was just sitting there. Some people were moving to the beat, but most were just watching him, like they would a monkey at the zoo.

But when Manuel did a fancy dance step, there was a burst of applause and some girls screamed. Manuel tried another dance step. He heard more applause and screams and started getting into the groove as he shivered and snaked like Michael Jackson around the stage. But the record got stuck, and he had to sing

Para bailar la bamba
Para bailar la bamba
Para bailar la bamba
Para bailar la bamba

again and again.

Manuel couldn't believe his bad luck. The audience began to laugh and stand up in their chairs. Manuel remembered how the forty-five record had dropped from his hand and rolled across the cafeteria floor. It probably got scratched, he thought, and now it was stuck, and he was stuck dancing and moving his lips to the same words over and over. He had never been so embarrassed. He would have to ask his parents to move the family out of town.

After Mr. Roybal ripped the needle across the record, Manuel slowed his dance steps to a halt. He didn't know what to do except bow to the audience, which applauded wildly, and scoot off the stage, on the verge of tears. This was worse than the homemade flashlight. At least no one laughed then, they just snickered.

Manuel stood alone, trying hard to hold back the tears as Benny, center stage, played his trumpet. Manuel was jealous because he sounded great, then mad as he recalled that it was Benny's loud trumpet playing that made the forty-five record fly out of his hands. But when the entire cast lined up for a curtain call, Manuel received a burst of applause that was so loud it shook the walls of the cafeteria. Later, as

---

Vocabulary

classic (klas′ ik) *adj.* serving as a standard, model, or guide, because of excellence or lasting appeal

intently (in tent′ lē) *adv.* in a focused way; with attention

Untitled painting. Gil Mayers (b. 1947). Private collection.

Viewing the painting: What musical instruments can you see in this painting? Do you think the music these musicians are playing is like "La Bamba"?

he mingled with the kids and parents, everyone patted him on the shoulder and told him, "Way to go. You were really funny."

Funny? Manuel thought. Did he do something funny?

Funny. Crazy. Hilarious. These were the words people said to him. He was confused, but beyond caring. All he knew was that people were paying attention to him, and his brother and sisters looked at him with a mixture of jealousy and awe. He was going to pull Mario aside and punch him in the arm for wearing his shirt, but he cooled it. He was enjoying the limelight. A teacher brought him cookies and punch, and the popular kids who had never before given him the time of day now clustered around him. Ricardo, the editor of the school bulletin, asked him how he made the needle stick.

"It just happened," Manuel said, crunching on a star-shaped cookie.

At home that night his father, eager to undo the buttons on his shirt and ease into his La-Z-Boy recliner, asked Manuel the same thing, how

He was enjoying the limelight.

he managed to make the song stick on the words *"Para bailar la bamba."*

Manuel thought quickly and reached for scientific jargon he had read in magazines. "Easy, Dad. I used laser tracking with high optics and low functional decibels per channel." His proud but confused father told him to be quiet and go to bed.

"Ah, *que niños tan truchas*,"[5] he said as he walked to the kitchen for a glass of milk. "I don't know how you kids nowadays get so smart."

Manuel, feeling happy, went to his bedroom, undressed, and slipped into his pajamas. He looked in the mirror and began to pantomime "La Bamba," but stopped because he was tired of the song. He crawled into bed. The sheets were as cold as the moon that stood over the peach tree in their backyard.

He was relieved that the day was over. Next year, when they asked for volunteers for the talent show, he wouldn't raise his hand. Probably.

---

5. *Que niños tan truchas* (kä nēn′ yos tän trōō′ chəs) means "These kids are so sharp!"

Vocabulary

mingle (ming′ gəl) *v.* to join together; mix

jargon (jär′ gən) *n.* terms used in certain art, science, or other field that may not be understood by outsiders

Responding to Literature

PERSONAL RESPONSE

- ◆ What moment in the story do you think is the most tense for Manuel?
- ◆ Look back at your notes from the **Focus Activity** on page 216. Did Manuel express any of the feelings you've had about performing?

Analyzing Literature

RECALL

1. What had Manuel volunteered to do? Why?
2. What happens during rehearsal?
3. How is Manuel's performance different from what he imagined it would be?
4. How does Manuel feel about his performance after it is over?

INTERPRET

5. At the beginning of the story, how does Manuel feel about having volunteered? How can you tell?
6. Why, do you think, does the author describe the problem that arises during rehearsal?
7. How does the author show that Manuel does not know how the audience responds to his act?
8. Do you think that Manuel will volunteer next year? Why or why not?

EVALUATE AND CONNECT

9. Why does the author have Manuel remember his experience in first grade during Science Week? What does this show about Manuel? If you were Manuel and you were remembering this, how would you feel?
10. Theme Connection   The author shows Manuel being very embarrassed in front of everyone. What might Manuel learn from this experience?

LITERARY ELEMENTS

Similes

When Manuel crawls into a bed with sheets "as cold as the moon," the reader quickly imagines how cold those sheets are—very cold! The author is not saying that the sheets are a certain number of degrees below zero. He is comparing the feel of the sheets with the moon. Sheets and the moon are very different, but readers know what Gary Soto means. His comparison makes the cold sheets easy to imagine. Such a comparison of two unlike things using the word *like* or *as* is a **simile.**

1. Find another simile in "La Bamba." Tell what is being compared.

2. Explain what you imagine from reading the comparison.

● See **Literary Terms Handbook,** p. R8.

Literature and Writing

Writing About Literature

Point of View   Write a paragraph or two describing the show from the point of view of another performer or a member of Manuel's family.

Creative Writing

Alternative Ending   What might have happened in the story if the record had not skipped? Imagine a different ending and then write it. Present your new story ending to a small group.

Extending Your Response

Literature Groups

What's So Funny?   Which parts of the story are the funniest? Are they things that *happen,* things Manuel *says,* or things he *thinks?* List the things in the story that made group members laugh. Share your list with the class.

Performing

Rock 'n' Roll Revisited   With a small group, take turns acting out Manuel's performance. Remember that you will be acting as a person who is acting out his idea of being a rock star. As a group, evaluate how well each member portrays Manuel.

Listening and Speaking

The Entertainers   How did other performers feel about the show? Take the role of one of the people in the talent show, and have other students take the roles of others. Take turns interviewing each other. Ask how the performers feel just before the show, during their performances, and after their performances.

Reading Further

If you'd like to read more by Gary Soto, you might enjoy these books:
Baseball in April and Other Stories
Local News

 Save your work for your portfolio.

Learning for Life

Radio Ad   Create a radio ad announcing the school talent show. First write the script for the ad and practice reading it. Then tape-record the ad and play it back for the class.

Skill Minilessons

GRAMMAR AND LANGUAGE • APOSTROPHES IN POSSESSIVES

How do you know that the song "La Bamba" that Manuel wants to sing is the version Ritchie Valens sang? The writer places an 's at the end of the name Valens. Thus it becomes "Ritchie Valens's 'La Bamba.'"

To show ownership with a plural noun ending in s, add only the apostrophe. Thus the song of several brothers becomes the "brothers' song." If the plural noun does not end in s, then add 's. The song of the women is the "women's song."

PRACTICE Rewrite the following as possessives by adding either 's or just the apostrophe.

1. the song of the three girls
2. the nervousness of Manuel
3. the record player of Mr. Roybal
4. the applause of the audience
5. the hit of Valens

● For more on apostrophes, see **Language Handbook,** p. R36.

READING AND THINKING • VERIFYING PREDICTIONS

When Mr. Roybal had trouble with the record player during rehearsal, readers could **predict** there might be trouble during the show. Reread the talent show section to verify whether Mr. Roybal's record player caused trouble. Predicting during reading means thinking ahead about how things might turn out. It adds interest to what you are reading and helps you remember important ideas. When you read how

events actually turn out, you are verifying your prediction.

PRACTICE Look through the story and write another prediction readers could make. Write the outcome from the story next to your prediction.

● For more on verifying predictions, see **Reading Handbook,** p. R76.

VOCABULARY • PRONUNCIATION

Pronouncing a word properly is important. If you don't know how to pronounce it, you won't say it, and saying a word is a way of getting used to it.

Next to each word in a dictionary, the pronunciation is given with letters and symbols. For example, the word gem would appear like this: (jem). That tells you to pronounce the g like a j and to pronounce the e with its regular short-vowel sound. If the vowel is supposed to be pronounced with its long vowel sound, it has a straight line over it. So game would look like this: (gām).

An accent mark points to the syllable you should stress. (Don't di zurt' a friend in the dez'ərt.) The

strange ə symbol in dez'ərt represents the unstressed vowel sound found in many words.

PRACTICE Use the pronunciation given for each word to answer the question that follows it.

1. **debut** (dā bū') Does the second syllable of debut rhyme with few, cute, or nut?
2. **jargon** (jär' gən) Does jargon rhyme with upon, bargain, or throne?
3. **hygiene** (hī' jēn) Does the first syllable of hygiene rhyme with ridge, buy, or pig?
4. **flail** (flāl) Does flail rhyme with tale or partial?
5. **coordinator** (kō ôr' də nā' tər) Which syllables are accented in coordinator?

Mariachi Music

Before it became a rock-and-roll hit in the United States, "La Bamba" was a familiar folk song in Mexico. There, well-known songs are played in restaurants and on street corners by musicians called *mariachis* (ma rē äch' ēz). People stop to listen or to sing along as violins, guitars, a six-string guitar with a large, round belly called a *guitarron* (gē' tär ōn), and a smaller, five-string guitar called a *vihela* (vē hā' lə) weave their sounds around the trumpet melody.

Mariachi music began in western Mexico during the 1850s. Then, rural musicians played a variety of stringed instruments—guitars, lutes, violins, and even harps. They played folk music for weddings, festivals, and other important ceremonies.

Today, mariachi musicians look different and sound different. The simple shirts, pants, and straw hats of rural mariachis have been replaced by the *trajes de charros* (trä' hās də char' ōs). This is the traditional costume of the Mexican cowboy or rancher—tight trousers with silver buttons, short embroidered jacket, silk bow tie, and large sombrero. During the 1930s, the trumpet joined the stringed instruments and changed the traditional mariachi sound.

Because listeners might request favorite songs from different regions of Mexico, mariachi musicians learn a wide range of songs. A *son,* one of the most important styles, features a heavy beat and sometimes humorous lyrics. In 1987 Linda Ronstadt recorded "Y Andale," a song almost every mariachi knows. She won a Grammy award for her 1987 album, *Canciones de mi Padre,* and she helped to make mariachi music popular in the United States.

ACTIVITY

Within a group, create a pantomime band to celebrate the heritage of one or more students in the group. What kinds of music will you play? What clothes might you wear? What will you name the band? Find a recording of a song that reflects the heritage you have chosen. Share the song, along with your group's pantomime performance, with the class.

SONG LYRICS

Carl Perkins and Elvis Presley knew how important shoes could be.

Blue Suede Shoes

by Carl Perkins, as performed by Elvis Presley

Well, it's one for the money, two for the
show, three to get ready, now go, cat, go
But don't you step on my Blue Suede
Shoes.
You can do anything but lay off of my Blue
Suede Shoes.

Well, you can knock me down, step on my
face, slander my name all over the place;
Do anything that you want to do, but
uh uh, honey, lay off of my shoes
Don't you step on my Blue Suede Shoes,
You can do anything but lay off of my Blue
Suede Shoes.

[Well, it's blue, blue, blue suede shoes
Blue, blue, blue suede shoes
Blue, blue, blue suede shoes
Blue, blue, blue suede shoes
Well, you can do anything, but lay off
of my blue suede shoes.]

© 1956 Hi-Lo Music, Inc.

Respond

1. How does Elvis feel about his blue suede shoes?

2. Do you have any clothing that makes you feel this way?

Before You Read
Shoes for Hector

MEET
NICHOLASA MOHR

From the moment my mother handed me some scrap paper, a pencil, and a few crayons, I decided that by making pictures and writing letters I could create my own world, like 'magic'," says Nicholasa Mohr (nē kō lä′ sä   mōr). "In the small, crowded apartment I shared with my large family . . . 'making magic' permitted me all the space and freedom my imagination could handle." Mohr grew up to become a successful painter, printmaker, and storyteller. The characters in her stories are often Puerto Rican people.

Nicholasa Mohr was born in 1935. This story was published in 1975.

FOCUS ACTIVITY

Imagine that you are going to an important event and you want to look your best. What clothes will you wear?

QuickWrite
Write a quick description of the ideal shoes to wear, whether or not you own such a pair. How do they look? What color and style are they?

Setting a Purpose
Read "Shoes for Hector" to find out what shoes Hector wears for an important occasion.

BACKGROUND

Did You Know?   From early in history, people have been wearing shoes to protect their feet. They may have begun by tying leaves, bark, or animal hides to the bottom of their feet. Various kinds of shoes developed around the world. People in warm climates wore sandals. People in colder or harsher regions wore boots. Until the mid-1800s, all types of shoes were made by hand. Because a shoemaker could make only about one pair a day, shoes were expensive. Today, a shoe-making machine can make more than one thousand pairs a day, so shoes have become more affordable.

VOCABULARY PREVIEW

sulking (sulk′ ing) *adj.* silent and unfriendly; bad-tempered; p. 233

resigned (ri zīnd′) *adj.* accepting or giving in unhappily but without resistance or complaint; p. 234

inscription (in skrip′ shən) *n.* something that is written, carved, or marked on a surface; p. 235

Shoes for Hector

Nicholasa Mohr ~

Hector's mother had gone to see Uncle Luis the day before graduation, and he had come by the same evening. Everyone sat in the living room watching Uncle Luis as he took a white box out of a brown paper bag. Opening the box, he removed a pair of shiny, light-caramel-colored shoes with tall heels and narrow, pointed toes. Holding them up proudly, he said, "Set me back twelve bucks, boy!"

Shoes for Hector

Everyone looked at Hector and then back at Uncle Luis.

"Here you go, my boy. . . ." He gestured toward Hector. "Try them on."

"I'm not gonna try those things on!" Hector said.

"Why not?" asked Uncle Luis. "What's wrong with them? They are the latest style, man. Listen, boy, you will be a la moda[1] with these."

"They . . . they're just not my type. Besides, they don't go with my suit—it's navy blue. Those shoes are orange!" Hector's younger brothers and sister looked at each other and began to giggle and laugh.

"Shut up, you dummies!" Hector shouted angrily.

"Hector, what is the matter with you?" his mother asked. "That's no way to behave."

"I'd rather wear my sneakers than those, Mami. You and Papi promised to buy me shoes. You didn't say nothing about wearing Uncle Luis's shoes."

"Wait a minute, now. Just wait a minute," Hector's father said. "We know, but we just couldn't manage it now. Since your Uncle Luis has the same size foot like you, and he was nice enough to lend you his new shoes, what's the difference? We done what we could, son; you have to be satisfied."

Hector felt the blood rushing to his face and tried to control his embarrassment and anger. His parents had been preparing his graduation party now for more than a week. They should have spent the money on my shoes instead of on a dumb party, he thought. Hector had used up all the earnings from his part-time job. He had bought his suit, tie, shirt, socks, and handkerchief. His parents had promised to buy him the shoes. Not one cent left, he thought, and it was just too late now.

"It's not my fault that they lay me off for three days," his father said, "and that Petie got sick and that Georgie needed a winter jacket and Juanito some . . ."

As his father spoke, Hector wanted to say a few things. Like, No, it's my fault that you have to spend the money for shoes on a party and a cake and everything to impress the neighbors and the familia. Stupid dinner! But instead he remained quiet, and did not say a word.

"Hector . . . come on, my son. Hector, try them on, bendito.[2] Uncle Luis was nice enough to bring them," he heard his mother plead. "Please, for me."

"Maybe I can get into Papi's shoes," Hector answered.

"My shoes don't fit you. And your brothers are all younger and smaller than you. There's nobody else. You are lucky Uncle Luis has the same size foot," his father responded.

"O.K., I'll just wear my sneakers," said Hector.

"Oh, no . . . no, never mind. You don't wear no sneakers, so that people can call us a bunch of jíbaros![3] You wear them shoes!" his mother said.

---

1. The Spanish expression *a la moda* (ä′ lə mō′də) means "in fashion; stylish."

2. *Bendito* (ben dē′ tō) means "saint" or "blessed one." Hector's mother is expressing affection.

3. A *jíbaro* (hē′ bə rō) is someone whose parents come from different countries or cultures. Hector's mother is afraid people will think the family is ignorant.

New Shoes for H., 1973–74. Don Eddy. Acrylic on canvas, 117.7 x 121.9 cm. The Cleveland Museum of Art.

Viewing the painting: How do you think Hector feels when he looks in a window like this?

"Mami, they are orange!" Hector responded. "And look at them pointed fronts—they go on for a mile. I'm not wearing them."

"Come on, please," his mother coaxed. "They look nice and brand new, too."

"Hector!" his father said loudly. "Now, your Uncle Luis was nice enough to bring them, and you are going to try them on." Everyone was silent and Hector sat sulking. His mother took the shoes from Uncle Luis and over to Hector.

"Here, son, try them on, at least. See?" She held them up. "Look at them. They are not orange, just a light-brown color, that's all. Only a very light brown."

Without looking at anyone, Hector took the shoes and slowly put them on. No doubt about it, they felt like a perfect fit.

"How about that?" Uncle Luis smiled. "Now you look sharp. Right in style, boy!"

Hector stood up and walked a few paces. He knew what the kids called these shoes; he could hear them. "Roach killers. Man,

Vocabulary

sulking (sulk´ ing) *adj.* silent and unfriendly; bad-tempered

Shoes for Hector

the greenhorns[4] wear them shoes to attack the cockroaches that hide in the corners. Man, they go right in there with them points and zap . . . zap . . . and snap . . . they're dead! Mata-cucaracha[5] shoes." In spite of all the smiling faces in the living room, Hector still heard all the remarks he was sure his friends would make if he wore those shoes.

"O.K., you look wonderful. And it's only for one morning. You can take them off right after graduation," his mother said gently.

Hector removed the shoes and put them back in the box, <u>resigned</u> that there was just no way out. At that moment he even found himself wishing that he had not been selected as valedictorian[6] and wasn't receiving any honors.

"Take your time, Hector. You don't have to give them back to me right away. Wear the shoes for the party. So you look good," he heard Uncle Luis calling out as he walked into his bedroom.

"That stupid party!" Hector whispered out loud.

With a pained expression on his face the next morning, Hector left the apartment wearing Uncle Luis's shoes. His mother and father walked proudly with him.

Hector arrived at the school auditorium and took his place on line. Smiling and waving at him, his parents sat in the audience.

"Hector López . . ." He walked up the long aisle onto the stage. He finished his speech and sat on a chair provided for him on the stage. They called his name again several times, and each time Hector received an honor or prize. Included were a wrist-watch and a check for cash. Whenever Hector stood up and walked to the podium,[7] he prayed that no one would notice his shoes.

Finally, graduation exercises were over and Hector hurried off the stage, looking for his parents. People stopped him and congratulated him on his many honors and on his speech. His school friends shook his hand and they exchanged addresses. Hector found himself engaged in long good-byes. Slowly, people began to leave the large auditorium, and Hector and his parents headed for home.

Hector sat on his bed and took off Uncle Luis's shoes. "Good-bye," he said out loud, making a face, and dropped them into the box. He sighed with relief. No one had even mentioned the shoes, he thought. Man . . . I bet they didn't even notice them. Boy! Was I ever lucky. . . . Nobody said a word. How about that? he said to himself. Reaching under the bed, he took out his sneakers and happily put them on. Never again, he continued, if I can help it. No, sir. I'm gonna make sure I got me shoes to wear! He remembered all the things he won at graduation. Looking at

---

4. Here, Hector uses *greenhorns* to mean "fools." The word usually refers to beginners.
5. *Mata* (mä′ tä) means "killer," and *cucaracha* (ko͞o′ kə rä′ chə) means "cockroach."
6. A class's highest-ranked student is called the *valedictorian*, and he or she often gives a speech during the graduation ceremony.
7. A *podium* can be either a small, raised platform or a stand with a slanted shelf for holding a speaker's papers.

Vocabulary
resigned (ri zīnd′) *adj.* accepting or giving in unhappily but without resistance or complaint

his new wristwatch, he put it on. That's really something, he thought. He took out the check for cash he had received and read, "*Pay to the Order of Hector López . . . The Sum of Twenty-Five Dollars and 00/100 Cents.*" I can't wait to show everybody, he said to himself.

Hector left his room and looked into the kitchen. His mother and grandmother were busily preparing more food. He heard voices and music in the living room and quickly walked in that direction. When his younger brothers and sister saw him, they jumped up and down.

"Here's Hector!" Petie yelled.

"Happy Graduation Day, Hector!" everyone shouted.

The living room was full of people. His father was talking to Uncle Luis and some neighbors. Uncle Luis called out, "There he is. Hector! . . . There's my man now."

"Look." Hector's father pointed to a table that was loaded with platters of food and a large cake. The cake had the inscription "Happy Graduation to Hector." Behind the cake was a large placard printed in bright colors:

HAPPY GRADUATION DAY, HECTOR
FROM ALL YOUR FAMILY
Mami, Papi, Abuelita,[8] *Petie, Georgie, Juanito, and Millie*

8. *Abuelita* (ä′ bwə lē′ tə) means "grandmother."

Rows of multi-colored crepe-paper streamers were strung across the ceiling and walls. Lots of balloons had been blown up and attached to each streamer. A big bell made of bright-red crepe paper and cardboard was set up under the center ceiling light. The record player was going full blast with a loud merengue;[9] some of the kids were busy dancing. Hector's face flushed when he saw Gloria. He had hoped she would come to the party, and there she was. Looking great, he thought.

Some neighbors came over and congratulated Hector. His friends began to gather around, asking him lots of questions and admiring his wristwatch.

"Show them the check, Hector," his father said proudly. "That's some smart boy; he just kept getting honors! Imagine, they even give him money. . . ."

Hector reached into his jacket pocket and took out the check for twenty-five dollars. He passed it around so that everyone could see it. Impressed, they asked him, "Hey, man. Hector, what you gonna do with all that money?"

"Yeah. Tell us, Hector, what you gonna do?"

Hector smiled and shrugged his shoulders. "Buy me a pair of shoes! Any color except orange!" he replied.

9. *Merengue* (mä reng′ gä) is the name of a dance.

Vocabulary
inscription (in skrip′ shən) *n.* something that is written, carved, or marked on a surface

Responding to Literature

PERSONAL RESPONSE

- ◆ While you were reading the story, what did you think would happen? Were you surprised by the ending of the story? Explain.
- ◆ What kind of new shoes would you get if you were Hector? Use your ideas from the **Focus Activity** on page 230.

Analyzing Literature

RECALL

1. What is the important occasion that is about to be celebrated?
2. How does Hector react to being given his uncle's shoes? Why?
3. How does Hector feel about his party at the beginning of the story?
4. How will Hector use his check for twenty-five dollars?

INTERPRET

5. Why are Hector's shoes more visible than those of other students during the ceremony?
6. Do Hector's parents and uncle understand how he feels about the shoes? Support your answer with information from the story.
7. Do Hector's feelings about his party change by the end of the story? How do you know?
8. After the ceremony, do you think Hector is glad he wore the shoes? Why or why not?

EVALUATE AND CONNECT

9. Do you think Hector learns something from this experience? If so, what?
10. In your opinion, should Hector's parents have bought him the shoes he wanted? Why or why not?

LITERARY ELEMENTS

Theme

Theme is the main idea of a story. Sometimes an author states the theme of a story in a sentence or two. More often, the reader figures out the theme by thinking about the characters and events and then deciding whether the story has a *message*. All the elements of a story, including characters, plot, setting, and mood, can work together to reveal the theme. Showing how a character handles a problem is one way the author can reveal the theme or message of a story.

1. Hector wears shoes he thinks are ugly even though he'd rather not wear them. What does this show about him?

2. Based on Hector's action, what would you say is the theme of "Shoes for Hector"?

● See **Literary Terms Handbook,** p. R9.

Extending Your Response

Writing About Literature

Visualize a Scene   How do you picture Hector's graduation and his party? Use information in the story and your imagination to draw one of these scenes. Write a paragraph describing your picture and point out details you used from the story.

Creative Writing

Dear Hector   Write a letter to Hector. Explain how you would have handled his situation, sympathize with him about his problem, or describe a similar experience you have had.

Literature Groups

Living in Two Worlds   Hector is afraid of what his friends will think if he does what his family wants him to do. "In spite of all the smiling faces [of his family] in the living room, Hector still heard all the remarks he was sure his friends would make if he wore those shoes." Discuss how Hector deals with this conflict. Does he make the right choices? What else could he do?

Learning for Life

Shoe Store Ad   Create an advertisement for a pair of shoes that you would like to own. Draw the shoes. Then choose just the right words—one or two words, or a sentence at most—to add to the poster. Use your notes from the **Focus Activity.** Can you excite someone about the shoes and cause them to see the shoes as you do?

Save your work for your portfolio.

Skill Minilesson

VOCABULARY • MULTIPLE-MEANING WORDS

Building a vocabulary means more than learning new words. It is just as important to learn new meanings of familiar words. The word *favor,* for example, has at least eleven different meanings.

   If you read that a woman *resigned* from her job, you would probably know she quit. However, *resigned* is an adjective in "Shoes for Hector," and it means "accepting or giving in unhappily but without resistance." You will often come across a word that you think you know but that doesn't make sense in the sentence you're reading. That's a clue that it has another, less familiar meaning.

PRACTICE   Each pair of phrases below uses the same word. In one phrase, the meaning is probably familiar to you. In the other one, it may not be. For each phrase, write a synonym or short meaning for the underlined word. Use a dictionary to find any meanings you don't know.

1. a. a home <u>address</u>   b. a graduation <u>address</u>
2. a. play a <u>game</u>   b. have a <u>game</u> leg
3. a. to have a <u>rash</u>   b. a <u>rash</u> action
4. a. to <u>lead</u>   b. pencil <u>lead</u>
5. a. <u>close</u> the door   b. not too <u>close</u>

Before You Read
Eleven

MEET
SANDRA CISNEROS

Growing up in a family with six brothers, Sandra Cisneros (sis ner′ ōs′) learned to speak up to get noticed. "You had to be fast and you had to be funny—you had to be a *storyteller*," she says. Her family moved often between Chicago and Mexico City, and Cisneros went to several different schools. Now a resident of San Antonio, she often writes about children from Latino cultures living in the United States. She has said of her writing, "Anything that is truly powerful comes from here," pointing to her heart.

Sandra Cisneros was born in 1954. This story was first published in 1991.

FOCUS ACTIVITY

What were you like five years ago? What did you like to do? What made you laugh?

Make a Web
Make a web around your name and write all the things you think of when you think of yourself as five years younger. How have you changed? Share ideas with a partner.

Setting a Purpose
Think about yourself at different ages as you read "Eleven."

BACKGROUND

Did You Know?   Memories are triggered by all of our senses. For example, when we hear a song, we might have a memory about when we last heard it. An old song can remind listeners of thoughts and feelings they had back when the song was popular. When you are older, you may hear a song that is popular now and be reminded of yourself as you are now. However, the strongest trigger for memory is not sound or even sight, as you might expect. The strongest trigger for memory is smell.

Sandra Cisneros ~

What they don't understand about birthdays

and what they never tell you is that when you're eleven,
you're also ten, and nine, and eight, and seven, and six, and
five, and four, and three, and two, and one. And when you
wake up on your eleventh birthday you expect to feel
eleven, but you don't. You open your eyes and everything's
just like yesterday, only it's today. And you don't feel eleven
at all. You feel like you're still ten. And you are—underneath the year that makes you eleven.

Like some days you might say something stupid, and
that's the part of you that's still ten. Or maybe some days
you might need to sit on your mama's lap because you're
scared, and that's the part of you that's five. And maybe one
day when you're all grown up maybe you will need to cry
like if you're three, and that's okay. That's what I tell Mama
when she's sad and needs to cry. Maybe she's feeling three.

Carmela Bertagna, c. 1880. John Singer Sargent. Oil on canvas, 23½ x 19½ in. Columbus Museum of Art, OH. Bequest of Frederick W. Schumacher.

Viewing the painting: What qualities might the girl in this painting share with the narrator of "Eleven"?

Because the way you grow old is kind of like an onion or like the rings inside a tree trunk or like my little wooden dolls that fit one inside the other, each year inside the next one. That's how being eleven years old is.

You don't feel eleven. Not right away. It takes a few days, weeks even, sometimes even months before you say Eleven when they ask you. And you don't feel smart eleven, not until you're almost twelve. That's the way it is.

Only today I wish I didn't have only eleven years rattling inside me like pennies in a tin Band-Aid box. Today I wish I was one hundred and two instead of eleven because if I was one hundred and two I'd have known what to say when Mrs. Price put the red sweater on my desk. I would've known how to tell her it wasn't mine instead of just sitting there with that look on my face and nothing coming out of my mouth.

"Whose is this?" Mrs. Price says, and she holds the red sweater up in the air for all the class to see. "Whose? It's been sitting in the coatroom for a month."

"Not mine," says everybody. "Not me."

"It has to belong to somebody," Mrs. Price keeps saying, but nobody can remember. It's an ugly sweater with red plastic buttons and a collar and sleeves all stretched out like you could use it for a jump rope. It's maybe a thousand years old and even if it belonged to me I wouldn't say so.

Maybe because I'm skinny, maybe because she doesn't like me, that stupid Sylvia Saldívar[1] says, "I think it belongs to

Rachel." An ugly sweater like that, all raggedy and old, but Mrs. Price believes her. Mrs. Price takes the sweater and puts it right on my desk, but when I open my mouth nothing comes out.

"That's not, I don't, you're not . . . Not mine," I finally say in a little voice that was maybe me when I was four.

"Of course it's yours," Mrs. Price says. "I remember you wearing it once." Because she's older and the teacher, she's right and I'm not.

Not mine, not mine, not mine, but Mrs. Price is already turning to page thirty-two, and math problem number four. I don't know why but all of a sudden I'm feeling sick inside, like the part of me that's three wants to come out of my eyes, only I squeeze them shut tight and bite down on my teeth real hard and try to remember today I am eleven, eleven. Mama is making a cake for me for tonight, and when Papa comes home everybody will sing Happy birthday, happy birthday to you.

But when the sick feeling goes away and I open my eyes, the red sweater's still sitting there like a big red mountain. I move the red sweater to the corner of my desk with my ruler. I move my pencil and books and eraser as far from it as possible. I even move my chair a little to the right. Not mine, not mine, not mine.

In my head I'm thinking how long till lunchtime, how long till I can take the red sweater and throw it over the schoolyard fence, or leave it hanging on a parking meter, or bunch it up into a little ball and toss it in the alley. Except when math period ends Mrs. Price says loud and in

---

1. *Saldívar* (säl dē′ vär)

Eleven

front of everybody, "Now, Rachel, that's enough," because she sees I've shoved the red sweater to the tippy-tip corner of my desk and it's hanging all over the edge like a waterfall, but I don't care.

"Rachel," Mrs. Price says. She says it like she's getting mad. "You put that sweater on right now and no more nonsense."

"But it's not—"

"Now!" Mrs. Price says.

This is when I wish I wasn't eleven, because all the years inside of me—ten, nine, eight, seven, six, five, four, three, two, and one—are pushing at the back of my eyes when I put one arm through one sleeve of the sweater that smells like cottage cheese, and then the other arm through the other and stand there with my arms apart like if the sweater hurts me and it does, all itchy and full of germs that aren't even mine.

That's when everything I've been holding in since this morning, since when Mrs. Price put the sweater on my desk, finally lets go, and all of a sudden I'm crying in front of everybody. I wish I was invisible but I'm not. I'm eleven and it's my birthday today and I'm crying like I'm three in front of everybody. I put my head down on

the desk and bury my face in my stupid clown-sweater arms. My face all hot and spit coming out of my mouth because I can't stop the little animal noises from coming out of me, until there aren't any more tears left in my eyes, and it's just my body shaking like when you have the hiccups, and my whole head hurts like when you drink milk too fast.

I wish I was invisible but I'm not.

But the worst part is right before the bell rings for lunch. That stupid Phyllis Lopez, who is even dumber than Sylvia Saldívar, says she remembers the red sweater is hers! I take it off right away and give it to her, only Mrs. Price pretends like everything's okay.

Today I'm eleven. There's a cake Mama's making for tonight, and when Papa comes home from work we'll eat it. There'll be candles and presents and everybody will sing Happy birthday, happy birthday to you, Rachel, only it's too late.

I'm eleven today. I'm eleven, ten, nine, eight, seven, six, five, four, three, two, and one, but I wish I was one hundred and two. I wish I was anything but eleven, because I want today to be far away already, far away like a runaway balloon, like a tiny *o* in the sky, so tiny-tiny you have to close your eyes to see it.

Responding to Literature

PERSONAL RESPONSE
- ◆ Do you understand how Rachel feels?
- ◆ What would you tell Rachel to make her feel better about what happened?

Analyzing Literature

RECALL AND INTERPRET
1. What special day is it for Rachel, the narrator? How does she feel about it?
2. Why does the teacher think the red sweater belongs to Rachel?
3. What does the teacher make Rachel do? Does Rachel feel better after the mix-up is resolved? Why or why not?

EVALUATE AND CONNECT
4. Why does the narrator say that she spoke in a voice from age four? Have you ever used a voice like that? Explain.
5. The narrator repeats the idea that a birthday party at home later should make her feel better. Do you think it will? Would it make you feel better, if you were in her situation?
6. The author uses the **first-person point of view** (see page R6) to tell this story. How does this affect you as you read the story?

LITERARY ELEMENTS

Repetition
Rachel believes that people are made up of every age they have ever been. She thinks, "[W]hen you're eleven, you're also ten, and nine, and eight, and seven, and six, and five, and four, and three, and two, and one." This **repetition** of ages going down from eleven shows how important age is to Rachel. Readers also see, as Rachel decides what age she feels, how upset she is.

1. Rachel mentions different ages throughout the story. What reasons does she have for thinking about her age?
2. Find another example of repetition and tell what it adds to the story.

● See **Literary Terms Handbook**, p. R7.

Extending Your Response

Literature Groups
Analyzing Theme   Rachel compares getting older to the layers of an onion and the rings of a tree. What does she mean? Discuss examples from the story as well as your own ideas. Use your notes from the **Focus Activity** on page 238.

Writing About Literature
Sensory Images   The sweater is described using images that appeal to readers' senses. Find images in the story that tell how the sweater looks, smells, and feels. Then write your own description of the sweater based on these images.

Shoes for Hector **and** Eleven

COMPARE **CHARACTERS**

In "Shoes for Hector" and "Eleven," both main characters face an embarrassing situation.

1. How does each character handle an embarrassing situation?
2. Which character feels better about the outcome? Why?
3. Which character do you think handles the situation better? Why?

COMPARE **PROBLEMS**

How are the characters' problems alike? How could they have solved their problems? Complete one of the assignments below.

- Write an advice column. Include two letters, one from Rachel and one from Hector, describing their problems. Write one letter of advice to both.

- Draw a Venn diagram and compare and contrast the problems of the two main characters. Ask yourself: In what ways are the problems of the main characters alike? Are the ways the main characters solve their problems similar? Do other people help solve the problems? How does each character's personality affect how he or she deals with the problem?

COMPARE **THEMES**

Evaluate what the two main characters in these two stories may have learned from their experiences. In the future, would each handle a similar situation in the same way? What did *you* learn from reading about their experiences?

Writing Skills

Defining Audience and Purpose

In "Shoes for Hector," Hector's mother persuades him to wear Uncle Luis's shoes. She uses emotion as well as reason. She finally succeeds because she understands her audience—Hector—and his views.

> "Come on, my son. . . . Uncle Luis was nice enough to bring them. . . . Please, for me. . . . And it's only for one morning. You can take them off right after graduation."

When you write to persuade, you can better understand your **audience**—your readers—by asking yourself the questions below.

◆ What do my readers already know about this issue? What facts might help them understand it better?

◆ What are my readers' views on this issue? What reasoning might make sense to them, considering their views?

◆ What are my readers' personal concerns? What emotional appeals might touch their concerns?

This chart shows how to use questions and answers to plan persuasive writing.

Audience: Senator Jasper	Task: a letter persuading her to draft a clean-air bill for our area	
What she knows: knows this area; used to live here	**Her views:** supports more factories, businesses, public health	**Personal concerns:** getting re-elected being respected
Facts she might need: air pollution statistics for area; number of new factories here	**Reasoning:** clean air will attract newcomers, cleaner air = less lung disease	**Appeals to concerns:** grateful local citizens will vote for her; chance to earn respect, be a hero

ACTIVITIES

1. Imagine writing a talk persuading first graders to take action against a litter problem in your area. Make a planning chart like the one above.

2. Imagine writing a second talk on the same subject. This time your audience is the parents and teachers in your school district. Fill in a second chart.

Before You Read

The Sidewalk Racer or *On the Skateboard*, and *Daydreamers*

MEET LILLIAN MORRISON

Lillian Morrison was a librarian for over forty years. She wrote and edited several books of poetry about sports.

Lillian Morrison was born in 1917. This poem was published in 1965.

MEET ELOISE GREENFIELD

"I believe everyone spends time daydreaming," says Eloise Greenfield. "With writing, sometimes an idea will come, or a word will come, or a title, or an opening sentence, or an image, and then it may be months or years later before it really develops into a story. I think it's all working in the subconscious or somewhere in your daydreaming during the period that it's developing."

Eloise Greenfield was born in 1929. This poem was published in 1981.

FOCUS ACTIVITY

Do you like playing hard? What are some of your favorite activities or games? Do you like sitting quietly doing nothing at all? Why?

Partners
Tell a partner how you feel about playing actively and sitting quietly. Then share your ideas with another pair.

Setting a Purpose
Read "The Sidewalk Racer" and "Daydreamers" to discover the experiences and feelings of the speakers.

BACKGROUND

Skateboarding was probably invented in the late 1950s by someone who enjoyed both roller-skating and surfing. Early skateboards had clay wheels. The wheels tended to stop dead when they hit stones and to slip during turns, throwing the rider off the board.

In the 1970s, plastic wheels came into use. These gripped the ground better than clay wheels, making skateboards easier to control. Riders began wearing helmets and elbow and knee pads to prevent injuries from falls.

Today, skateboarding is an international sport in which experts perform stunts in specially designed "parks."

The Sidewalk Racer

or On the Skateboard

Lillian Morrison ᵔ

Skimming
an asphalt sea
I swerve, I curve, I
sway; I speed to whirring
5 sound an inch above the
ground; I'm the sailor
and the sail, I'm the
driver and the wheel
I'm the one and only
10 single engine
human auto
mobile.

Daydreamers

Eloise Greenfield

Daydreamers . . .

holding their bodies still
for a time
letting the world turn around them

5   while their dreams hopscotch,
doubledutch,° dance,

thoughts rollerskate,
crisscross,
bump into hopes and wishes.

10   Dreamers
thinking up new ways,
looking toward new days,

planning new tries,
asking new whys.
15   Before long,
hands will start to move again,
eyes turn outward,
bodies shift for action,
but for this moment they are still,

20   they are
the daydreamers,
letting the world dizzy itself
without them.

Scenes passing through their minds
25   make no sound
glide from hiding places
promenade and return
silently

the children watch their memories
30   with spirit-eyes
seeing more than they saw before

feeling more
or maybe less
than they felt the time before
35   reaching with spirit-hands
to touch the dreams
drawn from their yesterdays

They will not be the same
after this growing time,
40   this dreaming.
In their stillness they have moved
forward

toward womanhood
toward manhood.
45   This dreaming has made them
new.

---

6 *Doubledutch* is a jump-rope game using two
ropes swung crisscross by two turners.

Responding to Literature

PERSONAL RESPONSE

Make a word web with the title of the poem you liked best in the center. Attach thoughts and feelings you had while reading the poem.

Analyzing Literature

RECALL

1. What words in "The Sidewalk Racer" let you feel the movement of someone on a skateboard?

2. How do daydreamers look? According to the poet, how do their dreams and thoughts "move"?

INTERPRET

3. In "The Sidewalk Racer," Morrison refers to an "asphalt sea." What does she mean?

4. According to the speaker of "Daydreamers," why is daydreaming important?

EVALUATE AND CONNECT

5. Why, do you think, do the lines of "The Sidewalk Racer" appear as they do on the page?

6. In "The Sidewalk Racer," the skateboarder becomes both the "driver and the wheel." What does this mean? Have you ever felt this way?

7. Do you think that sports or athletic activities are good subjects for poems? Explain.

8. How do dreams "hopscotch, doubledutch, dance"? Do yours do that?

9. How can daydreaming help people to "move forward"?

10. If daydreaming is a good thing, as Greenfield implies, why do people sometimes discourage others from daydreaming too much?

LITERARY ELEMENTS

Metaphor

A **metaphor** is a figure of speech that compares two seemingly unlike things to create a fresh, new way of looking at something.
   For example, in "The Sidewalk Racer," Morrison says that the person on the skateboard is "the sailor / and the sail." Morrison creates a clear picture for readers of the skateboarder moving across the sidewalk as swiftly and smoothly as a sailboat gliding on water.

1. What other metaphors does Morrison include in "The Sidewalk Racer"? What things are being compared?

2. When Greenfield says that thoughts "bump into hopes and wishes," what does she mean?

● See **Literary Terms Handbook,** p. R5.

Extending Your Response

Writing About Literature

Speakers   Each poem tells about an activity, skateboarding or daydreaming. What role does the speaker play in each poem? Is the speaker observing or participating? Write a paragraph about the speakers in these poems. Describe what the speaker's role adds to the meaning of each poem.

Creative Writing

Creating a Shape Poem   Printed on the page, Lillian Morrison's poem could suggest the shape of its subject: a skateboard. Write a shape poem of your own. You may want to describe one of the games or activities you discussed during the **Focus Activity** on page 246.

Art Activity

Draw an Impression   Within a small group, pretend that you are watching clouds pass overhead. Close your eyes, let your mind go blank, and take turns describing the clouds you see. After a few moments of silence, take turns sharing any daydreams you had as you relaxed. Draw a picture to represent your daydream.

Learning for Life

Safety First   In a school announcement, recommend safety gear for a sport you enjoy. If possible, check with a coach for equipment suggestions. To interest your listeners, include a quote from the coach or an anecdote about how such sports equipment has helped you or others.

Reading Further

You might enjoy these books by the poets:

The Sidewalk Racer and Other Poems of Sports and Motion by Lillian Morrison

Childtimes: A Three-Generation Memoir by Eloise Greenfield and Lessie Jones Little

📖 **Save your work for your portfolio.**

Skill Minilesson

GRAMMAR AND LANGUAGE • VIVID VERBS

One reason that Morrison's poem creates such a clear picture of a skateboard racing along is her choice of lively verbs. See how flat and dull her poem would be if the first lines of "The Sidewalk Racer" were written as follows:

Moving on / an asphalt sea / I move, I turn, I / go back and forth.

PRACTICE   Use a thesaurus to find three vivid substitutes for the following verbs:

1. talk   4. eat
2. go   5. run
3. sit

● For more on verbs, see **Language Handbook,** p. R28.

Technology Skills

Database: Getting Organized

An electronic database is a software program that allows you to organize, store, and retrieve information. Data is organized into a table of columns and rows. Each single piece of information is called a field, and a group of fields in a row is called a record.

Field Columns (Categories)

Name	Address	City	State	Zip
Brown, Charlene	12814 South Emerald	Chicago	IL	60601
Evans, Daryl	1829 West 45th Street	New York	NY	10021
Huchinson, Bill	6754 South Park Place	St. Petersburg	FL	33716
Michowski, Dan	2032 Third Avenue	New York	NY	10017
Sanchez, Gloria	2 Billings Road	Laredo	TX	78040
Watanabe, Sarah	3404 Camino Road	Santa Clara	CA	95051
Whitney, Peter	1209 East Maple Street	Chicago	IL	60611

← Record (the Evans, Daryl row)

← Field (the Laredo / TX / 78040 cell)

Once the information is in your database, you can recall it in a number of useful ways. For example, you can tell an address-book database to show you all the names of people who live in a certain city, or even a particular zip code.

Can you think of ways in which you could use a database? Here's an example. Imagine that you have a large CD collection. Some friends come over to listen to music, and they like female country-and-western singers. If your CDs are organized on a database, you could quickly discover which CDs have female country-and-western singers by doing a simple keyword search.

Music Collection

CD Title	Music Category	Artist(s)	Artists' Description
All I Have to Give	Pop	Backstreet Boys	male group
Blues on the Bayou	Rhythm & Blues	B. B. King	male vocalist, guitarist
Sittin' on Top of the World	Country & Western	LeAnn Rimes	female vocalist
Never Say Never	Pop	Brandy	female vocalist
Double Live	Country & Western	Garth Brooks	male vocalist

Create a Database

1. Open the database program on your computer. Go to the **File** menu and select **New Database.** The computer will ask you to name and create the database. In the space marked File Name type in Music Collection. If the program asks you to define a primary key, click **No.**

2. The computer will ask what type of database you want to create. Select **Table.** Then select **Design** view.

3. The program will ask you to create and describe your field names. In the top cell of the Field column, type CD Title.

4. Below that entry, type in Music Category. Continue in the same manner with the categories: Artist(s) and Artists' Description. (In the description field, you can use such terms as *male/female vocalist, chorus, solo piano,* and so on.)

5. Now go to the column labeled Data Type and choose **Text** for each of your named fields. Leave the column labeled Description blank.

6. Using the View menu, select **Table View.** You will now see that each field you named has a column in the table. Fill in the information for at least five records (rows). When you are finished, click **Save** in the File menu. At this point, you may print your table and save it in your portfolio.

Forms

A database with a great many fields can be difficult to read. You need to scroll a good deal because the table is much wider than your monitor's screen. Database programs allow you to create forms that make viewing your information easier. A form puts each record in a database on a "card" that you can design with the help of your software. Use the tutorial or manual that came with your database software or the Help function to learn how to create forms.

CD Title	My Love Is Your love
Music Category	Soul/R&B
Artist(s)	Whitney Houston
Artists' Description	female vocalist
Record Label/Number	BMG/Arista 19037

band: title:

| Bands | 1 | It's Not Right But It's Okay | ▼ |

ACTIVITIES

1. To put your records in alphabetical order, pull down the **Records** menu to **Sort,** and then to **Sort Ascending.**

2. Create a new database for the names, addresses, and phone numbers of your friends and family. You could also include in it additional fields for E-mail addresses and birthdays. If you wish, create a form to view your information.

Before You Read

Concha and *The Southpaw*

MEET MARY HELEN PONCE

Mary Helen Ponce (pôn' sā) grew up in a Mexican American com-munity in California. She says, "We feared few things in the barrio [neighborhood]. We knew everyone; everyone knew us. We belonged."

Mary Helen Ponce was born in 1938. "Concha" was published in 1988.

MEET JUDITH VIORST

Judith Viorst (vyôrst) raised three sons, and their worries and concerns have often been sub-jects for her writing. Viorst says, "Four of the books . . . I con-sciously sat down and wrote because one child or another of mine had a problem. . . . I hoped it might help my boys to laugh at their problems."

Judith Viorst was born in 1931. "The Southpaw" was published in 1974.

FOCUS ACTIVITY

What outdoor games do you like to play? Which ones were favorites when you were younger? Did you ever make up games?

Roundrobin
In a small group, take turns telling about outside games. Jot down a list of games, including those you made up.

Setting a Purpose
Read "Concha" and "The Southpaw" to find out about games the characters play.

BACKGROUND

Did You Know? Ants have been around for at least the last 100 million years. Ants are cooper-ative insects that live together in large colonies. Within a colony, ants have specialized jobs. Some take care of the young. Others guard the nest entrance, keep the nest clean, or store food.

Interior view of ant colony.

VOCABULARY PREVIEW

amass (ə mas') *v.* to pile up; collect or gather (a great quantity); p. 255

pelt (pelt) *v.* to strike repeatedly by throwing something; p. 256

camouflaged (kam' ə fläzhd') *adj.* concealed by a disguise that blends in with the surroundings; p. 256

treacherous (trech' ər əs) *adj.* dangerous; p. 256

retreat (ri trēt') *v.* to withdraw, as from battle; pull back; p. 257

cavity (kav' ə tē) *n.* a hollow space in a tooth, caused by decay; any hollow place or hole; p. 259

laughingstock (laf' ing stok') *n.* a person or thing that is made fun of; p. 260

254   THEME 3

CONCHA

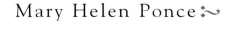

Mary Helen Ponce ∾

WHILE GROWING UP in the small barrio of Pacoima,[1] my younger brother Joey and I were left alone to find ways *para divertirnos*,[2] to keep ourselves busy—and out of our mother's way. One way in which we whiled away long summer days was by making pea shooters. These were made from a hollow reed which we first cleaned with a piece of wire. We then collected berries from *los pirules*,[3] the pepper trees that lined our driveway. Once we <u>amassed</u> enough dry berries we put them in our mouths and spat them out at each other through the pea shooter.

---

1. *Pacoima* (pä′ kō ē′ mə)
2. *Para divertirnos* (pär′ ə dē′ vər tēr′ nōs) means "to amuse ourselves" or, as the narrator says, "to keep ourselves busy."
3. *Los pirules* (lōs pē rōō′ lās) means "the pepper trees."

Vocabulary
amass (ə mas′) *v.* to pile up; collect or gather (a great quantity)

The berries had a terrible taste—they were even said to be poison! I was most careful not to swallow them. We selected only the hard, firm peas. The soft ones, we knew, would get mushy, crumble in our mouths and force us to gag—and lose a fight. During an important battle a short pause could spell defeat. Oftentimes while playing with Joey I watched closely. When he appeared to gag I dashed back to the pepper tree to load up on ammunition. I <u>pelted</u> him without mercy until he begged me to stop.

"No more. Ya no," Joey cried as he bent over to spit berries. "No more!"

"Ha, ha I got you now." I spat berries at Joey until, exhausted, we called a truce and slumped onto a wooden bench.

In fall our game came to a halt—the trees dried up; the berries fell to the ground. This was a sign for us to begin other games.

Our games were seasonal. During early spring we made whistles from the long blades of grass that grew in the open field behind our house. In winter we made dams, forts and canals from the soft mud that was our street. We tied burnt matchsticks together with string. These were our men. We positioned them along the forts (<u>camouflaged</u> with small branches). We also played kick the can, but our most challenging game was playing with red ants.

The ants were of the common variety: red, round and <u>treacherous</u>. They invaded our yard and the *llano*[4] every summer. We

4. *Llano* (yä′ nō) means "flat ground."

Playtime. Diana Ong (b. 1940). Computer graphics, 5 x 4 mm chrome.

Viewing the painting: What are the boys and girls in this painting doing? How are they like the characters in the story?

Vocabulary

pelt (pelt) *v.* to strike repeatedly by throwing something
camouflaged (kam′ ə fläzhd′) *adj.* concealed by a disguise that blends in with the surroundings
treacherous (trech′ ər əs) *adj.* dangerous

always knew where ants could be found, *donde habia hormigas*.[5] We liked to build mud and grass forts smack in the middle of ant territory. The ants were the enemy, the matchstickmen the heroes, or good guys.

Playing with ants was a real challenge! While placing our men in battle positions we timed it so as not to get bitten. We delighted in beating the ants at their own game.

Sometimes we got really brave and picked up ants with a stick, then twirled the stick around until the ants got dizzy-drunk (or so we thought)—and fell to the ground. We made ridges of dirt and pushed the ants inside, covered them with dirt and made bets as to how long it would take them to dig their way out.

Concha, my best friend and neighbor, was quite timid at school. She avoided all rough games such as kickball and Red Rover. When it came to playing with ants however, Concha held first place for brav-ery. She could stand with her feet atop an anthill for the longest time! We stood trembling as ants crawled up our shoes, then quickly stomped our feet to scare them off. But Concha never lost her nerve.

One time we decided to have an ant con-test. The prize was a candy bar—a Sugar Daddy sucker. We first found an anthill, lined up, then took turns standing beside the anthill while the juicy red ants climbed over our shoes. We dared not move—but when the first ant moved towards our ankles we stomped away, our Oxfords making swirls of dust that allowed us

Did You Know?
Oxfords are ankle-high shoes with laces.

to retreat to the sidelines. But not Concha. She remained in place as big red ants crept up her shoes. One, five, ten! We stood and counted, holding our breath as the ants con-tinued to climb. Fifteen, twenty! Twenty ants were crawling over Concha!

"*Ujule*, she sure ain't scared," cried Mundo in a hushed voice. "*No le tiene miedo a las hormigas.*"[6]

"Uhhhhh," answered Beto, his eyes wide.

". . . I mean for a girl," added Mundo as he poked Beto in the ribs. We knew Beto liked Concha—and always came to her rescue.

We stood and counted ants. We were so caught up in this feat that we failed to notice the twenty-first ant that climbed up the back of Concha's sock . . . and bit her!

"Ay, ay, ay," screeched Concha.

---

5. *Donde habia hormigas* (dōn′ dā ä′ bē ə ôr mē′ gəs) means "where ants lived."

6. *Ujule. No le tiene miedo* (ōō hōō′ lā nō lā tye′ nā mē ā′ dō) *a las hormigas* means "She's not afraid of the ants."

Vocabulary
retreat (ri trēt′) *v.* to withdraw, as from battle; pull back

"Gosh, she's gonna die," cried an alarmed Virgie as she helped stomp out ants. "She's gonna die!"

"She's too stupid to die," laughed Mundo, busy brushing ants off his feet. "She's too stupid."

"But sometimes people die when ants bite them," insisted Virgie, her face pale. "They gets real sick."

"The ants will probably die," Mundo snickered, holding his stomach and laughing loudly. "Ah, ha, ha."

"Gosh you're mean," said a shocked Virgie, hands on hips. "You are so mean."

"Yeah, but I ain't stupid."

"Come on you guys, let's get her to the *mangera*,"[7] Beto cried as he reached out to Concha who by now had decided she would live. "Come on, let's take her to the faucet."

We held Concha by the waist as she hobbled to the water faucet. Her cries were now mere whimpers as no grownup had come out to investigate. From experience we knew that if a first cry did not bring someone to our aid we should stop crying—or go home.

We helped Concha to the faucet, turned it on and began to mix water with dirt. We knew the best remedy for insect bites was *lodo*.[8] We applied mud to all bug stings to stop the swelling. Mud was especially good for wasp stings, the yellowjackets we so feared—and from which we ran away at top speed. Whenever bees came close we stood still until they flew away, but there were no set rules on how to get rid of *avispas*.[9] We hit out at them, and tried to scare them off but the yellowjackets were fierce! In desperation we flung dirt at them, screamed and ran home.

Not long after the ant incident Concha decided she was not about to run when a huge wasp broke up our game of jacks. She stood still, so still the wasp remained on her dark head for what seemed like hours. We stood and watched, thinking perhaps the wasp had mistaken Concha's curly hair for a bush! We watched—and waited.

"*Ujule*, she sure is brave," exclaimed Virgie as she sucked on a popsicle. "She sure is brave."

"She's stupid," grunted Mundo, trying to be indifferent. "She's just a big show-off who thinks she's so big."

"So are you," began Virgie, backing off. "So are you."

"Yeah? Ya wanna make something outta it?"

"Let's go," interrupted Beto in his soft voice. "*Ya vamonos*."[10] He smiled at Concha—who smiled back.

In time the wasp flew away. Concha immediately began to brag about how a "real big wasp" sat on her hair for hours. She never mentioned the ant contest—nor the twenty-first ant that led her to *el lodo*.

---

7. *Mangera* (män gä′ rə) means "faucet."
8. *Lodo* (lō′ dō) means "mud."

9. *Avispas* (ə vēs′ pəs) means "wasps."
10. *Ya vamonos* (yä vä′ mə nōs) means "Let's go."

The Southpaw

Judith Viorst

Dear Richard,

    Don't invite me to your birthday party because I'm not coming. And give back the Disneyland sweatshirt I said you could wear. If I'm not good enough to play on your team, I'm not good enough to be friends with.

                  Your former friend,
                  Janet

P.S. I hope when you go to the dentist he finds twenty <u>cavities</u>.

Dear Janet,

Here is your stupid Disneyland sweatshirt, if that's how you're going to be. I want my comic books now—finished or not. No girl has ever played on the Mapes Street baseball team, and as long as I'm captain, no girl ever will.

                  Your former friend,
                  Richard

P.S. I hope when you go for your checkup you need a tetanus[1] shot.

---

1. *Tetanus* (tet′ ən əs) is a disease caused by bacteria that usually enters the body through a wound.

Vocabulary
cavity (kav′ ə tē) *n.* a hollow space in a tooth, caused by decay; any hollow place or hole

Dear Richard,

I'm changing my goldfish's name from Richard to Stanley. Don't count on my vote for class president next year. Just because I'm a member of the ballet club doesn't mean I'm not a terrific ballplayer.

Your former friend,
Janet

P.S. I see you lost your first game, 28–0.

Dear Janet,

I'm not saving any more seats for you on the bus. For all I care you can stand the whole way to school. Why don't you forget about baseball and learn something nice like knitting?

Your former friend,
Richard

P.S. Wait until Wednesday.

Dear Richard,

My father said I could call someone to go with us for a ride and hot-fudge sundaes. In case you didn't notice, I didn't call you.

Your former friend,
Janet

P.S. I see you lost your second game, 34–0.

Dear Janet,

Remember when I took the laces out of my blue-and-white sneakers and gave them to you? I want them back.

Your former friend,
Richard

P.S. Wait until Friday.

Dear Richard,

Congratulations on your unbroken record. Eight straight losses, wow! I understand you're the laughingstock of New Jersey.

Your former friend,
Janet

P.S. Why don't you and your team forget about baseball and learn something nice like knitting maybe.

Dear Janet,

Here's the silver horseback-riding trophy that you gave me. I don't think I want to keep it anymore.

Your former friend,
Richard

P.S. I didn't think you'd be the kind who'd kick a man when he's down.[2]

---

2. The expression *kick a man when he's down* means "to be unkind to a person who already has a lot of problems."

Vocabulary

laughingstock (laf′ ing stok′) *n.* a person or thing that is made fun of

Dear Richard,

I wasn't kicking exactly. I was kicking <u>back</u>.

Your former friend,
Janet

P.S. In case you were wondering, my batting average is .345.

Dear Janet,

Alfie is having his tonsils out tomorrow. We might be able to let you catch next week.

Richard

Dear Richard,

I pitch.

Janet

Dear Janet,

Joel is moving to Kansas and Danny sprained his wrist. How about a permanent place in the outfield?

Richard

Dear Richard,

I pitch.

Janet

Dear Janet,

Ronnie caught the chicken pox and Leo broke his toe and Elwood has these stupid violin lessons. I'll give you first base, and that's my final offer.

Richard

Dear Richard,

Susan Reilly plays first base, Marilyn Jackson catches, Ethel Kahn plays center field, I pitch. It's a package deal.

Janet

P.S. Sorry about your 12-game losing streak.

Dear Janet,

Please! Not Marilyn Jackson.

Richard

Dear Richard,

Nobody ever said that I was unreasonable. How about Lizzie Martindale instead?

Janet

Dear Janet,

At least could you call your goldfish Richard again?

Your friend,
Richard

Responding to Literature

PERSONAL RESPONSE

What images from each selection linger in your mind? Share your impressions with others in the group.

Analyzing Literature

RECALL

1. In "Concha" what games do the narrator's friends play?
2. Who is the bravest at playing with the ants? How does she show her bravery?
3. In "The Southpaw," what is Janet's disagreement with Richard about?
4. Who wins this conflict? How?

INTERPRET

5. Why, do you think, do Concha and her friends find the ants so fascinating?
6. What does the author show about Concha by contrasting the way she acts at school with the way she deals with ants?
7. In the dispute between Janet and Richard, which character do you feel is right? Explain your answer.
8. When do Richard and Janet start trying to understand each other? Which note shows the change?

EVALUATE AND CONNECT

9. Does "Concha" seem true to life? Are the games like any you have played? Use notes from the **Focus Activity** to explain.
10. In "Concha," Ponce uses words like "ain't" in the dialogue. Does this make the story seem more real? Why or why not?

LITERARY ELEMENTS

Characterization

Characterization is the way a writer reveals the personality of a character. Which character in either selection interests you most? Why? Write at least two paragraphs about that character, telling what you know about the character based on the story and what you find interesting about him or her.

1. Based on what you know from the stories, compare Janet and Concha as characters.
2. "The Southpaw" is told entirely through notes. How does this affect what we know about the characters?

● See **Literary Terms Handbook,** p. R2.

Extending Your Response

Writing About Literature

Point of View Retell the ant contest episode in Ponce's story from Concha's point of view. How would Concha describe the scene in which she is bitten? Share your version with the class.

Creative Writing

And Another Thing . . . What do you think will happen to Richard's team and to Janet and Richard's friendship? Write two more exchanges of notes between the friends over the next few weeks.

Literature Groups

Debate Was Concha really brave? Debate both sides of this question. Discuss her actions. Was Concha brave before she was bitten? What about directly after? How did she react later to the wasp? Be prepared to share your group's opinions.

Learning for Life

Rules of the Game
Think about a game you made up as a younger child. Check your list from the **Focus Activity** on page 254. Write down the rules of the game as you remember them. How many people are needed? Are props important? Where should the game be played? If possible, use the rules to play the game with a small group.

💼 **Save your work for your portfolio.**

Skill Minilesson

VOCABULARY • THE SUFFIX *-ous*

A **suffix** is a word part added to the end of a word. Sometimes adding a suffix greatly changes the meaning of the word. For example, *joyless* is the opposite of *joyful.* Often, though, a suffix changes the meaning just a little. Many suffixes just change words from one part of speech to another.

The suffix *-ous* means "having, full of, or characterized by." Adding it to a noun creates an adjective. So, land that has *mountains* is *mountainous.* If the noun ends with an *e,* the *e* disappears. So, a day of *adventure* is *adventurous.* If the noun ends with a *y,* the *y* may change to

an *i* or an *e. Glory* becomes *glorious,* "full of glory." Sometimes, the *y* just disappears, as when *treachery* becomes *treacherous.*

PRACTICE Match each word on the left to its meaning on the right.

1. plenteous	a. big and empty
2. torturous	b. smelly
3. cavernous	c. not trustworthy
4. traitorous	d. more than enough
5. odorous	e. causing great pain

● For more about adding suffixes, see **Language Handbook,** Spelling, p. R40.

NEWSPAPER ARTICLE

A generation ago, few girls took part in school sports.

Blowing the Whistle on Inequality for Girls

by Kymberli Hagelberg and Christine Marn—*Sun Newspapers*, September 11, 1997

If you let me play . . . If you let me play sports, I will like myself more. I will have more self-confidence. . . . I will learn what it means to be strong. If you let me play sports . . .
—*(Nike television advertisement. Created by Weiden & Kennedy, Portland, OR.)*

The ad's claim of benefits to girls who are active in childhood athletics have been well documented. According to studies cited by the U.S. Department of Education Office for Civil Rights, girls involved in athletics do better in school, do not drop out, and have a better chance to complete college.

Until the 1970s, few young women participated in school sports. Then in 1972 the playing field was leveled with the institution of Title IX. This federal law prohibits discrimination based on gender in any activity that receives federal funding. Little League baseball saw the first ponytail invasion shortly after Title IX was adopted. From there, girls' participation in track, soccer, basketball, and other sports grew.

In broad terms, the law requires schools to meet the interests and abilities of a student athlete regardless of gender. In some cases, this has meant that a girl may play on a boys' team when no comparable program for girls exists in her school.

Schools must also make sure girls' sports programs have like equipment, access to practice facilities, locker rooms, and medical and training facilities.

Respond

1. Has playing a sport improved your life? How?

2. Are girls' sports as important as boys' sports in your community? Explain.

GRAMMAR LINK

Using Apostrophes Correctly

Possessive nouns and **possessive pronouns** tell who or what has something. They can be singular or plural. In the sentences on the left, however, it is difficult to tell who possesses what. For example, is it possible to tell from the second example whether the dishes belong to one, or more than one, pet? Correct use of **apostrophes** makes ownership and possession clear.

PROBLEM	SOLUTION
We will visit Lewis classroom and Emilys classroom.	Use an apostrophe and an *s* to form the possessive of a singular noun. • We will visit Lewis's classroom and Emily's classroom.
Remember to fill the pets dishes.	Use an apostrophe alone to form the possessive of a plural noun that ends in *s*. • Remember to fill the pets' dishes.
The womens children are waiting.	Use an apostrophe and an *s* to form the possessive of a plural noun that does not end in *s*. • The women's children are waiting.
The dog wants food in it's dish.	Do not use an apostrophe with a possessive pronoun. • The dog wants food in its dish.

In addition to being used in possessives, apostrophes are used in **contractions.** A contraction is a word made by combining two words and leaving out one or more letters. An apostrophe replaces the missing letter or letters—for example, *can't* for *cannot, isn't* for *is not, who's* for *who is,* and *it's* for *it is.*

● For more about apostrophes, see **Language Handbook,** p. R36–R37.

EXERCISES

1. Write the possessive form of each word.
   - **a.** Jim
   - **b.** James
   - **c.** man
   - **d.** men
   - **e.** lady
   - **f.** ladies
   - **g.** leaf
   - **h.** leaves
   - **i.** you
   - **j.** we
   - **k.** dress
   - **l.** dresses
   - **m.** city
   - **n.** cities
   - **o.** horses

2. Write each contraction correctly by putting the apostrophe where it belongs.
   - **a.** you + are = youre
   - **b.** she + will = shell
   - **c.** we + have = weve
   - **d.** she + had = shed
   - **e.** they + would = theyd
   - **f.** should + not = shouldnt

BIOGRAPHY

A **biography** is the story of a person's life written by someone other than the subject. Most biographies are written about people who have influenced or inspired others. These examples from Carl Sandburg's biography *Abe Lincoln Grows Up* illustrate elements you will find in all biographies.

BIOGRAPHY ELEMENTS

MODEL: *Abe Lincoln Grows Up*

FACTS Biographies are based on facts. Biographers must be accurate when stating names, dates, and reasons for events. Biographers interview people involved or use journal entries, letters, newspaper accounts, or public records.

> . . . in the courthouse at Springfield in Washington County, . . . the bond gave notice: "There is a marriage shortly intended between Thomas Lincoln and Nancy Hanks." It was June 10, 1806.

CHARACTERS In a biography, the most important character is the subject of the biography. The author lets the reader learn about the subject and other characters by telling about events that really happened and conversations that really took place.

> One of the neighbors said he [Lincoln] was strong as three men. Another said, "He can sink an ax deeper into wood than any man I ever saw."

SETTING A biography must accurately show the times in which the subject lived. Setting sometimes explains why subjects act as they do. Here Sandburg provides details about the Lincolns' cabin.

> . . . two trees about fourteen feet apart . . . formed the two strong corner-posts of a sort of cabin with three sides, the fourth side open. . . .

GENERALIZATIONS Authors of biographies often make broad statements, or generalizations, about their subjects. These statements are supported by incidents from the subject's life.

> Sally Bush, the stepmother, was all of a good mother to Abe. If he broke out laughing when others saw nothing to laugh at, she let it pass as a sign of his thoughts working their own way.

Active Reading Strategies

Tips for Reading Biographies

Good readers actively take part in the process of reading by using a number of different strategies. Some strategies are especially helpful when you read a biography.

● For more about reading strategies, see **Reading Handbook,** pp. R79–R94.

REVIEW

Biographies can present many facts, names, and dates all at once. When a lot of information has been presented, review what you have read. By looking back over several paragraphs or pages, you can see how the information fits together.

Ask yourself . . . What have I learned about the subject? How does this relate to what I knew before?

APPLYING THE STRATEGIES

Read "Alexander the Great King" by Olivia Coolidge. Use the Active Reading Model notes in the margins as you read. Write your responses on a separate piece of paper.

RESPOND

Try to imagine the people and places described in the biography, and think about why they are important. Form your own opinion about the subject of the biography.

Ask yourself . . . Would I have liked to know this person? Do I want to imitate the person in any way? Do I admire or feel sorry for the subject?

Before You Read
Alexander the Great King

MEET OLIVIA COOLIDGE

"Facts are the bricks with which a biographer builds," Olivia Coolidge says. One of the hardest parts of writing biographies, she adds, is finding out which "facts" are really facts and not judgments. Coolidge was born in London, England. Over the years, she has taught English, Latin, and Greek in Europe and in the United States and has published biographies, histories, and retellings of myths.

Olivia Coolidge was born in 1908. This selection, which comes from The Golden Days of Greece, *was first published in 1968.*

FOCUS ACTIVITY

Who are some of the world's greatest leaders, past and present? What do you think made or makes them great?

Brainstorm
With your classmates, brainstorm qualities you think are important for great rulers or leaders. Record your conclusions.

Setting a Purpose
Read "Alexander the Great King" to find out about one famous leader of ancient times.

BACKGROUND

The Time and Place   The events in this selection begin in ancient Macedon, a kingdom on the Balkan Peninsula of southeastern Europe. Philip II, the father of Alexander the Great, ruled Macedon from 359 to 336 B.C. When Philip was killed, his son Alexander became king and ruled from 336 to 323 B.C.

VOCABULARY PREVIEW

conquest (kon′ kwest) *n.* the act of taking control over people or territory; p. 269

impudence (im′ pyə dəns) *n.* speech or behavior that is offensively forward or rude; p. 270

bolt (bōlt) *v.* to dash away suddenly; p. 270

contempt (kən tempt′) *n.* a feeling toward something or someone considered to be low or worthless; scorn; p. 273

hover (huv′ ər) *v.* to remain as if suspended in the air over a particular spot; p. 274

superb (soo purb′) *adj.* of superior quality; fine; first-rate; p. 275

procession (prə sesh′ ən) *n.* a steady forward movement, especially in a grand, formal manner; p. 277

lofty (lôf′ tē) *adj.* high in rank, character, or quality; elevated; p. 278

Alexander
the Great King

Olivia Coolidge ⁓

The Battle of Issus. c. 200–0 B.C. Mosaic, 3.42 x 5.92 m. National Archaeological Museum, Naples. This mosaic covered the floor of a room in a Roman house. It was copied from a Greek painting.

Alexander was the only son of King Philip of Macedon[1] by the queen Olympias. The queen soon quarreled with Philip over his custom of taking extra wives like the king of Persia. Partly for this reason, and partly because Philip was busy with his wars of conquest, the boy's education was left to his mother, who chose for him a stern tutor. Leonidas would allow no softness in the boy.

ACTIVE READING MODEL

QUESTION

Who is Alexander's tutor? What is he like?

---

1. *Macedon* (mas′ ə don′) or *Macedonia* (mas′ ə dō′ nē ə) was an ancient kingdom of southeastern Europe that included the area of the modern-day country of Macedonia as well as parts of Greece and Bulgaria.

Vocabulary
conquest (kon′ kwest) *n.* the act of taking control over people or territory

He used to look through the chest where Alexander kept his clothes and blankets to be sure that the queen had not provided anything costly. He only allowed the plainest food, and he taught the prince that the best "cook" for a good breakfast was an all-night walk, and for a good dinner was a light breakfast. In fact, he gave Alexander the sort of training which Xenophon[2] praised in *The Education of Cyrus*.

When Alexander was about twelve, legend says, an incident attracted Philip's attention. A dealer had a great black horse for sale, which he called Bucephalus,[3] or Bull's-head, because of the shape of a white mark on his forehead. He was indeed a splendid creature, but he would let nobody mount him. Philip told the owner to take him away, but Alexander said it was a shame to lose such an animal because nobody had the skill to ride him.

Philip was angry at his impudence, but the boy offered to bet the price of the horse that he could ride it. He had noticed that Bucephalus was frightened by his own shadow dancing on the ground in front of him. He turned him to face the sun and patted him until he quieted down. Suddenly he sprang on his back, and the horse bolted madly. Philip, who had never thought the boy would mount, was afraid for him now. Alexander, however, clung on until Bucephalus was tired enough to be guided safely home.

We shall never know if the story of how Alexander won his horse is a true one, but it gives a good picture of his cleverness and daring. Philip began to take interest in the boy, and shortly afterward he arranged another tutor for him who was in his own way the most famous man in the Greek world.

Aristotle had come to Plato's Academy when he was seventeen and had proved himself the best pupil Plato had.[4] He had stayed there another seventeen years, learning and teaching, until Plato died. At this point he left the Academy to form a school of his own. Aristotle was a different kind of man from Plato. He did not have as much imagination, but he was more practical. When Plato, for instance, wanted to know what the ideal government might be, he started to consider what the

EVALUATE

Do you think this story of Bucephalus is based on facts?

EVALUATE

Which of the author's comments about Aristotle are facts, and which are opinions?

---

2. In this book, the Greek historian *Xenophon* (zen′ ə fən) wrote about the man who founded the Persian Empire in the sixth century B.C.
3. *Bucephalus* (bōō sef′ ə ləs)
4. The *Academy* was the school where the Greek thinker and writer *Plato* taught until his death in 347 B.C. *Aristotle* is considered one of the greatest thinkers ever.

Vocabulary

impudence (im′ pyə dəns) *n.* speech or behavior that is offensively forward or rude
bolt (bōlt) *v.* to dash away suddenly

<>
</>

Olivia Coolidge ～

soul of a man was like. When Aristotle asked himself the same question, he collected a hundred and fifty-eight different constitutions which had been set up by the Greek states;[5] and he tried to compare them.

Now Aristotle, as it chanced, had been born in one of the Greek towns on the Macedonian coast. His father had been a doctor and was actually court physician to King Amyntas of Macedonia, Philip's father. Philip and he were about the same age, and shared childhood memories. Since then, Aristotle had learned in the Academy that Plato's purpose was to train the rulers of the future. For both these reasons, Aristotle was willing to tutor Alexander. Thus on top of the education described by Xenophon, Alexander received some of the training of Plato.

He never became a philosopher, but he was clever and eager to learn. Aristotle's position as tutor gave a special interest to the young heir of Macedon, as many remembered Plato saying that the ruler of the future must have this sort of education. Statesmen like Demosthenes[6] who visited the court of King Philip thought it worthwhile to meet the boy.

REVIEW

What do you know about Alexander's education and training so far?

They were nearly all impressed. Alexander was striking-looking, with blue eyes and golden curls. He was tall for his age, and good at every sport. He loved poetry and music; and he liked to compare himself with his legendary ancestor Achilles, hero of the *Iliad*,[7] who won great glory from his earliest years.

Philip soon gave his son military training. When Alexander commanded a wing in the battle of Chaeronea,[8] he was only eighteen years old; but he had been fighting since he was sixteen, and he had also governed Macedonia while his father was absent.

Alexander the Great.
Roman sculpture.

---

5. Ancient Greece was really a group of "city-states," each made up of a city and the surrounding villages and farmland.
6. *Demosthenes* (də mos′ thə nēz′)
7. The adventures of the great warrior Achilles (ə kil′ ēz) are described in the *Iliad* by Homer.
8. In 338 B.C., Philip's army defeated Greek forces at *Chaeronea* (ker′ ə nē′ ə), and Greece came under the control of Macedon.

Alexander the Great Cutting the Gordian Knot. Perino del Vaga. Fresco. Castel Sant'Angelo, Rome.

Viewing the painting: According to an old legend, the Gordian knot could be untied only by the person who would rule Asia. Unable to untie it, Alexander is said to have cut it with his sword. What does this legend say about Alexander?

Olivia Coolidge ∿

ACTIVE READING MODEL

When Philip was murdered, his son was only twenty. Demosthenes urged the Athenians[9] to regain their freedom. But his plans were upset by the energy of Alexander. The Athenians were forced to receive him as their master. They did not like him. Philip at least, many felt, had been a great man. The Athenians, who were unused to kings, sneered at this untried boy who wanted to be treated like a hero. When Alexander went on to Corinth, everyone laughed at what happened to him there.

There was a philosopher in Corinth called Diogenes[10] who felt that nothing mattered except a man's own soul. To show his <u>contempt</u> for the world, he dressed in rags, was unshaven and dirty, and had no home but a big tub laid on its side in which he took shelter when the weather forced him to do so. He lost no chance of telling the Corinthians what he thought of them for caring about useless things, and he had become famous for his rude remarks.

Curious, Alexander went to see him. They made a strange contrast as the golden-haired young man in the royal costume stood looking down at the rough philosopher who was squatting in front of his tub. Diogenes took no notice of the king until Alexander asked if he could do anything for him.

There probably was no one in Corinth who would not have been glad to ask a favor of the master of all Greece. Diogenes looked up frowning at the tall young man in front of him and said, "Yes. Stop standing between me and the sun."

The Greeks laughed, but Alexander was not angry. He admired the philosopher's spirit and said to his friends, "If I were not Alexander I should have liked to be Diogenes."

The war which Philip had planned against Persia was only delayed two years by his death. In 334, Alexander invaded Asia Minor with about thirty-five thousand troops. Nearly half were Macedonians, the rest hired soldiers or troops sent by the Greek cities. The army took with it engineers for making bridges or siege towers, well diggers, surveyors to find out about routes and camp grounds, geographers to make maps, botanists and other

QUESTION

What happened to Alexander at Corinth that made people laugh?

CONNECT

Would you like to be Diogenes? Would you rather be Alexander?

---

9. Two of the formerly independent city-states were *Athens* and *Corinth*. The *Athenians* were citizens of Athens.
10. *Philosophers* discuss the meaning and purpose of life and the universe. *Diogenes* (dī oj′ ə nēz′), Plato, and Aristotle were three of the better-known philosophers of ancient Greece.

Vocabulary
contempt (kən tempt′) *n.* a feeling toward something or someone considered to be low or worthless; scorn

Alexander the Great King

ACTIVE READING MODEL

learned men to collect specimens[11] and find out more about the country they conquered. There was a baggage train, of course, and a military council of high officers trained by Philip. Everything was planned to go like clockwork.

Philip had merely meant to conquer Asia Minor. The Greek cities on the coast would be easily won over, and they would dry up the stream of hired soldiers on which the Persians relied. The great landowners of the country districts made splendid cavalry in the Persian style; but the peasants, though loyal to their lords and personally warlike, were too poor to afford the armor of Greek infantry. Hard fighting lay ahead of Alexander, but he was victorious.

After a while he found that he could not hold his gains without going further. Control of Asia Minor with its long seacoast depended on a fleet. The fleet of the Persians came from Egypt and the great Phoenician city of Tyre[12] on the Syrian coast. Alexander advanced against Tyre because he had to, descending from mountainous country into the plain where Asia Minor borders on Syria.

QUESTION

Why did Alexander decide to continue to try to conquer other lands?

Darius III, who had succeeded Artaxerxes,[13] was a weak ruler, but he came of fighting stock and knew that he must battle for his kingdom. He could not, however, get together an army which was larger than the countryside would support. His native infantry was not equal to the Greeks, and his leadership was poor. When he met Alexander at the battle of the Issus, the Macedonian charged at the head of his men, while the Persian hovered in a chariot in the rear and speedily fled. Darius's leaderless men were cut to pieces, and Alexander found himself master of Syria.

He hurried to blockade Tyre, but found it difficult. The Tyrians kept his warships off by piling great boulders under water. Alexander sent merchant ships to haul these away, but the Tyrians

Alexander the Great. Greek coins.

---

11. Alexander often used *sieges* (sēj′ əs) to conquer cities. His forces would surround a city and build *siege towers* along key roads. From the towers, his men could attack the city repeatedly and cut off its supplies. *Botanists* are scientists who study plants. Scientists collect *specimens*, or samples, that can be examined later.
12. *Phoenicia* was the Greek name for the coastal areas of what are now Syria, Lebanon, and Israel. In Alexander's time, this area was part of the Persian Empire, and *Tyre* was an important center of commerce.
13. *Darius* and *Artaxerxes* (är′ tə zerk′ sēz) were Persian kings.

Vocabulary

hover (huv′ ər) *v.* to remain as if suspended in the air over a particular spot

ventured out in their own warships to attack them. Alexander brought up his fleet to protect his dredgers,[14] but Tyrian divers cut their cables under water. Meanwhile, on the land side his engineers were unable for a long while to make the slightest progress. Tyre held out for seven months, but King Darius did not dare face Alexander again. Unaided, the city fell at last in July, 332. By November, Alexander was in Egypt, where he was received with joy, since the Egyptians had long desired to be free from the Persians. Alexander controlled the whole eastern end of the Mediterranean.

Once more his only defense lay in attack. The true center of the Persian empire lay across the Euphrates, in Media, Babylonia, and Persia.[15] In Susa, long the capital, and in Persepolis, where the kings had built their palaces in the days of their pride, lay uncounted treasure piled up from the tribute[16] of two hundred years. For this even Darius must fight. Eighteen months had gone by since his defeat, and he had by now refitted his forces. The cavalry, which had always been superb, was better armed. For the infantry less could be done, seeing that to make new equipment took much time, and to drill fighters even longer. Darius was relying on chariots whose wheels had long knives sticking out. A few hundred of these might well be able to break up massed infantry if skillfully handled.

Darius gave battle on the flat plain of Gaugamela, since he was anxious to give his chariots a chance. There on the first of October, 331, Alexander found him. The chariots made their charge, but Alexander had screened his infantry by javelin men and slingers. For the sake of speed, the chariots had little armor. Men and horses crashed to the ground, and very few of them reached the infantry. The rest of the battle swayed back and forth. The Persians had the greater numbers, but the Greeks the better army. They had a tradition of victory, too, and a finer commander.

Once more Darius took to flight. He might have spared himself the effort, for he had lost his kingdom by now and even his life. The Persian

Alexander the Great. Bactrian coin of 2nd century B.C.

VISUALIZE

What did this treasure look like?

REVIEW

Why did the Persians lose this battle?

---

14. Here, *dredgers* refers to the ships Alexander sent to remove the underwater boulders.
15. The *Euphrates* River runs through present-day Turkey, Syria, and Iraq. *Media* and *Babylonia* were regions of the Persian Empire. *Persia* itself was a small country within what is now Iran.
16. Here, *tribute* refers to payments that one nation is forced to pay to a more powerful nation.

Vocabulary
superb (soo purb′) *adj.* of superior quality; fine; first-rate

nobles whom he had twice deserted in battle were finished with him. He was arrested; and as the pursuit of Alexander came close, he was finally murdered.

There was now no king in the empire but Alexander. The men of Babylon came out to surrender. The satrap[17] of Persia tried to keep him from entering his homeland but was swept aside. Alexander took Susa and Persepolis. He sat on the Great King's throne and seized his treasure. As a sign to the whole East, he set fire to the palace of King Xerxes and burned it to the ground. The miracle had come to pass. Greece had conquered the empire.

QUESTION

Why does the author change focus here?

We need not follow Alexander farther east across the steppes of Turkestan,[18] through the foothills of the Himalayas, into India. Susa had been only the center of an empire which stretched as far east as it did west. There were adventures ahead for Alexander with tribes, by lands and rivers which he had never heard of. But before he pursued his way, he had to face the problem of holding what he had won. It is what Alexander did to found an empire as much as his generalship that made him great.

Greeks generally thought that barbarians, which is what they called non-Greeks, were fit to be plundered or made slaves, rather than to rule. Alexander, however, was half barbarian[19] himself; and he had seen the wonders of Babylonia and Egypt, as well as the splendor of Persian kings. He understood that East and West must be mingled into a greater whole and that he, Alexander, must have a share in both.

EVALUATE

Was this a good way to begin uniting East and West?

The first thing that he did was found many cities through the eastern world where homeless Greek soldiers found a new place to live and build their temples. Those cities acted as market places for country villages or stages on the trade routes which had run far in Persian times and were soon to be thronged[20] with travelers. Alexandria in Egypt has always been the greatest of the towns that Alexander founded, but there were many others, including one called after Bucephalus, his horse. From these cities Greek ways spread all over the East. When the Romans came to rule two hundred years later, they found that Greek had become a second language through the eastern part of their whole

---

17. The Persian Empire was divided into provinces, each ruled by an official called a *satrap* (sā′ trap).
18. *Turkestan* is an old name for the region of central Asia that includes parts of modern Russia, Afghanistan, and China.
19. *Plundered* means robbed by force, especially during a war; Alexander was *half barbarian* because his mother, Olympias, was Greek, but Philip was a Macedonian—a non-Greek.
20. Here, *thronged* means "crowded."

Olivia Coolidge

empire. They were content to let it remain so and to speak it themselves; for the Romans, like the eastern peoples, had much to learn from the Greeks.

All this Alexander did, but in actually governing the peoples of the East he relied on themselves. He split up the power of the satraps, to be sure; and he left trusty Macedonian generals here and there with troops. All the same, he tried to employ the great Persian nobles, got to know them, dressed in eastern clothes himself, and liked his friends to do so. He married an eastern princess called Roxana and encouraged his friends to follow his example.

He did not want men to think of him as a conqueror, but rather as a godlike hero, born to rule. There is often something of this feeling about kingship. Philip's image had been carried in <u>procession</u> with those of the

REVIEW

How did Alexander do things in a unique way?

Vocabulary

procession (prə sesh′ ən) *n.* a steady forward movement, especially in a grand, formal manner

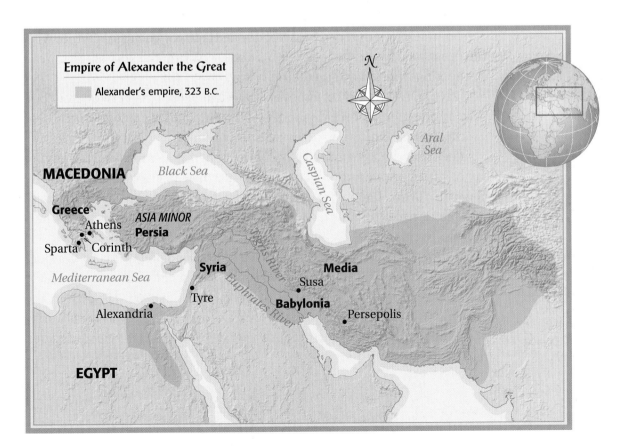

Empire of Alexander the Great in 323 B.C.

Viewing the map: Across how many continents did Alexander's empire stretch?

gods. Egyptian kings were thought divine, and the Persians could claim at least to be God's servants. Alexander had found these ideas in the East and was eager to adopt them because he needed loyalty. They meant something special to him, too. Achilles, his ancestor, was half divine. During the quarrels between his mother and Philip, Queen Olympias made a mystery of his birth, pretending that he was more than Philip's son. It is likely also that his victories had gone to his head. No one had ever done what he had done, and he was not yet thirty. Alexander gave out that he was not really Philip's son, but was born of a god.

It was a wise political stroke, but his Macedonian friends did not like it. They were many years away from home and they may have been tired of adventures. Perhaps they had their ambitions, too; and they did not wish Alexander to show favor to native princes. At all events, there were plots against him.

Alexander was noble and trusting by nature. Early in his campaigns his doctor was mixing a drink of medicine for him when a letter was brought in. He read it. It warned him that the doctor was planning to poison him. Alexander stretched out one hand for the drink, while with the other he offered the letter to his doctor. While the startled man read it, the king drained the medicine down.

RESPOND

What do you think about Alexander's changing attitudes?

After this, it is sad to discover that years later this very doctor took part in an attempt on Alexander's life. Alexander's new position was making him so lofty that he could trust no one.

The strain had begun to tell on him. If he made mistakes, his empire might collapse even more quickly than it had been won. At feasts he began to drink deeply, as his father had once done. His royal rages became terrible to endure. But victory followed him all the same wherever he went.

EVALUATE

Do you feel that you know Alexander? What stands out about him? Do you admire him?

In 323, he was back from India in Babylon, preparing to conquer Arabia; but his amazing career was over at last. He fell sick of a fever and, weakened by battle wounds, could not throw it off. He died in the palace of the kings of Babylon on June 13, 323 B.C. He was only thirty-two years old and in the thirteenth year of his reign. He had conquered nearly all of the known world.

Vocabulary
lofty (lôf′ tē) *adj.* high in rank, character, or quality; elevated

Responding to Literature

Alexander the Great.

PERSONAL RESPONSE

After reading this selection, do you think Alexander was a great leader? Look back at your notes from the **Focus Activity** on page 268.

Active Reading Response

Look back at the strategies in the **Active Reading Model** notes. Did reviewing help you think about and remember important details? Find three additional places in the story where you could apply this strategy.

Analyzing Literature

RECALL

1. How did Alexander get his horse, Bucephalus?
2. Who was Alexander's famous tutor? Why was he willing to tutor Alexander?
3. According to the ancient Greeks, what was a barbarian? How should a barbarian be treated?
4. How and when did Alexander finally die?

INTERPRET

5. What did you learn about the young Alexander by the way in which he got his horse?
6. From childhood on, what legendary hero did Alexander compare himself to? Do you think this helped him or hurt him?
7. How did Alexander view barbarians? How did it affect how he governed those he conquered?
8. Why were there death plots against Alexander from his own people?

EVALUATE AND CONNECT

9. **Character** What would you say was Alexander's greatest strength? greatest weakness? Explain your answers.
10. What did you enjoy reading about more—Alexander's battles or events in his personal life? Why?

LITERARY ELEMENTS

Characterization

Characterization, revealing the personality of a character, is as important in biography as it is in fiction. Because biography is a true account of someone's life, it is important that the main character is revealed through incidents that really happened or words that were really spoken. Biographers of historic people can no longer interview their subject, or his or her friends, family, and coworkers. Biographers rely instead on such sources as letters, journals, newspaper accounts, legal documents, and other recorded reports of the day.

1. Describe the meeting between Alexander and Diogenes. What does this reveal about Alexander?

2. What sources might the biographer have used to find out about this meeting?

● See **Literary Terms Handbook,** p. R2.

Literature and Writing

Writing About Literature

Summarize   Darius III was one of Alexander's enemies. Look back in the selection at the clashes between them. Write a paragraph or two summarizing the battles and telling about their outcome.

Personal Writing

A Leader in the Making?   Would you like to be president of the United States? Write in your journal about the qualities you possess that most qualify you to be our country's leader.

Extending Your Response

Literature Groups

Discussing Power   Harry S. Truman, president of the United States from 1945 to 1953, said, "If a man can accept a situation in a place of power with the thought that it's only temporary, he comes out all right. But when he thinks that he is the *cause* of the power, that can be his ruination." Do you agree? Do you think Truman's words can be applied to Alexander the Great? Support your answer with examples from the selection.

Detail of Alexander from *Craterus Lion-Hunting with Alexander.* c. 200 B.C. Mosaic. Archaeological Museum, Pella, Greece.

Interdisciplinary Activity

History   With a partner, research the legacy of Alexander the Great. What did he begin that lived on long after he was dead? Has he influenced today's world? Share your findings with the class.

Learning for Life

Fashion Statement   As Alexander learned about the culture of the East, he began to dress in Eastern-style clothing. He wanted his friends to do so, too. Investigate the clothing styles of ancient Persia and ancient Greece. Then plan an ad campaign to make the clothing of the East appealing to the Greeks.

Reading Further

If you'd like to read more by Olivia Coolidge, you might enjoy these books:
The Golden Days of Greece
Greek Myths

📖 **Save your work for your portfolio.**

Skill Minilessons

GRAMMAR AND LANGUAGE • COMMAS

Commas tell the reader when to pause, and they make the meaning of a sentence clearer. A comma is usually used to separate items in a series of three or more items.

Examples:
- Alexander fought battles near Granicus, at Issus, *and* on the Gaugamelan plain.
- Alexander never asked what he should do, where he should go, *or* how he should fight.

PRACTICE Copy the following sentences, adding commas where needed.

1. Alexander was noble trusting and brave.
2. Philip bought a horse tried to ride it and then wanted to sell it.
3. Along with the army, Alexander took engineers diggers surveyors geographers and botanists.
4. Alexander took his armies across the steppes of Turkestan through the Himalayan foothills and into India.
5. Alexander caught a fever became extremely weak and died.

● For more on commas, see **Language Handbook,** p. R33–R34.

READING AND THINKING • FACT AND OPINION

When you read a biography, you should always question whether what you are reading is **fact,** a statement that can be proved, or the author's **opinion,** a personal belief or feeling. A *valid opinion* is an opinion that is supported by facts.
- *Alexander's horse was Bucephalus* is a fact. This can be found in historical sources.
- *Horses are beautiful animals* is an opinion. It shows the feelings of the author toward horses.
- *The Greeks had a better army than the Persians had* is a valid opinion because the facts show that the Greek army had many more victories than the Persian army did.

PRACTICE Identify each of the following as a fact or opinion.

1. Alexander was the son of King Philip.
2. Alexander was Philip's smartest child.
3. At age twenty, Alexander became king.
4. Alexander defeated Darius III twice.
5. Alexander was one of the greatest miltary leaders in ancient history.

● For more on distinguishing fact and opinion, see **Reading Handbook,** p. R83.

VOCABULARY • ANTONYMS

A word may have a perfect **antonym**—another word that means exactly the opposite. For example, the exact opposite of *past* is *future.* Some words, such as *plunder,* don't have any antonyms at all. Most words, however, are in between. They don't have perfect antonyms, but they have reasonable ones. Thinking about what could be an antonym for a word makes you think about what that word really means.

PRACTICE Match each word in the left column to its antonym in the right column.

1. bolt	a. low
2. conquest	b. respect
3. superb	c. stay
4. lofty	d. surrender
5. contempt	e. horrible

Reading and Thinking Skills

Using Text Structures

Good readers use the overall organization of nonfiction articles and books to better follow and understand writers' ideas. Nonfiction may be organized in different ways, depending on an author's subject and purpose:

Sequence of Events A writer tells events in the order they happened.

Cause and Effect A writer explains cause-and-effect connections between events.

Steps in a Process A writer explains how to do something or how something happens, step by step.

Elaboration A writer states an idea and then gives details or examples that help explain it.

Comparison and Contrast A writer compares topics point by point.

Problem and Solution A writer explains a problem and suggests a solution.

Read this paragraph from "A Backwoods Boy." It is organized by *elaboration*, the statement of an idea followed by examples.

> Mostly, he educated himself by borrowing books and newspapers. There are many stories about Lincoln's efforts to find enough books to satisfy him in that backwoods country. Those he liked he read again and again, losing himself in the adventures of *Robinson Crusoe* or the magical tales of *The Arabian Nights*. He was thrilled by a biography of George Washington, with its stirring account of the Revolutionary War.

● For more on text structures, see **Reading Handbook,** p. R78–R79.

ACTIVITY

Read several paragraphs from "Alexander the Great King" by Olivia Coolidge or another work of nonfiction. Look for ways the writer organizes information. Discuss your ideas in a group. Then share the group's conclusions with the class.

Vo·cab·u·lar·y Skills

Recognizing Roots

A **root** is the most important part of a word, the part that tells what the word means. Knowing the meaning of a root can help you figure out an unfamiliar word.

A root can be a whole word, such as *friend.* Prefixes, suffixes, or other word parts can be attached to *friend* to make new words, such as *friendly, unfriendliness, friend-ship,* and *befriend.* A root that's a whole word is sometimes called a "base word."

Most roots are not whole words; they are parts of words. They may originally have been Latin words or Greek words or words from another language. For example, the root of *recognize* is *cogn.* It comes from a Latin word that means "to know." When you *recognize* something, you "re-know" it, or know it again. Here are a few roots you may recognize.

ROOT	MEANING	EXAMPLES
aud	hear	audience, auditorium, audio
dict	speak	dictate, predict, verdict
div	divide	division, indivisible, divorce
loc	place	location, dislocate, locomotion
nov	new	novel, renovate, novelty
port	carry	portable, transport, import
spec	see	spectator, inspect, suspect
terr	land	territory, terrestrial, terrace
vac	empty	vacuum, vacate, vacant

EXERCISE

Use the list of roots above to figure out the answer to each question.
1. If Alexander evacuated a city, he made the people
   a. move in.   **b.** pay taxes.   **c.** leave.
2. If Alexander wanted an order to be audible, he probably
   a. spoke loudly.   **b.** wrote it down.   **c.** kept it secret.
3. Saying that Alexander was quite a spectacle refers to his
   a. bravery.   **b.** intelligence.   **c.** appearance.
4. Alexander was a novice at battle when he was
   a. wounded.   **b.** a beginner.   **c.** experienced.
5. Alexander's problems with terrain could have been caused by
   a. weapons.   **b.** disloyalty.   **c.** hills or valleys.

Before You Read

A Backwoods Boy

MEET
RUSSELL FREEDMAN

After receiving the Newbery Medal for *Lincoln: A Photobiography*, Russell Freedman said, "I was never tempted to write an idealized, hero-worshiping account. A knowledge of Lincoln's weaknesses throws his strengths, and his greatness, into sharper relief." Freedman was the first nonfiction writer in thirty-two years to win the Newbery Award. He is the author of more than thirty-five nonfiction books.

Russell Freedman was born in 1929. This selection is the second chapter of Lincoln: A Photobiography, *which was published in 1987.*

FOCUS ACTIVITY

What do you know about the early life of Abraham Lincoln? What do you think he was like as a boy?

Make a List
As a class, make a list on the chalkboard. Record ideas about Lincoln's early life.

Setting a Purpose
Read "A Backwoods Boy" to find out more about Lincoln's growing-up years.

BACKGROUND

The Time and Place
This selection begins near Hodgenville, Kentucky, on February 12, 1809, the day Abraham Lincoln was born. It ends in 1837, the year Lincoln moved to Springfield, Illinois.

VOCABULARY PREVIEW

forlorn (fôr lôrn′) *adj.* sad because of being abandoned; p. 287

luminous (lōō′ mə nəs) *adj.* shining; bright; p. 288

reflective (ri flek′ tiv) *adj.* showing serious and careful thinking; thoughtful; p. 289

intellectual (int′ əl ek′ chōō əl) *n.* one who tries to know and understand things mainly through thinking; p. 290

meager (mē′ gər) *adj.* not enough in amount or quantity; p. 292

aptitude (ap′ tə tōōd′) *n.* a natural ability; talent; p. 293

intrigue (in trēg′) *v.* to arouse the curiosity or interest of; fascinate; p. 294

decline (di klīn′) *v.* to become less; fall into a worse condition; p. 294

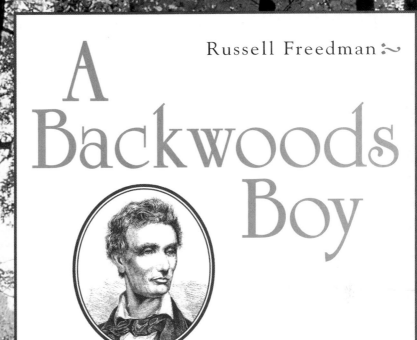

A Backwoods Boy

Russell Freedman :~

Abraham Lincoln never liked to talk much about his early life. A poor backwoods farm boy, he grew up swinging an ax on frontier homesteads in Kentucky, Indiana, and Illinois.

He was born near Hodgenville, Kentucky, on February 12, 1809, in a log cabin with one window, one door, a chimney, and a hard-packed dirt floor. His parents named him after his pioneer grandfather. The first Abraham Lincoln had been shot dead by hostile Indians in 1786, while planting a field of corn in the Kentucky wilderness.

Young Abraham was still a toddler when his family packed their belongings and moved to another log-cabin farm a few miles north, on Knob Creek. That was the first home he could remember, the place where he ran and played as a barefoot boy.

He remembered the bright waters of Knob Creek as it tumbled past the Lincoln cabin and disappeared into the Kentucky hills. Once he fell into the rushing creek and almost drowned before he was pulled out by a neighbor boy. Another time he caught a fish and gave it to a passing soldier.

Lincoln never forgot the names of his first teachers—Zachariah Riney followed by Caleb Hazel—who ran a windowless log schoolhouse two miles away. It was called a "blab school." Pupils of all ages sat on rough wooden benches and bawled out their lessons aloud. Abraham went there with his sister Sarah, who was two years older, when they could be spared from their chores at home. Holding hands, they would walk through scrub trees and across creek bottoms to the schoolhouse door. They learned their numbers from one to ten, and a smattering[1] of reading, writing, and spelling.

Their parents couldn't read or write at all. Abraham's mother, Nancy, signed her name by making a shakily drawn mark. He would remember her as a thin, sad-eyed woman who labored beside her husband in the fields. She liked to gather the children around her in the evening to recite prayers and Bible stories she had memorized.

His father, Thomas, was a burly, barrel-chested farmer and carpenter who had worked hard at homesteading since marrying Nancy Hanks in 1806. A sociable fellow, his greatest pleasure was to crack jokes and swap stories with his chums. With

---

1. *Smattering* means "very limited knowledge."

Replica of Lincoln's Illinois home.
Viewing the photograph: What do you think the inside of this log cabin might look like?

painful effort, Thomas Lincoln could scrawl his name. Like his wife, he had grown up without education, but that wasn't unusual in those days. He supported his family by living off his own land, and he watched for a chance to better himself.

In 1816, Thomas decided to pull up stakes again and move north to Indiana, which was about to join the Union as the nation's nineteenth state. Abraham was seven. He remembered the one hundred-mile journey as the hardest experience of his life. The family set out on a cold morning in December, loading all their possessions on two horses. They crossed the Ohio River on a makeshift ferry, traveled through towering forests, then hacked a path through tangled under-brush until they reached their new home-site near the backwoods community of Little Pigeon Creek.

Thomas put up a temporary winter shelter—a crude, three-sided lean-to of logs and branches. At the open end, he kept a fire burning to take the edge off the cold and scare off the wild animals. At night, wrapped in bearskins and huddled by the fire, Abraham and Sarah listened to wolves howl and panthers scream.

Abraham passed his eighth birthday in the lean-to. He was big for his age, "a tall spider of a boy," and old enough to handle an ax. He helped his father clear the land. They planted corn and pumpkin seeds between the tree stumps. And they built a new log cabin, the biggest one yet, where Abraham climbed a ladder and slept in a loft beneath the roof.

Soon after the cabin was finished, some of Nancy's kinfolk arrived. Her aunt and uncle with their adopted son Dennis had decided to follow the Lincolns to Indiana. Dennis Hanks became an extra hand for Thomas and a big brother for Abraham, someone to run and wrestle with.

A year later, Nancy's aunt and uncle lay dead, victims of the dreaded "milk sick-ness" (now known to be caused by a poiso-nous plant called white snake root). An epidemic of the disease swept through the Indiana woods in the summer of 1818. Nancy had nursed her relatives until the end, and then she too came down with the disease. Abraham watched his mother toss in bed with chills, fever, and pain for seven days before she died at the age of thirty-four. "She knew she was going to die," Dennis Hanks recalled. "She called up the children to her dying side and told them to be good and kind to their father, to one another, and to the world."

Thomas built a coffin from black cherry wood, and nine-year-old Abraham whittled the pegs that held the wooden planks together. They buried Nancy on a wind-swept hill, next to her aunt and uncle. Sarah, now eleven, took her mother's place, cooking, cleaning, and mending clothes for her father, brother, and cousin Dennis in the forlorn and lonely cabin.

Thomas Lincoln waited for a year. Then he went back to Kentucky to find himself a new wife. He returned in a four-horse wagon with a widow named Sarah Bush Johnston, her three children, and all her household goods. Abraham and his sister were

---

Vocabulary
forlorn (fôr lôrn′) *adj.* sad because of being abandoned

Lincoln's father, Thomas Lincoln.

fortunate, for their step-mother was a warm and loving person. She took the motherless children to her heart and raised them as her own. She also spruced up the neglected Lincoln cabin, now shared by eight people who lived, ate, and slept in a single smoky room with a loft.

Abraham was growing fast, shooting up like a sunflower, a spindly[2] youngster with big bony hands, unruly black hair, a dark complexion, and luminous gray eyes. He became an expert with the ax, working alongside his father, who also hired him out to work for others. For twenty-five cents a day, the boy dug wells, built pig-pens, split fence rails, felled[3] trees. "My how he could chop!" exclaimed a friend. "His ax would flash and bite into a sugar tree or a sycamore, and down it would come. If you heard him felling trees in a clearing, you would say there were three men at work, the way the trees fell."

Meanwhile, he went to school "by littles," a few weeks one winter, maybe a month the next. Lincoln said later that all his schooling together "did not amount to one year." Some fragments of his schoolwork still survive, including a verse that he wrote in his homemade arithmetic book: "Abraham Lincoln / his hand and pen / he will be good but / god knows When."

Mostly, he educated himself by borrowing books and newspapers. There are many stories about Lincoln's efforts to find enough books to satisfy him in that backwoods country. Those he liked he read again and again, losing himself in the adventures of *Robinson Crusoe* or the magical tales of *The Arabian Nights*. He was thrilled by a biography of George Washington, with its stirring account of the Revolutionary War. And he came to love the rhyme and rhythm of poetry, reciting passages from Shakespeare or the Scottish poet Robert Burns at the drop of a hat. He would carry a book out to the field with him, so he could read at the end of each plow furrow, while the horse was getting its breath. When noon came, he would sit under a tree and read while he ate. "I never saw Abe after he was twelve that he didn't have a book in his hand or in his pocket," Dennis Hanks remembered. "It didn't seem natural to see a feller[4] read like that."

By the time he was sixteen, Abraham was six feet tall—"the gangliest awkwardest feller . . . he appeared to be all joints," said a neighbor. He may have looked awkward, but hard physical labor had given him a tough, lean body with muscular arms like steel cables. He could grab a woodsman's ax by the handle and hold it straight out at arm's length. And he

---

2. Here, *spindly* means tall and very thin.
3. *Felled* means "cut down."

---

4. *Feller* is how Hanks says "fellow."

Vocabulary
luminous (lōō′ mə nəs) *adj.* shining; bright

was one of the best wrestlers and runners around.

He also had a reputation as a comic and storyteller. Like his father, Abraham was fond of talking and listening to talk. About this time he had found a book called *Lessons in Elocution*, which offered advice on public speaking. He practiced before his friends, standing on a tree stump as he entertained them with fiery imitations of the roving preachers and politicians who often visited Little Pigeon Creek.

Folks liked young Lincoln. They regarded him as a good-humored, easygoing boy—a bookworm maybe, but smart and willing to oblige. Yet even then, people noticed that he could be moody and withdrawn. As a friend put it, he was "witty, sad, and reflective by turns."

At the age of seventeen, Abraham left home for a few months to work as a ferryman's helper on the Ohio River. He was eighteen when his sister Sarah died early in 1828, while giving birth to her first child.

That spring, Abraham had a chance to get away from the backwoods and see something of the world. A local merchant named James Gentry hired Lincoln to accompany his son Allen on a twelve hundred-mile flatboat voyage to New Orleans. With their cargo of country produce, the two boys floated down the Ohio River and into the Mississippi, maneuvering with long poles to

Sarah Bush Lincoln at seventy-seven.

avoid snags and sandbars, and to navigate in the busy river traffic.

New Orleans was the first real city they had ever seen. Their eyes must have popped as the great harbor came into view, jammed with the masts of sailing ships from distant ports all over the world. The city's cobblestone streets teemed with sailors, traders, and adventurers speaking strange languages. And there were gangs of slaves everywhere. Lincoln would never forget the sight of black men, women, and children being driven along in chains and auctioned off like cattle. In those days, New Orleans had more than two hundred slave dealers.

The boys sold their cargo and their flatboat and returned upriver by steamboat. Abraham earned twenty-four dollars—a good bit of money at the time—for the three-month trip. He handed the money over to his father, according to law and custom.

Thomas Lincoln was thinking about moving on again. Lately he had heard glowing reports about Illinois, where instead of forests there were endless prairies with plenty of rich black soil. Early in 1830, Thomas sold his Indiana farm. The Lincolns piled everything they owned into two ox-drawn wagons and set out over muddy roads, with Abraham, just turned twenty-one, driving one of the wagons himself.

Vocabulary
reflective (ri flek′ tiv) *adj.* showing serious and careful thinking; thoughtful

They traveled west to their new homesite in central Illinois, not far from Decatur. Once again, Abraham helped his father build a cabin and start a new farm.

He stayed with his family through their first prairie winter, but he was getting restless. He had met an enterprising fellow named Denton Offutt, who wanted him to take another boatload of cargo down the river to New Orleans. Abraham agreed to make the trip with his stepbrother, John Johnston, and a cousin, John Hanks.

When he returned to Illinois three months later, he paid a quick farewell visit to his father and stepmother. Abraham was twenty-two now, of legal age, free to do what he wanted. His parents were settled and could get along without him. Denton Offutt was planning to open a general store in the flourishing[5] village of New Salem, Illinois, and he had promised Lincoln a steady job.

Lincoln arrived in New Salem in July 1831 wearing a faded cotton shirt and blue jeans too short for his long legs—a "friendless, uneducated, penniless boy," as he later described himself. He tended the counter at Denton Offutt's store and slept in a room at the back.

The village stood in a wooded grove on a bluff above the Sangamon[6] River. Founded just two years earlier, it had about one hundred people living in one- and two-room log houses. Cattle grazed behind split-rail

Lincoln the Rail Splitter. J. L. G. Ferris.
Viewing the painting: What do you think the artist was trying to say about Lincoln?

fences, hogs snuffled along dusty lanes, and chickens and geese flapped about underfoot. New Salem was still a small place, but it was growing. The settlers expected it to become a frontier boom town.[7]

With his gifts for swapping stories and making friends, Lincoln fit easily into the life of the village. He showed off his skill with an ax, competed in footraces, and got along with everyone from Mentor Graham, the schoolmaster, to Jack Armstrong, the leader of a rowdy gang called the Clary's Grove boys. Armstrong was the wrestling champion of New Salem. He quickly challenged Lincoln to a match.

On the appointed day, an excited crowd gathered down by the river, placing bets as the wrestlers stripped to the waist for combat. They circled each other, then came to grips, twisting and tugging until they crashed to the ground with Lincoln on top. As he pinned Armstrong's shoulders to the ground, the other Clary's Grove boys dived in to join the scuffle. Lincoln broke away, backed against a cliff, and defiantly offered to take them all on—one at a time. Impressed, Armstrong jumped to his feet and offered Lincoln his hand, declaring the match a draw. After that, they were fast friends.

Lincoln also found a place among the town's <u>intellectuals</u>. He joined the New

---

5. *Flourishing* means growing or developing successfully; doing very well.
6. *Sangamon* (sang′ gə mən)

---

7. A *boom town* is one that has grown quickly because of economic opportunities.

Vocabulary
intellectual (int′ əl ek′ chōo əl) *n.* one who tries to know and understand things mainly through thinking

Interior scene of general store owned by Abraham Lincoln and William Berry.

Viewing the photograph: List as many details as you can about this photograph. Which detail do you think is most important? Why?

Salem Debating Society, which met once a week in James Rutledge's tavern. The first time he debated, he seemed nervous. But as he began to speak in his high, reedy voice, he surprised everyone with the force and logic of his argument. "He was already a fine speaker," one debater recalled. "All he lacked was culture."

Lincoln was self-conscious about his meager education, and ambitious to improve himself. Mentor Graham, the schoolmaster and a fellow debater, took a liking to the young man, lent him books, and offered to coach him in the fine points of English grammar. Lincoln had plenty of time to study. There wasn't much business at Offutt's store, so he could spend long hours reading as he sat behind the counter.

When the store failed in 1832, Offutt moved on to other schemes. Lincoln had to find something else to do. At the age of twenty-three, he decided to run for the Illinois state legislature. Why not? He knew everyone in town, people liked him, and he was rapidly gaining confidence as a public speaker. His friends urged him to run, saying that a bright young man could go far in politics. So Lincoln announced his candidacy and his political platform.[8] He was in favor of local improvements, like better roads and canals. He had made a study of the Sangamon River, and he proposed that it be dredged and cleared so steamboats could call at New Salem— insuring a glorious future for the town.

Before he could start his campaign, an Indian war flared up in northern Illinois.

8. In politics a candidate's *platform* is a public statement of his or her beliefs, ideas, and goals.

Vocabulary
meager (mē' gər) *adj.* not enough in amount or quantity

Chief Black Hawk of the Sauk and Fox tribes had crossed the Mississippi, intending, he said, to raise corn on land that had been taken from his people thirty years earlier. The white settlers were alarmed, and the governor called for volunteers to stop the invasion. Lincoln enlisted in a militia[9] company made up of his friends and neighbors. He was surprised and pleased when the men elected him as their captain, with Jack Armstrong as first sergeant. His troops drilled and marched, but they never did sight any hostile Indians. Years later, Lincoln would joke about his three-month stint as a military man, telling how he survived "a good many bloody battles with mosquitoes."

By the time he returned to New Salem, election day was just two weeks off. He jumped into the campaign—pitching horseshoes with voters, speaking at barbecues, chatting with farmers in the fields, joking with customers at country stores. He lost, finishing eighth in a field of thirteen. But in his own precinct, where folks knew him, he received 227 votes out of 300 cast.

Defeated as a politician, he decided to try his luck as a frontier merchant. With a fellow named William Berry as his partner, Lincoln operated a general store that sold everything from axes to beeswax. But the two men showed little aptitude for business, and their store finally "winked out," as Lincoln put it. Then Berry died, leaving Lincoln saddled with a $1,100 debt—a gigantic amount for someone who had never

earned more than a few dollars a month. Lincoln called it "the National Debt," but he vowed to repay every cent. He spent the next fifteen years doing so.

To support himself, he worked at all sorts of odd jobs. He split fence rails, hired himself out as a farmhand, helped at the local gristmill. With the help of friends, he was appointed postmaster of New Salem, a part-time job that paid about fifty dollars a year. Then he was offered a chance to become deputy to the local surveyor. He knew nothing about surveying, so he bought a compass, a chain, and a couple of textbooks on the subject. Within six weeks, he had taught himself enough to start work—laying out roads and townsites, and marking off property boundaries.

As he traveled about the county, making surveys and delivering mail to faraway farms, people came to know him as an honest and dependable fellow. Lincoln could be counted on to witness a contract, settle a boundary dispute, or compose a letter for folks who couldn't write much themselves. For the first time, his neighbors began to call him "Abe."

In 1834, Lincoln ran for the state legislature again. This time he placed second in a field of thirteen candidates, and was one of four men elected to the Illinois House of Representatives from Sangamon County. In November, wearing a sixty-dollar tailor-made suit he had bought on credit, the first suit he had ever owned, the twenty-five-year-old legislator climbed into a stagecoach and set out for the state capital in Vandalia.

In those days, Illinois lawmakers were paid three dollars a day to cover their

---

9. A *militia* (mi lish′ ə) is a military force made up of civilians who serve as soldiers during a time of emergency.

Vocabulary
aptitude (ap′ tə tōōd′) *n.* a natural ability; talent

expenses, but only while the legislature was in session. Lincoln still had to earn a living. One of his fellow representatives, a rising young attorney named John Todd Stuart, urged Lincoln to take up the study of law. As Stuart pointed out, it was an ideal profession for anyone with political ambitions.

And in fact, Lincoln had been toying with the idea of becoming a lawyer. For years he had hung around frontier courthouses, watching country lawyers bluster and strut as they cross-examined witnesses and delivered impassioned[10] speeches before juries. He had sat on juries himself, appeared as a witness, drawn up legal documents for his neighbors. He had even argued a few cases before the local justice of the peace.

Yes, the law <u>intrigued</u> him. It would give him a chance to rise in the world, to earn a respected place in the community, to live by his wits instead of by hard physical labor.

Yet Lincoln hesitated, unsure of himself because he had so little formal education. That was no great obstacle, his friend Stuart kept telling him. In the 1830s, few American lawyers had ever seen the inside of a law school. Instead, they "read law" in the office of a practicing attorney until they knew enough to pass their exams.

Lincoln decided to study entirely on his own. He borrowed some law books from Stuart, bought others at an auction, and began to read and memorize legal codes and precedents.[11] Back in New Salem, folks would see him walking down the road, reciting aloud from one of his law books, or lying under a tree as he read, his long legs stretched up the trunk. He studied for nearly three years before passing his exams and being admitted to practice on March 1, 1837.

By then, the state legislature was planning to move from Vandalia to Springfield, which had been named the new capital of Illinois. Lincoln had been elected to a second term in the legislature. And he had accepted a job as junior partner in John Todd Stuart's Springfield law office.

In April, he went back to New Salem for the last time to pack his belongings and say good-bye to his friends. The little village was <u>declining</u> now. Its hopes for growth and prosperity had vanished when the Sangamon River proved too treacherous for steamboat travel. Settlers were moving away, seeking brighter prospects[12] elsewhere.

By 1840, New Salem was a ghost town. It would have been forgotten completely if Abraham Lincoln hadn't gone there to live when he was young, penniless, and ambitious.

---

10. An *impassioned* speech expresses strong, sincere feelings and can produce equally strong responses in the listeners.

11. The sets of laws passed by various units of government are called *legal codes. Precedents* (pres′ ə dənts) are court decisions that serve as examples for deciding future cases.
12. *Prospects* are chances for future success.

Vocabulary
intrigue (in trēg′) *v.* to arouse the curiosity or interest of; fascinate
decline (di klīn′) *v.* to become less; fall into a worse condition

Responding to Literature

PERSONAL RESPONSE

◆ What anecdote or piece of information about Lincoln's early life do you find most interesting?

◆ Look back at the list from the **Focus Activity** on page 284. With classmates, add new ideas and correct any inaccuracies.

Analyzing Literature

RECALL

1. In what places did Abraham Lincoln grow up? Who raised him?

2. How much formal schooling did Lincoln have?

3. What did Lincoln see in New Orleans that he never forgot?

4. What kinds of work did Lincoln do as a boy and as a young adult?

INTERPRET

5. What were some hardships Lincoln faced while growing up?

6. How can you tell that schooling was important to Lincoln?

7. In your opinion, what qualities did Lincoln have to make him a good legislator? Support your ideas with information from the selection.

8. In what ways did life in Lincoln's day differ from life today? Use information from the selection.

EVALUATE AND CONNECT

9. Events in the selection are told in **chronological order**—the order in which they occurred. Is the sequence of events clear? What are some words or phrases Freedman uses to indicate time order?

10. Based on this selection, are you interested in reading the rest of *Lincoln: A Photobiography*? Why or why not?

Abraham Lincoln. Matthew Wilson. U.S. Naval Academy.

LITERARY ELEMENTS

Source Material in Biography

To gather information for *Lincoln: A Photobiography,* Russell Freedman traveled to Lincoln's birthplace in Kentucky. He saw Ford's Theater in Washington, D.C., where Lincoln was shot in 1865. He visited the Illinois State Historical Library and read Lincoln's handwritten letters and other documents, including first-draft notes of the Emancipation Proclamation, the document that freed the slaves. By using these sources in his research, Freedman found many facts and could better sort fact from fiction about Lincoln's life.

1. What are some sources you would use for researching a book on Lincoln?

2. What are some sources Freedman may have used in this selection?

● See **Literary Terms Handbook,** p. R1.

Literature and Writing

Writing About Literature

Author's Purpose   Authors usually write for one or more of the following purposes: to entertain, to inform readers about a subject, or to persuade readers to believe something. Explain in a paragraph or two what you think Freedman's purposes were for writing this biography. Use examples from the selection.

Personal Writing

Experience Is the Best Teacher   Lincoln had an eventful life, even as a boy. Some experiences, such as the loss of his mother, must have been hard. Others, such as storytelling and practicing speeches before his friends, may have been great fun. Pick an experience from Lincoln's growing-up years. Write two or three paragraphs telling how you would handle such an experience, and how it would change you.

Extending Your Response

Literature Groups

"Mr. President"   If you could interview Abraham Lincoln today, what would you ask him? Brainstorm a list of interview questions. Think about how he lived, the times he lived in, what he thought was right or wrong, his goals, his feelings, or his worries.

interNET CONNECTION

Tour the historic sites of Lincoln's life in New Salem and Springfield. Browse under the entries *Abraham Lincoln* and *Springfield, Illinois,* to see what photos and historic information you can find.

Art Activity

Illustrating History   As a class, decide on a list of important events to include on a time line of Lincoln's early life. Draw a time line and create a colorful mural to illustrate the events.

Listening and Speaking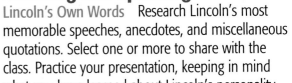

Lincoln's Own Words   Research Lincoln's most memorable speeches, anecdotes, and miscellaneous quotations. Select one or more to share with the class. Practice your presentation, keeping in mind what you have learned about Lincoln's personality. Then share your presentation with the class.

Reading Further

If you'd like to read more by Russell Freedman, you might enjoy these books:
Indian Chiefs
Eleanor Roosevelt: A Life of Discovery

📑 **Save your work for your portfolio.**

Skill Minilessons

GRAMMAR AND LANGUAGE • DEMONSTRATIVE PRONOUNS

This, that, these, and *those* are **demonstrative pronouns.** They are used with nouns or by themselves to point out people, places, or things. *This* and *these* point out something that is close to the speaker. *That* and *those* point out something that is far from the speaker. *This* and *that* are singular and are used with singular verbs. *These* and *those* are plural and are used with plural verbs.

These books are about Lincoln.
That is Lincoln's portrait.

PRACTICE For each sentence, write the correct demonstrative pronoun.

1. ___ book I'm holding is about Lincoln.
2. ___ were hard times when Lincoln grew up.
3. Which of the photographs in ___ selection are of Lincoln?
4. How many of ___ books we read last year were biographies?
5. ___ room over there is Lincoln's bedroom.

● For more on pronouns, see **Language Handbook,** p. R27.

READING AND THINKING • MAIN IDEA

Authors often state one important idea in a paragraph. The other sentences in the paragraph add information or lend support to this **main idea.**

The main idea can be stated directly. An example on page 294 is "the law intrigued him." The other sentences in the paragraph contain details that tell why the law intrigued Lincoln.

Sometimes the main idea of a paragraph is not stated. You can discover it by asking yourself what

the largest, most important idea in the paragraph is. The other sentences often add details and facts that support that idea.

PRACTICE Choose a paragraph in "A Backwoods Boy." Write the main idea of the paragraph. Then list the supporting details.

● For more on main idea, see **Reading Handbook,** p. R79–R80.

VOCABULARY • UNLOCKING MEANING

When you learn a new word, you also learn something about any other word that has the same base word or comes from the same root.

PRACTICE Use what you know about the clue words to figure out the answers to the questions.

1. Clue: *aptitude*
   If a boy is an apt student, he is
   a. lazy.　　　c. quick to learn.
   b. talkative.
2. Clue: *intellectual*
   A girl's intellect is her
   a. beauty.　　　c. kindness.
   b. mental ability.

3. Clue: *reflective*
   To reflect on what he said, you
   a. repeat it.　　　c. argue about it.
   b. think about it.
4. Clue: *luminous*
   An insect with luminescence is a
   a. firefly.　　　c. ladybug.
   b. cicada.
5. Clue: *forlorn*
   A lovelorn man loves someone who
   a. left him.　　　c. agreed to a date.
   b. married him.

Writing WORKSHOP

Persuasive Writing: A Letter

What problems do you and your friends struggle with? What problems do you see in your school or your community? Maybe you worry about pollution or endangered animals. Have you ever had an idea that could make things better, if only somebody would listen? A letter just might make a difference.

Assignment: Using the steps in this workshop, write a letter to a government office or a company with suggestions for solving a problem.

● As you write your persuasive letter, refer to the **Writing Handbook,** pp. R43–R47.

The Writing Process

PREWRITING

PREWRITING TIP
For more ideas, talk with classmates. What bothers them? What would they like to change?

● **Explore Problems**

You might write to a real person about a real-life problem or to a fictional or historical character from a selection in this theme. (Could you help Manuel in "La Bamba" make friends with Petra Lopez? Could you comfort Rachel in "Eleven"?) You may prefer to write about a community or an ecological concern. An idea tree like the one below is one way to explore a topic.

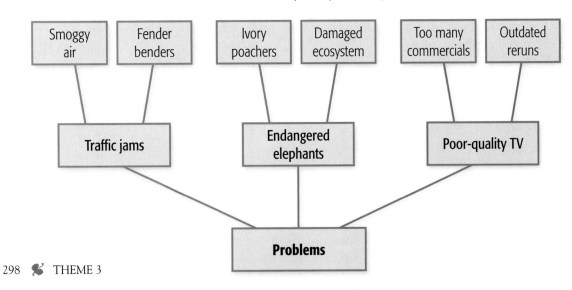

● Make Choices

Which problems do you have solutions for? Which problem do you care about most? Decide whom you will write to. Choose an audience who can make the changes you will suggest.

● Think About Your Audience and Purpose

Since your purpose is to persuade, put yourself in your reader's place. How might you help your reader see the problem as you do? How might you persuade your reader to try your solution? Think of ways to appeal to your reader's interests and concerns. The Writing Skills activity on page 245 may help you.

● Organize Your Thoughts

Your letter will have four main parts. Filling in a form like the one below can help you plan them.

PROBLEM	SOLUTION
Too many commercials on TV.	Put all commercials between shorter shows. Have only one or two breaks in movies; show all commercials then.
BACKGROUND	**PERSUASION**
Why is it a problem? • Viewers tired of having shows interrupted. • The closer to the end of a movie, the more commercials there are. • Viewers end up channel-surfing. What causes it? • Station needs to make money.	Why will it work? • Having fewer commercials would attract more viewers. • Happy viewers more likely to buy products. • Station would make more money. What makes it good? • Everyone wins.

Writing WORKSHOP

DRAFTING

DRAFTING TIP
To persuade your reader, try showing how things could get worse if the problem continues.

● Spotlight the Problem

To catch your reader's interest, try opening with a brief scene or story showing the problem. Go on to state the problem clearly. In a new paragraph, explain more about the problem. Use the background section of your prewriting notes.

● Sell Your Solution

In your next paragraphs, explain your solution. Show how and why it will work, and convince your reader that your idea is worthwhile. Answer any objections that your reader might have. End by urging your reader to try your idea.

MODEL · DRAFTING

If you make these changes, I think we would all be happier. Viewers would not have their shows interrupted, and they would watch your station more. Everyone would win. Isn't it worth a try?

REVISING

REVISING TIP
See page R52 for letter forms. To an adult you have never met, write a business letter.

● Rework Your Letter

To see your letter with new eyes, imagine that you are the one receiving it. Mark any parts that might be confusing. Then make changes. The **Questions for Revising** can help.

Next, ask a partner to read your letter and go over the **Questions for Revising** with you. Keep changing your letter until it is as persuasive as you can make it.

QUESTIONS FOR REVISING

☑ How might I change the first lines of my letter to interest my reader more?

☑ What facts could make the problem clearer to my reader?

☑ What details could I add to help explain my solution and persuade my reader?

☑ Where do I deal with objections that my reader might have?

☑ How do the last lines of my letter encourage my reader to try my plan?

EDITING/PROOFREADING

After revising your letter, use the **Proofreading Checklist** to help find errors in grammar and mechanics. The **Grammar Link** on page 265 shows you how to spot and correct problems with apostrophes.

Grammar Hint

Remember not to use an apostrophe in *its* (meaning "belonging to it"). Use an apostrophe only when you mean "it is." It's clear that something must be done. A wild animal has a right to its freedom.

PROOFREADING CHECKLIST

☑ Each sentence has a complete subject and predicate.

☑ Punctuation marks, including apostrophes, are used correctly. (Double-check *its* and *it's*.)

☑ Capitalization is correct.

☑ Spelling is correct.

☑ The letter follows a standard form.

MODEL · EDITING/PROOFREADING

I don't mind watching a commercial if it's at the end of the show.

PUBLISHING/PRESENTING

Try role-playing in a small group. "Send" your letter, and ask classmates to take on the character of your reader and "phone" you in response. Do the same for them. If appropriate, consider mailing your letter. Get your teacher's permission and help with finding the right address. Then check your mailbox for a reply!

TECHNOLOGY TIP
E-mail is a fast way to send your letter. Most businesses and government offices have E-mail addresses.

Reflecting

Use your journal to explore your thoughts about this writing experience.
- What was the hardest part of writing your letter? How did you handle it?
- For this kind of writing, would you rather work with others or alone? Explain.

📖 **Save your work for your portfolio.**

Theme Wrap-Up

Responding to the Theme

1. Which selection in this theme best helped you understand feelings and thoughts of other people your age? Explain your answer.

2. What new ideas do you have about the following as a result of reading this theme?
   - how people deal with problems of growing up
   - experiences and feelings shared by young people

3. Present your theme project to the class.

Analyzing Literature

COMPARE BIOGRAPHIES

Think about the biographical selections that you read in this theme. Which of the two selections would you like to read in full? Why? Choose one of the selections from this theme, and tell why you like it. Discuss characters, setting, and author's viewpoint in the selection.

Evaluate and Set Goals

1. Which of the following was most enjoyable to you? Which was most difficult?
   - reading and thinking about the selections
   - doing independent writing
   - analyzing the selections in discussions
   - making presentations
   - doing research

2. How would you assess your work in this theme, using the following scale? Give at least two reasons for your assessment.
   4 = outstanding   2 = fair
   3 = good   1 = weak

3. Based on what you found difficult in this theme, choose a goal to work toward in the next theme.
   - Write down your goal and three steps you will take to help you reach it.
   - Meet with your teacher to review your goal and your plan for achieving it.

Build Your Portfolio

SELECT

Choose two pieces of work you did in this theme to include in your portfolio. Use these questions to help you choose.

- ✦ Which do you consider your best work?
- ✦ Which challenged you the most?
- ✦ Which did you learn the most from?
- ✦ Which did you enjoy the most?

REFLECT

Write some notes to accompany the pieces you selected. Use these questions to guide you.

- ✦ What do you like best about the piece?
- ✦ What did you learn from creating it?
- ✦ What might you do differently if you were beginning this piece again?

Reading on Your Own

If you have enjoyed the literature in this theme, you might also be interested in the following books.

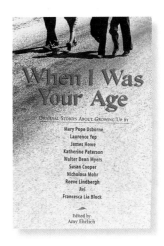

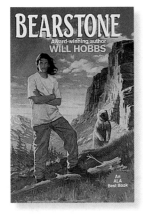

Bearstone
by Will Hobbs An elderly Colorado rancher helps a fourteen-year-old Ute boy to grow up.

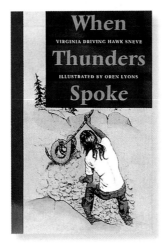

When Thunders Spoke
by Virginia Driving Hawk Sneve A boy discovers the value of a Sioux tradition.

When I Was Your Age: Original Stories About Growing Up
edited by Amy Ehrlich This collection of stories by ten popular writers includes fiction and autobiography.

Harriet Tubman: Conductor on the Underground Railroad
by Ann Petry This biography tells the exciting story of a woman who helped hundreds of enslaved people escape to freedom.

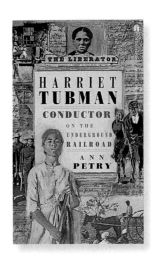

Standardized Test Practice

Read the passage and decide which type of error, if any, appears in each underlined section. Mark the letter for that answer on your paper.

Everyone knows that Benjamin Franklin signed the declaration of indepen-
(1)
dence. But many people don't know that Franklins involvement with that docu-
(2)
ment extended far beyond putting his name on it. In addition to his work as a

statesman, Benjamin Franklin was an ingenious inventor, a briliant journalist,
(3)
and a man of wisdom.

Franklin published many great American Journals, including *Poor Richard's*
(4)
Almanack and *The Pennsylvania Gazette.* Franklin is credited with inventing the
(5)
lightning rod, a new kind of eyeglasses, and a more efficient stove. Franklin's
(6)
many accomplishments show that he lived by his own words "Well done is

better than well said."

---

1 A Spelling error
   B Capitalization error
   C Punctuation error
   D No error

2 F Spelling error
   G Capitalization error
   H Punctuation error
   J No error

3 A Spelling error
   B Capitalization error
   C Punctuation error
   D No error

4 F Spelling error
   G Capitalization error
   H Punctuation error
   J No error

5 A Spelling error
   B Capitalization error
   C Punctuation error
   D No error

6 F Spelling error
   G Capitalization error
   H Punctuation error
   J No error

Read the passage and choose the word or group of words that belongs in each space. Mark the letter for your answer on your paper.

One summer, my father decided to start a vegetable garden in our backyard. He __(1)__ tomatoes, zucchini, and green peppers. He watered the plants every day. One afternoon, when I didn't have __(2)__ to do, my father asked me to help him with the watering. I __(3)__ the hose over the tomatoes while he inspected the progress of the zucchini plants. The zucchini had grown the most __(4)__ of all of the vegetables. The tomatoes were doing __(5)__, also. Once the vegetables were big enough to pick and eat, __(6)__ had a wonderful home-grown meal.

---

1 **A** has been planted
   B plants
   C is planting
   D planted

2 **F** nothing
   G anything
   H hardly nothing
   J hardly anything

3 **A** was holding
   B hold
   C held
   D have held

4 **F** quickest
   G quick
   H quickly
   J quicker

5 **A** good
   B well
   C best
   D most well

6 **F** him and me
   G he and I
   H he and me
   J him and I

STOP

What's Most Important

> ❝ Happiness is not a goal. It is a by-product. ❞
>
> —Eleanor Roosevelt

THEME CONTENTS

GENRE FOCUS *SHORT STORY*

Exploring the Theme

What's Most Important

When your team is about to score, it's easy to tell what's important—winning! Sometimes what's important to us isn't obvious. The selections in this theme explore what we value. Check out the activity below to help you start thinking about the theme.

Starting Points

BEAUTY IN THE EYE OF THE BEHOLDER

Jon and his cat Garfield share something each one values. In a small group, exchange ideas about these questions:

- What would you share with someone you wanted to be friends with?
- What does your choice for sharing show about what you value and what you hope your new friend may value too?

Garfield
by Jim Davis

Theme Projects

Choose a project listed below to complete as you read the selections in this theme. Work on your own, with a partner, or with a group.

CRITICAL VIEWING
Adding Up Ads

1. Collect newspaper and magazine ads that you think have important messages dealing with such topics as fire prevention or recycling.

2. Mount the ads on construction paper, using one piece of paper for each ad. Number the back of each.

3. Ask classmates to place the ads in order by putting the message that seems most important first and the message that seems least important last. Record the order of each person's choices.

4. What are the most important issues to your classmates?

5. Share your results with the class.

interNET CONNECTION

Check out the Web for more project ideas or more books related to the theme. For example, try typing the keyword *volunteers* into a search engine. You may also want to check out the Glencoe Web site (lit.glencoe.com).

LEARNING FOR LIFE
Job Descriptions

1. List places in your community where people can volunteer their time. Include such places as a food pantry or a pet shelter.

2. Talk to a person in charge of one such place. Ask what volunteers do there. Find out what qualities are important for volunteers.

3. Write job descriptions for volunteers.

MULTIMEDIA PROJECT
Movie Messages

1. List movies you think have messages that could help or encourage people.

2. Select one movie and create a jingle to promote it. Emphasize what you hope people will learn from the movie.

3. Make a poster with a slogan for the movie.

4. Present your poster and jingle to the class.

Before You Read

The Stone

MEET LLOYD ALEXANDER

L loyd Alexander is best known for his adventure stories based on history and legend. After serving in the army in World War II, Alexander worked as a cartoonist, an advertising copywriter, and an editor. He wrote stories in his free time. "One thing I had learned during . . . those years . . . was to write about things I knew and loved," he says. ". . . I learned a writer could know and love a fantasy world as much as his real one."

Lloyd Alexander was born in 1924. This story, which appears in The Foundling, and Other Tales of Prydain, *was published in 1973.*

FOCUS ACTIVITY

Imagine that you are a character in a fairy tale and have been granted one wish. Your wish cannot be for more wishes. What would you wish for? What would help you decide?

Make a List
Write a wish. Then add it to a class list of wishes. Which wishes are the most popular?

Setting a Purpose
Read "The Stone" to see how a character uses a wish.

BACKGROUND

The Time and Place   Like traditional fairy tales, this story is set sometime in the long ago and faraway past.

Did You Know?   Lloyd Alexander's *Prydain Chronicles*—like *The Lord of the Rings* books by J. R. R. Tolkien and *The Chronicles of Narnia* by C. S. Lewis—are called high fantasy. They are connected stories that take place in imaginary worlds. The plots of high fantasy often involve life-and-death situations and contests between good and evil.

VOCABULARY PREVIEW

frail (frāl) *adj.* lacking in strength; weak; p. 311
threadbare (thred′ bār′) *adj.* shabby; worn-out; p. 312
gape (gāp) *v.* to stare in wonder or surprise, often with the mouth open; p. 312
plight (plīt) *n.* an unfortunate, distressing, or dangerous situation; difficulty; p. 312
retort (ri tôrt′) *v.* to reply, especially in a sharp, witty, or clever manner; p. 315
heed (hēd) *n.* careful attention; notice; p. 315
vainly (vān′ lē) *adv.* without success; p. 317
laden (lād′ ən) *adj.* loaded; weighed down; burdened; p. 318

The Stone

Lloyd Alexander ~

There was a cottager named Maibon, and one day he was driving down the road in his horse and cart when he saw an old man hobbling along, so frail and feeble he doubted the poor soul could go many more steps. Though Maibon offered to take him in the cart, the old man refused; and Maibon went his way home, shaking his head over such a pitiful sight, and said to his wife, Modrona:

"Ah, ah, what a sorry thing it is to have your bones creaking and crack- ing, and dim eyes, and dull wits. When I think this might come to me, too! A fine, strong-armed, sturdy-legged fellow like me? One day to go tottering, and have his teeth rattling in his head, and live on porridge, like a baby? There's no fate worse in all the world."

"There is," answered Modrona, "and that would be to have neither teeth nor porridge. Get on with you, Maibon, and stop borrowing trouble.[1] Hoe your field or you'll have no crop to harvest, and no food for you, nor me, nor the little ones."

---

1. Modrona means that it's best not to worry about troubles that might come up in the future.

Vocabulary
frail (frāl) *adj.* lacking in strength; weak

The Stone

Sighing and grumbling, Maibon did as his wife bade him.[2] Although the day was fair and cloudless, he took no pleasure in it. His ax-blade was notched, the wooden handle splintery; his saw had lost its edge; and his hoe, once shining new, had begun to rust. None of his tools, it seemed to him, cut or chopped or delved[3] as well as they once had done.

"They're as worn out as that old codger[4] I saw on the road," Maibon said to himself. He squinted up at the sky. "Even the sun isn't as bright as it used to be, and doesn't warm me half as well. It's gone threadbare as my cloak. And no wonder, for it's been there longer than I can remember. Come to think of it, the moon's been looking a little wilted around the edges, too.

"As for me," went on Maibon, in dismay, "I'm in even a worse state. My appetite's faded, especially after meals. Mornings, when I wake, I can hardly keep myself from yawning. And at night, when I go to bed, my eyes are so heavy I can't hold them open. If that's the way things are now, the older I grow, the worse it will be!"

In the midst of his complaining, Maibon glimpsed something bouncing and tossing back and forth beside a fallen tree in a corner of the field. Wondering if one of his piglets had squeezed out of the sty and gone rooting for acorns, Maibon hurried across the turf. Then he dropped his ax and gaped in astonishment.

There, struggling to free his leg which had been caught under the log, lay a short, thickset figure: a dwarf with red hair bristling in all directions beneath his round, close-fitting leather cap. At the sight of Maibon, the dwarf squeezed shut his bright red eyes and began holding his breath. After a moment, the dwarf's face went redder than his hair; his cheeks puffed out and soon turned purple. Then he opened one eye and blinked rapidly at Maibon, who was staring at him, speechless.

"What," snapped the dwarf, "you can still see me?"

"That I can," replied Maibon, more than ever puzzled, "and I can see very well you've got yourself tight as a wedge under that log, and all your kicking only makes it worse."

At this, the dwarf blew out his breath and shook his fists. "I can't do it!" he shouted. "No matter how I try! I can't make myself invisible! Everyone in my family can disappear—Poof! Gone! Vanished! But not me! Not Doli! Believe me, if I could have done, you never would have found me in such a plight. Worse luck! Well, come on. Don't stand there goggling like an idiot. Help me get loose!"

At this sharp command, Maibon began tugging and heaving at the log. Then he stopped, wrinkled his brow, and scratched his head, saying:

---

2. *Bade* is the past tense of *bid,* which means "to order or ask."
3. *Delved* is the past tense of *delve,* which means, here, "to dig."
4. A *codger* is a person, especially an old man, who's odd and a bit grumpy.

Vocabulary

threadbare (thred′ bār′) *adj.* shabby; worn-out
gape (gāp) *v.* to stare in wonder or surprise, often with the mouth open
plight (plīt) *n.* an unfortunate, distressing, or dangerous situation; difficulty

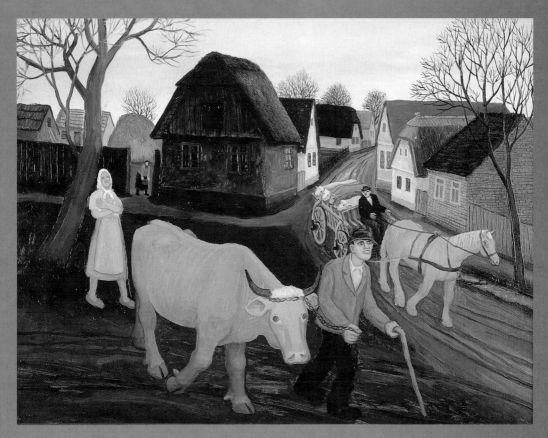

Untitled. Franjo Mraz (b. 1910).

Viewing the painting: What might Maibon think about the people in the painting?

"Well, now, just a moment, friend. The way you look, and all your talk about turning yourself invisible—I'm thinking you might be one of the Fair Folk."[5]

"Oh, clever!" Doli retorted. "Oh, brilliant! Great clodhopper! Giant beanpole! Of course I am! What else! Enough gabbling. Get a move on. My leg's going to sleep."

"If a man does the Fair Folk a good turn," cried Maibon, his excitement growing, "it's told they must do one for him."

"I knew sooner or later you'd come round to that," grumbled the dwarf. "That's the way of it with you ham-handed, heavy-footed oafs. Time was, you humans got along well with us. But nowadays, you no

sooner see a Fair Folk than it's grab, grab, grab! Gobble, gobble, gobble! Grant my wish! Give me this, give me that! As if we had nothing better to do!

"Yes, I'll give you a favor," Doli went on. "That's the rule, I'm obliged[6] to. Now, get on with it."

Hearing this, Maibon pulled and pried and chopped away at the log as fast as he could, and soon freed the dwarf.

Doli heaved a sigh of relief, rubbed his shin, and cocked a red eye at Maibon, saying:

"All right. You've done your work, you'll have your reward. What do you want? Gold, I suppose. That's the usual. Jewels? Fine clothes? Take my advice, go for something

---

5. *Fair Folk* is another name for fairies or fairylike beings who have magical powers.

6. Here, *obliged* means "required."

practical. A hazelwood twig to help you find water if your well ever goes dry? An ax that never needs sharpening? A cook pot always brimming with food?"

"None of those!" cried Maibon. He bent down to the dwarf and whispered eagerly, "But I've heard tell that you Fair Folk have magic stones that can keep a man young forever. That's what I want. I claim one for my reward."

Doli snorted. "I might have known you'd pick something like that. As to be expected, you humans have it all muddled. There's nothing can make a man young again. That's even beyond the best of our skills. Those stones you're babbling about? Well, yes, there are such things. But greatly overrated. All they'll do is keep you from growing any older."

"Just as good!" Maibon exclaimed. "I want no more than that!"

Doli hesitated and frowned. "Ah— between the two of us, take the cook pot. Better all around. Those stones— we'd sooner not give them away. There's a difficulty—"

"Because you'd rather keep them for yourselves," Maibon broke in. "No, no, you shan't

cheat me of my due. Don't put me off with excuses. I told you what I want, and that's what I'll have. Come, hand it over and not another word."

Doli shrugged and opened a leather pouch that hung from his belt. He spilled a number of brightly colored pebbles into his palm, picked out one of the larger stones, and handed it to Maibon. The dwarf then jumped up, took to his heels, raced across the field, and disappeared into a thicket.

Laughing and crowing over his good fortune and his cleverness, Maibon hurried back to the cottage. There, he told his wife what had happened, and showed her the stone he had claimed from the Fair Folk.

"As I am now, so I'll always be!" Maibon declared, flexing his arms and thumping his chest. "A fine figure of a man! Oho, no gray beard and wrinkled brow for me!"

Instead of sharing her husband's jubilation,[7] Modrona flung up her hands and burst out:

"Maibon, you're a greater fool than ever I supposed! And selfish into the bargain! You've turned down treasures! You didn't even ask that dwarf for so much as new jackets for the children! Nor a new apron for me! You could have had the roof mended. Or the walls plastered. No, a stone is what you ask for! A bit of rock no better than you'll dig up in the cow pasture!"

Crestfallen and sheepish,[8] Maibon began thinking his wife was right, and the dwarf had indeed given him no more than a common field stone.

"Eh, well, it's true," he stammered, "I feel no different than I did this morning, no better nor worse, but every way the same. That redheaded little wretch! He'll rue[9] the day if I ever find him again!"

So saying, Maibon threw the stone into the fireplace. That night he grumbled his way to bed, dreaming revenge on the dishonest dwarf.

Next morning, after a restless night, he yawned, rubbed his eyes, and scratched his chin. Then he sat bolt upright in bed, patting his cheeks in amazement.

"My beard!" he cried, tumbling out and hurrying to tell his wife. "It hasn't grown! Not by a hair! Can it be the dwarf didn't cheat me after all?"

"Don't talk to me about beards," declared his wife as Maibon went to the fireplace, picked out the stone, and clutched it safely in both hands. "There's trouble enough in the chicken roost. Those eggs should have hatched by now, but the hen is still brooding on her nest."

"Let the chickens worry about that," answered Maibon. "Wife, don't you see what a grand thing's happened to me? I'm not a minute older than I was yesterday. Bless that generous-hearted dwarf!"

"Let me lay hands on him and I'll bless him," retorted Modrona. "That's all well and good for you. But what of me? You'll stay as you are, but I'll turn old and gray, and worn and wrinkled, and go doddering[10] into my grave! And what of our little ones? They'll grow up and have children of their own. And grandchildren, and great-grandchildren. And you, younger than any of them. What a foolish sight you'll be!"

But Maibon, gleeful over his good luck, paid his wife no heed, and only tucked the stone deeper into his pocket. Next day, however, the eggs had still not hatched.

"And the cow!" Modrona cried. "She's long past due to calve, and no sign of a young one ready to be born!"

"Don't bother me with cows and chickens," replied Maibon. "They'll all come right, in time. As for time, I've got all the time in the world!"

Having no appetite for breakfast, Maibon went out into his field. Of all the

---

7. *Jubilation* means "great joy and excitement."
8. Maibon feels discouraged (*crestfallen*) and embarrassed (*sheepish*).
9. To *rue* is to regret or be sorry for.

10. Here, *doddering* means "trembling with old age."

Vocabulary
retort (ri tôrt´) *v.* to reply, especially in a sharp, witty, or clever manner
heed (hēd) *n.* careful attention; notice

seeds he had sown there, however, he was surprised to see not one had sprouted. The field, which by now should have been covered with green shoots, lay bare and empty.

"Eh, things do seem a little late these days," Maibon said to himself. "Well, no hurry. It's that much less for me to do. The wheat isn't growing, but neither are the weeds."

Some days went by and still the eggs had not hatched, the cow had not calved, the wheat had not sprouted. And now Maibon saw that his apple tree showed no sign of even the smallest, greenest fruit.

"Maibon, it's the fault of that stone!" wailed his wife. "Get rid of the thing!"

"Nonsense," replied Maibon. "The season's slow, that's all."

Nevertheless, his wife kept at him and kept at him so much that Maibon at last, and very reluctantly, threw the stone out the cottage window. Not too far, though, for he had it in the back of his mind to go later and find it again.

Next morning he had no need to go looking for it, for there was the stone sitting on the window ledge.

A Rural Scene (detail). Konstantin Rodko (b. 1908).

Viewing the painting: How is this farm different from Maibon's farm while he has the stone?

"You see?" said Maibon to his wife. "Here it is back again. So, it's a gift meant for me to keep."

"Maibon!" cried his wife. "Will you get rid of it! We've had nothing but trouble since you brought it into the house. Now the baby's fretting and fuming. Teething, poor little thing. But not a tooth to be seen! Maibon, that stone's bad luck and I want no part of it!"

Protesting it was none of his doing that the stone had come back, Maibon carried it into the vegetable patch. He dug a hole, not a very deep one, and put the stone into it.

Next day, there was the stone above ground, winking and glittering.

"Maibon!" cried his wife. "Once and for all, if you care for your family, get rid of that cursed thing!"

Seeing no other way to keep peace in the household, Maibon regretfully and unwillingly took the stone and threw it down the well, where it splashed into the water and sank from sight.

But that night, while he was trying vainly to sleep, there came such a rattling and clattering that Maibon clapped his hands over his ears, jumped out of bed, and went stumbling into the yard. At the well, the bucket was jiggling back and forth and up and down at the end of the rope; and in the bottom of the bucket was the stone.

Now Maibon began to be truly distressed, not only for the toothless baby, the calfless cow, the fruitless tree, and the hen sitting desperately on her eggs, but for himself as well.

"Nothing's moving along as it should," he groaned. "I can't tell one day from another. Nothing changes, there's nothing to look forward to, nothing to show for my work. Why sow if the seeds don't sprout? Why plant if there's never a harvest? Why eat if I don't get hungry? Why go to bed at night, or get up in the morning, or do anything at all? And the way it looks, so it will stay for ever and ever! I'll shrivel from boredom if nothing else!"

"Maibon," pleaded his wife, "for all our sakes, destroy the dreadful thing!"

Maibon tried now to pound the stone to dust with his heaviest mallet; but he could not so much as knock a chip from it. He put it against his grindstone without so much as scratching it. He set it on his anvil and belabored it with hammer and tongs, all to no avail.[11]

At last he decided to bury the stone again, this time deeper than before. Picking up his shovel, he hurried to the field. But he suddenly halted and the shovel dropped from his hands. There, sitting cross-legged on a stump, was the dwarf.

"You!" shouted Maibon, shaking his fist. "Cheat! Villain! Trickster! I did you a good turn, and see how you've repaid it!"

Did You Know?
An *anvil* is an iron or steel block on which heated metals are hammered into desired shapes. *Tongs* are the tool used to grasp the metal while it's being hammered.

---

11. Here, *avail* means "help" or "advantage."

The Stone

The dwarf blinked at the furious Maibon. "You mortals[12] are an ungrateful crew. I gave you what you wanted."

"You should have warned me!" burst out Maibon.

"I did," Doli snapped back. "You wouldn't listen. No, you yapped and yammered, bound to have your way. I told you we didn't like to give away those stones. When you mortals get hold of one, you stay just as you are—but so does everything around you. Before you know it, you're mired[13] in time like a rock in the mud. You take my advice. Get rid of that stone as fast as you can."

"What do you think I've been trying to do?" blurted Maibon. "I've buried it, thrown it down the well, pounded it with a hammer—it keeps coming back to me!"

"That's because you really didn't want to give it up," Doli said. "In the back of your mind and the bottom of your heart, you didn't want to change along with the rest of the world. So long as you feel that way, the stone is yours."

"No, no!" cried Maibon. "I want no more of it. Whatever may happen, let it happen. That's better than nothing happening at all. I've had my share of being young, I'll take my share of being old. And when I come to the end of my days, at least I can say I've lived each one of them."

"If you mean that," answered Doli, "toss the stone onto the ground, right there at the stump. Then get home and be about your business."

Maibon flung down the stone, spun around, and set off as fast as he could. When he dared at last to glance back over his shoulder, fearful the stone might be bouncing along at his heels, he saw no sign of it, nor of the redheaded dwarf.

Maibon gave a joyful cry, for at that same instant the fallow[14] field was covered with green blades of wheat, the branches of the apple tree bent to the ground, so laden they were with fruit. He ran to the cottage, threw his arms around his wife and children, and told them the good news. The hen hatched her chicks, the cow bore her calf. And Maibon laughed with glee when he saw the first tooth in the baby's mouth.

Never again did Maibon meet any of the Fair Folk, and he was just as glad of it. He and his wife and children and grand-children lived many years, and Maibon was proud of his white hair and long beard as he had been of his sturdy arms and legs.

"Stones are all right, in their way," said Maibon. "But the trouble with them is, they don't grow."

---

12. *Mortals* refers to humans.
13. To be *mired* is to be stuck.

14. Maibon's fields had appeared to be *fallow*—not planted or farmed for at least one growing season.

Vocabulary

laden (lād' ən) *adj.* loaded; weighed down; burdened

Responding to Literature

PERSONAL RESPONSE

- ◆ Were you surprised at the way Maibon's wish turned out?
- ◆ Look back at your wishes in the class list from the **Focus Activity** on page 310. Do you think any of those wishes would have turned out as Maibon's wish did? Why or why not?

Analyzing Literature

RECALL

1. What does Maibon see as he drives down the road? How does he feel about what he sees?
2. How does Maibon get to make a wish?
3. What is Maibon's wish?
4. What problems develop because of his wish?

INTERPRET

5. How does Maibon feel about growing older? Why does he feel this way?
6. Why is Maibon's wife unhappy with his choice of a wish?
7. Why does Maibon want to get rid of the stone?
8. Why does the stone keep coming back?

EVALUATE AND CONNECT

9. Authors commonly provide hints about what will happen in a story. This kind of hint is called **foreshadowing**. How does Doli's reaction to Maibon's wish foreshadow what is to come?
10. Theme Connection   How do you picture yourself as an older person? What qualities do you hope you will have?

LITERARY ELEMENTS

Themes and Morals

The main idea of a story is called the story's **theme.** The theme is a general statement about life and living. A traditional tale often teaches a lesson about correct behavior. This kind of theme is called a **moral.** Do you remember how Aesop's fable "The Hare and the Tortoise" illustrated this moral: Slow and steady wins the race?

To think about the theme, or moral, for "The Stone," ask yourself what the main character learned and how his thinking changed by the end of the story.

1. In a sentence, what is the moral of "The Stone"?

2. What happens in the story that illustrates this moral?

● See **Literary Terms Handbook,** p. R9.

Literature and Writing

Writing About Literature

Compare and Contrast At the beginning of the story, Maibon has a vivid picture of what it is like to be old. In a paragraph or two, compare and contrast his view on old age at the beginning of the story with his view on old age when he actually becomes old. Use words from the story.

Creative Writing

Creating a Fantasy Select a wish from the list you made for the **Focus Activity** on page 310. Write a paragraph or two describing what happens when someone receives that wish.

Extending Your Response

Literature Groups

Winning Big Winning a lottery seems like a modern-day wish come true. Share stories you have read or heard about people who win a million dollars in a lottery. How do you think it might change them? How might their experiences be similar to those of Maibon?

Performing

Scripting In a small group, rewrite this story as a play with parts for a narrator, Maibon, his wife, Doli, and the old man. Then assign parts and rehearse together. Perform your play for another group of students.

*inter*NET
CONNECTION

Among Lloyd Alexander's most highly honored works are the *Prydain Chronicles.* The author has suggested that these fantasies take place in an imaginary place not unlike fifth-century Wales. Find out about *castles of Wales,* as well as *Welsh mythology,* on the Internet.

Learning for Life

Taking a Wish Survey Ask at least fifteen people what they would wish if they could have only one wish. Include family members, friends, teachers, and neighbors. Take notes and compare wishes. What are the most common wishes? Share your findings with the class.

Reading Further

You might enjoy these fantasies about wishes and immortality:
Tuck Everlasting by Natalie Babbitt
Bright Shadow by Avi

 Save your work for your portfolio.

Skill Minilessons

GRAMMAR AND LANGUAGE • CAPITALIZATION IN DIALOGUE

All words spoken directly by a character or by a real person must be enclosed in quotation marks. Sentences within quotation marks begin with a capital letter, as in the following examples:

"Everyone in my family can disappear," Doli said.

Doli said, "Everyone in my family can disappear."

PRACTICE Add capital letters and quotation marks as needed in the following sentences.

1. Maibon said, don't put me off with excuses.
2. that's the wish I want, Maibon said.
3. Doli said, you're a great fool, Maibon.
4. you're very selfish, too, Doli added.
5. today is like yesterday, Maibon said.

● For more about capitalization, see **Language Handbook,** p. R30.

READING AND THINKING • CLASSIFYING

Classifying is forming groups based on similar attributes or qualities. Lloyd Alexander uses two kinds of details in "The Stone." **Fantastic details** describe things that do not exist or

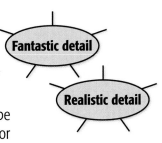

happen in the real world, and **realistic details** describe events or things that are true-to-life and could happen.

PRACTICE Classify details from "The Stone." Add examples of each kind of detail to clusters like those shown.

● For more about reading and thinking strategies, see **Reading Handbook,** pp. R75–R83.

VOCABULARY • DICTIONARY DEFINITIONS

Dictionaries can be a big help if you know how to use them. First you have to find the word you want. Then you have to figure out which meaning is the right one for your situation. For example, "The Stone" uses the word *vainly.* Since *vainly* is an adverb made from *vain,* the dictionary may give meanings for *vain,* but not for *vainly.* So, you look up *vain* and then use what you know about adverbs to understand *vainly.* Here is a set of meanings for *vain:*

vain *adj.* **1.** too interested in, or proud of, one's own abilities, appearance, or accomplishments: *a vain actor* **2.** not successful or effective: *a vain effort* **3.** of no real value or meaning; empty: *a vain promise*

PRACTICE Decide which meaning of *vain* (or *vainly*) is used in each sentence below and write the number of that meaning.

1. Clara tried *vainly* to be heard over the noise of the siren.
2. If you don't want people to think you're *vain,* don't brag so much!
3. Dad made several *vain* attempts to keep the dog off my bed.
4. Rick looked *vainly* in every mirror he passed so he could admire himself.
5. Mom won't really take away my allowance; that's just a *vain* threat.

Making Inferences

A skillful short story writer must be sure to provide all the details the reader needs to understand the story. There are times, however, when the reader must fill in some of the information. Read the following passage from "The Stone":

> At the sight of Maibon, the dwarf squeezed shut his bright red eyes and began holding his breath. After a moment, the dwarf's face went redder than his hair; his cheeks puffed out and soon turned purple. Then he opened one eye and blinked rapidly at Maibon, who was staring at him, speechless.
>
> "What," snapped the dwarf, "you can still see me?"

Lloyd Alexander does not state directly that Maibon is amazed at the sight of the dwarf or that the dwarf is trying to make himself invisible. A good reader, however, **makes inferences** about what is happening. An inference is a logical guess based on evidence in the story and on what readers know from experience. As you read on, you may find additional information to confirm your inferences. In "The Stone," for example, you learn that the dwarf was, indeed, trying to disappear.

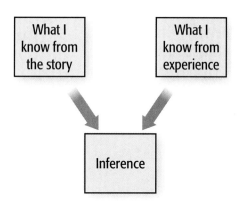

- For more about making inferences, see **Reading Handbook,** p. R82.

EXERCISE

Find two places in "The Stone" where you can make inferences about characters. Then answer these questions.

1. What details did the story provide that helped you make these inferences?

2. What information did you provide from your own experience?

3. Were these inferences confirmed by information as you continued reading?

Using Pronouns

A **pronoun** is a word that takes the place of one or more nouns. The noun that a pronoun refers to is called its **antecedent.** It must be clear exactly which antecedent a pronoun refers to, and the correct pronoun must be used.

PROBLEMS	SOLUTIONS
A pronoun that can refer to more than one antecedent 　While Maibon was helping Doli, he was very rude. 　[*He* could refer to *Maibon* or *Doli.*]	Rewrite the sentence so that it is clear to whom the pronoun refers. 　Doli was very rude, even though Maibon was helping him.
Object pronouns used as subjects of the sentence 　Maibon and him talked about magic stones.	In the subject part of a sentence, use a subject pronoun. 　Maibon and he talked about magic stones.
Subject pronouns used as objects of verbs or prepositions 　Maibon's wish caused problems for his wife and he.	Use an object pronoun as the object of a verb or preposition. 　Maibon's wish caused problems for his wife and him.

● For more about using pronouns, see **Language Handbook,** p. R27.

EXERCISES

1. Revise the sentences to make clear the antecedent of each pronoun.
   a. Doli asked Maibon if he was invisible.
   b. Maibon told Doli that he was ungrateful.
   c. When Maibon asked Doli for a magic stone, he thought it was a foolish wish.
   d. Several days after Doli gave Maibon the stone, he regretted it.
   e. The stone made the baby fuss, so Maibon decided to get rid of it.

2. Write the correct pronoun for each sentence.
   a. Both Rico and (I, me) read "The Stone."
   b. The story made sense to both (he, him) and (I, me).
   c. "You and (I, me) can learn from this," Rico said.
   d. I agreed that people have to accept changes that happen to (they, them).
   e. "Life without growth is impossible for (we, us) and for all creatures," I said.

Before You Read

April Rain Song and *in Just—*

It was during a lonely period in his childhood, Langston Hughes said, that "books began to happen to me, and I began to believe in nothing but books and the wonderful world in books."

Langston Hughes was born in 1902 and died in 1967. This poem was published in 1932.

MEET
E. E. CUMMINGS

Writing poems that surprise by their unusual punctuation, capitalization, and arrangement made E. E. Cummings one of the best known poets of his time. He believed that breaking accepted rules of composition helped him to express his ideas in a more original way.

E. E. Cummings was born in 1894 and died in 1962. "in Just—" was published in 1923.

FOCUS ACTIVITY

Do you like rain? How do you react when you hear that showers are forecast? Does the weather affect your mood?

FreeWrite
Write your impressions of rain. How do you feel when you hear it? How does rain feel? How does it look, taste, and smell?

Setting a Purpose
Read the poems to see how important weather can be.

BACKGROUND

Langston Hughes has been called the poet laureate of Harlem. He often wrote about people and life in Harlem, a section of New York City.

In his autobiography, *The Big Sea,* Langston Hughes explained how he wrote poetry: "There are seldom many changes in my poems once they're down [on paper]. Generally, the first two or three lines come to me from something I'm thinking about, or looking at, or doing, and the rest of the poem . . . flows from those first few lines, usually right away. If there is a chance to put the poem down then, I write it down. If not, I try to remember it until I get to a pencil and paper; for poems are like rainbows: They escape you quickly."

Black Girls Walking in a Sunny Shower, Washington, 1979. David Alan Redpath Michie. Oil on board. 44.4 x 42 cm. Robert Fleming Holdings Limited, London.

April Rain Song

Langston Hughes

Let the rain kiss you.
Let the rain beat upon your head with silver liquid drops.
Let the rain sing you a lullaby.

The rain makes still pools on the sidewalk.
The rain makes running pools in the gutter.
The rain plays a little sleep-song on our roof at night—

And I love the rain.

in Just—

E. E. Cummings

in Just-
spring   when the world is mud-
luscious° the little
lame balloonman

5   whistles   far   and wee°

and eddieandbill come
running from marbles and
piracies° and it's
spring

10   when the world is puddle-wonderful

the queer
old balloonman whistles
far   and   wee
and bettyandisbel come dancing

15   from hop-scotch and jump-rope and

it's
spring
and
        the

20   goat-footed°

balloonMan   whistles
far
and
wee

---

3 Something that's *luscious* is delightful to the senses.
5 *Wee* means "very small."
8 Eddie and Bill have been playing at being pirates.
20 One of the gods in Greek myths was Pan, who played an instrument called a panpipe. He had a man's body down to the waist, but his lower body and legs were a goat's. He was associated with forests, fields, and nature in general.

Responding to Literature

PERSONAL RESPONSE

- ◆ Which poem do you like best? Why?
- ◆ Look at your own writing about rain from the **Focus Activity,** on page 324. Do you see rain in the same way as it is described in "April Rain Song"?

Analyzing Literature

RECALL

1. What three things should we let rain do, according to "April Rain Song"?
2. In "in Just—" what games have the children been playing?

INTERPRET

3. What is the difference in the way rain is shown in the first and second stanzas of "April Rain Song"?
4. Why are the children's names run together in "in Just—"?

EVALUATE AND CONNECT

5. In "April Rain Song," rain is a "lullaby" and plays a "sleep-song." Does rain sometimes have the same effect on you?
6. The speaker expresses feelings about rain in the last line of "April Rain Song." What might you say in such a line to express your feelings about rain?
7. How do you picture the balloonman in "in Just—"?
8. From whose point of view is spring described in "in Just—": from a child's or an adult's? How do you know?
9. What season is it in these poems? What do the poets make you feel or remember?
10. Theme Connection What do you think the speaker of each poem values? Why?

Pan of Rohallion, 1894. Frederick William MacMonnies.

LITERARY ELEMENTS

Personification

"Let the rain kiss you," says the speaker in "April Rain Song." Notice that rain is personified, or given a human ability—to kiss. **Personification** is a figure of speech in which an animal, object, or idea is given human form or characteristics. The poet creates a feeling of safety and security by suggesting that the rain can give a gentle kiss, as a parent would.

1. Find another example of personification in "April Rain Song."
2. How does the personification affect how you think about the rain?

● See **Literary Terms Handbook,** p. R6.

Extending Your Response

Writing About Literature

Repetition In these poems, Langston Hughes and E. E. Cummings use repetition. Find an example of repetition in one of the poems. Write a paragraph telling what is repeated and what the repetition adds to the poem.

Literature Groups

Poetry Critics Here is what critic Harriet Monroe said about E. E. Cummings's poetry:

> Mr. Cummings has an eccentric system of typography which, in our opinion, has nothing to do with the poem, but intrudes itself irritatingly, like scratched or blurred spectacles, between it and the reader's mind.

By *typography* Monroe means the way words appear on the page. Find examples of strange typography in "in Just—." Then discuss Monroe's comment and decide whether you agree.

Creative Writing

Word Games E. E. Cummings creates two new words in "in Just—" by combining a noun with an adjective: *mud-luscious* and *puddle-wonderful.* These words help him describe spring in a fresh way. Create a few new words of your own to describe a favorite season. Use your new words in a short paragraph.

Art Activity

Words for Games Think of a favorite game or activity. Draw a simple sketch of it, or of part of it, such as a basketball hoop. Then write words along the outline of your sketch that describe your feelings about playing the game or doing the activity. You might want to arrange your words into a shape poem, as described on page 251.

📖 **Save your work for your portfolio.**

Skill Minilesson

GRAMMAR AND LANGUAGE • PARTS OF A SENTENCE

The way E. E. Cummings arranges the words in "in Just—" makes the poem look difficult to understand. Writing the poem out in ordinary sentences and adding punctuation where it belongs may help you make sense of the poem.

- Put a capital letter at the beginning of each sentence, and a period at the end.
- Look for the subjects and predicates in each sentence. (Poems can contain fragments as well.)
- Reread what you have written to see if the meaning of the poem is clearer.

PRACTICE Write the following parts of the poem as sentences. Underline the subject of each sentence.

1. the little lame balloonman whistles far and wee
2. eddieandbill come running from marbles and piracies
3. the world is puddle-wonderful
4. bettyandisbel come dancing from hop-scotch and jump-rope
5. it's spring

● For more about sentences, see **Language Handbook,** pp. R27–R28.

MEDIA Connection

MAGAZINE ARTICLE

Leonardo da Vinci, the artist who painted the *Mona Lisa,* is famous for his inventions as well as for his paintings.

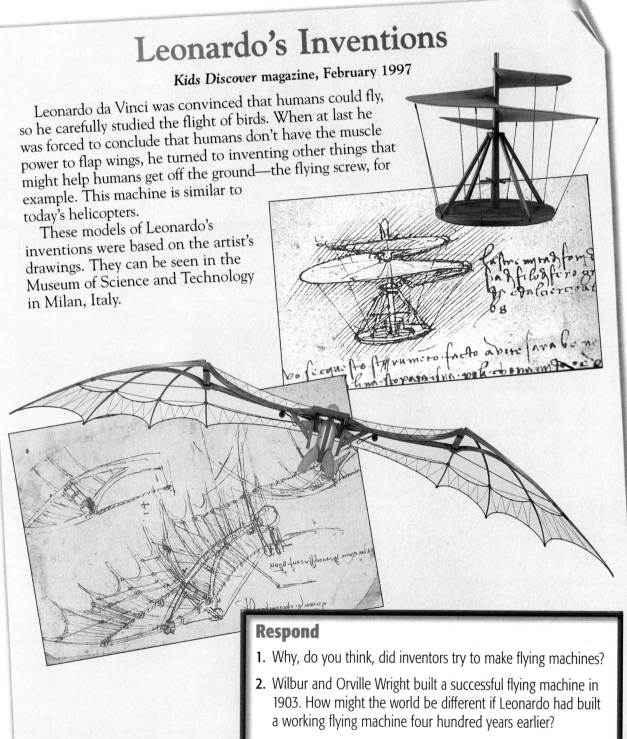

Leonardo's Inventions

Kids Discover magazine, February 1997

Leonardo da Vinci was convinced that humans could fly, so he carefully studied the flight of birds. When at last he was forced to conclude that humans don't have the muscle power to flap wings, he turned to inventing other things that might help humans get off the ground—the flying screw, for example. This machine is similar to today's helicopters.

These models of Leonardo's inventions were based on the artist's drawings. They can be seen in the Museum of Science and Technology in Milan, Italy.

Respond

1. Why, do you think, did inventors try to make flying machines?

2. Wilbur and Orville Wright built a successful flying machine in 1903. How might the world be different if Leonardo had built a working flying machine four hundred years earlier?

Before You Read

Wings

MEET JANE YOLEN

Jane Yolen enjoys telling old stories that highlight modern problems. "I think the worst thing in the world is the child who grows up without any connection to folk tradition," she says. "This is our connection with our history, and with human mystery too. These are the stories that carry the morality of generations." Yolen has written almost two hundred books, including nonfiction and poetry, but is known especially for her original fairy tales. She also heads Jane Yolen Books, which publishes science fiction and fantasy for young people.

Jane Yolen was born in 1939. This story was published in 1991.

FOCUS ACTIVITY

Think of different meanings for the words *proud* and *pride*. How can pride be both good and bad?

Journal
In your journal, write an example of a situation when pride is encouraged and respected. Then write an example of a situation when pride could create problems. Share your ideas with the class.

Setting a Purpose
Read "Wings" to see how an old story teaches a lesson.

BACKGROUND

The Time and Place
The story begins in ancient Greece, and then moves to Crete and Sicily. Daedalus is believed to have been a real person.

VOCABULARY PREVIEW

consequence (kon′ sə kwens′) *n.* the result of an earlier action or condition; effect; p. 332

exile (eg′ zīl) *n.* one who is forced to leave his or her home, community, or country; p. 332

devise (di vīz′) *v.* to think out; invent; plan; p. 333

devour (di vour′) *v.* to eat up greedily; p. 334

bemoan (bi mōn′) *v.* to express grief; cry out; p. 335

realm (relm) *n.* a kingdom; any area of knowledge, power, or control; p. 337

singe (sinj) *n.* a burning or scorching, especially at the tip or edge; p. 337

lure (loor) *n.* a powerful attraction that is hard to resist; temptation; p. 337

Wings

Jane Yolen

Once in ancient Greece, when the gods dwelt[1] on a high mountain overseeing the world, there lived a man named Daedalus[2] who was known for the things he made.

He invented the axe, the bevel, and the awl.[3] He built statues that were so lifelike they seemed ready to move. He designed a maze[4] whose winding passages opened one into another as if without beginning, as if without end.

---

1. In Greek myths, the gods lived *(dwelt)* on Mount Olympus.
2. *Daedalus* (ded′ əl əs)
3. The *bevel* is a tool for measuring and marking angles. The pointed *awl* is used to make small holes or designs in materials.
4. In Daedalus's *maze,* footpaths were separated by high walls that made it difficult for a person to find the way out.

331

Did You Know?
A maze is also called a
labyrinth (lab′ ə rinth′).

But Daedalus never understood the labyrinth of his own heart. He was clever but he was not always kind. He was full of pride but he did not give others praise. He was a maker—but he was a taker, too.

The gods always punish such a man.

Athens[5] was the queen of cities and she had her princes. Daedalus was one. He was a prince and he was an artist, and he was proud of being both.

The very elements[6] were his friends, and the people of Athens praised him.

"The gods will love you forever, Daedalus," they cried out to him as he walked through the city streets.

The gods listened and did not like to be told what to do.

A man who hears only praise becomes deaf. A man who sees no rival to his art becomes blind. Though he grew rich and he grew famous in the city, Daedalus also grew lazy and careless. And one day, without thought for the consequences, he caused the death of his young nephew, Prince Talos, who fell from a tall temple.

Even a prince cannot kill a prince. The king of Athens punished Daedalus by sending him away, away from all he loved: away from the colorful pillars of the temples, away from the noisy, winding streets, away from the bustling shops and stalls, away from his smithy,[7] away from the sound of the dark sea. He would never be allowed to return.

And the gods watched the exile from on high.

Many days and nights Daedalus fled from his past. He crossed strange lands. He crossed strange seas. All he carried with him was a goatskin flask, the clothes on his back, and the knowledge in his hands. All he carried with him was grief that he had caused a child's death and grief that Athens was now dead to him.

He traveled a year and a day until he came at last to the island of Crete, where the powerful King Minos ruled.

The sands of Crete were different from his beloved Athens, the trees in the meadow were different, the flowers and the houses and the little, dark-eyed people were different. Only the birds seemed the same to Daedalus, and the sky—the vast, open, empty road of the sky.

But the gods found nothing below them strange.

---

5. *Athens* was one of the greatest city-states of ancient Greece.
6. The ancient Greeks thought that fire, water, air, and earth were the *elements,* or basic materials, from which everything was made.

7. Here, *smithy* means "workshop."

Vocabulary
consequence (kon′ sə kwens′) *n.* the result of an earlier action or condition; effect
exile (eg′ zīl) *n.* one who is forced to leave his or her home, community, or country

Daedalus knew nothing of Crete but Crete knew much of Daedalus, for his reputation had flown on wings before him. King Minos did not care that Daedalus was an exile or that he had been judged guilty of a terrible crime.

"You are the world's greatest builder, Daedalus," King Minos said. "Build me a labyrinth in which to hide a beast."

"A cage would be simpler," said Daedalus.

"This is no ordinary beast," said the king. "This is a monster. This is a prince. His name is Minotaur[8] and he is my wife's own son. He has a bull's head but a man's body. He eats human flesh. I cannot kill the queen's child. Even a king cannot kill a prince. And I cannot put him in a cage. But in a maze such as you might build, I could keep him hidden forever."

Daedalus bowed his head, but he smiled at the king's praise. He built a labyrinth for the king with countless corridors and winding ways. He devised such cunning passages that only he knew the secret pathway to its heart—he, and the Minotaur who lived there.

Yet the gods marked the secret way as well.

For many years Daedalus lived on the island of Crete, delighting in the praise he received from king and court. He made hundreds of new things for them. He made dolls with moving parts and a dancing floor inlaid with wood and stone for the princess Ariadne.[9] He made iron gates for the king and queen wrought[10] with cunning designs. He grew fond of the little dark-eyed islanders, and he married a Cretan[11] wife. A son was born to them whom Daedalus named Icarus.[12] The boy was small like his mother but he had his father's quick, bright ways.

Daedalus taught Icarus many things, yet the one Daedalus valued most was the language of his lost Athens. Though he had a grand house and servants to do his bidding, though he had a wife he loved and a son he adored, Daedalus was not entirely happy. His heart still lay in Athens, the land of his youth, and the words he spoke with his son helped keep the memory of Athens alive.

One night a handsome young man came to Daedalus' house, led by a lovesick Princess Ariadne. The young man spoke with Daedalus in that Athenian tongue.

"I am Theseus,[13] a prince of Athens, where your name is still remembered with praise. It is said that Daedalus was more than a prince, that he had the gods in his hands. Surely such a man has not forgotten Athens."

Daedalus shook his head. "I thought Athens had forgotten me."

"Athens remembers and Athens needs your help, O prince," said Theseus.

"Help? What help can I give Athens, when I am so far from home?"

---

8. *Minotaur* (min′ ə tôr′)

9. *Ariadne* (ar′ ē ad′ nē)
10. *Wrought* means "formed or decorated with care."
11. *Cretan* refers to people or things from Crete.
12. *Icarus* (ik′ ər əs)
13. *Theseus* (thē′ sē əs)

Vocabulary
devise (di vīz′) *v.* to think out; invent; plan

"Then you do not know . . . ," Theseus began.

"Know what?"

"That every seven years Athens must send a tribute[14] of boys and girls to King Minos. He puts them into the labyrinth you devised and the monster Minotaur devours them there."

Horrified, Daedalus thought of the bright-eyed boys and girls he had known in Athens. He thought of his own dark-eyed son asleep in his cot. He remembered his nephew, Talos, whose eyes had been closed by death. "How can I help?"

"Only you know the way through the maze," said Theseus. "Show me the way that I may slay the monster."

"I will show you," said Daedalus thoughtfully, "but Princess Ariadne must go as well. The Minotaur is her half-brother. He will not hurt her. She will be able to lead you to him, right into the heart of the maze."

The gods listened to the plan and nodded gravely.

Daedalus drew them a map and gave Princess Ariadne a thread to tie at her waist, that she might unwind it as they went and so find the way back out of the twisting corridors.

Hand in hand, Theseus and Ariadne left and Daedalus went into his son's room. He looked down at the sleeping boy.

"I am a prince of Athens," he whispered. "I did what must be done."

If Icarus heard his father's voice, he did not stir. He was dreaming still as Ariadne and Theseus threaded their way to the very center of the maze. And before he awakened, they had killed the Minotaur and fled from Crete, taking the boys and girls of Athens with them. They took all hope of Daedalus' safety as well.

Then the gods looked thoughtful and they did not smile.

When King Minos heard that the Minotaur had been slain and Ariadne taken, he guessed that Daedalus had betrayed him, for no one else knew the secret of the maze. He ordered Daedalus thrown into a high prison tower.

"Thus do kings reward traitors!" cried Minos. Then he added, "See that you care for your own son better than you cared for my wife's unfortunate child." He threw Icarus into the tower, too, and slammed the great iron gate shut with his own hand.

The tiny tower room, with its single window overlooking the sea, was Daedalus' home now. Gone was Athens where he had been a prince, gone was Crete where he had been a rich man. All he had left was one small room, with a wooden bench and straw pallets[15] on the floor.

Day after day young Icarus stood on the bench and watched through the

---

14. *Tribute* is a payment that one nation is forced to pay to a more powerful nation.

15. A *pallet* is a crude bed or mattress.

Vocabulary
devour (di vour´) *v.* to eat up greedily

334

window as the seabirds dipped and soared over the waves.

"Father!" Icarus called each day. "Come and watch the birds."

But Daedalus would not. Day after day, he leaned against the wall or lay on a pallet bemoaning his fate and cursing the gods who had done this thing to him.

The gods heard his curses and they grew angry.

One bright day Icarus took his father by the hand, leading him to the window.

"Look, Father," he said, pointing to the birds. "See how beautiful their wings are. See how easily they fly."

Just to please the boy, Daedalus looked. Then he clapped his hands to his eyes. "What a fool I have been," he whispered. "What a fool. Minos may have forbidden me sea and land, but he has left me the air. Oh, my son, though the king is ever so great and powerful, he does not rule the sky. It is the gods' own road and I am a favorite of the gods. To think a child has shown me the way!"

Every day after that, Daedalus and Icarus coaxed the birds to their window with bread crumbs saved from their meager meals. And every day gulls, gannets, and petrels, cormorants and pelicans, shearwaters and grebes,[16] came to the sill. Daedalus stroked the feeding birds with his clever hands and harvested handfuls of feathers. And Icarus, as if playing a game, grouped the feathers on the floor in order of size, just as his father instructed.

But it was no game. Soon the small piles of feathers became big piles, the big piles, great heaps. Then clever Daedalus, using a needle he had shaped from a bit of bone left over from dinner and thread pulled out of his own shirt, sewed together small feathers, overlapping them with the larger, gently curving them in great arcs. He fastened the ends with molded candle wax and made straps with the leather from their sandals.

At last Icarus understood. "Wings, Father!" he cried, clapping his hands together in delight. "Wings!"

At that the gods laughed, and it was thunder over water.

They made four wings in all, a pair for each of them. Icarus had the smaller pair, for he was still a boy. They practiced for days in the tower, slipping their arms through the straps, raising and lowering the wings, until their arms had grown strong and used to the weight. They hid the wings beneath their pallets whenever the guards came by.

At last they were ready. Daedalus kneeled before his son.

"Your arms are strong now, Icarus," he said, "but do not forget my warning."

The boy nodded solemnly, his dark eyes wide. "I must not fly too low or the water will soak the feathers. I must not fly too high or the sun will melt the wax."

---

16. [gulls . . . grebes] These are all sea birds.

Vocabulary
bemoan (bi mōn´) v. to express grief; cry out

"Remember," his father said. "Remember."

The gods trembled, causing birds to fall through the bright air.

Daedalus climbed onto the sill. The wings made him clumsy but he did not fall. He helped Icarus up.

First the child, then the man, leaped out into the air. They pumped once and then twice with their arms. The wind caught the feathers of the wings and pushed them upward into the Cretan sky.

Wingtip to wingtip they flew, writing the lines of their escape on the air. Some watchers below took them for eagles. Most took them for gods.

As they flew, Daedalus concentrated on long, steady strokes. He remembered earlier days, when the elements had been his friends: fire and water and air. Now, it seemed, they were his friends once more.

But young Icarus had no such memories to steady his wings. He beat them with abandon, glorying in his freedom. He slipped away from his father's careful pattern along a wild stream of wind.

"Icarus, my son—remember!" Daedalus cried out.

But Icarus spiraled[17] higher and higher and higher still. He did not hear his father's voice. He heard only the music of the wind; he heard only the sighing of the gods.

_____

17. A *spiral* is a curve that moves in a circle away from or closer to a fixed, central point. To *spiral* is to move along this kind of curve.

The Fall of Icarus. Abraham Rattner (1895–1978). Private collection.
Viewing the painting: How does this painting make you feel about Icarus's flight?

He passed the birds. He passed the clouds. He passed into the realm of the sun. Too late he felt the wax run down his arms; too late he smelled the singe of feathers. Surprised, he hung solid in the air. Then, like a star in nova,[18] he tumbled from the sky, down, down, down into the waiting sea.

And the gods wept bitterly for the child.

"Where are you, my son?" Daedalus called. He circled the water, looking desperately for some sign. All he saw were seven feathers afloat on the sea, spinning into different patterns with each passing wave.

Weeping, he flew away over the dark sea to the isle of Sicily. There he built a temple to the god Apollo,[19] for Apollo stood for life and light and never grew old but remained a beautiful boy forever. On the temple walls Daedalus hung up his beautiful wings as an offering to the bitter wisdom of the gods.

So Daedalus' story ended—and yet it did not. For in Sicily he was received kindly by King Cocalus,[20] who was well pleased with his skills.

Meanwhile, back in Crete, enraged at his prisoners' escape, King Minos was determined to find and punish them. He proclaimed a great reward for anyone skilled enough to pass a silken thread through the closed spiral of a seashell. He knew that if Daedalus was alive, he could not resist the lure of such a game.

Daedalus was sure he could easily solve the puzzle. He bored a small hole in one end of a shell, moistened it with a bit of honey, then closed up the hole. Fastening a thread to an ant, he put the insect into the shell. The ant scurried through the twisting labyrinth toward the sweet smell, running as easily as Princess Ariadne had run through the maze with the thread unwinding at her waist. When the ant emerged from the other end, it had pulled the silken thread through the spirals of the shell.

Though he used a false name to claim the prize, Daedalus did not fool King Minos. Minos knew the winner was his old enemy. So, with a mighty army, Minos sailed to Sicily to bring Daedalus back.

But King Cocalus would not give up Daedalus to the foreign invaders, and a great battle was fought. With Daedalus' help, King Cocalus was victorious and King Minos was killed. Minos was clever but he was not kind. He had a heart scabbed over with old remembered wounds.

The gods always punish such a man.

---

18. A *nova* is a star that suddenly increases in brightness and then, over weeks or years, fades back to the way it was.
19. The sun god *Apollo* was also the god of light, truth, healing, manly beauty, music, and poetry.
20. *Cocalus* (kō′ kə ləs)

Vocabulary
realm (relm) *n.* a kingdom; any area of knowledge, power, or control
singe (sinj) *n.* a burning or scorching, especially at the tip or edge
lure (loor) *n.* a powerful attraction that is hard to resist; temptation

Responding to Literature

PERSONAL RESPONSE

- ◆ Are you surprised by the ending?
- ◆ What problems does pride cause for Daedalus? How would you define his kind of pride? Check your notes from the **Focus Activity** on page 330.

Analyzing Literature

RECALL

1. Why is Daedalus famous?
2. Why does Daedalus go to Crete? What does he do there?
3. What does Daedalus do that makes King Minos angry? How does King Minos respond?
4. What does Daedalus invent in prison? Why?

INTERPRET

5. What personality traits of Daedalus lead to his being sent away from Greece and to many of his other problems? Give examples from the story to support your answer.
6. Throughout the story, in what ways does King Minos show that he thinks Daedalus is clever?
7. Why does Daedalus agree to help Theseus?
8. Why does Daedalus hang his wings in a temple he built to honor Apollo?

EVALUATE AND CONNECT

9. If you were Icarus, what would you have done after you had leaped from the prison tower?
10. Why, do you think, does the author include the reactions of the gods? How do these affect you as you read the story?

LITERARY ELEMENTS

Myth and Legend

A **myth** is an ancient, anonymous story that explains how something came to be as it is. It usually involves gods and goddesses. A **legend** is a story that may have some basis in history. Both kinds of stories were thought to be true by many of the people who told them. Myths and legends convey the beliefs and ideals of a culture and often provide examples of how humans should behave. These stories were told and retold, and thus handed down from generation to generation.

1. In "Wings," how do you know what the gods think?

2. Do the gods intervene during the course of the story? Support your response.

3. What do you think ancient people learned about how to behave from this story?

● See **Literary Terms Handbook**, p. R5.

Extending Your Response

Writing About Literature

Foreshadowing   **Foreshadowing** is hinting about what will happen later in a story. How do readers know that something terrible may happen to Daedalus and Icarus? Find clues in the story. Write a paragraph explaining how the author foreshadows what is going to happen.

Personal Writing

Who I Am Like . . .   Are you like Icarus? Do you understand what he felt as he flew? Do you understand why he acted as he did? Or are you more like Daedalus, the great builder and inventor who was filled with imagination? Compare yourself to one of these characters in your journal.

Literature Groups

Amazing Secrets   When Daedalus gave away the secrets of the maze, was he brave or foolish? Talk about the consequences both for the people of Athens and for Daedalus and his family. What motivated Daedalus? Did he act out of self-interest or self-sacrifice? Did he know the penalty he would face?

Interdisciplinary Activity

Math   With a small group, create on paper a maze worthy of concealing the Minotaur. You might want to make individual mazes and then interweave them into a master maze. It might be helpful to plan and lay out your maze by using yarn or craft sticks. Invite another group to solve your maze.

Save your work for your portfolio.

Skill Minilesson

VOCABULARY • PRONUNCIATION

A dictionary pronunciation for the word *singe* looks like this: sinj. The word has been respelled to show how it should be pronounced. When *g* has a "soft" sound, it is respelled as a *j*, because a soft *g* has the same sound that *j* has. The pronunciation for *gate* looks like this: gāt. This shows that the *g* has a "hard" *g* sound and the *a* has a long *a* sound.

Another consonant that can be pronounced in various ways is *c*. Dictionary pronunciations never use *c*. They substitute *s* or *k*, because the letter *c* is almost always pronounced like either *s* or *k*.

PRACTICE   Use the pronunciation chart to figure out the answers to the questions.

SYMBOLS	SOUND
g	g as in **game, ago, fog**
j	j as in **joke**, g as in **gem**, dge as in **bridge**
k	k as in **kit**, ck as in **tack**, c as in cat
s	s as in **sat**, c as in **cent**, ss as in **pass**

1. (kāj): Is this word *keg, cage,* or *catch?*
2. (pās): Is this word *pace, pack,* or *pass?*
3. (pēs): Is this word *peek, peas,* or *peace?*
4. (ej): Is this word *egg, each,* or *edge?*
5. (rāj): Is this word *rage, rag,* or *ridge?*

Before You Read

The Flying Machine

MEET
RAY BRADBURY

I'm a . . . teller of cautionary tales," Ray Bradbury says, "someone who looks at the machines we have now and says if this is true, ten years from now that will be true, and thirty years from now the other thing will be true. I've had a lot of fun growing up in this age." Bradbury is one of the world's best-known science fiction writers. He has written novels; scripts for radio, television, and movies; poetry; and more than four hundred short stories.

Ray Bradbury was born in 1920. This story was first published in 1953.

FOCUS ACTIVITY

What kinds of music boxes have you seen? Did any include a figure that danced or moved? What music played? How did the music boxes work? What else did you notice about them?

Share
Share your experiences with your classmates.

Setting a Purpose
Read "The Flying Machine" to enjoy a fantasy set in ancient China.

BACKGROUND

Did You Know? About 214 B.C., Emperor Shih Huang Ti, the first emperor of a united China, connected a number of defensive walls to form a "Great Wall" that would protect his empire from invasion by fierce Mongol horsemen. To accomplish this project, he had his army round up 700,000 people and force them to work. The resulting wall stood about thirty feet high and twenty feet wide and extended about 1,700 miles. Additions and improvements were made by other emperors as late as A.D. 1644. Today the Great Wall of China extends 3,750 miles.

VOCABULARY PREVIEW

dominion (də min′ yən) *n.* the territory or country under the authority of a particular ruler or government; p. 341
writhe (rīth) *v.* to move with a twisting motion; p. 342
horde (hôrd) *n.* a large group; crowd; p. 342
apparatus (ap′ ə rat′ əs) *n.* something created or invented for a particular purpose; p. 343
serene (sə rēn′) *adj.* calm; peaceful; undisturbed; p. 344
solace (sol′ is) *n.* relief from sorrow; comfort; p. 345

The Flying Machine

Ray Bradbury ∿

Quang Hsing, Manchu Dynasty. Artist unknown. Metropolitan Museum of Art, New York.

*I*n the year A.D. 400, the Emperor Yuan held his throne by the Great Wall of China, and the land was green with rain, readying itself toward the harvest, at peace, the people in his <u>dominion</u> neither too happy nor too sad.

Early on the morning of the first day of the first week of the second month of the new year, the Emperor Yuan was sipping tea and fanning himself against a warm breeze when a servant ran across the scarlet and blue garden tiles, calling, "Oh, Emperor, Emperor, a miracle!"

Vocabulary

dominion (də min′ yən) *n.* the territory or country under the authority of a particular ruler or government

"Yes," said the Emperor, "the air *is* sweet this morning."

"No, no, a miracle!" said the servant, bowing quickly.

"And this tea is good in my mouth, surely that is a miracle."

"No, no, Your Excellency."

"Let me guess then—the sun has risen and a new day is upon us. Or the sea is blue. *That* now is the finest of all miracles."

"Excellency, a man is flying!"

"What?" The Emperor stopped his fan.

"I saw him in the air, a man flying with wings. I heard a voice call out of the sky, and when I looked up, there he was, a dragon in the heavens with a man in its mouth, a dragon of paper and bamboo, colored like the sun and the grass."

"It is early," said the Emperor, "and you have just wakened from a dream."

"It is early, but I have seen what I have seen! Come, and you will see it too."

"Sit down with me here," said the Emperor. "Drink some tea. It must be a strange thing, if it is true, to see a man fly. You must have time to think of it, even as I must have time to prepare myself for the sight."

They drank tea.

"Please," said the servant at last, "or he will be gone."

The Emperor rose thoughtfully. "Now you may show me what you have seen."

"Excellency, a man is flying!"

They walked into a garden, across a meadow of grass, over a small bridge, through a grove of trees, and up a tiny hill.

"There!" said the servant.

The Emperor looked into the sky.

And in the sky, laughing so high that you could hardly hear him laugh, was a man; and the man was clothed in bright papers and reeds to make wings and a beautiful yellow tail, and he was soaring all about like the largest bird in a universe of birds, like a new dragon in a land of ancient dragons.

The man called down to them from high in the cool winds of morning, "I fly, I fly!"

The servant waved to him. "Yes, yes!"

The Emperor Yuan did not move. Instead he looked at the Great Wall of China now taking shape out of the farthest mist in the green hills, that splendid snake of stones which writhed with majesty across the entire land. That wonderful wall which had protected them for a timeless time from enemy hordes and preserved peace for years without number. He saw the town, nestled to itself by a river and a road and a hill, beginning to waken.

"Tell me," he said to his servant, "has anyone else seen this flying man?"

"I am the only one, Excellency," said the servant, smiling at the sky, waving.

Vocabulary

writhe (rīth) *v.* to move with a twisting motion
horde (hôrd) *n.* a large group; crowd

The Emperor watched the heavens another minute and then said, "Call him down to me."

"Ho, come down, come down! The Emperor wishes to see you!" called the servant, hands cupped to his shouting mouth.

The Emperor glanced in all directions while the flying man soared down the morning wind. He saw a farmer, early in his fields, watching the sky, and he noted where the farmer stood.

The flying man alit[1] with a rustle of paper and a creak of bamboo reeds. He came proudly to the Emperor, clumsy in his rig, at last bowing before the old man.

"What have you done?" demanded the Emperor.

"I have flown in the sky, Your Excellency," replied the man.

"What *have* you done?" said the Emperor again.

"I have just told you!" cried the flier.

"You have told me nothing at all." The Emperor reached out a thin hand to touch the pretty paper and the birdlike keel of the <u>apparatus</u>. It smelled cool, of the wind.

"Is it not beautiful, Excellency?"

Did You Know?
On a boat or plane, the *keel* is the main timber or steel piece that runs lengthwise along the bottom and supports the rest of the frame.

"Yes, too beautiful."

"It is the only one in the world!" smiled the man. "And I am the inventor."

"The *only* one in the world?"

"I swear it!"

"Who else knows of this?"

"No one. Not even my wife, who would think me mad with the sun. She thought I was making a kite. I rose in the night and walked to the cliffs far away. And when the morning breezes blew and the sun rose, I gathered my courage, Excellency, and leaped from the cliff. I flew! But my wife does not know of it."

"Well for her, then," said the Emperor. "Come along."

They walked back to the great house. The sun was full in the sky now, and the smell of the grass was refreshing. The Emperor, the servant, and the flier paused within the huge garden.

The Emperor clapped his hands. "Ho, guards!"

The guards came running.

"Hold this man."

The guards seized the flier.

"Call the executioner,"[2] said the Emperor.

"What's this!" cried the flier, bewildered. "What have I done?" He began to weep, so that the beautiful paper apparatus rustled.

"Here is the man who has made a certain machine," said the Emperor, "and yet asks us what he has created. He does not know himself. It is only necessary that he

---

1. This is a past-tense form of *alight*, meaning "to land, step down, or get off."

2. An *executioner* is one who kills another according to an official death sentence.

Vocabulary
apparatus (ap′ ə rat′ əs) *n.* something created or invented for a particular purpose

create, without knowing why he has done so, or what this thing will do."

The executioner came running with a sharp silver ax. He stood with his naked, large-muscled arms ready, his face covered with a <u>serene</u> white mask.

"One moment," said the Emperor. He turned to a nearby table upon which sat a machine that he himself had created. The Emperor took a tiny golden key from his own neck. He fitted this key to the tiny, delicate machine and wound it up. Then he set the machine going.

The machine was a garden of metal and jewels. Set in motion, birds sang in tiny metal trees, wolves walked through miniature forests, and tiny people ran in and out of sun and shadow, fanning themselves with miniature fans, listening to the tiny emerald birds, and standing by impossibly small but tinkling fountains.

"Is *it* not beautiful?" said the Emperor. "If you asked me what I have done here, I could answer you well. I have made birds sing, I have made forests murmur, I have set people to walking in this woodland, enjoying the leaves and shadows and songs. That is what I have done."

"But, oh, Emperor!" pleaded the flier, on his knees, the tears pouring down his face. "I have done a similar thing! I have found beauty. I have flown on the morning wind. I have looked down on all the sleeping houses and gardens. I have smelled the sea and and even *seen* it, beyond the hills, from my high place. And I have soared like a bird; oh, I cannot say how beautiful it is up there, in the sky, with the wind about me, the wind blowing me here like a feather, there like a fan, the way the sky smells in the morning! And how free one feels! *That* is beautiful, Emperor, that is beautiful too!"

"Yes," said the Emperor sadly, "I know it must be true. For I felt my heart move with you in the air and I wondered: What is it like? How does it feel? How do the distant

Antique mechanical box. French vermeil, enamel, emeralds, sapphires, and opal.

Vocabulary
serene (sə rēn′) *adj.* calm; peaceful; undisturbed

pools look from so high? And how my houses and servants? Like ants? And how the distant towns not yet awake?"

"Then spare me!"

"But there are times," said the Emperor, more sadly still, "when one must lose a little beauty if one is to keep what little beauty one already has. I do not fear you, yourself, but I fear another man."

"What man?"

"Some other man who, seeing you, will build a thing of bright papers and bamboo like this. But the other man will have an evil face and an evil heart, and the beauty will be gone. It is this man I fear."

"Why? Why?"

"Who is to say that someday just such a man, in just such an apparatus of paper and reed, might not fly in the sky and drop huge stones upon the Great Wall of China?" said the Emperor.

No one moved or said a word.

"Off with his head," said the Emperor.

The executioner whirled his silver ax.

"Burn the kite and the inventor's body and bury their ashes together," said the Emperor.

The servants retreated to obey.

The Emperor turned to his handservant, who had seen the man flying. "Hold your tongue. It was all a dream, a

> ## "Off with his head," said the Emperor.

most sorrowful and beautiful dream. And that farmer in the distant field who also saw, tell him it would pay him to consider it only a vision. If ever the word passes around, you and the farmer die within the hour."

"You are merciful, Emperor."

"No, not merciful," said the old man. Beyond the garden wall he saw the guards burning the beautiful machine of paper and reeds that smelled of the morning wind. He saw the dark smoke climb into the sky. "No, only very much bewildered and afraid." He saw the guards digging a tiny pit wherein to bury the ashes. "What is the life of one man against those of a million others? I must take solace from that thought."

He took the key from its chain about his neck and once more wound up the beautiful miniature garden. He stood looking out across the land at the Great Wall, the peaceful town, the green fields, the rivers and streams. He sighed. The tiny garden whirred its hidden and delicate machinery and set itself in motion; tiny people walked in forests, tiny foxes loped through sunspeckled glades in beautiful shining pelts, and among the tiny trees flew little bits of high song and bright blue and yellow color, flying, flying, flying in that small sky.

"Oh," said the Emperor, closing his eyes, "look at the birds, look at the birds!"

Vocabulary
solace (sol′ is) *n.* relief from sorrow; comfort

Responding to Literature

PERSONAL RESPONSE

- ◆ Do you agree with the emperor's decision?
- ◆ Compare the mechanical box in the story with the ones described in the **Focus Activity** on page 340. How are they alike and different?

Analyzing Literature

RECALL AND INTERPRET

1. What two inventions are described? How are they different?
2. What does the emperor do with the inventor and his invention? Do you think these were easy decisions for him? Why?
3. How does the emperor's treatment of the inventor differ from his treatment of the two witnesses? Why is this?

EVALUATE AND CONNECT

4. Theme Connection   What would you have done if you were the emperor? Why?
5. Why, do you think, did Bradbury write this story?
6. Does this story remind you of any stories you have seen or read in the news? In what ways?

LITERARY ELEMENTS

Setting

Setting is the time and place of a story. Knowing the setting helps readers understand a story by "placing" the events—connecting them to other things they know about that time and that place. Sometimes authors give the time and place at the beginning of the story. At other times, the author tells the setting later or reveals it with clues throughout the story.

1. At what point in the story does Bradbury describe the setting?
2. How does knowing the setting help you understand the story?

● See **Literary Terms Handbook,** p. R8.

Extending Your Response

Literature Groups

Beyond Compare   Which invention did you like best, the flier's or the emperor's? Why? What does each invention show about the character who valued it? In the end, which character was more dangerous, the flier or the emperor? Defend your point of view.

Creative Writing

See What I See   Imagine that you are the inventor of the flying machine. Write a letter to your wife, telling her your impressions of flying. How does the Great Wall of China look? How about the homes and gardens and the sea? Use ideas from the story and your own imagination.

COMPARING SELECTIONS

Wings and The Flying Machine

COMPARE **CHARACTERS**

These stories have powerful rulers, as well as characters who experiment with flight.

1. What are the goals of the characters who want to fly in these stories?

2. Would you say that the inventor in "The Flying Machine" is more like Icarus or Daedalus? Use information in the stories to support your answer.

3. In what ways are the emperor and King Minos alike? Are both opposed to flight in general? Whom do you respect more? Why?

COMPARE **THEME**

Think about how the flights end up for Daedalus, Icarus, and the inventor. What do you think these characters would say that they learned from their experiences? Discuss the lessons they might have learned. In a group, write guidelines based on these lessons that might have protected one or more of the characters.

COMPARE **EXPERIENCES**

Remember how flight felt to Icarus and to the inventor? Think of a time when you felt excited. Was it because of something you did or made? Did it involve going on a scary ride or doing something that required courage?

- Find words that describe the feeling of flight in both stories.
- Share with a partner an experience of your own that gave you a feeling of joy and excitement.

Vo·cab·u·lar·y Skills

Understanding Homophones

Some words sound the same even though they are spelled differently and have different meanings. These words are called **homophones,** and they are handy for making up jokes called puns.

Question: Why were the Middle Ages also called the Dark Ages?

Answer: Because it was knight time.

Question: Should a pony wear a scarf around its throat?

Answer: Of course, since it's a little hoarse.

Some homophones are familiar. An ordinary jet is a *plain plane.* A sailor who looks at oceans *sees seas.* Others are not so familiar. In "The Flying Machine," the emperor worries about enemy *hordes* that might invade his country. A *horde* is a large group. If the emperor were worried about enemy *hoards,* his concern would be different. A *hoard* is something that's been stored up. So enemy *hordes* would be particularly dangerous if they had *hoards* of weapons.

Homophones may cause problems in writing. Even a computer spell-check can't correct *threw* instead of *through,* because *threw* is not misspelled.

EXERCISE

If the underlined word is the correct one to use, write *Correct.* If it is a homophone for the correct word, write the word that should have been used.

1. Above the trees and flours, enjoying the beauty and piece, a man flew on wings
   <u>1</u>   <u>2</u>   <u>3</u>

   he had maid himself. He herd someone call him and thought the emperor
   <u>4</u>   <u>5</u>

   wanted to meet him and here about flying, sew he came down. How could he
   <u>6</u>   <u>7</u>   <u>8</u>

   have guest what the emperor would do?
   <u>9</u>   <u>10</u>

2. Daedalus was used to hearing prays from the people of Athens. Then, one day,
   <u>1</u>   <u>2</u>

   his nephew dyed because Daedalus was careless. Daedalus was cent away, forced
   <u>3</u>   <u>4</u>

   to flee, and was not aloud to return home. Still, he loved Athens, and he
   <u>5</u>   <u>6</u>

   remembered the passed. When he got the chance to help Athens, he did,
   <u>7</u>

   although he new that he and his son might suffer four it.
   <u>8</u>   <u>9</u>   <u>10</u>

King Minos and Art on the Palace Walls

Crete, an island in the Mediterranean and Aegean seas, was home to a thriving culture from around 3000 B.C. to 1200 B.C. This culture is called the Minoan civilization, after the legendary King Minos. After about 1400 B.C., it steadily declined. Fires—perhaps set by plundering invaders—left many Minoan settlements in ruins. These lay buried and all but forgotten until the 1900s, when scholars began unearthing palaces decorated with delicate, lively frescoes—paintings made on plaster walls.

Dolphin fresco from the apartment of the queen. Knossos, Crete.

Many Minoan frescoes show scenes of animals or plants framed by geometrical patterns. Some are filled with leaping fish, octopuses, and other sea life. On others, a lion walks regally and monkeys chase each other through reeds. Paintings of human figures commonly show them from the side—men in brown and women in white. Red was a popular background color.

A number of frescoes featured bulls, recalling the legend of the Minotaur. Bulls probably held religious meaning for the people of ancient Crete. One fresco shows the sport of bull-leaping. In this sport, young acrobats vaulted over the backs of charging bulls.

ACTIVITY

Create a painting that resembles a Cretan fresco. Paint a long mural on bulletin board paper. You might show how you imagine bull-leaping. Decorate the borders of your "fresco" with geometrical patterns.

SHORT STORY

If you are reading a short piece of fiction, you are probably reading a short story. The short story form has roots in the fables and folktales that people have told since before recorded time. However, the short story as we know it is only about 150 years old.

Most fiction includes the same five literary elements. These pages discuss the five elements in a children's story you probably know: "Goldilocks and the Three Bears."

Goldilocks is hungry, tired, and lost in the woods. The three bears leave their cottage to go for a walk while their porridge cools.

1 **EXPOSITION** is background information about characters and setting. It sets the scene for the conflict.

SHORT STORY ELEMENTS	**MODEL:** "Goldilocks and the Three Bears"
SETTING is the time and place of the story's action. Setting can also include customs, values, and beliefs of a place or an era.	The setting of the story is an imaginary forest long ago.
CHARACTERS are the actors in the story. They can be people, animals, robots, or whatever the writer chooses. The main character is called the **protagonist.**	The characters are the mother bear, the father bear, the baby bear, and Goldilocks. Goldilocks is the protagonist, because she carries out the main action.

Most plots develop in five stages.

3 CLIMAX is the point of highest interest, conflict, or suspense in the story.

The bears find Goldilocks asleep in the baby bear's bed.

4 FALLING ACTION shows what happens to the characters after the climax.

The bears' shouting wakes Goldilocks, and she runs out of the cottage.

Goldilocks takes a nap in one of the beds.

Goldilocks sees the cottage and knocks on the door. No one is home, so she walks in.

The three bears return to their cottage. They notice the eaten porridge and broken chair.

Goldilocks escapes from the three bears unharmed.

Goldilocks eats the porridge and sits in the chairs, breaking one.

2 RISING ACTION develops the conflict.

5 RESOLUTION shows how the conflict is resolved or the problem solved.

POINT OF VIEW is the vantage point from which a story is told. The person telling the story is the **narrator**. In **first-person point of view**, the narrator is a character in the story. In **third-person point of view**, the narrator is outside the story.

"Goldilocks and the Three Bears" is told from the third-person point of view, by a narrator outside the story.

THEME is the main message that the reader can take from the story. A theme may be stated directly in the story or in its title. However, most stories have **implied** themes, suggested by what the characters learn or by what their experiences illustrate. Readers' ideas about implied themes may vary.

The theme of "Goldilocks and the Three Bears" is implied. A reader might find this theme: It's important to respect others' property.

PLOT is the basic structure of the story. It is a series of related events in which a problem is explored and then solved. Plot is created through **conflict**—a struggle between people, between ideas, or between other forces.

The conflict is between Goldilocks and the three bears. The diagram on these pages shows how the plot develops.

Active Reading Strategies

Tips for Reading a Short Story

As you have learned, effective readers are active readers. They interact with the text as they read. They have conversations with themselves about points in the story. Use the strategies below to help you read the short stories in this theme.

● For more about these and other reading strategies, see **Reading Handbook,** pp. R63–R94.

PREDICT

Predicting what will come next helps you stay alert for details you might otherwise miss. Combine clues in the text with what you already know to make educated guesses about what will come next.

Ask Yourself . . .

● How do I think this character is going to act?

● Do I have a good idea about what will happen next?

● Do I see where the action in this story is leading?

QUESTION

Questioning helps you clarify your understanding of the text as you go along.

Ask Yourself . . .

● Do I understand what I just read?

● Does what happened make sense to me?

● Do I understand how each character is acting?

● Do the actions and words of the characters match?

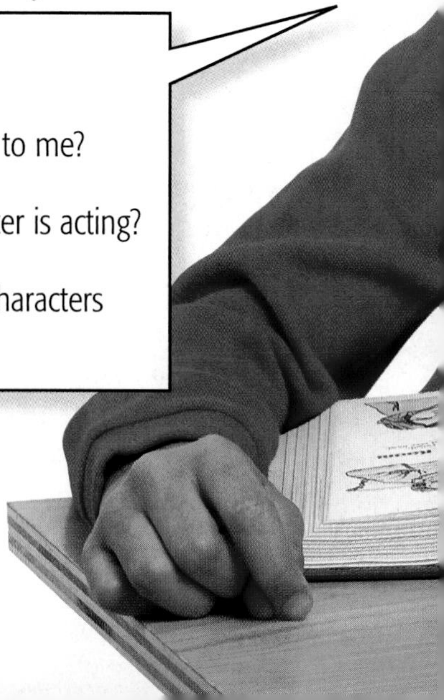

VISUALIZE

Form pictures in your mind. Pay attention to the details the writer gives you, and combine them with your own experiences to visualize the scene.

RESPOND

Respond during and after reading. Think about what the story means to you. Notice the emotions you feel as you read.

Ask Yourself . . .

- How do I picture this scene?

- Which details do I focus on?

- What else do I understand about the story or characters from picturing this scene?

Ask Yourself . . .

- What do I feel at this point in the story? Why?

- Do this character's actions surprise me? Why?

- What did I learn from reading this?

- Does this story remind me of any other stories I've read?

APPLYING THE STRATEGIES

Read the following selection, "The White Umbrella." Use the **Active Reading Model** notes in the margins as you read. Write your responses on a separate piece of paper or use stick-on notes.

353

Before You Read
The White Umbrella

MEET GISH JEN

MEET GISH JEN

Gish Jen (gish jin) was born with the first name Lillian, but in high school, she changed her first name to the last name of the famous silent-film actor Lillian Gish. "It was part of becoming a writer," Jen says, "not becoming the person I was supposed to be." Jen is the daughter of Chinese immigrants. As a child in one of the few Asian American families in her town, Jen dealt with some hurtful experiences. Nonetheless, she writes of her childhood with humor.

Gish Jen was born in 1955. This story was first published in 1984.

FOCUS ACTIVITY

Think about a television program or movie in which a relative of the main character does something that embarrasses the main character. What does the relative do? Why does it embarrass the main character?

QuickWrite

Briefly write your responses to these questions. Then share your recollection with a small group.

Setting a Purpose

Read "The White Umbrella" to see how the narrator handles embarrassment.

BACKGROUND

The Time and Place   This story takes place in the United States during the 1960s. This was a time when most mothers did not work outside the home. Children were used to finding their mothers at home when they came home from school.

VOCABULARY PREVIEW

audible (ô′ də bəl) *adj.* capable of being heard; loud enough to be heard; p. 356

discreet (dis krēt′) *adj.* showing care and good judgment; cautious; p. 356

credibility (kred′ ə bil′ ə tē) *n.* the power to encourage or inspire belief; believability; p. 357

stupendous (stoo pen′ dəs) *adj.* causing surprise or amazement; p. 357

rendition (ren dish′ ən) *n.* a performance; p. 357

revelation (rev′ ə lā′ shən) *n.* information that had been unknown or secret and is now revealed; p. 363

divert (di vurt′) *v.* to draw the attention away; distract; p. 364

confirm (kən furm′) *v.* to uphold the truth of something; remove all doubts or suspicion; p. 364

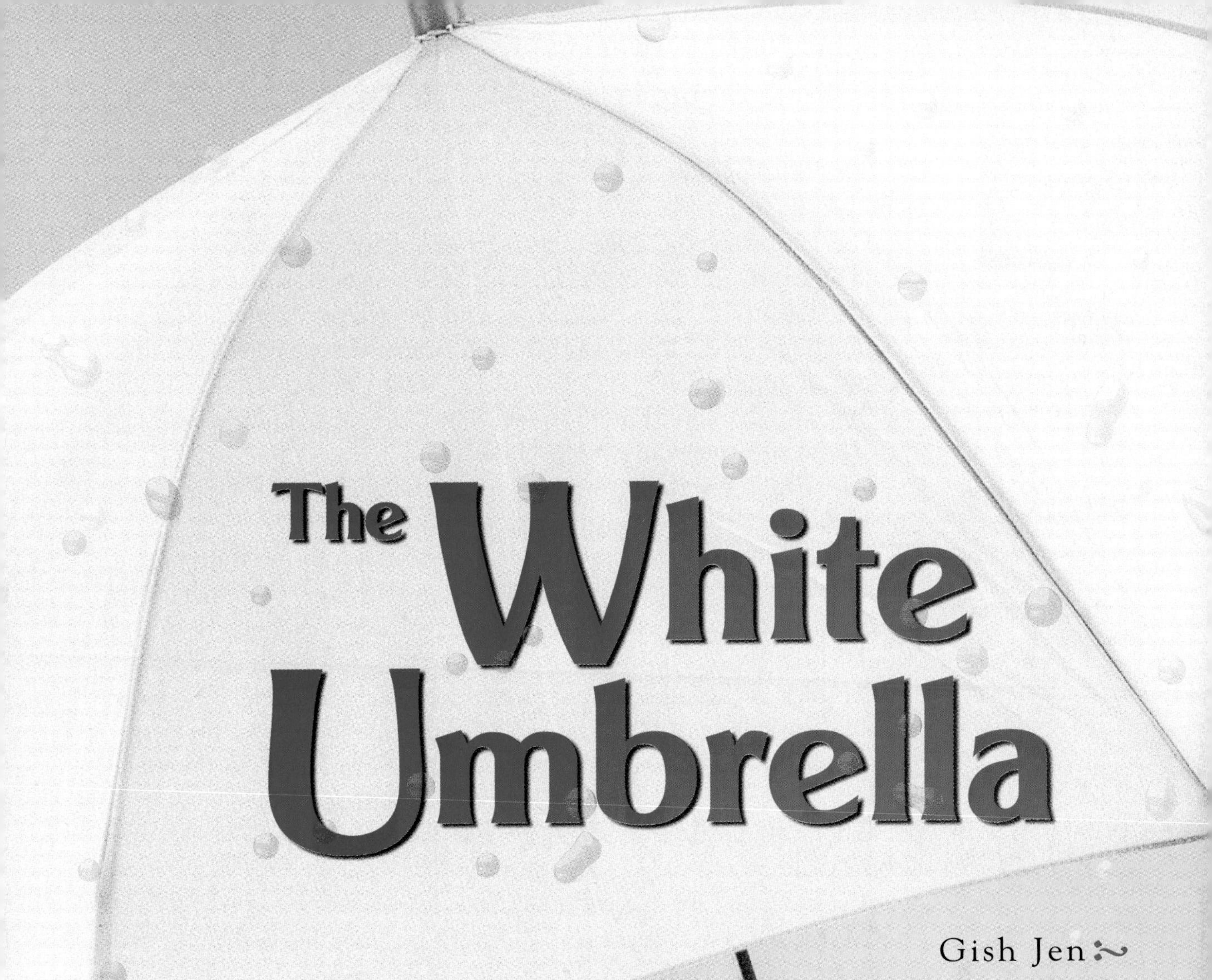

The White Umbrella

Gish Jen

ACTIVE
READING
MODEL

QUESTION

Why wouldn't the narrator's mother explain that she is working?

When I was twelve, my mother went to work without telling me or my little sister.

"Not that we need the second income." The lilt[1] of her accent drifted from the kitchen up to the top of the stairs, where Mona and I were listening.

---

1. A *lilt* is a light, lively quality of voice.

The White Umbrella

ACTIVE READING MODEL

QUESTION

Why does the narrator's father talk so quietly?

PREDICT

What does it mean to be "discreet"? Will this be important to the story?

"No," said my father, in a barely <u>audible</u> voice. "Not like the Lee family."

The Lees were the only other Chinese family in town. I remembered how sorry my parents had felt for Mrs. Lee when she started waitressing downtown the year before; and so when my mother began coming home late, I didn't say anything, and tried to keep Mona from saying anything either.

"But why shouldn't I?" she argued. "Lots of people's mothers work."

"Those are American people," I said.

"So what do you think we are? I can do the pledge of allegiance with my eyes closed."

Nevertheless, she tried to be <u>discreet</u>; and if my mother wasn't home by 5:30, we would start cooking by ourselves, to make sure dinner would be on time. Mona would wash the vegetables and put on the rice; I would chop.

For weeks we wondered what kind of work she was doing. I imagined that she was selling perfume, testing dessert recipes for the local newspaper. Or maybe she was working for the florist. Now that she had learned to drive, she might be delivering boxes of roses to people.

"I don't think so," said Mona as we walked to our piano lesson after school. "She would've hit something by now."

A gust of wind littered the street with leaves.

"Maybe we better hurry up," she went on, looking at the sky. "It's going to pour."

"But we're too early." Her lesson didn't begin until 4:00, mine until 4:30, so we usually tried to walk as slowly as we could. "And anyway, those aren't the kind of clouds that rain. Those are cumulus clouds."

We arrived out of breath and wet.

"Oh, you poor, poor dears," said old Miss Crosman. "Why don't you call me the next time it's like this out? If your mother won't drive you, I can come pick you up."

"No, that's okay," I answered. Mona wrung her hair out on Miss Crosman's rug. "We just couldn't get the roof of our car to close, is all. We took it to the beach last summer and got

Did You Know?
Cumulus (kū′ myə ləs) clouds are big and pillowy with flat bases.

Vocabulary
audible (ô′ də bəl) *adj.* capable of being heard; loud enough to be heard
discreet (dis krēt′) *adj.* showing care and good judgment; cautious

sand in the mechanism."[2] I pronounced this last word carefully, as if the credibility of my lie depended on its middle syllable. "It's never been the same." I thought for a second. "It's a convertible."

"Well then make yourselves at home." She exchanged looks with Eugenie Roberts, whose lesson we were interrupting. Eugenie smiled good-naturedly. "The towels are in the closet across from the bathroom."

Huddling at the end of Miss Crosman's nine-foot leatherette couch, Mona and I watched Eugenie play. She was a grade ahead of me and, according to school rumor, had a boyfriend in high school. I believed it. . . . She had auburn hair, blue eyes, and, I noted with a particular pang, a pure white folding umbrella.

"I can't see," whispered Mona.

"So clean your glasses."

"My glasses *are* clean. You're in the way."

I looked at her. "They look dirty to me."

"That's because *your* glasses are dirty."

Eugenie came bouncing to the end of her piece.

"Oh! Just stupendous!" Miss Crosman hugged her, then looked up as Eugenie's mother walked in. "Stupendous!" she said again. "Oh! Mrs. Roberts! Your daughter has a gift, a real gift. It's an honor to teach her."

Mrs. Roberts, radiant with pride, swept her daughter out of the room as if she were royalty, born to the piano bench. Watching the way Eugenie carried herself, I sat up, and concentrated so hard on sucking in my stomach that I did not realize until the Robertses were gone that Eugenie had left her umbrella. As Mona began to play, I jumped and ran to the window, meaning to call to them—only to see their brake lights flash then fade at the stop sign at the corner. As if to allow them passage, the rain had let up; a quivering sun lit their way.

The umbrella glowed like a scepter on the blue carpet while Mona, slumping over the keyboard, managed to eke out[3] a fair rendition of a catfight. At the end of the piece, Miss Crosman asked her to stand up.

---

2. The working parts of a machine are its *mechanism*. On the roof of a convertible car, the mechanism is the set of gears that make the roof go up or down.

3. The phrase *eke out* means "to barely manage to make or supply."

Vocabulary

credibility (kred′ ə bil′ ə tē) *n.* the power to encourage or inspire belief; believability

stupendous (stoo pen′ dəs) *adj.* causing surprise or amazement

rendition (ren dish′ ən) *n.* a performance

ACTIVE READING MODEL

QUESTION

Why does the narrator lie?

QUESTION

How does the narrator feel about Eugenie?

VISUALIZE

How do you picture this umbrella?

The White Umbrella

ACTIVE READING MODEL

QUESTION

Who is trying to tell the truth?

VISUALIZE

How do you picture the narrator with the umbrella?

"Stay right there," she said, then came back a minute later with a towel to cover the bench. "You must be cold," she continued. "Shall I call your mother and have her bring over some dry clothes?"

"No," answered Mona. "She won't come because she . . ."

"She's too busy," I broke in from the back of the room.

"I see." Miss Crosman sighed and shook her head a little. "Your glasses are filthy, honey," she said to Mona. "Shall I clean them for you?"

Sisterly embarrassment seized me. Why hadn't Mona wiped her lenses when I told her to? As she resumed abuse of the piano, I stared at the umbrella. I wanted to open it, twirl it around by its slender silver handle; I wanted to dangle it from my wrist on the way to school the way the other girls did. I wondered what Miss Crosman would say if I offered to bring it to Eugenie at school tomorrow. She would be impressed with my consideration for others; Eugenie would be pleased to have it back; and I would have possession of the umbrella for an entire night. I looked at it again, toying with the idea of asking for one for Christmas. I knew, however, how my mother would react.

"Things," she would say. "What's the matter with a raincoat? All you want is things, just like an American."

Sitting down for my lesson, I was careful to keep the towel under me and sit up straight.

"I'll bet you can't see a thing either," said Miss Crosman, reaching for my glasses. "And you can relax, you poor dear." She touched my chest, in an area where she never would have touched Eugenie Roberts. "This isn't a boot camp."

When Miss Crosman finally allowed me to start playing I played extra well, as well as I possibly could. See, I told her with my fingers. You don't have to feel sorry for me.

"That was wonderful," said Miss Crosman. "Oh! Just wonderful."

An entire constellation[4] rose in my heart.

"And guess what," I announced proudly. "I have a surprise for you."

Then I played a second piece for her, a much more difficult one that she had not assigned.

"Oh! That was stupendous," she said without hugging me. "Stupendous! You are a genius, young lady. If your mother had started you younger, you'd be playing like Eugenie Roberts by now!"

QUESTION

Why did the narrator learn a second, more difficult, piece?

---

4. A *constellation* is a group of stars, such as the Big Dipper, that is seen as representing a character or object.

Viewing the photograph: How, do you think, are this girl's feelings about playing the piano like those of the narrator?

I looked at the keyboard, wishing that I had still a third, even more difficult piece to play for her. I wanted to tell her that I was the school spelling bee champion, that I wasn't ticklish, that I could do karate.

"My mother is a concert pianist," I said.

She looked at me for a long moment, then finally, without saying anything, hugged me. I didn't say anything about bringing the umbrella to Eugenie at school.

The steps were dry when Mona and I sat down to wait for my mother.

"Do you want to wait inside?" Miss Crosman looked anxiously at the sky.

"No," I said. "Our mother will be here any minute."

"In a while," said Mona.

"Any minute," I said again, even though my mother had been at least twenty minutes late every week since she started working.

QUESTION

Why does Miss Crosman hug the narrator?

QUESTION

Does the narrator really believe this?

The White Umbrella

ACTIVE READING MODEL

According to the church clock across the street we had been waiting twenty-five minutes when Miss Crosman came out again.

"Shall I give you ladies a ride home?"

"No," I said. "Our mother is coming any minute."

"Shall I at least give her a call and remind her you're here? Maybe she forgot about you."

"I don't think she *forgot*," said Mona.

"Shall I give her a call anyway? Just to be safe?"

"I bet she already left," I said. "How could she forget about us?"

Miss Crosman went in to call.

"There's no answer," she said, coming back out.

"See, she's on her way," I said.

"Are you sure you wouldn't like to come in?"

"No," said Mona.

"Yes," I said. I pointed at my sister. "She meant yes too. She meant no, she wouldn't like to go in."

Miss Crosman looked at her watch. "It's 5:30 now, ladies. My pot roast will be coming out in fifteen minutes. Maybe you'd like to come in and have some then?"

"My mother's almost here," I said. "She's on her way."

We watched and watched the street. I tried to imagine what my mother was doing; I tried to imagine her writing messages in the sky, even though I knew she was afraid of planes. I watched as the branches of Miss Crosman's big willow tree started to sway; they had all been trimmed to exactly the same height off the ground, so that they looked beautiful, like hair in the wind.

It started to rain.

"Miss Crosman is coming out again," said Mona.

"Don't let her talk you into going inside," I whispered.

"Why not?"

"Because that would mean that Mom isn't really coming any minute."

"But she isn't," said Mona. "She's *working*."

"Shhh! Miss Crosman is going to hear you."

"She's working! She's working! She's working!"

I put my hand over her mouth, but she licked it, and so I was wiping my hand on my wet dress when the front door opened.

"We're getting even *wetter*," said Mona right away. "Wetter and wetter."

"Shall we all go in?" Miss Crosman pulled Mona to her feet. "Before you young ladies catch pneumonia? You've been out here an hour already."

QUESTION

Why does Mona act this way?

"We're *freezing*." Mona looked up at Miss Crosman. "Do you have any hot chocolate? We're going to catch *pneumonia*."

"I'm not going in," I said. "My mother's coming any minute."

"Come on," said Mona. "Use your *noggin*."

"Any minute."

"Come on, Mona." Miss Crosman opened the door. "Shall we get you inside first?"

"See you in the hospital," said Mona as she went in. "See you in the hospital with *pneumonia*."

I stared out into the empty street. The rain was pricking me all over; I was cold; I wanted to go inside. I wanted to be able to let myself go inside. If Miss Crosman came out again, I decided, I would go in.

She came out with a blanket and the white umbrella.

I could not believe that I was actually holding the umbrella, opening it. It sprang up by itself as if it were alive, as if that were what it wanted to do—as if it belonged in my hands, above my head. I stared up at the network of silver spokes, then spun the umbrella around and around and around. It was so clean and white that it seemed to glow, to illuminate everything around it.

"It's beautiful," I said.

Miss Crosman sat down next to me, on one end of the blanket. I moved the umbrella over so that it covered her too. I could feel the rain on my left shoulder and shivered. She put her arm around me.

"You poor, poor dear."

I knew that I was in store for another bolt of sympathy, and braced myself by staring up into the umbrella.

"You know, I very much wanted to have children when I was younger," she continued.

"You did?"

She stared at me a minute. Her face looked dry and crusty, like day-old frosting.

"I did. But then I never got married."

I twirled the umbrella around again.

"This is the most beautiful umbrella I have ever seen," I said. "Ever, in my whole life."

"Do you have an umbrella?"

"No. But my mother's going to get me one just like this for Christmas."

"Is she? I tell you what. You don't have to wait until Christmas. You can have this one."

The White Umbrella

ACTIVE
READING
MODEL

PREDICT

Do you think owning
the umbrella will
change anything for
the narrator?

"But this one belongs to Eugenie Roberts," I protested. "I have to give it back to her tomorrow in school."

"Who told you it belongs to Eugenie? It's not Eugenie's. It's mine. And now I'm giving it to you, so it's yours."

"It is?"

She hugged me tighter. "That's right. It's all yours."

"It's mine?" I didn't know what to say. "Mine?" Suddenly I was jumping up and down in the rain. "It's beautiful! Oh! It's beautiful!" I laughed.

Miss Crosman laughed too, even though she was getting all wet.

"Thank you, Miss Crosman. Thank you very much. Thanks a zillion. It's beautiful. It's *stupendous!*"

"You're quite welcome," she said.

"Thank you," I said again, but that didn't seem like enough. Suddenly I knew just what she wanted to hear. "I wish you were my mother."

Illustrated by Jacqueline Osborn. Stockworks.

Viewing the illustration: Is this person's piano playing like the narrator's, Mona's, or Eugenie Roberts's? Why do you think so?

Gish Jen

Right away I felt bad.

"You shouldn't say that," she said, but her face was opening into a huge smile as the lights of my mother's car cautiously turned the corner. I quickly collapsed the umbrella and put it up my skirt, holding onto it from the outside, through the material.

"Mona!" I shouted into the house. "Mona! Hurry up! Mom's here! I told you she was coming!"

Then I ran away from Miss Crosman, down to the curb. Mona came tearing up to my side as my mother neared the house. We both backed up a few feet, so that in case she went onto the curb, she wouldn't run us over.

"But why didn't you go inside with Mona?" my mother asked on the way home. She had taken off her own coat to put over me, and had the heat on high.

"She wasn't using her noggin," said Mona, next to me in the back seat.

"I should call next time," said my mother. "I just don't like to say where I am."

That was when she finally told us that she was working as a check-out clerk in the A&P.[5] She was supposed to be on the day shift, but the other employees were unreliable, and her boss had promised her a promotion if she would stay until the evening shift filled in.

For a moment no one said anything. Even Mona seemed to find the <u>revelation</u> disappointing.

"A promotion already!" she said, finally.

I listened to the windshield wipers.

"You're so quiet." My mother looked at me in the rear view mirror. "What's the matter?"

"I wish you would quit," I said after a moment.

She sighed. "The Chinese have a saying: one beam cannot hold the roof up."

"But Eugenie Roberts's father supports their family."

She sighed once more. "Eugenie Roberts's father is Eugenie Roberts's father," she said.

As we entered the downtown area, Mona started leaning hard against me every time the car turned right, trying to push me over. Remembering what I had said to Miss Crosman, I tried to maneuver the umbrella under my leg so she wouldn't feel it.

ACTIVE READING MODEL

QUESTION

Why does the narrator feel bad?

RESPOND

How do you feel to learn at last about the mother's job?

QUESTION

What do you think this Chinese saying means?

---

5. *A&P* is short for Atlantic and Pacific Tea Company, a chain of grocery stores.

Vocabulary

revelation (rev′ ə lā′ shən) *n.* information that had been unknown or secret and is now revealed

WHAT'S MOST IMPORTANT 363

The White Umbrella

ACTIVE
READING
MODEL

RESPOND

How do you feel about the man's behavior toward the narrator's family?

PREDICT

What do you think will happen next?

RESPOND

What overall feeling do you have as you finish the story?

"What's under your skirt?" Mona wanted to know as we came to a traffic light. My mother, watching us in the rear view mirror again, rolled slowly to a stop.

"What's the matter?" she asked.

"There's something under her skirt!" said Mona, pulling at me. "Under her skirt!"

Meanwhile, a man crossing the street started to yell at us. "Who do you think you are, lady?" he said. "You're blocking the whole damn crosswalk."

We all froze. Other people walking by stopped to watch.

"Didn't you hear me?" he went on, starting to thump on the hood with his fist. "Don't you speak English?"

My mother began to back up, but the car behind us honked. Luckily, the light turned green right after that. She sighed in relief.

"What were you saying, Mona?" she asked.

We wouldn't have hit the car behind us that hard if he hadn't been moving too, but as it was our car bucked violently, throwing us all first back and then forward.

"Uh oh," said Mona when we stopped. "*Another* accident."

I was relieved to have attention <u>diverted</u> from the umbrella. Then I noticed my mother's head, tilted back onto the seat. Her eyes were closed.

"Mom!" I screamed. "Mom! Wake up!"

She opened her eyes. "Please don't yell," she said. "Enough people are going to yell already."

"I thought you were dead," I said, starting to cry. "I thought you were dead."

She turned around, looked at me intently, then put her hand to my forehead.

"Sick," she <u>confirmed</u>. "Some kind of sick is giving you crazy ideas."

As the man from the car behind us started tapping on the window, I moved the umbrella away from my leg. Then Mona and my mother were getting out of the car. I got out after them; and while everyone else was inspecting the damage we'd done, I threw the umbrella down a sewer.

Vocabulary

divert (di vurt´) v. to draw the attention away; distract

confirm (kən furm´) v. to uphold the truth of something; remove all doubts or suspicion

Responding to Literature

PERSONAL RESPONSE

How did you respond to the end of the story? Did you feel the same way the main character does?

Active Reading Response

Look back at the strategies described in the **Active Reading Model** notes on pages 352 and 353. Choose a strategy and find three additional places in the story where you could apply it.

Analyzing Literature

RECALL

1. Why doesn't the narrator's mother drive the girls to and from their piano lessons?
2. What does the narrator tell her teacher about her mother?
3. Why does the narrator admire the white umbrella?
4. How does the narrator get the white umbrella?

INTERPRET

5. How does each member of the narrator's family feel about the changes in their routines? Support your answers.
6. How does the narrator show that she wants Miss Crosman to admire her?
7. Theme Connection   How does the narrator feel about getting the white umbrella? Use information from the story to explain your answer.
8. What chain of events leads up to the accident?

EVALUATE AND CONNECT

9. When her sister says, "Lots of people's mothers work," the narrator responds, "Those are American people." What do you think she means?
10. Through the use of **foreshadowing**, authors provide clues to events that will happen later in a story. What clues foreshadow the accident at the end of the story?

LITERARY ELEMENTS

Symbolism

A **symbol** is something that stands for something beyond itself. An object may stand for an idea. For example, a diamond ring is a symbol for an engagement; and a red, white, and blue flag is a symbol for the United States.

Authors of short stories often use symbols to suggest themes. In "The Flying Machine," for example, the emperor's music box symbolizes the orderly world that the emperor tries to protect. The theme of the story might be stated this way: It is impossible and undesirable for the real world to be as unchanging as a music box world.

1. What do you think the white umbrella in the story stands for?

2. What does this symbol suggest about the theme of the story?

● See **Literary Terms Handbook,** p. R8.

Literature and Writing

Writing About Literature

Description   Write a paragraph explaining how the following passage from the story helps you picture the scene: "Mrs. Roberts, radiant with pride, swept her daughter out of the room as if she were royalty, born to the piano bench."

Creative Writing

Dear Diary   Look back at your notes from the **Focus Activity** on page 354 about characters in embarrassing situations. Then write a diary entry as if you were the narrator describing an incident that embarrassed her.

Extending Your Response

Literature Groups

Compare   "The umbrella glowed like a scepter on the blue carpet." Compare the way the narrator felt about the umbrella at first with the way she felt about it at the end of the story. Look at the words the author uses. What does the narrator learn about what she values?

Interdisciplinary Activity

Social Studies   Why did the family have so many negative feelings about the mother going to work? Should the mother have taken a job? Should she have kept it a secret? Should her husband and daughters have reacted as they did? Discuss these issues.

Learning for Life

Accident Report   Write a report on the car accident of the narrator's mother. Include details explaining what happened, as well as statements each driver makes about what happened. Draw one or more diagrams to show where each car was.

Performing

Music   Do you know how to play a musical instrument? If possible, bring your instrument to class. Play a musical piece for a small group. Explain how you make sounds on your instrument, such as by blowing, plucking, or hitting. Also, share a few tips on how the instrument is played.

Reading Further

If you would like to read more stories about people testing their values, try these:
On My Honor by Marion Dane Bauer
Shiloh by Phyllis Reynolds Naylor

Save your work for your portfolio.

Skill Minilessons

GRAMMAR AND LANGUAGE • IMPERATIVE SENTENCES

"Wake up!" the narrator screamed when she saw her mother's closed eyes. Her short sentence is called an imperative sentence. An imperative sentence gives a command or makes a request. The subject is not stated—it is understood to be "you," the person spoken to.

PRACTICE Label the imperative sentences. If a sentence is <u>not</u> imperative, change it to an imperative sentence by removing the subject. You might also have to change some other words and punctuation.

1. Why don't you call me?
2. Well, then, make yourselves at home.
3. So, clean your glasses.
4. Stay right there.
5. You can relax, you poor dear.
6. Do you want to wait inside?
7. Maybe you'd like to come in.
8. Come on, Mona.
9. Hurry up!
10. Please don't yell.

⦿ For more about imperative sentences, see **Language Handbook,** p. R28.

READING AND THINKING • MAKING INFERENCES

Important information in a story isn't always stated directly. To figure it out, you must make **inferences** based on clues in the story or from your own experience. For example, when the narrator's father speaks "in a barely audible voice" about a family he feels sorry for, you might infer that he feels badly about his own family's situation.

PRACTICE What inference can you make about the narrator when she wishes she had a more difficult piece to play and wants to tell Miss Crosman that she is the spelling bee champion?

⦿ For more about inferences, see **Reading Handbook,** p. R82.

VOCABULARY • THE ROOT *vert*

The **root** of a word is the word or part of a word that is used as the base in making other words. The root of *divert* is *vert,* which means "to turn." If you *divert* someone's attention, you turn it away from its focus. Most words that contain *vert* have something to do with turning. *Extroverts* are people who turn their attention outward, away from themselves. They are friendly and outgoing. *Introverts* turn their attention inward. They are quiet and shy.

PRACTICE Use your knowledge of the root *vert* to answer the following questions.

1. If you *divert* a stream, do you dam it up, make it deeper, or change its direction?
2. Do *vertebrae* make your back strong, allow it to bend, or hold your shoulders in place?
3. If you suffer from *vertigo,* are you dizzy, grouchy, or itchy?
4. If a wolf that has been tamed *reverts,* does it start acting sleepy, wild, or gentle? (Hint: In this word, the prefix *re-* means "back.")
5. If a photograph is *inverted,* is it cloudy, upside down, or broken into bits?

Technology Skills

Comfortable Computing

If you spend just 3 hours a week at the computer, you'll point, click, and type away 156 hours a year. That's more than 1,000 hours by the time you finish high school. All that sitting and wrist rotation, not to mention staring at a flickering monitor, can take its toll. If you develop a sore neck, a stiff back, and an ache in your wrists after a while, chances are you need to take a long, hard look at how you operate your computer.

The next time you sit down to do a bit of Web surfing, take a minute to notice how you work at the computer. How far away from the screen are you sitting? Where are your feet? Where do you place your wrists when you type? How do you operate the mouse? These things may not seem important now, but hour after hour of incorrect posture or poor hand movements while you use a computer can do serious harm.

Warm Up

If you go out for the track team, your coach will have you stretch before and after every practice. That's because muscles work better and recover faster when they're warm and limber. Now think about the muscles and tendons in your fingers, wrists, neck, and back. Long-term computer use puts a strain on those muscles similar to that of an intense, repetitive workout. Warm up before a long day of Net surfing or gaming by slowly rotating your neck, touching your toes, and stretching your fingers. Don't work or play nonstop for hours. Take a fifteen-minute break every couple of hours. Here are some further hints.

At least 16 inches between eyes and screen

Top of screen at or below eye level

Forearms horizontal

Feet flat on floor

Back straight and supported by chair

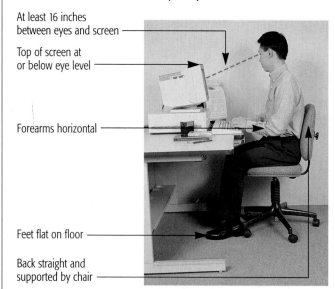

Posture

- Adjust your chair so your feet stay flat on the floor.
- Sit up straight, and keep the small of your back against the back of the chair.
- Keep your elbows on the same level as your wrists and your forearms approximately parallel to the floor.
- If the chair has armrests that force your elbows too high, try a chair without armrests.

Arms and Wrists

- Don't rest your wrists on the desk or keyboard while you type. If possible, use a wrist pad.
- When you move your mouse back and forth, use your entire hand, not just your wrist.
- Don't clutch the mouse tightly; keep your hand and fingers as relaxed as possible, and click gently.

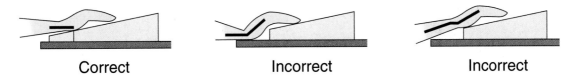

Correct Incorrect Incorrect

Monitor

- Avoid harsh lighting that produces a glare on the computer screen. If ceiling lights cause reflections, try tilting the screen down a bit.
- Adjust your monitor for a comfortable contrast and brightness.
- Keep your screen clean.
- Adjust your monitor so that the screen is at, or just below, eye level. Keep about 16–20 inches between your head and the monitor screen.

TAKE A BREAK

Don't work nonstop at your computer hour after hour, no matter how exciting the game you're playing may seem. Use your breaks wisely. Here are some tips.

- Staring at a close object for a long time tires the eyes. Take frequent breaks to focus your eyes on something distant—the farther, the better.
- Every hour or so, stretch your neck muscles by looking over your right and left shoulders.
- Give your hands and fingers a break too. Make a fist, and hold it for a few seconds. Then spread your fingers as far apart as possible. Repeat this several times.

EXERCISES

1. Do a Web search using the keywords *health* and *computing* or *computer injuries*. Share what you discover with your class.

2. In a small group, design a new look for your computer lab based on what you've learned about healthy computing. Sketch a diagram that illustrates how workstations should be set up, and submit it to your lab instructor for review.

Before You Read
Becky and the Wheels-and-Brake Boys

MEET JAMES BERRY

J ames Berry grew up in Jamaica, and he writes about life there and elsewhere in the Caribbean region. "In the Caribbean, we were the last outpost of the [British] Empire," he says. "No one has reported our stories, or the way we saw things. It's the function of writers and poets to bring in the left-out side of the human family." Berry, who now lives in England, is a well-known poet and literary critic. His books for young people include *Ajeemah and His Son* and *The Future-Telling Lady*.

James Berry was born in 1925. This story was first published in 1987.

FOCUS ACTIVITY

Have you ever wanted something you were told you couldn't have? What did you want? Why did you want it? Why couldn't you have it?

Think/Pair/Share
Tell a partner about an experience in which you really wanted something. Then share experiences with the class.

Setting a Purpose
Read "Becky and the Wheels-and-Brake Boys" to see how the narrator tries to get something she wants.

BACKGROUND

Did You Know?
In 1494 Spanish explorers led by Columbus landed on an island in the Caribbean Sea called Xaymaca by the people who lived there, the Arawak Indians. In 1655 England

captured Jamaica from Spain. Enslaved Africans were brought in to work on Jamaican sugar plantations. In 1962 the island won independence. Jamaica's official language is English, but most people speak a mixture of English and languages originating in Africa.

VOCABULARY PREVIEW

veranda (və ran′ də) *n.* a long porch, usually with a roof, along one or more sides of a house; p. 372

overseer (ō′ vər sē′ ər) *n.* one who watches over and directs the work of laborers; p. 373

scruffy (skruf′ ē) *adj.* worn or dirty; shabby; p. 374

straightaway (strāt′ ə wā′) *adv.* at once; immediately; p. 375

Becky and the Wheels-and-Brake Boys

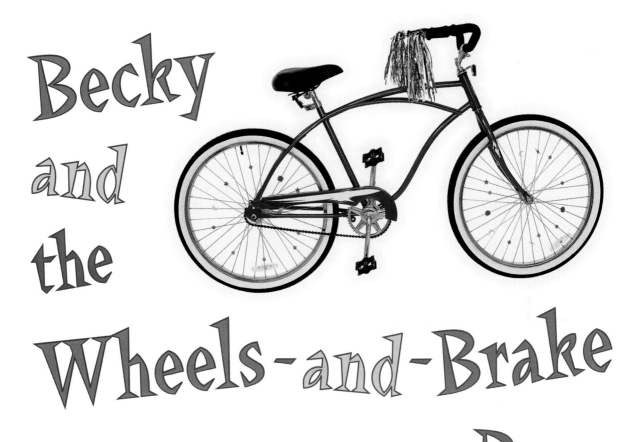

James Berry

Even my own cousin Ben was there—riding away, in the ringing of bicycle bells down the road. Every time I came to watch them—see them riding round and round enjoying themselves—they scooted off like crazy on their bikes.

They can't keep doing that. They'll see!

I only want to be with Nat, Aldo, Jimmy, and Ben. It's no fair reason they don't want to be with me. Anybody could go off their head[1] for that. Anybody! A girl can not, not, let boys get away with it all the time.

---

1. Here, *go off their head* means "go crazy."

Bother! I have to walk back home, alone.

I know total-total that if I had my own bike, the Wheels-and-Brake Boys wouldn't treat me like that. I'd just ride away with them, wouldn't I?

Over and over I told my mum I wanted a bike. Over and over she looked at me as if I was crazy. "Becky, d'you think you're a boy? Eh? D'you think you're a boy? In any case, where's the money to come from? Eh?"

Of course I know I'm not a boy. Of course I know I'm not crazy. Of course I know all that's no reason why I can't have a bike. No reason! As soon as I get indoors I'll just have to ask again—ask Mum once more.

At home, indoors, I didn't ask my mum.

It was evening time, but sunshine was still big patches in yards and on housetops. My two younger brothers, Lenny and Vin, played marbles in the road. Mum was taking measurements of a boy I knew, for his new trousers and shirt. Mum made clothes for people. Meggie, my sister two years younger than me, was helping Mum on the veranda. Nobody would be pleased with me not helping. I began to help.

Granny-Liz would always stop fanning herself to drink up a glass of ice water. I gave my granny a glass of ice water, there in her rocking chair. I looked in the kitchen to find shelled coconut pieces to cut into small cubes for the fowls' morning feed. But Granny-Liz had done it. I came

and started tidying up bits and pieces of cut-off material around my mum on the floor. My sister got nasty, saying she was already helping Mum. Not a single good thing was happening for me.

With me even being all so thoughtful of Granny's need of a cool drink, she started up some botheration[2] against me.

Listen to Granny-Liz: "Becky, with you moving about me here on the veranda, I hope you dohn[3] have any centipedes or scorpions[4] in a jam jar in your pocket."

"No, mam," I said sighing, trying to be calm. "Granny-Liz," I went on, "you forgot. My centipede and scorpion died." All the same, storm broke against me.

"Becky," my mum said. "You know I don't like you wandering off after dinner. Haven't I told you I don't want you keeping company with those awful riding-about bicycle boys? Eh?"

"Yes, mam."

"Those boys are a menace. Riding bicycles on sidewalks and narrow paths together, ringing bicycle bells and braking at people's feet like wild bulls charging anybody, they're heading for trouble."

2. *Botheration* means "trouble, worry, or complaint."
3. This is Granny-Liz's way of saying *don't*.
4. A *centipede* is a long, flat insect with many sets of legs, and a *scorpion* is related to the spider but has a stinger at the end of a long tail.

Vocabulary
veranda (və ran′ də) *n.* a long porch, usually with a roof, along one or more sides of a house

"They're the Wheels-and-Brake Boys, mam."

"The what?"

"The Wheels-and-Brake Boys."

"Oh! Given themselves a name as well, have they? Well, Becky, answer this. How d'you always manage to look like you just escaped from a hair-pulling battle? Eh? And don't I tell you not to break the backs down and wear your canvas shoes like slippers? Don't you ever hear what I say?"

"Yes, mam."

"D'you want to end up a field laborer? Like where your father used to be overseer?"

"No, mam."

"Well, Becky, will you please go off and do your homework?"

Everybody did everything to stop me. I was allowed no chance whatsoever. No chance to talk to Mum about the bike I dream of day and night. And I knew exactly the bike I wanted. I wanted a bike like Ben's bike. Oh, I wished I still had even my scorpion on a string to run up and down somebody's back!

I answered my mum. "Yes, mam." I went off into Meg's and my bedroom.

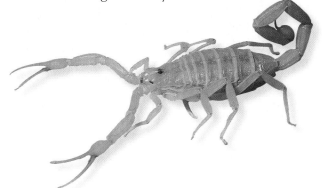

I sat down at the little table, as well as I might. Could homework stay in anybody's head in broad daylight outside? No. Could I keep a bike like Ben's out of my head? Not one bit. That bike took me all over the place. My beautiful bike jumped every log, every rock, every fence. My beautiful bike did everything cleverer than a clever cowboy's horse, with me in the saddle. And the bell, the bell was such a glorious gong of a ring!

If Dad was alive, I could talk to him. If Dad was alive, he'd give me money for the bike like a shot.

I sighed. It was amazing what a sigh could do. I sighed and tumbled on a great idea. Tomorrow evening I'd get Shirnette to come with me. Both of us together would be sure to get the boys interested to teach us to ride. Wow! With Shirnette they can't just ride away!

Next day at school, everything went sour. For the first time, Shirnette and me had a real fight, because of what I hated most.

Shirnette brought a cockroach to school in a shoe-polish tin. At playtime she opened the tin and let the cockroach fly into my blouse. Pure panic and disgust nearly killed me. I crushed up the cockroach in my clothes and practically ripped my blouse off, there in open sunlight. Oh, the smell of a cockroach is the nastiest ever to block your nose! I started running with my blouse to go and wash it. Twice I had to stop and be sick.

I washed away the crushed cockroach stain from my blouse. Then the stupid

Vocabulary
overseer (ō′ vər sē′ ər) *n.* one who watches over and directs the work of laborers

Shirnette had to come into the toilet, falling about laughing. All right, I knew the cockroach treatment was for the time when I made my centipede on a string crawl up Shirnette's back. But you put fair-is-fair aside. I just barged into Shirnette.

When it was all over, I had on a wet blouse, but Shirnette had one on, too.

Then, going home with the noisy flock of children from school, I had such a new, new idea. If Mum thought I was scruffy, Nat, Aldo, Jimmy, and Ben might think so, too. I didn't like that.

After dinner I combed my hair in the bedroom. Mum did her machining on the veranda. Meggie helped Mum. Granny sat there, wishing she could take on any job, as usual.

I told Mum I was going to make up a quarrel with Shirnette. I went, but my friend wouldn't speak to me, let alone come out to keep my company. I stood alone and watched the Wheels-and-Brake Boys again.

This time the boys didn't race away past me. I stood leaning against the tall coconut palm tree. People passed up and down. The nearby main road was busy with traffic. But I didn't mind. I watched the boys. Riding round and round the big

Sisy. Diana Ong (b. 1940).

Viewing the painting: How might the friendship between these girls be like that between Becky and Shirnette?

Vocabulary
scruffy (skruf′ē) *adj.* worn or dirty; shabby

Did You Know?
The bright, red-and-orange flowers of the *flame tree* give it this name.

flame tree, Nat, Aldo, Jimmy, and Ben looked marvelous.

At first each boy rode round the tree alone. Then each boy raced each other round the tree, going round three times. As he won, the winner rang his bell on and on, till he stopped panting and could laugh and talk properly. Next, most reckless and fierce, all the boys raced against each other. And, leaning against their bicycles, talking and joking, the boys popped soft drinks open, drank, and ate chipped bananas.

I walked up to Nat, Aldo, Jimmy, and Ben and said, "Can somebody teach me to ride?"

"Why don't you stay indoors and learn to cook and sew and wash clothes?" Jimmy said.

I grinned. "I know all that already," I said. "And one day perhaps I'll even be mum to a boy child, like all of you. Can you cook and sew and wash clothes, Jimmy? All I want is to learn to ride. I want you to teach me."

I didn't know why I said what I said. But everybody went silent and serious.

One after the other, Nat, Aldo, Jimmy, and Ben got on their bikes and rode off. I wasn't at all cross with them. I only wanted to be riding out of the playground with them. I knew they'd be heading into

the town to have ice cream and things and talk and laugh.

Mum was sitting alone on the veranda. She sewed buttons onto a white shirt she'd made. I sat down next to Mum. Straightaway, "Mum," I said, "I still want to have a bike badly."

"Oh, Becky, you still have that foolishness in your head? What am I going to do?"

Mum talked with some sympathy. Mum knew I was honest. "I can't get rid of it, mam," I said.

Mum stopped sewing. "Becky," she said, staring in my face, "how many girls around here do you see with bicycles?"

"Janice Gordon has a bike," I reminded her.

"Janice Gordon's dad has acres and acres of coconuts and bananas, with a business in the town as well."

I knew Mum was just about to give in. Then my granny had to come out onto the veranda and interfere. Listen to that Granny-Liz. "Becky, I heard you mother tell you over and over she cahn⁵ afford to buy you a bike. Yet you keep on and on. Child, you're a girl."

"But I don't want a bike because I'm a girl."

"D'you want it because you feel like a bwoy?" Granny said.

"No. I only want a bike because I want it and want it and want it."

Granny just carried on. "A tomboy's like a whistling woman and a crowing

---

5. When Granny-Liz says "*you* mother" and "*cahn* afford," she means *your* and *can't*.

Vocabulary
straightaway (strāt′ ə wā′) *adv.* at once; immediately

Schoolboys, 1986. Frané Lessac. Oil on canvas, 30 x 25 in. Collection of the artist.

Viewing the painting: In what ways might these boys be like Nat, Aldo, Jimmy, and Ben?

hen, who can only come to a bad end. D'you understand?"

I didn't want to understand. I knew Granny's speech was an awful speech. I went and sat down with Lenny and Vin, who were making a kite.

By Saturday morning I felt real sorry for Mum. I could see Mum really had it hard for money. I had to try and help. I knew anything of Dad's—anything–would be worth a great mighty hundred dollars.

I found myself in the center of town, going through the busy Saturday crowd. I hoped Mum wouldn't be too cross. I went into the fire station. With lots of luck I came face to face with a round-faced man in uniform. He talked to me. "Little miss, can I help you?"

I told him I'd like to talk to the head man. He took me into the office and gave me a chair. I sat down. I opened out my brown paper parcel. I showed him my dad's sun helmet. I told him I thought it would make a good fireman's hat. I wanted to sell the helmet for some money toward a bike, I told him.

The fireman laughed a lot. I began to laugh, too. The fireman put me in a car and drove me back home.

Mum's eyes popped to see me bringing home the fireman. The round-faced

Did You Know?
A *sun helmet* is a sturdy hat with a wide brim all around. It is also called a pith helmet.

fireman laughed at my adventure. Mum laughed, too, which was really good. The fireman gave Mum my dad's hat back. Then—mystery, mystery—Mum sent me outside while they talked.

My mum was only a little cross with me. Then—mystery and more mystery—my mum took me with the fireman in his car to his house.

The fireman brought out what? A bicycle! A beautiful, shining bicycle! His nephew's bike. His nephew had been taken away, all the way to America. The bike had been left with the fireman-uncle for him to sell it. And the good, kind fireman-uncle decided we could have the bike—on small payments. My mum looked uncertain. But in a big, big way, the fireman knew it was all right. And Mum smiled a little. My mum had good sense to know it was all right. My mum took the bike from the fireman Mr. Dean.

And guess what? Seeing my bike much, much newer than his, my cousin Ben's eyes popped with envy. But he took on the big job. He taught me to ride. Then he taught Shirnette.

I ride into town with the Wheels-and-Brake Boys now. When she can borrow a bike, Shirnette comes too. We all sit together. We have patties and ice cream and drink drinks together. We talk and joke. We ride about, all over the place.

And, again, guess what? Fireman Mr. Dean became our best friend, and Mum's especially. He started coming around almost every day.

Responding to Literature

PERSONAL RESPONSE

- ◆ Are you surprised by the ending of the story? Why or why not?
- ◆ Think about the experience you shared in the **Focus Activity** on page 370. Were you satisfied with the outcome in your own situation? Explain.

Analyzing Literature

RECALL

1. What does Becky want? Why?
2. How do Becky's mother and grandmother react to her desire?
3. What happens when Becky tries to convince the boys to teach her to ride?
4. What does Becky finally do to get what she wants? What finally happens?

INTERPRET

5. Theme Connection   In what ways does Becky think getting what she wants will change her life?
6. How do you know that Becky's family is struggling to make a living?
7. How are boys and girls supposed to act in Becky's culture? How do you know this?
8. How important is the memory of Becky's father in this story? Explain.

EVALUATE AND CONNECT

9. Do you recall when you learned to ride a bike? Did it change your life as much as it changed Becky's?
10. The **resolution** is the part of the plot that reveals the outcome or solves the problem in the story. What is this story's resolution? Is it satisfying? If so, in what ways?

Extending Your Response

Writing About Literature

Goal   Becky's goal in the story is to ride a bike and join the Wheels-and-Brake Boys. How does this group behave in the story? What appeals to Becky about them? How does her mother see them? Write a paragraph describing this group and its appeal to Becky.

Creative Writing

Road Trip   Becky pictures her bike jumping "every log, every rock, every fence." Imagine yourself on a bike. Where would you go? What would you see? Write a paragraph to describe what you see around you as you take an imaginary bike ride.

Literature Groups

Need It, Want It, Got to Have It   What different plans does Becky come up with to get a bike and to learn to ride? What character traits in Becky help her achieve her goals? Brainstorm for other ways she might have been able to get a bike or learn to ride. Share your group's ideas with the class.

Learning for Life

Planning Interviews   Do Granny-Liz and the Wheels-and-Brake Boys have any of the same views about why Becky shouldn't ride a bike? "Interview" them by asking questions of students who role-play these characters. Write questions that will draw out their opinions on Becky wanting a bike and on the roles of boys and girls in general. Share interview results with classmates.

Save your work for your portfolio.

Skill Minilesson

VOCABULARY • COMPOUND WORDS

Becky's father was an *overseer,* someone who watches over the work other people do. *Overseer* is a **compound word**—two or more words put together to make one. *Over* is easy. A *seer* is "one who sees." *Over* plus *seer* equals *overseer.*

You can often get a good idea of what an unfamiliar compound word means by thinking about the meanings of the words that are joined.

PRACTICE Match each compound word with its definition.

1. backslide
2. endmost
3. pushover
4. pigeonhole
5. blameworthy

   a. guilty
   b. farthest away
   c. small compartment
   d. easy to defeat
   e. to return to earlier, less good, ways

LISTENING, SPEAKING, and VIEWING

Holding a Group Discussion

In "Becky and the Wheels-and-Brake Boys," Becky tells the boys she wants to learn to ride, but they don't even listen. If the boys had listened, perhaps the group could have worked out a solution for Becky. When you discuss things in a group, listen to each person's opinions and comments. Ideas from one person often trigger new ideas in others, and the knowledge of the group continues to grow. In your group, try to make sure that everyone has a chance to speak. The following tips can help.

Group Discussion Tips

- Listen carefully. Make mental notes of others' points. Be ready to interject your own ideas when it is appropriate.
- When you speak, limit yourself to one or two points. Be receptive to others' comments on your ideas.
- Keep the discussion on track; make sure your comments deal directly with the topic.

- Let other speakers finish; avoid interrupting.
- When someone criticizes your ideas, listen without comment. Pause to give the criticism careful thought. Before you respond, try repeating the criticism, to be sure you have understood. You may need to discourage some group members from interrupting others and encourage quiet people to give their ideas.

ACTIVITIES

1. Listen to a panel discussion, either in person or on television. Notice how panel members follow (or ignore) each tip listed above. Jot down examples, and share them with classmates.

2. Join in a group discussion of opinions. Afterward, rate your group's performance on each tip listed above. Compare your results with those of others in your group.

MEDIA Connection

SONG LYRICS

The song "Brother, Can You Spare a Dime?" expressed some of the frustrations facing people who lived during the Great Depression.

Brother, Can You Spare a Dime?

by E. Y. Harburg and Jay Cornay

They used to tell me I was building
   a dream,
And so I followed the mob
When there was earth to plough or
   guns to bear
I was always there—right there on
   the job.
They used to tell me I was building
   a dream
With peace and glory ahead
Why should I be standing in line
Just waiting for bread?

Once I built a railroad, made it run,
Made it race against time.
Once I built a railroad,
Now it's done
Brother, can you spare a dime?

Once I built a tower, to the sun.
Brick and rivet and lime,
Once I built a tower,
Now it's done
Brother, can you spare a dime?

© 1932 Harms, Inc.

These men are standing in what was known as a "bread line." Charitable organizations and individuals provided free bread, soup, coffee, and doughnuts to jobless workers and to the families who depended on them. For many, these "soup kitchens" provided the only food they would eat all day.

Respond

1. What are some of the feelings expressed in this song?

2. How might your life be different if you were living during the Depression?

Before You Read

President Cleveland, Where Are You?

MEET ROBERT CORMIER

Like the main character in this story, Robert Cormier (kôr mēr´) was a boy during the 1930s. "The streets were terrible," he says about this time. "It was [the] Depression and it was bleak, but home was warm." Cormier grew up in Leominster, Massachusetts, and still lives there. He often uses the town as the setting for his stories: "I've invented, out of necessity, a place called Monument, which really is my home town of Leominster and also part of Fitchburg."

Robert Cormier was born in 1925. This story was published in 1980 in the collection Eight Plus One.

FOCUS ACTIVITY

Have you ever tried to collect all of something? What was the hardest part of completing your collection?

Brainstorming
In a small group, discuss things you have collected. How might you get the things needed to complete the collection?

Setting a Purpose
Read "President Cleveland, Where Are You?" to find out about some things young people collected during the 1930s.

Collector's cards of Presidents Benjamin Harrison and Grover Cleveland.

BACKGROUND

The Time and Place   This story takes place during the Great Depression in a town called Monument. The Great Depression began in late 1929 and lasted through the 1930s. It was a time of hardship for many people. Banks closed, and so did many other businesses. Thousands of people lost their savings. Millions lost their jobs.

VOCABULARY PREVIEW

allot (ə lot´) *v.* to distribute or give out; p. 384

skirmish (skur´ mish) *n.* a brief or minor conflict; p. 385

console (kən sōl´) *v.* to comfort or cheer someone who is sad or disappointed; p. 386

splurge (splurj) *v.* to spend money without worrying; p. 386

obsessed (əb sest´) *adj.* concentrating too much on a single emotion or idea; p. 389

dismal (diz´ məl) *adj.* gloomy; miserable; cheerless; p. 389

compassion (kəm pash´ ən) *n.* sympathy for another's suffering combined with a desire to help; p. 390

dominant (dom´ ə nənt) *adj.* having the greatest power or force; controlling; p. 390

dejection (di jek´ shən) *n.* sadness; low spirits; p. 391

blissfully (blis´ fə lē) *adv.* in an extremely happy way; joyfully; p. 391

President Cleveland,

22nd PRESIDENT

GROVER CLEVELAND

Where Are You?

Robert Cormier ~

That was the autumn of the cowboy cards—

Buck Jones and Tom Tyler and Hoot Gibson and especially Ken
Maynard.[1] The cards were available in those five-cent packages of
gum: pink sticks, three together, covered with a sweet white powder.
You couldn't blow bubbles with that particular gum, but it couldn't
have mattered less. The cowboy cards were important—the pictures
of those rock-faced men with eyes of blue steel.

On those wind-swept, leaf-tumbling afternoons we gathered
after school on the sidewalk in front of Lemire's Drugstore,
across from St. Jude's Parochial School,[2] and we swapped and
bargained and matched for the cards. Because a Ken Maynard
serial[3] was playing at the Globe every Saturday afternoon, he was the most popular cowboy of all, and one
of his cards was worth at least ten of any other kind.

Collector's cards of
Presidents Benjamin Harrison
and Warren Harding.

---

1. These were all popular stars of cowboy movies in the 1930s.
2. A *parochial* (pə rō′ kē əl) *school* is run by a church or another religious organization rather than by a city or state government.
3. In the 1930s, moviegoers watched *serials,* long stories that were shown in episodes.

President Cleveland, Where Are You?

Rollie Tremaine had a treasure of thirty or so, and he guarded them jealously. He'd match you for the other cards, but he risked his Ken Maynards only when the other kids threatened to leave him out of the competition altogether.

You could almost hate Rollie Tremaine. In the first place, he was the only son of Auguste Tremaine, who operated the Uptown Dry Goods Store, and he did not live in a tenement[4] but in a big white birthday cake of a house on Laurel Street. He was too fat to be effective in the football games between the Frenchtown Tigers and the North Side Knights, and he made us constantly aware of the jingle of coins in his pockets. He was able to stroll into Lemire's and casually select a quarter's worth of cowboy cards while the rest of us watched, aching with envy.

Once in a while I earned a nickel or dime by running errands or washing windows for blind old Mrs. Belander, or by finding pieces of copper, brass, and other valuable metals at the dump and selling them to the junkman. The coins clutched in my hand, I would race to Lemire's to buy a cowboy card or two, hoping that Ken Maynard would stare boldly out at me as I opened the pack. At one time, before a disastrous matching session with Roger Lussier (my best friend, except where the cards were involved), I owned five Ken Maynards and considered myself a millionaire, of sorts.

One week I was particularly lucky; I had spent two afternoons washing floors for Mrs. Belander and received a quarter. Because my father had worked a full week at the shop, where a rush order for fancy combs had been received, he allotted my brothers and sisters and me an extra dime along with the usual ten cents for the Saturday-afternoon movie. Setting aside the movie fare, I found myself with a bonus of thirty-five cents, and I then planned to put Rollie Tremaine to shame the following Monday afternoon.

Monday was the best day to buy the cards because the candy man stopped at Lemire's every Monday morning to deliver the new assortments. There was nothing more exciting in the world than a fresh batch of card boxes. I rushed home from school that day and hurriedly changed my clothes, eager to set off for the store. As I burst through the doorway, letting the screen door slam behind me, my brother Armand blocked my way.

He was fourteen, three years older than I, and a freshman at Monument High School. He had recently become a stranger to me in many ways—indifferent to such matters as cowboy cards and the Frenchtown Tigers—and he carried himself with a mysterious dignity that was fractured now and then when his voice began shooting off in all directions like some kind of vocal fireworks.

"Wait a minute, Jerry," he said. "I want to talk to you." He motioned me out of earshot

---

4. Here, *tenement* (ten′ ə mənt) means "apartment building."

Vocabulary
allot (ə lot′) *v.* to distribute or give out

of my mother, who was busy supervising the usual after-school skirmish in the kitchen.

I sighed with impatience. In recent months Armand had become a figure of authority, siding with my father and mother occasionally. As the oldest son he sometimes took advantage of his age and experience to issue rules and regulations.

"How much money have you got?" he whispered.

"You in some kind of trouble?" I asked, excitement rising in me as I remembered the blackmail plot of a movie at the Globe a month before.

He shook his head in annoyance. "Look," he said, "it's Pa's birthday tomorrow. I think we ought to chip in and buy him something . . ."

I reached into my pocket and caressed the coins. "Here," I said carefully, pulling out a nickel. "If we all give a nickel we should have enough to buy him something pretty nice."

He regarded me with contempt. "Rita already gave me fifteen cents, and I'm throwing in a quarter. Albert handed over a dime—all that's left of his birthday money. Is that all you can do—a nickel?"

"Aw, come on," I protested. "I haven't got a single Ken Maynard left, and I was going to buy some cards this afternoon."

"Ken Maynard!" he snorted. "Who's more important—him or your father?"

His question was unfair because he knew that there was no possible choice— "my father" had to be the only answer. My father was a huge man who believed in the things of the spirit, although my mother often maintained that the spirits[5] he believed in came in bottles. He had worked at the Monument Comb Shop since the age of fourteen; his booming laugh—or grumble—greeted us each night when he returned from the factory. A steady worker when the shop had enough work, he quickened with gaiety on Friday nights and weekends, a bottle of beer at his elbow, and he was fond of making long speeches about the good things in life. In the middle of the Depression, for instance, he paid cash for a piano, of all things, and insisted that

---

5. Spiritual matters are often called *things of the spirit,* but bottled *spirits* are alcoholic beverages.

Vocabulary
skirmish (skur′ mish) *n.* a brief or minor conflict

President Cleveland, Where Are You?

my twin sisters, Yolande and Yvette, take lessons once a week.

I took a dime from my pocket and handed it to Armand.

"Thanks, Jerry," he said. "I hate to take your last cent."

"That's all right," I replied, turning away and consoling myself with the thought that twenty cents was better than nothing at all.

When I arrived at Lemire's I sensed disaster in the air. Roger Lussier was kicking disconsolately[6] at a tin can in the gutter, and Rollie Tremaine sat sullenly on the steps in front of the store.

"Save your money," Roger said. He had known about my plans to splurge on the cards.

"What's the matter?" I asked.

"There's no more cowboy cards," Rollie Tremaine said. "The company's not making any more."

"They're going to have President cards," Roger said, his face twisting with disgust. He pointed to the store window. "Look!"

A placard in the window announced: "Attention, Boys. Watch for the New Series. Presidents of the United States. Free in Each 5-Cent Package of Caramel Chew."

Viewing the photograph: What might these young people be looking at? How are they like Jerry and his friends at Lemire's Drugstore?

6. *Disconsolately* means that Roger is so hopelessly unhappy that nothing can help and no one can console him.

Vocabulary

console (kən sōl′) *v.* to comfort or cheer someone who is sad or disappointed
splurge (splurj) *v.* to spend money without worrying

"President cards?" I asked, dismayed.

I read on: "Collect a Complete Set and Receive an Official Imitation Major League Baseball Glove, Embossed with Lefty Grove's Autograph."[7]

Glove or no glove, who could become excited about Presidents, of all things?

Rollie Tremaine stared at the sign. "Benjamin Harrison, for crying out loud," he said. "Why would I want Benjamin Harrison when I've got twenty-two Ken Maynards?"

I felt the warmth of guilt creep over me. I jingled the coins in my pocket, but the sound was hollow. No more Ken Maynards to buy.

"I'm going to buy a Mr. Goodbar," Rollie Tremaine decided.

I was without appetite, indifferent even to a Baby Ruth, which was my favorite. I thought of how I had betrayed Armand and, worst of all, my father.

"I'll see you after supper," I called over my shoulder to Roger as I hurried away toward home. I took the shortcut behind the church, although it involved leaping over a tall wooden fence, and I zigzagged recklessly through Mr. Thibodeau's garden, trying to outrace my guilt. I pounded up the steps and into the house, only to learn that Armand had already taken Yolande and Yvette uptown to shop for the birthday present.

I pedaled my bike furiously through the streets, ignoring the indignant[8] horns of automobiles as I sliced through the traffic. Finally I saw Armand and my sisters emerge from the Monument Men's Shop. My heart sank when I spied the long, slim package that Armand was holding.

"Did you buy the present yet?" I asked, although I knew it was too late.

"Just now. A blue tie," Armand said. "What's the matter?"

"Nothing," I replied, my chest hurting.

He looked at me for a long moment. At first his eyes were hard, but then they softened. He smiled at me, almost sadly, and touched my arm. I turned away from him because I felt naked and exposed.

"It's all right," he said gently. "Maybe you've learned something." The words were gentle, but they held a curious dignity, the dignity remaining even when his voice suddenly cracked on the last syllable.

I wondered what was happening to me, because I did not know whether to laugh or cry.

Sister Angela was amazed when, a week before Christmas vacation, everybody in the class submitted a history essay worthy of a high mark—in some cases as high as A-minus. (Sister Angela did not believe that anyone in the world ever deserved an A.) She never learned—or at least she never let on that she knew—we all had become experts on the Presidents because of the cards we purchased at Lemire's. Each card contained a picture of a President, and on the reverse side, a summary of his career. We looked at those cards so often that the biographies imprinted themselves on our minds without effort. Even our street-corner

---

7. Robert *Grove* (1900–1970) was an outstanding pitcher for the Philadelphia Athletics and the Boston Red Sox between 1925 and 1941. A machine carved his *embossed* autograph by making a shallow cut in the glove's leather.

8. If the car horns sound *indignant* (in dig´ nənt), it's because the drivers are annoyed with the narrator's behavior in traffic.

conversations were filled with such information as the fact that James Madison was called "The Father of the Constitution," or that John Adams had intended to become a minister.

The President cards were a roaring success and the cowboy cards were quickly forgotten. In the first place we did not receive gum with the cards, but a kind of chewy caramel. The caramel could be tucked into a corner of your mouth, bulging your cheek in much the same manner as wads of tobacco bulged the mouths of baseball stars. In the second place the competition for collecting the cards was fierce and frustrating—fierce because everyone was intent on being the first to send away for a baseball glove and frustrating because although there were only thirty-two Presidents, including Franklin Delano Roosevelt, the variety at Lemire's was at a minimum. When the deliveryman left the boxes of cards at the store each Monday, we often discovered that one entire box was devoted to a single President—two weeks in a row the boxes contained nothing but Abraham Lincoln. One week Roger Lussier and I were the heroes of Frenchtown. We journeyed on our bicycles to the North Side, engaged three boys in a matching bout and returned with five new Presidents, including Chester Alan Arthur, who up to that time had been missing.

Viewing the photograph: What does this photograph tell you about the 1930s?

Perhaps to sharpen our desire, the card company sent a sample glove to Mr. Lemire, and it dangled, orange and sleek, in the window. I was half sick with longing, thinking of my old glove at home, which I had inherited from Armand. But Rollie Tremaine's desire for the glove outdistanced my own. He even got Mr. Lemire to agree to give the glove in the window to the first person to get a complete set of cards, so that precious time wouldn't be wasted waiting for the postman.

We were delighted at Rollie Tremaine's frustration, especially since he was only a substitute player for the Tigers. Once after spending fifty cents on cards—all of which turned out to be Calvin Coolidge—he threw them to the ground, pulled some dollar bills out of his pocket and said, "The heck with it. I'm going to buy a glove!"

"Not that glove," Roger Lussier said. "Not a glove with Lefty Grove's autograph. Look what it says at the bottom of the sign."

We all looked, although we knew the words by heart: "This Glove Is Not For Sale Anywhere."

Rollie Tremaine scrambled to pick up the cards from the sidewalk, pouting more than ever. After that he was quietly obsessed with the Presidents, hugging the cards close to his chest and refusing to tell us how many more he needed to complete his set.

I too was obsessed with the cards, because they had become things of comfort in a world that had suddenly grown dismal. After Christmas a layoff at the shop had thrown my father out of work. He received no paycheck for four weeks, and the only income we had was from Armand's after-school job at the Blue and White Grocery Store—a job he lost finally when business dwindled as the layoff continued.

Although we had enough food and clothing—my father's credit had always been good, a matter of pride with him—the inactivity made my father restless and irritable. He did not drink any beer at all, and laughed loudly, but not convincingly, after gulping down a glass of water and saying, "Lent[9] came early this year." The twins fell sick and went to the hospital to have their tonsils removed. My father was confident that he would return to work eventually and pay off his debts, but he seemed to age before our eyes.

When orders again were received at the comb shop and he returned to work, another disaster occurred, although I was the only one aware of it. Armand fell in love.

I discovered his situation by accident, when I happened to pick up a piece of paper that had fallen to the floor in the bedroom he and I shared. I frowned at the paper, puzzled.

"Dear Sally, When I look into your eyes the world stands still . . ."

The letter was snatched from my hands before I finished reading it.

"What's the big idea, snooping around?" Armand asked, his face crimson. "Can't a guy have any privacy?"

He had never mentioned privacy before. "It was on the floor," I said. "I didn't know it was a letter. Who's Sally?"

He flung himself across the bed. "You tell anybody and I'll muckalize[10] you," he threatened. "Sally Knowlton."

Nobody in Frenchtown had a name like Knowlton.

"A girl from the North Side?" I asked, incredulous.[11]

He rolled over and faced me, anger in his eyes, and a kind of despair too.

"What's the matter with that? Think she's too good for me?" he asked. "I'm warning you, Jerry, if you tell anybody . . ."

"Don't worry," I said. Love had no particular place in my life; it seemed an

---

9. *Lent* is the period including the forty weekdays before Easter. During Lent, some Christians show sorrow for their sins by giving up something they enjoy.
10. *Muckalize* is a made-up word. Muck is dirty, sticky, slimy mud, or anything that's messy and disgusting.
11. To be *incredulous* (in kre′ jə ləs) is to be unwilling or unable to believe something.

Vocabulary

obsessed (əb sest′) *adj.* concentrating too much on a single emotion or idea
dismal (diz′ məl) *adj.* gloomy; miserable; cheerless

unnecessary waste of time. And a girl from the North Side was so remote that for all practical purposes she did not exist. But I was curious. "What are you writing her a letter for? Did she leave town, or something?"

"She hasn't left town," he answered. "I wasn't going to send it. I just felt like writing to her."

I was glad that I had never become involved with love—love that brought desperation[12] to your eyes, that caused you to write letters you did not plan to send. Shrugging with indifference, I began to search in the closet for the old baseball glove. I found it on the shelf, under some old sneakers. The webbing was torn and the padding gone. I thought of the sting I would feel when a sharp grounder slapped into the glove, and I winced.

"You tell anybody about me and Sally and I'll—"

"I know. You'll muckalize me."

I did not divulge[13] his secret and often shared his agony, particularly when he sat at the supper table and left my mother's special butterscotch pie untouched. I had never realized before how terrible love could be. But my compassion was short-lived because I had other things to worry about: report cards due at Eastertime; the loss of income from old Mrs. Belander,

who had gone to live with a daughter in Boston; and, of course, the Presidents.

Because a stalemate[14] had been reached, the President cards were the dominant force in our lives—mine, Roger Lussier's and Rollie Tremaine's. For three weeks, as the baseball season approached, each of us had a complete set—complete except for one President, Grover Cleveland. Each time a box of cards arrived at the store we hurriedly bought them (as hurriedly as our funds allowed) and tore off the wrappers, only to be confronted by James Monroe or Martin Van Buren or someone else. But never Grover Cleveland, never the man who had been the twenty-second *and* the twenty-fourth President of the United States. We argued about Grover Cleveland. Should he be placed between Chester Alan Arthur and Benjamin Harrison as the twenty-second President or did he belong between Benjamin Harrison and William McKinley as the twenty-fourth President? Was the card company playing fair? Roger Lussier brought up a horrifying possibility—did we need *two* Grover Clevelands to complete the set?

Indignant, we stormed Lemire's and protested to the harassed[15] storeowner, who had long since vowed never to stock a new series. Muttering angrily, he searched his bills and receipts for a list of rules.

---

12. *Desperation* means "distress caused by great need or loss of hope."
13. To *divulge* a secret is to reveal it or make it known, so that it's no longer a secret.

14. The chess term *stalemate* refers to a situation in which no further action is possible.
15. Someone who is *harassed* (har′ əsd) is repeatedly bothered or annoyed by someone else.

Vocabulary

compassion (kəm pash′ ən) *n.* sympathy for another's suffering combined with a desire to help

dominant (dom′ ə nənt) *adj.* having the greatest power or force; controlling

"All right," he announced. "Says here you only need one Grover Cleveland to finish the set. Now get out, all of you, unless you've got money to spend."

Outside the store, Rollie Tremaine picked up an empty tobacco tin and scaled it across the street. "Boy," he said. "I'd give five dollars for a Grover Cleveland."

When I returned home I found Armand sitting on the piazza steps, his chin in his hands. His mood of dejection mirrored my own, and I sat down beside him. We did not say anything for a while.

Did You Know?
A *piazza* (pē az′ ə) is a large covered porch.

"Want to throw the ball around?" I asked.

He sighed, not bothering to answer.

"You sick?" I asked.

He stood up and hitched up his trousers, pulled at his ear and finally told me what the matter was—there was a big dance next week at the high school, the Spring Promenade,[16] and Sally had asked him to be her escort.

I shook my head at the folly of love. "Well, what's so bad about that?"

"How can I take Sally to a fancy dance?" he asked desperately. "I'd have to buy her a corsage . . . And my shoes are practically falling apart. Pa's got too many worries now to buy me new shoes or give me money for flowers for a girl."

I nodded in sympathy. "Yeah," I said. "Look at me. Baseball time is almost here, and all I've got is that old glove. And no Grover Cleveland card yet . . ."

"Grover Cleveland?" he asked. "They've got some of those up on the North Side. Some kid was telling me there's a store that's got them. He says they're looking for Warren G. Harding."

"Holy Smoke!" I said. "I've got an extra Warren G. Harding!" Pure joy sang in my veins. I ran to my bicycle, swung into the seat—and found that the front tire was flat.

"I'll help you fix it," Armand said.

Within half an hour I was at the North Side Drugstore, where several boys were matching cards on the sidewalk. Silently but blissfully I shouted: President Grover Cleveland, here I come!

Did You Know?
A *corsage* (kôr säzh′) is a flower or small bunch of flowers worn by a woman, usually at the shoulder or on the wrist.

After Armand had left for the dance, all dressed up as if it were Sunday, the small green box containing the corsage under his arm, I sat on the railing of the piazza, letting my feet dangle. The neighborhood was

16. A formal dance or ball used to be called a *promenade* (prom′ ə nād′). Today it's usually shortened to *prom*.

Vocabulary
dejection (di jek′ shən) *n.* sadness; low spirits
blissfully (blis′ fə lē) *adv.* in an extremely happy way; joyfully

quiet because the Frenchtown Tigers were at Daggett's Field, practicing for the first baseball game of the season.

I thought of Armand and the ridiculous expression on his face when he'd stood before the mirror in the bedroom. I'd avoided looking at his new black shoes. "Love," I muttered.

Spring had arrived in a sudden stampede of apple blossoms and fragrant breezes. Windows had been thrown open and dust mops had banged on the sills all day long as the women busied themselves with housecleaning. I was puzzled by my lethargy.[17] Wasn't spring supposed to make everything bright and gay?

I turned at the sound of footsteps on the stairs. Roger Lussier greeted me with a sour face.

"I thought you were practicing with the Tigers," I said.

"Rollie Tremaine," he said. "I just couldn't stand him." He slammed his fist against the railing. "Jeez, why did he have to be the one to get a Grover Cleveland? You should see him showing off. He won't let anybody even touch that glove . . ."

I felt like Benedict Arnold[18] and knew that I had to confess what I had done.

"Roger," I said, "I got a Grover Cleveland card up on the North Side. I sold it to Rollie Tremaine for five dollars."

"Are you crazy?" he asked.

---

17. *Lethargy* (leth′ ər jē) is a feeling or condition of laziness or drowsiness.
18. During the Revolutionary War, this American general turned traitor.

"I needed that five dollars. It was an—an emergency."

"Boy!" he said, looking down at the ground and shaking his head. "What did you have to do a thing like that for?"

I watched him as he turned away and began walking down the stairs.

"Hey, Roger!" I called.

He squinted up at me as if I were a stranger, someone he'd never seen before.

"What?" he asked, his voice flat.

"I had to do it," I said. "Honest."

He didn't answer. He headed toward the fence, searching for the board we had loosened to give us a secret passage.

I thought of my father and Armand and Rollie Tremaine and Grover Cleveland and wished that I could go away someplace far away. But there was no place to go.

Roger found the loose slat in the fence and slipped through. I felt betrayed: weren't you supposed to feel good when you did something fine and noble?

A moment later two hands gripped the top of the fence and Roger's face appeared. "Was it a real emergency?" he yelled.

"A real one!" I called. "Something important!"

His face dropped from sight and his voice reached me across the yard: "All right."

"See you tomorrow!" I yelled.

I swung my legs over the railing again. The gathering dusk began to soften the sharp edges of the fence, the rooftops, the distant church steeple. I sat there a long time, waiting for the good feeling to come.

Responding to Literature

PERSONAL RESPONSE

Do you find this story humorous? serious? both? Describe your impressions.

Analyzing Literature

RECALL

1. After the cowboy cards, what do Jerry and his friends collect? Why?
2. Why do the boys enjoy collecting the cards?
3. Why does Armand ask Jerry for money?
4. How does Jerry finally help Armand?

INTERPRET

5. Why is collecting the cards difficult?
6. Do all the boys have the same opportunities to collect the cards? Explain.
7. How does Jerry let down his father and Armand?
8. As the story ends, why isn't Jerry feeling good about helping Armand?

EVALUATE AND CONNECT

9. *Theme Connection* What values do you think Jerry is learning from Armand?
10. In your opinion, why are readers left to imagine the scene in which Jerry gives Armand what he needs for the dance?

LITERARY ELEMENTS

Plot

The **plot** is the sequence of events in a story. Each event causes or leads to the next. The situation and characters are introduced in **exposition.** Events of the plot reveal a problem, called the **conflict.** Tension builds through **rising action** as events caused by the problem develop and sharpen the problem. Everything comes to a head in the **climax,** the point of greatest interest and emotion. Then the action in the story falls off and the tension drops. The **resolution** shows how the problem is solved.

1. What is the main conflict or problem in this story?

2. What are two events that add to the rising action?

3. What event occurs at the climax of the story? Explain.

● See **Literary Terms Handbook,** p. R6.

Presidents Benjamin Harrison, Grover Cleveland, and Franklin Delano Roosevelt.

Literature and Writing

Writing About Literature

Figures of Speech Robert Cormier says, "I use a lot of similes and metaphors when I work, simply because it's the best way of describing a building or a scene." Find at least three figures of speech in the story and write a paragraph telling why they are effective.

Personal Writing

Collector's Corner In your journal, describe a collection you own or would like to begin. Use your notes from the **Focus Activity** on page 382 for ideas. Explain why you chose the collection. Do the pieces have meaning? Which do you think would be more fun—collecting the pieces or owning the collection?

Extending Your Response

Learning for Life

Oral History Interview people who lived through the Great Depression. In a small group, prepare a list of questions on what life was like then. You might ask how young people earned money, what they did for fun, or how they spent time with their families. Then complete your interviews and share what you have learned with the class.

Literature Groups

Growing and Changing After Jerry's sacrifice for Armand, he feels betrayed: "Weren't you supposed to feel good when you did something fine and noble?" Discuss the conflicting feelings Jerry experiences. Why, do you think, does he decide to help Armand? Why does he feel betrayed afterward? Do you think Jerry will feel differently as time goes on?

Listening and Speaking

Readers Theater With a partner or small group, practice reading a section of the story and then present it to the class.

Interdisciplinary Activity

Math Prices during the Great Depression were obviously much lower than today's prices. A movie ticket cost ten cents, and a packet of gum and cards cost five. A corsage and new shoes cost five dollars. Assume that the corsage cost one dollar and the shoes cost four. Find 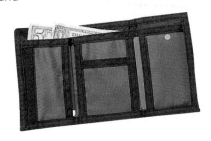 out present-day prices of all these items and compute the percentage increase for each one.

Reading Further

If you would like to read more by Robert Cormier, try this book:
I Am the Cheese

📖 **Save your work for your portfolio.**

Skill Minilessons

GRAMMAR AND LANGUAGE • PUNCTUATING DIALOGUE

When Armand asks for money, Jerry asks him, "You in some kind of trouble?" Later, when Jerry tells Roger that he had an emergency, he says, "Something important!" Notice that question marks and exclamation marks are placed inside the quotation marks in dialogue. Sentences of dialogue can end with a comma if a speaker tag is added at the end, as when Jerry reassures Armand: "Don't worry," I said.

PRACTICE Place quotation marks around the dialogue and add commas or periods that are needed.

1. Hey, Roger! I called.
2. I'll help you fix it Armand said.
3. How can I take Sally to a fancy dance? he asked desperately.
4. I needed that five dollars I told him. It was an— an emergency
5. Holy smoke! I said I've got an extra Warren G. Harding

● For more about punctuating dialogue, see **Language Handbook,** p. R35–R36.

READING AND THINKING • GENERALIZING

When you **generalize,** you think of a broad, general statement that applies to many facts or situations. Jerry's family did not have much money due to the Depression. You may know true or fictional stories about other people during the Depression. When you think about all the stories, you may notice that most of their families had little money and that many fathers were out of work. You might make this generalization: Many people didn't have much money during the Depression.

PRACTICE Write a generalization based on the following information.

In Monument, young people collect president cards. In Fayette, they collect cowboy cards. In Olympia, they collect baseball cards.

● For more about generalizing, see **Reading Handbook,** p. R82.

VOCABULARY • ANALOGIES

"A finger is to a hand as a toe is to a foot" is an **analogy.** The relationship between *finger* and *hand* is the same as the relationship between *toe* and *foot.* The analogy can be written as

finger : hand :: toe : foot.

One possible relationship between words is that they mean the same thing; they are synonyms. Another relationship is that they mean the opposite; they are antonyms.

PRACTICE Choose the word that best completes each analogy.

1. slowly : quickly :: blissfully :
   a. sadly   b. proudly   c. carefully
2. power : strength :: compassion :
   a. feeling   b. cruelty   c. pity
3. speech : talk :: dejection :
   a. repetition   b. joy   c. sadness
4. argue : disagree :: allot :
   a. distribute   b. collect   c. lend
5. simple : difficult :: dismal :
   a. warm   b. gloomy   c. cheerful

Writing WORKSHOP

Expository Writing: Character Evaluation

Think about the characters you met in the stories of this theme, What's Most Important. Choose one character that you remember clearly. How do you feel about the character's actions? If you were in the character's place, would you act as he or she does? When you judge, or **evaluate**, a character's actions, you get a closer look at the character. You also get a closer look at your own ideas.

Assignment: In an essay, evaluate the actions of one character from Theme 4. Use the process shown in this workshop.

● As you write your character evaluation, refer to the **Writing Handbook,** pp. R43–R47.

The Writing Process

PREWRITING

PREWRITING TIP
For more insight, write a dialogue between you and your character. Ask about things you don't understand. Imagine how he or she might answer.

● **Explore Ideas**

To find a character to write about, skim your journal or talk with classmates. Another approach is to make a chart. Many characters in this theme give up things that are of value to them. Chart their decisions and your responses. You might write about the character you understand best—or about the one you understand least.

Character	Story	What character gives up	Character's reasons	My response
Maibon	"The Stone"	magical stone	hidden drawbacks	Why not renegotiate?
Daedalus	"Wings"	secret of labyrinth	patriotism, remorse	Impossible choice!
Jerry	"President Cleveland . . ."	trading card		
narrator	"The White Umbrella"	white umbrella		

● Decide on Standards

An evaluation is based on **standards**—ideas about what is important. List some standards you will use. Write details from the story, showing how the character measures up.

● Think About Your Audience and Purpose

How will you shape your evaluation? Four of many possibilities are

- a personal essay to be shared with your teacher and classmates

- a letter to the character, explaining your views

- a speech to others in the story, supporting or condemning the character

- an article for your school newspaper, comparing the character to a real-life figure

● Look at the Big Picture

Your evaluation will share your overall response to the character's actions. Write your response now, in a sentence or two, to guide you as you draft. Then write the main points you will make in explaining your response. Be sure that you can find details in the story to illustrate each point.

My Response
Daedalus isn't unkind. He's a kind person with bad luck and hard choices.
Point 1: Daedalus doesn't purposely kill Talos.
Point 2: Choice between Minotaur and Athenian kids is no-win situation.
Point 3: Daedalus tries many ways to keep Icarus safe.

The Fall of Icarus. Carlo Saraceni (1585–1620). Museo di Capodimonte, Naples.

Writing WORKSHOP

DRAFTING

DRAFTING TIP
If you can't think of a strong opening sentence, leave a blank for it. Then go on to the rest of your draft. You can fill in the blank when you revise.

● Grab Your Audience

To catch your audience's interest, open with a sentence showing your character in action. If appropriate, tell your readers the title and author of the story in which the character appears. Include brief information about his or her role in the story.

● Draft Your Evaluation

You might state your response near the beginning, using the rest of the essay to explain it. An alternate plan: use the body paragraphs to build toward your response, and state your response at the end. Whichever plan you choose, write at least a paragraph about each of your main points. Use details from your prewriting notes.

> **MODEL · DRAFTING**
>
> Daedalus soars on handmade wings, but he can't escape the gods' anger. In Jane Yolen's "Wings," the gods think Daedalus is unkind. I think he is a kind person faced with bad luck and hard choices.

REVISING

REVISING TIP
Even if a story is set in the past, use the present tense to write about it.

● Take a Second Look

After a break, plan changes that will improve your draft. If you feel ready, ask a classmate to go over your draft with you. Use the **Questions for Revising** as a guide.

QUESTIONS FOR REVISING

☑ How might I change my opening sentences to better catch my audience's interest?

☑ Where do I state my overall response? How might I make it clearer?

☑ Where might I add details to make my points easier to understand?

☑ Where do I explain the standards that my evaluation is based on?

EDITING/PROOFREADING

When your essay says exactly what you want it to, go over it once more to correct errors in grammar, usage, and mechanics. Use the **Proofreading Checklist**. The information in the **Grammar Link** on page 323 can help you check for correct pronoun usage.

PROOFREADING CHECKLIST

☑ All pronoun usage is correct.

☑ There are no run-on sentences or sentence fragments.

☑ All subjects and verbs agree.

☑ Punctuation and capitalization are correct.

☑ All words are correctly spelled.

Grammar Hint

Everyone is singular and takes a singular possessive pronoun: *her* or *his*.
On the boys' team, *everyone* did *his* best.
If group members are male and female, use *his* or *her*.
Everyone knew *his* or *her* part.

MODEL · EDITING/PROOFREADING

In "The White Umbrella," everyone has ~~their~~ own <ins>his or her</ins> view of the situation.

TECHNOLOGY TIP
When you discover a misspelled word, use your computer's search function to check for repetitions of the error.

PUBLISHING/PRESENTING

Evaluations are great discussion starters. In a small group, read each other's work. Then discuss other ideas and interpretations.

PRESENTING TIP
In a panel discussion, compare responses.

Reflecting

Think about the following questions and write your responses in your journal.

- What was the most important change you made when you revised your draft? Why was it important?

- Did your view of the character change as you worked on your evaluation? If so, explain how. If not, explain why not.

👜 **Save your work for your portfolio.**

Theme Wrap-Up

Responding to the Theme

1. Which selection in this theme helped you think about what's most important? Explain your answer.

2. What new ideas do you have about the following as a result of your reading in this theme?
   - how a person decides what is most important
   - how people resolve conflicts involving values

3. Present your theme project to the class.

Analyzing Literature

COMPARE SHORT STORIES
Choose two short stories from this theme to compare. You may compare them in terms of plot, characters, themes, or point of view. Use examples and quotations from the short stories to support your opinions. If you compare plots, you might want to create your own plot diagram, like the one on pages 350–351.

Evaluate and Set Goals

1. Which of the following was most enjoyable to you? Which was most difficult?
   - reading and thinking about the selections
   - doing independent writing
   - analyzing the selections in discussions
   - making presentations
   - doing research

2. How would you assess your work in this theme, using the following scale? Give at least two reasons for your assessment.
   4 = outstanding   2 = fair
   3 = good   1 = weak

3. Based on what you found difficult in this theme, choose a goal to work toward in the next theme.
   - Write your goal and three steps you will take to help you reach it.
   - Meet with your teacher to review your goal and your plan for achieving it.

 ## Build Your Portfolio

SELECT
Choose two pieces of work you did in this theme to include in your portfolio. Use these questions to help you choose.

- Which do you consider your best work?
- Which challenged you the most?
- Which did you learn the most from?
- Which did you enjoy the most?

REFLECT
Write some notes to accompany the pieces you selected. Use these questions to guide you.

- What do you like best about the piece?
- What did you learn from creating it?
- What might you do differently if you were beginning this piece again?

Reading on Your Own

If you have enjoyed the literature in this theme, you might be interested in the following books.

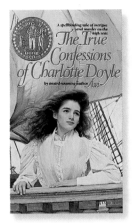

The True Confessions of Charlotte Doyle
by Avi The only passenger aboard an 1832 sailing ship, thirteen-year-old Charlotte must decide whether she will side with a tyrannical captain or a crew ready for mutiny.

But That's Another Story: Favorite Authors Introduce Popular Genres
edited by Sandy Asher Authors of thirteen short stories discuss writing in such genres as science fiction, fantasy, horror, and realistic fiction.

Bridge to Terabithia
by Katherine Paterson A boy learns the importance of friendship.

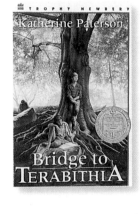

Our Stories: A Fiction Workshop for Young Authors
by Marion Dane Bauer An award-winning author gives advice to beginning writers.

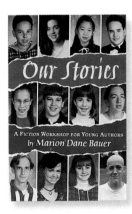

Standardized Test Practice

Read the following passage. Then read each question on page 403. Decide which is the best answer to each question. Mark the letter for that answer on your paper.

What Should Maya Do?

"Stop it, Josh! You know that's not true," Maya shouted.

"You are, too! Everyone knows you're a teacher's pet," Josh yelled back.

"That's not true at all. You are just spreading rumors because I am the only one who got a 100 on the science test."

"Sure, Maya."

Josh walked away, leaving Maya standing alone at recess. The other kids were having so much fun playing kickball that no one seemed to notice that she was standing by herself.

"I am *not* a teacher's pet," Maya kept saying to herself over and over again.

Susan, Maya's best friend, saw Maya and ran over to her.

"You look like you're about to cry, Maya. What's wrong?" Susan asked as she put her arm around Maya to comfort her.

"Josh keeps calling me names. He says I don't really deserve to get a 100 on the test we got back today, and that I only get good grades because I'm nice to Mrs. Smith."

"Maya, don't worry. Everyone knows that you deserve the grades you get—and everyone knows that Mrs. Smith grades fairly. Josh always tries to make trouble. Come play kickball with us and you'll feel better."

Maya really didn't want to play kickball, but she didn't want to stand there feeling sorry for herself, either. She looked across the playground and saw that Josh was standing there pointing at her and laughing. She couldn't hear what he was saying, but she knew that he was talking about her.

Susan noticed it, too. She grabbed Maya's arm and dragged her across the yard, right through a game of dodgeball and some girls playing jump rope.

When Susan and Maya approached Josh, he said loudly, "Look who it is: Little Miss Perfect."

The rest of the class stopped and looked at what was happening. Maya felt her face getting red, and she started to sweat. She knew that she had to stand up for herself and it had to be now. As Susan started to talk, Maya interrupted her.

"Josh, you'd better—," Susan started to say.

"No, that's okay, Susan. I'll handle this myself. Josh, I don't care what you say. I know that I did well on the test because I studied hard. I am not ashamed of being smart and getting As. Maybe if you got more As, you wouldn't be so mean to everyone. Go ahead and make fun of me if you want. I know the truth."

As twenty pairs of eyes looked at Maya and Josh, it was Josh's turn to get red and sweaty. Josh had bullied many kids in Mrs. Smith's class for one reason or another. Most kids were afraid of crossing him, so they went along with whatever he said because they feared they would be his next victims. They looked anxiously around. Josh finally broke the silence.

"Whatever, Maya. I was just saying stuff."

He looked around, and he knew that everyone was staring at him. This was the first time that anyone had stood up to him. He didn't quite know what to do.

Finally, Maya looked at all of her classmates. She knew she had to give Josh exactly what he deserved. She stuck her hand out for him to shake and said, "Truce."

Josh was so surprised that he didn't react, at first. Then, he put out his hand to shake hers. Just as he did, the bell rang and recess was over.

---

1 Why are Maya and Josh yelling at one another at the beginning of the story?

   A Josh took Maya's lunch.

   B Maya didn't want to play on Josh's kickball team.

   C Josh was calling Maya names.

   D Josh got Maya in trouble.

2 How did Maya feel after she stood up to Josh?

   F Nervous

   G Quiet

   H Cold

   J Proud

3 Which of the following is the best summary of this passage?

   A Maya gets punished for cheating.

   B Maya gets into a fight with Josh and then forgives him.

   C Maya gets a good grade on a test and talks to Susan at recess.

   D Maya is proud of her friends.

4 What did Josh feel when Maya finally confronted him in front of everyone?

   F Embarrassed

   G Happy

   H Bored

   J Excited

5 At the end of the passage, the word truce means —

   A we will be best friends

   B we will be enemies

   C we will continue to argue about this

   D we will stop arguing

6 Which of the following is most likely to happen on the way back to class?

   F The students in the class talk about what happened outside.

   G Susan tells Maya that she did the wrong thing.

   H Josh shakes Maya's hand.

   J Josh discovers that he got a 100 on his test, too.

7 The author probably wanted to help people understand that —

   A studying for tests can help you become a teacher's pet.

   B sometimes people need to stand up for themselves.

   C it's better to ignore a bully.

   D it pays to study and get good grades.

STOP

The Will to Win

Winning is not everything—but making the effort to win is.

—Vince Lombardi, former coach of the Green Bay Packers football team

The Runner. Ruben DeAnda (b. 1945). Dye/transfer, 16 x 20 in. Artist's collection.

THEME CONTENTS

GENRE FOCUS FOLKTALE

Exploring the Theme

The Will to Win

Do you remember learning how to ride a bike? The first day you tried, you probably fell several times. Perhaps you even scraped your knees. Finally, with practice and determination, you learned to keep your balance. As you'll discover in this theme, no matter who you are or what situation you face, it helps to have "the will to win."

Starting Points

IN YOUR OWN WORDS

Why is Calvin wearing extra pants in this cartoon?

- Create a word web using as many words as you can to describe what it means to be determined.

DEFINING DETERMINATION

With a partner, list activities that require extra effort to master, such as mountain climbing, skateboarding, swimming long distance, memorizing a speech, cooking, or learning to type. Why does trying your best matter? Discuss your ideas. Then put stars next to the activity each of you likes best.

CALVIN AND HOBBES ©1988 Watterson. Reprinted with permission of UNIVERSAL PRESS SYNDICATE. All rights reserved.

Theme Projects

Choose one of the projects below to complete as you read the selections in this theme. Work on your own, with a partner, or with a group.

LEARNING FOR LIFE
Stories of Success

1. Watch a movie about someone who faced a challenge but didn't give up.

2. Pick your favorite scene from the movie and create your own skit based on that scene. You might assign roles to other students or play all of them yourself. Practice and perform your version of the scene for your classmates.

3. Create a poster that advertises your performance and emphasizes the main character's determination.

MULTIMEDIA PROJECT
Finding Famous "Firsts"

Create a computer slideshow or a scrapbook celebrating stories of hard-earned success.

1. Research famous "firsts" achieved by people who had to overcome prejudice, disabilities, or other obstacles. For example, who was the first woman to climb Mt. Everest? Who was the first African American to win an Oscar?

2. Collect artwork or photos of the people you find.

3. Use a software program to scan the images into a computer, or mount each image on paper. Add a caption to each image.

4. Share your project with your classmates.

interNET CONNECTION

Check out the World Wide Web for more project ideas or more books related to this theme. Try typing the keywords *prizewinners, goals,* or *awards* into a search engine. For more about this theme, check out the Glencoe Web site at lit.glencoe.com

INTERDISCIPLINARY/MATH
Charting Progress

Choose a sports team that has shown improvement. Then track the team's game statistics in the newspaper or online.

1. Collect specific numbers to show how much the team has improved over a single season or over several years.

2. Use your research to make a chart of the team's progress.

3. What was the team's record during the time you charted?

4. Write a short story or a news article about this team's "will to win."

Before You Read

Satchel Paige

MEET BILL LITTLEFIELD

"People like to tell their stories to folks inclined to listen, and I'm one of those folks." So says Bill Littlefield, radio host, teacher, and author. In his book *Champions: Stories of Ten Remarkable Athletes*, Littlefield emphasizes the courage shown by players who had to overcome such difficult problems as discrimination, poverty, and physical handicaps. Littlefield is a professor at Curry College in Milton, Massachusetts, and the host and writer for a weekly sports show on public radio. He has won five broadcast awards from the Associated Press.

Bill Littlefield was born in 1948. This biography was published in 1993.

FOCUS ACTIVITY

Have you ever set a goal for yourself? What obstacles came up as you pursued your goal? Did you succeed?

QuickWrite
Jot down the answers to these questions.

Setting a Purpose
Read "Satchel Paige" to find out about obstacles an athlete overcame.

BACKGROUND

Did You Know?
Baseball, "the national pastime," is considered the national sport of the United States. The game may have come from an English game called *rounders*, which was played on a dia-

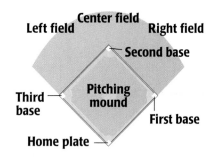

mond-shaped field with four bases. In 1845 a group of amateur players in New York City formulated rules for a similar game they called New York baseball.

VOCABULARY PREVIEW

makeshift (māk′ shift′) *adj.* suitable as a temporary substitute for the proper or desired thing; p. 411

potential (pə ten′ shəl) *adj.* capable of being; p. 411

confrontation (kon′ frun tā′ shən) *n.* a face-to-face meeting; p. 413

prejudice (prej′ ə dis) *n.* an unfavorable opinion or a judgment formed unfairly; p. 413

characterize (kar′ ik tə rīz′) *v.* to be a quality of; p. 413

perspective (pər spek′ tiv) *n.* the ability to see things in relationship to one another; point of view; p. 413

exploit (eks′ ploit) *n.* a heroic deed; p. 415

Satchel Paige

Bill Littlefield

Late in the afternoon of July 9, 1948, Leroy "Satchel" Paige began the long walk from the bullpen to the mound at Cleveland's Municipal Stadium. He didn't hurry. He never hurried. As he said himself, he "kept the juices flowing by jangling gently" as he moved. The crowd roared its appreciation. This was the fellow they'd come to see.

Satchel Paige

When Satchel finally reached the mound, Cleveland manager Lou Boudreau took the ball from starting pitcher Bob Lemon, who would eventually be voted into the Hall of Fame but had tired that day, and gave it to Paige. Probably he said something like, "Shut 'em down, Satchel." Whatever he said, Paige had no doubt heard the words a thousand times. Though he was a rookie with the Indians that year, no pitcher in the history of baseball had ever been more thoroughly prepared for a job. He kicked at the rubber, looked in for the sign, and got set to throw. In a moment, twenty-odd years later than it should have happened, Satchel Paige would deliver his first pitch in the big leagues.

The tall, skinny kid named Leroy Paige became Satchel Paige one day at the rail-road station in Mobile, Alabama. He was carrying bags for the folks getting on and off the trains, earning all the nickels and dimes he could to help feed his ten brothers and sisters. Eventually it occurred to him that if he slung a pole across his narrow shoulders and hung the bags, or satchels, on the ends of the pole, he could carry for more people at once and collect more nickels and dimes. It worked, but it looked a little funny. "You look like some kind of ol' satchel tree," one of his friends told him, and the nickname stuck.

Even in those days, before he was a teenager, Satchel Paige could throw hard and accurately. Years later, Paige swore that when his mother would send him out into the yard to get a chicken for dinner, he would brain the bird with a rock. "I used to kill *flying* birds with rocks, too,"

he said. "Most people need shotguns to do what I did with rocks."

It was not a talent that would go unnoticed for long. He was pitching for the semipro[1] Mobile Tigers before he was eighteen . . . or maybe before he was sixteen, or before he was twelve. There is some confusion about exactly when Satchel Paige was born, and Satchel never did much to clarify the matter. But there never has been any confusion about whether he could pitch. His first steady job in baseball was with the Chattanooga Black Lookouts. He was paid fifty dollars a month. In the seasons that followed he would also pitch for the Birmingham Black Barons, the Nashville Elite Giants, the Baltimore Black Sox, the Pittsburgh Crawfords, and the Kansas City Monarchs, among other teams.

If those names are not as familiar sounding as those of the New York Yankees, the Los Angeles Dodgers, or the Boston Red Sox, it's because they were all clubs in the Negro leagues, not the major leagues. Today the presence of black baseball players in the big leagues is taken for granted. Hank Aaron is the greatest of the home run hitters, and Rickey Henderson has stolen more bases than any other big leaguer. But before 1947, neither of them would have had the opportunity to do what they have done. Until Brooklyn Dodger general manager Branch Rickey signed Jackie Robinson, black players had no choice but to play for one of the all-black teams, and making that choice, they faced hardships no major-leaguer today could imagine.

---

1. The prefix *semi-* means "partly; half." A member of a *semipro* team is paid to play part-time and may have another, full-time job; a *professional* player receives a full-time salary.

Players in the Negro leagues crowded into broken-down cars and bumped over rutted roads to <u>makeshift</u> ball fields with lights so bad that every pitch was a <u>potential</u> weapon. Then they drove all night for an afternoon game three hundred miles away. On good days they played before big, appreciative crowds in parks they'd rented from the major league teams in Chicago, New York, or Pittsburgh. On bad days they learned that the team they were playing for was too broke to finish the season, and they would have to look for a healthier team that could use them, or else find a factory job.

It took talent, hard work, and a sense of humor to survive in the Negro leagues, and Satchel Paige had a lot of all three. But he didn't just survive. He prospered. Everybody knows about the fastball, the curve, and the slider. But Satchel threw a "bee" ball, which, he said, "would always *be* where I wanted it

---

Vocabulary
makeshift (māk′ shift′) *adj.* suitable as a temporary substitute for the proper or desired thing
potential (pə ten′ shəl) *adj.* capable of being

Satchel Paige

to *be*." He featured a trouble ball, which, of course, gave the hitters a lot of trouble. Even the few who could see it couldn't hit it. Sometimes he'd come at them with his hesitation pitch, a delivery so mysterious that the man at the plate would sometimes swing before the ball left Satchel's hand.

Nor was pitching his sole triumph. Early in his career Satchel Paige began building a reputation as a storyteller, a spinner of tall tales as well as shutouts. He particularly liked to recall an occasion upon which he was asked to come on in relief of a pitcher who'd left men on first and third with nobody out. "It was a tight situation," Satchel would say.

We only had a one-run lead, and that was looking mighty slim. But I had an idea. When I left the bench, I stuck a baseball in my pocket, so when the manager gave me the game ball on the mound, I had two. I went into my stretch just like usual. Then I threw one ball to first and the other to third. It was a good pick-off move, you see, and it fooled the batter, too. He swung, even though there was no ball to swing at. Those boys at first and third were both out, of course, and the umpire called strike three on the batter, so that was it for the inning. It's always good to save your strength when you can.

Major-leaguers today make enough money so that they don't have to work over the winter, but it hasn't always been so. Big-leaguers and Negro-leaguers alike used to

make extra money after their regular seasons ended by putting together makeshift teams and playing each other wherever they could draw a paying crowd. This practice was called barnstorming, and Satchel Paige was the world champion at it. For thirty years, from 1929 to 1958, he played baseball summer and winter. When it was too cold to play in the Negro league cities, he played in Cuba, Mexico, and the Dominican Republic. In Venezuela he battled a boa constrictor in the outfield, or so he said, and in Ciudad Trujillo[2] he dodged the machine-gun fire of fans who'd bet on the losing team.

Throughout the early years of these adventures, the years of Satchel's prime, he

---

2. *Ciudad Trujillo* (sē′ oo däd′ troo hē′ yō) is the Spanish name for a city in northwestern Venezuela.

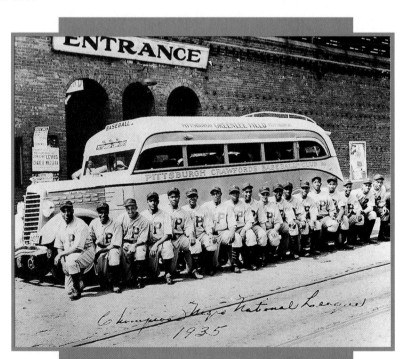

Viewing the photograph: Satchel Paige and his teammates on the Pittsburgh Crawfords pose as the champions of the Negro National League in 1935. How might one of these ballplayers explain the will to win?

often barnstormed against the best white ballplayers of his day. St. Louis Cardinal great Dizzy Dean once told him, "You're a better pitcher than I ever hope to be." Paige beat Bob Feller and struck out Babe Ruth. And when Joe DiMaggio, considered by some the most multi-talented ballplayer ever, beat out an infield hit against Paige in 1936, DiMaggio turned to his team-mates and said, "Now I know I can make it with the Yankees. I finally got a hit off of ol' Satch."

Everywhere these confrontations took place, Satchel Paige would hear the same thing: "If only you were white, you'd be a star in the big leagues." The fault, of course, was not with Satchel. The fault and the shame were with major league baseball, which stubbornly, stupidly clung to the same prejudice that characterized many institutions in the United States besides baseball. Prejudice has not yet disappeared from the game. Black players are far less likely than their white counterparts[3] to be hired as managers or general managers. But today's black players can thank Robinson, Paige, and a handful of other pioneers for the opportunities they enjoy.

Though the color line prevented Satchel Paige from pitching in the company his talent and hard work should have earned for him, he was not bitter or defeated. Ignorant white fans would sometimes taunt him, but he kept their insults in perspective. "Some of them would call you names," he said of his early years on the road, "but most of them would cheer you." Years later he worked to shrug off the pain caused by the restaurants that would not serve him, the hotels that would not rent him a room, the fans who would roar for his bee ball but would not acknowledge him on the street the next day. "Fans all holler the same at a ball game," he would say, as if the racists[4] and the racist system had never touched him at all.

When he finally got the chance to become the first black pitcher in the American League at age forty-two (or forty-six, or forty-eight), he made the most of it. On that first day in Cleveland, Satchel Paige did the job he'd never doubted he could do. First he smiled for all the photographers. Then he told the butterflies in his stomach to leave off their flapping around. Then he shut down the St. Louis Browns for two innings before being lifted for a pinch hitter.

And still there were doubters. "Sure," they said to each other the next day when they read the sports section. "The old man could work two innings against the Browns. Who couldn't?"

But Satchel Paige fooled 'em, as he'd been fooling hitters for twenty-five years and more. He won a game in relief six days

---

3. Here, *counterparts* refers to people who hold similar positions.

4. *Racists* believe that differences between races make their own race better than others.

Vocabulary
confrontation (kon′ frun tā′ shən) *n.* a face-to-face meeting
prejudice (prej′ ə dis) *n.* an unfavorable opinion or a judgment formed unfairly
characterize (kar′ ik tə rīz′) *v.* to be a quality of
perspective (pər spek′ tiv) *n.* the ability to see things in relationship to one another; point of view

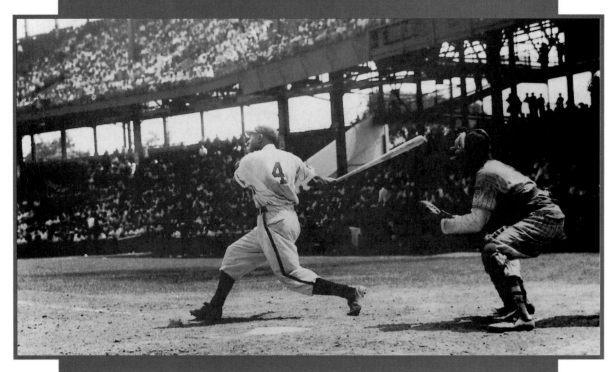

Viewing the photograph: What had just happened when this photograph was taken?

later, his first major league win. Then on August 3 he started a game against the Washington Senators before 72,000 people. Paige went seven innings and won. In his next two starts he threw shutouts against the Chicago White Sox, and through the waning[5] months of that summer, his only complaint was that he was "a little tired from underwork." The routine on the major league level must have been pretty leisurely for a fellow who'd previously pitched four or five times a week.

Satchel Paige finished the 1948 season with six wins and only one loss. He'd allowed the opposing teams an average of just over two runs a game. Paige was named Rookie of the Year, an honor he might well have achieved twenty years earlier if he'd had the chance. The sportswriters of the day agreed that without Satchel's contribution, the Indians, who won the pennant, would have finished second at best. Many of the writers were dismayed when Satchel appeared for only two-thirds of an inning in the World Series that fall. Paige, too, was disappointed that the manager hadn't chosen to use him more, but he was calm in the face of what others might have considered an insult. The writers told him, "You sure take things good." Satchel smiled and said, "Ain't no other way to take them."

Satchel Paige outlasted the rule that said he couldn't play in the big leagues because he was black. Then he made fools of the people who said he couldn't get major league hitters out because he was too old. But his big league numbers over several years—twenty-eight wins and thirty-two saves—don't begin to tell the story of Paige's unparalleled[6] career. Playing for teams that

---

5. Here, *waning* means "nearing the end of."

6. If something is *unparalleled,* nothing is equal to it or better than it.

no longer exist in leagues that came and went with the seasons, Satchel Paige pitched in some 2,500 baseball games. Nobody has ever pitched in more. And he had such fun at it. Sometimes he'd accept offers to pitch in two cities on the same day. He'd strike out the side for three innings in one game, then fold his long legs into his car and race down the road toward the next ballpark. If the police could catch him, they would stop him for speeding. But when they recognized him, as often as not they'd escort him to the second game with sirens howling, well aware that there might be a riot in the park if Satchel Paige didn't show up as advertised. Once he'd arrived, he'd instruct his infielders and outfielders to sit down for an inning, then he'd strike out the side again.

For his talent, his energy, and his showmanship, Satchel Paige was the most famous of the Negro league players, but when he got some measure of recognition in the majors, he urged the writers to remember that there had been lots of other great ballplayers in those Negro league games. He named them, and he told their stories. He made their <u>exploits</u> alive and real for generations of fans who'd never have known.

In 1971, the Baseball Hall of Fame in Cooperstown, New York, inducted[7] Satchel Paige. The action was part of the Hall's attempt to remedy baseball's shame, the color line. The idea was to honor Paige and some of the other great Negro league players like Josh Gibson and Cool Papa Bell, however late that honor might come. Satchel Paige could have rejected that gesture. He could have told the baseball establishment that what it was doing was too little, too late. But when the time came for Satchel Paige to speak to the crowd gathered in front of the Hall of Fame to celebrate his triumphs, he told the people, "I am the proudest man on the face of the earth today."

Satchel Paige, whose autobiography was entitled *Maybe I'll Pitch Forever*, died in Kansas City in 1982. He left behind a legend as large as that of anyone who ever played the game, as well as a long list of achievements celebrated in story and song—and in at least one fine poem, by Samuel Allen:

To Satch

Sometimes I feel like I will *never* stop
Just go on forever
Till one fine mornin'
I'm gonna reach up and grab me a
   handfulla stars
Swing out my long lean leg
And whip three hot strikes burnin' down
   the heavens
And look over at God and say
How about that!

---

7. To be *inducted* is to be admitted or brought into a group. The *Baseball Hall of Fame* honors great players, managers, and broadcasters.

Vocabulary
exploit (eks′ ploit) *n.* a heroic deed

Responding to Literature

PERSONAL RESPONSE

- ◆ What is the most interesting thing you learned from the selection?
- ◆ Look back at your notes from the **Focus Activity** on page 408. Were the obstacles to your goals within your power to change? Were Paige's?

Analyzing Literature

RECALL

1. In what baseball league did Satchel Paige play for most of his career? Why?
2. What are some pitches Paige was known for? Describe them.
3. What is "barnstorming" in baseball? Why did baseball players do it?
4. How did Paige feel about being inducted into the Baseball Hall of Fame?

INTERPRET

5. Did discrimination end for Paige after he began playing for the major leagues? Support your answer.
6. After joining the major leagues, what facts prove that Paige was a great pitcher?
7. How did barnstorming help Paige's reputation as a player? Give examples.
8. Paige was inducted late into the Baseball Hall of Fame. What feelings does the author have about this? How do you know the author's feelings?

EVALUATE AND CONNECT

9. The author tells much of the biography with **anecdotes.** An anecdote is a brief account of an event that illustrates some point about the subject. How do you think the author decided which anecdotes to include?
10. What would you ask or tell Satchel Paige if you could meet him?

LITERARY ELEMENTS

Biography

Many people admire the achievements of sports figures and want to know about their lives. A **biography** is the true story of a person's life written by someone other than the subject.

Facts and characters are essential elements of biography, but setting and generalizations are also important. For example, Littlefield explains about the segregated society of Paige's time and generalizes that Satchel Paige ". . . was not bitter or defeated."

1. Find two incidents that show that Paige was not bitter.
2. Find a detail that tells about the times in which Paige lived.

● See **Literary Terms Handbook,** p. R1.

Paige's hat from the Kansas City Royals.

Extending Your Response

Writing About Literature

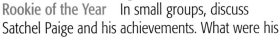

Critical Thinking   The author says of Paige's induction into the Hall of Fame, "The action was part of the Hall's attempt to remedy baseball's shame, the color line." Based on what you have read and your own knowledge, what was "the color line"? Write a definition. Then, in a paragraph, describe one incident that shows how the color line affected Paige.

Creative Writing

The Sports Page   Write a headline for the sports page on the day that Satchel Paige was on the mound to pitch in his first major-league game. Use your imagination and what you know of him to describe his movements and how his pitch looked as it sailed across the plate.

Literature Groups

Rookie of the Year   In small groups, discuss Satchel Paige and his achievements. What were his biggest accomplishments? Do you think Paige would name the same accomplishments you do, in the same order? What were his most difficult setbacks? What stands out about his personality? How do you think he saw himself?

Performing

A Song for Satch   With a partner, make up a song that tells the highlights of Satchel Paige's life—from how he received his nickname to when he entered the Baseball Hall of Fame. If you need a tune, you might want to use a familiar song or the theme of a television show. Practice your song, and then perform it for the class.

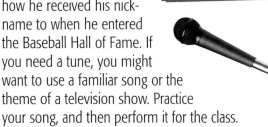

💼 **Save your work for your portfolio.**

Skill Minilesson

VOCABULARY   • THE PREFIXES *com-* and *con-*

Prefixes are word parts that are added to the beginning of a whole word or a root to form a new word. *Com-* and *con-* are really the same prefix, just spelled a little differently. Both can mean "together with." A *confrontation* happens when two or more people *confront* each other. They meet face to face, or "front to front." Enemies may *confront* each other on a battlefield. Baseball teams *confront* each other on a diamond.

PRACTICE   Think about the prefixes and the base words they are attached to in the list below. Then match each word to its definition.

1. conform   a. a joining together
2. compress   b. to make or become the same
3. compatriot   c. to make smaller by pushing
4. conjunction   parts together
5. concurrent   d. happening at the same time
                  e. one from the same country

MEDIA Connection

WEB SITE

Several Web sites include information about the Negro leagues and the integration of the major leagues. Read the one below.

Shadowball

Address: ▼ www.negro-league.columbus.oh.us

The first professional black team was the Cuban Giants, originally a group of waiters from the Argyle Hotel in Babylon, Long Island. They called themselves "Cuban" to hide the fact that they were African Americans, and "Giants" after the popular all-white New York Giants.

Pennants of Negro league teams.

Jackie Robinson's debut in major league baseball was a revolution in several ways. Of course, he was the first black player in the modern majors. But also, his Negro league style of play had an immediate impact on the game. Player and manager **Buck O'Neil** recalls: "At that time, [major league] baseball was a base-to-base thing. You hit the ball, you wait on first base until somebody hit it again. But in our baseball you got on base

if you walked, you stole second, you'd try to steal, they'd bunt you over to third and you'd actually score runs without a hit. This was our baseball."

COOL QUOTES

Satchel Paige

"I ain't never throwed an illegal pitch. . . . Just once in a while I used to toss one that ain't never been seen by this generation!"

"I never had a job. I always played baseball."

"Don't look back. Something might be gaining on you."

"If your stomach disputes you, lie down and pacify it with your cool thoughts."

"Keep the juices flowing by jiggling around gently as you move."

Buck O'Neil

"Baseball fulfilled me like music. I played most of my life and loved it. Waste no tears for me. I wasn't born too early— I was right on time."

Respond

1. What were some differences between major league baseball and Negro league baseball, according to Buck O'Neil?

2. Which of the Cool Quotes do you find meaningful? Why?

Batting Averages

When you're reading about sports, numbers can be almost as important as words. For example, you may know that Ty Cobb was a great batter, but how great was he? Well, his career batting average was .366, the best ever recorded in Major League Baseball.

If you're a baseball fan, a number like that probably sounds familiar, but do you know where it comes from? A **batting average** is the number you get when you divide the total hits a batter made by his or her total turns at bat. Here is the formula for a player's batting average:

$$\text{total hits} \div \text{total at-bats} = \text{batting average}$$

Let's say a player steps up to the plate 50 times and hits the ball 10 times. That means you would divide 50 into 10. Your answer is .200.

Every player earns a batting average for each season, and each year the player's average for his or her entire career is calculated and recorded. However, every turn at bat does not count toward a player's average. If the batter walks, sacrifices (hits an out intentionally), or is hit by a pitch, then that turn does not count toward the batter's total at-bats.

In baseball, .400 is considered an excellent average. Ted Williams was the last player to bat over .400 during a single season of Major League Baseball. His average was .406 in 1941. Numbers like that show how hard it is for even the best baseball players to hit a professional pitch. But if you think about it, .400, forty percent, means a batter made only four good hits during ten trips to the plate. If the player hit the ball every time at bat, the average would be 1.00, one hundred percent. Do you know of any other sport that celebrates a 60 percent failure rate for its greatest athletes?

ACTIVITY

You know Ty Cobb's career batting average was .366. With 11,448 at-bats, how many hits did Cobb make?

These baseball players were also famous for their batting averages. What players do you know about who have good batting averages?

Player	Career Batting Average
Hank Aaron	.305
Wade Boggs	.346*
Lou Gehrig	.340
Tony Gwynn	.329*
Babe Ruth	.342
Ted Williams	.344
	* Active

MEDIA Connection

WEB SITE

The Iditarod is a 1,100-mile race between Anchorage and Nome, Alaska. The winner of the first long race in 1973 took about twenty days to run the course, but in recent years winning times have been about ten days.

Junior Iditarod

Address: www.iditarod.com

In order to enter "The Last Great Race," the Iditarod Trail Sled Dog Race, one must be 18 years old. In 1977, a number of younger mushers wanted to "mush the Iditarod Trail." A group of these young people got together and organized the first Iditarod for junior mushers.

The Junior Iditarod trail is 130 miles long. Mushers travel the 65 miles from Wasilla to Yentna, where race rules require that they stay with their dogs and care for them just as the mushers in the adult Iditarod do. The next day they return to Wasilla. Mushers between the ages of 14 and 18 are eligible to compete in the Junior Iditarod. These young people often have their own teams and are totally responsible for training them. Many of the young mushers have gone on to compete in the Iditarod.

Around 15 junior mushers are expected to participate in the 1998 race. Here are two of them:

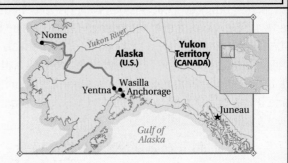

Faren Okray— North Pole, AK
Faren Okray was born in Louisiana but has lived in Alaska for the last eight years. Faren did a unit study on dog mushing in 1990 and "fell in love with the sport." She's been mushing since 1993. Her enthusiasm has spread to her younger brothers who are all mushing with her now.

Dan Seavey— Sterling, AK

Dan Seavey says, "I have been mushing all my life, racing since 1992. Both my dad and grandpa have run the Iditarod multiple times and I have helped my dad train for the Iditarod the last three years." He also helps his folks operate summer tours, so he runs dogs year round. Dan ran his first Junior Iditarod in 1997 and finished second. A home-schooled eleventh grader, he plans to go to college after high school and says he may become a veterinarian.

Respond
1. What would be difficult about mushing?
2. What would be fun?

Before You Read

The King of Mazy May

MEET JACK LONDON

Like his character Walt Masters, London had "seen the sun at midnight, watched the ice-jams on one of the mightiest of rivers, and played beneath the northern lights. . . ." At age twenty-one, Jack London was living the rough life of a gold prospector in Canada's Klondike territory. Although he did not find gold, his experiences gave him a "gold mine" of ideas for stories. By the time he died at age forty, London had written over fifty books of stories, novels, and political essays.

Jack London was born in San Francisco in 1876 and died in 1916. This story was published in 1899.

FOCUS ACTIVITY

Have you ever had an outdoor adventure? Have you camped or fished or hiked? What exciting or unusual things happened?

Three-Step Interview
With a partner, interview other pairs about experiences in "the great outdoors." Take notes, and share the information you gather with the group.

Setting a Purpose
Read "The King of Mazy May" to share a wilderness adventure.

BACKGROUND

The Time and Place   This story takes place in the late 1800s in the Klondike region of the Yukon Territory. The Klondike is a remote wilderness area of northwestern Canada, near Alaska.

Gold was discovered there in 1896, and about one hundred thousand people set out for the gold fields over the next seven years. Most did not find gold. By 1904 most of the surface gold had been mined, and the exciting days of the Klondike Gold Rush were over.

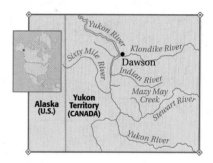

VOCABULARY PREVIEW

endure (en door´) *v.* to hold up under (pain or other hardship); put up with; p. 424

industrious (in dus´ trē əs) *adj.* steady, hard-working; p. 424

adjoining (ə joi´ ning) *adj.* located next to; p. 425

evidently (ev´ ə dent´ lē) *adv.* clearly; p. 426

perilously (per´ ə ləs lē) *adv.* dangerously; riskily; p. 428

capsize (kap´ sīz) *v.* to overturn; p. 429

flounder (floun´ dər) *v.* to move in an awkward way; p. 430

antic (an´ tik) *n.* an odd, silly, or comical action; p. 431

The King of

Mazy May

Jack London

Walt Masters is not a very large boy,
but there is manliness in his make-up, and he himself,
although he does not know a great deal that most boys
know, knows much that other boys do not know.

He can . . . drive the wild wolf-dogs fifty miles a day on the packed trail.

He has never seen a train of cars or an elevator in his life, and for that matter, he has never once looked upon a corn-field, a plow, a cow, or even a chicken. He has never had a pair of shoes on his feet, or gone to a picnic or a party, or talked to a girl. But he has seen the sun at midnight, watched the ice-jams on one of the mightiest of rivers, and played beneath the northern lights, the one white child in thousands of square miles of frozen wilderness.

Walt has walked all the fourteen years of his life in sun-tanned, moose-hide moccasins, and he can go to the Indian camps and "talk big" with the men, and trade calico and beads with them for their precious furs. He can make bread without baking-powder, yeast or hops,[1] shoot a moose at three hundred yards, and drive the wild wolf-dogs fifty miles a day on the packed trail.

Last of all, he has a good heart, and is not afraid of the darkness and loneliness, of man or beast or thing. His father is a good man, strong and brave, and Walt is growing up like him.

Walt was born a thousand miles or so down the Yukon, in a trading-post below the Ramparts.[2] After his mother died, his father and he came on up the river, step by step, from camp to camp, till now they are settled down on the Mazy May Creek in the Klondike[3] country. Last year they and several others had spent much toil and time on the Mazy May, and endured great hardships; the creek, in turn, was just beginning to show up its richness and to reward them for their heavy labor. But with the news of their discoveries, strange men began to come and go through the short days and long nights, and many unjust things they did to the men who had worked so long upon the creek.

Si Hartman had gone away on a moose-hunt, to return and find new stakes driven and his claim jumped. George Lukens and his brother had lost their claims in a like manner, having delayed too long on the way to Dawson[4] to record them. In short, it was an old story, and quite a number of the earnest, industrious prospectors had suffered similar losses.

---

1. *Calico* is a cotton cloth with a pattern. Bakers usually use *yeast* to make bread dough rise, but either *baking powder* or *hops* is a possible substitute.

2. The *Yukon* River begins in Canada's Yukon Territory and flows west to the Bering Sea. In central Alaska, the river passes through a deep, narrow, steep-sided valley called the *Ramparts.*

3. The *Klondike* is the name of both a river and a gold-mining region in the Yukon Territory near the Alaskan border.

4. A *claim* was the piece of land that a *prospector,* or gold-seeker, claimed to own. The prospector drove wooden *stakes* into the ground to mark its boundaries and recorded the claim with officials. A prospector who *jumped* a claim took possession of land already claimed by someone else. In the late 1890s, *Dawson* was capital of the Yukon Territory.

Vocabulary

endure (en door´) *v.* to hold up under (pain or other hardship); put up with
industrious (in dus´ trē əs) *adj.* steady, hard-working

But Walt Masters's father had recorded his claim at the start, so Walt had nothing to fear, now that his father had gone on a short trip up the White River prospecting for quartz. Walt was well able to stay by himself in the cabin, cook his three meals a day, and look after things. Not only did he look after his father's claim, but he had agreed to keep an eye on the <u>adjoining</u> one of Loren Hall, who had started for Dawson to record it.

Loren Hall was an old man, and he had no dogs, so he had to travel very slowly. After he had been gone some time, word came up the river that he had broken through the ice at Rosebud Creek, and frozen his feet so badly that he would not be able to travel for a couple of weeks. Then Walt Masters received the news that old Loren was nearly all right again, and about to move on afoot for Dawson, as fast as a weakened man could.

Walt was worried, however; the claim was liable to be jumped at any moment because of this delay, and a fresh stampede had started in on the Mazy May. He did

The result of the year's "wash up": A sketch in the Bank of British North America, Dawson City, 1898. Jules M. Price. Illustration from *From Euston to Klondike.*

Viewing the print: What do you think the man is weighing? How important is the measurement?

Vocabulary
adjoining (ə joi′ ning) *adj.* located next to

not like the looks of the newcomers, and one day, when five of them came by with crack[5] dog-teams and the lightest of camping outfits, he could see that they were prepared to make speed, and resolved to keep an eye on them. So he locked up the cabin and followed them, being at the same time careful to remain hidden.

He had not watched them long before he was sure that they were professional stampeders, bent on jumping all the claims in sight. Walt crept along the snow at the rim of the creek and saw them change many stakes, destroy old ones, and set up new ones.

In the afternoon, with Walt always trailing on their heels, they came back down the creek, unharnessed their dogs, and went into camp within two claims of his cabin. When he saw them make preparations to cook, he hurried home to get something to eat himself, and then hurried back. He crept so close that he could hear them talking quite plainly, and by pushing the underbrush aside he could catch occasional glimpses of them. They had finished eating and were smoking around the fire.

"The creek is all right, boys," a large, black-bearded man, evidently the leader said, "and I think the best thing we can do is to pull out tonight. The dogs can follow the trail; besides, it's going to be moonlight. What say you?"

"But it's going to be beastly cold," objected one of the party. "It's forty below zero now."

"An' sure, can't ye keep warm by jumpin' off the sleds an' runnin' after the dogs?" cried an Irishman. "An' who wouldn't? The creek as rich as a United States mint! Faith, it's an ilegant chanst[6] to be gettin' a run fer yer money! An' if ye don't run, it's mebbe you'll not get the money at all, at all."

"That's it," said the leader. "If we can get to Dawson and record, we're rich men; and there is no telling who's been sneaking along in our tracks, watching us, and perhaps now off to give the alarm. The thing for us to do is to rest the dogs a bit, and then hit the trail as hard as we can. What do you say?"

Evidently the men had agreed with their leader, for Walt Masters could hear nothing but the rattle of the tin dishes which were being washed. Peering out cautiously, he could see the leader studying a piece of paper. Walt knew what it was at a glance—a list of all the unrecorded claims on Mazy May. Any man could get these lists by applying to the gold commissioner at Dawson.

"Thirty-two," the leader said, lifting his face to the men. "Thirty-two isn't recorded, and this is thirty-three. Come on; let's take a look at it. I saw somebody had been working on it when we came up this morning."

Three of the men went with him, leaving one man to remain in camp. Walt crept carefully after them till they came to Loren Hall's shaft. One of the men went down and built a fire on the bottom to thaw out

---

5. Here, *crack* means "excellent; first-rate."

6. This is the Irishman's way of saying "elegant chance," meaning "excellent opportunity."

Vocabulary
evidently (ev′ ə dent′ lē) *adv.* clearly

On the Klondike. 1890s. Roper.

Viewing the painting: Compare the men in this painting with the stampeders.

the frozen gravel, while the others built another fire on the dump and melted water in a couple of gold-pans. This they poured into a piece of canvas stretched between two logs, used by Loren Hall in which to wash his gold.

In a short time a couple of buckets of dirt were sent up by the man in the shaft, and Walt could see the others grouped anxiously about their leader as he proceeded to wash it. When this was finished, they stared at the broad streak of black sand and yellow gold-grains on the bottom of the pan, and one of them called excitedly for the man who had

remained in camp to come. Loren Hall had struck it rich, and his claim was not yet recorded. It was plain that they were going to jump it.

Walt lay in the snow, thinking rapidly. He was only a boy, but in the face of the threatened injustice against old lame Loren Hall he felt that he must do something. He waited and watched, with his mind made up, till he saw the men begin to square up new stakes. Then he crawled away till out of hearing, and broke into a run for the camp of the stampeders. Walt's father had taken their own dogs with him prospecting, and the boy knew how impossible it was for him to undertake the seventy miles to Dawson without the aid of dogs.

Gaining the camp, he picked out, with an experienced eye, the easiest running sled and started to harness up the stampeders' dogs. There were three teams of six each, and from these he chose ten of the best. Realizing how necessary it was to have a good head-dog, he strove[7] to discover a leader amongst them; but he had little time in which to do it, for he could hear the voices of the returning men. By the time the team was in shape and everything ready, the claim-jumpers came into sight in an open place not more than a hundred yards from the trail, which ran down the bed of the creek. They cried out to him, but he gave no heed, grabbing up one of their fur sleeping-robes which lay loosely in the snow, and leaping upon the sled.

"Mush! Hi! Mush on!"[8] he cried to the animals, snapping the keen-lashed whip among them.

The dogs sprang against the yoke-straps, and the sled jerked under way so suddenly as to almost throw him off. Then it curved into the creek, poising <u>perilously</u> on one runner. He was almost breathless with suspense, when it finally righted with a bound and sprang ahead again. The creek bank was high and he could not see, although he could hear the cries of the men and knew they were running to cut him off. He did not dare to think what would happen if they caught him; he only clung to the sled, his heart beating wildly, and watched the snow-rim of the bank above him.

Suddenly, over this snow-rim came the flying body of the Irishman, who had leaped straight for the sled in a desperate attempt to capture it; but he was an instant too late. Striking on the very rear of it, he was thrown from his feet, backward, into the snow. Yet, with the quickness of a cat, he had clutched the end of the sled with one hand, turned over, and was dragging behind on his breast, swearing at the boy and threatening all kinds of terrible things if he did not stop the dogs; but Walt cracked him sharply across the knuckles with the butt of the dog-whip till he let go.

It was eight miles from Walt's claim to the Yukon—eight very crooked miles, for the creek wound back and forth like a snake, "tying knots in itself," as George Lukens said. And because it was so crooked, the dogs could not get up their best speed, while the sled ground heavily on its side against the curves, now to the right, now to the left.

Travelers who had come up and down the Mazy May on foot, with packs on their backs, had declined to go around all the bends, and instead had made short cuts across the narrow necks of creek bottom. Two of his pursuers had gone back to harness the remaining dogs, but the others took advantage of these short cuts, running

---

7. *Strove* is the past tense of *strive* and means "made a hard, serious effort."
8. Dog-sled drivers say "Mush!" to order their dogs to begin pulling or to move faster. Early French fur traders in Canada used the command "Marchons!" (meaning "March! Go!"), but English and American dog-sledders mispronounced it, saying "Mush on!"

Vocabulary
perilously (per′ ə ləs lē) *adv.* dangerously; riskily

on foot, and before he knew it they had almost overtaken him.

"Halt!" they cried after him. "Stop, or we'll shoot!"

But Walt only yelled the harder at the dogs, and dashed round the bend with a couple of revolver bullets singing after him. At the next bend they had drawn up closer still, and the bullets struck uncomfortably near to him; but at this point the Mazy May straightened out and ran for half a mile as the crow flies. Here the dogs stretched out in their long wolf-swing, and the stampeders, quickly winded, slowed down and waited for their own sled to come up.

Looking over his shoulder, Walt reasoned that they had not given up the chase for good, and that they would soon be after him again. So he wrapped the fur robe about him to shut out the stinging air, and lay flat on the empty sled, encouraging the dogs, as he well knew how.

At last, twisting abruptly between two river islands, he came upon the mighty Yukon sweeping grandly to the north. He could not see from bank to bank, and in the quick-falling twilight it loomed[9] a great white sea of frozen stillness. There was not a sound, save the breathing of the dogs, and the churn of the steel-shod sled.

No snow had fallen for several weeks, and the traffic had packed the main-river trail till it was hard and glassy as glare ice. Over this the sled flew along, and the dogs kept the trail fairly well, although Walt quickly discovered that he had made a mistake in choosing the leader. As they were driven in single file, without reins, he had to guide them by his voice, and it was evident the head-dog had never learned the meaning of "gee" and "haw."[10] He hugged the inside of the curves too closely, often forcing his comrades behind him into the soft snow, while several times he thus capsized the sled.

There was no wind, but the speed at which he traveled created a bitter blast, and with the thermometer down to forty below, this bit through fur and flesh to the very bones. Aware that if he remained constantly upon the sled he would freeze to death, and knowing the practice of Arctic travelers, Walt shortened up one of the lashing-thongs, and whenever he felt chilled, seized hold of it, jumped off, and ran behind till warmth was restored. Then he would climb on and rest till the process had to be repeated.

> **There was not a sound, save the breathing of the dogs, and the churn of the steel-shod sled.**

---

9. To *loom* is to come into view in a way that seems large and, often, threatening.
10. These are commands used to direct dogs, horses, and some other animals. *Gee* is "to the right," and *haw* is "to the left."

Vocabulary
capsize (kap′ sīz) *v.* to overturn

Looking back he could see the sled of his pursuers, drawn by eight dogs, rising and falling over the ice hummocks[11] like a boat in a seaway. The Irishman and the black-bearded leader were with it, taking turns in running and riding.

Night fell, and in the blackness of the first hour or so, Walt toiled desperately with his dogs. On account of the poor lead-dog, they were constantly floundering off the beaten track into the soft snow, and the sled was as often riding on its side or top as it was in the proper way. This work and strain tried his strength sorely. Had he not been in such haste he could have avoided much of it, but he feared the stampeders would creep up in the darkness and overtake him. However, he could hear them occasionally yelling to their dogs, and knew from the sounds that they were coming up very slowly.

When the moon rose he was off Sixty Mile, and Dawson was only fifty miles away. He was almost exhausted, and breathed a sigh of relief as he climbed on the sled again. Looking back, he saw his enemies had crawled up within four hundred yards. At this space they remained, a black speck of motion on the white river-breast. Strive as they would, they could not shorten this distance, and strive as he would he could not increase it.

He had now discovered the proper lead-dog, and he knew he could easily run away from them if he could only change the bad leader for the good one. But this was impossible, for a moment's delay, at

How to reach the

KLONDIKE.

COLUMBIA NAVIGATION AND TRADING COMPANY.

S. S. City of Columbia (1900 tons) will depart from the Old Dominion Line Pier 26, North River,

Wednesday, Dec. 1st, for

ST. MICHAEL,

connecting with Company's river steamers for

DAWSON CITY.

Fare to Dawson City, including 1000 pounds of baggage, $680.00 up, according to accommodation. Passengers desiring to meet the ship at San Francisco or Seattle will be provided with transportation by rail to either point at same rate.

For passage tickets and further information apply to the agents,

RAYMOND & WHITCOMB,
31 East Fourteenth Street, New York.

296 Washington St., Boston, Mass.
1005 Chestnut St., Philadelphia, Pa.
95 Adams St., Chicago, Ill.

An advertisement for a steamship company.

the speed they were running, would bring the men behind upon him.

When he got off the mouth of Rosebud Creek, just as he was topping a rise, the ping of a bullet on the ice beside him, and the report[12] of a gun, told him that they were this time shooting at him with a rifle. And from then on, as he cleared the summit of each ice-jam, he stretched flat on the leaping sled till the rifle-shot from the rear warned him that he was safe till the next ice-jam.

Now it is very hard to lie on a moving sled, jumping and plunging and yawing[13] like a boat before the wind, and to shoot through the deceiving moonlight at an

---

11. The *hummocks* are bumps or ridges.

---

12. A gun's *report* is the explosive noise of its being fired.
13. To *yaw* is to turn from a straight course without meaning to.

Vocabulary
flounder (floun′ dər) *v.* to move in an awkward way

object four hundred yards away on another moving sled performing equally wild antics. So it is not to be wondered at that the black-bearded leader did not hit him.

After several hours of this, during which, perhaps, a score[14] of bullets had struck about him, their ammunition began to give out and their fire slackened. They took greater care, and only whipped a shot at him at the most favorable opportunities. He was also beginning to leave them behind, the distance slowly increasing to six hundred yards.

Lifting clear on the crest of a great jam off Indian River, Walt Masters met his first accident. A bullet sang past his ears, and struck the bad lead-dog.

The poor brute plunged in a heap, with the rest of the team on top of him.

Like a flash, Walt was by the leader. Cutting the traces with his hunting knife, he dragged the dying animal to one side and straightened out the team.

He glanced back. The other sled was coming up like an express-train. With half the dogs still over their traces, he cried, "Mush on!" and leaped upon the sled just as the pursuing team dashed abreast of him.

The Irishman was just preparing to spring for him,—they were so sure they had him that they did not shoot,—when Walt turned fiercely upon them with his whip.

He struck at their faces, and men must save their faces with their hands. So there was no shooting just then. Before they could recover from the hot rain of blows, Walt reached out from his sled, catching their wheel-dog[15] by the fore legs in mid-spring, and throwing him heavily. This brought the whole team into a snarl, capsizing the sled and tangling his enemies up beautifully.

Away Walt flew, the runners of his sled fairly screaming as they bounded over the frozen surface. And what had seemed an accident proved to be a blessing in disguise. The proper lead-dog was now to the fore, and he stretched low to the trail and whined with joy as he jerked his comrades along.

By the time he reached Ainslie's Creek, seventeen miles from Dawson, Walt had left his pursuers, a tiny speck, far behind. At Monte Cristo Island he could no longer see them. And at Swede Creek, just as daylight was silvering the pines, he ran plump into the camp of old Loren Hall.

Almost as quick as it takes to tell it, Loren had his sleeping-furs rolled up, and had joined Walt on the sled. They permitted the dogs to travel more slowly, as there was no sign of the chase in the rear, and just as they pulled up at the gold commissioner's office in Dawson, Walt, who had kept his eyes open to the last, fell asleep.

And because of what Walt Masters did on this night, the men of the Yukon have become very proud of him, and always speak of him now as the King of Mazy May.

---

14. A *score* is twenty.

15. The *wheel-dog* is the one nearest the front end of the sled. The term was borrowed from horse teams, in which the wheel-horse is nearest the front wheels of a wagon or carriage.

Vocabulary
antic (an´ tik) *n.* an odd, silly, or comical action

Responding to Literature

PERSONAL RESPONSE

What part of the story did you find most exciting? Why? Share
your feelings about this part of the story with the group.

Analyzing Literature

RECALL

1. What are Walt Masters and his father doing in the Klondike?
2. What are the five newcomers trying to do?
3. What does Walt do to protect his neighbor's claim?
4. How does Walt manage to keep ahead of the men?

INTERPRET

5. Even before the chase begins, how do Walt's actions show
   that he has good skills for surviving outdoors?
6. Does Walt feel justified in taking the sled and dogs and using
   violence? Do you think his actions are justified? Explain.
7. Walt's father asked him to keep an eye on his neighbor's
   claim. Why do you think his father trusted him with this task?
8. Why is Walt called the King of Mazy May?

EVALUATE AND CONNECT

9. Would you call Walt's actions heroic? Why or why not?
10. How does the setting of the Klondike add to the tension in the
    story? Use examples from the selection.

LITERARY ELEMENTS

Suspense

Writers interest their readers
when they create **suspense**—they
raise questions about the outcome of events in a story. As
Walt's lead dog causes the team
to continually flounder ". . . off
the beaten track into the soft
snow," readers share Walt's fear
and tension. The uncertainty
about what will happen to Walt
spurs readers to quickly read on.
Suspense is part of the rising
action of the story. Each additional problem, setback, and danger raises the story's level of
suspense.

1. Does the chase itself create a
   situation of suspense? Explain.

2. What will be resolved by the
   outcome of the chase?

3. What are two problems, setbacks, or dangers Walt
   encounters?

● See **Literary Terms
  Handbook,** p. R8.

Extending Your Response

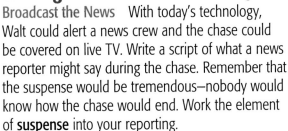

Writing About Literature

Broadcast the News   With today's technology, Walt could alert a news crew and the chase could be covered on live TV. Write a script of what a news reporter might say during the chase. Remember that the suspense would be tremendous—nobody would know how the chase would end. Work the element of **suspense** into your reporting.

Personal Writing

Diary Entry   Write a diary entry about an adventure, especially one in the wilderness. You may find ideas in your notes on outdoor experiences from the **Focus Activity** on page 421. Be sure to include information about the setting, such as the weather or terrain. Also remember to mention the roles others played in your adventure.

Literature Groups

What Went Right, What Went Wrong   As a group, make a list of the things Walt had in his favor or that went his way during the chase. Make another list of the problems, setbacks, and disadvantages he faced. Discuss the reasons Walt succeeded and whether he could just as easily have failed.

Interdisciplinary Activity

Art/Geography   Work with a partner to copy onto poster board the map of the Mazy May Creek, the Yukon River, and Dawson on page 421. Then devise a board game. Draw or create two dog sled markers. Use incidents from the story and your own imagination to write cards that will advance the two "dog sleds" along the route to Dawson.

Save your work for your portfolio.

Skill Minilesson

VOCABULARY • DENOTATION AND CONNOTATION

The dictionary definition of a word is its **denotation.** A word may also have an added meaning, a meaning that suggests certain feelings associated with the word. This is its **connotation.** Two words may have similar denotations but very different connotations. For example, *sobbing* suggests pitiful crying, while *blubbering* suggests foolish, silly crying. Several of the vocabulary words in "The King of Mazy May" have connotations that are important to know.

PRACTICE   Use the information given about connotations to answer the questions.

1. *Industrious* suggests being active in a careful and steady way because of a feeling that the task is important.

   Both a bird building a nest and a puppy playing with a ball are busy. Which is *industrious?*

2. *Endure* suggests continuing or lasting even though it is very hard to do so.
   Both Rick and Nick continue to do their homework. Rick's is easy. Nick's is difficult. Which one *endures* the task?

3. An *antic* is an odd, silly, or comical action.
   Joe and John played tricks on one another. John's trick was mean, but Joe's was fun. Which could be called an *antic?*

● For more about denotation and connotation, see **Reading Handbook,** p. R74.

Before You Read

Priscilla and the Wimps

MEET RICHARD PECK

Richard Peck says that he tries to give readers "leading characters they can look up to and reasons to believe that problems can be solved." When Peck began writing as a full-time career, he wrote about problems he had seen as a high school teacher. He has written more than fifteen novels for teenagers. Some of his most popular are ghost stories featuring Blossom Culp, the science fiction story *Lost in Cyberspace*, and the satire *Secrets of the Shopping Mall*.

Richard Peck was born in 1934. This story was first published in 1984.

FOCUS ACTIVITY

What is a typical situation involving a bully? How do such situations usually turn out?

Journal
List five ways to deal with bullies. Share your ideas in a group.

Setting a Purpose
Read "Priscilla and the Wimps" to enjoy a humorous tale about a bully who meets his match.

BACKGROUND

Did You Know?   There are plenty of individual differences in people as they grow up. However, girls between ten and fourteen are often taller than boys of the same age. By the end of high school, most boys have grown taller than most girls.

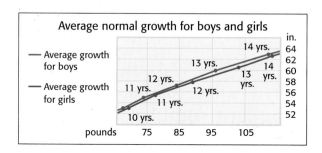

Average normal growth for boys and girls

— Average growth for boys
— Average growth for girls

14 yrs. — 64 in.
13 yrs. — 62
12 yrs. — 60
11 yrs. — 58
— 56
— 54
10 yrs. — 52

pounds   75   85   95   105

VOCABULARY PREVIEW

slither (sli<u>th</u>′ ər) *v.* to move along with a sliding or gliding motion, as a snake; p. 436

swagger (swag′ ər) *v.* to walk or behave in a bold, rude, or proud way; p. 437

immense (i mens′) *adj.* of great size; huge; p. 438

wedge (wej) *v.* to push or crowd into a narrow space; p. 438

straggler (strag′ lər) *n.* one who lags behind the main group; p. 438

fate (fāt) *n.* a power that determines events before they happen; p. 438

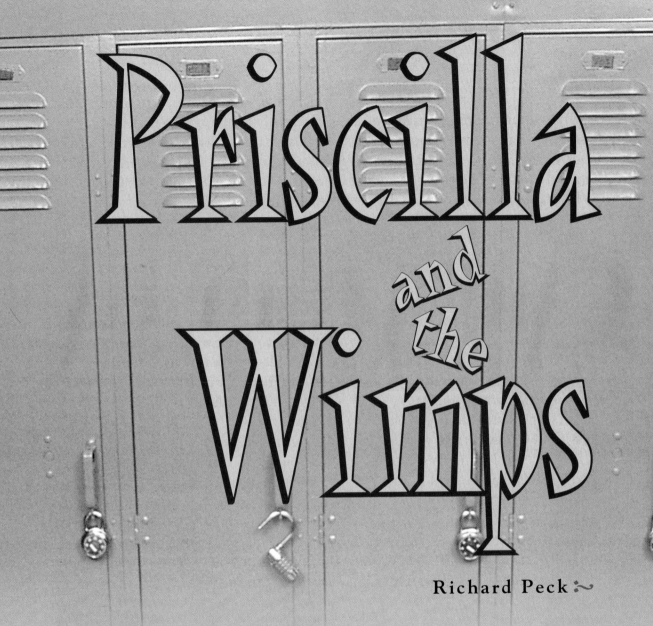

Priscilla and the Wimps

Richard Peck

Listen, there was a time when you couldn't even go to the *rest room* around this school without a pass. And I'm not talking about those little pink tickets made out by some teacher. I'm talking about a pass that could cost anywhere up to a buck, sold by Monk Klutter.

Not that Mighty Monk ever touched money, not in public. The gang he ran, which ran the school for him, was his collection agency.[1] They were Klutter's Kobras, a name spelled out in nailheads on six well-known black plastic windbreakers.

---

1. A *collection agency* is a company that forces people to pay their debts.

Priscilla and the Wimps

Monk's threads were more . . . subtle.[2] A pile-lined suede battle jacket with lizard-skin flaps over tailored Levis and a pair of ostrich-skin boots, brassed-toed and suitable for kicking people around. One of his Kobras did nothing all day but walk a half step behind Monk, carrying a fitted bag with Monk's gym shoes, a roll of rest-room passes, a cashbox, and a switchblade[3] that Monk gave himself manicures with at lunch over at the Kobras' table.

Speaking of lunch, there were a few cases of advanced malnutrition among the newer kids. The ones who were a little slow in handing over a cut of their lunch money and were therefore barred from the cafeteria. Monk ran a tight ship.[4]

I admit it. I'm five foot five, and when the Kobras slithered by, with or without Monk, I shrank. And I admit this, too: I paid up on a regular basis. And I might add: so would you.

This school was old Monk's Garden of Eden. Unfortunately for him, there was a serpent[5] in it. The reason Monk didn't recognize trouble when it was staring him in the face is that the serpent in the Kobras' Eden was a girl.

Practically every guy in school could show you his scars. Fang marks from Kobras, you might say. And they were all highly visible in the shower room: lumps, lacerations,[6] blue bruises, you name it. But girls usually got off with a warning.

Except there was this one girl named Priscilla Roseberry. Picture a girl named Priscilla Roseberry, and you'll be light years[7] off. Priscilla was, hands down, the largest student in our particular institution of learning. I'm not talking fat. I'm talking big. Even beautiful, in a bionic[8] way. Priscilla wasn't inclined toward organized crime. Otherwise, she could have put together a gang that would turn Klutter's Kobras into garter snakes.

Priscilla was basically a loner except she had one friend. A little guy named Melvin Detweiler. You talk about The Odd Couple. Melvin's one of the smallest guys above midget status ever seen. A really nice guy, but, you know—little. They even had lockers next to each other, in the same bank as mine. I don't know what they had going. I'm not saying this was a romance. After all, people deserve their privacy.

Priscilla was sort of above everything, if you'll pardon a pun.[9] And very calm, as only the very big can be. If there was anybody who didn't notice Klutter's Kobras, it was Priscilla.

Until one winter day after school when we were all grabbing our coats out

---

2. *Threads* is a slang word for "clothes." *Subtle* means "not very noticeable." Of course, Monk's outfits are not really subtle.
3. A *switchblade* is a knife with a switch that releases the blade.
4. *Advanced malnutrition* comes from a severe shortage of food. Running a *tight ship* means being strict.
5. In a Bible story, Adam and Eve live happily in the *Garden of Eden* until a *serpent* causes them to be sent away.

6. *Lacerations* are cuts or wounds.
7. A *light year* is the distance light travels through space in one year—about 5.9 trillion miles. So if you're "light years off," you're about as wrong as you could be.
8. Here, *bionic* refers to characters in science fiction stories who have artificial body parts that make them unusually strong.
9. A *pun* is a joke in which a word has two meanings. Priscilla is *above everything* in two ways.

Vocabulary

slither (slith′ ər) *v.* to move along with a sliding or gliding motion, as a snake

of our lockers. And hurrying, since Klutter's Kobras made sweeps of the halls for after-school shakedowns.[10]

Anyway, up to Melvin's locker <u>swaggers</u> one of the Kobras. Never mind his name. Gang members don't need names. They've got group identity. He reaches down and grabs little Melvin by the neck and slams his head against his locker door. The sound of skull against steel rippled all the way down the locker row, speeding the crowds on their way.

"Okay, let's see your pass," snarls the Kobra.

"A pass for what this time?" Melvin asks, probably still dazed.

"Let's call it a pass for very short people," says the Kobra, "a dwarf tax." He wheezes a little Kobra chuckle at his own wittiness. And already he's reaching for Melvin's wallet with the hand that isn't circling Melvin's windpipe. All this time, of course, Melvin and the Kobra are standing in Priscilla's big shadow.

She's taking her time shoving her books into her locker and pulling on a very large-size coat. Then, quicker than the eye, she brings the side of her enormous hand down in a chop that breaks the Kobra's hold on Melvin's throat. You could hear a pin drop in that hallway. Nobody'd ever laid a finger on a Kobra, let alone a hand the size of Priscilla's.

Then Priscilla, who hardly ever says anything to anybody except to

---

10. A *shakedown* is a kind of repeated robbery in which threats are used against the victim.

Vocabulary
swagger (swag′ ər) *v.* to walk or behave in a bold, rude, or proud way

Priscilla and the Wimps

Melvin, says to the Kobra, "Who's your leader, wimp?"

This practically blows the Kobra away. First he's chopped by a girl, and now she's acting like she doesn't know Monk Klutter, the Head Honcho of the World. He's so amazed, he tells her. "Monk Klutter."

"Never heard of him," Priscilla mentions. "Send him to see me." The Kobra just backs away from her like the whole situation is too big for him, which it is.

Pretty soon Monk himself slides up. He jerks his head once, and his Kobras slither off down the hall. He's going to handle this interesting case personally. "Who is it around here doesn't know Monk Klutter?"

He's standing inches from Priscilla, but since he'd have to look up at her, he doesn't. "Never heard of him," says Priscilla.

Monk's not happy with this answer, but by now he's spotted Melvin, who's grown smaller in spite of himself. Monk breaks his own rule by reaching for Melvin with his own hands. "Kid," he says, "you're going to have to educate your girl friend."

His hands never quite make it to Melvin. In a move of pure poetry Priscilla has Monk in a hammerlock. His neck's popping like gunfire, and his head's bowed under the immense weight of her forearm. His suede jacket's peeling back, showing pile.

Did You Know?
In wrestling, a *hammerlock* is a hold in which one person twists the opponent's arm behind his or her back.

Priscilla's behind him in another easy motion. And with a single mighty thrust forward, frog-marches[11] Monk into her own locker. It's incredible. His ostrich-skin boots click once in the air. And suddenly he's gone, neatly wedged into the locker, a perfect fit. Priscilla bangs the door shut, twirls the lock, and strolls out of school. Melvin goes with her, of course, trotting along below her shoulder. The last stragglers leave quietly.

Well, this is where fate, an even bigger force than Priscilla, steps in. It snows all that night, a blizzard. The whole town ices up. And school closes for a week.

---

11. When Priscilla *frog-marches* Monk, she seizes him from behind and forces him to march in front of her.

Vocabulary
immense (i mens′) *adj.* of great size; huge
wedge (wej) *v.* to push or crowd into a narrow space
straggler (strag′ lər) *n.* one who lags behind the main group
fate (fāt) *n.* a power that determines events before they happen

Responding to Literature

PERSONAL RESPONSE

How does the ending of the story compare with real-life situations involving bullies? Use your ideas from the **Focus Activity** on page 434.

Analyzing Literature

RECALL AND INTERPRET

1. Who causes problems for most of the boys at the narrator's school? Which group usually doesn't have trouble? Support your answer.
2. In what ways does Monk show his power? Why do you think he acts as he does?
3. How does Priscilla handle Monk? What does the narrator feel about Priscilla's actions? Support your answer.

EVALUATE AND CONNECT

4. The author uses a **first-person narrator.** How does this technique draw the reader into the story? Use examples from the story.
5. Were you surprised by the ending? Why or why not?
6. Based on your own experiences, do you think a real person in Priscilla's situation would have acted as she did? Explain your answer.

Extending Your Response

Literature Groups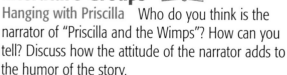

Hanging with Priscilla Who do you think is the narrator of "Priscilla and the Wimps"? How can you tell? Discuss how the attitude of the narrator adds to the humor of the story.

Learning for Life

Rules of Conduct Imagine that Priscilla has broken the power of the gang and has been asked to help create a new code of conduct for the school. Write a code of conduct that Priscilla might write and that you think is appropriate.

The King of Mazy May and

Priscilla and the Wimps

COMPARE **SITUATIONS**

Think about the situation of the main character in each story.

- Who causes the problems in each story? In what ways are these characters alike?
- What dangers are part of each problem?
- Who, if anyone, helps the main character in each story solve the problem?

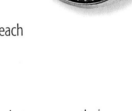

COMPARE **CHARACTERS**

Share ideas about the characters in the two stories.

- Are the good and the bad characters easy to identify in each story?
- What qualities do the two main characters share?
- Why does each main character "get involved"?
- How does each main character handle the problem? In what ways are their methods alike or different?

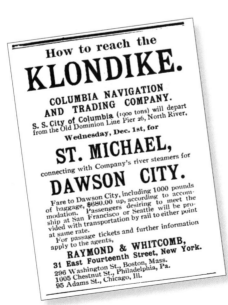

How to reach the

KLONDIKE.

COLUMBIA NAVIGATION AND TRADING COMPANY.

S. S. City of Columbia (1900 tons) will depart from the Old Dominion Line Pier 26, North River,

Wednesday, Dec. 1st, for

ST. MICHAEL,

connecting with Company's river steamers for

DAWSON CITY.

Fare to Dawson City, including 1000 pounds of baggage, $680.00 up, according to accommodation. Passengers desiring to meet the ship at San Francisco or Seattle will be provided with transportation by rail to either point at same rate.

For passage tickets and further information apply to the agents,

RAYMOND & WHITCOMB,
31 East Fourteenth Street, New York.
296 Washington St., Boston, Mass.
1005 Chestnut St., Philadelphia, Pa.
95 Adams St., Chicago, Ill.

COMPARE **OUTCOMES**

Write an incident report—a detailed account of exactly what happened—from the point of view of an authority who could become involved in either story situation. It might be the gold commissioner in Dawson, or the principal in Priscilla's school. In your report, describe the unfair practices of some characters, and what the main character did to overcome the problem. Include the final outcome, and make recommendations about what to do with those who have violated the rules and laws.

Vo·cab·u·lar·y *Skills*

Understanding Homographs

In "The King of Mazy May," the dogs pulling Walt's sled *flounder,* or struggle to move, in the deep snow. But *flounder* is also a kind of fish. These words are **homographs.** They are two different words with the same spelling. Sometimes homographs are pronounced differently but look the same. The *winds* in Klondike country are icy cold. The river bed *winds* back and forth like a snake.

How can a reader tell which meaning for a word is the right one? The best clues are found in the sentence or paragraph the word is in. When Walt hears "the ping of a bullet on the ice beside him, and the *report* of a gun," the *report* has to be a sound, not a paper written for school.

You might read a sentence and think you understand all the words in it, but the sentence doesn't make sense. In "Priscilla and the Wimps," the narrator describes the friendship between Priscilla and Melvin. He says, "They even had lockers next to each other, in the same *bank* as mine." If you think that a *bank* has to be either a place for savings or the land along a river, this sentence is confusing. If you realize that *bank* can also mean "a row of objects," the sentence makes sense.

EXERCISES

◆ Look at the definition for each word. Then choose the sentence that uses a *different* meaning for the word.

1. *down: soft feathers*
   a. That pillow is filled with down.
   b. Sheep grazed on the down.

2. *fresh: rude, sassy*
   a. We need some fresh ideas.
   b. If you make fresh remarks, you'll get in trouble.

3. *spell: say or write the letters of a word*
   a. Please spell me for awhile.
   b. Some words are hard to spell.

◆ Choose the meaning for the underlined word that is more likely to be correct.

1. "The sergeant was a seasoned soldier." *Seasoned* probably means
   a. experienced.
   b. salted or spiced.

2. "For this kind of shot, most players use an iron." *Iron* probably means
   a. an object used for pressing cloth.
   b. a kind of golf club.

3. The pioneers cured meat so it would last a long time." *Cured* probably means
   a. made healthy again.
   b. preserved by salting or smoking.

FOLKTALE

Every group of people has its own **folklore**—the customs, songs, dances, and tales that have been passed down from one generation to the next. For most of history, folklore was passed along through word of mouth, with one person teaching it to another. Very little was written down.

Today, people are able to share old stories and customs. One type of folklore that is enjoyed all over the world is the **folktale.** In his story "The Stone" on page 311, Lloyd Alexander imitates an old story of this type. You will find the following elements in a typical folktale.

MODEL: "The Stone"

SETTING Folktales are often set in the past, in a land far removed from modern life. The few details that are mentioned do not clearly place the action in a particular place and time. Because the setting is vague, as in the following example from "The Stone," readers can use their imaginations to create the setting that makes the most sense to them.

> There was a cottager named Maibon, and one day he was driving down the road in his horse and cart when he saw an old man hobbling along, so frail and feeble he doubted the poor soul could go many more steps.

CHARACTERS Often the main character in a folktale is a simple, common person who is facing an everyday problem. For example, he or she may not have enough money or, like Maibon in "The Stone," may be afraid of growing old.

> "Ah, ah, what a sorry thing it is to have your bones creaking and cracking, and dim eyes, and dull wits. When I think this might come to me, too! A fine, strong-armed, sturdy-legged fellow like me? One day to go tottering, and have his teeth rattling in his head, and live on porridge, like a baby? There's no fate worse in all the world."

Untitled.
Franza Mraz (b. 1910).

MAGIC Some folktales include magic, but many do not. For example, in tall tales like "Pecos Bill" (page 447) or **trickster tales** like "The Toad and the Donkey" (page 477), animals may talk, but they do not change into other animals, lay golden eggs, or live in magic lamps. A special kind of folktale that uses magic is the **fairy tale.** These tales include magical events such as a pumpkin turning into a coach and magical figures such as Fair Folk who can grant wishes.

Doli heaved a sigh of relief, rubbed his shin, and cocked a red eye at Maibon, saying:

"All right. You've done your work, you'll have your reward. What do you want? Gold, I suppose. That's the usual. Jewels? Fine clothes? Take my advice, go for something practical. A hazelwood twig to help you find water if your well ever goes dry? An ax that never needs sharpening? A cook pot always brimming with food?"

MORAL People have used folktales to teach lessons about life and human nature for thousands of years. Such a lesson is called the *moral* of the story. Sometimes the main characters learn to value something they always had but didn't appreciate. See how Maibon in "The Stone" finally realizes that natural change is good, after all.

Never again did Maibon meet any of the Fair Folk, and he was just as glad of it. He and his wife and children and grandchildren lived many years, and Maibon was proud of his white hair and long beard as he had been of his sturdy arms and legs.

"Stones are all right, in their way," said Maibon. "But the trouble with them is, they don't grow."

Active Reading Strategies

Tips for Reading a Folktale

A folktale is a story that is simple enough to be understood by a child. But even adults enjoy its creativity and the truths it shares. When you read a folktale, you need to recapture the attitude of a child who believes in magic and the impossible. Use the strategies below as you read.

- For more about these and other reading strategies, see **Reading Handbook,** pp. R63–R94.

PREDICT

You predict when you use clues in the story, as well as your own knowledge, to make a good guess about what will happen next. Predicting is useful in reading many stories but is especially useful for folktales, where events can be repeated or may be similar to what has happened before.

Ask Yourself . . .

- Has something like this happened to this character before?
- How did the character handle it?
- What do I expect to happen now?

QUESTION

When you come across a piece of information that doesn't make sense, stop and question what you have read.

Ask Yourself . . .

- Does this make sense?
- What exactly is giving me a problem?
- If I reread the sentence before this, or read on, can I make sense of this?

VISUALIZE

Some folktales, such as tall tales, use exaggeration for humor. You can enjoy the exaggeration by picturing what is being described. Try to imagine the sights and sounds that the characters are experiencing, no matter how far-fetched they may be.

Ask Yourself . . .

- Can I picture this in my mind?

- Which details help me form pictures of this scene?

- Would I be able to describe this scene to someone else?

CONNECT

When you pull together what you have read and what you know, you are connecting. One way to connect is to notice the qualities you admire in various characters.

Ask Yourself . . .

- Does what I've just read match up with what I know about this?

- Have I read other versions of this story? How are they like this one?

- Am I like the main character? Would I like to be? If so, in what ways?

APPLYING THE STRATEGIES

Read the tall tale that follows, "Pecos Bill." As you read, use the Active Reading Model notes in the margins to help you enjoy the tale.

Before You Read

Pecos Bill

MEET MARY POPE OSBORNE

My childhood was spent on different Army posts with my parents, two brothers, and sister," says Mary Pope Osborne. As the daughter of a United States Army colonel, moving and traveling were part of her life. She lived mostly in the southern United States and, for three years, in Austria. She says, "I feel that the years I spent traveling . . . , the different jobs I've held . . . and my interests in philosophy and mythology have all informed and shaped my work."

Mary Pope Osborne was born in 1949. This story was published in 1991.

FOCUS ACTIVITY

Think about one of the funniest things you have seen lately on television or in a movie. What was so funny about it? Did others around you think it was funny too?

FreeWrite
Write about several things you have seen recently that are funny. Compare responses in a small group.

Setting a Purpose
Read "Pecos Bill" to enjoy a funny story.

BACKGROUND

Did You Know? Where do tall tale heroes come from? Some tall tale heroes were real people, like Casey Jones, a train engineer on the Illinois Central Railroad who died heroically holding his brake during a crash. On the other hand, the Paul Bunyan stories were probably made up by loggers. Pecos Bill had a different kind of beginning. He was not a real person, and he wasn't made up by a special group. In 1923 Edward O'Reilly wrote a magazine story with a cowboy hero named Pecos Bill. Other writers picked up the character and wrote more and more fantastic adventures for him.

VOCABULARY PREVIEW

desolate (des′ ə lit) *adj.* deserted or uninhabited; p. 449
parched (pärcht) *adj.* severely in need of rain; very dry; p. 452
barren (bar′ ən) *adj.* having little or no plant life; empty; p. 454
revert (ri vurt′) *v.* to return to an earlier condition, behavior, or belief; p. 454
catastrophe (kə tas′ trə fē′) *n.* a great and sudden disaster; p. 454

PECOS BILL

Mary Pope Osborne

Pecos Bill Watching Girl on Flying Fish (detail). Donald A. Daily. Watercolor.

PECOS BILL

ACTIVE READING MODEL

Ask any coyote near the Pecos River in western Texas who was the best cowboy who ever lived, and he'll throw back his head and howl, "Ah-hooo!" If you didn't know already, that's coyote language for *Pecos Bill*.

When Pecos Bill was a little baby, he was as tough as a pine knot. He teethed on horseshoes instead of teething rings and played with grizzly bears instead of teddy bears. He could have grown up just fine in the untamed land of eastern Texas. But one day his pappy ran in from the fields, hollering, "Pack up, Ma! Neighbors movin' in fifty miles away! It's gettin' too crowded!"

Before sundown Bill's folks loaded their fifteen kids and all their belongings into their covered wagon and started west.

PREDICT

What kind of story do you expect?

Pecos Bill as Young Child with Coyotes. Donald A. Daily. Watercolor.

Viewing the illustration: What does this illustration tell you about how the coyotes feel about Bill?

Mary Pope Osborne ∾

As they clattered across the <u>desolate</u> land of western Texas, the crushing heat nearly drove them all crazy. Baby Bill got so hot and cross that he began to wallop his big brothers. Pretty soon all fifteen kids were going at one another tooth and nail. Before they turned each other into catfish bait, Bill fell out of the wagon and landed *ker-plop* on the sun-scorched desert.

The others were so busy fighting that they didn't even notice the baby was missing until it was too late to do anything about it.

Well, tough little Bill just sat there in the dirt, watching his family rattle off in a cloud of dust, until an old coyote walked over and sniffed him.

"Goo-goo!" Bill said.

Now it's an amazing coincidence, but "Goo-goo" happens to mean something similar to "Glad to meet you" in coyote language. Naturally the old coyote figured he'd come across one of his own kind. He gave Bill a big lick and picked him up by the scruff of the neck and carried him home to his den.

Bill soon discovered the coyote's kinfolk were about the wildest, roughest bunch you could imagine. Before he knew it, he was roaming the prairies with the pack. He howled at the moon, sniffed the brush, and chased lizards across the sand. He was having such a good time, scuttling about naked and dirty on all fours, that he completely forgot what it was like to be a human.

Pecos Bill's coyote days came to an end about seventeen years later. One evening as he was sniffing the sagebrush, a cowpoke came loping by on a big horse. "Hey, you!" he shouted. "What in the world are you?"

Bill sat on his haunches[1] and stared at the feller.

"What *are* you?" asked the cowpoke again.

"Varmint,"[2] said Bill hoarsely, for he hadn't used his human voice in seventeen years.

"No, you ain't!"

"Yeah, I am. I got fleas, don't I?"

"Well, that don't mean nothing. A lot of Texans got fleas. The thing varmints got that you ain't got is a tail."

VISUALIZE

How do you picture this?

QUESTION

What happened to Bill?

CONNECT

What other stories does this remind you of?

QUESTION

How old is Bill?

QUESTION

Why did Bill think he was a "varmint"?

---

1. To sit on your *haunches* is to squat.
2. A *varmint* is a pesky, annoying insect, animal, or person.

Vocabulary
desolate (des′ ə lit) *adj.* deserted or uninhabited

PECOS BILL

"Oh, yes, I do have a tail," said Pecos Bill.

"Lemme see it then," said the cowpoke.

Bill turned around to look at his rear end, and for the first time in his life he realized he didn't have a tail.

"Dang," he said. "But if I'm not a varmint, what am I?"

"You're a cowboy! So start acting like one!"

Bill just growled at the feller like any coyote worth his salt would. But deep down in his heart of hearts he knew the cowpoke was right. For the last seventeen years he'd had a sneaking suspicion that he was different from that pack of coyotes. For one thing, none of them seemed to smell quite as bad as he did.

So with a heavy heart he said good-bye to his four-legged friends and took off with the cowpoke for the nearest ranch.

Acting like a human wasn't all that easy for Pecos Bill. Even though he soon started dressing right, he never bothered to shave or comb his hair. He'd just throw some water on his face in the morning and go around the rest of the day looking like a wet dog. Ignorant cowpokes claimed Bill wasn't too smart. Some of the meaner ones liked to joke that he wore a ten-dollar hat on a five-cent head.

The truth was Pecos Bill would soon prove to be one of the greatest cowboys who ever lived. He just needed to find the kind of folks who'd appreciate him. One night when he was licking his dinner plate, his ears perked up. A couple of ranch hands were going on about a gang of wild cowboys.

"Yep. Those fellas are more animal than human," one ranch hand was saying.

"Yep. Them's the toughest bunch I ever come across. Heck, they're so tough, they can kick fire out of flint rock with their bare toes!"

"Yep. 'N' they like to bite nails in half for fun!"

"Who are these fellers?" asked Bill.

"The Hell's Gate Gang," said the ranch hand. "The mangiest,[3] meanest, most low-down bunch of low-life varmints that ever grew hair."

"Sounds like my kind of folks," said Bill, and before anyone could holler whoa, he jumped on his horse and took off for Hell's Gate Canyon.

Bill hadn't gone far when disaster struck. His horse stepped in a hole and broke its ankle.

"Dang!" said Bill as he stumbled up from the spill. He draped the lame critter around his neck and hurried on.

---

3. To be *mangiest* (mān′ jē əst) is to be the most *mangy*—worn, dirty, and shabby in appearance.

After he'd walked about a hundred more miles, Bill heard some mean rattling. Then a fifty-foot rattlesnake reared up its ugly head and stuck out its long, forked tongue, ready to fight.

"Knock it off, you scaly-hided fool. I'm in a hurry," Bill said.

The snake didn't give a spit for Bill's plans. He just rattled on.

Before the cussed varmint could strike, Bill had no choice but to knock him cross-eyed. "Hey, feller," he said, holding up the dazed snake. "I like your spunk.[4] Come go with us." Then he wrapped the rattler around his arm and continued on his way.

After Bill had hiked another hundred miles with his horse around his neck and his snake around his arm, he heard a terrible growl. A huge mountain lion was crouching on a cliff, getting ready to leap on top of him.

"Don't jump, you mangy bobtailed fleabag!" Bill said.

Well, call any mountain lion a mangy bobtailed fleabag, and he'll jump on your back for sure. After this one leaped onto Bill, so much fur began to fly that it darkened the sky. Bill wrestled that mountain lion into a headlock, then squeezed him so tight that the big cat had to cry uncle.

When the embarrassed old critter started to slink off, Bill felt sorry for him. "Aw, c'mon, you big silly," he said. "You're more like me than most humans I meet."

He saddled up the cat, jumped on his back, and the four of them headed for the canyon, with the mountain lion screeching, the horse neighing, the rattler rattling, and Pecos Bill hollering a wild war whoop.

When the Hell's Gate Gang heard those noises coming from the prairie, they nearly fainted. They dropped their dinner plates, and their faces turned as white as bleached desert bones. Their knees knocked and their six-guns shook.

"Hey, there!" Bill said as he sidled[5] up to their campfire, grinning. "Who's the boss around here?"

A nine-foot feller with ten pistols at his sides stepped forward and in a shaky voice said, "Stranger, I was. But from now on, it'll be you."

"Well, thanky, pardner," said Bill. "Get on with your dinner, boys. Don't let me interrupt."

Once Bill settled down with the Hell's Gate Gang, his true genius revealed itself. With his gang's help, he put together the biggest ranch in the southwest. He used New Mexico as a corral and Arizona as a pasture.

---

4. Bill likes the snake's courage, spirit, and determination.
5. Bill moved sideways in a cautious way that didn't cause alarm or disturbance.

ACTIVE READING MODEL

PREDICT

Based on similar incidents, what do you think will happen now?

PREDICT

What kind of impression do you think this group will make on the Hell's Gate Gang?

PREDICT

Were you right in your prediction? What impression did Bill make?

PECOS BILL

CONNECT

What do you know about these things that Bill "invented"?

VISUALIZE

How dry was it? Use the details to visualize this scene.

He invented tarantulas and scorpions as practical jokes. He also invented roping. Some say his rope was exactly as long as the equator; others argue it was two feet shorter.

Things were going fine for Bill until Texas began to suffer the worst drought in its history. It was so dry that all the rivers turned as powdery as biscuit flour. The <u>parched</u> grass was catching fire everywhere. For a while Bill and his gang managed to lasso water from the Rio Grande.[6] When that river dried up, they lassoed water from the Gulf of Mexico.

Did You Know?
The *tarantula* (tə ran' chə lə) is a large, hairy spider. Its sting can be painful but is not usually dangerous to humans.

No matter what he did, though, Bill couldn't get enough water to stay ahead of the drought. All his horses and cows were starting to dry up and blow away like balls of tumbleweed. It was horrible.

Just when the end seemed near, the sky turned a deep shade of purple. From the distant mountains came a terrible roar. The cattle began to stampede, and a huge black funnel of a cyclone appeared, heading straight for Bill's ranch.

The rest of the Hell's Gate Gang shouted, "Help!" and ran.

But Pecos Bill wasn't scared in the least. "Yahoo!" he hollered, and he swung his lariat and lassoed that cyclone around its neck.

QUESTION

How would you summarize what happened?

CONNECT

What do you know about Death Valley and what it is like there? How accurate is this description?

Bill held on tight as he got sucked up into the middle of the swirling cloud. He grabbed the cyclone by the ears and pulled himself onto her back. Then he let out a whoop and headed that twister across Texas.

The mighty cyclone bucked, arched, and screamed like a wild bronco. But Pecos Bill just held on with his legs and used his strong hands to wring the rain out of her wind. He wrung out rain that flooded Texas, New Mexico, and Arizona, until finally he slid off the shriveled-up funnel and fell into California. The earth sank about two hundred feet below sea level in the spot where Bill landed, creating the area known today as Death Valley.

"There. That little waterin' should hold things for a while," he said, brushing himself off.

---

6. A *drought* (drout) is a long period of very dry weather. The *Rio Grande,* or "Grand River," forms part of the border between Texas and Mexico.

Vocabulary
parched (pärcht) *adj.* severely in need of rain; very dry

Mary Pope Osborne 〜

After his cyclone ride, no horse was too wild for Pecos Bill. He soon found a young colt that was as tough as a tiger and as crazy as a streak of lightning. He named the colt Widow Maker and raised him on barbed wire[7] and dynamite. Whenever the two rode together, they back-flipped and somersaulted all over Texas, loving every minute of it.

One day when Bill and Widow Maker were bouncing around the Pecos River, they came across an awesome sight: a wild-looking, red-haired woman riding on the back of the biggest catfish Bill had ever seen. The woman looked like she was having a ball, screeching, "Ride 'em, cowgirl!" as the catfish whipped her around in the air.

"What's your name?" Bill shouted.

"Slue-foot Sue! What's it to you?" she said. Then she war-whooped away over the windy water.

---

7. A *barb* is any sharp, thornlike point. On the plains, fences were made from *barbed wire*.

Pecos Bill Lassos a Tornado. Donald A. Daily. Watercolor.
Viewing the illustration: How does Bill appear to feel about riding the cyclone, or tornado?

Thereafter all Pecos Bill could think of was Slue-foot Sue. He spent more and more time away from the Hell's Gate Gang as he wandered the <u>barren</u> cattle-lands, looking for her. When he finally found her lonely little cabin, he was so love-struck he <u>reverted</u> to some of his old coyote ways. He sat on his haunches in the moonlight and began a-howling and ah-hooing.

Well, the good news was that Sue had a bit of coyote in her too, so she completely understood Bill's language. She stuck her head out her window and ah-hooed back to him that she loved him, too. Consequently Bill and Sue decided to get married.

On the day of the wedding Sue wore a beautiful white dress with a steel-spring bustle, and Bill appeared in an elegant buckskin suit.

But after a lovely ceremony, a terrible <u>catastrophe</u> occurred. Slue-foot Sue got it into her head that she just had to have a ride on Bill's wild bronco, Widow Maker.

Did You Know?

A *bustle* is a pad or frame that used to be worn by women at the back of a skirt just below the waist. The bustle look was fashionable for much of the 1800s.

"You can't do that, honey," Bill said. "He won't let any human toss a leg over him but me."

"Don't worry," said Sue. "You know I can ride anything on four legs, not to mention what flies or swims."

Bill tried his best to talk Sue out of it, but she wouldn't listen. She was dying to buck on the back of that bronco. Wearing her white wedding dress with the bustle, she jumped on Widow Maker and kicked him with her spurs.

Well, that bronco didn't need any thorns in his side to start bucking to beat the band. He bounded up in the air with such amazing force that suddenly Sue was flying high into the Texas sky. She flew over plains and mesas, over canyons, deserts, and prairies. She flew so high that she looped over the new moon and fell back to earth.

But when Sue landed on her steel-spring bustle, she rebounded right back into the heavens! As she bounced back and forth between heaven and earth, Bill whirled his lariat above his head,

Did You Know?

A *mesa* (mā′ sə) is a flat-topped hill or mountain with steep, rocky sides.

Vocabulary

barren (bar′ ən) *adj.* having little or no plant life; empty
revert (ri vurt′) *v.* to return to an earlier condition, behavior, or belief
catastrophe (kə tas′ trə fē′) *n.* a great and sudden disaster

Pecos Bill Watching Girl on Flying Fish. Donald A. Daily. Watercolor.

Viewing the illustration: Why do you think Bill finds Slue-foot Sue so irresistible?

then lassoed her. But instead of bringing Sue back down to earth, he got yanked into the night sky alongside her!

Together Pecos Bill and Slue-foot Sue bounced off the earth and went flying to the moon. And at that point Bill must have gotten some sort of foothold in a moon crater—because neither he nor Sue returned to earth. Not ever.

Folks figure those two must have dug their boot heels into some moon cheese and raised a pack of wild coyotes just like themselves. Texans'll tell you that every time you hear thunder rolling over the desolate land near the Pecos River, it's just Bill's family having a good laugh upstairs. When you hear a strange ah-hooing in the dark night, don't be fooled—that's the sound of Bill howling *on* the moon instead of *at* it. And when lights flash across the midnight sky, you can bet it's Bill and Sue riding the backs of some white-hot shooting stars.

CONNECT

What other sayings or little stories do you know that tell where thunder comes from?

QUESTION

Where are Bill and Sue?

Responding to Literature

PERSONAL RESPONSE

What was your favorite part of this story? Why?

Active Reading Response
Which scene was the most humorous to visualize?
Describe how you pictured the scene.

Analyzing Literature

RECALL

1. Who raised Pecos Bill and why?
2. How does Bill look when the Hell's Gate Gang first sees him?
3. How does Bill use his lasso to save the ranch?
4. What is Sue doing when Bill first sees her?

INTERPRET

5. What qualities do you think Bill picked up from his childhood that make him a good cowboy?
6. How do Bill and his gang change the West?
7. How are Bill's horse, Widow Maker, and the cyclone alike?
8. Where do Bill and Sue live after their wedding? Do you think this is a good ending to the story? Explain your answer.

EVALUATE AND CONNECT

9. What personality traits of Pecos Bill do you admire? Why?
10. **Exaggeration** is an overstatement. What does exaggeration add to this story?

LITERARY ELEMENTS

Tall Tale

A **tall tale** is a humorous, highly exaggerated story, often about a legendary hero. Many American tall tales were created during the 1800s as the United States grew westward. People made up stories with heroes who handled, with strength and style, the same problems they faced. The larger-than-life heroes could outsmart or outwork or outfight anyone. People added their own exaggerations to the stories, making them more humorous, more impossible to believe, and more fun to listen to with each retelling.

1. Who might be most interested in tall tales about Pecos Bill? Why?

2. Based on this story, what were some hardships of life in the West in the 1800s?

● See **Literary Terms Handbook,** p. R9.

Literature and Writing

Writing About Literature

Exaggeration An **exaggeration** that describes the Hell's Gate Gang is: "They're so tough, they can kick fire out of flint rock with their bare toes!" Use this sentence framework (He's/She's so _____ , he/she can _____ .) to write two or three of your own exaggerations about characters in the story.

Creative Writing

Creating a Tall Tale Hero Think about the unique challenges and problems of people your age, and create a **tall tale hero** who can handle them. Describe the personality traits of the hero or heroine in a paragraph. Then show in another paragraph a tricky situation–it can be exaggerated or silly–that the hero handles with ease.

Extending Your Response

Literature Groups

Stretching the Truth Read aloud and discuss examples of exaggeration in the story. What do you picture from what you read? Do the exaggerations make you laugh? Look back at your notes from the **Focus Activity** on page 446 about what makes you laugh. Was exaggeration one of the reasons you found some situations to be humorous?

Art Activity

No Place Like Home Use your imagination to draw a picture of the home of Pecos Bill and Slue-foot Sue at the end of the story. Include items that each character would want around their home, based on what they like and how they act in the story.

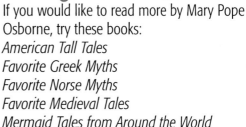

Reading Further

If you would like to read more by Mary Pope Osborne, try these books:
American Tall Tales
Favorite Greek Myths
Favorite Norse Myths
Favorite Medieval Tales
Mermaid Tales from Around the World

 Save your work for your portfolio.

Performing

From Pecos Bill Himself Rewrite a section from "Pecos Bill" as if he were telling the story himself. Include as much Western **dialect** (see page R2) as you can. Practice your presentation. Then share it with the class as if you were Pecos Bill.

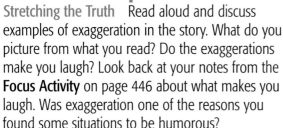

Skill Minilessons

GRAMMAR AND LANGUAGE • MODIFIERS

Descriptions in tall tales often include **comparative** and **superlative adjectives.** Something is not just *tall,* but the *tallest.* Pecos Bill's ranch is not just *big,* but "the *biggest* ranch in the southwest."

The comparative form of an adjective compares two things or people. The superlative form compares more than two things or people. Most adjectives of one syllable are made into comparatives and superlatives by adding *-er* and *-est.* Most adjectives of two or more syllables are made into comparatives and superlatives by adding *more* and *most:*

adjective	comparative	superlative
love-struck	more love-struck	most love-struck
impatient	more impatient	most impatient

PRACTICE Write the following adjectives in all three forms–the adjective, comparative adjective, and superlative adjective forms.

1. stronger
2. meanest
3. tough
4. bravest
5. elegant

● For more about adjectives, see **Language Handbook,** p. R24.

READING AND THINKING • ESTABLISHING CRITERIA

Tall tales are part of the folktale tradition. They have some characteristics that make them unique from other folktales. You can think about these characteristics when trying to decide if a folktale is a tall tale.

Tall tales use all or most of these elements:

- exaggeration
- humor
- a larger-than-life hero
- unbelievable situations
- dialect

PRACTICE Decide whether "Pecos Bill" is a tall tale, based on the criteria given here. Then write one or two paragraphs, giving an example from the story of each characteristic.

● For more about reading strategies, see **Reading Handbook,** pp. R63–R94.

VOCABULARY • ANALOGIES

"Big is to *huge* as *scary* is to *terrifying."* That is an example of a particular kind of **analogy.** An analogy compares two pairs of things or ideas. A short way to write an analogy is:

big : huge :: scary : terrifying

Something very *big* is *huge* just as something very *scary* is *terrifying.* The words in each pair have similar meanings, but the second word is stronger.

To finish an analogy, think of a sentence that describes the relationship between the first pair of words. Then find another pair of words that would fit into that same sentence.

PRACTICE Choose the pair of words that best completes each analogy. These analogies are similar to the example on the left.

1. thirsty : parched ::
   a. tall : thin
   b. dry : damp
   c. hungry : starving
   d. small : young
   e. loud : rude
2. misfortune : catastrophe ::
   a. snowfall : blizzard
   b. nose : face
   c. smile : frown
   d. song : music
   e. mistake : error

● For more about analogies, see **Communications Skills Handbook,** p. R58.

LISTENING, SPEAKING, and VIEWING

Listening to Instructions

Pecos Bill, the story goes, showed cowboys how to use the lariat. You can imagine what might have happened if the cowboys hadn't paid careful attention—especially since in some versions of the story, the first lariat was a rattlesnake!

When someone explains how to do something, pay careful attention. The following guidelines can help you get the most out of instructions.

Listening to Instructions

- To set your focus, be sure exactly what the instructions are for. Instructions for *twirling* a lariat, for example, will be very different from instructions for *making* a lariat.

- Keep your eyes on the speaker or look carefully at the illustrations. Picture yourself doing each step. Do you have enough information? Do you know what materials you'll need?

- Stay alert for word clues, such as *the basic parts, most importantly,* or *above all.* These signal key points in the instructions.

- Notice any points you don't understand. Jot down your questions. After the instructions have been given, ask any questions that have not been cleared up.

ACTIVITIES

1. Listen to a classmate read a set of instructions that he or she has written. Use the guidelines for listening above. Then discuss with your classmate what you heard, and compare it with what he or she read.

2. Take turns giving and listening to instructions for doing familiar activities, such as folding a paper airplane or tying a bow. When you are the listener, use the guidelines above. Then try following the instructions exactly as they were given.

Technology Skills

Internet: Communicating Around the World

The Internet is a network that links computers all over the world. With a computer linked to the Internet, you can access Web sites on the World Wide Web and exchange electronic messages with E-mail software.

Using a Web Browser

To move around the World Wide Web, you must use your computer's Web browser–software that helps you go from site to site. When you open your Web browser, your computer will take you to a starting point called **Home.** You can always get back to this point by clicking on your toolbar icon that resembles a house. Explore the other icons on your Web browser. Your teacher or lab instructor can help you understand what each one does. You can also use the **Help** button to learn about them. Make sure you can find and use the icons that allow you to **Search,** move **Back,** move **Forward, Stop,** and **Refresh** (or **Reload**) the screen.

Getting to a Web Site

Web sites have addresses called URLs (Uniform Resource Locators). The URL of most sites you will encounter begin with http://. Http stands for HyperText Transfer Protocol. You can reach a Web site by typing its URL into the address bar at the top of your browser screen. Try it. After http://, type www.sg/. Then press the Enter key on your keyboard (the Return key on a Macintosh). In a matter of seconds you'll find yourself at a site in Singapore, halfway around the world. Take a few minutes to explore the site.

Using a Search Engine

Usually, you won't know the URLs of the sites you want to find. You'll only know that you need a certain kind of site–for example, one that will tell you about schools in a different country. You will need to use a search engine, a tool that allows you to use keywords to find information on the Web.

Open your search engine. Somewhere near the top, you'll find a white box you can type into. Next to it will be a button that in most engines says "Search." Try searching for Web sites in another country. For keywords try: "sites in ___ ." In place of the blank, fill in the name of a country. The quotation marks tell the search engine to look for the whole phrase rather than for each word by itself. Visit a few of the sites your search engine comes up with by clicking on their underlined titles or descriptors.

TECHNOLOGY TIP

You can tell if a site is from a particular country by looking at its URL. Sites outside the United States have two-letter extensions that identify the country. The abbreviation for Singapore is *sg.* You used it in the URL *www.sg.* The country abbreviation always comes in the position where you usually find *.com, .org,* or *.gov.* For example, www.museums.or.ke/ is a site in Kenya, Africa. You can find a list of these country abbreviations by using the keywords "Internet country abbreviations."

Finding a School

Use the Internet to search for and find sixth-grade students in another country. Once you find a school, start an E-mail discussion about differences and similarities between your school and your "E-pal's" school.

1. With a group, compose a model for an E-mail letter you could send to an overseas school. In your message, introduce yourself, explain your assignment, and courteously ask permission to correspond with a student there. Include your E-mail address so that the student can contact you. Have your teacher look over your letter and make any suggested revisions.

2. To find lists of schools in a different country, use the keywords "elementary schools" or "middle schools" and the name of a country. Another way to find a school is through the Route 66 site: http://Web66.coled.umn.edu/schools.html.

3. You may have to visit several sites before you find an elementary or middle school that includes an E-mail address. Look for an address for the head of the school, the head of the English or Humanities department, or a sixth-grade teacher of English.

4. If you receive an E-mail response within a few days, begin your correspondence by describing your school environment. Perhaps you can tell about your classes, the activities your school offers, and your school's social life. Ask your E-pal to do the same for his or her school.

5. After several exchanges of E-mail, you should have some idea of what school is like for your E-pal. Take a few minutes, and think about what you've discovered. In your journal, describe the school environment of your E-pal, and compare it with your own. What do you like about your E-pal's school? What do you like better at your own school? Discuss your findings with a classmate. Did she or he reach similar conclusions?

ACTIVITIES

1. Keep a list of cultural differences and similarities you find as you write to others via E-mail. Save the list in your portfolio.

2. Demonstrate World Wide Web searching to younger kids at a nearby elementary school.

Before You Read

Baker's Bluejay Yarn

MEET MARK TWAIN

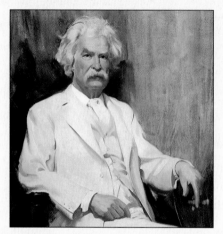

As a boy, Samuel Langhorne Clemens made rafts to sail on the Mississippi River, played pirates in caves and woods near his home in Hannibal, Missouri, and got into trouble at school and at home. "I was born excited," he later said of himself. As an adult, Clemens worked as a riverboat pilot on the Mississippi. Then he joined the California gold rush and worked as a correspondent for various newspapers. In 1862, using the name "Mark Twain," he published his first successful story.

Mark Twain was born in 1835 and died in 1910. This story was first published in 1880.

FOCUS ACTIVITY

Do you think birds and other animals communicate with each other? If so, how? Do you think animals of the same species are able to "talk" to each other?

Sharing

With a classmate, discuss animal communication, and share your ideas and observations. Make notes of your ideas.

Setting a Purpose

Read "Baker's Bluejay Yarn" to enjoy a tale about how blue jays communicate.

BACKGROUND

Did You Know? With blue and white feathers, crested heads, and long blue tails, blue jays are easy to recognize. They are known for their loud, harsh voices. The blue jay seems to say "Thief! Thief!" or "Jay! Jay!" or even "Cat! Cat!" Crows and magpies are fellow-noisemakers, and are related to blue jays.

VOCABULARY PREVIEW

fluent (flōō′ ənt) *adj.* spoken or written smoothly and effortlessly; p. 464

commonplace (kom′ ən plās′) *adj.* ordinary; not original or interesting; p. 464

principle (prin′ sə pəl) *n.* a basic law, truth, or belief; rule of personal conduct; p. 465

signify (sig′ nə fī′) *v.* to represent; mean; p. 465

gratification (grat′ ə fi kā′ shən) *n.* the condition of being pleased or satisfied; p. 465

absurdity (ab sur′ də tē) *n.* something ridiculous; nonsense; p. 467

Baker's Bluejay Yarn

Mark Twain

Tin Roof, 1977. Herbert Shuptrine. Watercolor, 21 x 28¾ in. Collection Mrs. Mary S. Jolley.

Animals talk to each other, of course.

There can be no question about that; but I suppose there are very few people who can understand them. I never knew but one man who could. I knew he could, however, because he told me so himself. He was a middle-aged, simple-hearted miner who had lived in a lonely corner of California, among the woods and mountains, a good many years, and had studied the ways of his only neighbors, the beasts and the birds, until he believed he could accurately translate any remark which they made. This was Jim Baker.

According to Jim Baker, some animals have only a limited education, and use only very simple words, and scarcely ever a comparison or a flowery figure;[1] whereas, certain other animals have a large vocabulary, a fine command of language and a ready and <u>fluent</u> delivery; consequently these latter talk a great deal; they like it; they are conscious of their talent, and they enjoy "showing off." Baker said, that after long and careful observation, he had come to the conclusion that the bluejays were the best talkers he had found among birds and beasts. Said he:

"There's more *to* a bluejay than any other creature. He has got more moods, and more different kinds of feelings than other creatures; and, mind you, whatever a bluejay feels, he can put into language. And no mere <u>commonplace</u> language, either, but rattling, out-and-out book-talk—and bristling with metaphor,[2] too—just bristling! And as for command of language—why *you* never see a bluejay get stuck for a word. No man ever did. They just boil out of him! And another thing: I've noticed a good deal, and there's no bird, or cow, or anything that uses as good grammar as a bluejay. You may say a cat uses good grammar. Well, a cat does—but you let a cat get excited once; you let a cat get to pulling fur with

Steller's Jay, 1989. Carl Brenders. Mixed media on board, 18 x 12 in. Private collection.

Viewing the art: What might this jay be thinking?

another cat on a shed, nights, and you'll hear grammar that will give you the lockjaw. Ignorant people think it's the *noise* which fighting cats make that is so aggravating, but it ain't so; it's the sickening grammar they use. Now I've never heard a jay use bad grammar but very seldom; and when they do, they are as ashamed as a human; they shut right down and leave.

"You may call a jay a bird. Well, so he is, in a measure—because he's got feathers on him, and don't belong to no church, perhaps; but otherwise he is just as much a

---

1. A *flowery figure* is a fancy expression.
2. The expression *bristling with* means "full of." A *metaphor* is a comparison in which one thing is said to be another.

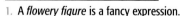

Vocabulary

fluent (flōō′ ənt) *adj.* spoken or written smoothly and effortlessly
commonplace (kom′ ən plās′) *adj.* ordinary; not original or interesting

human as you be. And I'll tell you for why. A jay's gifts, and instincts, and feelings, and interests, cover the whole ground. A jay hasn't got any more <u>principle</u> than a Congressman. A jay will lie, a jay will steal, a jay will deceive, a jay will betray; and four times out of five, a jay will go back on his solemnest promise. The sacredness of an obligation[3] is a thing which you can't cram into no bluejay's head. Now, on top of all this, there's another thing; a jay can out-swear any gentleman in the mines. You think a cat can swear. Well, a cat can; but you give a bluejay a subject that calls for his reserve-powers, and where is your cat? Don't talk to me—I know too much about this thing. And there's yet another thing; in the one little particular of scolding—just good, clean, out-and-out scolding—a bluejay can lay over anything, human or divine. Yes, sir, a jay is everything that a man is. A jay can cry, a jay can laugh, a jay can feel shame, a jay can reason and plan and discuss, a jay likes gossip and scandal,[4] a jay has got a sense of humor, a jay knows when he is an ass just as well as you do—maybe better. If a jay ain't human, he better take in his sign, that's all. Now I'm going to tell you a per-fectly true fact about some bluejays.

"When I first begun to understand jay language correctly, there was a little incident happened here. Seven years ago,

the last man in this region but me moved away. There stands his house—been empty ever since; a log house, with a plank roof—just one big room, and no more; no ceiling—nothing between the rafters and the floor. Well, one Sunday morning I was sitting out here in front of my cabin, with my cat, taking the sun, and looking at the blue hills, and listening to the leaves rustling so lonely in the trees, and think-ing of the home away yonder in the states, that I hadn't heard from in thirteen years, when a bluejay lit on that house, with an acorn in his mouth, and says, 'Hello, I reckon I've struck something.' When he spoke, the acorn dropped out of his mouth and rolled down the roof, of course, but he didn't care; his mind was all on the thing he had struck. It was a knot-hole in the roof. He cocked his head to one side, shut one eye and put the other one to the hole, like a possum looking down a jug; then he glanced up with his bright eyes, gave a wink or two with his wings—which <u>signifies</u> <u>gratification</u>, you understand—and says, 'It looks like a hole, it's located like a hole—blamed if I don't believe it *is* a hole!'

"Then he cocked his head down and took another look; he glances up perfectly joyful, this time; winks his wings and his tail both, and says, 'Oh, no, this ain't no fat thing, I reckon! If I ain't in luck!—why it's a perfectly elegant hole!' So he flew down and got that acorn, and fetched it up and dropped it in, and was

---

3. Something that's *sacred* is holy, or deserving of great respect. Here, *obligation* means "a promise."
4. *Scandal* is shocking behavior.

Vocabulary
principle (prin′ sə pəl) *n.* a basic law, truth, or belief; rule of personal conduct
signify (sig′ nə fī′) *v.* to represent; mean
gratification (grat′ ə fi kā′ shən) *n.* the condition of being pleased or satisfied

just tilting his head back, with the heavenliest smile on his face, when all of a sudden he was paralyzed into a listening attitude and that smile faded gradually out of his countenance[5] like breath off'n a razor, and the queerest look of surprise took its place. Then he says, 'Why, I didn't hear it fall!' He cocked his eye at the hole again, and took a long look; raised up and shook his head; stepped around to the other side of the hole and took another look from that side; shook his head again. He studied a while, then he just went into the *details*—walked round and round the hole and spied into it from every point of the compass. No use. Now he took a thinking attitude on the comb of the roof[6] and scratched the back of his head with his right foot a minute, and finally says, 'Well, it's too many for *me*, that's certain; must be a mighty long hole; however, I ain't got no time to fool around here, I got to 'tend to business; I reckon it's all right—chance it, anyway.'

"So he flew off and fetched another acorn and dropped it in, and tried to flirt his eye to the hole quick enough to see what become of it, but he was too late. He held his eye there as much as a minute; then he raised up and sighed, and says, 'Confound it, I don't seem to understand this thing, no way; however, I'll tackle her again.' He fetched another acorn, and done his level best to see what become of it, but he couldn't. He says, 'Well, *I* never struck no such a hole as this before; I'm of the opinion it's a totally new kind of a hole.' Then he begun to get mad. He held in for a spell, walking up and down the comb of the roof and shaking his head

and muttering to himself; but his feelings got the upper hand of him, presently, and he broke loose and cussed himself black in the face. I never see a bird take on so about a little thing. When he got through he walks to the hole and looks in again for half a minute; then he says, 'Well, you're a long hole, and a deep hole, and a mighty singular[7] hole altogether—but I've started in to fill you, and I'm d—d if I *don't* fill you, if it takes a hundred years!'

"And with that, away he went. You never see a bird work so since you was born. He laid into his work, and the way he hove[8] acorns into that hole for about two hours and a half was one of the most exciting and astonishing spectacles I ever struck. He never stopped to take a look any more—he just hove 'em in and went for more. Well, at last he could hardly flop his wings, he was so tuckered out. He comes a-drooping down, once more, sweating like an ice-pitcher, drops his acorn in and says, '*Now* I guess I've got the bulge on you by this time!' So he bent down for a look. If you'll believe me, when his head come up again he was just pale with rage. He says, 'I've shoveled acorns enough in there to keep the family thirty years, and if I can see a sign of one of 'em I wish I may land in a museum with a belly full of sawdust in two minutes!'

"He just had strength enough to crawl up on to the comb and lean his back agin the chimbly, and then he collected his impressions and begun to

---

5. Someone's *countenance* is his or her face.
6. The *comb of the roof* is the ridge along the highest part.

7. If a thing is *singular,* it's unusual, remarkable, or one-of-a-kind.
8. *Hove* is a past tense of *heave,* meaning "to lift and throw."

free his mind. I see in a second that what I had mistook for profanity in the mines was only just the rudiments,[9] as you may say.

"Another jay was going by, and heard him doing his devotions, and stops to inquire what was up. The sufferer told him the whole circumstance, and says, 'Now yonder's the hole, and if you don't believe me, go and look for yourself.' So this fellow went and looked, and comes back and says, 'How many did you say you put in there?' 'Not any less than two tons,' says the sufferer. The other jay went and looked again. He couldn't seem to make it out, so he raised a yell, and three more jays come. They all examined the hole, they all made the sufferer tell it over again, then they all discussed it, and got off as many leather-headed opinions about it as an average crowd of humans could have done.

"They called in more jays; then more and more, till pretty soon this whole region 'peared to have a blue flush about it. There must have been five thousand of them; and such another jawing and disputing and ripping and cussing, you never heard. Every jay in the whole lot put his eye to the hole and delivered a more chuckle-headed opinion about the mystery than the jay that went there before him. They examined the house all over, too. The door was standing half open, and at last one old jay happened to go and light on it and look in. Of course, that knocked the mystery galley-west[10] in a second. There lay the acorns, scattered all over the floor. He flopped his wings and raised a whoop. 'Come here!' he says, 'Come here, everybody; hang'd if this fool hasn't been trying to fill up a house with acorns!' They all came a-swooping down like a blue cloud, and as each fellow lit on the door and took a glance, the whole absurdity of the contract that that first jay had tackled hit him home and he fell over backward suffocating with laughter, and the next jay took his place and done the same.

"Well, sir, they roosted around here on the housetop and the trees for an hour, and guffawed over that thing like human beings. It ain't any use to tell me a bluejay hasn't got a sense of humor, because I know better. And memory, too. They brought jays here from all over the United States to look down that hole, every summer for three years. Other birds, too. And they could all see the point, except an owl that come from Nova Scotia to visit the Yo Semite,[11] and he took this thing in on his way back. He said he couldn't see anything funny in it. But then he was a good deal disappointed about Yo Semite, too."

---

9. The blue jay's bad language *(profanity)* earlier had been only the beginning (the *rudiments*) of its knowledge of cursing.

10. To knock something *galley-west* is to knock it into complete ruin.

11. *Nova Scotia* is a province of eastern Canada. Across the continent, *Yo Semite* (usually spelled *Yosemite*) is the valley and national park in east central California.

Vocabulary
absurdity (ab sur′ də tē) *n.* something ridiculous; nonsense

Responding to Literature

PERSONAL RESPONSE

Do you react to the story more as a blue jay would, or as the owl did? Explain your answer.

Analyzing Literature

RECALL

1. Who is Jim Baker? What is his special talent?
2. According to Jim Baker, what are some characteristics of blue jays? What are they best at?
3. Where does the blue jay put the acorns?
4. Why is the blue jay alarmed after dropping the first acorn?

INTERPRET

5. How do readers know about the incident that happened among the blue jays?
6. What characteristics that Baker mentions does the blue jay display when it continues to bring and drop acorns?
7. Why can't the blue jay complete his task?
8. In what ways do the birds act like humans as they try to help the blue jay solve his problem?

EVALUATE AND CONNECT

9. A **yarn** is a far-fetched tale that uses exaggeration to create humor. What are some examples of exaggeration in this story?
10. Theme Connection How does the blue jay show his determination? Have you ever known a person like this? Explain.

LITERARY ELEMENTS

Dialect

People living in the West during the 1800s had their own way of speaking. It was English, but with special expressions and unique ways of using words. It was a **dialect.** Dialect is a variation of language based on the way people speak in different regions. Mark Twain tells the story as though it was spoken by his character, Jim Baker. For example, Twain uses *get to pulling fur* to mean "start fighting" and *I reckon* to mean "I suppose."

1. List five expressions from the story that are examples of dialect, and tell what each expression means.

2. How would the story be different if Twain had told it in ordinary, standard English instead of in a dialect?

● See **Literary Terms Handbook,** p. R2.

A miner's tools: shovel, gold pan, pick.

Literature and Writing

Writing About Literature

Summary Write a paragraph summarizing what happens in "Baker's Bluejay Yarn." What does the blue jay do? What does he think he is doing? When he realizes he has a problem, what do the other birds do? How does the story end?

Creative Writing

Talking Among Themselves Look back at your notes from the **Focus Activity** on page 462. Imagine that the chirping of birds or the barking of dogs is actually conversation. Choose one type of animal and write an animal conversation. You may want to have the animals give their opinions of the blue jays and how they handled their problem.

Extending Your Response

Literature Groups

Story in a Story How many storytellers are involved in "Baker's Bluejay Yarn"? See if you can identify them. What elements of a good story are used in telling this tale? Make a list of these qualities and compare your list with that of another literature group.

inter**NET**
C O N N E C T I O N

On the Internet, find more information about birds, especially blue jays. Try browsing under *National Audubon Society, blue jays,* or *Roger Tory Peterson.* (Peterson wrote the guidebooks many bird-watchers use to identify birds.)

Interdisciplinary Activity

Science Find out about birds in your area and what they eat. Make a bird feeder for them by cutting an opening in a clean, one-gallon plastic bottle, such as a milk bottle. With an adult's help, cut in about 1¼ inches from the bottom of the bottle and make an opening about 5 inches by 4 inches. Tie a piece of twine around the handle or neck of the bottle. Fill the feeder with seed and hang it in a place where you can watch the birds come to eat.

Reading Further

If you would like to read more by Mark Twain, try these books:
The Adventures of Tom Sawyer
A Connecticut Yankee in King Arthur's Court
The Prince and the Pauper

Save your work for your portfolio.

Skill Minilessons

GRAMMAR AND LANGUAGE • PREPOSITIONAL PHRASES

Prepositional phrases function as adjectives and adverbs because they describe or modify other words. As adjectives, prepositional phrases modify nouns or pronouns. As adverbs, prepositional phrases modify verbs, adjectives, or other adverbs.

The jay walked around the hole. (Around the hole is a prepositional phrase telling where the jay walked. The phrase acts as an adverb describing the verb walked.)

I read a book about birds. (About birds is a prepositional phrase describing the noun book. The phrase acts as an adjective.)

PRACTICE List the prepositional phrases in each of these sentences from the story, along with the word each phrase modifies. Write "adj" for a phrase that acts as an adjective and "adv" for one that acts as an adverb.

1. . . . the queerest look of surprise took its place.
2. He cocked his head to one side. . .
3. Now I'm going to tell you a perfectly true fact about some bluejays.
4. The sacredness of an obligation is a thing which you can't cram into no bluejay's head.
5. The acorn dropped from his mouth.

● For more about prepositions, see **Language Handbook,** p. R26.

READING AND THINKING • STEPS IN A PROCESS

Instructions and directions often list steps and show them in a certain order. Whether you are putting together a model or baking brownies, following the steps in the correct order is necessary. Otherwise, you may end up with a model that is missing pieces or brownies stuck to a pan that was never greased. Sometimes steps are numbered. These are easy to follow. At other times, steps are included in a paragraph or two of text. The order in which the

steps are mentioned can guide you. Also, keywords such as *then, next,* and *finally* can help you follow the correct order.

PRACTICE Skim "Baker's Bluejay Yarn" to identify the step-by-step instructions for completing the task of the blue jay.

● For more about steps in a process and skimming, see **Reading Handbook,** p. R80 and p. R67.

VOCABULARY • THE SUFFIX *-ity*

It is *absurd* to try to fill up a house with acorns. The jay falls down laughing over the *absurdity* of the situation. The suffix *-ity* doesn't change the basic meaning of *absurd;* it makes it into a noun. If you see that two things are *similar,* you notice a *similarity.* The blue jay uses *profane* language, so what he says is *profanity.* (A word that ends with a vowel, such as *profane,* usually drops the vowel when *-ity* is added.)

PRACTICE Use what you know about familiar words and the suffix *-ity* to match each word to its definition.

1. totality
2. solidity
3. severity
4. rarity
5. liquidity

a. the quality of flowing
b. seriousness or strictness
c. hardness or firmness
d. something that is whole or complete
e. something that is uncommon

Using Adjectives

If you want to describe something, you use adjectives. "Blue jays have a *large* vocabulary, maybe because they are *intelligent.*" If you want to compare two things, you use the **comparative form:** "Blue jays have a *larger* vocabulary than cats, maybe because they are *more intelligent.*" The comparative form is made by adding *-er* or the word *more.* When you compare more than two things, you use the **superlative form:** The members of the Hell's Gate Gang are "the *mangiest, meanest, most low-down* bunch." The superlative form is made by adding *-est* or the word *most.*

PROBLEMS	SOLUTIONS
Good and *bad* have irregular comparative and superlative forms.	Use *better* and *best* as the comparative and superlative forms of *good* and *worse* and *worst* as the comparative and superlative forms of *bad.*
INCORRECT: Blue jays have a gooder sense of humor than you might think.	Blue jays have a better sense of humor than you might think.
INCORRECT: Bill solved the baddest drought in Texas's history.	Bill solved the worst drought in Texas's history.
It is incorrect to use both *-er* and *more* or *-est* and *most* at the same time.	Learn which adjectives require *-er* and *-est* and which require *more* and *most,* and form their comparatives and superlatives correctly.
INCORRECT: Paige was the most fastest pitcher of his day.	Paige was the fastest pitcher of his day.

● For more about adjectives, see **Language Handbook,** p. R24.

EXERCISE

Write the correct comparative or superlative form of the adjective in parentheses.

1. Some folks say that Pecos Bill was the (great) cowboy who ever lived.
2. Insulting a mountain lion is the (bad) thing a person can do.
3. Luckily for Bill, his fighting was (good) than the mountain lion's.
4. A dry spell created a situation (horrible) than you can imagine.
5. Bill lassoed a cyclone and proved he was (strong) than it was.
6. Bill thought Slue-foot Sue was the (wonderful) woman he'd ever seen.
7. He used his (good) arguments to keep Sue off Widow Maker.

Before You Read

Doc Rabbit, Bruh Fox, and Tar Baby and The Toad and the Donkey

MEET VIRGINIA HAMILTON

"I grew up within the warmth of loving aunts and uncles, all reluctant farmers but great storytellers," Virginia Hamilton says. She is proud to be descended from Levi Perry, who escaped from slavery and settled in Ohio.

Virginia Hamilton was born in 1936. This story was published in 1985.

MEET TONI CADE BAMBARA

Toni Cade added "Bambara" to her name after she found the name on a sketchbook in her great-grandmother's trunk. She became a college professor, a writer, and an activist for African American women.

Toni Cade Bambara was born in 1939 and died in 1995. This story was published in 1971.

FOCUS ACTIVITY

Have you ever enjoyed a television program, movie, or story in which one character plays a trick on another? What was it? How did it turn out?

Make a List

As a class, list stories you know in which a character is tricked by another character. Which character comes out ahead in each story—the trickster or the character who is tricked?

Setting a Purpose

Read these folktales to see how things turn out for two tricksters.

BACKGROUND

Did You Know?   Some folktales are told in slightly different versions in different countries. In *The People Could Fly,* Virginia Hamilton writes, "There are some three hundred versions of the Tar Baby tale. . . . In the Bahamas the elephant creates the tar baby; in Brazil an old woman or man traps a monkey in a sticky wax [doll]. There is a version from India, and there are African versions among the Ewes and Yorubas, all showing the great . . . universality of this tale."

Doc Rabbit, Bruh Fox, and Tar Baby

Virginia Hamilton ～

Heard tell about Doctor Rabbit and Brother Fox. They were buildin a house. And they kept a crock of cream in the bubbly brook down below the house they were buildin. Every once in a while, Doc Rabbit got thirsty. And he hollered aside so Bruh Fox wouldn't know who it was, "Whooo-hooo, whooo-hooo, whooo-hooo," like that. Scared Bruh Fox to death.

"Who is it there?" Bruh Fox say.

"Sounds like somebody callin bad," said Doc Rabbit.

"Well, can you tell what they want?" Bruh Fox say.

"Can't tell nothin and I'm not lookin to see," said Doc.

"Oh, but yer the doctor. Yer the doctor, you'd better go see," says Bruh Fox.

So Doc Rabbit went off down to the bubbly brook where the water ribbled, keepin the cream cold. He drank a long drink of sweet cream. Then he went back to help Bruh Fox with the house.

"Who was it callin?" asks Bruh Fox.

"Just started callin me, was all it was," said Doc Rabbit.

So Doc Rabbit got down to work. But the sun was hot and he came thirsty again. He went about callin out the side of his mouth:

"Whoo-ahhh, whooo-ahhh, whoo-ahhh!"

"Who is callin so scared?" says Bruh Fox, trembly all over.

"Somebody callin me for help, I expect," Doc Rabbit said. "But I am sure not goin this time, me."

"You have to go. You have to, yer the only doctor. Go ahead on, you," Bruh Fox say.

Big Doc Rabbit went down to the brook again. The water was so cool and ribbly and it kept the crock of cream so fresh and cold. Doc Rabbit drank about half of the cream this time. Then he went back up to help Brother Fox with the hard labor of raisin the roof.

Bruh Fox says, "What was the name of the one callin you this time?"

"Name of about half done callin," mumbled Doc Rabbit. "Whew! This work is hard labor."

The rabbit toiled and sweated until his fur was wringin wet. He took off his fur coat, too. He wrung it dry and put it back on. But that didn't even cool him any. He says over his shoulder, says, "Whooo-wheee, whooo-wheee!" like that.

The fox says, lookin all around, "Somebody else callin you, Rabbit."

"I sure am not goin this time," Doc Rabbit said. "I'll just stay right here this time."

"You go on," says Bruh Fox. "Go ahead on, folks needin you today."

So Doc Rabbit scurried[1] down to the ribblin brook. It was nice by the water. He sat himself down, took up the crock of cream. He drank it all down. Then he ran off.

Fox feel a suspicion. He went down there, saw the cream was all gone. He filled up the crock with some lemon and sugar water he had. He knew Rabbit was after anything cold and sweet.

---

1. *Scurried* means "ran quickly."

"Think I'll catch me a doctor and a hare together," Fox says to himself.

Next, he made a little baby out of the tar there. The baby lookin just like a baby rabbit. He named it Tar Baby and sat it right there on the waterside. Bruh Fox went back up the hill and he worked on his house. He thought he might keep the house to himself. Doc Rabbit was bein bad so and not workin atall.

Doc Rabbit came back for a drink. He spied the new crock full. And he spied Tar Baby just sittin, gazin out on the water.

"What you doin here, baby rabbit?" Rabbit asked Tar Baby.

Tar Baby wouldn't say. Too stuck up.

"You better speak to me," Doc Rabbit said, "or I'll have to hurt you."

But the Tar Baby wasn't gone speak to a stranger.

So Doc Rabbit kicked Tar Baby with his left hind foot. Foot got stuck, it did. "Whoa, turn me loose!" the rabbit cried. "Turn me loose!"

Tar Baby stayed still. Gazin at the water. Lookin out over the ribbly water.

Brer Rabbit stuck on the Tar Baby. Engraving.

Viewing the illustration: Who seems to be having the last laugh? What might Doc Rabbit do next?

So Doc Rabbit kicked hard with his right hind foot. "Oh, oh, I'm stuck again. You'd better let me loose, baby," Doc Rabbit said. "I got another good foot to hit you with."

Tar Baby said nothin. Gazin at the water. Lookin far on by the waterside.

Doc Rabbit kicked Tar Baby with another foot, and that foot got stuck way deep. "Better turn me loose," Rabbit hollered, gettin scared now. Shakin now. Says, "I got one foot left and here it comes!"

He kicked that tar baby with the one foot left, and that got stuck just like the other three.

"Well, well, well," said Doc Rabbit, shakin his head and lookin at Tar Baby.

Tar Baby gazin on the water. Watchin out for the pretty birds.

"Well, I still got my head," Doc Rabbit said. "I'm mad, now! I'm agone use my head, too."

He used his head on the little tar baby. Butted his head in the tar baby's stomach as hard as he could. Doc Rabbit's head got stuck clear up to his eyes. His big rabbit ears went whole in the tar of Tar Baby.

That was the way Bruh Fox found him. Doc Rabbit was stuck in Tar Baby. Bruh Fox got him loose.

"What must I do with you?" Bruh Fox said. He led Rabbit along to the house they were buildin. "You the one drank up my crock of cream. I didn't get one taste. Have a mind to burn you in a fire, too."

"Oh, I like fires," Doc Rabbit said. "Do go on burn me up, Bruh Fox, for it's my pleasure to have my coat on fire."

"Well, then, I won't burn you," said the fox. "Burnin up is too good for you."

"Huh," grunted Doc Rabbit. He said no more. Bruh Fox had him in his mouth, a-danglin down his back. Then he laid the rabbit under his paws so he could speak.

"Well, think I'll throw you in that thorny briar patch," Bruh Fox said. "How you like that?"

"Oh, mercy, don't do that!" cried Doc Rabbit. "Whatever you do with me, don't dare throw me in those thorny briars!"

"That's what I'll do, then," Bruh Fox said.

And that's what Brother Fox did. He sure did. Took Doc Rabbit by the short hair and threw him—*Whippit! Whappit!*—right in the briar patch.

"Hot lettuce pie! This is where I want to be," Doc Rabbit hollered for happiness. He was square in the middle of the briar patch. "Here is where my mama and papa had me born and raised. Safe at last!"

"Didn't know rabbits have they homes in the briars," Bruh Fox said, scratching his tail.

He knows it now.

The Toad and the Donkey

Toni Cade Bambara ～

One day Brother Spider didn't have nothing better to do so he asked ole Toad and ole Donkey to have a race across the island.

The donkey said, "What? You want me, the fastest dude around here, to race that little old hop frog. I've got a reputation, you know."

And the toad said, "Never mind all that, Big Mouth—let's race."

The donkey thought to himself, this is ridiculous. But since Brother Spider always had good prizes (Brother Spider was a terrific thief), he agreed.

"O.K.," said Spider. "The only rule is that Brother Donkey has to howl every mile so we can know where you all are."

Toad says, "Fine with me. Let's set the race for Saturday."

"Oh no," says Donkey, for he suspected something trickified. "Tomorrow morning."

So Toad went home for dinner and put it to the family like so: "Listen here, we spread out along the path in the bushes, then at every milepost when Mr. Donkey howls out, one of you steps out and howls too." So they each packed a little breakfast of gungo peas and sweet potato bread and bakes all wrapped up in tanya leaves and took up their positions along the road.

So the race began. And Spider lit a cigar and lay back.

Brother Donkey took off at a light trot, his tail stuck up in the air to match his nose, stopping every now and then to stick his face through somebody's fence to munch on some grass. And when he got to the first milepost, he sang out, "La, la, la. Here I am. Where are you? Ha, ha."

And way in front of him Uncle Julius Toad sang back, "Up here. La, la, la," and licked his fingers.

Which really surprised Donkey. So he cut out the grass eating and got a move on. But then he passed a well and decided he had time for a drink, for how much hopping can a toad do. And at the next post he sang out, "Tra, la, la. Here I am. Where are you?"

And way up ahead Aunt Minnie Toad sang back, "Up here. Ha, ha."

By the fifth post, Donkey started getting a little worried so he slashed himself with his tail like a horsewhip and started galloping. But Cousins Emery, Walter and Cecil Toad were on the case. And it's the same story each time. "Tra la la, I'm up the road ahead of you, Donkey."

And Donkey began to get sad in his mind when he realized he was not going to beat Toad. And he decided before he even got to the finish line that he would never race again. And donkeys have been kind of stubborn about running ever since.

Responding to Literature

PERSONAL RESPONSE

◆ In the two stories, which trick did you like best? Why?

◆ Think back to the **Focus Activity** on page 472. Did a trickster character triumph in each of the stories you just read? Explain.

Analyzing Literature

RECALL

1. What are Doc Rabbit and Bruh Fox doing at the beginning of the story?

2. Who expects to win the race in "The Toad and the Donkey"? Why?

3. Who tricks whom in each story?

4. How does each trick work out?

INTERPRET

5. Would you expect Doc Rabbit and Bruh Fox to be able to work together successfully? Why or why not?

6. Why, do you think, does the Donkey decide not to race again? What does this show about him?

7. Do you think any character in these two stories has a "right" to trick the other? If so, who and why?

8. Which **character** in the two stories do you find most clever? most foolish? Why?

EVALUATE AND CONNECT

9. What qualities of human nature do these characters show?

10. Theme Connection   Which character from these two stories has the greatest will to win? Explain.

LITERARY ELEMENTS

Trickster Tale

In a **trickster tale,** the trickster is usually a smaller, weaker character, while the opponent is larger and more powerful. In African American and Native American folktales, the trickster is often a rabbit. The rabbit seems small and helpless, but it wins by being quick and smart. Clever tricksters get themselves out of trouble, but in many stories they get right back into it. Tricksters who try to take advantage of others and change the rules to favor themselves usually end up caught in their own mischief.

1. Which character in each story is the trickster? How do you know?

2. Are the outcomes of these stories satisfying? Why or why not?

● See **Literary Terms Handbook,** pp. R3–R4.

Extending Your Response

Writing About Literature

Take a Message?   What was funny about each story? Was there something serious about each as well? What kind of messages do you carry away? In a paragraph, tell what lesson each story teaches.

Creative Writing

Tell a Tale   Write a short tale of your own. Use animal characters to tell your story. You may want to tell a story that teaches a lesson and end your story with a **moral,** or statement of the lesson the story illustrates.

Literature Groups

Natural Behavior   Brainstorm a list of animal characteristics for each of these animals: donkey, toad, fox, and rabbit. Then check off the qualities that hold true about each animal as a character in these stories. Does each character's behavior make sense based on the kind of animal it is?

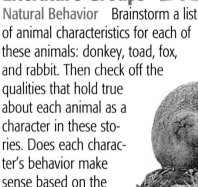

Learning for Life

Real Estate Listing   Use the details from the story and your own imagination to write a real estate listing for Doc Rabbit's Briar Patch. What good points about the patch will make it appeal to other buyers? Draw a picture of the Briar Patch, list its best selling points, and include a fair selling price.

Performing

Begin Again   With a partner, reread the last two paragraphs of one of the stories. Use the story ending as a springboard to another adventure for the trickster character. Write down your new adventure and then practice telling it together. You may want to videotape your performance.

Reading Further

If you enjoyed her story, try these books by Virginia Hamilton:
Folktales   *The All Jahdu Storybook*
The People Could Fly: American Black Folktales
Novels   *Cousins*
The House of Dies Drear

📖 **Save your work for your portfolio.**

Skill Minilesson

GRAMMAR AND LANGUAGE   • LEVELS OF USAGE

These stories use **dialect,** variations in language spoken in different regions. Dialects differ from **Standard English** in spelling, word use, and pronunciation. In these stories, for example, characters use words and expressions such as *dude, yer* for *you're,* and *can't tell nothin.*

PRACTICE   In each of the two stories, find five sentences that include dialect. Rewrite each sentence in Standard English. Which sentences fit best in the story? Why?

● For more about dialect, see **Literary Terms Handbook,** p. R2.

Making Generalizations

A **generalization** is a broad statement based on a group of facts or experiences. "Dogs make good pets" is a generalization. The statement describes the experiences of many people with dogs.

You can recognize some generalizations by noticing clue words such as *most, many, usually, sometimes, few, seldom, all,* and *generally.* Notice the clue word in the following example: "*Most* dogs play 'fetch.'"

Once you have recognized a generalization, it is important to figure out if the generalization is valid. Generalizations tend to sound true. However, people often make broad, general statements based only on their own experiences or on unconvincing information. If a postal carrier says, "All dogs bite," ask yourself if the generalization makes sense, based on what you know. Also, think about the facts or experiences that the generalization is based on. The postal carrier may be generalizing based on only a few personal experiences.

Find the generalization in the paragraph below from "The Toad and the Donkey." Do you think it is a valid generalization? Why or why not?

> And Donkey began to get sad in his mind when he realized he was not going to beat Toad. And he decided before he even got to the finish line that he would never race again. And donkeys have been kind of stubborn about running ever since.

● For more about generalizations, see **Reading Handbook,** p. R82.

ACTIVITIES

1. With a partner, review the ending of "Doc Rabbit, Bruh Fox, and Tar Baby." Find a generalization, and decide whether it is valid. Justify your response.

2. In a small group, write three generalizations about determination. Share your generalizations with the class. Decide if the generalizations are valid.

Writing WORKSHOP

Expository Writing: "How-To" Essay

What are you good at? Don't be modest—maybe you have a great jump shot, make mouth-watering cookies, or know a surefire chess strategy. Picture yourself doing something you know well. How do you do it? How would you explain the process to someone else? This is your chance to share your expertise.

Assignment: Write a step-by-step explanation that tells others how to do something.

● As you write your "how-to" essay, refer to **Writing Handbook,** pp. R43–R47.

The Writing Process

PREWRITING

PREWRITING TIP
Since this will be a short piece of writing, choose a simple process rather than a complicated one: choose how to shoot a free throw rather than how to play basketball.

● **Find a Topic**

You may have taken lessons in a special skill, or you may have learned by doing. Can you fix a bike tire, calm a fussy toddler, or travel across town on city buses? Not everyone can. Brainstorm a list of things you've done this week. Include some activities you were required to do as well as some that were just for fun. Then choose one activity that you'd like to write about.

fed Kyle's iguana
math homework: square roots
trombone practice
bought new shoes
played a computer game

made dinner Saturday
read a magazine
cleaned my half of bedroom
E-mailed Sayon

● Consider Audience and Purpose

Will your approach be serious or humorous? Will you write for younger children, for people your age, for older people, or for a mixed audience? Will you aim at readers who already know a bit about your topic, or at total beginners? As you plan, keep in mind your readers' needs. For example, beginners will need basic terms explained in detail. Young children might need short, simple words and sentences.

● Choose a Format

Your how-to writing might be in essay form or in the form of a letter to a friend. You may choose to create a pamphlet, an illustrated guide, a photo essay, an audiotape, a videotape, or a multimedia presentation. Within your teacher's guidelines, choose a format that fits your audience and purpose.

● Rough Out Your Plan

Break down your process into steps. (To do this, try "walking through" the process in your mind. You might also actually perform the steps.) As you work, list materials and equipment needed in order to complete each step. You might fill in a graphic like the one below.

How to: Make pizza dough
Materials needed: Small bowl, large covered bowl, mixing fork, pizza pan, 2 c. flour, 3 T. oil, 1 t. salt, 5 T. warm milk, 1 pkg. dry yeast, 1 t. sugar, 1 egg

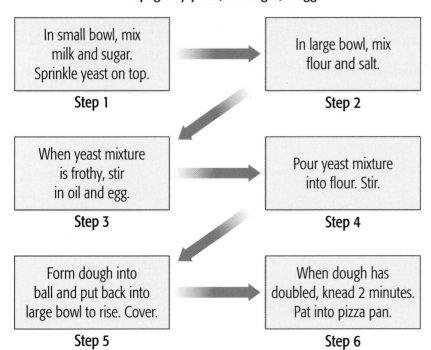

In small bowl, mix milk and sugar. Sprinkle yeast on top. **Step 1**	In large bowl, mix flour and salt. **Step 2**
When yeast mixture is frothy, stir in oil and egg. **Step 3**	Pour yeast mixture into flour. Stir. **Step 4**
Form dough into ball and put back into large bowl to rise. Cover. **Step 5**	When dough has doubled, knead 2 minutes. Pat into pizza pan. **Step 6**

DRAFTING

● Invite Interest

A surprising statement or question can invite your audience into your writing. (Which do you find more inviting: *Making fresh, crisp pizza dough–homemade, from scratch–is easier than you think,* or *Making pizza dough is a six-step process*?) Include your list of needed materials in your opening paragraph.

● Make Each Step Clear

You might write one short paragraph for each step. Follow your sequence chart to keep the steps in order, and use transitions such as *first, next, meanwhile,* or *after an hour.* Include any tips, advice, or comparisons that might help your audience. At the end, add a "wrap-up" statement: *Your pizza dough is now ready to use.*

> **MODEL · DRAFTING**
>
> Finally, take the dough out and knead it for two minutes. Knead means press it down with your hands, fold it double, press it again, and so on. Don't worry about technique.

REVISING

● Rework Your Draft

Read your draft, making any changes needed for clarity and completeness. Then ask a friend to listen to your draft and to imagine following the process. Would it work? Together, use the **Questions for Revising** to troubleshoot.

QUESTIONS FOR REVISING

☑ What surprising statement or question might make my opening more inviting?

☑ What, if anything, should I add to my list of materials?

☑ How do I make the order of my steps clear? Where might I reorganize or add transitions for more clarity?

☑ Where might I change the wording or add information to help my audience understand?

☑ How have I "wrapped up" my draft?

EDITING/PROOFREADING

After revising, go over your draft once more. Use the **Proofreading Checklist** to help you find and correct problems with grammar, usage, and mechanics. Pay special attention to modifiers, as shown in the **Grammar Link** on page 471.

Grammar Hint

Remember that *good*, an adjective, can never modify a verb. Use *well* with verbs. To bake well, the dough must rise first.

PROOFREADING CHECKLIST
- ☑ Modifiers are correctly used. (Double-check *good* and *well.*)
- ☑ All pronoun forms are correct, and pronouns agree with their antecedents.
- ☑ All verbs agree with their subjects.
- ☑ There are no run-ons or fragments.
- ☑ End marks, capitalization, and spelling are correct.

MODEL · EDITING/PROOFREADING

Practice these steps, and you will soon cook as
well
good as a professional pizza chef.
^

TECHNOLOGY TIP
On a computer, use the "Find" command to locate all uses of the words *good* and *well.* Check that each word is used correctly.

PUBLISHING/PRESENTING

Create a design for your work. For example, you might use numerals, headings, boxes, or a combination to set off your steps. If you chose a format that includes audio or visual portions, add them. Share your final product with your classmates.

PRESENTING TIP
You might combine your work with classmates' work to create a "How-To" booklet or display.

Reflecting

Think over your experiences with this Workshop. Then answer these questions.

- Which parts of your process were hardest to put into words?
- How is explaining a process like writing a narrative, and how is it different? Which kind of writing do you prefer? Why?

📖 **Save your work for your portfolio.**

Theme Wrap-Up

Responding to the Theme

1. Which selections in this theme helped you think about determination and winning? Explain your answer.

2. What new ideas do you have about the following as a result of your reading in this theme?
   - the importance of determination in achieving success
   - different attitudes toward competition

3. Present your theme project to the class.

Analyzing Literature

EVALUATE FOLKTALES
Choose a folktale from this theme to evaluate. Consider these questions.
   - How effectively does the folktale illustrate a moral or theme?
   - How entertaining is the tale?
   - How well are literary elements such as setting and characterization used in the tale?

Evaluate and Set Goals

1. Which of the following was most enjoyable to you? Which was most difficult?
   - reading and thinking about the selections
   - doing independent writing
   - analyzing the selections in discussions
   - making presentations
   - doing research

2. How would you assess your work in this theme, using the following scale? Give at least two reasons for your assessment.
   4 = outstanding   2 = fair
   3 = good   1 = weak

3. Based on what you found difficult in this theme, choose a goal to work toward in the next theme.
   - Write down your goal and three steps you will take to help you reach it.
   - Meet with your teacher to review your goal and your plan for achieving it.

Build Your Portfolio

SELECT
Choose two pieces of work you did in this theme to include in your portfolio. Use these questions to help you choose.

   - Which do you consider your best work?
   - Which challenged you the most?
   - Which did you learn the most from?
   - Which did you enjoy the most?

REFLECT
Write some notes to accompany the pieces you selected. Use these questions to guide you.

   - What do you like best about the piece?
   - What did you learn from creating it?
   - What might you do differently if you were beginning this piece again?

Reading on Your Own

If you have enjoyed the literature in this theme, you might be interested in the following books.

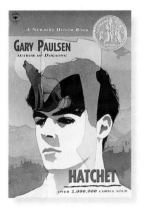

Hatchet
by Gary Paulsen
Stranded in the Canadian wilderness after a plane crash, thirteen-year-old Brian must learn how to survive on his own.

Cut from the Same Cloth: American Women of Myth, Legend, and Tall Tale
by Robert D. San Souci
Fifteen stories from various parts of the United States, including Alaska and Hawaii, tell of heroic women. Native American, African American, and Hispanic American are represented in this collection.

The Wanderings of Odysseus: The Story of the Odyssey
by Rosemary Sutcliff This prose retelling of the Greek classic is beautifully illustrated by Alan Lee. Odysseus, who struggles for ten years to reach his home, is one trickster-hero who succeeds.

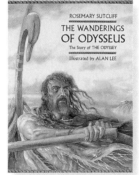

Island of the Blue Dolphins
by Scott O'Dell A Native American girl, accidentally left behind by her people, spends eighteen years on a lonely island.

Standardized Test Practice

Read the following passage. Then read each question on page 489. Decide which is the best answer to each question. Mark the letter for that answer on your paper.

Roberto Clemente: A Man of Talent and Charity

Roberto Clemente was one of the greatest baseball players of all time. He was born in Carolina, Puerto Rico, in 1934. Carolina was a poor community in Puerto Rico, and Roberto's family worked hard to make enough money to live on. Roberto was lucky to have received an education at all. He was especially lucky to have met a woman named Maria Isabela Cáceres, a teacher who dedicated her life to helping Roberto and other students like him. Roberto became a man who had not only tremendous talent, but also compassion for those in need.

The Baseball Player The record books show that Roberto Clemente collected 3,000 hits during his major-league career. He came to bat 9,454 times, drove in 1,305 runs, and played 2,433 games over an eighteen-year career. These are quite impressive statistics for a baseball player of any time period. He played for the Pittsburgh Pirates for his entire career. In 1971, the Pirates won the World Series, with Clemente leading the team to victory. He was a superstar in this particular series against the Baltimore Orioles, even being named the MVP (Most Valuable Player). It was an accomplishment he had worked diligently for, and all his hard work paid off. He was confident that he would continue to excel on the playing field.

The Man However, Roberto Clemente had a love beyond baseball. He met a woman named Vera when he was back in Carolina for a visit, after he had become a famous baseball player. Vera walked into a pharmacy where Roberto was sitting with his teacher, Senora Cáceres. Roberto and his teacher were reminiscing about the past when Vera caught his eye. She was also a student of Cáceres's, and Clemente wanted an introduction. However, his teacher did not think it was proper to introduce them, so Roberto did it himself. He and Vera were married in 1964.

The Humanitarian Besides being a baseball player and a devoted husband, Roberto Clemente always wanted to help those in need. In 1972, there was a deadly earthquake in Managua, Nicaragua. It was the worst earthquake the Western Hemisphere had had in a long time. Roberto had just been to Nicaragua two weeks earlier with a junior baseball team, and he had made many friends there during this time. He was saddened to hear the news, and he wanted to help. Roberto knew he could get the people of Puerto Rico to listen to him. He went on television to ask for their assistance in this time of crisis.

He asked them to donate medicine, clothes, food, and shoes to the people of Nicaragua. Roberto took the supplies with him on a plane on December 31, 1972. It was an old plane, and the pilot had trouble getting the engine to work properly. The flight was delayed while a mechanic made adjustments to the engine. Finally, the plane left San Juan Airport. Ninety seconds later, the pilot radioed the airport to tell them that the plane was coming back to the airport. Yet the plane never came back. A radio report informed the people of Puerto Rico and the United States that Roberto's plane was missing. For three days people waited and searched, but to no avail. Roberto Clemente died at the age of 38.

Although Roberto Clemente lived a short life, he accomplished many goals and was well loved. He touched the hearts of the Puerto Rican people, and he helped change people's lives throughout his travels. He died wanting to help others and will always be remembered for his kindness and generosity. In 1973, he was elected to the National Baseball Hall of Fame. Yet, besides being honored for his baseball ability, he was a man honored for his charity and desire to help those in need. The world lost not only a fine athlete but also a fine man.

---

1   The author of the passage believes that Roberto Clemente lived a —

   A   short but full life

   B   long and full life

   C   rewarding but disappointing life

   D   fast and confusing life

2   In the passage, the word <u>diligently</u> means —

   F   in a lazy manner

   G   in a playful, fun-loving manner

   H   by chance

   J   in a hard-working manner

3   This passage gives you reason to believe that Roberto Clemente —

   A   is remembered for his educational and athletic abilities at school

   B   had helped other people before his flight to Nicaragua

   C   was voted to the Hall of Fame in 1985

   D   was a teacher back in Puerto Rico

4   How can you tell that Roberto Clemente and his teacher in Puerto Rico had a good relationship?

   F   He liked her so much that he married her.

   G   He was able to fly her to the United States to watch him play baseball.

   H   They would spend time together talking about the past when he was back home.

   J   She encouraged him to start playing baseball and later tried to teach him proper manners.

5   How did Roberto Clemente and his wife meet?

   A   They met on one of Roberto's trips to Puerto Rico.

   B   They were introduced to one another by their teacher, Maria Isabela Cáceres.

   C   She came to many of his games, and finally they went out on a date.

   D   She was a volunteer on his trip to Nicaragua.

Getting Through Hard Times

> 66 The best way out is always through. 99
>
> —Robert Frost

THEME 6

THEME CONTENTS

GENRE FOCUS EXPOSITORY NONFICTION

Exploring the Theme

Getting Through Hard Times

How do you handle tough situations? With courage? With determination? In the selections in this theme, you will see people responding to different kinds of challenges. Some difficult situations bring out the best in people. After reading these selections, you may find yourself inspired to meet your own challenges in new ways, or you may develop a new attitude toward a tough situation.

Starting Points

AN IMAGE FROM A HARD TIME
The photograph on the right was taken at a time when many people in the United States were unemployed and homeless. What do you think this mother is thinking or feeling? What might happen to her and her children? What do you think the photographer wanted to communicate in this photograph?

LOOKING AT HARD TIMES
- Share other photographs, drawings, or paintings that show people who are dealing with difficult situations. Notice their facial expressions and posture.
- Discuss the emotions each person may be experiencing. Do you find strength and perseverance in a face? What other inner strengths do you see? What might each person say to himself or herself to help get through this difficult time?

Migrant Mother, Nipoma, California, 1936. Dorothea Lange.

Theme Projects

As you read the selections in this theme, try one of the projects below. Work on your own, with a partner, or with a group.

MULTIMEDIA PROJECT
Presentation on Courage
Many admirable people faced hard problems in their lives. Martin Luther King Jr., Helen Keller, Anne Frank, and Jackie Robinson are a few.

1. List well-known people you admire. Choose one who has faced hard times.
2. Use the Web and library to create a list of plays, songs, videos, films, Web sites, and books on your subject.
3. Explore several resources from your list.
4. Using pictures, words, music, or video, re-create for the class the highlights of what you learned.

CRITICAL VIEWING
Judging the News
The news is filled with stories of people facing problems or setbacks.

1. Take notes on a story on the television news.
2. Check the same story on the Web and in the newspaper. Does each version use the same pictures and information? Does each tell the story in the same way?
3. Repeat the procedure for several days or longer.
4. List the pros and cons of each type of media coverage. Which did you like best? Why? Share your results with the class.

interNET CONNECTION

Check out the Web for more project ideas. Search the *School Bell* directory for on-line clubs and organizations at *Yahooligans.* Also, contact the Glencoe Web site to explore more about this theme: lit.glencoe.com

LEARNING FOR LIFE
Musical Solutions
Music often helps people deal with hard times.

1. In a small group, research lyrics in songbooks or from CDs. Gather a list of songs and lyrics about people facing difficulties or about how to face troubles.
2. Play the music or read the lyrics of songs your group finds most meaningful for the class. Share what the music means to you.

Before You Read

Whatif and *Life Doesn't Frighten Me*

MEET SHEL SILVERSTEIN

"When I was a kid—twelve, fourteen, around there—I would much rather have been a good baseball player or a hit with the girls," said Shel Silverstein. "But I couldn't play ball, I couldn't dance. . . . So, I started to draw and to write." Besides writing and illustrating poetry and prose, Silverstein was a cartoonist and songwriter.

Shel Silverstein was born in 1932 and died in 1999. "Whatif" was published in 1981.

MEET MAYA ANGELOU

"I believe all things are possible for a human being, and I don't think there is anything in the world I can't do," claims Maya Angelou (mī yə an' jə lo).

Maya Angelou was born in 1928. This poem was published in 1978.

FOCUS ACTIVITY

What is a worrywart? What kinds of things does a worrywart worry about? Are these worries worth worrying about?

Think/Pair/Share

Write a list of worries that might be important to a worrywart. They can be about school or life in general. Underline the worries you think make sense. Compare your list with a partner's. Share ideas with the class.

Setting a Purpose

Read to discover the worries expressed in these poems.

BACKGROUND

During the 1950s Shel Silverstein served in the army and worked for the U.S. armed forces newspaper *Stars and Stripes* as a cartoonist. Later, he wrote cartoons, songs, humorous poetry for adults, and children's stories. His books of humorous poetry for young people continue to be very popular.

After finishing high school, Maya Angelou worked as a dancer, a singer, an actor, an editor, and a teacher. She has received awards for her autobiographical works and her poetry. In 1996 she received a Grammy for her reading of her poem "On the Pulse of Morning" at the inauguration of President Bill Clinton.

Some of Silverstein's books.

Whatif

Shel Silverstein

Last night, while I lay thinking here,
Some Whatifs crawled inside my ear
And pranced and partied all night long
And sang their same old Whatif song:
5   Whatif I'm dumb in school?
Whatif they've closed the swimming pool?
Whatif I get beat up?
Whatif there's poison in my cup?
Whatif I start to cry?
10   Whatif I get sick and die?
Whatif I flunk that test?
Whatif green hair grows on my chest?
Whatif nobody likes me?
Whatif a bolt of lightning strikes me?
15   Whatif I don't grow taller?
Whatif my head starts getting smaller?
Whatif the fish won't bite?
Whatif the wind tears up my kite?
Whatif they start a war?
20   Whatif my parents get divorced?
Whatif the bus is late?
Whatif my teeth don't grow in straight?
Whatif I tear my pants?
Whatif I never learn to dance?
25   Everything seems swell, and then
The nighttime Whatifs strike again!

Life Doesn't Frighten Me

Maya Angelou

Shadows on the wall
Noises down the hall
Life doesn't frighten me at all
Bad dogs barking loud
5 Big ghosts in a cloud
Life doesn't frighten me at all.

Mean old Mother Goose
Lions on the loose
They don't frighten me at all
10 Dragons breathing flame
On my counterpane°
That doesn't frighten me at all

I go boo
Make them shoo
15 I make fun
Way they run
I won't cry
So they fly
I just smile
20 They go wild
Life doesn't frighten me at all.

Tough guys in a fight
All alone at night
Life doesn't frighten me at all.

25 Panthers in the park
Strangers in the dark
No, they don't frighten me at all.

That new classroom where
Boys all pull my hair
30 (Kissy little girls
With their hair in curls)
They don't frighten me at all.

Don't show me frogs and snakes
And listen for my scream,
35 If I'm afraid at all
It's only in my dreams.

I've got a magic charm
That I keep up my sleeve,
I can walk the ocean floor
40 And never have to breathe.

Life doesn't frighten me at all
Not at all
Not at all.
Life doesn't frighten me at all.

---

11 A *counterpane* is a quilt or bedspread.

Portrait in Orange, c. 1989. Diana Ong. Acrylic on canvas, 36 x 24 in. Superstock, Inc. Collection, Jacksonville, FL.

Viewing the painting: How do you think this young person would handle her worries and concerns? What makes you think so?

Responding to Literature

PERSONAL RESPONSE

Look at your list from the **Focus Activity** on page 494. Which worries on your list were also in the poems?

Analyzing Literature

RECALL

1. According to the poem, how long does the speaker suffer from the "Whatifs"?
2. In the first two stanzas, what exactly *doesn't* frighten the speaker of "Life Doesn't Frighten Me"?

INTERPRET

3. What does the speaker mean by the sentence "Some Whatifs crawled inside my ear"?
4. Do you think the speaker in "Life Doesn't Frighten Me" is really brave? Explain.

EVALUATE AND CONNECT

5. Why does Silverstein run together the words "What" and "if"? How does it affect the reader?
6. Do you think "Whatifs" happen to everyone? Explain your answer.
7. From "Life Doesn't Frighten Me," give examples of realistic fears and imagined fears. Which worries do you think are worse, the realistic ones or the imagined ones? Explain.
8. A **refrain** is a phrase or a line that is repeated over and over again. What is the refrain in "Life Doesn't Frighten Me"? Why do you think Angelou chose to make this into a refrain?
9. Which poem most closely expresses how you feel about worries?
10. Theme Connection   What common worry or "Whatif" would you add to either poem?

LITERARY ELEMENTS

Speaker

As you read a poem, notice the characteristics of the **speaker,** the person who says the words of the poem. Sometimes the speaker of a poem is the poet. This is not true, however, of "Life Doesn't Frighten Me." If you read the poem closely, you'll notice that the speaker is a young girl, not Maya Angelou as an adult. For example, in lines 28–29, the speaker says that she is not frightened of little boys pulling her hair.

1. Why is it important to understand that the speaker of "Life Doesn't Frighten Me" is a young girl?

2. How would you describe the speaker of "Whatif"? Explain.

● See **Literary Terms Handbook,** p. R8.

Extending Your Response

Writing About Literature

Line Lengths Notice the line lengths in each poem. Choose one poem and write a paragraph explaining why, in your opinion, the poet used different line lengths within the poem. How do the changing line lengths help the poet express the meaning of the poem?

Personal Writing

Prescription Write a prescription for getting rid of everyday worries. Think of two or three sentences of advice and reassurance that can help "chase away" such fears. Write them in your journal.

Literature Groups

Worry List Discuss and then list the worries in the poems into the categories Reasonable, Somewhat Reasonable, and Unreasonable. How does mixing different kinds of worries affect how you feel as you read each poem? Share your group's opinions.

Performing

Sidewalk Chants Remember chanting children's rhymes like "A Sailor Went to Sea-Sea-Sea"? Make up a rhyming chant about silly fears. Repetition can create a rhythm. Here's an example: "Not afraid of spiders, Not afraid of webs, Not afraid of crackers, Eaten in my bed." Compose your chant with a partner and present it to the class.

Art Activity

Comic Strip Choose one or more of the worries expressed in either poem, and illustrate the worry in a comic strip. Include one or more lines or phrases from the poem in your work.

Save your work for your portfolio.

Skill Minilesson

GRAMMAR AND LANGUAGE • PREPOSITIONAL PHRASES

Maya Angelou uses many **prepositional phrases** in "Life Doesn't Frighten Me." They add details to the fears that the speaker pictures. A prepositional phrase begins with a preposition and ends with a noun or pronoun.

PRACTICE On a separate piece of paper, copy each fragment or sentence from Angelou's poem, and underline the prepositional phrase.

1. Shadows on the wall
2. Noises down the hall
3. Big ghosts in a cloud
4. Tough guys in a fight
5. All alone at night
6. Panthers in the park
7. Strangers in the dark
8. And listen for my scream
9. It's only in my dreams.
10. I keep up my sleeve

● For more on prepositional phrases, see **Language Handbook,** p. R26.

Before You Read

Abd al-Rahman Ibrahima

MEET WALTER DEAN MYERS

"I wrote fiction . . . from the time I was ten or eleven, filling up notebooks," Walter Dean Myers says. As a teenager, he won several literary contests, but he never thought he could be a writer. To his parents, it just wasn't a practical way to make a living. "When I was a kid, my people didn't think of being a writer as legitimate kind of work." After serving in the army and trying several jobs, he took up writing as a career. Myers's books are praised for their sensitive portrayals of young people.

Walter Dean Myers was born in 1937. This selection is from the book Now Is Your Time!, *which was published in 1991.*

FOCUS ACTIVITY

The refrain of an old African American spiritual is, "Free at last! Free at last! Thank God Almighty, we're free at last!"

Freewrite
Imagine how you would feel if suddenly you "belonged" to someone, and all your rights and freedoms were taken away. Freewrite anything that comes to mind.

Setting a Purpose
Read "Abd al-Rahman Ibrahima" to discover one man's journey into bondage.

BACKGROUND

The Time and Place
This biography begins in 1762 when the son of an African chief is born in Fouta Djallon, a district in what is now Guinea.

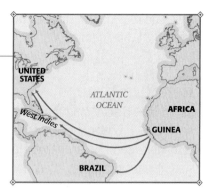

Routes by which enslaved Africans reached the Americas.

VOCABULARY PREVIEW

warily (wār′ ə lē) *adv.* in a cautious manner; p. 502
destined (des′ tind) *adj.* fixed or decided beforehand; p. 502
dominate (dom′ ə nāt) *v.* to rule or control; p. 502
bearing (bār′ ing) *n.* way of carrying oneself and behaving; manner; p. 503
agony (ag′ ə nē) *n.* great pain and suffering of the mind or body; p. 504
trek (trek) *n.* a journey, especially one that is slow and difficult; p. 505
bondage (bon′ dij) *n.* slavery; p. 507
prosper (pros′ pər) *v.* to grow, especially in wealth; to succeed; p. 508

Abd al-Rahman Ibrahima

Walter Dean Myers ∿

Who were the Africans brought to the New World? What was their African world like? There is no single answer. The Africans came from many countries, and from many cultures. Like the Native Americans, they established their territories based on centuries of tradition. Most, but not all, of the Africans who were brought to the colonies came from central and west Africa. Among them was a man named Abd al-Rahman Ibrahima.

Abd al-Rahman Ibrahima

The European invaders, along with those Africans who cooperated with them, had made the times dangerous. African nations that had lived peacefully together for centuries now eyed each other <u>warily</u>. Slight insults led to major battles. Bands of outlaws roamed the countryside attacking the small villages, kidnaping those unfortunate enough to have wandered from the protection of their people. The stories that came from the coast were frightening. Those kidnaped were taken to the sea and sold to whites, put on boats, and taken across the sea. No one knew what happened then.

Abd al-Rahman Ibrahima was born in 1762 in Fouta Djallon,[1] a district of the present country of Guinea. It is a beautiful land of green mountains rising majestically from grassy plains, a land rich with minerals, especially bauxite.[2]

Ibrahima was a member of the powerful and influential Fula people and a son of one of their chieftains. The religion of Islam had swept across Africa centuries before, and the young Ibrahima was raised in the tradition of the Moslems.

The Fula were taller and lighter in complexion than the other inhabitants of Africa's west coast; they had silky hair, which they often wore long. A pastoral[3] people, the Fula had a complex system of government, with the state divided into nine provinces and each province divided again into smaller districts. Each province had its chief and its subchiefs.

As the son of a chief Ibrahima was expected to assume a role of political leadership when he came of age. He would also be expected to set a moral example, and to be well versed in his religion. When he reached twelve he was sent to Timbuktu to study.

Under the Songhai dynasty[4] leader Askia the Great, Timbuktu had become a center of learning and one of the largest cities in the Songhai Empire. The young Ibrahima knew he was privileged to attend the best-known school in west Africa. Large and sophisticated, with wide, tree-lined streets, the city attracted scholars from Africa, Europe, and Asia. Islamic[5] law, medicine, and mathematics were taught to the young men <u>destined</u> to become the leaders of their nations. It was a good place for a young man to be. The city was well guarded, too. It had to be, to prevent the chaos that, more and more, <u>dominated</u> African life nearer the coast.

Ibrahima learned first to recite from the Koran,[6] the Moslem holy book, and then to read it in Arabic. From the Koran, it was felt, came all other knowledge. After Ibrahima had finished his studies in Timbuktu, he returned to Fouta Djallon to continue to prepare himself to be a chief.

---

1. *Fouta Djallon* (fōō′ tä   jä lōn′)
2. *Bauxite* is a claylike substance from which we get aluminum.
3. Here, *pastoral* means that the Fula raised herds of animals.

4. The word *dynasty* refers to a series of rulers who are members of the same family.
5. The religion based on the teachings of Muhammad is Islam, and things that have to do with this religion are referred to as *Islamic, Moslem,* or *Muslim.*
6. *Koran* (kō rän′)

Vocabulary
warily (wâr′ ə lē) *adv.* in a cautious manner
destined (des′ tind) *adj.* fixed or decided beforehand
dominate (dom′ ə nāt) *v.* to rule or control

Early engraving of Timbuktu.

Viewing the print: What details do you notice about the city where Ibrahima attended school?

The Fula had little contact with whites, and what little contact they did have was filled with danger. So when, in 1781, a white man claiming to be a ship's surgeon[7]

---

7. A *ship's surgeon* was not what we call a surgeon today but a physician who provided care for all sorts of health problems.

stumbled into one of their villages, they were greatly surprised.

John Coates Cox hardly appeared to be a threat. A slight man, blind in one eye, he had been lost for days in the forested regions bordering the mountains. He had injured his leg, and it had become badly infected as he tried to find help. By the time he was found and brought to the Fula chiefs, he was more dead than alive.

Dr. Cox, an Irishman, told of being separated from a hunting party that had left from a ship on which he had sailed as ship's surgeon. The Fula chief decided that he would help Cox. He was taken into a hut, and a healer was assigned the task of curing his infected leg.

During the months Dr. Cox stayed with the Fula, he met Ibrahima, now a tall, brown-skinned youth who had reached manhood. His <u>bearing</u> reflected his status as the son of a major chief. Dr. Cox had learned some Fulani, the Fula language, and the two men spoke. Ibrahima was doubtless curious about the white man's world, and Dr. Cox was as impressed by Ibrahima's education as he had been by the kindness of his people.

Vocabulary
bearing (bār′ ing) *n.* way of carrying oneself and behaving; manner

Abd al-Rahman Ibrahima

When Dr. Cox was well enough to leave, he was provided with a guard; but before he left, he warned the Fula about the danger of venturing too near the ships that docked off the coast of Guinea. The white doctor knew that the ships were there to take captives.

Cox and Ibrahima embraced fondly and said their good-byes, thinking they would never meet again.

Ibrahima married and became the father of several children. He was in his mid-twenties when he found himself leading the Fula cavalry in their war with the Mandingo.[8]

The first battles went well, with the enemy retreating before the advancing Fula. The foot warriors attacked first, breaking the enemy's ranks and making them easy prey for the well-trained Fula cavalry. With the enemy in full rout[9] the infantry returned to their towns while the horsemen, led by Ibrahima, chased the remaining stragglers. The Fula fought their enemies with spears, bows, slings, swords, and courage.

The path of pursuit led along a path that narrowed sharply as the forests thickened. The fleeing warriors disappeared into the forest that covered a sharply rising mountain. Thinking the enemy had gone for good, Ibrahima felt it would be useless to chase them further.

"We could not see them," he would write later.

But against his better judgment, he decided to look for them. The horsemen dismounted at the foot of a hill and began the steep climb on foot. Halfway up the hill the Fula realized they had been lured into a trap! Ibrahima heard the rifles firing, saw the smoke from the powder and the men about him falling to the ground, screaming in <u>agony</u>. Some died instantly. Many horses, hit by the gunfire, thrashed about in pain and panic. The firing was coming from both sides, and Ibrahima ordered his men to the top of the hill, where they could, if time and Allah permitted it, try a charge using the speed and momentum[10] of their remaining horses.

Ibrahima was among the first to mount, and urged his animal onward. The enemy warriors came out of the forests, some with bows and arrows, others with muskets that he knew they had obtained from the Europeans. The courage of the Fula could not match the fury of the guns. Ibrahima called out to his men to save themselves, to flee as they could. Many tried to escape, rushing madly past the guns. Few survived.

Did You Know?
The *musket* is a type of gun used before the invention of the rifle. Muskets were six to seven feet long and weighed twenty pounds or more. They fired either single round balls or many smaller balls called buckshot.

---

8. The *Mandingo* were another people of western Africa.
9. The expression *in full rout* means "in disorderly retreat."

10. *Allah* means "God." *Momentum,* here, means "force resulting from movement."

Vocabulary
agony (agʹ ə nē) *n.* great pain and suffering of the mind or body

Those who did clustered about their young leader, determined to make one last, desperate stand. Ibrahima was hit in the back by an arrow, but the aim was not true and the arrow merely cut his broad shoulder. Then something smashed against his head from the rear.

The next thing Ibrahima knew was that he was choking. Then he felt himself being lifted from water. He tried to move his arms, but they had been fastened securely behind his back. He had been captured.

When he came to his full senses, he looked around him. Those of his noble cavalry who had not been captured were already dead. Ibrahima was unsteady on his legs as his clothes and sandals were stripped from him. The victorious Mandingo warriors now pushed him roughly into file with his men. They began the long trek that would lead them to the sea.

In Fouta Djallon being captured by the enemy meant being forced to do someone else's bidding, sometimes for years. If you could get a message to your people, you could, perhaps, buy your freedom. Otherwise, it was only if you were well liked, or if you married one of your captor's women, that you would be allowed to go free, or to live like a free person.

Ibrahima sensed that things would not go well for him.

The journey to the sea took weeks. Ibrahima was tied to other men, with ropes around their necks. Each day they walked from dawn to dusk. Those who were slow were knocked brutally to the ground. Some of those who could no

longer walk were speared and left to die in agony. It was the lucky ones who were killed outright if they fell.

When they reached the sea, they remained bound hand and foot. There were men and women tied together. Small children clung to their mothers as they waited for the boats to come and the bargaining to begin.

Ibrahima, listening to the conversations of the men who held him captive, could understand those who spoke Arabic. These Africans were a low class of men, made powerful by the guns they had been given, made evil by the white man's goods. But it didn't matter who was evil and who was good. It only mattered who held the gun.

Ibrahima was inspected on the shore, then put into irons and herded into a small boat that took him out to a ship that was larger than any he had ever seen.

The ship onto which Ibrahima was taken was already crowded with black captives. Some shook in fear; others, still tied, fought by hurling their bodies at their captors. The beating and the killing continued until the ones who were left knew that their lot[11] was hopeless.

On board the ship there were more whites with guns, who shoved them toward the open hatch. Some of the Africans hesitated at the hatch, and were clubbed down and pushed below-decks.

It was dark beneath the deck, and difficult to breathe. Bodies were pressed close

11. Here, *lot* means "fate; final outcome."

Vocabulary
trek (trek) *n.* a journey, especially one that is slow and difficult

against other bodies. In the section of the ship he was in, men prayed to various gods in various languages. It seemed that the whites would never stop pushing men into the already crowded space. Two sailors pushed the Africans into position so that each would lie in the smallest space possible. The sailors panted and sweated as they untied the men and then chained them to a railing that ran the length of the ship.

The ship rolled against its mooring[12] as the anchor was lifted, and the journey began. The boards of the ship creaked and moaned as it lifted and fell in the sea. Some of the men got sick, vomiting upon themselves in the wretched darkness. They lay cramped, muscles aching, irons cutting into their legs and wrists, gasping for air.

Once a day they would be brought out on deck and made to jump about for exercise. They were each given a handful of either beans or rice cooked with yams and water from a cask. The white sailors looked hardly better than the Africans, but it was they who held the guns.

Illness and the stifling[13] conditions on the ships caused many deaths. How many depended largely on how fast the ships could be loaded with Africans and how long the voyage from Africa took. It was not unusual for 10 percent of the Africans to die if the trip took longer than the usual twenty-five to thirty-five days.

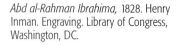

Abd al-Rahman Ibrahima, 1828. Henry Inman. Engraving. Library of Congress, Washington, DC.

Ibrahima, now twenty-six years old, reached Mississippi in 1788. As the ship approached land, the Africans were brought onto the deck and fed. Some had oil put on their skins so they would look better; their sores were treated or covered with pitch.[14] Then they were given garments to wear in an obvious effort to improve their appearance.

Although Ibrahima could not speak English, he understood he was being bargained for. The white man who stood on the platform with him made him turn around, and several other white men neared him, touched his limbs, examined his teeth, looked into his eyes, and made him move about.

Thomas Foster, a tobacco grower and a hard-working man, had come from South Carolina with his family and had settled on the rich lands that took their minerals from the Mississippi River. He already held one captive, a young boy. In August 1788 he bought two more. One of them was named Sambo, which means "second son." The other was Ibrahima.

Foster agreed to pay $930 for the two Africans. He paid $150 down and signed an agreement to pay another $250 the following January and the remaining $530 in January of the following year.

When Ibrahima arrived at Foster's farm, he tried to find someone who could explain

---

12. A ship's *mooring* is the place where it is docked.
13. The conditions were suffocating or smothering (*stifling*).

14. The *pitch* used here was a thick, dark, sticky substance from trees.

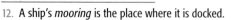

to the white man who he was—the son of a chief. He wanted to offer a ransom for his own release, but Foster wasn't interested. He understood, perhaps from the boy whom he had purchased previously, that this new African was claiming to be an important person. Foster had probably never heard of the Fula or their culture; he had paid good money for the African, and wasn't about to give him up. Foster gave Ibrahima a new name: He called him Prince.

For Ibrahima there was confusion and pain. What was he to do? A few months before, he had been a learned man and a leader among his people. Now he was a captive in a strange land where he neither spoke the language nor understood the customs. Was he never to see his family again? Were his sons forever lost to him?

As a Fula, Ibrahima wore his hair long; Foster insisted that it be cut. Ibrahima's clothing had been taken from him, and his sandals. Now the last remaining symbol of his people, his long hair, had been taken as well.

He was told to work in the fields. He refused, and he was tied and whipped. The sting of the whip across his naked flesh was terribly painful, but it was nothing like the pain he felt within. The whippings forced him to work.

For Ibrahima this was not life, but a mockery of life. There was the waking in the morning and the sleeping at night; he worked, he ate, but this was not life. What was more, he could not see an end to it. It was this feeling that made him attempt to escape.

Ibrahima escaped to the backwoods regions of Natchez. He hid there, eating wild berries and fruit, not daring to show his face to any man, white or black. There was no telling who could be trusted. Sometimes he saw men with dogs and knew they were searching for runaways, perhaps him.

Where was he to run? What was he to do? He didn't know the country, he didn't know how far it was from Fouta Djallon, or how to get back to his homeland. He could tell that this place was ruled by white men who held him in captivity. The other blacks he had seen were from all parts of Africa. Some he recognized by their tribal markings, some he did not. None were allowed to speak their native tongues around the white men. Some already knew nothing of the languages of their people.

As time passed Ibrahima's despair deepened. His choices were simple. He could stay in the woods and probably die, or he could submit his body back into bondage. There is no place in Islamic law for a man to take his own life. Ibrahima returned to Thomas Foster.

Foster still owed money to the man from whom he had purchased Ibrahima. The debt would remain whether he still possessed the African or not. Foster was undoubtedly glad to see that the African had returned. Thin, nearly starving, Ibrahima was put to work.

Ibrahima submitted himself to the will of Thomas Foster. He was a captive, held in bondage not only by Foster but by the society in which he found himself. Ibrahima maintained his beliefs in the

---

Vocabulary
bondage (bon′ dij) *n.* slavery

religion of Islam and kept its rituals as best he could. He was determined to be the same person he had always been: Abd al-Rahman Ibrahima of Fouta Djallon and of the proud Fula people.

By 1807 the area had become the Mississippi Territory. Ibrahima was forty-five and had been in bondage for twenty years. During those years he met and married a woman whom Foster had purchased, and they began to raise a family. Fouta Djallon was more and more distant, and he had become resigned to the idea that he would never see it or his family again.

Thomas Foster had grown wealthy and had become an important man in the territory. At forty-five Ibrahima was considered old. He was less useful to Foster, who now let the tall African grow a few vegetables on a side plot and sell them in town, since there was nowhere in the territory that the black man could go where he would not be captured by some other white man and returned.

It was during one of these visits to town that Ibrahima saw a white man who looked familiar. The smallish man walked slowly and with a limp. Ibrahima cautiously approached the man and spoke to him. The man looked closely at Ibrahima, then spoke his name. It was Dr. Cox.

The two men shook hands and Dr. Cox, who now lived in the territory, took Ibrahima to his home. John Cox had not prospered over the years, but he was still hopeful. He listened carefully as Ibrahima told his story—the battle near Fouta Djallon, the defeat, the long journey across the Atlantic Ocean, and, finally, his sale to Thomas Foster and the years of labor.

Dr. Cox and Ibrahima went to the Foster plantation. Meeting with Foster, he explained how he had met the tall black man. Surely, he reasoned, knowing that Ibrahima was of royal blood, Foster would free him? The answer was a firm, but polite, no. No amount of pleading would make Foster change his mind. It didn't matter that Dr. Cox had supported what Ibrahima had told Foster so many years before, that he was a prince. To Foster the man was merely his property.

Dr. Cox had to leave the man whose people had saved his life, but he told Ibrahima that he would never stop working for his freedom.

Andrew Marschalk, the son of a Dutch baker, was a printer, a pioneer in his field, and a man of great curiosity. By the time Marschalk heard about it, Cox had told a great many people in the Natchez district the story of African royalty being held in slavery in America. Marschalk was fascinated. He suggested that Ibrahima write a letter to his people, telling them of his whereabouts and asking them to ransom him. But Ibrahima had not been to his homeland in twenty years. The people there were still being captured by slave traders. He would have to send a messenger who knew the countryside, and who knew the Fula. Where would he find such a man?

For a long time Ibrahima did nothing. Finally, some time after the death of Dr. Cox in 1816, Ibrahima wrote the letter that Marschalk suggested. He had little

---

Vocabulary

prosper (pros' pər) v. to grow, especially in wealth; to succeed

faith in the procedure but felt he had nothing to lose. Marschalk was surprised when Ibrahima appeared with the letter written neatly in Arabic. Since one place in Africa was the same as the next to Marschalk, he sent the letter not to Fouta Djallon but to Morocco.[15]

The government of Morocco did not know Ibrahima but understood from his letter that he was a Moslem. Moroccan officials, in a letter to President James Monroe, pleaded for the release of Ibrahima. The letter reached Henry Clay, the American Secretary of State.

The United States had recently ended a bitter war with Tripoli[16] in north Africa, and welcomed the idea of establishing good relations with Morocco, another north African country. Clay wrote to Foster about Ibrahima.

Foster resented the idea of releasing Ibrahima. The very idea that the government of Morocco had written to Clay and discussed a religion that Ibrahima shared with other Africans gave Ibrahima a past that Foster had long denied, a past as honorable as Foster's. This idea challenged a basic premise[17] of slavery—a premise that Foster must have believed without reservation: that the Africans had been nothing but savages, with no humanity or human feelings, and therefore it was all right to enslave them. But after more letters and pressure from the State Department, Foster agreed to release Ibrahima if he could be assured that Ibrahima would leave the country and return to Fouta Djallon.

Many people who believed that slavery was wrong also believed that Africans could not live among white Americans. The American Colonization Society had been formed expressly to send freed Africans back to Africa. The society bought land, and a colony called Liberia was established on the west coast of Africa. Foster was assured that Ibrahima would be sent there.

By then Ibrahima's cause had been taken up by a number of abolitionist[18] groups in the north as well as by many free Africans. They raised money to buy his wife's freedom as well.

On February 7, 1829, Ibrahima and his wife sailed on the ship *Harriet* for Africa. The ship reached Liberia, and Ibrahima now had to find a way to reach his people again. He never found that way. Abd al-Rahman Ibrahima died in Liberia in July 1829.

Who was Ibrahima? He was one of millions of Africans taken by force from their native lands. He was the son of a chief, a warrior, and a scholar. But to Ibrahima the only thing that mattered was that he had lost his freedom. If he had been a herder in Fouta Djallon, or an artist in Benin, or a farmer along the Gambia,[19] it would have been the same. Ibrahima was an African who loved freedom no less than other beings on earth. And he was denied that freedom.

---

15. *Morocco* is a nation in northern Africa.
16. *Tripoli* (trip′ ə lē) is a region of what is now the country of Libya; it's also the name of a city.
17. A *premise* is a statement that is accepted as true even though it hasn't been proven.
18. The movement to abolish, or do away with, slavery was called abolitionism, and people who supported this cause were *abolitionists.*
19. *Benin* (ben in′) is a country in western Africa. The *Gambia* River flows from Fouta Djallon to the Atlantic.

Responding to Literature

PERSONAL RESPONSE

- ◆ How did you react to this selection? Were you surprised? Angry? Sad?
- ◆ Was Ibrahima's experience of slavery different from what you had imagined it would be like? If so, in what ways? Look at your ideas from the **Focus Activity** on page 500.

Charleston, South Carolina, identification tag for free African Americans.

Identification tag for enslaved African Americans.

Analyzing Literature

RECALL

1. What was Ibrahima's life like before he was captured?
2. How did Ibrahima and Dr. Cox happen to meet the first time?
3. How did Ibrahima come to live at Thomas Foster's farm?
4. How did the U.S. Secretary of State get involved in Ibrahima's release?

INTERPRET

5. Do you think Foster believed that Ibrahima was an important person in his home country? Is it likely he would have cared? Why or why not?
6. Why does Ibrahima return to Foster after successfully running away?
7. Do you think Dr. Cox was successful in helping Ibrahima become free? Explain.
8. Once Foster agreed to let Ibrahima go, why did he insist that Ibrahima go back to Africa?

EVALUATE AND CONNECT

9. Myers begins the selection with two questions. How do these questions help you know the **author's purpose** for writing?
10. Theme Connection   Ibrahima was finally released after being enslaved for forty years. How would you react if something you had wanted desperately for a long time, and given up on, suddenly became possible? Explain.

LITERARY ELEMENTS

Biography

In the **biography** of a historical figure, the time and place in which the events happen may be completely unfamiliar to readers. Readers need a context, or framework, to understand what happens to the characters and why it is significant. The framework lets readers know about the way people lived and their customs, beliefs, and attitudes.

1. What do you learn about the Fula people and their government? How do these details help you to understand Ibrahima?

2. How does knowing about Ibrahima's people affect how you feel about his becoming enslaved?

● See **Literary Terms Handbook,** p. R1.

Literature and Writing

Writing About Literature

Character Sketch In this selection, the author asks, "Who was Ibrahima?" Think about Ibrahima's life before and after he was enslaved. In a paragraph, summarize the two or three things you think are most important to know about him. Support your ideas with specific details from the selection.

Creative Writing

Here I Am Andrew Marschalk, the printer, encouraged Ibrahima to "write a letter to his people, telling them of his whereabouts and asking them to ransom him." By then, Ibrahima had been away from home for twenty years. Imagine you are Ibrahima. What letter would you write?

Extending Your Response

Performing

News Report Imagine that you are a news reporter. As the ship *Harriet* is preparing to leave for Africa, you observe Ibrahima and his wife about to board. Perhaps they speak to the crowd. Role-play a hurried interview with Ibrahima. Then write a report based on your interview and what you know about Ibrahima's release. Present your news report to the class.

Literature Groups

Author's Purpose What might the author hope that Ibrahima's life can teach those who read about it? Why does he use one man's life story to speak about a larger issue? Is his technique effective? Do you think Ibrahima would be pleased or displeased that his life story was used in this way? Support your opinion, and share your group's ideas with the class.

Interdisciplinary Activity

Geography
Ibrahima's ship probably departed from what is now Guinea and traveled to Mississippi. On a map of the world, trace with a finger the probable route and use the mileage scale to tell how many miles the difficult journey was.

Reading Further

If you'd like to read more by Walter Dean Myers, you might enjoy these books:
Me, Mop, and the Moondance Kid
Tales of a Dead King

 Save your work for your portfolio.

Skill Minilessons

GRAMMAR AND LANGUAGE • COMMAS TO SEPARATE INTERRUPTING ELEMENTS

Commas are used to set off information that interrupts the flow of thought in a sentence. The interruption may be an expression, a comment, a definition, a clarification, additional information, or even a name. Notice how commas help make the following sentence clearer.

The European invaders, along with those Africans who cooperated with them, had made the times dangerous.

PRACTICE Copy these sentences from the selection. Add commas to set off interrupting elements.

1. Most but not all of the Africans who were brought to the colonies came from central and west Africa.
2. From the Koran it was felt came all other knowledge.
3. . . . you could perhaps buy your freedom.
4. Dr. Cox an Irishman told of being separated from a hunting party . . .
5. Andrew Marschalk the son of a Dutch baker was a printer . . .

● For more about commas, see **Language Handbook,** pp. R33–R34.

READING AND THINKING • SUMMARIZING

A **summary** is a brief retelling of important events and ideas. Ibrahima gave Dr. Cox a summary of his life since they last met:

. . . Ibrahima told his story—the battle near Fouta Djallon, the defeat, the long journey across the Atlantic Ocean, and, finally, his sale to Thomas Foster and the years of labor.

PRACTICE Write a summary about the efforts made to free Ibrahima. Reread the story beginning at the point at which Ibrahima runs into Dr. Cox again. Take notes, and then use your notes to write a summary of how Ibrahima regained his freedom.

● For more about summarizing, see **Reading Handbook,** p. R81.

VOCABULARY • THE SUFFIX -age

A **suffix** is a word part added to the end of a word that changes the word's meaning. The change in meaning may be big, such as when *hope* becomes *hopeless,* or it may be small, such as when *marry* becomes *marriage. Bondage* also contains the suffix *-age.* The verb *bond* means "hold together," and *bondage* means "being bound" or "captivity."

You can often figure out what a word with the suffix *-age* means by looking for a "base word," that is, a whole word inside the bigger one. The spelling may be a little different, as when the *y* in *marry* changes to an *i.*

PRACTICE Use what you know about base words and the suffix *-age* to match each word to its meaning.

1. stoppage
2. usage
3. percentage
4. pilgrimage
5. breakage

a. how something is treated
b. an ending or quitting
c. a journey for a religious reason
d. the result of smashing, splitting, or crushing
e. part in relation to every hundred

● For more about adding suffixes, see **Language Handbook,** Spelling, p. R40.

MAGAZINE ADVERTISEMENT

Advertisements sometimes suggest that only a particular brand can make buyers happy.

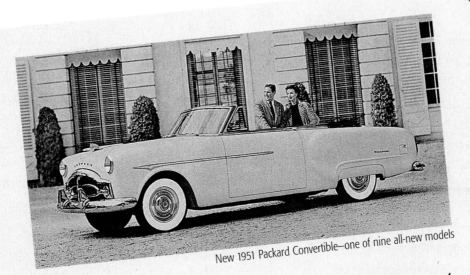

New 1951 Packard Convertible—one of nine all-new models

Pride of Possession is Standard Equipment

How can we put a price tag on your neighbors' look of envy . . . or on your own feeling of well-being . . . as you drive your new 1951 Packard home for the first time?

We can't, of course. So—Pride of Possession is Standard Equipment. Like the exclusiveness of Packard beauty—and the years-ahead superiority of Packard engineering—you can't buy a new 1951 Packard without it. And you never can match it— no matter how much you may be willing to pay— in any other car!

It's more than a car . . . it's a

PACKARD

ASK THE MAN WHO OWNS ONE

Before You Read
The Gold Cadillac

MEET MILDRED D. TAYLOR

I n my early years, the trip
was a marvelous adventure,
a twenty-hour picnic," says
Mildred D. Taylor, describing a
yearly trip to visit relatives in
the South. Her family had
moved north from Mississippi
when she was a baby. Each
year the family packed a huge
picnic for a visit south. Taylor
did not know then that they
had to pack food. As African
Americans, her family was not
welcome in many Southern
restaurants in those days.
Taylor grew up to become an
accomplished writer and won
the Newbery Medal for *Roll of
Thunder, Hear My Cry.*

*Mildred D. Taylor was born in 1943.
This story was published in 1987.*

FOCUS ACTIVITY

Have you or someone you know ever been denied something
that someone else was allowed to have? Was the situation fair?
Were you left out for a reason that you understood?

Sharing Ideas
Briefly write down what happened. Describe what it's like to
be left out. If you wish, share experiences with the class.

Setting a Purpose
Find out whether the characters in *The Gold Cadillac* are
treated fairly.

BACKGROUND

Did You Know?   The story takes place in 1950. At that time,
segregation was legal in many states. For example, drinking
fountains might have
been labeled "White
Only" or "Colored." City
parks might have had
signs reading "Whites
Only." On city buses, an
African American was
required to sit at the
back of the bus and had
to give up a seat if a
white person wanted it.

Man drinking from water container marked "Colored."

VOCABULARY PREVIEW

feature (fē′ chər) *n.* a part or quality that makes a thing outstanding or different from similar things; p. 516
practical (prak′ ti kəl) *adj.* sensible about everyday activities,
work, and so on; p. 516
caravan (kar′ ə van′) *n.* a number of people or vehicles
traveling together, especially for safety through dangerous
regions; p. 518
heedful (hēd′ fəl) *adj.* giving careful attention (to); mindful;
p. 521

My sister and I were playing out on the front lawn when the gold Cadillac rolled up and my father stepped from behind the wheel. We ran to him, our eyes filled with wonder. "Daddy, whose Cadillac?" I asked.

And Wilma demanded, "Where's our Mercury?"

My father grinned. "Go get your mother and I'll tell you all about it."

"Is it ours?" I cried. "Daddy, is it ours?"

"Get your mother!" he laughed. "And tell her to hurry!" Wilma and I ran off to obey as Mr. Pondexter next door came from his house to see what this new Cadillac was all about. We threw open the front door, ran through the downstairs front parlor and straight through the house to the kitchen where my mother was cooking and one of my aunts was helping her. "Come on, Mother-Dear!" we cried together. "Daddy say come on out and see this new car!"

The Gold Cadillac

Mildred D. Taylor ∾

"What?" said my mother, her face showing her surprise. "What're you talking about?"

"A Cadillac!" I cried.

"He said hurry up!" relayed Wilma.

And then we took off again, up the back stairs to the second floor of the duplex.[1] Running down the hall, we banged on all the apartment doors. My uncles and their wives stepped to the doors. It was good it was a Saturday morning. Everybody was home.

"We got us a Cadillac! We got us a Cadillac!" Wilma and I proclaimed in unison.[2] We had decided that the Cadillac had to be ours if our father was driving it and holding on to the keys. "Come on see!" Then we raced on, through the upstairs sunroom, down the front steps, through the downstairs sunroom, and out to the Cadillac. Mr. Pondexter was still there. Mr. LeRoy and Mr. Courtland from down the street were there too and all were admiring the Cadillac as my father stood proudly by, pointing out the various features.

"Brand-new 1950 Coupe deVille!"[3] I heard one of the men saying.

"Just off the showroom floor!" my father said. "I just couldn't resist it."

My sister and I eased up to the car and peeked in. It was all gold inside. Gold leather seats. Gold carpeting. Gold dashboard. It was like no car we had owned before. It looked like a car for rich folks.

"Daddy, are we rich?" I asked. My father laughed.

"Daddy, it's ours, isn't it?" asked Wilma, who was older and more practical than I. She didn't intend to give her heart too quickly to something that wasn't hers.

"You like it?"

"Oh, Daddy, yes!"

He looked at me. "What 'bout you, 'lois?"

"Yes, sir!"

My father laughed again. "Then I expect I can't much disappoint my girls, can I? It's ours all right!"

Wilma and I hugged our father with our joy. My uncles came from the house and my aunts, carrying their babies, came out too. Everybody surrounded the car and owwed and ahhed. Nobody could believe it.

Then my mother came out.

Everybody stood back grinning as she approached the car. There was no smile on her face. We all waited for her to speak. She stared at the car, then looked at my father, standing there as proud as he could be. Finally she said, "You didn't buy this car, did you, Wilbert?"

"Gotta admit I did. Couldn't resist it."

"But . . . but what about our Mercury? It was perfectly good!"

"Don't you like the Cadillac, Dee?"

"That Mercury wasn't even a year old!"

---

1. *Duplex* means "double." A duplex apartment has rooms on two floors, and a duplex house has two separate units for two families.
2. Here, *proclaim* means "announce publicly," and *in unison* means "speaking the same words at the same time."
3. *Coupe de Ville* (kōōp′ də vil′)

My father nodded. "And I'm sure whoever buys it is going to get themselves a good car. But we've got ourselves a better one. Now stop frowning, honey, and let's take ourselves a ride in our brand-new Cadillac!"

My mother shook her head. "I've got food on the stove," she said and turning away walked back to the house.

There was an awkward silence and then my father said, "You know Dee never did much like surprises. Guess this here Cadillac was a bit too much for her. I best go smooth things out with her."

Everybody watched as he went after my mother. But when he came back, he was alone.

"Well, what she say?" asked one of my uncles.

My father shrugged and smiled. "Told me I bought this Cadillac alone, I could just ride in it alone."

Another uncle laughed. "Uh-oh! Guess she told you!"

"Oh, she'll come around," said one of my aunts. "Any woman would be proud to ride in this car."

"That's what I'm banking on," said my father as he went around to the street side of the car and opened the door. "All right! Who's for a ride?"

"We are!" Wilma and I cried.

All three of my uncles and one of my aunts, still holding her baby, and Mr.

Dolly and Rach, c. 1930. John Wesley Hardrick. Oil on board, 38 x 33 in. Collection of Georgia A. Hardrick Rhea.

Viewing the painting: In what ways does the relationship between the girls in the painting reflect that between Wilma and 'lois?

Pondexter climbed in with us and we took off for the first ride in the gold Cadillac. It was a glorious ride and we drove all through the city of Toledo. We rode past the church and past the school. We rode through Ottawa Hills where the rich folks lived and on into Walbridge Park and past the zoo, then along the Maumee River. But none us had had enough of the car so my father put the car on the road and we drove all the way to Detroit. We had plenty of family there and everybody was just as pleased as could be about the Cadillac. My father told our Detroit relatives that he was in the doghouse with my mother about buying the Cadillac. My uncles told them she wouldn't ride in the car. All the Detroit family thought that was funny and everybody, including my father, laughed about it and said my mother would come around.

It was early evening by the time we got back home, and I could see from my mother's face she had not come around. She was angry now not only about the car, but that we had been gone so long. I didn't understand that, since my father had called her as soon as we reached Detroit to let her know where we were. I had heard him myself. I didn't understand either why she did not like that fine Cadillac and thought she was being terribly disagreeable with my father. That night as she tucked Wilma and me in bed I told her that too.

"Is this your business?" she asked.

"Well, I just think you ought to be nice to Daddy. I think you ought to ride in that car with him! It'd sure make him happy."

"I think you ought to go to sleep," she said and turned out the light.

Later I heard her arguing with my father. "We're supposed to be saving for a house!" she said.

"We've already got a house!" said my father.

"But you said you wanted a house in a better neighborhood. I thought that's what we both said!"

"I haven't changed my mind."

"Well, you have a mighty funny way of saving for it, then. Your brothers are saving for houses of their own and you don't see them out buying new cars every year!"

"We'll still get the house, Dee. That's a promise!"

"Not with new Cadillacs we won't!" said my mother and then she said a very loud good night and all was quiet.

The next day was Sunday and everybody figured that my mother would be sure to give in and ride in the Cadillac. After all, the family always went to church together on Sunday. But she didn't give in. What was worse she wouldn't let Wilma and me ride in the Cadillac either. She took us each by the hand, walked past the Cadillac where my father stood waiting and headed on toward the church, three blocks away. I was really mad at her now. I had been looking forward to driving up to the church in that gold Cadillac and having everybody see.

On most Sunday afternoons during the summertime, my mother, my father, Wilma, and I would go for a ride. Sometimes we just rode around the city and visited friends and family. Sometimes we made short trips over to Chicago or Peoria or Detroit to see relatives there or to Cleveland where we had relatives too, but we could also see the Cleveland Indians play. Sometimes we joined our aunts and uncles and drove in a caravan out to the park or to the beach. At the park or the beach Wilma and I would run and play. My mother and my aunts would spread a picnic and my father and my uncles would shine their cars.

Vocabulary

caravan (kar′ ə van′) *n.* a number of people or vehicles traveling together, especially for safety through dangerous regions

But on this Sunday afternoon my mother refused to ride anywhere. She told Wilma and me that we could go. So we left her alone in the big, empty house, and the family cars, led by the gold Cadillac, headed for the park. For a while I played and had a good time, but then I stopped playing and went to sit with my father. Despite his laughter he seemed sad to me. I think he was missing my mother as much as I was.

That evening my father took my mother to dinner down at the corner café. They walked. Wilma and I stayed at the house chasing fireflies in the backyard. My aunts and uncles sat in the yard and on the porch, talking and laughing about the day and watching us. It was a soft summer's evening, the kind that came every day and was expected. The smell of charcoal and of barbecue drifting from up the block, the sound of laughter and music and talk drifting from yard to yard were all a part of it. Soon one of my uncles joined Wilma and me in our chase of fireflies and when my mother and father came home we were at it still. My mother and father watched us for awhile, while everybody else watched them to see if my father would take out the Cadillac and if my mother would slide in beside him to take a ride. But it soon became evident that the dinner had not changed my mother's mind. She still refused to ride in the Cadillac. I just couldn't understand her objection to it.

Though my mother didn't like the Cadillac, everybody else in the neighborhood certainly did. That meant quite a few folks too, since we lived on a very busy block. On one corner was a grocery store, a cleaner's, and a gas station. Across the street was a beauty shop and a fish market, and down the street was a bar, another grocery store, the Dixie Theater, the café, and a drugstore. There were always people strolling to or from one of these places and because our house was right in the middle of the block just about everybody had to pass our house and the gold Cadillac. Sometimes people took in the Cadillac as they walked, their heads turning for a longer look as they passed. Then there were people who just outright stopped and took a good look before continuing on their way. I was proud to say that car belonged to my family. I felt mighty important as people called to me as I ran down the street. "'Ey, 'lois! How's that Cadillac, girl? Riding fine?" I told my mother how much everybody liked that car. She was not impressed and made no comment.

> *Though my mother didn't like the Cadillac, everybody else in the neighborhood certainly did.*

Since just about everybody on the block knew everybody else, most folks knew that my mother wouldn't ride in the Cadillac. Because of that, my father took a lot of good-natured kidding from the men. My mother got kidded too as the women said if she didn't ride in that car, maybe some other woman would. And everybody laughed about it and began to bet on who would give

Springtime (Portrait of Ella Mae Moore), 1933. John Wesley Hardrick. Oil on board, 48 x 32 in. Private collection.

Viewing the painting: Does this woman remind you of 'lois's mother? Why or why not?

it where I please. Even down to Mississippi."

My uncles argued with him and tried to talk him out of driving the car south. So did my aunts and so did the neighbors, Mr. LeRoy, Mr. Courtland, and Mr. Pondexter. They said it was a dangerous thing, a mighty dangerous thing, for a black man to drive an expensive car into the rural South.

"Not much those folks hate more'n to see a northern Negro coming down there in a fine car," said Mr. Pondexter. "They see those Ohio license plates, they'll figure you coming down uppity, trying to lord[4] your fine car over them!"

I listened, but I didn't understand. I didn't understand why they didn't want my father to drive that car south. It was his.

in first, my mother or my father. But then my father said he was going to drive the car south into Mississippi to visit my grandparents and everybody stopped laughing.

My uncles stopped.

So did my aunts.

Everybody.

"Look here, Wilbert," said one of my uncles, "it's too dangerous. It's like putting a loaded gun to your head."

"I paid good money for that car," said my father. "That gives me a right to drive

"Listen to Pondexter, Wilbert!" cried another uncle. "We might've fought a war to free people overseas, but we're not free here! Man, those white folks down south'll lynch[5] you soon's look at you. You know that!"

---

4. The expression *lord (it) over* refers to behaving in a grand, overly proud manner.
5. *Lynch* means "to murder (an accused person), usually by hanging, through the action of a mob." Someone who is *lynched* does not get a lawful trial and, often, is put to death because of racial hatred.

Wilma and I looked at each other. Neither one of us knew what *lynch* meant, but the word sent a shiver through us. We held each other's hand.

My father was silent, then he said: "All my life I've had to be heedful of what white folks thought. Well, I'm tired of that. I worked hard for everything I got. Got it honest, too. Now I got that Cadillac because I liked it and because it meant something to me that somebody like me from Mississippi could go and buy it. It's my car, I paid for it, and I'm driving it south."

My mother, who had said nothing through all this, now stood. "Then the girls and I'll be going too," she said.

"No!" said my father.

My mother only looked at him and went off to the kitchen.

My father shook his head. It seemed he didn't want us to go. My uncles looked at each other, then at my father. "You set on doing this, we'll all go," they said. "That way we can watch out for each other." My father took a moment and nodded. Then my aunts got up and went off to their kitchens too.

All the next day my aunts and my mother cooked and the house was filled with delicious smells. They fried chicken and baked hams and cakes and sweet potato pies and mixed potato salad. They filled jugs with water and punch and coffee. Then they packed everything in huge picnic baskets along with bread and boiled eggs, oranges and apples, plates and napkins, spoons and forks and cups. They placed all that food on the back seats of the cars. It was like a grand, grand picnic we were

going on, and Wilma and I were mighty excited. We could hardly wait to start.

My father, my mother, Wilma, and I got into the Cadillac. My uncles, my aunts, my cousins got into the Ford, the Buick, and the Chevrolet, and we rolled off in our caravan headed south. Though my mother was finally riding in the Cadillac, she had no praise for it. In fact, she said nothing about it at all. She still seemed upset and since she still seemed to feel the same about the car, I wondered why she had insisted upon making this trip with my father.

We left the city of Toledo behind, drove through Bowling Green and down through the Ohio countryside of farms and small towns, through Dayton and Cincinnati, and across the Ohio River into Kentucky. On the other side of the river my father stopped the car and looked back at Wilma and me and said, "Now from here on, whenever we stop and there're white people around, I don't want either one of you to say a word. *Not one word!* Your mother and I'll do all the talking. That understood?"

"Yes, sir," Wilma and I both said, though we didn't truly understand why.

My father nodded, looked at my mother and started the car again. We rolled on, down Highway 25 and through the blue-grass hills of Kentucky. Soon we began to see signs. Signs that read: WHITE ONLY, COLORED NOT ALLOWED. Hours later, we left the Bluegrass State and crossed into Tennessee. Now we saw even more of the signs saying: WHITE ONLY, COLORED NOT ALLOWED. We saw the signs above water fountains and in restaurant windows. We

---

Vocabulary
heedful (hēd′ fəl) *adj.* giving careful attention (to); mindful

saw them in ice cream parlors and at hamburger stands. We saw them in front of hotels and motels, and on the restroom doors of filling stations. I didn't like the signs. I felt as if I were in a foreign land.

I couldn't understand why the signs were there and I asked my father what the signs meant. He said they meant we couldn't drink from the water fountains. He said they meant we couldn't stop to sleep in the motels. He said they meant we couldn't stop to eat in the restaurants. I looked at the grand picnic basket I had been enjoying so much. Now I understood why my mother had packed it. Suddenly the picnic did not seem so grand.

Finally we reached Memphis. We got there at a bad time. Traffic was heavy and we got separated from the rest of the family. We tried to find them but it was no use. We had to go on alone. We reached the Mississippi state line and soon after we heard a police siren. A police car came up behind us. My father slowed the Cadillac, then stopped. Two white policemen got out of their car. They eyeballed the Cadillac and told my father to get out.

"Whose car is this, boy?" they asked.

I saw anger in my father's eyes. "It's mine," he said.

"You're a liar," said one of the policemen. "You stole this car."

"Turn around, put your hands on top of that car and spread eagle,"[6] said the other policeman.

My father did as he was told. They searched him and I didn't understand why. I didn't understand either why they had called my father a liar and didn't believe that the Cadillac was his. I wanted to ask but I remembered my father's warning not to say a word and I obeyed that warning.

The policemen told my father to get in the back of the police car. My father did. One policeman got back into the police car. The other policeman slid behind the wheel of our Cadillac. The police car started off. The Cadillac followed. Wilma and I looked at each other and at our mother. We didn't know what to think. We were scared.

The Cadillac followed the police car into a small town and stopped in front of the police station. The policeman stepped out of our Cadillac and took the keys. The other policeman took my father into the police station.

"Mother-Dear!" Wilma and I cried. "What're they going to do to our daddy? They going to hurt him?"

"He'll be all right," said my mother. "He'll be all right." But she didn't sound so sure of that. She seemed worried.

We waited. More than three hours we waited. Finally my father came out of the police station. We had lots of questions to ask him. He said the police had given him a ticket for speeding and locked him up. But then the judge had come. My father had paid the ticket and they had let him go.

He started the Cadillac and drove slowly out of the town, below the speed limit. The police car followed us. People standing on steps and sitting on porches and in front of stores stared at us as we

---

6. To stand *spread eagle* is to stand with the arms and legs spread wide. In this position, a suspect cannot surprise the police officer by drawing a hidden weapon. The expression comes from the fact that this posture suggests the appearance of an eagle swooping down to grasp its victim.

passed. Finally we were out of the town. The police car still followed. Dusk was falling. The night grew black and finally the police car turned around and left us.

We drove and drove. But my father was tired now and my grandparents' farm was still far away. My father said he had to get some sleep and since my mother didn't drive, he pulled into a grove of trees at the side of the road and stopped.

"I'll keep watch," said my mother.

"Wake me if you see anybody," said my father.

"Just rest," said my mother.

So my father slept. But that bothered me. I needed him awake. I was afraid of the dark and of the woods and of whatever lurked there. My father was the one who kept us safe, he and my uncles. But already the police had taken my father away from us once today and my uncles were lost.

"Go to sleep, baby," said my mother. "Go to sleep."

> *When he came back and started the motor, he turned the Cadillac north, not south.*

But I was afraid to sleep until my father woke. I had to help my mother keep watch. I figured I had to help protect us too, in case the police came back and tried to take my father away again. There was a long,

sharp knife in the picnic basket and I took hold of it, clutching it tightly in my hand. Ready to strike, I sat there in the back of the car, eyes wide, searching the blackness outside the Cadillac. Wilma, for a while, searched the night too, then she fell asleep. I didn't want to sleep, but soon I found I couldn't help myself as an unwelcome drowsiness came over me. I had an uneasy sleep and when I woke it was dawn and my father was gently shaking me. I woke with a start and my hand went up, but the knife wasn't there. My mother had it.

My father took my hand. "Why were you holding the knife, 'lois?" he asked.

I looked at him and at my mother. "I—I was scared," I said.

My father was thoughtful. "No need to be scared now, sugar," he said. "Daddy's here and so is Mother-Dear." Then after a glance at my mother, he got out of the car, walked to the road, looked down it one way, then the other. When he came back and started the motor, he turned the Cadillac north, not south.

"What're you doing?" asked my mother.

"Heading back to Memphis," said my father. "Cousin Halton's there. We'll leave the Cadillac and get his car. Driving this car any farther south with you and the girls in the car, it's just not worth the risk."

And so that's what we did. Instead of driving through Mississippi in golden splendor, we traveled its streets and roads and highways in Cousin Halton's solid, yet not so splendid, four-year-old Chevy. When we reached my grandparents' farm, my uncles and aunts were already there. Everybody was glad to see us. They had

The Gold Cadillac

been worried. They asked about the Cadillac. My father told them what had happened, and they nodded and said he had done the best thing.

We stayed one week in Mississippi. During that week I often saw my father, looking deep in thought, walk off alone across the family land. I saw my mother watching him. One day I ran after my father, took his hand, and walked the land with him. I asked him all the questions that were on my mind. I asked him why the policemen had treated him the way they had and why people didn't want us to eat in the restaurants or drink from the water fountains or sleep in the hotels. I told him I just didn't understand all that.

My father looked at me and said that it all was a difficult thing to understand and he didn't really understand it himself. He said it all had to do with the fact that black people had once been forced to be slaves. He said it had to do with our skins being colored. He said it had to do with stupidity and ignorance. He said it had to do with the law, the law that said we could be treated like this here in the South. And for that matter, he added, any other place in these United States where folks thought the same as so many folks did here in the South. But he also said, "I'm hoping one day though we can drive that long road down here and there won't be any signs. I'm hoping one day

the police won't stop us just because of the color of our skins and we're riding in a gold Cadillac with northern plates."

When the week ended, we said a sad good-bye to my grandparents and all the Mississippi family and headed in a caravan back toward Memphis. In Memphis we returned Cousin Halton's car and got our Cadillac. Once we were home my father put the Cadillac in the garage and didn't drive it. I didn't hear my mother say any more about the Cadillac. I didn't hear my father speak of it either.

Some days passed and then on a bright Saturday afternoon while Wilma and I were playing in the backyard, I saw my father go into the garage. He opened the garage doors wide so the sunshine streamed in, and began to shine the Cadillac. I saw my mother at the kitchen window staring out across the yard at my father. For a long time, she stood there watching my father shine his car. Then she came out and crossed the yard to the garage and I heard her say, "Wilbert, you keep the car."

He looked at her as if he had not heard.

"You keep it," she repeated and turned and walked back to the house.

My father watched her until the back door had shut behind her. Then he went on shining the car and soon began to sing. About an hour later he got into the car and drove away. That evening when he came back he was walking. The Cadillac was nowhere in sight.

"Daddy, where's our new Cadillac?" I demanded to know. So did Wilma.

He smiled and put his hand on my head. "Sold it," he said as my mother came into the room.

"But how come?" I asked. "We poor now?"

"No, sugar. We've got more money towards our new house now and we're all together. I figure that makes us about the richest folks in the world." He smiled at my mother and she smiled too and came into his arms.

After that we drove around in an old 1930s Model A Ford my father had. He said he'd factory ordered us another Mercury, this time with my mother's approval. Despite that, most folks on the block figured we had fallen on hard times after such a splashy showing of good times and some folks even laughed at us as the Ford rattled around the city. I must admit that at first I was pretty much embarrassed to be riding around in that old Ford after the splendor of the Cadillac. But my father said to hold my head high. We and the family knew the truth. As fine as the Cadillac had been, he said, it had pulled us apart for awhile. Now, as ragged and noisy as that old Ford was, we all rode in it together and we were a family again. So I held my head high.

Still though, I thought often of that Cadillac. We had had the Cadillac only a little more than a month, but I wouldn't soon forget its splendor or how I'd felt riding around inside it. I wouldn't soon forget either the ride we had taken south in it. I wouldn't soon forget the signs, the policemen, or my fear. I would remember that ride and the gold Cadillac all my life.

Responding to Literature

PERSONAL RESPONSE

◆ Were you afraid for any of the characters as you read? Explain.

◆ Were your own feelings, as described in the **Focus Activity** on page 514, like those of any character in this story? Explain.

Analyzing Literature

RECALL

1. How does 'lois's mother react to the new Cadillac?

2. What do 'lois's uncles, aunts, and neighbors think about driving the Cadillac to the South?

3. What do the police first accuse 'lois's father of? What is their final charge?

4. How do 'lois and her family finally get to relatives' homes in Mississippi?

INTERPRET

5. When does 'lois's mother decide to ride in the car after all? Why does she make this decision?

6. Theme Connection   How do you think the trip to Mississippi changes 'lois? How does it change her father?

7. Do you think the final charge of the police against 'lois's father is a fair one? Explain.

8. Why do you think 'lois's father sells the Cadillac?

EVALUATE AND CONNECT

9. What purpose (to inform, to entertain, or to persuade), or combination of purposes, do you think Taylor had in mind when she wrote this selection? Explain. (See page R1.)

10. Would you have sold the Cadillac? Why or why not?

Extending Your Response

Writing About Literature

Conflict The girls' parents have different feelings about the Cadillac. In two paragraphs, describe each parent's view of the car at the beginning of the story. How does each parent show his or her feelings about the car? Then explain how and why each parent's view changes as a result of the trip to Mississippi.

Personal Writing

Coup de Ville! Reread the description of the gold Cadillac. Ask yourself how you would feel to be riding in such a car. Write a paragraph, using your feelings and reactions to describe how you picture it.

Literature Groups

Driving Around Owning the Cadillac almost surely did not turn out as 'lois's father imagined it would. Discuss in what ways owning the Cadillac was good or bad for the family. Share your group's ideas with the class.

Learning for Life

Write an Ad If 'lois's father had sold the Cadillac by listing it in the newspaper, what ad might he have written? Study the automobile ads in the newspaper. Using details from the story that describe the Cadillac, write your own ad to sell this car.

93 CHEVY BERETTA, 1-owner, 2dr, 5-spd, a/c, am/fm, cruise, green w/grey int, airbag, only 54K miles, $4950

Reading Further

If you'd like to read more by Mildred D. Taylor, you might enjoy these books:
Song of the Trees
Mississippi Bridge

Save your work for your portfolio.

Skill Minilesson

GRAMMAR AND LANGUAGE • POSSESSIVE PRONOUNS

Possessive pronouns are used to show ownership or possession. An apostrophe is never used with a possessive pronoun: *Is that gold Cadillac ours?*

	Singular	**Plural**
lst person:	my, mine	our, ours
2nd person:	your, yours	your, yours
3rd person:	his, her, hers, its	their, theirs

PRACTICE Copy just the possessive pronouns in the following sentences.

1. My sister and I were playing outside.
2. We saw Dad in his new car.
3. The Cadillac had to be ours if our father was driving it.
4. Its gold leather seats and carpeting were brand new.

● For more on possessive pronouns, see **Language Handbook,** p. R27.

Using Commas Correctly

When people speak, they can use small pauses to help their words make sense. In writing, we use **commas** to substitute for those pauses.

Commas are needed in any kind of series. The series might be a list of people or things, such as "I saw Tom, Rita, Mr. Hawkins, and a spider." It might include a number of events, such as "Tom saw me, smiled, noticed the spider, and let out a yelp." It might be a list of descriptions, such as "The spider was large, brown, and hairy."

Commas are also used to separate *what* someone said from *who* said it (the speaker tag). "That kind of spider," I said, "is big but harmless."

Problem 1 Missing commas in a series

> *My mother, my father Wilma, and I would go for a ride.*
>
> *I ran after my father took his hand, and walked the land with him.*

Solution Use commas to separate three or more items in a series.

> *My mother, my father, Wilma, and I would go for a ride.*
>
> *I ran after my father, took his hand, and walked the land with him.*

Problem 2 Missing commas with direct quotations

> *"Look here, Wilbert" said one of my uncles "it's too dangerous."*

Solution Put a comma inside the quotation marks after the first part of a quotation and also right after the speaker tag.

> *"Look here, Wilbert," said one of my uncles, "it's too dangerous."*

● For more on commas, see **Language Handbook,** pp. R33–R34.

EXERCISE

Rewrite the sentences, adding commas wherever they are needed.

1. "Daddy" 'lois asked "are we rich?"
2. My uncles aunts and cousins gathered around the new car.
3. "What we need to do" said Daddy "is to go on a trip!"
4. We packed ham cake pie and potato salad.
5. "We're all together" said Daddy "and that makes us rich."

Vo·cab·u·lar·y *Skills*

Understanding Idioms

In "The Gold Cadillac," an aunt tells the girls' father that his wife will change her mind about riding in the car. The father says, "That's what I'm banking on." He does not, of course, mean that he's going anywhere near a bank. The phrase *to bank on* means "to depend on."

Every language uses words or phrases in ways that have special meanings, different from what they usually mean. These words or phrases are called **idioms.** Someone who is *on the ball* isn't actually balancing on a ball. You might *take a stand* about something even while you're sitting down. People sometimes *crack up* when they hear a good joke, but they're not at all injured.

You can often figure out what an unfamiliar idiom means. One way is to think about what the literal meanings of the words suggest. Another way is to use context clues to figure out what an idiom means.

> My father told our Detroit relatives that he was *in the doghouse* with my mother about buying the Cadillac. (*In the doghouse* means "in trouble.")

EXERCISE

Think about the meaning of the idiom in each sentence. Then write a short definition or a phrase that could be substituted for each idiom.

1. The gold Cadillac is a big fancy car that must have *cost an arm and a leg.*

2. It *makes a big splash* in the neighborhood, and everyone stops to admire it.

3. The mother wants to save money for a house and *does not hold with* buying a new car instead.

4. She refuses to ride in the car, but the father keeps hoping she will *come around.*

5. After the family is stopped by the police, the father realizes that driving the Cadillac into the rural South at that time is *playing with fire.*

Before You Read

The Horse Snake

MEET HUYNH QUANG NHUONG

"I always planned to return to my hamlet . . . ," writes Huynh Quang Nhuong (hwin kwän nōōn). "But war disrupted my dreams. The land I love was lost to me forever." Huynh grew up in Vietnam. When he was a child, he wanted one day to be a teacher in his village. After attending Saigon University, Huynh was drafted into the South Vietnamese army. He was wounded in battle and permanently paralyzed. Huynh now lives in Missouri.

Huynh Quang Nhuong was born in 1946. "The Horse Snake" is from Huynh's autobiography, The Land I Lost, *which was published in 1982.*

FOCUS ACTIVITY

What do you know about snakes? How do they look and feel? How do they move? What sounds do they make? How do they catch their food and eat it?

Make a Web

Write *snake* in the center of a web. Attach ideas that tell what you know and how you feel about this animal. Compare your responses in a small group.

Setting a Purpose

Read the selection to find out what a "horse snake" is.

BACKGROUND

The Time and Place   Huynh Quang Nhuong's family lived in a small village in Vietnam. His family raised rice and other crops. One of Huynh's chores was to take care of the family's water buffalo, Tank, who liked to nibble on the rice plants when he could. When the author was twelve, he was allowed to hunt with his father in the jungle. The animals most feared in his village were the tiger, the wild hog, the crocodile, and the horse snake.

VOCABULARY PREVIEW

nocturnal (nok turn′ əl) *adj.* active at night; p. 532
succumb (sə kum′) *v.* to yield to a wound or disease; die; p. 533
petrify (pet′ rə fī′) *v.* to paralyze with astonishment, fear, or horror; p. 535
perish (per′ ish) *v.* to die, especially in a violent way or unexpectedly; p. 535

THE HORSE SNAKE

Huynh Quang Nhuong ∼

Despite all his courage there was one creature in the jungle that Tank always tried to avoid—the snake. And there was one kind of snake that was more dangerous than other snakes—the horse snake. In some areas people called it the bamboo snake because it was as long as a full-grown bamboo tree.[1] In other regions, the people called it the thunder or lightning snake, because it attacked so fast and with such power that its victim had neither time to escape nor strength to fight it. In our area, we called it the horse snake because it could move as fast as a thoroughbred. One night a frightened friend of our family's banged on our door and asked us to let him in. When crossing the rice field in front of our house on his way home from a wedding, he had heard the unmistakable hiss of a horse snake. We became very worried; not only for us and our friend, but also for the cattle and other animals we raised.

---

1. This statement is an exaggeration, since *bamboo trees* can grow to a height of 120 feet.

It was too far into the night to rouse all our neighbors and go to search for the snake. But my father told my cousin to blow three times on his buffalo horn, the signal that a dangerous wild beast was loose in the hamlet.[2] A few seconds later we heard three long quivering sounds of a horn at the far end of the hamlet answering our warning. We presumed that the whole hamlet was now on guard.

I stayed up that night, listening to all the sounds outside, while my father and my cousin sharpened their hunting knives. Shortly after midnight we were startled by the frightened neighing of a horse in the rice field. Then the night was still, except for a few sad calls of <u>nocturnal</u> birds and the occasional roaring of tigers in the jungle.

The next day early in the morning all the able-bodied men of the hamlet gathered in front of our house and divided into groups of four to go and look for the snake. My father and my cousin grabbed their lunch and joined a searching party.

They found the old horse that had neighed the night before in the rice field. The snake had squeezed it to death. Its chest was smashed, and all its ribs broken. But the snake had disappeared.

Everybody agreed that it was the work of one of the giant horse snakes which had terrorized our area as far back as anyone could remember. The horse snake usually eats small game, such as turkeys, monkeys, chickens, and ducks, but for unknown reasons sometimes it will attack people and cattle.

A fully grown horse snake can reach the size of a king python. But, unlike pythons, horse snakes have an extremely poisonous bite. Because of their bone-breaking 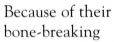 squeeze and fatal bite they are one of the most dangerous creatures of the uplands.

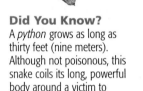

Did You Know?
A *python* grows as long as thirty feet (nine meters). Although not poisonous, this snake coils its long, powerful body around a victim to suffocate it.

The men searched all day, but at nightfall they gave up and went home. My father and my cousin looked very tired when they returned. My grandmother told them to go right to bed after their dinner and that she would wake them up if she or my mother heard any unusual sounds.

The men went to bed and the women prepared to stay up all night. My mother sewed torn clothing and my grandmother read a novel she had just borrowed from a friend. And for the second night in a row, they allowed my little sister and me to stay awake and listen with them for as long as we could. But hours later, seeing the worry on our faces, my grandmother put aside her novel and told us a story:

---

2. A small country village is a *hamlet*.

Vocabulary
nocturnal (nok turn′ əl) *adj.* active at night

Once upon a time a happy family lived in a small village on the shore of the South China Sea. They respected the laws of the land and loved their neighbors very much. The father and his oldest son were woodcutters. The father was quite old, but he still could carry home a heavy load of wood.

One day on his way home from the jungle he was happier than usual. He and his son had discovered a wild chicken nest containing twelve eggs. Now he would have something special to give to his grandchildren when they pulled his shirtsleeves and danced around him to greet him when he came home.

The father looked at the broad shoulders of his son and his steady gait under a very heavy load of wood. He smiled. His son was a good son, and he had no doubt that when he became even older still his son would take good care of him and his wife.

As he was thinking this he saw his son suddenly throw the load of wood at a charging horse snake that had come out of nowhere. The heavy load of wood crashed into the snake's head and stunned it. That gave them enough time to draw their sharp woodcutting knives. But instead of attacking the horse snake from the front, the elder shouted to his son to run behind the big bush of elephant grass nearby while he, who was a little too old to run fast, jumped into the front end of the bush.

Each time the snake passed by him the old man managed to hit it with his knife. He struck the snake many times. Finally it became weak and slowed down; so he came out of his hiding place and attacked the snake's tail, while his son attacked the snake's head. The snake fought back furiously, but finally it succumbed to the well-coordinated attack of father and son.

When the snake was dead, they grabbed its tail and proudly dragged it to the edge of their village. Everyone rushed out to see their prize. They all argued over who would have the honor of carrying the snake to their house for them.

The old woodcutter and his son had to tell the story of how they had killed the snake at least ten times, but the people never tired of hearing it, again and again. They all agreed that the old woodcutter and his son were not only brave but clever as well. Then and there the villagers decided that when their chief, also a brave and clever man, died, the old woodcutter was the only one who deserved the honor of replacing him.

When my grandmother finished the story, my little sister and I became a bit more cheerful. People could defeat this dangerous snake after all. The silent darkness outside became less threatening. Nevertheless, we were still too scared to sleep in our room, so my mother made a

---

Vocabulary

succumb (sə kum′) *v.* to yield to a wound or disease; die

makeshift bed in the sitting room, close to her and our grandmother.

When we woke up the next morning, life in the hamlet had almost returned to normal. The snake had not struck again that night, and the farmers, in groups of three or four, slowly filtered back to their fields. Then, late in the afternoon, hysterical cries for help were heard in the direction of the western part of the ham-let. My cousin and my father grabbed their knives and rushed off to help.

It was Minh, a farmer, who was crying for help. Minh, like most farmers in the area, stored the fish he had caught in the rice field at the end of the rainy season in a small pond. That day Minh's wife had wanted a good fish for dinner. When Minh approached his fish pond he heard what sounded like someone trying to steal his fish by using a bucket to empty water from the pond. Minh was very angry and rushed over to catch the thief, but when he reached the pond, what he saw so

Shadow. Pham Duc Cuong. Private collection.
Viewing the painting: In what ways might this scene be similar to Huynh's village?

petrified him that he fell over backward, speechless. When he regained control he crawled away as fast as he could and yelled loudly for help.

The thief he saw was not a person but a huge horse snake, perhaps the same one that had squeezed the old horse to death two nights before. The snake had hooked its head to the branch of one tree and its tail to another and was splashing the water out of the pond by swinging its body back and forth, like a hammock. Thus, when the shallow pond became dry, it planned to swallow all the fish.

All the villagers rushed to the scene to help Minh, and our village chief quickly organized an attack. He ordered all the men to surround the pond. Then two strong young men approached the snake, one at its tail and the other at its head. As they crept closer and closer, the snake assumed a striking position, its head about one meter above the pond, and its tail swaying from side to side. It was ready to strike in either direction. As the two young men moved in closer, the snake watched them. Each man tried to draw the attention of the snake, while a third man crept stealthily to its side. Suddenly he struck the snake with his long knife. The surprised snake shot out of the pond like an arrow and knocked the young man unconscious as it rushed by. It broke through the circle of men and went into an open rice field. But it received two more wounds on its way out.

The village chief ordered all the women and children to form a long line between the open rice field and the jungle and to yell as loudly as they could, hoping to scare the snake so that it would not flee into the jungle. It would be far easier for the men to fight the wounded snake in an open field than to follow it there.

But now there was a new difficulty. The snake started heading toward the river. Normally a horse snake could beat any man in a race, but since this one was badly wounded, our chief was able to cut off its escape by sending half his men running to the river. Blocked off from the river and jungle, the snake decided to stay and fight.

The hunting party surrounded the snake again, and this time four of the best men attacked the snake from four different directions. The snake fought bravely, but it perished. During the struggle one of the men received a dislocated shoulder, two had bruised ribs, and three were momentarily blinded by dirt thrown by the snake. Luckily all of them succeeded in avoiding the fatal bite of the snake.

We rejoiced that the danger was over. But we knew it would only be a matter of time until we would once again have to face our most dangerous natural enemy—the horse snake.

Vocabulary
petrify (pet′ rə fī′) *v.* to paralyze with astonishment, fear, or horror
perish (per′ ish) *v.* to die, especially in a violent way or unexpectedly

Responding to Literature

PERSONAL RESPONSE

- ◆ Did anything in this selection surprise you? If so, what?
- ◆ Review your web on snakes from the **Focus Activity** on page 530. Does the horse snake possess the qualities you recorded? Is the horse snake unique in any way? Explain.

Analyzing Literature

RECALL

1. Why is the kind of snake in the selection given each of these names: bamboo snake, lightning snake, and horse snake?
2. How do the villagers send messages to each other? What is the signal for danger?
3. What are the two ways that the horse snake kills its prey?
4. What are the important events in the story that the grandmother tells the children?

INTERPRET

5. What is the most important reason that the villagers fear the horse snake?
6. Why don't the villagers rush out at night when they hear the horse neigh?
7. Do you think the horse snake is intelligent? Explain.
8. Why, do you think, does the grandmother tell the story about the horse snake?

EVALUATE AND CONNECT

9. An **autobiography** is the story of a person's life written by that person. Why do you think Huynh includes the incident about the horse snake in his autobiography?
10. Theme Connection   The villagers kill the snake by working together. What problem in your school or community might be solved if people worked together? Explain.

LITERARY ELEMENTS

Author's Purpose

An **author's purpose** may be to inform, to entertain, or to persuade—or a combination of these things. Writers present factual information when they wish to inform. Writers who want to entertain may tell a story. Writers who hope to persuade present ideas to influence readers.

1. What purpose or purposes do you think Huynh had for writing this piece? Why do you think so?

2. How well did he achieve these purposes?

● See **Literary Terms Handbook,** p. R1.

Farmhouse and rice fields on the Mekong Delta, Vietnam.

Extending Your Response

Writing About Literature

Visualize Reread the scene in which the snake is emptying the fish pond. Then close your eyes and picture the scene. Use the author's words and your own visualization to write a paragraph describing this scene.

Creative Writing

Horror Movie Star With a few additional physical features and abilities, the horse snake could easily be the star of a horror movie. Write a brief description of this potential superstar.

Literature Groups

Snake List Reread together sections of the selection that tell why the people of the village fear the horse snake. How do they react to it being near their village? Note how the snake acts. Decide what qualities the snake has. Make a list of attributes, or qualities, of the horse snake. Compare your group's list with that of another group.

*inter*NET CONNECTION

Find out about the history, culture, land, and people of Vietnam by browsing under the country's name. View on-line photos of the country's jungles and rivers.

Interdisciplinary Activity

Science Find out about snakes that live in your region. Research these types of snakes in the library or on the Web. Present your information, along with any available pictures, to the class.

Save your work for your portfolio.

Skill Minilesson

VOCABULARY • MULTIPLE-MEANING WORDS

Most words have more than one meaning. For example, the horse snake *petrified* a man in the story. It paralyzed him with fear. However, *petrified* wood is not frightened; it has been turned to stone.

PRACTICE Use context clues to decide which meaning of *snake* is the right one in each sentence.

a. *noun:* a legless reptile
b. *noun:* a sneaky, disloyal person
c. *noun:* a long, bendable, metal tool
d. *verb:* to move or twist like a snake

1. A plumber may use a *snake* to clear a drain.
2. Cowboys wore boots as protection against *snakes.*
3. I thought he was my friend, but he turned out to be a *snake.*
4. If we *snake* along on the ground, the enemy may not see us.

Before You Read

from *Woodsong*

MEET GARY PAULSEN

"School was a nightmare because I was unbelievably shy and terrible at sports," recalls Gary Paulsen. "I had no friends." As the son of an army officer, Paulsen moved often while growing up. Though changing schools often made him uncomfortable and unhappy, he discovered the library. A librarian took an interest in him and guided him toward subjects that he enjoyed. A talented, award-winning author, Paulsen often writes about nature and survival. His books *Dogsong* and *Hatchet* are Newbery Honor Books.

Gary Paulsen was born in 1939. Woodsong was published in 1990.

FOCUS ACTIVITY

Imagine someone hiking alone in a cold, snowy wilderness area. The hiker has no radio or other communication devices. What are some dangers that the hiker might face?

List Ideas
List everything you can think of as a possible danger.

Setting a Purpose
Read the selection to experience a dangerous situation with the author.

BACKGROUND

Did You Know?   In *Woodsong* Gary Paulsen writes about working as a trapper, mostly of coyotes and beavers, deep in the forests of Minnesota. A friend offered him a dog team to help him with his work. One night in the moonlight, he was crossing Clear Water Lake. He recalls, "There was no one around, and all I could hear was the rhythm of the dogs' breathing as they pulled the sled. . . . [T]he steam from the dogs' breath all but hid their bodies—the entire world seemed to glisten. It almost stopped my heart; I'd never seen anything so beautiful." Paulsen has written about his experiences with dog teams in some of his most popular books.

VOCABULARY PREVIEW

virtually (vur′ chōō ə lē) *adv.* for all practical purposes; truthfully; p. 539
snowball (snō′ bôl) *v.* to grow rapidly larger in size or importance; p. 540
well (wel) *v.* to flow up or out; gush; rise; p. 540
contrary (kon′ trer ē) *adj.* opposite; entirely different; p. 540
chagrin (shə grin′) *n.* a feeling of annoyance or distress arising from disappointment, failure, or embarrassment; p. 540
literally (lit′ ər ə lē) *adv.* without exaggeration; actually; p. 541
persist (pər sist′) *v.* to continue firmly and steadily, especially in the face of difficulty; p. 541

from

Woodsong

Gary Paulsen

There was a point where an old logging trail went through a small, sharp-sided gully—a tiny canyon. The trail came down one wall of the gully—a drop of fifty or so feet—then scooted across a frozen stream and up the other side. It might have been a game trail that was slightly widened, or an old foot trail that had not caved in. Whatever it was, I came onto it in the middle of January. The dogs were very excited. New trails always get them tuned up and they were fairly smoking as we came to the edge of the gully.

I did not know it was there and had been letting them run, not riding the sled brake to slow them, and we virtually shot off the edge.

The dogs stayed on the trail but I immediately lost all control and went flying out into space with the sled. As I did, I kicked sideways and caught my knee on a sharp snag, felt the wood enter under the kneecap and tear it loose.

Vocabulary
virtually (vur′ chōō ə lē) *adv.* for all practical purposes; truthfully

I may have screamed then.

The dogs ran out on the ice of the stream but I fell onto it. As these things often seem to happen, the disaster snowballed.

The trail crossed the stream directly at the top of a small, frozen waterfall with about a twenty-foot drop. Later I saw the beauty of it, the falling lobes[1] of blue ice that had grown as the water froze and refroze, layering on itself. . . .

But at the time I saw nothing. I hit the ice of the stream bed like dropped meat, bounced once, then slithered over the edge of the waterfall and dropped another twenty feet onto the frozen pond below, landing on the torn and separated kneecap.

I have been injured several times running dogs—cracked ribs, a broken left leg, a broken left wrist, various parts frozen or cut or bitten while trying to stop fights—but nothing ever felt like landing on that knee.

I don't think I passed out so much as my brain simply exploded.

Again, I'm relatively certain I must have screamed or grunted, and then I wasn't aware of much for two, perhaps three minutes as I squirmed around trying to regain some part of my mind.

When things settled down to something I could control, I opened my eyes and saw that my snow pants and the jeans beneath were ripped in a jagged line for about a foot. Blood was welling out of the tear, soaking the cloth and the ice underneath the wound.

Shock and pain came in waves and I had to close my eyes several times. All of this was in minutes that seemed like hours and I realized that I was in serious trouble. Contrary to popular belief, dog teams generally do not stop and wait for a musher[2] who falls off. They keep going, often for many miles.

Lying there on the ice I knew I could not walk. I didn't think I could stand without some kind of crutch, but I knew I couldn't walk. I was a good twenty miles from home, at least eight or nine miles from any kind of farm or dwelling.

It may as well have been ten thousand miles.

There was some self-pity creeping in, and not a little chagrin at being stupid enough to just let them run when I didn't know the country. I was trying to skootch myself up to the bank of the gully to get into a more comfortable position when I heard a sound over my head.

I looked up and there was Obeah looking over the top of the waterfall, down at me.

---

1. A *lobe* is a rounded object or the rounded part that sticks out from the surface of an object. Your ears, for example, each have a lobe.

2. A dog-sled driver is called a *musher* because the command "Mush!" is used to order the dogs to begin pulling or to move faster.

Vocabulary
snowball (snō′ bôl) *v.* to grow rapidly larger in size or importance
well (wel) *v.* to flow up or out; gush; rise
contrary (kon′ trer ē) *adj.* opposite; entirely different
chagrin (shə grin′) *n.* a feeling of annoyance or distress arising from disappointment, failure, or embarrassment

I couldn't at first believe it.

He whined a couple of times, moved back and forth as if he might be going to drag the team over the edge, then disappeared from view. I heard some more whining and growling, then a scrabbling sound, and was amazed to see that he had taken the team back up the side of the gully and dragged them past the waterfall to get on the gully wall just over me.

They were in a horrible tangle but he dragged them along the top until he was well below the waterfall, where he scrambled down the bank with the team almost literally falling on him. They dragged the sled up the frozen stream bed to where I was lying.

On the scramble down the bank Obeah had taken them through a thick stand of cockleburs. Great clumps of burrs wadded between their ears and down their backs.

Did You Know?

A dog's *ruff* is the longer hair that forms a sort of wide collar around its neck.

He pulled them up to me, concern in his eyes and making a soft whine, and I reached into his ruff and pulled his head down and hugged him and was never so happy to see anybody probably in my life. Then I felt something and looked down to see one of the other dogs—named Duberry—licking the wound in my leg.

She was not licking with the excitement that prey blood would cause, but with the gentle licking that she would use when cleaning a pup, a wound lick.

I brushed her head away, fearing infection, but she persisted. After a moment I lay back and let her clean it, still holding onto Obeah's ruff, holding onto a friend.

And later I dragged myself around and untangled them and unloaded part of the sled and crawled in and tied my leg down. We made it home that way, with me sitting in the sled: and later when my leg was sewed up and healing and I was sitting in my cabin with the leg propped up on pillows by the wood stove; later when all the pain was gone and I had all the time I needed to think of it . . . later I thought of the dogs.

How they came back to help me, perhaps to save me. I knew that somewhere in the dogs, in their humor and the way they thought, they had great, old knowledge; they had something we had lost.

And the dogs could teach me.

Vocabulary

literally (lit′ ər ə lē) *adv.* without exaggeration; actually
persist (pər sist′) *v.* to continue firmly and steadily, especially in the face of difficulty

Responding to Literature

PERSONAL RESPONSE

- ◆ Which images from the story stay in your mind? Briefly write them down and share them with a partner.
- ◆ How similar was the author's experience to the dangers you imagined in the **Focus Activity?** Share ideas with the class.

Analyzing Literature

RECALL AND INTERPRET

1. What disaster happens to Paulsen? Whose fault is it, do you think?
2. What does Paulsen expect to happen after the disaster? What does happen?
3. Why does Paulsen say that the dogs "had great, old knowledge; they had something we had lost"?

EVALUATE AND CONNECT

4. How does the author "hook" you to read this selection, especially in the opening paragraphs?
5. What "human" traits does Paulsen seem to find in dogs? Do you feel the same way as Paulsen does? Explain.
6. What details show Paulsen's knowledge of dogs and dog behavior?

Extending Your Response

Literature Groups

Problem   Use details in the story to describe the problem Paulsen faces after his sled goes off the trail. What exactly is his situation? Can you think of any possible solutions for him? Is he likely to survive? Discuss the difficulty he faces.

Personal Writing

Faithfully Yours   Think about the surprise Paulsen feels as the dogs act in an unexpected way. Recall the bond he feels with the dogs. Think about your own or a friend's pet. Do you feel a bond with the animal? Why, or why not? Write a paragraph about the pet, describing it and explaining in what ways its behavior is surprising.

COMPARING SELECTIONS

THE HORSE SNAKE **and** *from* **Woodsong**

COMPARE DANGERS

The narrator of each selection faces danger.

1. Who or what causes the danger in each selection?
2. Does each selection describe a special situation, or do the characters face such a danger every day? Explain.

COMPARE RESPONSES

The characters in each selection have different responses to the dangerous situations they face. Compare the narrators' responses to their problems.

1. How does the narrator's response compare with the responses of other characters in the selection?
2. Do the narrator's feelings change as the story continues? Why?
3. What is the solution to the problem in each selection? Explain.

COMPARE AUTHORS' PURPOSES

Each of these selections is from an **autobiography,** a narrative about a person's life written by the person who lived it.

1. What does each narrator learn from his experience?
2. Why, do you think, does each writer want to share this episode of his life?
3. What connections did you make between each author's experience and your own life?

![MEDIA Connection]

MAGAZINE ARTICLE
Almost two thousand years ago, the city of Pompeii was totally destroyed by an unexpected disaster.

Violent Vesuvius

Kids Discover, August/September 1995

People who lived near Vesuvius in A.D. 79 thought of it as simply a very big hill. However, Vesuvius was really a sleeping volcano, silently and slowly building up pressure until it would one day explode.

On August 24, A.D. 79, after a series of small steam explosions made an opening at the top of the mountain, Vesuvius erupted. The blast shot pumice and ash toward the sky. After about half an hour, the pumice and ash rained down and began to blanket the city. The sleeping giant had awakened, with a deafening roar.

What caused Vesuvius to erupt? The earth's surface is made up of huge rocks, called plates. When the plates move apart or hit each other, molten (melted, liquid) rock, called magma, from deep within the earth is pushed to the surface by pressure from hot underground gases. The magma in Vesuvius was so hot and steam-filled that it turned to pumice. There was no lava in this eruption because the magma was too explosive and steam-filled to form lava.

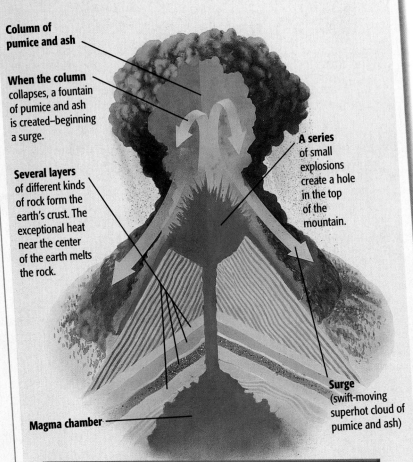

Column of pumice and ash

When the column collapses, a fountain of pumice and ash is created–beginning a surge.

Several layers of different kinds of rock form the earth's crust. The exceptional heat near the center of the earth melts the rock.

A series of small explosions create a hole in the top of the mountain.

Surge (swift-moving superhot cloud of pumice and ash)

Magma chamber

Respond

1. What happened just before Vesuvius erupted?

2. Why was the area around Vesuvius buried by pumice and ash rather than by lava?

Before You Read
The Dog of Pompeii

MEET LOUIS UNTERMEYER

"At ten I fancied myself a storyteller," Louis Untermeyer remembered. "My brother was a rewarding listener." Untermeyer made up adventures based on his favorite stories, such as "The Arabian Nights" and "Jason and the Golden Fleece," as he and his brother fell asleep at night. As for school, Untermeyer could only say, "I excelled in nothing." As an adult, Untermeyer became a jeweler. He also wrote poetry and edited poetry anthologies. Eventually he became a full-time writer and editor.

Louis Untermeyer was born in 1885 and died in 1977. This story was published in 1932.

FOCUS ACTIVITY

Have you ever responded to a weather emergency, such as a warning of a flood, tornado, or hurricane?

Small-Group Discussion
How did you (or would you) prepare for the emergency?

Setting a Purpose
Read "The Dog of Pompeii" to find out about an emergency in Pompeii.

BACKGROUND

The Time and Place
In A.D. 79, Pompeii was a city of around 20,000 people. Wealthy Romans liked its closeness to the Mediterranean Sea. Mount Vesuvius, the volcano that overlooked the city, had not erupted in several hundred years.

ITALY
Rome
Via Appia
Naples
Pompeii
Mediterranean Sea

VOCABULARY PREVIEW

sham (sham) *adj.* pretended or staged; fake; imitation; p. 547
stodgy (stoj′ē) *adj.* heavy and slow in movement; dull and lacking interest; p. 547
bazaar (bə zär′) *n.* a place for the sale of a variety of goods; marketplace; p. 548
corrupt (kə rupt′) *v.* to change from good to bad; make spoiled, evil, dishonest; p. 549
pondering (pon′ dər ing) *n.* the act of thinking over carefully; serious thought; p. 551
keen (kēn) *adj.* highly sensitive; sharp; p. 551
lurch (lurch) *v.* to move suddenly in an uneven manner; plunge forward or to the side; p. 552
dislodge (dis loj′) *v.* to move or force out of a place or position; p. 552

The Dog of Pompeii

Louis Untermeyer

Tito and his dog Bimbo lived (if you could call
it living) under the wall where it joined the inner gate. They
really didn't live there; they just slept there. They lived anywhere.
Pompeii was one of the gayest of the old Latin towns, but although
Tito was never an unhappy boy, he was not exactly a merry one.

The streets were always lively with shining chariots and bright red trappings;[1] the open-air theaters rocked with laughing crowds; sham-battles and athletic sports were free for the asking in the great stadium. Once a year the Caesar visited the pleasure-city and the fire-works lasted for days; the sacrifices in the Forum were better than a show. But Tito saw none of these things. He was blind—had been blind from birth. He was known to every one in the poorer quarters. But no one could say how old he was, no one remembered his parents, no one could tell where he came from. Bimbo was another mystery. As long as people could remember seeing Tito—about twelve or thirteen years—they had seen Bimbo. Bimbo had never left his side. He was not only dog, but nurse, pillow, playmate, mother and father to Tito.

Did I say Bimbo never left his master? (Perhaps I had better say comrade, for if any one was the master, it was Bimbo.) I was wrong. Bimbo did trust Tito alone exactly three times a day. It was a fixed routine, a custom understood between boy and dog since the beginning of their friendship, and the way it worked was this: Early in the morning, shortly after dawn, while Tito was still dreaming, Bimbo would disappear. When Tito awoke, Bimbo would be sitting quietly at his side, his ears cocked, his stump of a tail tapping the ground, and a fresh-baked bread—more like a large round roll—at his feet. Tito would stretch himself;

Bimbo would yawn; then they would break-fast. At noon, no matter where they happened to be, Bimbo would put his paw on Tito's knee and the two of them would return to the inner gate. Tito would curl up in the corner (almost like a dog) and go to sleep, while Bimbo, looking quite important (almost like a boy) would disappear again. In half an hour he'd be back with their lunch. Sometimes it would be a piece of fruit or a scrap of meat, often it was nothing but a dry crust. But sometimes there would be one of those flat rich cakes, sprinkled with raisins and sugar, that Tito liked so much. At supper-time the same thing happened, although there was a little less of everything, for things were hard to snatch in the evening with the streets full of people. Besides, Bimbo didn't approve of too much food before going to sleep. A heavy supper made boys too restless and dogs too stodgy—and it was the business of a dog to sleep lightly with one ear open and muscles ready for action.

But, whether there was much or little, hot or cold, fresh or dry, food was always there. Tito never asked where it came from and Bimbo never told him. There was plenty of rain-water in the hollows of soft stones; the old egg-woman at the corner sometimes gave him a cupful of strong goat's milk; in the grape-season the fat wine-maker let him have drippings of the mild juice. So there was no danger of going hungry or thirsty. There was plenty of everything in Pompeii—if you knew where to find it—and if you had a dog like Bimbo.

---

1. A chariot's *trappings* would be a decorated cloth spread over the horse.

Vocabulary

sham (sham) *adj.* pretended or staged; fake; imitation
stodgy (stoj′ ē) *adj.* heavy and slow in movement; dull and lacking interest

The Dog of Pompeii

As I said before, Tito was not the merriest boy in Pompeii. He could not romp with the other youngsters and play Hare-and-Hounds and I-spy and Follow-your-Master and Ball-against-the-Building and Jack-stones and Kings-and-Robbers with them. But that did not make him sorry for himself. If he could not see the sights that delighted the lads of Pompeii he could hear and smell things they never noticed. He could really see more with his ears and nose than they could with their eyes. When he and Bimbo went out walking he knew just where they were going and exactly what was happening.

"Ah," he'd sniff and say, as they passed a handsome villa,[2] "Glaucus Pansa is giving a grand dinner tonight. They're going to have three kinds of bread, and roast pigling, and stuffed goose, and a great stew—I think bear-stew—and a fig-pie." And Bimbo would note that this would be a good place to visit tomorrow.

Or, "H'm," Tito would murmur, half through his lips, half through his nostrils. "The wife of Marcus Lucretius is expecting her mother. She's shaking out every piece of goods in the house; she's going to use the best clothes—the ones she's been keeping in pine-needles and camphor[3]—and there's an extra girl in the kitchen. Come, Bimbo, let's get out of the dust!"

Or, as they passed a small but elegant dwelling opposite the public-baths, "Too bad! The tragic poet is ill again. It must be a bad fever this time, for they're trying smoke-fumes instead of medicine. Whew! I'm glad I'm not a tragic poet!"

Or, as they neared the Forum, "Mm-m! What good things they have in the Macellum today!" (It really was a sort of butcher-grocer-market-place, but Tito didn't know any better. He called it the Macellum.) "Dates from Africa, and salt oysters from sea-caves, and cuttlefish, and new honey, and sweet onions, and— ugh!—water-buffalo steaks. Come, let's see what's what in the Forum." And Bimbo, just as curious as his comrade, hurried on. Being a dog, he trusted his ears and nose (like Tito) more than his eyes. And so the two of them entered the center of Pompeii.

The Forum was the part of the town to which everybody came at least once during each day. It was the Central Square and everything happened here. There were no private houses; all was public—the chief temples, the gold and red bazaars, the silk-shops, the town-hall, the booths belonging to the weavers and jewel-merchants, the wealthy woolen market, the shrine of the household gods. Everything glittered here. The buildings looked as if they were new— which, in a sense, they were. The earthquake of twelve years ago had brought down all the old structures and, since the citizens of Pompeii were ambitious to rival Naples and even Rome, they had seized the opportunity to rebuild the whole town. And they had done it all within a dozen years. There was scarcely a building that was older than Tito.

---

2. A *villa* is a house, especially one in the country or at the seashore.
3. *Pine-needles* and *camphor* are used to keep moths out of the clothes.

Vocabulary

bazaar (bə zär´) *n.* a place for the sale of a variety of goods; marketplace

Tito had heard a great deal about the earthquake though, being about a year old at the time, he could scarcely remember it. This particular quake had been a light one—as earthquakes go. The weaker houses had been shaken down, parts of the out-worn wall had been wrecked; but there was little loss of life, and the brilliant new Pompeii had taken the place of the old. No one knew what caused these earthquakes. Records showed they had happened in the neighborhood since the beginning of time. Sailors said that it was to teach the lazy city-folk a lesson and make them appreciate those who risked the dangers of the sea to bring them luxuries and protect their town from invaders. The priests said that the gods took this way of showing their anger to those who refused to worship properly and who failed to bring enough sacrifices to the altars and (though they didn't say it in so many words) presents to the priests. The tradesmen said that the foreign merchants had corrupted the ground and it was no longer safe to traffic in[4] imported goods that came from strange places and carried a curse with them. Every one had a different

4. The expression *traffic in* means "trade or do business with."

Round mills for grinding grain, a brick oven, and one of the 81 loaves of bread found in the oven in a Pompeii bakery.

Vocabulary
corrupt (kə rupt′) *v.* to change from good to bad; make spoiled, evil, dishonest

The Dog of Pompeii

explanation—and every one's explanation was louder and sillier than his neighbor's.

They were talking about it this afternoon as Tito and Bimbo came out of the side-street into the public square. The Forum was the favorite promenade[5] for rich and poor. What with the priests arguing with the politicians, servants doing the day's shopping, tradesmen crying their wares, women displaying the latest fashions from Greece and Egypt, children playing hide-and-seek among the marble columns, knots of soldiers, sailors, peasants from the provinces—to say nothing of those who merely came to lounge and look on—the square was crowded to its last inch. His ears even more than his nose guided Tito to the place where the talk was loudest. It was in front of the Shrine of the Household Gods that, naturally enough, the householders were arguing.

"I tell you," rumbled a voice which Tito recognized as bathmaster Rufus's, "there won't be another earthquake in my lifetime or yours. There may be a tremble or two, but earthquakes, like lightnings, never strike twice in the same place."

"Do they not?" asked a thin voice Tito had never heard. It had a high, sharp ring to it and Tito knew it as the accent of a stranger. "How about the two towns of Sicily that have been ruined three times within fifteen years by the eruptions of Mount Etna? And were they not warned? And does that column of smoke above Vesuvius mean nothing?"

"That?" Tito could hear the grunt with which one question answered another.

"That's always there. We use it for our weather-guide. When the smoke stands up straight we know we'll have fair weather; when it flattens out it's sure to be foggy; when it drifts to the east—"

"Yes, yes," cut in the edged voice. "I've heard about your mountain barometer.[6] But the column of smoke seems hundreds of feet higher than usual and it's thickening and spreading like a shadowy tree. They say in Naples—"

"Oh, Naples!"

Tito knew this voice by the little squeak that went with it. It was Attilio, the cameo-cutter. "*They* talk while we suffer. Little help we got from them last time. Naples commits the crimes and Pompeii pays the price. It's become a proverb with us. Let them mind their own business."

Did You Know?
A *cameo* (kam′ ē ō′) is a piece of jewelry made from ivory, a precious or semi-precious stone, or a shell that is carved in layers to produce a raised design, which is often a woman's profile.

"Yes," grumbled Rufus, "and others, too."

"Very well, my confident friends," responded the thin voice which now sounded curiously flat. "We also have a proverb—and it is this: Those who will not listen to men must be taught by the gods. I say no more. But I leave a last warning. Remember the holy ones. Look to your temples. And when the smoke-tree

---

5. A *promenade* is a public walkway where people can take long strolls.

6. The people of Pompeii used the mountain's smoke as a *barometer*—something that indicates changes—to predict the weather. Modern weather forecasters use an instrument called a barometer to measure atmospheric pressure.

Did You Know?

The *toga* (tō′ gə) was the loose outer garment worn by men of the Roman Empire. A long cloth was draped over the entire body, covering the left arm and leaving the right arm exposed. The color and design of a man's toga indicated his social position.

above Vesuvius grows to the shape of an umbrella-pine, look to your lives."

Tito could hear the air whistle as the speaker drew his toga about him and the quick shuffle of feet told him the stranger had gone.

"Now what," said the cameo-cutter, "did he mean by that?"

"I wonder," grunted Rufus, "I wonder."

Tito wondered, too. And Bimbo, his head at a thoughtful angle, looked as if he had been doing a heavy piece of <u>pondering</u>. By nightfall the argument had been forgotten. If the smoke had increased no one saw it in the dark. Besides, it was Caesar's birthday and the town was in holiday mood. Tito and Bimbo were among the merry-makers, dodging the charioteers who shouted at them. A dozen times they almost upset baskets of sweets and jars of Vesuvian wine, said to be as fiery as the streams inside the volcano, and a dozen times they were cursed and cuffed. But Tito never missed his footing. He was thankful for his <u>keen</u> ears and quick instinct—most thankful of all for Bimbo.

They visited the uncovered theater and, though Tito could not see the faces of the actors, he could follow the play better than most of the audience, for their attention wandered—they were distracted by the scenery, the costumes, the by-play,[7] even by themselves—while Tito's whole attention was centered in what he heard. Then to the city-walls, where the people of Pompeii watched a mock naval-battle in which the city was attacked by the sea and saved after thousands of flaming arrows had been exchanged and countless colored torches had been burned. Though the thrill of flaring ships and lighted skies was lost to Tito, the shouts and cheers excited him as much as any and he cried out with the loudest of them.

The next morning there were *two* of the beloved raisin and sugar cakes for his breakfast. Bimbo was unusually active and thumped his bit of a tail until Tito was afraid he would wear it out. The boy could not imagine whether Bimbo was urging him to some sort of game or was trying to tell something. After a while, he ceased to notice Bimbo. He felt drowsy. Last night's late hours had tired him. Besides, there was a heavy mist in the air—no, a thick fog rather than a mist—a fog that got into his throat and scraped it and made him cough. He walked as far as the marine gate to get a breath of the sea. But the blanket of haze had spread all over the bay and even the salt air seemed smoky.

He went to bed before dusk and slept. But he did not sleep well. He had too

---

7. *By-play* refers to actions or conversations that take place apart from the main action or conversation, especially in a theatrical production.

Vocabulary

pondering (pon′ dər ing) *n.* the act of thinking over carefully; serious thought
keen (kēn) *adj.* highly sensitive; sharp

The Dog of Pompeii

many dreams—dreams of ships lurching in the Forum, of losing his way in a screaming crowd, of armies marching across his chest, of being pulled over every rough pavement of Pompeii.

He woke early. Or, rather, he was pulled awake. Bimbo was doing the pulling. The dog had dragged Tito to his feet and was urging the boy along. Somewhere. Where, Tito did not know. His feet stumbled uncertainly; he was still half asleep. For a while he noticed nothing except the fact that it was hard to breathe. The air was hot. And heavy. So heavy that he could taste it. The air, it seemed, had turned to powder, a warm powder that stung his nostrils and burned his sightless eyes.

Then he began to hear sounds. Peculiar sounds. Like animals under the earth. Hissings and groanings and muffled cries that a dying creature might make dislodging the stones of his underground cave. There was no doubt of it now. The noises came from underneath. He not only heard them—he could feel them. The earth twitched; the twitching changed to an uneven shrugging of the soil. Then, as Bimbo half-pulled, half-coaxed him across, the ground jerked away from his feet and he was thrown against a stone-fountain.

The water—hot water—splashing in his face revived him. He got to his feet, Bimbo steadying him, helping him on again. The noises grew louder; they came closer. The cries were even more animal-like than before, but now they came from human throats. A few people, quicker of foot and more hurried by fear, began to rush by. A family or two—then a section—then, it seemed, an army broken out of bounds. Tito, bewildered though he was, could recognize Rufus as he bellowed past him, like a water-buffalo gone mad. Time was lost in a nightmare.

It was then the crashing began. First a

Excavators working in Pompeii uncover houses and streets ten to twenty feet underground.
Viewing the photograph: What does this photograph from the 1890s tell you about the excavators' methods?

sharp crackling, like a monstrous snapping of twigs; then a roar like the fall of a whole forest of trees; then an explosion that tore earth and sky. The heavens, though Tito could not see them, were shot through with continual flickerings of fire. Lightnings above were answered by thunders beneath. A house fell. Then another. By a miracle the two companions had escaped the dangerous side-streets and were in a more open space. It was the Forum. They rested here a while—how long he did not know.

Tito had no idea of the time of day. He could *feel* it was black—an unnatural black-ness. Something inside—perhaps the lack of breakfast and lunch—told him it was past noon. But it didn't matter. Nothing seemed to matter. He was getting drowsy, too drowsy to walk. But walk he must. He knew it. And Bimbo knew it; the sharp tugs told him so. Nor was it a moment too soon. The sacred ground of the Forum was safe no longer. It was beginning to rock, then to pitch, then to split. As they stumbled out of the square, the earth wriggled like a caught snake and all the columns of the temple of Jupiter came down. It was the end of the world—or so it seemed. To walk was not enough now. They must run. Tito was too frightened to know what to do or where to go. He had lost all sense of direction. He started to go back to the inner gate; but Bimbo, straining his back to the last inch, almost pulled his clothes from him. What did the creature want? Had the dog gone mad?

Then, suddenly, he understood. Bimbo was telling him the way out—urging him there. The sea-gate of course. The sea-gate—and then the sea. Far from falling buildings, heaving ground. He turned,

Bimbo guiding him across open pits and dangerous pools of bubbling mud, away from buildings that had caught fire and were dropping their burning beams. Tito could no longer tell whether the noises were made by the shrieking sky or the agonized[8] people. He and Bimbo ran on— the only silent beings in a howling world.

New dangers threatened. All Pompeii seemed to be thronging toward the marine-gate and, squeezing among the crowds, there was the chance of being trampled to death. But the chance had to be taken. It was growing harder and harder to breathe. What air there was choked him. It was all dust now—dust and peb-bles, pebbles as large as beans. They fell on his head, his hands—pumice-stones[9] from the black heart of Vesuvius. The mountain was turning itself inside out. Tito remem-bered a phrase that the stranger had said in the Forum two days ago: "Those who will not listen to men must be taught by the gods." The people of Pompeii had refused to heed the warnings; they were being taught now—if it was not too late.

Suddenly it seemed too late for Tito. The red hot ashes blistered his skin, the stinging vapors tore his throat. He could not go on. He staggered toward a small tree at the side of the road and fell. In a moment Bimbo was beside him. He coaxed. But there was no answer. He licked Tito's hands, his feet, his face. The boy did not stir. Then Bimbo did the last thing he could—the last thing he wanted to do. He bit his comrade, bit him deep in the arm. With a cry of pain, Tito

---

8. To be *agonized* is to be in great pain.

9. Pumice (pum′ is) is light rock formed by volcanic activity.

The Dog of Pompeii

jumped to his feet, Bimbo after him. Tito was in despair, but Bimbo was determined. He drove the boy on, snapping at his heels, worrying his way through the crowd; barking, baring his teeth, heedless of kicks or falling stones. Sick with hunger, half-dead with fear and sulphur-fumes, Tito pounded on, pursued by Bimbo. How long he never knew. At last he staggered through the marine-gate and felt soft sand under him. Then Tito fainted. . . .

Some one was dashing sea-water over him. Some one was carrying him toward a boat.

"Bimbo," he called. And then louder, "Bimbo!" But Bimbo had disappeared.

Voices jarred against each other. "Hurry—hurry!" "To the boats!" "Can't you see the child's frightened and starving!" "He keeps calling for some one!" "Poor boy, he's out of his mind." "Here, child—take this!"

They tucked him in among them. The oar-locks creaked; the oars splashed; the boat rode over toppling waves. Tito was safe. But he wept continually.

"Bimbo!" he wailed. "Bimbo! Bimbo!"

He could not be comforted.

Eighteen hundred years passed. Scientists were restoring the ancient city; excavators[10] were working their way through the stones and trash that had buried the entire town. Much had already been brought to light—statues, bronze instruments, bright mosaics, household articles; even delicate paintings had been preserved by the fall of ashes that had taken over two thousand lives. Columns were dug up and the Forum was beginning to emerge.

Did You Know?
A *mosaic* (mō zā′ ik) is a design made of variously colored bits of glass or stone set in plaster.

It was at a place where the ruins lay deepest that the Director paused.

"Come here," he called to his assistant. "I think we've discovered the remains of a building in good shape. Here are four huge millstones that were most likely turned by slaves or mules—and here is a whole wall standing with shelves inside it. Why! It must have been a bakery. And here's a curious thing. What do you think I found under this heap where the ashes were thickest? The skeleton of a dog!"

"Amazing!" gasped his assistant. "You'd think a dog would have had sense enough to run away at the time. And what is that flat thing he's holding between his teeth? It can't be a stone."

"No. It must have come from this bakery. You know it looks to me like some sort of cake hardened with the years. And, bless me, if those little black pebbles aren't raisins. A raisin-cake almost two thousand years old! I wonder what made him want it at such a moment?"

"I wonder," murmured the assistant.

---

10. To *excavate* is to uncover or remove something by digging. *Excavator* often refers to a digging machine, but the scientists who dig through ruins using small hand tools so they won't damage the artifacts are also excavators.

Responding to Literature

PERSONAL RESPONSE

◆ If you could change one thing in the outcome of the story, what would you change?
◆ Think back to the discussion in the **Focus Activity** on page 545. Were your reactions to the emergency similar to those of Tito?

Analyzing Literature

RECALL

1. In Pompeii, where does Tito live and with whom? Why? What is his disability?
2. What do some people in Pompeii say causes earthquakes?
3. How does Bimbo save Tito's life?
4. Hundreds of years later, why are scientists surprised to find a dog in the ruins?

INTERPRET

5. What does Tito notice through his other senses during the eruption?
6. What are the warnings that the volcano will erupt?
7. Why, do you think, does Bimbo leave Tito?
8. What do Bimbo's actions throughout the story suggest about him?

Wall painting of a Pompeii street scene.

EVALUATE AND CONNECT

9. Do you think you would have liked Tito or Bimbo? Explain.
10. When authors give human characteristics to an animal or object, they are using **anthropomorphism.** What human traits does Bimbo have? Use examples from the selection.

LITERARY ELEMENTS

Historical Fiction

In **historical fiction,** an author tells a fictionalized story about a real historical figure or event. Authors may describe an event through made-up characters, and may also make up dialogue and incidents in the plot. However, they keep the historical event, the setting, and the customs and times, as true to the facts as possible. Authors re-create the event, using the tools of fiction. In this way, authors help readers experience the event or understand it in a more personal way.

1. Why does the author tell the story of Pompeii through Tito and Bimbo?

2. Do you think the places described in Pompeii, such as the Macellum and the Forum, are real places? How could you find out?

● See **Literary Terms Handbook,** p. R4.

Literature and Writing

Writing About Literature

Sensory Details   Find a section of the story that contains many sensory details–words and phrases that appeal to your senses of sight, hearing, touch, taste, and smell. Then write a paragraph describing how the sensory details help you sense the character, scene, or action.

Creative Writing

Can You Dig It?   Imagine that it is A.D. 3500. Archaeologists excavate the site where your school now stands. Describe three things they might find, and tell what meaning the archaeologists might give to each object. Based on these things, how might archaeologists describe school life at the turn of the twenty-first century? Write a short archaeologist's report about these "artifacts."

Extending Your Response

Interdisciplinary Activity

History   What exactly did archaeologists find at Pompeii? How does this city look now? How did archaeologists "discover" the city? Which places mentioned in this selection have been uncovered in Pompeii? Present your findings to the class.

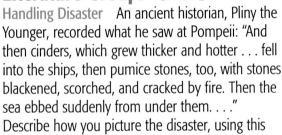

interNET
CONNECTION

Has Mount Vesuvius "slept" since A.D. 79? Search the Web using the phrase *Mount Vesuvius.* View photographs and learn more about this volcano. Share your findings with the class.

Literature Groups

Handling Disaster   An ancient historian, Pliny the Younger, recorded what he saw at Pompeii: "And then cinders, which grew thicker and hotter . . . fell into the ships, then pumice stones, too, with stones blackened, scorched, and cracked by fire. Then the sea ebbed suddenly from under them. . . ." Describe how you picture the disaster, using this quotation and examples from the story. Share your group's ideas with the class.

Reading Further

If you'd like to read other historical fiction, try these books:
Across Five Aprils by Irene Hunt
Number the Stars by Lois Lowry
Sign of the Beaver by Elizabeth Speare

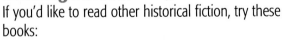 **Save your work for your portfolio.**

Skill Minilessons

GRAMMAR AND LANGUAGE • VARYING SENTENCE PATTERNS

Writers vary sentence patterns to keep readers' interest. Here are some ways to vary sentence patterns:

- Vary the lengths of sentences mixing shorter and longer sentences in a paragraph.
- Combine sentences to avoid repeating phrases.
- Begin sentences in different ways so that all sentences don't sound the same.

● For more on sentence patterns, see **Language Handbook,** p. R11.

PRACTICE Copy the following sentences. Combine short sentences. Eliminate repeated words.

1. Tito was blind. Tito relied on Bimbo to "see."
2. Bimbo and Tito bumped into the fence. Bimbo and Tito returned to the gate.
3. The air was hot. The air was heavy.
4. Bimbo pulled the boy and pushed the boy into the street.
5. A man carried him and the man dropped him into the boat.

READING AND THINKING • SPATIAL RELATIONSHIPS

Readers are able to picture Tito during the eruption as he is thrown against the stone-fountain and falls to the ground. Hot water from the fountain splashes him, and Bimbo helps him regain his balance after he rises to his feet. The information in the story helps us "see" this scene. Phrases such as "thrown against," "got to his feet," and "Bimbo steadying him" help you picture where the boy and the dog are in relation to each other and to the fountain.

● For more on spatial relationships, see **Reading Handbook,** p. R80.

PRACTICE Reread the following passage. Then answer the questions.

The villagers tucked Tito in among them. The oar-locks creaked; the oars splashed; the boat rode over the toppling waves. . . .

"Bimbo!" Tito wailed. "Bimbo! Bimbo!"

1. Where is Tito? How do you know?
2. Who is with him?
3. How do you picture Tito in relation to the others?

VOCABULARY • ANALOGIES

An **analogy** is a type of comparison based on relationships (see pages 395 and 458). Some analogies have to do with how things are done.

gulping : drinking :: gobbling : eating

Gulping is *drinking* in a fast, eager way just as *gobbling* is *eating* in a fast, eager way. The relationship between each pair of words is the same.

PRACTICE Complete each analogy. The first analogy has to do with how things are done. The others have to do with either synonyms or antonyms.

1. inspecting : looking :: pondering :
   a. walking   b. thinking   c. staring
2. give : take :: sham :
   a. genuine   b. safe   c. tired
3. assist : help :: corrupt :
   a. pollute   b. cheat   c. support
4. enormous : huge :: keen :
   a. lucky   b. fair   c. sharp
5. stop : start :: lurch :
   a. push   b. stumble   c. glide

● For more on analogies, see **Communications Skills Handbook,** p. R58.

Technology Skills

Multimedia: Electronic Slide Shows

Frequently, you may be called upon to present your work to your classmates, to teachers, and perhaps to audiences outside of school. You can use a computer with presentation software to get your point across in an interesting way.

Think about the advertisements you can recall seeing in magazines. What elements do they include? Photographs? Artwork? Catchy phrases? Advertisers generally design their promotions to attract and hold the attention of consumers. You can attract and hold the attention of *your* audiences by using presentation software on your computer.

A Multimedia Presentation

In a multimedia presentation, each screen a viewer sees is called a slide. Generally, a slide consists of text–not too much of it–and an image of some kind. Each slide should be limited to a single idea with a few supporting details.

Main idea

- **Supporting point**

- **Supporting point**

- **Supporting point**

Because you need to get your point across quickly, it's important that you choose your words and images carefully. Most presentation software packages have "wizard" or template features that can assist you in creating effective slides.

Practice

1. Think about your favorite movie. On a sheet of paper, write down three reasons you enjoy this film. Then sketch an image that you remember from the movie. Don't worry about the quality of your artwork. Just try to portray a scene you think captures the spirit of the movie.

2. Open your presentation software.

   - Click on **File/New.**
   - Select a slide template that includes spaces for a title, text, and a picture.
   - Click in the title text box, and type in the title of your favorite movie.
   - Click in the body text box, and type in the three reasons you like the film.
   - Using a search engine, try to find on the Internet a picture from the movie that you can download and insert into the picture box. If you can't find a photo from your chosen movie, find a piece of clip art that most resembles the image you drew. (Check with your teacher or lab instructor to find out if photos or clip art are available on your school network.)
   - When your slide is completed, click on **File/Save.** (Your teacher or lab instructor will tell you where you should save your work.)

3. Share your work with your classmates. To show your slide, select **Slide Show/View Show.**

4. That's all there is to making a single slide in a simple multimedia presentation!

   - To add additional slides, select **Insert/New Slide.**
   - To see a group of slides, select **View/Slide Sorter.** In this view, you can move slides to rearrange their order.
   - To move from sorter view to a single slide, click on the slide you want, and then select **View/Slide** (or just double click on the slide).

5. You can also decorate your slides with a variety of background colors and patterns. Add a new slide, and experiment with the features you'll find in the **Format** menu.

TECHNOLOGY TIP

When you see an instruction that includes two or more items separated by slashes, you will need to combine a set of actions. For example, "Select **File/New**" is a shortened way of saying that you should open the **File** menu by clicking on it and—without releasing the mouse button—pull down to **New** and select it by releasing the mouse button.

ACTIVITIES

1. Working with a partner, choose another movie or a television show as the basis for a complete slide show. Include a title slide and at least six additional slides. Add several appropriate pictures to your slides.

2. The next time you're assigned a paper, ask your teacher if you can present it as a multimedia slide show.

3. Working with a group, create a slide show for some school event, such as a charity drive or an upcoming sports event.

Mount St. Helens in April, 1980.

EXPOSITORY NONFICTION

Newspaper articles give information about the day's events, but they don't often give much explanation about them. For example, a newspaper may report that a volcano has erupted, or that a new medicine is curing a sickness. It may not explain, however, what caused the eruption, or how the medicine works. The special kind of writing that *explains* is **expository writing.**

Look for these characteristics in expository nonfiction.

TOPIC AND PURPOSE
A piece of expository writing may identify its topic and purpose more than once. As the article presents information, different statements tell where the article is headed and why.

SUBHEADS A subhead is a short line of type, usually in boldface (darker) type. It acts as a title for only the section of the article that follows.

CHRONOLOGICAL ORDER
Most explanations report events in the order that they occur. Sometimes an explanation must take a jump backwards to give more information about an event. After the jump back in time, the explanation moves forward again.

LOGICAL ORDER Often, explaining involves sorting different types of events that happen at the same time. At other times, it requires ordering events, ideas, or causes from most important to least important, or according to some other order.

1 This passage is from the middle of the article "Volcano." It follows the description of a particular volcanic eruption. This paragraph makes it clear that the article will now explain scientific reasons for the eruption.

2 Questions 2 and 3 point out different results of the eruption that will be examined separately.

4 This subhead sets off the scientific description of the eruption.

MODEL

The other job was to find out exactly what had happened on May 18. Most volcanic eruptions start slowly. Why had Mount St. Helens erupted suddenly? What events had caused the big fan-shaped area of destruction? What had become of the mountain top, which was now 1,200 feet lower?

The answers to these questions came slowly as geologists studied instrument records and photographs, interviewed witnesses, and studied the clues left by the eruption itself. But in time they pieced together a story that surprised them. . . .

The Big Blast

The May 18 eruption began with an earthquake that triggered an avalanche. . . .

The avalanche tore open the mountain. A scalding blast shot sideways out of the opening. It was a blast of steam, from water heated by rising magma.

Normally water cannot be heated beyond its boiling point, which is 212 degrees Fahrenheit at sea level. At boiling point, water turns to a gas, which we call steam. . . .

3 The article follows time order when it says that (1) scientists did research about the eruption, and (2) they found answers. Then it jumps back to the eruption to explain that event.

5 Here, *steam* is defined.

6 To understand what happened to water inside the volcano, readers need to understand what happens when water boils.

BACKGROUND FACTS
In expository writing, background facts often interrupt the chronological reporting of events. The background information helps make sense of the events.

DEFINITIONS OF TERMS
Often, important words or words with special meanings are defined in the text of an expository article.

Active Reading Strategies

Tips for Reading Expository Nonfiction

Because expository writing may present unfamiliar ideas and use unusual words, it demands careful reading. You can't afford to skip a strange word or a difficult sentence—that word or sentence might be a key to understanding the rest of the article. Use the strategies suggested here to take control of an information article.

● For more about reading strategies, see **Reading Handbook,** pp. R63–R94.

PREVIEW

Look over the article to discover what you can expect from it. Read the title and any subtitles. Examine photographs, charts, and other illustrations, and read their captions. What do these elements tell you about the article's topic, purpose, and organization?

Ask Yourself . . .

● What does the title tell me about the general topic?

● From the length of the article, can I guess whether it will go into great detail?

● Do the subtitles suggest anything about the order of ideas or events?

● From the illustrations, what points can I expect the article to focus on?

QUESTION

Expository writing contains facts, figures, names, dates, and other data. An expository writer may explain a complex idea, describe a detailed scene, or present a complicated sequence of events. It is important to ask questions while you are reading to check that you understand the information and concepts presented.

Ask Yourself . . .

● What does this term mean?

● How does this fact relate to the ideas in this paragraph?

● Why did the writer include this paragraph?

VISUALIZE

Use the author's descriptions to visualize as you read. You may find yourself picturing an object or scene so completely that facts you read further on fall right into place in your mind.

Ask Yourself . . .

- Can I picture this object?

- What details in the text help me picture this?

- Do later facts add to my visualization of the scene?

REVIEW

As authors explore topics in expository writing, ideas are built upon each other like the blocks of a pyramid. As you read, think back to what you have already read about the subject in the selection. You may want to reread sections to see how the ideas are connected and developed.

Ask Yourself . . .

- What have I already read about this in the selection?

- Can I summarize what I've already read?

- How does this new information fit in with what I read before?

- What did I learn about the topic that I didn't know before?

APPLYING THE STRATEGIES

Read "Volcano" from Patricia Lauber's *Volcano: The Eruption and Healing of Mount St. Helens.* Use the **Active Reading Model** notes in the margins as you read. Write your responses on a separate piece of paper to look over when you have finished reading.

Before You Read

from *Volcano*

MEET PATRICIA LAUBER

I had not thought of doing a book specifically on Mount St. Helens—until I saw the photo," says Patricia Lauber. "It was a close-up of a hardy green plant that had pushed its way up through a crack in the crust of ash and put out a pink flower. It made me think about doing a book that would explain not only why and how the volcano erupted but also how life came back to a region as barren as the moon." Lauber has written many award-winning books and has edited several science publications.

Patricia Lauber was born in 1924. Volcano: The Eruption and Healing of Mount St. Helens was published in 1986.

FOCUS ACTIVITY

What do you know about volcanoes? What do they look like? What signs warn of an eruption?

K-W-L Chart

With a partner, record what you know and what you would like to find out about volcanoes in the first and second sections of a K-W-L chart (**K**now, **W**ant to Know, Have **L**earned chart; see page 574). Then share ideas with the class.

Setting a Purpose

Read to find out what happens when a volcano erupts.

BACKGROUND

The Time and Place   In 1982 the U.S. government named 110,000 acres of land around the volcano as the Mount St. Helens National Volcanic Monument. The land was left as it was so that scientists can study the changes caused by the eruptions. They can also record the return to life as plants and animals reestablish themselves on the mountain.

VOCABULARY PREVIEW

fell (fel) *v.* to cut down; chop; p. 566
yield (yēld) *v.* to give forth; produce; p. 568
avalanche (av′ ə lanch′) *n.* the swift, sudden fall of a mass of snow, ice, earth, or rocks down a mountain slope; p. 569
register (rej′ is tər) *v.* to show or record, as on a scale; indicate; p. 569
relieve (ri lēv′) *v.* to remove or make easier to bear; lessen; reduce; p. 569

from Volcano

Patricia Lauber

The Volcano Wakes

FOR MANY YEARS THE VOLCANO SLEPT. It was silent and still, big and beautiful. Then the volcano, which was named Mount St. Helens, began to stir. On March 20, 1980, it was shaken by a strong earthquake. The quake was a sign of movement inside St. Helens. It was a sign of a waking volcano that might soon erupt again.

from Volcano

ACTIVE READING MODEL

QUESTION

What do the words *molten, magma,* and *lava* mean?

QUESTION

How was the mountain built?

VISUALIZE

How do you picture the mountain?

Mount St. Helens was built by many eruptions over thousands of years. In each eruption hot rock from inside the earth forced its way to the surface. The rock was so hot that it was molten, or melted, and it had gases trapped in it. The name for such rock is magma. Once the molten rock reaches the surface it is called lava. In some eruptions the magma was fairly liquid. Its gases escaped gently. Lava flowed out of the volcano, cooled, and hardened. In other eruptions the magma was thick and sticky. Its gases burst out violently, carrying along sprays of molten rock. As it blasted into the sky, the rock cooled and hardened. Some of it rained down as ash—tiny bits of rock. Some rained down as pumice—frothy rock puffed up by gases.

Together the lava flows, ash, and pumice built a mountain with a bowl-shaped crater at its top. St. Helens grew to a height of 9,677 feet, so high that its peak was often hidden by clouds. Its big neighbors were built in the same way. Mount St. Helens is part of the Cascade Range, a chain of volcanoes that runs from northern California into British Columbia.

In the middle 1800s a number of small eruptions took place. Between 1832 and 1857 St. Helens puffed out clouds of steam and ash from time to time. It also gave off small flows of lava. Then the mountain fell still.

For well over a hundred years the volcano slept. Each spring, as winter snows melted, its slopes seemed to come alive. Wildflowers bloomed in meadows. Bees gathered pollen and nectar. Birds fed, found mates, and built nests. Bears lumbered out of their dens. Herds of elk and deer feasted on fresh green shoots. Thousands of people came to hike, picnic, camp, fish, paint, bird-watch, or just enjoy the scenery. Logging crews felled tall trees and planted seedlings.

These people knew that Mount St. Helens was a volcano, but they did not fear it. To them it was simply a green and pleasant mountain, where forests of firs stretched up the slopes and streams ran clear and cold.

The mountain did not seem so trustworthy to geologists, scientists who study the earth. They knew that Mount St. Helens was dangerous. It was a young volcano and one of the most active in the Cascade Range. In 1975 two geologists finished a study of the volcano's past

Vocabulary
fell (fel) *v.* to cut down; chop

A hillside near Mount St. Helens after the eruption.

Viewing the photograph: This was once a forest of huge fir trees. Can you picture the mountain before the eruption?

eruptions. They predicted that Mount St. Helens would erupt again within 100 years, perhaps before the year 2000.

The geologists were right. With the earthquake of March 20, 1980, Mount St. Helens woke from a sleep of 123 years. Magma had forced its way into the mountain, tearing apart solid rock. The snapping of that rock set off the shock waves that shook St. Helens. That quake was followed by many others. Most of them were smaller, but they came so fast and so often that it was hard to tell when one quake ended and another began.

On March 27 people near Mount St. Helens heard a tremendous explosion. The volcano began to blow out steam and ash that stained its snow-white peak. Small explosions went on into late April, stopped, started again on May 7, and stopped on May 14.

The explosions of late March opened up two new craters at the top of the mountain. One formed inside the old crater. The other formed nearby. The two new craters grew bigger. Soon they joined, forming one large crater that continued to grow during the next few weeks. Meanwhile, the north face of the mountaintop was swelling and cracking. The swelling formed a bulge that grew outward at a rate of five to six feet a day.

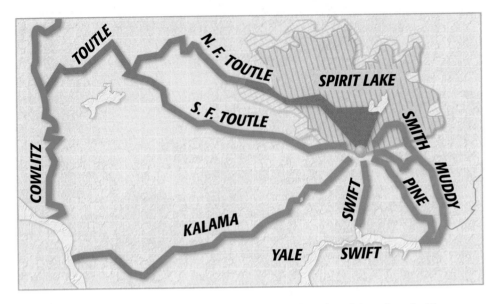

This small circle on the right side of the map represents Mount St. Helens. The red shows the path of the avalanche. Everything in the red-striped area, which represents about 230 square miles, was destroyed. In the yellow-striped area, the trees stood but were killed by the heat.

QUESTION

What were the geologists doing?

Geologists were hard at work on the waking volcano. They took samples of ash and gases, hoping to find clues to what was happening inside. They placed instruments on the mountain to record earthquakes and the tilting of ground. They kept measuring the bulge. A sudden change in its rate of growth might be a sign that the volcano was about to erupt. But the bulge grew steadily, and the ash and gases yielded no clues.

By mid-May the bulge was huge. Half a mile wide and more than a mile long, it had swelled out 300 feet.

On Sunday morning, May 18, the sun inched up behind the Cascades, turning the sky pink. By 8 A.M. the sun was above the mountains, the sky blue, the air cool. There was not one hint of what was to come.

VISUALIZE

How do you visualize the scene around the mountain just before and just after the eruption?

At 8:32 Mount St. Helens erupted. Billowing clouds of smoke, steam, and ash hid the mountain frow view and darkened the sky for miles.

The eruption went on until evening. By its end a fan-shaped area of destruction stretched out to the north, covering some 230 square miles. Within that area 57 people and countless plants and animals had died.

Geologists now faced two big jobs. One was to keep watch on the mountain, to find out if more eruptions were building up. If so, they hoped to learn how to predict the eruptions.

The other job was to find out exactly what had happened on May 18. Most volcanic eruptions start slowly. Why had Mount St. Helens

Vocabulary
yield (yēld) v. to give forth; produce

erupted suddenly? What events had caused the big fan-shaped area of destruction? What had become of the mountaintop, which was now 1,200 feet lower?

The answers to these questions came slowly as geologists studied instrument records and photographs, interviewed witnesses, and studied the clues left by the eruption itself. But in time they pieced together a story that surprised them. This eruption turned out to be very different from the ones that built Mount St. Helens.

The Big Blast

The May 18 eruption began with an earthquake that triggered an avalanche. At 8:32 A.M. instruments that were miles away registered a strong earthquake. The pilot and passengers of a small plane saw the north side of the mountain rippling and churning. Shaken by the quake, the bulge was tearing loose. It began to slide, in a huge avalanche that carried along rock ripped from deep inside Mount St. Helens.

The avalanche tore open the mountain. A scalding blast shot sideways out of the opening. It was a blast of steam, from water heated by rising magma.

Normally water cannot be heated beyond its boiling point, which is 212 degrees Fahrenheit at sea level. At boiling point, water turns to a gas, which we call steam. But if water is kept under pressure, it can be heated far beyond its boiling point and still stay liquid. (That is how a pressure cooker works.) If the pressure is removed, this superheated water suddenly turns, or flashes, to steam. As steam it takes up much more room—it expands. The sudden change to steam can cause an explosion.

Before the eruption Mount St. Helens was like a giant pressure cooker. The rock inside it held superheated water. The water stayed liquid because it was under great pressure, sealed in the mountain. When the mountain was torn open, the pressure was suddenly relieved. The superheated water flashed to steam. Expanding violently, it shattered rock inside the mountain and exploded out the opening, traveling at speeds of up to 200 miles an hour.

The blast flattened whole forests of 180-foot-high firs. It snapped off or uprooted the trees, scattering the trunks as if they were straws. At

ACTIVE READING MODEL

REVIEW

What were the geologists doing after the eruption? Is this what they did before?

VISUALIZE

What might you have seen from the airplane?

QUESTION

Why was the water so hot?

QUESTION

What happens when the hot water becomes steam?

Vocabulary

avalanche (av′ ə lanch′) *n.* the swift, sudden fall of a mass of snow, ice, earth, or rocks down a mountain slope
register (rej′ is tər) *v.* to show or record, as on a scale; indicate
relieve (ri lēv′) *v.* to remove or make easier to bear; lessen; reduce

from Volcano

ACTIVE READING MODEL

first, this damage was puzzling. A wind of 200 miles an hour is not strong enough to level forests of giant trees. The explanation, geologists later discovered, was that the wind carried rocks ranging in size from grains of sand to blocks as big as cars. As the blast roared out of the volcano, it swept up and carried along the rock it had shattered.

The result was what one geologist described as "a stone wind." It was a wind of steam and rocks, traveling at high speed. The rocks gave the blast its great force. Before it, trees snapped and fell. Their stumps looked as if they had been sandblasted. The wind of stone rushed on. It stripped bark and branches from trees and uprooted them, leveling 150 square miles of countryside. At the edge of this area other trees were left standing, but the heat of the blast scorched and killed them.

The stone wind was traveling so fast that it overtook and passed the avalanche. On its path was Spirit Lake, one of the most beautiful lakes in the Cascades. The blast stripped the trees from the slopes surrounding the lake and moved on.

Meanwhile the avalanche had hit a ridge and split. One part of it poured into Spirit Lake, adding a 180-foot layer of rock and dirt to the bottom of the lake. The slide of avalanche into the lake forced the water out. The water sloshed up the slopes, then fell back into the lake. With it came thousands of trees felled by the blast.

The main part of the avalanche swept down the valley of the North Fork of the Toutle[1] River. There, in the valley, most of the avalanche slowed and stopped. It covered 24 square miles and averaged 150 feet thick.

The blast itself continued for 10 to 15 minutes, then stopped. Minutes later Mount St. Helens began to erupt upwards. A dark column of ash and ground-up rock rose miles into the sky. Winds blew the ash eastward. Lightning flashed in the ash cloud and started forest fires. In Yakima,[2] Washington, some 80 miles away, the sky turned so dark that street lights went on at noon. Ash fell like snow that would not melt. This eruption continued for nine hours.

Shortly after noon the color of the ash column changed. It became lighter, a sign that the volcano

RESPOND

How do you react as you read about the "stone wind"?

QUESTION

What happens when the avalanche reaches Spirit Lake?

---

1. *Toutle* (tü′ təl)
2. *Yakima* (yäk′ ə mô)

Patricia Lauber~

was now throwing out mostly new magma. Until then much of the ash had been made of old rock.

At the same time the volcano began giving off huge flows of pumice and ash. The material was very hot, with temperatures of about 1,000 degrees Fahrenheit, and it traveled down the mountain at speeds of 100 miles an hour. The flows went on until 5:30 in the afternoon. They formed a wedge-shaped plain of pumice on the side of the mountain. Two weeks later temperatures in the pumice were still 780 degrees.

Finally, there were the mudflows, which started when heat from the blast melted ice and snow on the mountaintop. The water mixed with ash, pumice, ground-up rock, and dirt and rocks of the avalanche. The

ACTIVE READING MODEL

QUESTION

What did the lighter color of the ash column show?

Months after the eruptions, new life appears near Mount St. Helens.
Viewing the photograph: What kinds of plants do you recognize?

from *Volcano*

result was a thick mixture that was like wet concrete, a mudflow. The mudflows traveled fast, scouring the landscape and sweeping down the slopes into river valleys. Together their speed and thickness did great damage.

The largest mudflow was made of avalanche material from the valley of the North Fork of the Toutle River. It churned down the river valley, tearing out steel bridges, ripping houses apart, picking up boulders and trucks and carrying them along. Miles away it choked the Cowlitz River and blocked shipping channels in the Columbia River.

When the sun rose on May 19, it showed a greatly changed St. Helens. The mountain was 1,200 feet shorter than it had been the morning before. Most of the old top had slid down the mountain in the avalanche. The rest had erupted out as shattered rock. Geologists later figured that the volcano had lost three quarters of a cubic mile of old rock.

The north side of the mountain had changed from a green and lovely slope to a fan-shaped wasteland.

At the top of Mount St. Helens was a big, new crater with the shape of a horseshoe. Inside the crater was the vent, the opening through which rock and gases erupted from time to time over the next few years.

In 1980 St. Helens erupted six more times. Most of these eruptions were explosive—ash soared into the air, pumice swept down the north side of the mountain. In the eruptions of June and August, thick pasty lava oozed out of the vent and built a dome. But both domes were destroyed by the next eruptions. In October the pattern changed. The explosions stopped, and thick lava built a dome that was not destroyed. Later eruptions added to the dome, making it bigger and bigger.

During this time, geologists were learning to read the clues found before eruptions. They learned to predict what St. Helens was going to do. The predictions helped to protect people who were on and near the mountain.

Among these people were many natural scientists. They had come to look for survivors, for plants and animals that had lived through the eruption. They had come to look for colonizers, for plants and animals that would move in. Mount St. Helens had erupted many times before. Each time life had returned. Now scientists would have a chance to see how it did. They would see how nature healed itself.

Responding to Literature

PERSONAL RESPONSE

What images from the selection stay in your mind? Why?

Active Reading Response
Which reading strategy most helped you add to what you already knew about volcanoes? Use the K-W-L chart you began in the **Focus Activity** on page 564.

Mount St. Helens on May 19, 1980.

Analyzing Literature

RECALL

1. What does Mount St. Helens look like before the May 18, 1980, eruption? How is the mountain being used by various living things?
2. What is the "bulge"? How fast does it grow? How big is it before the eruption?
3. What causes the avalanche? Where does each part of the avalanche end up?
4. What is a "stone wind"? What causes it? What does it do?

INTERPRET

5. Do geologists view the mountain in the same way as the people in the area do? Explain.
6. What is the role of the geologists at Mount St. Helens? Do they control the volcano in any way?
7. How are the mudflows created? How do you know their destructive force?
8. In what ways is the mountain, before the explosion, "like a giant pressure-cooker"?

EVALUATE AND CONNECT

9. Would you want to be a geologist studying this volcano? Why or why not?
10. Nonfiction writing depends upon facts and true information. How do the facts in this selection help capture the reader's interest? Give examples.

LITERARY ELEMENTS

Nonfiction

Expository writing is **nonfiction** that informs or explains about a subject. Information about a subject can be complex, so authors use different **text structures** to present ideas clearly and logically. One text structure shows the cause-and-effect relationships between events. Lauber uses this technique to explain what happened during the eruption: *Because* magma forced its way into Mount St. Helens, rock within the mountain broke off. The act of breaking off rock *caused* shock waves that shook the land.

1. Reread the first paragraph in "The Big Blast." What causes the bulge to tear loose?
2. What is the instant effect of the bulge tearing loose?

● See **Literary Terms Handbook,** p. R6.

Literature and Writing

Writing About Literature

Compare and Contrast Write two paragraphs describing the volcano. In the first paragraph, describe the appearance of the mountain before the eruption on May 18. In the second paragraph, describe the changed mountain after the eruption and tell specifically how the scene has changed.

Personal Writing

Volcanic Reactions How did you react to the power and destructiveness of the volcano? Were you filled with awe? Were you frightened? Were you saddened because so much of nature seemed to be ruined? Are you interested in the scientific aspects of what occurred? Write two paragraphs in your journal responding to what you have read.

Extending Your Response

Art Activity

Volcanic Views Use your imagination and the text and pictures of the selection to draw two illustrations. In the first, show how you think the local people viewed Mount St. Helens before the eruption. In the second, portray what the geologists saw when they looked at the same mountain.

Literature Groups

Explosive Knowledge Look over your K-W-L chart from the **Focus Activity.** Discuss what you learned about volcanoes from this selection. What especially stood out to you about the Mount St. Helens eruptions? In your chart, write what you learned. Check whether you found out what you wanted to know, based on your chart. If not, decide how you can explore the topic further. Then share ideas with the class.

K	W	L

*inter*NET
C O N N E C T I O N

Do you want to take a virtual hike up Mount St. Helens? Search the Web using the phrase *VolcanoWorld-Kids' Door.* For additional information, search under *Mount St. Helens* and *USGS/Cascades Volcano Observatory.*

Reading Further

If you'd like to read more by Patricia Lauber, you might enjoy these books:
Summer of Fire: Yellowstone 1988
Flood: Wrestling with the Mississippi
Seeing Earth from Space

 **Save your work for your portfolio.**

Skill Minilessons

GRAMMAR AND LANGUAGE • COMMAS

Authors of expository writing sometimes include definitions in their sentences to make their ideas clearer. In the following example, *melted* is used to define *molten.* Because the definition is an interrupting element, it is set off with **commas:** *The rock was so hot that it was molten, or melted, and it had gases trapped in it.*

PRACTICE Copy these sentences from the selection, adding commas as needed.

1. The mountain did not seem so trustworthy to geologists scientists who study the earth.

2. Mount St. Helens is part of the Cascade Range a chain of volcanoes that runs from northern California into British Columbia.

3. The result was a thick mixture that was like wet concrete or a mudflow.

4. They had come to look for survivors for plants and animals that had lived through the eruption.

5. They had come to look for colonizers for plants and animals that would move in.

● For more on commas, see **Language Handbook,** pp. R33–R34.

READING AND THINKING • USING GRAPHIC AIDS

Graphic aids—**charts, tables, graphs,** or **diagrams**—can present information that would take many paragraphs to describe in words.

PRACTICE Use the diagram to answer the questions.

1. What kind of rock is at the deepest level?
2. What material flows over the volcano?
3. What materials make up the mountain itself?
4. What material rises in the volcano?

● For more on graphic aids, see **Reading Handbook,** p. R90.

Diagram labels: pumice, lava, and ash layers; sedimentary rock; conduits to surface; lava flow; igneous and metamorphic rock; basalt; magma

VOCABULARY • CONTEXT CLUES

You can often discover the meaning of an unfamiliar word by looking at its **context**—the words and sentences that surround it.

Logging crews *felled* tall trees and planted seedlings.

Since logging crews did this action, and the action was done to tall trees, you would conclude that *felled* probably means "chopped down."

PRACTICE Use clues in the sentences to define the underlined words.

1. A scalding blast of steam and hot ash shot from the mouth of the volcano.
2. The remaining trees were scorched. They were blackened and dead.
3. Many uprooted trees, with their broken roots trailing, floated down the river.

Reading and Thinking Skills

Identifying Main Ideas and Supporting Details

A piece of informative writing has a topic. Each paragraph that develops the topic has a **main idea.** Writers may state the main idea of a paragraph directly, or they may let readers figure it out for themselves. When a main idea is stated, it often appears as a general statement about the subject at the beginning of a selection. The sentence that states the main idea is called a **topic sentence.** The other sentences in the paragraph add **supporting details** to the main idea. These supporting details are facts, examples, incidents, or quotations that illustrate and develop the main idea.

What is the main idea in the paragraph below from *When Plague Strikes*? What details develop the main idea?

> Conditions in these medieval cities provided a splendid breeding ground for all types of vermin, including rats. There were no regular garbage collections, and refuse accumulated in piles in the streets. Rushes from wet or marshy places, not rugs, covered the floors in most homes. After a meal, it was customary to throw bits of leftover food onto the rushes for the dog or cat to eat. Rats and mice often got their share, too.

You can see that the main idea is stated in the first sentence—medieval cities were good breeding places for rats and other vermin. The details in the next four sentences illustrate this idea by providing supporting details.

● For more on identifying main ideas, see **Reading Handbook,** pp. R79–R80.

EXERCISE

Choose a paragraph from *Volcano* and answer the questions below. Compare your paragraph with those selected by others in your class.

1. What is the main idea of the paragraph?

2. What details support the main idea?

LISTENING, SPEAKING, and VIEWING

Presenting an Oral Report

When you learn new information about a subject that interests you, you want to share it with others. Giving an oral report can be exciting. Your interest and enthusiasm can be "catching." Your audience's response can fuel your own enthusiasm.

To be sure your oral report goes smoothly, practice ahead of time. If you practice in front of a mirror, you can check your posture and presentation. If you practice in front of friends or family, you can get a sense of how your audience will react. Use the following guidelines when you make an oral report.

Oral Presentation Guidelines

- Your voice carries best when you stand tall—but not stiff. Feel free to shift your stance to stay comfortable.
- Make eye contact with your listeners. As you speak, move your eyes from one person's face to the next.
- Speak at a normal pace—or even a little slowly. Don't let nervousness make you rush.
- Pause for a few seconds after each of your more important points. This lets listeners reflect on what you have said.

ACTIVITIES

1. With a partner, take turns explaining how to speak in front of a group. Use the **Oral Presentation Guidelines** above, and ask each other for helpful feedback on your informal presentations.

2. Orally present to your class a report you have written. Follow the guidelines above.

Before You Read

from *When Plague Strikes*

MEET
JAMES CROSS GIBLIN

I try to write books that I would have enjoyed reading when I was the age of my readers," says James Cross Giblin. Giblin has written award-winning nonfiction books on subjects ranging from hieroglyphics to skyscrapers. He explains, "Nonfiction books . . . [give] me the opportunity to pursue my research interests, meet interesting and stimulating experts in various fields, and share my enthusiasms with a young audience." Giblin has been a writer all of his life.

James Cross Giblin was born in 1933. When Plague Strikes *was published in 1995.*

FOCUS ACTIVITY

What do you think is the worst part of being sick?

Make a List

With a partner, make a list of symptoms that describe what it feels like to have the flu. Why is it important to stay home? How do you know when you are "back on your feet"? Share your ideas with the class.

Setting a Purpose

Read the selection to find out what plague is.

BACKGROUND

Did You Know?

Today, doctors wash their hands before examining each patient. They wear masks across their faces when they operate on patients. They wear thin, plastic gloves. These are all ways to prevent the spread of germs. However, people did not always understand where illnesses came from or how they were spread.

VOCABULARY PREVIEW

calamity (kə lam′ ə tē) *n.* great misfortune; disaster; p. 580

adaptable (ə dap′ tə bəl) *adj.* able to change to meet the needs of a certain situation; p. 581

tolerate (tol′ ə rāt′) *v.* to endure; put up with; p. 582

devastate (dev′ əs tāt′) *v.* to cause great pain, damage, or destruction; overwhelm; p. 583

futile (fū′ til) *adj.* useless or hopeless; not effective; p. 583

discredit (dis kred′ it) *v.* to reject as untrue; cause to be doubted or disbelieved; p. 587

imply (im plī′) *v.* to suggest without directly stating; p. 587

vulnerable (vul′ nər ə bəl) *adj.* capable of being damaged or wounded; easily hurt; p. 588

relentless (ri lent′ ləs) *adj.* unyielding; endless; p. 589

from
When Plague Strikes

James Cross Giblin ~

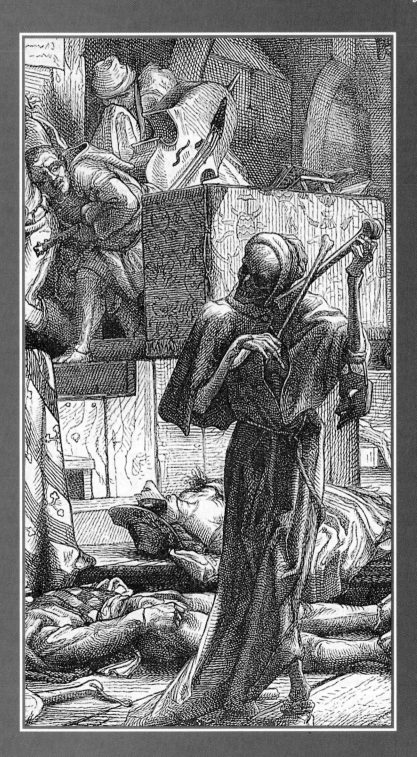

Out of the East

Early in 1347, a mysterious disease attacked people living near the Black Sea in what is now southern Ukraine. Its victims suffered from headaches, felt weak and tired, and staggered when they tried to walk.

By the third day, the lymph nodes[1] in the sufferers' groins, or occasionally their armpits, began to swell. Soon they reached the size of hens' eggs. These swellings became known as buboes, from the Greek word for groin, *boubon*. They gave the disease its official name: the bubonic[2] plague.

---

1. The *lymph nodes* are glands that filter out harmful substances.
2. *Buboes* (bū′ bōz), *bubonic* (bū bon′ ik)

The victim's heart beat wildly as it tried to pump blood through the swollen tissues. The nervous system started to collapse, causing dreadful pain and bizarre[3] movements of the arms and legs. Then, as death neared, the mouth gaped open and the skin blackened from internal bleeding. The end usually came on the fifth day.

Within weeks of the first reported cases, hundreds of people in the Black Sea region had sickened and died. Those who survived were terrified. They had no medicines with which to fight the disease. As it continued to spread, their fear changed to frustration, and then to anger. Someone— some outsider—must be responsible for bringing this calamity upon them.

The most likely candidates were the Italian traders who operated in the region. They bartered Italian goods for the silks and spices that came over the caravan routes from the Far East, then shipped the Eastern merchandise on to Italy. Although many of the traders had lived in the region for years, they were still thought of as being different. For one thing, they were Christians while most of the natives were Muslims.[4]

Deciding the Italians were to blame for the epidemic, the natives gathered an army and prepared to attack their trading post. The Italians fled to a fortress they had built on the coast of the Black Sea. There the natives besieged[5] them until the dread disease broke out in the Muslim army.

The natives were forced to withdraw. But before they did— according to one account—they gave the Italians a taste of the agony their people had been suffering. They loaded catapults with the bodies of some of their dead soldiers and hurled them over the high walls into the fortress. By doing so, they hoped to infect the Italians with the plague.

Did You Know?
The *catapult* (kat′ ə pult′) was a war machine that was used like a giant slingshot to hurl objects, such as large rocks. In the 1300s, soldiers often used catapults to attack castles surrounded by moats and cities surrounded by walls.

As fast as the bodies landed, the Italians dumped them into the sea. However, they did not move quickly enough, for the disease had already taken hold among them. In a panic, the traders loaded three ships and set sail for their home port of Genoa in Italy. They made it only as far as Messina,[6] on the island of Sicily, before the rapid spread of the disease forced them to stop.

This account of what happened in southern Ukraine may or may not be true. But it is a fact that the bubonic plague— the Black Death—arrived in Sicily in October 1347, carried by the crew of a fleet from the east. All the sailors on the

---

3. *Bizarre* means "extremely strange."
4. To *barter* is to trade goods for goods without using money. Traders traveled in groups, or *caravans*, along familiar roads for safety in deserts and dangerous regions. *Muslims* are people who follow Islam, the religion based on the teachings of Muhammad.

---

5. The natives *besieged* the Italians by surrounding their fortress with armed forces.
6. *Genoa* (jen′ ō ə), *Messina* (mi sē′ nə)

Vocabulary
calamity (kə lam′ ə tē) *n.* great misfortune; disaster

ships were dead or dying. In the words of a contemporary[7] historian, they had "sickness clinging to their very bones."

The harbormasters at the port of Messina ordered the sick sailors to remain on board, hoping in this way to prevent the disease from spreading to the town. They had no way of knowing that the actual carriers of the disease had already left the ships. Under cover of night, when no one could see them, they had scurried down the ropes that tied the ships to the dock and vanished into Messina.

---

7. *Contemporary* means "living or happening in the same period."

The carriers were black rats and the fleas that lived in their hair. Driven by an unending search for food, the rats' ancestors had migrated slowly westward along the caravan routes. They had traveled in bolts of cloth and bales of hay, and the fleas had come with them.

Although it was only an eighth of an inch long, the rat flea was a tough, adaptable creature. It depended for nourishment on the blood of its host, which it obtained through a daggerlike snout that could pierce the rat's skin. And in its stomach the flea often carried thousands of the deadly bacteria that caused the bubonic plague.

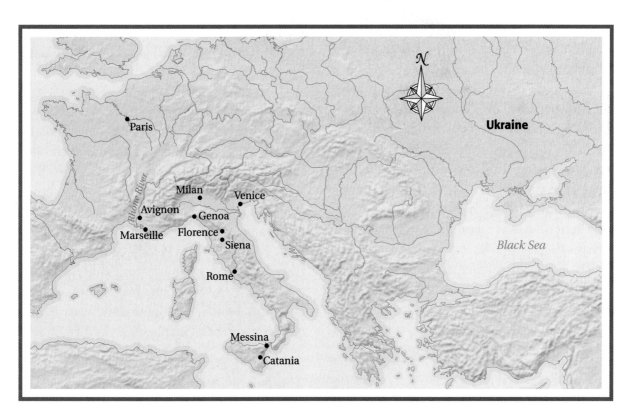

Some cities in Italy and France where the Black Death struck in 1347 and 1348.

Viewing the map: How did the plague travel the great distances shown on the map?

Vocabulary
adaptable (ə dap′ tə bəl) *adj.* able to change to meet the needs of a certain situation

The bacteria did no apparent harm to the flea, and a black rat could <u>tolerate</u> a moderate amount of them, too, without showing ill effects. But sometimes the flea contained so many bacteria that they invaded the rat's lungs or nervous system when the flea injected its snout. Then the rat died a swift and horrible death, and the flea had to find a new host.

Aiding the tiny flea in its search were its powerful legs, which could jump more than 150 times the creature's length. In most instances the flea landed on another black rat. Not always, though. If most of the rats in the vicinity were already dead or dying from the plague, the flea might leap to a human being instead. As soon as it had settled on the human's skin, the flea would begin to feed, and the whole process of infection would be repeated.

No doubt it was fleas, not Italian traders, that brought the bubonic plague to the Black Sea region, and other fleas that carried the disease on to Sicily. But no one at the time made the connection. To the people of the fourteenth century, the cause of the Black Death—which they called "the pestilence"[8]—was a complete and utter mystery.

When the first cases of the plague were reported in Messina, the authorities ordered the Italian fleet and all its sick crew members to leave the port at once. Their action came too late, however. Within days the disease had spread throughout the city and the surrounding countryside.

Some of the plague's victims fled to the nearby town of Catania, where they were treated kindly at first. But when the citizens of Catania realized how deadly the disease was, they refused to have anything more to do with anyone from Messina or even to speak to them. As was to happen wherever the plague struck, fear for one's own life usually outweighed any concern a person might have felt for the life of another.

On to Italy

From Sicily, trading ships loaded with infected flea-bearing rats carried the Black Death to ports on the mainland of Italy. Peddlers and other travelers helped spread it to inland cities such as Milan[9] and Florence.

Conditions in these medieval cities provided a splendid breeding ground for all types of vermin, including rats. There were no regular garbage collections, and refuse accumulated in piles in the streets. Rushes[10] from wet or marshy places, not rugs, covered the floors in most homes. After a meal, it was customary to throw bits of leftover food onto the rushes for the dog or cat to eat. Rats and mice often got their share, too.

Because the cities had no running water, even the wealthy seldom washed their heavy clothing, or their own bodies. As a result,

---

9. Milan (mi lan′)
10. *Medieval* (mē′ dē ē′ vəl) refers to the Middle Ages, roughly A.D. 500–1450. *Vermin* are any insects or animals that are troublesome or harmful. *Refuse* (ref′ ūs) is another word for garbage. *Rushes* are reedy, grasslike plants.

---

8. *Pestilence* (pes′ tə ləns) comes from a Latin word meaning "unhealthy" and refers to any highly infectious, widespread disease.

Vocabulary
tolerate (tol′ ə rāt′) *v.* to endure; put up with

both rich and poor were prime targets for lice and fleas and the diseases they carried—the most deadly being the bubonic plague.

Several Italian commentators noted an unusual number of dead rats in cities struck by the plague. It seems odd that no one linked this phenomenon[11] to the disease. Perhaps people were so used to being surrounded by vermin, dead and alive, that a few more didn't arouse that much concern. At any rate, the Italians sought other explanations for the terrible pestilence.

Some scholars thought the plague had been triggered by a series of earthquakes that had <u>devastated</u> large areas of Europe and Asia between 1345 and 1347. They said the quakes had released poisonous fumes from the Earth's core, and some believed the Devil was behind it all.

Others claimed that climatic changes had brought warmer, damper weather and strong southerly winds that carried the disease north. They tried to predict its course by studying the colors of the sky at twilight and the shapes of cloud formations. Meanwhile, the death toll in both city and countryside continued to mount.

At Venice, one of Italy's major ports, the city's leaders decreed that no one could leave an incoming ship for *quaranta giorni*—forty days—the length of time Christ was said to have suffered in the wilderness. From this decree comes the word *quarantine*,[12]

which means any isolation of restriction on travel intended to keep a contagious disease from spreading. But the quarantine in Venice proved no more effective than the one imposed earlier at Messina. When the Black Death struck in December 1347, Venice had a population of about 130,000. Eighteen months later, only about 70,000 Venetians were still alive.

Other Italian cities tried harsher measures to halt the spread of the disease. As soon as the first cases were reported in Milan, the authorities sent the city militia[13] to wall up the houses where the victims lived. All those inside, whether sick or well, were cut off from their friends and neighbors and left to die.

The most complete account of the Black Death in Italy was given by the writer Giovanni Boccaccio,[14] who lived in the city of Florence. In the preface to his classic book *The Decameron*, Boccaccio wrote: "Some say that the plague descended upon the human race through the influence of the heavenly bodies, others that it was a punishment signifying God's righteous anger at our wicked way of life."

After describing the disease's symptoms, Boccaccio went on to say: "Against these maladies, it seemed that all the advice of physicians and all the power of medicine were profitless and <u>futile</u>. Perhaps the nature of the illness was such

11. Anything that is extremely unusual is a *phenomenon* (fə nom′ ə non′).
12. To decree is to set forth an official rule, order, or decision. Venice (ven′ is), quarantine (kwôr′ ən tēn′)
13. A military force made up of civilians who serve as soldiers during a time of emergency is called a *militia* (mi lish′ ə).
14. *Giovanni Boccaccio* (jō vä′ nē   bō kä′ chē ō′)

Vocabulary
devastate (dev′ əs tāt′) *v.* to cause great pain, damage, or destruction; overwhelm
futile (fū′ til) *adj.* useless or hopeless; not effective

A doctor of the 1700s wears a mask during an outbreak of plague in Venice. The beak of the mask probably contained fragrant herbs.

Viewing the print: What kind of protection does the doctor think is provided by the mask?

that it allowed no remedy; or perhaps those people who were treating the illness, being ignorant of its causes, were not prescribing the appropriate cure."

One of the most alarming things about the bubonic plague was the way it struck. "It would rush upon its victims with the speed of a fire racing through dry or oily substances that happened to be placed within its reach," Boccaccio wrote. "Not only did it infect healthy persons who conversed or had any dealings with the sick . . . but it also seemed to transfer the sickness to anyone touching the clothes or the other objects which had been handled or used by the victims."

Boccaccio reported seeing two pigs in the street, rooting through the ragged clothes of a poor man who had died of the plague. Within a short time, the pigs began to writhe and squirm as though they had been poisoned. Then they both dropped dead, falling on the same rags they had been pulling and tugging a few minutes earlier.

How did the people of Florence react to this mysterious and fatal disease? Some isolated themselves in their homes, according to Boccaccio. They ate lightly, saw no outsiders, and refused to receive reports of the dead or sick. Others adopted an attitude of "play today for we die tomorrow." They drank heavily, stayed out late, and roamed through the streets singing and dancing as if the Black Death were an enormous joke. Still others, if they were rich enough, abandoned their homes in the city and fled to villas[15] in the countryside. They hoped in this way to escape the disease—but often it followed them.

Whatever steps they took, the same percentage of people in each group seemed to fall ill. So many died that the bodies piled up in the streets. A new occupation came into being: that of loading the bodies on carts and carrying them away for burial in mass graves. "No more respect was accorded to dead people," Boccaccio wrote, "than would be shown toward dead goats."

The town of Siena, thirty miles south of Florence, suffered severe losses also. A man named Agnolo di Tura[16] offered a vivid account of what happened there:

"The mortality[17] in Siena began in May. It was a horrible thing, and I do not know where to begin to tell of the cruelty. . . . Members of a household brought their dead to a ditch as best they could, without a priest, without any divine services. Nor did the death bell sound. . . . And as soon as those ditches were filled, more were dug. I, Agnolo di Tura, buried my five children with my own hands. . . . And no bells tolled, and nobody wept no matter what his loss because almost everyone expected death. . . . And people said and believed, 'This is the end of the world.'"

By the winter of 1348–49, a little more than a year after its first appearance in Sicily, the worst of the Black Death was over in Italy. No one knows exactly how many Italians died of the disease, because accurate medical records were not kept. Conservative[18] estimates put the loss at about a third of the population, but many scholars believe the death rate reached forty or fifty percent, especially in the cities.

In any case, it was the greatest loss of human life Italy had suffered in a comparable period of time—and a loss not equaled to the present day.

Meanwhile, the Black Death had swept on to France, entering that country via Marseilles and other southern ports. Before long it traveled inland and reached the city of Avignon,[19] where the Pope was then living.

---

15. A *villa* is a house, especially one in the country or at the seashore.
16. *Siena* (sē en′ ə), *Agnolo di Tura* (ä nyō′ lō di tōō′ rə)
17. Here, *mortality* means simply "deaths" or "the dying."
18. These estimates are cautious (*conservative*), meaning that the numbers are likely to be too low rather than too high.
19. *Marseilles* (mär sā′), *Avignon* (ä vē nyōn′)

Between Two Raging Fires

When the Black Death arrived in Avignon in the spring of 1348, this old walled city in southern France had been the home of the Pope and his College of Cardinals[20] for almost forty years. They had come there in 1309 to escape political unrest in Rome and had built a magnificent palace on the city's main square.

Pilgrims, priests, and diplomats crowded into Avignon from all over Europe to pay their respects to the Pope. Without meaning to, some of these visitors must have brought

---

20. *College of Cardinals* is the group of high-ranking priests who act as advisers to the Pope. (Here, *college* means "people who have the same purpose," not a school of higher learning.)

A doctor holding a vinegar-soaked sponge to his face treats a plague victim.

Viewing the woodcut: Why do you think the doctor holds the sponge to his face?

the pestilence with them. Between February and May, up to 400 people a day died of the plague in Avignon. When the graveyards were filled, the bodies of the dead had to be dumped into the Rhône River, which flowed through the heart of the city.

Many courageous priests ministered to the sick and dying even though they knew that they would probably become infected and die themselves. Meanwhile, Pope Clement VI decided it was his duty, as leader of the Roman Catholic Church on the Earth, to remain alive if at all possible. On the advice of his physician, he withdrew to his private rooms, saw nobody, and spent day and night between two fires that blazed on grates at opposite ends of his bedchamber.

What purpose were the fires supposed to serve? It was tied in with the theory of humors, which still dominated medical thought in the fourteenth century. This theory goes back to the Greek physician Hippocrates,[21] who lived from about 484 to 425 B.C. and is often called the "father of medicine."

Hippocrates examined sick persons carefully and honestly recorded the signs and symptoms of various diseases. But his knowledge of how the human body worked was extremely limited. He believed the body contained four basic liquids, which he called humors: blood, which came from the heart; phlegm, from the brain; yellow bile, from the liver; and black bile, from the spleen.[22]

---

21. *Hippocrates* (hi pok′ rə tēz)
22. Today, we know that *phlegm,* or mucus, is formed in the nose or throat, not the brain. *Bile* does come from the liver, and the body uses it to aid digestion. The *spleen* filters blood and produces white blood cells. The *heart,* of course, pumps blood but does not make it.

If these humors were in balance, Hippocrates wrote, a person would enjoy good health. But if one of them became more important than the others, the person was likely to feel pain and fall victim to a disease. A physician's main job, therefore, was to try to restore and maintain a proper balance among the four humors.

Blood and Bile

Another Greek physician, Galen (A.D. 130–200), took the ideas of Hippocrates a step further. Galen stated that the four humors in the human body reflected the four elements that people believed were the basis of all life: earth, air, fire, and water. Blood was hot and moist, like the air in summer. Phlegm was cold and moist, like water. Yellow bile was hot and dry, like fire, and black bile was cold and dry, like earth. In other words, according to Galen, the human body was a smaller, contained version of the wider natural world.

Galen recommended certain treatments to keep the humors in balance. For example, if a patient was too hot, various foods were prescribed to make him or her cooler. If this treatment failed, the physician might perform bloodletting to reduce the amount of hot blood in the patient's system.

Most of Galen's theories have been discredited in modern times, but for over a thousand years, until the sixteenth century, no physician thought of questioning them.

Most medieval physicians were actually scholar-priests. They spent their time analyzing the writings of Galen and Hippocrates and left the treatment of patients to surgeons and barber-surgeons.

Surgeons usually had some medical training in a university. They were regarded as skilled craftsmen, able to close wounds, set broken bones, and perform simple operations.

Most barber-surgeons were illiterate men whose only training came from serving as apprentices[23] to surgeons. As their name implies, they cut hair as well as setting simple fractures and bandaging wounds. Some say the traditional red-and-white-striped barber's pole comes from the time when barber-surgeons hung their bloody surgical rags in front of their shops to dry.

Did You Know?
The modern *barber's pole* has red, white, and blue stripes.

Two other groups of people played important roles in medieval medicine. Apothecaries[24] filled prescriptions and also prescribed herbs and drugs on their own. Nonprofessionals, many of them older women, provided medical care in rural areas where no surgeons or barber-surgeons were available. These nonprofessionals had no formal training and relied heavily on folk

---

23. Someone who is *illiterate* (i lit′ ər it) is unable to read or write. *Apprentices* are beginners who learn their skills from experienced professionals.
24. *Apothecaries* are druggists or pharmacists.

Vocabulary
discredit (dis kred′ it) *v.* to reject as untrue; cause to be doubted or disbelieved
imply (im plī′) *v.* to suggest without directly stating

remedies that had been handed down from generation to generation in the countryside.

Strange Treatments

This, then, was the medical scene when the Black Death raged through western Europe in the mid-fourteenth century. It helps to explain why physicians and surgeons were at such a loss to know what caused the epidemic, let alone how to treat it. It also answers the question of why the Pope's physician had him sit alone in his bedchamber between two raging fires.

Galen had written that diseases were transmitted from person to person by miasmas, poisonous vapors that arose from swamps and corrupted the air. The Pope's physician, who believed in Galen's theories, thought that hot air from the fires would combat any dangerous miasmas that got into the Pope's chamber and render[25] them harmless. (The Pope did survive, but it's doubtful whether the fires had anything to do with it except to make his chamber uncomfortable for rats and fleas.)

Other physicians and surgeons interpreted Galen's theories differently. Instead of fighting fire with fire, so to speak, they recommended fleeing from it. People were urged to leave warm, low, marshy places that were likely to produce miasmas and move to drier, cooler regions in the hills. If that was not possible, they were advised to stay indoors during the heat of the day, cover over any brightly lighted windows, and try to stay cool.

Hands and feet were to be washed regularly, but physicians warned against bathing the body because it opened the pores. This, they thought, made the body more vulnerable to attack by disease-bearing miasmas. Exercise was to be avoided for the same reason.

Sleep after eating and in the middle of the day was bad because the body was warmer then. And physicians cautioned their patients not to sleep on their backs at any time, because that made it easier for foul air to flow down their nostrils and get into their lungs.

To ward off[26] miasmas when one walked outside, physicians recommended carrying bouquets of sweet-smelling herbs and flowers and holding them up to the nose. Some say this practice was one of the inspirations for the old English nursery rhyme "Ring-a-ring o' roses." In the first published version it read as follows:

> Ring-a-ring o' roses,
>   A pocket full of posies,
> A-tishoo! A-tishoo!
>   We all fall down.

Those who link the rhyme to the plague think the ring o' roses was the rash that often signaled infection. The pocket full of posies referred to the flowers people carried to sweeten the air around them. A-tishoo! was the sound of sneezing, a common

---

25. To *transmit* a thing is to send it, or cause it to pass, from one person or place to another. To *render* a thing is to make or cause it to become. *Miasma* (mī az′ mə)

26. The expression *ward off* means "to turn back; keep away."

Vocabulary
vulnerable (vul′ nər ə bəl) *adj.* capable of being damaged or wounded; easily hurt

symptom of the disease, and "We all fall down" implied that all of its victims died.

Some prescribed treatments for the plague seem sensible or at least harmless: bed rest, drinking lots of liquids, and the application of salves made of herbs to the affected areas of the body. But other treatments hurt plague sufferers instead of helping them.

Surgeons who had studied Galen's theories believed that the Black Death interrupted the flow of the body's humors. Since the heart produced the most important of these liquids, blood, doctors thought one effective way to fight the plague and improve circulation was to bleed veins close to the heart.

The surgeons also thought that buboes, the swellings that characterized the disease, revealed where the body was being attacked, and they geared their treatment accordingly. If a buboe appeared in the region of the groin, for example, the surgeon drained blood from a vein leading to one of the organs in that area. By doing so, the surgeon meant to cool the body and help it fight the disease, but in fact bleeding only weakened the body's defenses.

St. Roch[27]

I n the face of treatments like these, it's no wonder that people lost faith in their physicians and came to rely more and more on prayer. Many directed their prayers to St. Roch, who had died in 1327 and was the particular saint associated with the plague.

According to the legends told about him in France and Italy, Roch inherited great wealth as a young man. Like St. Francis, he gave it away to the poor and then went on a religious pilgrimage[28] to Italy. He was in Rome when an epidemic struck, but instead of fleeing, Roch stayed on to nurse the sick. Eventually, he caught the disease himself.

Roch left the city and went to the countryside, where he expected to die alone in the woods. But a dog carrying a loaf of bread in its mouth miraculously found him. Each day the dog reappeared with a fresh loaf, and Roch gradually recovered.

He got home to France safely, but his relatives failed to recognize him and had Roch arrested as an impostor. He died in jail, filling his cell with a mysterious white light. After Roch's story spread and he was made a saint, it was thought he would come to the aid of plague victims just as the dog had come to his aid in the Roman woods.

Even prayers to St. Roch did not halt the relentless march of the Black Death through France, however. At the peak of the plague, the death rate in Paris was reported to be 800 a day. By the time the epidemic had run its course in 1349, over 50,000 Parisians had died—half the city's population.

---

27. *Roch* (rôk)

28. A *pilgrimage* is a long journey, especially to a holy place for a religious purpose.

Responding to Literature

PERSONAL RESPONSE

- ◆ What is the most surprising fact you discovered from reading this selection?
- ◆ Review the flu symptoms discussed in the **Focus Activity** on page 578. How might physicians of the 1300s have dealt with such symptoms?

Analyzing Literature

RECALL

1. What were the symptoms of the Black Death?
2. How did rats spread the plague?
3. How did Pope Clement VI try to protect himself from getting the plague? Did he survive?
4. What were health tips from physicians for preventing and treating plague?

INTERPRET

5. In addition to causing death, what made the plague so frightening?
6. What were three "explanations" for the Black Death that were believed among the people? What do these beliefs show about the people who held them?
7. What living conditions during the 1300s created a "breeding ground" for the plague?
8. Who was Roch? Why did some people feel that Roch could help them during the plague?

EVALUATE AND CONNECT

9. How could you find out whether the author has given an accurate account of what happened?
10. Theme Connection   How would you have protected yourself from the plague, knowing only what the people of the day knew?

Nonfiction

Authors of **nonfiction** organize information in different ways.

- **Chronological order.** Events are presented in the order in which they occur.
- **Order of importance.** The most important ideas are presented first, with less important ideas following.
- **Logical order.** Information is presented to show cause-effect, comparison-contrast, or problem-solution.
- **Spatial order.** Details are presented as they would be viewed—front to back, left to right, or in another order.

1. How are the first four paragraphs of the selection organized?
2. How is the section "Blood and Bile" organized?

● See **Literary Terms Handbook,** p. R6.

Literature and Writing

Writing About Literature

Explanation   The possible origins of the nursery rhyme "Ring-a-ring o' roses," the barber-pole, and the word *quarantine* are discussed in this selection. Find each item and reread these parts. Then write a paragraph telling the origin of one of these things. Be sure to paraphrase the author's words.

Creative Writing

By Decree   Write a decree, or order, from a town government to the people of the town. Announce the problem of the coming plague and advise the population on how to deal with the problem. Use ideas from the selection in the advice you offer.

Extending Your Response

Literature Groups

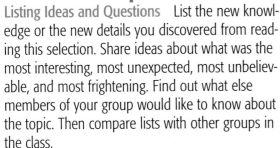

Listing Ideas and Questions   List the new knowledge or the new details you discovered from reading this selection. Share ideas about what was the most interesting, most unexpected, most unbelievable, and most frightening. Find out what else members of your group would like to know about the topic. Then compare lists with other groups in the class.

Learning for Life

Sanitation Workers   During the years of the Black Death, cities did not have systems for collecting trash. In a small group, find out about the trash collecting system used in your community. How often is trash collected? Where does the trash end up? Share your group's findings with classmates.

Interdisciplinary Activity

Health   Does the plague still exist? If so, is it as deadly as it once was? Investigate under *plague* in the encyclopedia and in nonfiction books. On the Web, search under the topic *plague* on the *World Health Organization* Web site. Share your findings with the class.

Reading Further

If you'd like to read more by James Cross Giblin, you might enjoy these books:

From Hand to Mouth, Or, How We Invented Knives, Forks, Spoons, and Chopsticks & the Table Manners to Go with Them

Milk: The Fight for Purity

Chimney Sweeps: Yesterday and Today

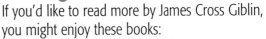

Save your work for your portfolio.

This engraving was meant to remind people that it was hopeless to try to escape death.

Skill Minilessons

GRAMMAR AND LANGUAGE • ACTION VERBS AND LINKING VERBS

Verbs can be either action verbs or linking verbs. An **action verb** names an action. In the following example, *examined* is the action verb.

The doctor examined sick patients.

The **direct object** receives the action of the verb. It answers the questions, "Whom?" or "What?" In this example, readers ask, "Whom did the doctor examine?" The answer is "sick patients." *Sick patients* is the direct object of *examine.*

A **linking verb** connects the subject of the sentence to a noun or adjective in the predicate.

The doctor is a barber.
The doctor is fearless.

In the first example, *doctor* is connected to *barber* by the linking verb *is. Barber* tells what the

doctor is. The second example shows a linking verb connecting the subject of the sentence with an adjective that describes the subject: *fearless* describes the doctor. Common linking verbs are *be, become, seem, appear, feel, taste, grow,* and *look.*

PRACTICE Tell whether the verb in each sentence is an action or a linking verb. Write the direct object of each action verb.
   1. Most medieval physicians were scholar-priests.
   2. Barber-surgeons were illiterate.
   3. Trading ships carried the Black Death.
   4. The flea was very adaptable.
   5. The disease attacked the nervous system.

● For more on verbs, see **Language Handbook,** pp. R28–R29.

READING AND THINKING • DRAWING CONCLUSIONS

Just as the people in the plague-infected cities drew conclusions about what caused the plague, readers often draw conclusions when they read. They use facts or events in the selection to come to an idea that is not directly stated.

PRACTICE Write a conclusion you can draw from these facts.
• Some thought earthquakes triggered the plague.
• Some thought the winds carried the disease.
• Some believed the devil caused the plague.

● For more on drawing conclusions, see **Reading Handbook,** p. R82.

VOCABULARY • DENOTATION AND CONNOTATION

Denotation is a word's dictionary definition. **Connotation** is the ideas a word suggests that go beyond its dictionary definition.

For example, *relentless* has the negative suggestion of a lack of pity or mercy. *Adaptable* has the positive suggestion of an admirable ability to change.

PRACTICE Use the information above to answer the questions.

   1. Both Al and Sal talked endlessly about my speech to the class. Al was making fun of me, and Sal was complimenting me. Which one was *relentless?*
   2. Both Polly and Molly can change their behavior. Molly does so if her old way of doing things doesn't work. Polly does so only when it is demanded of her. Which one is *adaptable?*

From the Common Cold to the Ebola Virus

A-ah-achoo! Every time you sneeze, you spray invisible viruses into the air. Sometimes a virus, such as a virus that causes the common cold, survives in the air long enough to spread to other people.

It's not easy to spot a virus. In fact, a virus is so small that you need a powerful electron microscope to see it. Viruses grow inside living cells and cause various diseases. A virus relies on another organism, called a *host*, to survive. The host may be a plant, an animal, or a human.

In 1976 scientists began looking for an especially dangerous virus that was killing people and animals living near African rain forests. This virus looks like a long, thin, knotted thread. Scientists named the virus *Ebola* (ē bō′ la) after a river in Africa. Ebola is so dangerous it kills nine out of every ten people it infects. Scientists feared Ebola might spread quickly and kill many other victims.

Researchers from the World Health Organization and the Centers for Disease Control were stumped by Ebola's mysterious patterns. Why does the virus appear and disappear so suddenly? Scientists have combed the rain forests in Africa where Ebola spread, searching for animals or plants hosting the virus. After much research, the scientists still have more questions than answers about this virus.

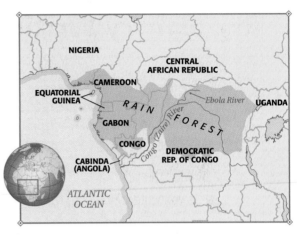

The African rain forest where Ebola first appeared.

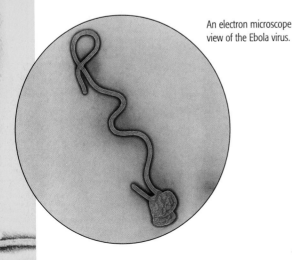

An electron microscope view of the Ebola virus.

ACTIVITY

"Looking at the Ebola under an electron microscope is like looking at a gorgeously wrought ice castle."
—*Karl Johnson, World Health Organization*

Why does Karl Johnson refer to a deadly virus as beautiful? Research shapes of various viruses. Draw a picture of a virus that interests you. Make your picture as colorful and artistic as you can. Then list a few details about the virus and its effects on humans.

Writing WORKSHOP

Expository Writing: Historical Report

Some things that you read are like time machines. They show what life was like in days gone by—and they make you curious to know more. One good way to learn about the past is to prepare a report. As you find information and think about what you've found, you bring the past into focus for your readers and for yourself.

Assignment: Follow the process in this workshop to write a historical report.

● As you write your report, refer to the **Writing Handbook,** pp. R48–R50.

The Writing Process

PREWRITING

PREWRITING TIP

To narrow a broad topic, look it up in the "Subject" part of the library's electronic catalog. Narrower subtopics may be listed under it.

● Find a Topic

What people, events, or places from the past arouse your curiosity? Brainstorm a list of things you'd like to know more about. The suggestions below can help.

● Skim "The Dog of Pompeii" (pages 546–554) again. What else might you like to know about life in ancient Roman times?

● Skim "When Plague Strikes" (pages 579–589) again. What else might you like to know about life in medieval Europe? Which region would you like to focus on?

● From what country do your ancestors come? What might you like to learn about its history?

● What do you know about the history of the area in which you live now? Which parts of its history interest you most?

Choose one topic, and narrow it until it is right for a two- to three-page report.

Gather Information

The encyclopedia can get you started. It may even lead you to other books—some encyclopedia articles list related books following the article. Don't stop there. Check magazine articles, history books, museums, and the Web. Try interviewing someone knowledgeable. Take notes as you go. On each card, write the name of the source, record facts in your own words, and put any quotations in quotation marks.

Know Your Audience and Purpose

For this report, your purpose is to inform: to organize your information and present it clearly. Your audience will be your teacher and classmates, so plan to highlight facts that will hold special interest for them.

Sundiata's childhood
David Wisniewski, Sundiata, Lion King of Mali, Clarion Books, 1992.

Sundiata couldn't walk until he was 7 yrs. old. He was teased & called names.

Organize Your Notes

Lay out your note cards so that you can see all of them. When you see what your information adds up to, you can decide on the main idea of your report. Then plan how to use your information to explain your main idea. An outline list, like the one shown, can help. Each part of your report will need facts or details to explain it.

Main Idea: Mali's King Sundiata met his hardest challenge when he was only seven.

Introduction: Meet a 7-year-old hero from 700 years ago

Body:
Part 1 Basic info. about Sundiata
Fact –Prince of Mali, born early 1200s
Fact –At age 18, saved Mali from invaders
Fact –Built Mali into huge African empire
Part 2 Sundiata's childhood
Fact –His father died & rivals took over.
Fact –Sundiata couldn't walk, was teased and insulted
Fact –At age 7, he started to walk.
Part 3 My ideas
Detail –Walking showed courage and strength.
Detail –Armies helped him in battles, but he had to walk on his own.

Conclusion: Sundiata at age 7 showed inner strength of a true hero.

DRAFTING

DRAFTING TIP
After you've used your notes, save them. You will need to check them again as you revise and proofread.

● Get a Good Start

Your introduction does not need to be long. You might write one sentence to spark your readers' interest, and another one to state your main idea. Then move on to the body of your report.

MODEL · DRAFTING

Over seven hundred years ago, a young boy in Africa became a hero. Mali's King Sundiata Keita met his hardest challenge when he was only seven years old.

Sundiata was born in the early 1200s. He was the son of King Maghan Kon Fatta of ancient Mali.

● Share Your Discoveries

Following your outline and notes draft the body and conclusion of your report. In the body of your report, you might devote one paragraph to each part listed on your outline. Give your readers the background and facts that they'll need to understand each part. For your conclusion, sum up what you have learned.

REVISING

REVISING TIP
Ask a partner to state your main idea in his or her own words. If your partner's idea doesn't reflect yours, you may need to rework your main idea sentence.

TECHNOLOGY TIP
If you use the Web as a source, download photos or art to illustrate your report.

● Plan Changes

Take a break—you've earned it! Then read your draft and plan how to make it better. Use the **Questions for Revising,** working on your own or with a partner. First, revise for clarity. Pencil in changes to make your information clearer. Next, revise for smoothness. Change your sentences and paragraphs to create the flow you want.

QUESTIONS FOR REVISING

☑ How can I change my first sentence to better catch my readers' interest?

☑ How could I make my main idea clearer?

☑ Where might I add facts or details to help readers understand my information?

EDITING/PROOFREADING

Before writing your final draft, proofread carefully for grammar, usage, and mechanics. Use the **Proofreading Checklist.** Pay special attention to commas, as in the **Grammar Link** on page 528.

Grammar Hint

Use a pair of commas to set off a quotation.

Crazy Horse said, "One does not sell the earth upon which the people walk," and I agree.

PROOFREADING CHECKLIST
- ☑ Commas and other punctuation marks are correctly used. (Double-check for commas with quotations.)
- ☑ Sentences are complete; there are no sentence fragments or run-ons.
- ☑ All pronouns agree with their antecedents.
- ☑ Spelling and capitalization are correct.

MODEL · EDITING/PROOFREADING

When Sundiata's friend shouted ˄"The lion is walking ˄" everyone rushed to see.

PUBLISHING/PRESENTING

Add drawings, photos, graphs, or other visuals to illustrate your report. Then present your report orally to your classmates. Use the guidelines on page 577.

PRESENTING TIP
Desktop publishing software can add headings, columns, and graphics.

Reflecting

Write well thought-out responses to the following questions.

- Which did you enjoy more, doing research or writing the report? Explain.
- What other topics would you like to explore in a report? What might you do differently to make writing your next report easier?

📖 **Save your work for your portfolio.**

Theme Wrap-Up

Responding to the Theme

1. Which selections in this theme helped you think about surviving difficult experiences? Explain your answer.

2. What new ideas do you have about the following as a result of your reading in this theme?
   - the kinds of difficult situations people have experienced in different periods of history
   - the complex causes for these problems
   - the difficulty of finding solutions
   - how different individuals respond to difficult situations

3. Present your theme project to the class.

Analyzing Literature

ANALYZE NONFICTION

Choose a nonfiction selection from this theme to analyze. Consider these questions as you write your analysis:

- How is information organized in the selection?
- How are facts used to support ideas?

Evaluate and Set Goals

1. Which of the following was most enjoyable to you? Which was most difficult?
   - reading and thinking about the selections
   - independent writing
   - analyzing the selections in discussions
   - making presentations
   - researching

2. How would you assess your work in this theme, using the following scale? Give at least two reasons for your assessment.

   4 = outstanding   2 = fair
   3 = good   1 = weak

3. Based on what you found difficult in this theme, choose a goal to work toward in the next theme.
   - Write down your goal and three steps you will take to try to reach it.
   - Meet with your teacher to review your goal and your plan for achieving it.

Build Your Portfolio

SELECT

Choose two pieces of work you did in this theme to include in your portfolio. Use these questions to help you choose.

- ✦ Which do you consider your best work?
- ✦ Which challenged you the most?
- ✦ Which did you learn the most from?
- ✦ Which did you enjoy the most?

REFLECT

Write some notes to accompany the pieces you selected. Use these questions to guide you.

- ✦ What do you like best about the piece?
- ✦ What did you learn from creating it?
- ✦ What might you do differently if you were beginning this piece again?

Reading on Your Own

If you have enjoyed the literature in this theme, you might be interested in the following books.

The Clay Marble
by Minfong Ho During the 1970s, twelve-year old Dara and her family struggle to survive in war-torn Cambodia.

The Invisible Thread
by Yoshiko Uchida The popular author describes growing up in Berkeley, California, as a Japanese American, and her family's internment in a Nevada concentration camp during World War II.

Hurricanes: Earth's Mightiest Storms
by Patricia Lauber Color photographs and scientific information will help you understand the disastrous effects of hurricanes.

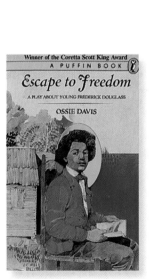

Escape to Freedom: A Play About Young Frederick Douglass
by Ossie Davis
Born enslaved, future orator and statesman Douglass endures cruelty and injustice before escaping to freedom.

Standardized Test Practice

Read the passage. Some sections are underlined. The underlined sections may be one of the following:

- Incomplete sentences
- Run-on sentences
- Correctly written sentences that should be combined
- Correctly written sentences that do not need to be rewritten

Choose the best way to write each underlined section. Mark the letter for your answer on your paper. If the underlined section needs no change, mark the choice "Correct as is."

Soccer originated in England, but games like soccer were played in ancient days in several places around the world. One soccer-like game was played in Central America. It consisted of one match that lasted for days. The playing
(1)
field was much different from the one we use for today's soccer. The field was longer the goals were stone rings placed high on a wall. The first team to get the
(2)
ball through a stone ring won the game. The whole community turned out to watch the event. The victors were hailed as champions; their names were often carved into the stone walls that surrounded the playing fields.

---

1 **A** One soccer-like game was played in Central America and consisted of one match that lasted for days.

B A soccer-like game, from Central America, was one match, but it lasted for days.

C The soccer-like game was a long one.

D Consisting of a single match, lasting for days, held in Central America, was a game like soccer.

2 **F** The field being longer and the goals stone rings placed high on a wall.

G The field was longer, and the goals were stone rings placed high on a wall.

H The field being longer; the goals being stone rings placed high on a wall.

J Correct as is

Read the passage and decide which type of error, if any, appears in each underlined section. Mark the letter for your answer on your paper.

Dear Tammy,

   It was so grate to meet you at camp this summer. I am glad we became such
   (1)
good friends. I hope that you will be able to visit me in Idaho sometime soon.

I think you would really, enjoy yourself here.
(2)
   If you come during the winter, we can go to Bogus Basin. It's a great place to

ski, and it's not far from my house. My parents' can drive us up to the lodge and
                                       (3)
pick us up again in a few hours. If you don't have skis, you can rent them.

   If you come in the summer, we can go to the rodeo. Have you ever heard of
                                                      (4)
the snake river stampede? It's a lot of fun! Some of my classmates ride their

horses in the parade before the rodeo begins.

Please write soon!

Your friend,

Patsy

---

1 A Spelling error
   B Capitalization error
   C Punctuation error
   D No error

2 F Spelling error
   G Capitalization error
   H Punctuation error
   J No error

3 A Spelling error
   B Capitalization error
   C Punctuation error
   D No error

4 F Spelling error
   G Capitalization error
   H Punctuation error
   J No error

Old Tales, New Twists

 A storyteller must be an entertainer of the spirit.

—Isaac Bashevis Singer

A Last Look Back. Celia Washington (b. 1959). Oil on canvas, 61 x 91 cm.
Private collection.

THEME 7

THEME CONTENTS

GENRE FOCUS **DRAMA**

Exploring the Theme

Old Tales, New Twists

People have told stories for as long as anyone can remember. You tell stories to your friends and family all the time—about what happened in gym class or about a new family moving in next door, for example. In this theme, you will read stories, some with a little twist, that people tell around the world.

Starting Points

BORROW A CLASSIC

The *Far Side* cartoon on the right assumes that readers know the fairy tale of Hansel and Gretel. The witch in the cartoon, however, is different from the witch in the fairy tale.

- With a partner, choose a favorite fairy tale or folktale. Together, retell the story, changing a few details to "modernize" it. Did you change the underlying meaning of the tale?

ADD A NEW ENDING

If you were baby-sitting or telling a story to a younger brother or sister, what folktale or fairy tale would you like to share?

- On your own, write a new ending for this favorite tale. Retell the story to a partner, adding your ending.

Theme Projects

Choose one of the projects below to complete as you read the selections in this theme. Work on your own, with a partner, or with a group.

CRITICAL VIEWING
Seeing Double
Authors retell folktales and fairy tales in different ways.

1. Read two illustrated versions of a popular fairy tale, such as "Beauty and the Beast."
2. If possible, view one or more movie versions of the tale.
3. Compare the ways the versions are told, illustrated, or performed. Share your conclusions.

LEARNING FOR LIFE
Write a Script
Recall a favorite story, fairy tale, or folktale, and consider how you could turn this story into a play. Write all or part of the tale in the form of a script.

1. Begin by listing the characters in the tale.
2. Then write the words each character will say.
3. Add notes telling the performers where to move and what to do.
4. Enlist "actors," and perform your story for the class.

MULTIMEDIA PROJECT
Do You See What I See?
Why do different people tell different stories about the same thing?

1. After a group activity, separately interview students who were present. Record the interviews on videotape or audiotape.
2. Ask the same questions about what each person saw and remembers. Have other students draw pictures or diagrams to represent what they remember best.
3. Did everyone recall the same details? Write your conclusions and present highlights to the class.

The Walt Disney Company.

interNET CONNECTION

Check out the World Wide Web or contact the Glencoe Web site lit.glencoe.com for more project ideas or selections related to the theme.

Before You Read

Creation and *Leyenda*

MEET SHONTO BEGAY

"All things are connected in the great cycle [of life]. . . . Everything in nature is related," says Shonto Begay (shon′ tō bə gā′). As the son of a Navajo spiritual leader, Begay learned this philosophy as a child. Begay is an artist as well as a writer, and his work reflects his Arizona and Navajo roots.

Shonto Begay was born in 1950. This poem was published in 1995.

MEET PAT MORA

"Many of my book ideas come from the desert where I grew up," says poet Pat Mora, "the open spaces, wide sky, all that sun, and all the animals that scurry across the hot sand or fly high over the mountains."

Pat Mora was born in 1942. This poem was published in 1984.

FOCUS ACTIVITY

Think about a favorite place. It could be a place in your home or neighborhood or a place you remember or imagine.

QuickWrite

Jot a few notes about how the place looks and what makes it special to you. Share your ideas with a partner.

Setting a Purpose

As you read, let yourself imagine and picture the images in "Creation" and "Leyenda."

BACKGROUND

The Time and Place

Shonto Begay's poem describes stories still told among Navajo people in New Mexico, Arizona, and Utah. Pat Mora's poem is about a group of people called the Toltecs, whose capital city was Tula.

Did You Know?   The Toltecs lived and prospered in what is now central Mexico from around A.D. 900 to 1200. They influenced later groups in central Mexico, including the Aztecs. Legends about the Toltecs and the amazing civilizations they developed were told among the Aztecs. The Spanish word for "legend" is *leyenda*.

Stone sculpture found at Tula.

Winter Stories, 1991 (detail). Shonto Begay. Acrylic on canvas, 20 x 28 in.

Creation

Shonto Begay ⁓

Many winter nights,
my father sat up and told us stories—
stories that came alive through voice and gesture.
Shadows from an old oil drum stove
5   danced on the hogan° wall.
The stove pipe rattled every once in a while
as the snow and wind whined outside.
Tiny drifts of snow sifted through
the cracks in the door.
10   The story hogan was warm,
the storytelling voice soothing.
He told us stories of creation, of the journey
through four worlds to get to the present one.

---

5 A *hogan* is a Navajo house or dwelling, especially one made of wood and
covered with earth.

Creation

First World was the dark world.
15 Insects lived in the cold.
Unhappiness drove them into the Second World,
the blue world. Birds lived there.
Jealousy ruled and the beings
of the Second World emerged into the Third.
20 The Third World was inhabited
by larger mammal beings,
Bear, Deer, Coyote, and Wolf,
and all of their cousins.
Life was good in the Third World for many years,
25 until slowly these beings began to argue
and fight among themselves.
Coyote stole Water-Being's baby
and the Third World was flooded.
The beings moved up to the Fourth World
30 through a reed.
Locust came up first. Turkey came up last.

First Man and First Woman were created
on the rim of the Fourth World.
The hero twins, Born-for-Water and Monster Slayer,
35 were born of their mother, Changing Woman,
and their father, the sun.
They were born for a purpose.
Monsters of great size and power roamed the land,
making life miserable for the first people.
40 The hero twins were to save the people
and the land from these monsters.
In a great battle, mountain ranges fell,
lakes dried up, and the earth trembled.
One by one, the great giants were felled.
45 These scars and places where Monster fell can still
be seen as mountains, volcanic plugs,° and gorges.
After the people of the Fourth World were saved,
they were instructed to rule wisely.
They were placed in charge of maintaining harmony.

---

46 A *volcanic plug* is the rock that fills or covers a volcano's vent, or opening, following
an eruption.

Our Chants, Their Songs, 1988. Shonto Begay. Acrylic on canvas, 48 x 32 in.

Viewing the painting: What kinds of stories might this storyteller tell? Why do you think so?

50 They were given the four sacred mountains
    as guardians of our holy land, *Diné taĥ.*

    The younger ones are usually asleep by now.
    My father ends his story for the night.
    There will be many more nights
55 this winter for stories. The fire in the stove roars,
    and shadows on the wall continue their dance.

Leyenda

Pat Mora ∾

They say there was magic at Tula.
Seeds burst overnight.
Plants danced out of the ground.
By dawn, green leaves swayed.

5   At Tula the Toltecs
picked giant ears of corn.
Mounds of soft cornsilk
became mattresses and pillows
for small, sleepy heads.

10   They say at Tula the Toltecs
picked green cotton, red cotton.
In fields that were ribbons of color,
Indians harvested rainbows.

They built palaces of jade, turquoise,
15   gold. They made a castle
of gleaming quetzal° plumage,°
and when the wind blew
small green and red feathers
landed on Indian heads.

16 A bird of Central America, the *quetzal* (ket säl′) has bright green
and red feathers, or *plumage* (plōō′ mij). The male quetzal can
measure up to four feet, including its four long tail feathers.

Responding to Literature

PERSONAL RESPONSE

In what ways do these poems remind you of special places? Use your ideas from the **Focus Activity** on page 606.

Analyzing Literature

RECALL

1. Who lived in each of the four worlds in "Creation"?
2. What are some ways that "magic" happens at Tula?

INTERPRET

3. What causes the second, third, and fourth worlds in "Creation" to develop?
4. Based on the poem, what might Tula really have looked like?

EVALUATE AND CONNECT

5. Theme Connection   Who is the speaker of "Creation"? How do you think the speaker feels about storytelling? Support your answer.
6. In your opinion, why does Mora tell about the Toltecs and Tula as if they were magical?
7. Which senses do the images in the poems appeal to?
8. Does either poem remind you of other poems or stories you have read? If so, which ones? In what ways?
9. Would you like to visit the "story hogan"? Why or why not?
10. Based on the descriptions in the poems, in which place would you choose to live—Tula or the Fourth World in "Creation"? Explain.

LITERARY ELEMENTS

Myths and Legends

Both myths and legends begin as stories that people tell and retell over generations. **Myths** explain some aspect of the natural world or explain human nature. Characters in myths may be gods, goddesses, or other superpowerful beings who create or change life on earth. **Legends** are stories with a connection to history. They usually focus on famous people or great deeds. Characters in legends may have been real people, and settings may be actual places.

1. Why might the stories referred to in "Creation" be called myths?

2. Why might the stories referred to in "Leyenda" be called legends?

● See **Literary Terms Handbook,** p. R5.

A Storyteller Doll. Helen Cordero. Cochiti Pueblo, NM.

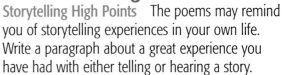

Extending Your Response

Writing About Literature

Identifying Lessons Both poems refer to stories that entertain, inform, and pass on knowledge. What values and beliefs might the stories referred to in each poem pass on to future generations?

Interdisciplinary Activity

Social Studies Many Navajo people live in domed homes called hogans. With a partner, research these homes at the library or on the Internet. Then design a hogan you would like to live in.

A hogan.

Personal Writing

Storytelling High Points The poems may remind you of storytelling experiences in your own life. Write a paragraph about a great experience you have had with either telling or hearing a story.

Literature Groups

Looking Back Both poems are about places from the past, whether real or mythical. Make a list of the most important images of the past in each poem. Share your ideas with other groups.

Reading Further

If you liked these poems, try these books:

Navajo: Visions and Voices Across the Mesa by Shonto Begay

The Desert Is My Mother by Pat Mora

🛍 **Save your work for your portfolio.**

Skill Minilesson

GRAMMAR AND LANGUAGE • PARTS OF SPEECH

Sometimes the same word can play a different role in different sentences.

The snow fell softly.

In this example, *snow* is a noun and the subject of the sentence.

The snow sculptures were gigantic.

Here, *snow* is an adjective describing *sculptures.*

It will snow tonight. It snowed yesterday.

Snow is a verb because it expresses an action.

PRACTICE Write *n.* if the underlined word is used as a noun, *v.* if it is used as a verb, or *adj.* if it is used as an adjective.

1. During the winter, my father told us stories.
2. We heard the whine of the winter winds.
3. The Third World flooded.
4. There was a great fight between monsters and the hero twins.

● For more about parts of speech, see **Language Handbook,** pp. R24–R29.

Ancient Civilizations in Mexico

Imagine climbing a 248-step pyramid built almost two thousand years ago. You can do just that in the ancient city of Teotihuacán (tā′ ō tē′ wə kän′) in central Mexico (see map on page 606).

Teotihuacán was once one of the largest cities in the world. For over eight hundred years, it was the largest city in Central America. By A.D. 500, as many as 200,000 people lived there. Teotihuacán had two grand pyramids, the Pyramid of the Sun and the Pyramid of the Moon, on a long, wide street the Aztecs later called the Avenue of the Dead.

Around A.D. 750, Teotihuacán was abandoned. By A.D. 950, the city of Tula dominated the region. About 40,000 people lived at Tula. Huge stone warriors were once the columns that held up the roof of a temple. Art that has been found at Tula shows the people were warriors and farmers. They grew beans and corn. The people of Tula were known for stone work, ceramics, and weaving. They traded with other people throughout a large area of Central America.

After these cities were abandoned, they were covered with blowing dirt and plants. Even the two hundred-foot-tall pyramids at Teotihuacán were covered. They looked more like hills than pyramids. To the Aztecs, who later settled the area, they looked like burial mounds.

Archaeologists are scientists who study past civilizations by digging up and exploring what was left behind. In the last hundred years or so, archaeologists have uncovered the pyramids, as well as palaces, temples, apartments, courtyards, streets, and craft shops at Teotihuacán and Tula. They have found pottery, stone and glass work, masks, and frescoes.

No one knows exactly what happened to end these cities. Archaeologists have found signs of a great fire in Teotihuacán. Around A.D. 1200, Tula may have been invaded by other tribes of people. Much of the history of these great cities, however, is still hidden by time.

A series of stone warrior columns was found on top of the Temple of the Morning Star in Tula.

ACTIVITY

Create a Pyramid of the Sun. View photographs of the pyramid on the Internet, browsing under *Teotihuacán* and *Pyramid of the Sun.* Use clay, papier-mâché, or other materials to build a three-dimensional structure.

The Pyramid of the Sun at Teotihuacán.

Before You Read

All Stories Are Anansi's and *The End of the World*

MEET HAROLD COURLANDER

Harold Courlander collected folktales from various parts of the world, especially Africa. He was most interested in tales that showed the values of the people from whom the stories came.

Harold Courlander was born in 1908 and died in 1996. "All Stories Are Anansi's" was published in 1957.

MEET JENNY LEADING CLOUD

Jenny Leading Cloud was a Sioux woman who told "The End of the World" to authors and editors Richard Erdoes and Alfonso Ortiz. Over a twenty-five-year period, these two men collected dozens of tales from eighty different groups of Native Americans.

This story was published in 1984.

FOCUS ACTIVITY

What kinds of stories make you want to sit down and start reading? Why?

Make a Web
With a partner, create a web around the word *stories*. Jot down as many different kinds of stories as you can and key words that tell about each kind.

Setting a Purpose
Read to enjoy two different kinds of tales.

BACKGROUND

Did You Know? Anansi is a favorite character in many African and Caribbean folktales. A spiderman, he is shown as either a spider or as a man with spider characteristics. Anansi is a trickster who tries to make everything turn out in the best possible way—for himself. His tricks are surprising, clever, and fun to read about.

Mask (gle). African (Liberia, Côte d'Ivoire, Dan). Wood, fiber, hair, vegetable colors, 17 x 8½ x 3¾ in. Harn Museum of Art Collection, University of Florida. Gift of Rod McGalliard. 1990.

VOCABULARY PREVIEW

dispute (dis pūt′) *n.* a difference of opinion; argument or quarrel; p. 616

merely (mēr′ lē) *adv.* no more than; only; p. 618

badlands (bad′ landz′) *n.* a dry region that has numerous ridges and peaks cut by erosion, but little plant life; the Badlands is a region of South Dakota; p. 619

feeble (fē′ bəl) *adj.* lacking physical strength; weak; p. 620

Untitled, 1990 (detail). Twins Seven-Seven. Ink on plywood with plywood collage, 244 x 122 cm. ©C.A.A.C.–The Pigozzi Collection, Geneva.

All Stories Are Anansi's

Retold by
Harold Courlander ❧

IN THE BEGINNING, ALL TALES and stories belonged to Nyame,[1] the Sky God. But Kwaku Anansi, the spider, yearned to be the owner of all the stories known in the world, and he went to Nyame and offered to buy them.

The Sky God said: "I am willing to sell the stories, but the price is high. Many people have come to me offering to buy, but the price was too high for them. Rich and powerful families have not been able to pay. Do you think you can do it?"

Anansi replied to the Sky God: "I can do it. What is the price?"

"My price is three things," the Sky God said. "I must first have Mmoboro, the hornets. I must then have Onini, the great python. I must then have Osebo, the leopard. For these things I will sell you the right to tell all stories."

Anansi said: "I will bring them."

He went home and made his plans. He first cut a gourd from a vine and made a small hole in it. He took a large calabash and filled it with water. He went to the tree where the hornets lived. He poured some of the water over himself, so that he was dripping. He threw some water over the hornets, so that

Did You Know?
A calabash (kal′ə bash′) is a gourd, or dried fruit, of a squash-like plant.

they too were dripping. Then he put the calabash on his head, as though to protect himself from a storm, and called out to the hornets: "Are you foolish people? Why do you stay in the rain that is falling?"

The hornets answered: "Where shall we go?"

"Go here, in this dry gourd," Anansi told them.

The hornets thanked him and flew into the gourd through the small hole. When the last of them had entered, Anansi plugged the hole with a ball of grass, saying: "Oh, yes, but you are really foolish people!"

He took his gourd full of hornets to Nyame, the Sky God. The Sky God accepted them. He said: "There are two more things."

Anansi returned to the forest and cut a long bamboo pole and some strong vines. Then he walked toward the house of Onini, the python, talking to himself. He said: "My wife is stupid. I say he is longer and stronger. My wife says he is shorter and weaker. I give him more respect. She gives him less respect. Is she right or am I right? I am right, he is longer. I am right, he is stronger."

When Onini, the python, heard Anansi talking to himself, he said: "Why are you arguing this way with yourself?"

The spider replied: "Ah, I have had a dispute with my wife. She says you are shorter and weaker than this bamboo pole. I say you are longer and stronger."

Onini said: "It's useless and silly to argue when you can find out the truth. Bring the pole and we will measure."

---

1. *Nyame* (en yä′ mä)

Vocabulary
dispute (dis pūt′) *n.* a difference of opinion; argument or quarrel

So Anansi laid the pole on the ground, and the python came and stretched himself out beside it.

"You seem a little short," Anansi said.

The python stretched further.

"A little more," Anansi said.

"I can stretch no more," Onini said.

"When you stretch at one end, you get shorter at the other end," Anansi said. "Let me tie you at the front so you don't slip."

He tied Onini's head to the pole. Then he went to the other end and tied the tail to the pole. He wrapped the vine all around Onini, until the python couldn't move.

"Onini," Anansi said, "it turns out that my wife was right and I was wrong. You are shorter than the pole and weaker. My opinion wasn't as good as my wife's. But you were even more foolish than I, and you are now my prisoner."

Anansi carried the python to Nyame, the Sky God, who said: "There is one thing more."

Osebo, the leopard, was next. Anansi went into the forest and dug a deep pit where the leopard was accustomed to walk. He covered it with small branches and leaves and put dust on it, so that it was impossible to tell where the pit was. Anansi went away and hid. When Osebo came prowling in the black of night, he stepped into the trap Anansi had prepared and fell to the bottom. Anansi heard the

Beaded stool with leopard design from Cameroon, Africa.
Viewing the artifact: This stool was intended for a king. Why might a leopard stool be appropriate for a king?

sound of the leopard falling, and he said: "Ah, Osebo, you are half-foolish!"

When morning came, Anansi went to the pit and saw the leopard there.

"Osebo," he asked, "what are you doing in this hole?"

"I have fallen into a trap," Osebo said. "Help me out."

"I would gladly help you," Anansi said. "But I'm sure that if I bring you out, I will have no thanks for it. You will get hungry,

Mask (Okorashi Oma). African (Nigeria, Southwestern Igbo). Wood and pigment, 10½ x 6¾ x 4 in. Harn Museum of Art Collection, University of Florida. Gift of Rod McGalliard. 1990.

Viewing the artifact: How might this mask reflect Anansi's attitude?

"Tie this to your tail," he said.

Osebo tied the rope to his tail.

"Is it well tied?" Anansi asked.

"Yes, it is well tied," the leopard said.

"In that case," Anansi said, "you are not merely half-foolish, you are all-foolish."

And he took his knife and cut the other rope, the one that held the tree bowed to the ground. The tree straightened up with a snap, pulling Osebo out of the hole. He hung in the air head downward, twisting and turning. And while he hung this way, Anansi killed him with his weapons.

Then he took the body of the leopard and carried it to Nyame, the Sky God, saying: "Here is the third thing. Now I have paid the price."

Nyame said to him: "Kwaku Anansi, great warriors and chiefs have tried, but they have been unable to do it. You have done it. Therefore, I will give you the stories. From this day onward, all stories belong to you. Whenever a man tells a story, he must acknowledge that it is Anansi's tale."

In this way Anansi, the spider, became the owner of all stories that are told. To Anansi all these tales belong.

and later on you will be wanting to eat me and my children."

"I swear it won't happen!" Osebo said.

"Very well. Since you swear it, I will take you out," Anansi said.

He bent a tall green tree toward the ground, so that its top was over the pit, and he tied it that way. Then he tied a rope to the top of the tree and dropped the other end of it into the pit.

Vocabulary
merely (mēr′ lē) *adv.* no more than; only

The End of the World

Jenny Leading Cloud

Somewhere, at a place where the prairie and the Mako Sica, the badlands, meet, there is a hidden cave. Not for many generations has anyone been able to find it. Even now, with so many cars and highways and tourists, no one has found this cave.

In the cave lives an old woman. She is so old that her face looks like a shriveled-up walnut. She is dressed in rawhide, the way people used to go around before the white people came to this country. She is sitting there—has been sitting there for a thousand years or more—working on a blanket strip for her buffalo robe. She is making that blanket strip out of dyed porcupine quills, the way our ancestors did before white traders brought glass beads to this turtle continent. Resting beside her, licking his paws, watching her all the time, is a Shunka Sapa, a huge black dog. His eyes never wander from the old woman whose teeth are worn flat, worn down to little stumps from using them to flatten numberless porcupine quills.

Vocabulary

badlands (bad' landz') *n.* a dry region that has numerous ridges and peaks cut by erosion, but little plant life; the Badlands is a region of South Dakota.

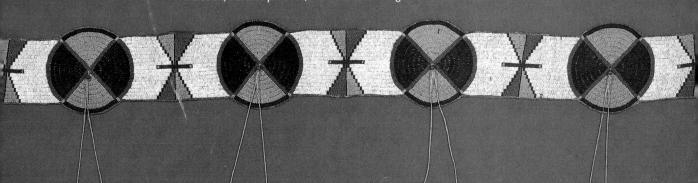

The End of the World

A few steps from where the old woman sits working on her blanket strip, a big fire is kept going. She lit this fire a thousand or more years ago and has kept it alive ever since. Over the fire hangs a big earthenware pot, the kind some Indian people used to make before the white man came with his kettles of iron. Inside the big pot, wojapi is boiling and bubbling. Wojapi is berry soup. It is good and sweet and red. That wojapi has been boiling in that pot for a long time, ever since the fire was lit.

Every now and then the old woman gets up to stir the wojapi in the huge earthenware pot. She is so old and <u>feeble</u> that it takes her a while to get up and hobble over to the fire. The moment the old woman's back is turned, the huge, black dog starts pulling out the porcupine quills from her blanket strip. This way, she never makes any progress, and her quillwork remains forever half finished. The Sioux people used to say that if the woman ever finished her blanket strip, in the very moment that she would thread the last porcupine quill to complete her design, the world would come to an end.

Vocabulary
feeble (fē′ bəl) *adj.* lacking physical strength; weak

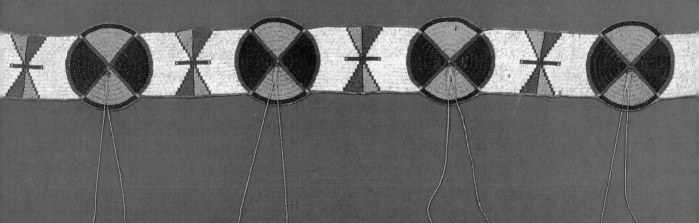

Responding to Literature

PERSONAL RESPONSE

Which story do you like best? Why? Is it the kind of story you thought you would like, based on the web you made for the **Focus Activity** on page 614.

Analyzing Literature

RECALL

1. In "All Stories Are Anansi's," how does Anansi capture the hornets, the python, and the leopard?
2. What risks does Anansi take to become the owner of all stories?
3. What tasks fill the days of the old woman in "The End of the World"?
4. What prevents the old woman from finishing her work?

INTERPRET

5. Why do you think Anansi is able to get the stories when so many others before him were not able to do so?
6. Why is it important to Anansi to own the stories?
7. Why do you think the storyteller presents the old woman doing ordinary tasks?
8. Why do you think no one can find the old woman's cave in "The End of the World"?

EVALUATE AND CONNECT

9. Theme Connection   Why do you think the people who first told the story of Anansi used a spider to represent a trickster character?
10. **Tone** shows an author's attitude toward the subject of a story. Does the tone of each story match what the story is about? Support your answer.

LITERARY ELEMENTS

Origin Tales

The earliest people must have looked at the untamed world around them and wondered, "How did this world come to be?" "What makes the sun rise each day?" They made up stories that explained what they saw, wondered about, or didn't understand. **Origin tales** are folktales that answer questions about how things began or how they came to be. Often the stories pass along a group's values and show how things fit together in the group's view of the plan of life.

1. What values does "The End of the World" teach?
2. What question might "All Stories Are Anansi's" answer?

● See **Literary Terms Handbook,** p. R3.

Literature and Writing

Writing About Literature

Preventing the End   Write a paragraph outlining the chain of causes and effects in "The End of the World" that allows the world to continue to exist. Then tell what fears and hopes this story addresses.

Creative Writing

Extra! Extra!   Write a headline and news story about Anansi's achievement. A good headline gives readers the idea of what happened while making them want to read the rest of the story. Then write a two-paragraph news story about Anansi's adventures. You may want to include a "news photo" or a diagram of where events took place. Share your article with a partner.

Extending Your Response

Literature Groups

Getting It Done   Examine Anansi's techniques of persuasion in the story. What does Anansi say and do to convince other characters to do what he wants? How does he "hook" his fellow creatures? List ideas and compare your group's ideas with those of other groups.

Performing

Choral Reading   In a small group, write a sentence, or **refrain,** that reminds readers of the message or an image from "The End of the World." Decide on a few places in the selection where the refrain will add feeling or drama. Then have one person read the story aloud while several others join in to read the refrain.

Art Activity

Make a Mural   The old woman in "The End of the World" is weaving a design in the blanket strip. In a small group, make a mural showing a design or scene that the old woman might weave that represents ongoing life.

Reading Further

If you liked these stories, you might enjoy these books:

The Hat-Shaking Dance, and Other Tales from the Gold Coast by Harold Courlander

The Cow-Tail Switch, and Other West African Stories by Harold Courlander

American Indian Myths and Legends collected and edited by Richard Erdoes and Alfonso Ortiz

Save your work for your portfolio.

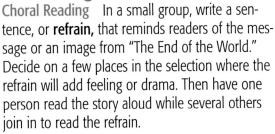

Skill Minilessons

GRAMMAR AND LANGUAGE • DOUBLING THE FINAL CONSONANT

The final letter in a word is sometimes doubled before a suffix is added. Double the consonant when the word ends in one consonant preceded by one vowel and when the word has an accent on the last syllable and the accent stays there after the suffix is added.

Examples: drip + ing = dri**pp**ing
re fer′ + ing = refe**rr**ing

PRACTICE Write the correct form of the following words.

1. offer + ing
2. plug + ed
3. wrap + ed
4. step + ed
5. bring + ing

● For more about adding suffixes, see **Language Handbook,** Spelling, p. R40–R41.

READING AND THINKING • VERIFYING PREDICTIONS

Did you expect Anansi to be able to "pay the price" for the stories from Nyame, the Sky God? Without even knowing it, you often make predictions about what will happen next as you read. **Predictions** are intelligent guesses based on clues authors provide in stories. You recall the clues and think ahead as you read. When you verify your predictions, you check to see whether your predictions were correct.

PRACTICE Write a logical prediction based on each sentence on the right. Then explain whether the prediction is verified by story events.

1. Even now, with so many cars and highways and tourists, no one has found this cave.
2. As the old woman works, the huge black dog's eyes never leave her.
3. Anansi questions how long the snake is and puts the pole on the ground next to the snake.

● For more about verifying predictions and other reading strategies, see **Reading Handbook,** pp. R63–R94.

VOCABULARY • COMPOUND WORDS

"The End of the World" says that an old woman lives in a cave where the prairie meets the badlands. The word *badlands* seems to say exactly what it means. Almost nothing grows there; it's rough; it's rocky. The *lands* are *bad.*

Many compound words make sense if you think about the meanings of the joined words. But don't try to figure out *butterfly* this way. It comes from an Old English word that names a yellow type of this insect–*buttorfleoge.*

PRACTICE Think about the words that form the compounds in the left column. Then match each one with its definition.

1. blockhead
2. faultfinder
3. cutback
4. bloodshed
5. mastermind

a. a reduction
b. violence that injures
c. a foolish person
d. a very smart person
e. someone who criticizes

Before You Read

Porcupine and the Sky Mirrors and *The Fly*

MEET
KATHERINE DAVISON

"Porcupine and the Sky Mirrors" is one of several tales that Katherine Davison retells in her book *Moon Magic: Stories from Asia.*

Katherine Davison was born in 1933. "Porcupine and the Sky Mirrors" was published in 1994.

MEET
MAI VO-DINH

"Like rural people every-where, the Vietnamese live close to animals, regarding them more often as friends and co-workers than as pets," writes Mai Vo-Dinh (mī vō′ dēn). Born in Hue, Vietnam, Mai Vo-Dinh came to the United States at twenty-seven. He is an artist and a writer.

Mai Vo-Dinh was born in 1933. "The Fly" was published in 1970.

FOCUS ACTIVITY

How important are manners or courtesy in getting along with others? When are you most likely to use your own best manners?

List Ideas
List six rules of manners that come to mind. Then share your list with a small group.

Setting a Purpose
Find out how important manners are in these stories.

BACKGROUND

The Time and Place
"Porcupine and the Sky Mirrors" is from Siberia. "The Fly" is from Vietnam (see map page 530).

Did You Know? People who borrow money must pay back the amount borrowed, plus a percentage of the amount of the loan, called interest. With a high rate of interest, this additional sum can be very large.

VOCABULARY PREVIEW

embrace (em brās′) *v.* to hug; p. 626
envious (en′ vē əs) *adj.* jealous; p. 627
confiscate (kon′ fis kāt′) *v.* to take away from a person or persons as a result of greater power or authority; p. 630
exasperated (ig zas′ pə rā′ tid) *adj.* angered or greatly annoyed; irritated; p. 631
alight (ə līt′) *v.* to come down after flight; land; p. 631
ensue (en sōō′) *v.* to come afterward or as a result; p. 631
insistence (in sis′ təns) *n.* the act of taking a stand and stick-ing strongly to it; determination; p. 632
insolent (in′ sə lənt) *adj.* boldly disrespectful; p. 632
majestic (mə jes′ tik) *adj.* impressive; grand; p. 632

Porcupine
and the
Sky Mirrors

Katherine Davison ~

Backdrop. G. Rigon. Private collection, Milan, Italy.

Long ago, when the world was new,
the people of Siberia knew that Porcupine was a wise little fellow
who could solve any problem. He was also a good neighbor and a
careful farmer.

Because Porcupine was so good-hearted and kind, he had a full
social life, as you can imagine. He was even a friend to the Sky
King, who lived above the clouds in his Sky House. One day,
Porcupine paid his friend a visit.

Porcupine and the Sky Mirrors

The Sky House was a splendid place. Its walls were slabs of sparkling ice, and ice bells tinkled cheerfully in every room. The blue floor was covered with fluffy, white rugs, and in the largest room, a great fire was always blazing. But the finest things of all were the two huge mirrors that stood on either side of the fire. One was made of gold and the other of silver, and they reflected the fire's light so brightly that it shone through the walls of ice and lighted the whole earth.

Did You Know?

A *samovar* (sam′ ə vär′) is a metal pot with a spigot and an internal heating tube. It's used to boil water for tea. In Russian, the word means "self-boiler."

Porcupine and the Sky King enjoyed themselves very much that afternoon. They drank hot, sweet tea poured from a shiny samovar. They ate a great many honey cakes and told funny stories. The king was a very amusing fellow when he could forget he was a king, and of course Porcupine was always good company.

At last, when it was time for Porcupine to go home, the Sky King said, "Friend Porcupine, take something with you so you will think of me and remember this wonderful visit." (It was very polite for a host to give something to his guests as they were leaving.)

"I don't need a gift to remember this enjoyable day," said Porcupine. "You've given me your fine hospitality, and that's enough. Save your gift."

The Sky King tugged at his long mustache and shook his head. "No, no, I insist!" he said firmly. "I want to give you something from the Sky House. It would be bad manners for you to refuse."

Porcupine said, "Well then, since I live a long way away, I'll take something to eat on the way home. Thank you."

The Sky King was pleased, and he gave Porcupine a leather bag full of delicious black bread. The king even walked part of the way home with him, to make the way seem shorter.

On the road, whom should they meet but the Earth King. "Hello, Brother," said the Sky King. "You're a long way from home today."

"I was just coming to visit you, Brother," said the Earth King, "but I got a late start. My goodness, how bright it is up here in the evening sky!"

"You see the light from my fire," answered the Sky King. Then he embraced his brother and said, "I'm delighted that you're here to visit me! Please stay for dinner! And perhaps my good friend Porcupine will come back and join us. It would be like a real party!"

Of course, Porcupine never liked to refuse a friend's request, and he could not resist the idea of a party, so the three of them went back through the cold northern sky to the Sky House.

When they got there, the Sky King laid out more good things to eat and drink. He built up the fire and set candles in every window until the northern lights flickered all over the sky. Everything was

---

Vocabulary

embrace (em brās′) *v.* to hug

so cheerful and beautiful that the Earth King became just a bit envious of his brother. His Earth House was a rather dark place, made of tree trunks and located in a gloomy forest.

In spite of this little stab of envy, the Earth King enjoyed himself very much. He sat beside the warm fire and feasted on tiny salted fish and rich red soup. He ate three kinds of black bread with two kinds of caviar[1] and four kinds of cheese. For dessert there were rosy apples and more honey cakes. He drank many glasses of hot tea and laughed at the funny stories told by Porcupine and the Sky King. He even told some stories of his own. But at the same time, he couldn't help wishing his house was as pretty and cheerful as his brother's.

The Sky King enjoyed the visit too, and when it was time for his guests to go home, he said, "Please take something to remember me by."

Porcupine answered, "No, nothing for me. I still have that nice black bread you gave me before."

"But you must have something more," said the Sky King. "I insist!"

So Porcupine took a little piece of goat's-milk cheese to go with the bread, and he promised to eat it on the way home.

Then the Sky King turned to the Earth King. "And you, Brother, what will you take to remember our visit?"

Now, all evening, as the Earth King admired the Sky House, the things he liked best of all were the shining mirrors on either side of the fire. More than anything else, the Earth King wanted those mirrors.

"Oh . . . I don't need a gift. Thank you, anyway," he said slowly, looking at the beautiful mirrors.

"But you must take something," the Sky King said. "I insist!"

"Well then, if I have to take something . . . give me those two mirrors. They will look very nice on each side of my own fireplace," said the Earth King.

"Oh," said the Sky King. "Oh, my goodness!"

He really didn't want to part with his sky mirrors. He had expected the Earth King to choose something small, the way Porcupine had done. But it would have been extremely bad manners to refuse, so very sadly he took down the mirrors and gave them to his brother.

The Earth King took the mirrors and went home. Porcupine went home too, but the Sky King didn't walk even a little part of the way with them. It took a long time to get home, because now that the Sky King had no sky mirrors to reflect the light of his fire onto the earth, it had become very dark, both in the sky and on the earth.

The next day, it was still dark, and the next day too. The Sky King sat by his fire feeling gloomy because his house seemed very dull without his sky mirrors. "Well, anyway, I did the right thing," the king said to himself. He said it several times, because it made him feel a little better to think about his good manners.

---

1. *Caviar* is fish eggs eaten as an appetizer; it is very expensive.

Vocabulary
envious (en′ vē əs) *adj.* jealous

Mask Child, 1944. Ian Paradine.

Viewing the painting: What might this sun and moon be saying to each other? Does anything about this painting remind you of the story?

On earth, Porcupine's farm was not doing well anymore, and all his neighbors' crops were dying too. "I'm worried about this," he thought to himself. "What if the world is never bright and warm again? The mirrors must be returned to the Sky House where they belong."

Porcupine considered the problem all day long, and the next day he went to pay a visit to his friend the Earth King. When Porcupine got to the Earth House, the Earth King was very glad to see him. "Sit down and have a glass of tea," he said. "How have you been, dear Porcupine?"

"Not as well as usual," Porcupine said truthfully. "It has been pretty dark at my house. Without the sky mirrors, I can no longer see the light of your brother's fire. And because there is no light, all the crops are dying."

The Earth King didn't like that answer. He pulled crossly on his mustache.

"Where are the mirrors, anyway?" asked Porcupine. "I thought you would have them standing by your fire."

"They are too beautiful to leave lying about. I put them away so nothing would happen to them," said the Earth King. (Really, he was afraid that his brother might come and take the mirrors back, so he had hidden them.)

Porcupine looked all around, but he couldn't see the mirrors anywhere.

The Earth King made tea in his big samovar, and he got out some honey cakes. The food was good, but somehow the stories they told each other didn't seem very funny, and the visit was a little sad. To tell the truth, the Earth King felt very sorry that the earth was now so dark and cold, but he couldn't bear to give back those beautiful mirrors.

When it was time for Porcupine to go, the Earth King said politely, "Please take something with you so that you will remember our visit."

"Oh no, nothing," said Porcupine.

"But I insist you take something. Perhaps some nice bread and cheese?"

"No, thank you," said Porcupine slowly. Then, just as he was speaking, he noticed something that gave him a wonderful idea. "But since you insist," Porcupine continued slowly, "I will ask you for a mirage[2]—one of those images in the air that look real, such as a lake in the middle of the desert. May I have one of those?"

The Earth King was surprised and unhappy at this request. "But a mirage is just a reflection of light on the air," he said. "I can't give you that!"

"Well, never mind," said Porcupine, pretending to be disappointed. "You have plenty of echoes in the Earth House. Will you give me an echo instead?"

The Earth King tugged on his mustache so hard that he had to stop very suddenly because he hurt himself. It was terrible manners to refuse something to a guest, but how could he give Porcupine an echo to take with him? "An echo is only a reflection of a sound," he said. "I just can't give you an echo, Porcupine! Ask me for something I can really give to you! Ask me for anything in my house, and it will be yours!"

Porcupine shrugged his shoulders and looked sad. But he was really very happy, because several minutes before, his sharp eyes had noticed something interesting. Beside the front door stood a large, old box. Under the lid, Porcupine could see a tiny sparkle of light. He had guessed that the sky mirrors were in that box, and now that the Earth King had refused him twice, he certainly could not refuse his third request!

"Well then," said Porcupine, "I guess I'll just take whatever is in that old box there—since I must take something."

The Earth King was furious! He pulled on his mustache so hard his eyes watered. How did Porcupine know the mirrors were in that box? The Earth King didn't want to give them back, but he couldn't refuse Porcupine a third time.

"I have good manners! I have very good manners!" he said, chewing on his mustache, his eyes watering terribly. He lifted the box and handed it to Porcupine. "Here, take it!" He tried to sound generous, but he slammed the door when Porcupine went out, and he did not offer to walk him any part of the way home.

Porcupine didn't go home, anyway. He ran all the way to the Sky House with the box in his arms. He was out of breath when he gave it to the Sky King, saying, "I have brought you (puff-puff) a present (puff-puff), old friend!"

When the Sky King opened the box and saw the mirrors, he was so happy he forgot his manners and didn't even remember to say, "Thank you."

He ran and set the mirrors beside his fire, and at once the firelight flashed all through the Sky House and down over the earth. Only then did the Sky King turn to Porcupine and say, "I thank you, old friend!"

If you look into the sky, you can see that the mirrors stand there still. The gold mirror is the warmest, and we call it the sun. The silver mirror is the moon that lights the night. If you go to the Sky House, you can see them there now.

---

2. A *mirage* (mi räzh') is an optical illusion caused by the bending of light rays through different layers of air.

The Fly

Mai Vo-Dinh

Everyone in the village knew the usurer, a rich and smart man. Having accumulated a fortune over the years, he settled down to a life of leisure in his big house surrounded by an immense garden and guarded by a pack of ferocious dogs.

But still unsatisfied with what he had acquired, the man went on making money by lending it to people all over the county at exorbitant[1] rates. The usurer reigned supreme in the area, for numerous were those who were in debt to him.

One day, the rich man set out for the house of one of his peasants. Despite repeated reminders, the poor laborer just could not manage to pay off his long-standing debt. Working himself to a shadow, the peasant barely succeeded in making ends meet. The moneylender was therefore determined that if he could not get his money back this time, he would

proceed to <u>confiscate</u> some of his debtor's most valuable belongings. But the rich man found no one at the peasant's house but a small boy of eight or nine playing alone in the dirt yard.

"Child, are your parents home?" the rich man asked.

"No, sir," the boy replied, then went on playing with his sticks and stones, paying no attention whatever to the man.

"Then, where are they?" the rich man asked, somewhat irritated, but the little boy went on playing and did not answer.

When the rich man repeated his query, the boy looked up and answered, with deliberate slowness, "Well, sir, my father has gone to cut living trees and plant dead ones and my mother is at the market place selling the wind and buying the moon."

---

1. A *usurer* (ū′ zhər ər) is someone who lends money, especially at a high interest rate. This man's *exorbitant* rates are beyond what is proper, reasonable, or usual.

Vocabulary
confiscate (kon′ fis kāt′) *v.* to take away from a person or persons as a result of greater power or authority

"What? What in heaven are you talking about?" the rich man commanded. "Quick, tell me where they are, or you will see what this stick can do to you!" The bamboo walking stick in the big man's hand looked indeed menacing.

After repeated questioning, however, the boy only gave the same reply. Exasperated, the rich man told him, "All right, little devil, listen to me! I came here today to take the money your parents owe me. But if you tell me where they really are and what they are doing, I will forget all about the debt. Is that clear to you?"

"Oh, sir, why are you joking with a poor little boy? Do you expect me to believe what you are saying?" For the first time the boy looked interested.

"Well, there is heaven and there is earth to witness my promise," the rich man said, pointing up to the sky and down to the ground.

But the boy only laughed. "Sir, heaven and earth cannot talk and therefore cannot testify. I want some living thing to be our witness."

Catching sight of a fly alighting on a bamboo pole nearby, and laughing inside because he was fooling the boy, the rich man proposed, "There is a fly. He can be our witness. Now, hurry and tell me what you mean when you say that your father is out cutting living trees and planting dead ones, while your mother is at the market selling the wind and buying the moon."

Looking at the fly on the pole, the boy said, "A fly is a good enough witness for me. Well, here it is, sir. My father has simply gone to cut down bamboos and make a fence with them for a man near the river. And my mother . . . oh, sir, you'll keep your promise, won't you? You will free my parents of all their debts? You really mean it?"

"Yes, yes, I do solemnly swear in front of this fly here." The rich man urged the boy to go on.

"Well, my mother, she has gone to the market to sell fans so she can buy oil for our lamps. Isn't that what you would call selling the wind to buy the moon?"

Shaking his head, the rich man had to admit inwardly that the boy was a clever one. However, he thought, the little genius still had much to learn, believing as he did that a fly could be a witness for anybody. Bidding the boy good-by, the man told him that he would soon return to make good his promise.

A few days had passed when the moneylender returned. This time he found the poor peasant couple at home, for it was late in the evening. A nasty scene ensued, the rich man claiming his money and the poor peasant apologizing and begging for another delay. Their argument awakened the little boy who ran to his father and told him, "Father, father, you don't have to pay your debt. This gentleman here has promised me that he would forget all about the money you owe him."

Vocabulary

exasperated (ig zas′ pə rā′ tid) *adj.* angered or greatly annoyed; irritated

alight (ə līt′) *v.* to come down after flight; land

ensue (en soo′) *v.* to come afterward or as a result

The Fly

"Nonsense," the rich man shook his walking stick at both father and son. "Nonsense, are you going to stand there and listen to a child's inventions? I never spoke a word to this boy. Now, tell me, are you going to pay or are you not?"

The whole affair ended by being brought before the mandarin[2] who governed the county. Not knowing what to believe, all the poor peasant and his wife could do was to bring their son with them when they went to court. The little boy's insistence about the rich man's promise was their only encouragement.

The mandarin began by asking the boy to relate exactly what had happened between himself and the moneylender. Happily, the boy hastened to tell about the explanations he gave the rich man in exchange for the debt.

"Well," the mandarin said to the boy, "if this man here has indeed made such a promise, we have only your word for it. How do we know that you have not invented the whole story yourself? In a case such as this, you need a witness to confirm it, and you have none." The boy remained calm and declared that naturally there was a witness to their conversation.

"Who is that, child?" the mandarin asked.

"A fly, Your Honor."

"A fly? What do you mean, a fly? Watch out, young man, fantasies are not to be tolerated in this place!" The mandarin's benevolent[3] face suddenly became stern.

"Yes, Your Honor, a fly. A fly which was alighting on this gentleman's nose!" The boy leapt from his seat.

"Insolent little devil, that's a pack of lies!" The rich man roared indignantly,[4] his face like a ripe tomato. "The fly was *not* on my nose; *he was on the housepole* . . ." But he stopped dead. It was, however, too late.

The majestic mandarin himself could not help bursting out laughing. Then the audience burst out laughing. The boy's parents too, although timidly, laughed. And the boy, and the rich man himself, also laughed. With one hand on his stomach, the mandarin waved the other hand toward the rich man:

"Now, now, that's all settled. You have indeed made your promises, dear sir, to the child. *Housepole or no housepole, your conversation did happen after all!* The court says you must keep your promise."

And still chuckling, he dismissed all parties.

---

2. When China was ruled by emperors, a high public official was called a *mandarin* (man' dər in).

3. *Benevolent* (bə nev' ə lənt) means "kindly and generous."
4. An *indignant* person is angry in response to meanness or injustice.

Vocabulary

insistence (in sis' təns) *n.* the act of taking a stand and sticking strongly to it; determination
insolent (in' sə lənt) *adj.* boldly disrespectful
majestic (mə jes' tik) *adj.* impressive; grand

Responding to Literature

PERSONAL RESPONSE

- ◆ Which story gives you a greater feeling of satisfaction? Why?
- ◆ Are the manners you listed in the **Focus Activity** on page 624 shown in the stories? Explain.

Analyzing Literature

RECALL

1. What happens when the Earth King visits the Sky King one day? What gift is given?
2. What does Porcupine accomplish when he later visits the Earth King? How does he do it?
3. Why does the rich man want to know where the boy's parents are in "The Fly"?
4. What does the rich man promise the boy? Who is the witness?

INTERPRET

5. Is the Sky King comfortable about the gift he gives his brother? Why or why not?
6. Why is it important for the animals in the forest that Porcupine accomplish his goal at the Earth King's house? Explain.
7. Why does the boy tell a riddle rather than explaining where his parents are?
8. How does the mandarin learn the truth about the rich man's promise?

EVALUATE AND CONNECT

9. Theme Connection   Why is **dialogue** important in the telling of these stories?
10. Do you wish you could meet a character in one of these stories? Which one? Why?

LITERARY ELEMENTS

Conflict

When one person goes against what others want, **conflict** is the natural result. In folktales, the conflict often surrounds an event that is unjust or unfair. The conflict is resolved by righting the wrong. A feeling of harmony is then restored. Sometimes good characters are rewarded, and bad characters are punished.

1. What is the conflict in "Porcupine and the Sky Mirrors"?

2. In "The Fly," what injustice is made right?

● See **Literary Terms Handbook**, p. R2.

A balance scale, symbol of justice, and a judge's gavel.

Literature and Writing

Writing About Literature

Riddles Reread the boy's riddle in "The Fly." Notice that while the riddle is true, it doesn't actually reveal information to the usurer. Using the boy's style, write a riddle that sums up the outcome of the case before the mandarin.

Creative Writing

When We Meet Again Will the Earth King try to get the mirrors back? Will the Sky King head off the problem? Will the Porcupine help? Write a few paragraphs describing what could happen the next time the two kings meet.

Extending Your Response

Performing

The Song Tells the Story With a partner, write song lyrics that tell the story of the sky mirrors or "The Fly." In the chorus, repeat the message or the most memorable part of the story. Make a tape-recording of your performance and play your song for the class.

*inter*NET CONNECTION

An *eclipse* is the apparent darkening of the sun or the moon as it passes through the shadow of the other or of the earth. View photographs of solar and lunar eclipses by browsing under *eclipse.*

Literature Groups

Folktale Characters The characters in folktales are often simple and one-dimensional. Each may have one main quality, such as foolishness. Also, most characters are either good or bad, or their actions are good or bad. For these stories, list which characters are good and which are bad. Then list one main quality for each.

Learning for Life

Petition Legally, to whom do the sky mirrors belong? Write a petition—a complaint and request for government action—as if you were the Earth King.

Reading Further

If you enjoyed these stories, try these books:

Moon Magic: Stories from Asia by Katherine Davison

The Toad Is the Emperor's Uncle by Mai Vo-Dinh

Save your work for your portfolio.

Skill Minilessons

GRAMMAR AND LANGUAGE • TROUBLESOME PAIRS

In the land where the Sky King, the Earth King, and Porcupine live, courtesy requires that a guest **choose** something before leaving. The Earth King **chose** the sky mirrors. *Choose* means "to select," while *chose* is the past-tense of *choose* and means "selected." The guest will then **accept** the gift, thanking the host. The Earth King shows good manners, **except** when he slams the door. To *accept* means "to receive," while *except* means "other than."

PRACTICE Select *choose* or *chose* for sentences 1–5. Select *accept* or *except* for sentences 6–10.

1. Which color will you _____ for your jacket?
2. The group _____ a new president.
3. I think I _____ the wrong assignment.
4. She won't _____ between her friends.
5. I may _____ not to go by myself.
6. The teacher won't _____ a torn paper.
7. Everyone came _____ the new student.
8. I brought snacks for everyone _____ Tom.
9. He had to _____ the way it turned out.
10. _____ for the rain, we had a great time!

● For more about troublesome pairs, see **Language Handbook,** p. R19–R23.

READING AND THINKING • IDENTIFYING FAULTY REASONING

Many characters in folktales are over-generalized and over-simplified–they are **stereotypes.** A stereotype is one general example that stands for a whole group. For example, in "The Fly" the usurer is an over-simplified picture of a rich man. Other common stereotypes are the mad scientist, the absent-minded professor, the beautiful princess, and the proud king. Stereotypes are avoided in most fiction, but they are useful in folktales for teaching lessons about life. In real life, thinking about people in terms of stereotypes and ignoring their individual differences is unfair.

PRACTICE Write a paragraph that explains how the usurer in "The Fly" could be considered a stereotype of a rich man.

● For more about reasoning, see **Reading Handbook,** p. R88.

VOCABULARY • THE SUFFIX -ic

When a word part is added to the end of a whole word that is familiar to you, you can often figure out what the new word means. The suffix *-ic* is often added to a whole word. A *majestic* person is one who has *majesty.* Sometimes *-atic* is added instead of just *-ic.* A *systematic* way of doing things uses a *system.*

PRACTICE Write the base word from which each of the following words was formed. Remember, the suffix may be *-ic* or *-atic,* and a vowel at the end of the base word may have been dropped.

  a. oceanic   f. comedic
  b. scenic   g. fanatic
  c. meteoric   h. angelic
  d. operatic   i. photographic
  e. climatic   j. problematic

● For more about adding suffixes, see **Language Handbook,** Spelling, p. R40.

Vo·cab·u·lar·y *Skills*

Using Dictionary Respellings

You can't always pronounce words correctly by just looking at how they are spelled. Some consonants and all vowels can be pronounced in different ways. Some letters are not pronounced at all: they are "silent." Dictionaries show how to pronounce a word with special letter symbols that stand for sounds.

In a **dictionary respelling,** *catch* appears like this: kach. *Gym* appears like this: jim. A vowel without any mark above it has its normal "short" sound, as in *pat, pet, pit, hot,* and *hut.* Other vowel sounds are shown by placing a mark above the vowel. For example, a straight line above a vowel shows that it is "long," such as the *a* in *crater.* (A long vowel "says its own name.")

In words of more than one syllable, space appears between the syllables, and accent marks (′) point to syllables spoken with extra stress, or emphasis.

● For more about using the dictionary, see **Reading Handbook,** p. R65.

symbol	meaning
ä	an **ah** sound, as in **father**
ô	an **aw** sound, as in **law**
oo	the vowel sound in **wood**
o͞o	the vowel sound in **fool**
oi	the vowel sound in **toy**
ou	an **ow** sound, as in **cow**
ə	the vowel sound at the end of **pencil, lemon, taken**
hw	**wh** as in white
th	**th** as in **thin**
<u>th</u>	**th** as in **this**
zh	the sound in the middle of **treasure** or at the end of **garage**

EXERCISES

◆ Use the pronunciation given for each word to answer the question that follows it.
1. *embrace* (em brās′) Does the second syllable rhyme with *pace* or *pass?*
2. *merely* (mēr′ lē) Does this word rhyme with *dearly, curly,* or *cheerily?*
3. *mirage* (mi räzh′) Does the *g* sound like the *g* in *package* or *garage?*

◆ Decide which word is represented by each dictionary pronunciation.
4. (di zurt′)	**a.** dessert	**b.** desert
5. (skat′ ər)	**a.** skater	**b.** scatter
6. (tôst)	**a.** tossed	**b.** toast
7. (od′ ər)	**a.** odor	**b.** odder
8. (bi lō′)	**a.** bellow	**b.** below
9. (ā′ jing)	**a.** again	**b.** aging
10. (found)	**a.** found	**b.** fond

GRAMMAR LINK

Avoiding Run-on Sentences

A **run-on sentence** is one that keeps going without pausing or stopping when it should. You can tell if a sentence has this problem by paying attention to main clauses. A **main clause** has a subject and a verb and can function as a sentence.

PROBLEM	SOLUTION
Two main clauses with no punctuation between them: *The mirrors reflect fire the reflection warms Earth.*	Separate the clauses into two sentences. *The mirrors reflect fire. The reflection warms Earth.* Separate the clauses with a comma and a coordinating conjunction. *The mirrors reflect fire, and the reflection warms Earth.* Separate closely related clauses with a semicolon. *The mirrors reflect fire; the reflection warms Earth.*
Main clauses joined by only a conjunction: *He gave away his mirrors but this made him sad.*	Add a comma before the conjunction. *He gave away his mirrors, but this made him sad.*

● For more about run-on sentences, see **Language Handbook,** p. R11.

EXERCISE

Write *C* if the sentence is correct. Write *R* if it is a run-on sentence, and rewrite the sentence to correct it.

1. The rich man wanted his money but the peasant couldn't pay it.

2. The rich man went to the peasant's house only a small boy was at home.

3. The rich man was looking for the boy's parents, the boy answered with a riddle.

4. The answer made no sense to the rich man, and he became angry.

5. The rich man made a promise to the boy and then the boy explained the riddle.

COMIC STRIP

Dragons appear in legends from the Viking age (around A.D. 700–1000) and in the comic strip about Vikings, *Hägar the Horrible*. Hägar himself has never slain a dragon and is not likely to do so.

Respond

1. How do Hägar and his friend escape the dragon?

2. Is this how dragon slayers are supposed to behave?

Before You Read
Dragon, Dragon

MEET JOHN GARDNER

"The house was full of books," John Gardner remembered of his childhood home. His mother, a former English teacher, and father, a farmer, loved to read aloud at home and at community gatherings. Gardner credited the Bible, Charles Dickens, and Walt Disney as important influences on his taste in literature as he grew up. As an adult, he became an expert on literature from the Middle Ages, and he used this knowledge in his fairy tales.

John Gardner was born in 1933 and died in 1982. This story was published in 1975 in Dragon, Dragon, and Other Timeless Tales.

FOCUS ACTIVITY

What do you know about fairy tale dragons?

Roundtable

Pass a piece of paper around a small group and list as many stories, movies, plays, songs, and video games with a dragon as you can. Then discuss how these dragons look and act.

Setting a Purpose

Read to enjoy a tale of a troublesome dragon.

BACKGROUND

The Time and Place The story takes place in an imaginary kingdom long, long ago.

Did You Know? In his book *Dragons: Truth, Myth, and Legend,* historian David Passes explains that dragon "sightings" were quite common several hundred years ago. He says, "Ordinary people saw them; so did kings, knights, archbishops, and monks." Today, scientists believe that dragons never existed.

An iguana.

VOCABULARY PREVIEW

ravage (rav′ ij) *v.* to destroy violently; ruin; p. 640
convenient (kən vēn′ yənt) *adj.* favorable to one's needs or purposes; providing advantage; p. 643
timidly (tim′ id lē) *adv.* lacking courage; shyly; p. 643
quest (kwest) *n.* a search; pursuit; p. 643
meekly (mēk′ lē) *adv.* in a patient and mild manner; gently; p. 643
lunge (lunj) *v.* to make a sudden forward movement; charge; p. 644
decent (dē′ sənt) *adj.* courteous, proper; p. 645

Dragon, Dragon

John Gardner

There was once a king whose kingdom was plagued[1] by a dragon. The king did not know which way to turn. The king's knights were all cowards who hid under their beds whenever the dragon came in sight, so they were of no use to the king at all. And the king's

wizard could not help either because, being old, he had forgotten his magic spells. Nor could the wizard look up the spells that had slipped his mind, for he had unfortunately misplaced his wizard's book many years before. The king was at his wit's end.

Every time there was a full moon the dragon came out of his lair and ravaged

---

1. *Plagued* means "greatly troubled or afflicted."

Vocabulary
ravage (rav′ ij) *v.* to destroy violently; ruin

St. George and the Dragon, 1456. Paolo Uccello. Oil on canvas, 57 x 73 in. National Gallery, London.

the countryside. He frightened maidens and stopped up chimneys and broke store windows and set people's clocks back and made dogs bark until no one could hear himself think.

He tipped over fences and robbed graves and put frogs in people's drinking water and tore the last chapters out of novels and changed house numbers around so that people crawled into bed with their neighbors' wives.

He stole spark plugs out of people's cars and put firecrackers in people's cigars and stole the clappers from all the church bells and sprung every bear trap for miles around so the bears could wander wherever they pleased.

And to top it all off, he changed around all the roads in the kingdom so that people could not get anywhere except by starting out in the wrong direction.

"That," said the king in a fury, "is enough!" And he called a meeting of everyone in the kingdom.

Now it happened that there lived in the kingdom a wise old cobbler who had a wife and three sons. The cobbler and his family came to the king's meeting and stood way in back by the door, for the cobbler had a feeling that since he was nobody important there had probably been some mistake, and no doubt the king had intended the meeting for everyone in the kingdom except his family and him.

"Ladies and gentlemen," said the king when everyone was present. "I've put up with that dragon as long as I can. He has got to be stopped."

All the people whispered amongst themselves, and the king smiled, pleased with the impression he had made.

But the wise cobbler said gloomily, "It's all very well to talk about it—but how are you going to do it?"

And now all the people smiled and winked as if to say, "Well, King, he's got you there!"

The king frowned.

"It's not that His Majesty hasn't tried," the queen spoke up loyally.

"Yes," said the king, "I've told my knights again and again that they ought to slay that dragon. But I can't *force* them to go. I'm not a tyrant."[2]

"Why doesn't the wizard say a magic spell?" asked the cobbler.

"He's done the best he can," said the king.

The wizard blushed and everyone looked embarrassed. "I used to do all sorts of spells and chants when I was younger," the wizard explained. "But I've lost my spell book, and I begin to fear I'm losing my memory too. For instance, I've been trying for days to recall one spell I used to do. I forget, just now, what the deuce[3] it was for. It went something like—

> Bimble
> Wimble
> Cha, Cha
> CHOOMPF!

Suddenly, to everyone's surprise, the queen turned into a rosebush.

"Oh dear," said the wizard.

"Now you've done it," groaned the king.

"Poor Mother," said the princess.

"I don't know what can have happened," the wizard said nervously, "but don't worry, I'll have her changed back in a jiffy." He shut his eyes and racked his brain for a spell that would change her back.

But the king said quickly, "You'd better leave well enough alone. If you change her into a rattlesnake we'll have to chop off her head."

Meanwhile the cobbler stood with his hands in his pockets, sighing at the waste of time. "About the dragon . . ." he began.

"Oh yes," said the king. "I'll tell you what I'll do. I'll give the princess' hand in marriage to anyone who can make the dragon stop."

"It's not enough," said the cobbler. "She's a nice enough girl, you understand. But how would an ordinary person support

---

2. A *tyrant* is a cruel, unjust ruler.

3. *What the deuce* (do͞os) is a questioning expression similar to "what on earth."

her? Also, what about those of us that are already married?"

"In that case," said the king, "I'll offer the princess' hand or half the kingdom or both—whichever is most convenient."

The cobbler scratched his chin and considered it. "It's not enough," he said at last. "It's a good enough kingdom, you understand, but it's too much responsibility."

"Take it or leave it," the king said.

"I'll leave it," said the cobbler. And he shrugged and went home.

But the cobbler's eldest son thought the bargain was a good one, for the princess was very beautiful and he liked the idea of having half the kingdom to run as he pleased. So he said to the king, "I'll accept those terms, Your Majesty. By tomorrow morning the dragon will be slain."

"Bless you!" cried the king.

"Hooray, hooray, hooray!" cried all the people, throwing their hats in the air.

The cobbler's eldest son beamed with pride, and the second eldest son looked at him enviously. The youngest son said timidly, "Excuse me, Your Majesty, but don't you think the queen looks a little unwell? If I were you I think I'd water her."

"Good heavens," cried the king, glancing at the queen who had been changed into a rosebush, "I'm glad you mentioned it!"

Now the cobbler's eldest son was very clever and was known far and wide for how quickly he could multiply fractions in his head. He was perfectly sure

he could slay the dragon by somehow or other playing a trick on him, and he didn't feel that he needed his wise old father's advice. But he thought it was only polite to ask, and so he went to his father, who was working as usual at his cobbler's bench, and said, "Well, Father, I'm off to slay the dragon. Have you any advice to give me?"

The cobbler thought a moment and replied, "When and if you come to the dragon's lair, recite the following poem.

Dragon, dragon, how do you do?
I've come from the king to murder you.

Say it very loudly and firmly and the dragon will fall, God willing, at your feet."

"How curious!" said the eldest son. And he thought to himself, "The old man is not as wise as I thought. If I say something like that to the dragon, he will eat me up in an instant. The way to kill a dragon is to outfox him." And keeping his opinion to himself, the eldest son set forth on his quest.

When he came at last to the dragon's lair, which was a cave, the eldest son slyly disguised himself as a peddler and knocked on the door and called out, "Hello there!"

"There's nobody home!" roared a voice.

The voice was as loud as an earthquake, and the eldest son's knees knocked together in terror.

"I don't come to trouble you," the eldest son said meekly. "I merely thought you might be interested in looking at some of our brushes. Or if you'd prefer,"

Vocabulary

convenient (kən vēn′ yənt) *adj.* favorable to one's needs or purposes; providing advantage
timidly (tim′ id lē) *adv.* lacking courage; shyly
quest (kwest) *n.* a search; pursuit
meekly (mēk′ lē) *adv.* in a patient and mild manner; gently

he added quickly, "I could leave our catalog with you and I could drop by again, say, early next week."

"I don't want any brushes," the voice roared, "and I especially don't want any brushes next week."

"Oh," said the eldest son. By now his knees were knocking together so badly that he had to sit down.

Suddenly a great shadow fell over him, and the eldest son looked up. It was the dragon. The eldest son drew his sword, but the dragon lunged and swallowed him in a single gulp, sword and all, and the eldest son found himself in the dark of the dragon's belly. "What a fool I was not to listen to my wise old father!" thought the eldest son. And he began to weep bitterly.

"Well," sighed the king the next morning, "I see the dragon has not been slain yet."

"I'm just as glad, personally," said the princess, sprinkling the queen. "I would have had to marry that eldest son, and he had warts."

Now the cobbler's middle son decided it was his turn to try. The middle son was very strong and was known far and wide for being able to lift up the corner of a church. He felt perfectly sure he could slay the dragon by simply laying into him, but he thought it would be only polite to ask his father's advice. So he went to his father and said to him, "Well, Father, I'm off to slay the dragon. Have you any advice for me?"

The cobbler told the middle son exactly what he'd told the eldest.

"When and if you come to the dragon's lair, recite the following poem.

Dragon, dragon, how do you do?
I've come from the king to murder you.

Say it very loudly and firmly, and the dragon will fall, God willing, at your feet."

"What an odd thing to say," thought the middle son. "The old man is not as wise as I thought. You have to take these dragons by surprise." But he kept his opinion to himself and set forth.

When he came in sight of the dragon's lair, the middle son spurred his horse to a gallop and thundered into the entrance swinging his sword with all his might.

But the dragon had seen him while he was still a long way off, and being very clever, the dragon had crawled up on top of the door so that when the son came charging in he went under the dragon and on to the back of the cave and slammed into the wall. Then the dragon chuckled and got down off the door, taking his time, and strolled back to where the man and the horse lay unconscious from the terrific blow. Opening his mouth as if for a yawn, the dragon swallowed the middle son in a single gulp and put the horse in the freezer to eat another day.

"What a fool I was not to listen to my wise old father," thought the middle son when he came to in the dragon's belly. And he too began to weep bitterly.

That night there was a full moon, and the dragon ravaged the countryside so

---

Vocabulary

lunge (lunj) *v.* to make a sudden forward movement; charge

Saint Georges, 1460. Andrea Mantegna. Oil on canvas. Galleria Dell' Academia, Venice, Italy.

Viewing the painting: Which of the cobbler's sons does this young knight resemble? Why?

terribly that several families moved to another kingdom.

"Well," sighed the king in the morning, "still no luck in this dragon business, I see."

"I'm just as glad, myself," said the princess, moving her mother, pot and all, to the window where the sun could get at her. "The cobbler's middle son was a kind of humpback."

Now the cobbler's youngest son saw that his turn had come. He was very upset and nervous, and he wished he had never been born. He was not clever, like his eldest brother, and he was not strong, like his second-eldest brother. He was a decent, honest boy who always minded his elders.

He borrowed a suit of armor from a friend of his who was a knight, and when the youngest son put the armor on it was so heavy he could hardly walk. From another knight he borrowed a sword, and that was so heavy that the only way the youngest son could get it to the dragon's lair was to drag it along behind his horse like a plow.

When everything was in readiness, the youngest son went for a last conversation with his father.

"Father, have you any advice to give me?" he asked.

"Only this," said the cobbler. "When and if you come to the dragon's lair, recite the following poem.

Vocabulary
decent (dē′ sənt) *adj.* courteous, proper

Mont St. Michel, 15th century. Limbourg Brothers. From *Tres Riches Heures du Duc de Berry.* MS 65/1284. Fol. 195r. Musée Condé, Chantilly, France.

Viewing the art: Why is the dragon able to fly? Why is Saint Michael?

dale and at last came to the dragon's cave.

The dragon, who had seen the cobbler's youngest son while he was still a long way off, was seated up above the door, inside the cave, waiting and smiling to himself. But minutes passed and no one came thundering in. The dragon frowned, puzzled, and was tempted to peek out. However, reflecting that patience seldom goes unrewarded, the dragon kept his head up out of sight and went on waiting. At last, when he could stand it no longer, the dragon craned his neck and looked. There at the entrance of the cave stood a trembling young man in a suit of armor twice his size, struggling with a sword so heavy he could lift only one end of it at a time.

At sight of the dragon, the cobbler's youngest son began to tremble so violently that his armor rattled like a house caving in. He heaved with all his might at the sword and got the handle up level with his chest, but even now the point was down in the dirt. As loudly and firmly as he could manage, the youngest son cried—

> *Dragon, dragon, how do you do?*
> *I've come from the king to murder you.*

"What?" cried the dragon, flabbergasted. "You? *You?* Murder *Me???*" All at once he began to laugh, pointing at the little

> *Dragon, dragon, how do you do?*
> *I've come from the king to murder you.*

Say it very loudly and firmly, and the dragon will fall, God willing, at your feet."

"Are you certain?" asked the youngest son uneasily.

"As certain as one can ever be in these matters," said the wise old cobbler.

And so the youngest son set forth on his quest. He traveled over hill and cobbler's son. "*He he he ho ha!*" he roared, shaking all over, and tears filled his eyes. "*He he he ho ho ho ha ha!*" laughed the dragon. He was laughing so hard he had to hang onto his sides, and he fell off the door and landed on his back, still laughing, kicking his legs helplessly, rolling from side to side, laughing and laughing and laughing.

The cobbler's son was annoyed. "I *do* come from the king to murder you," he said. "A person doesn't like to be laughed at for a thing like that."

"*He he he!*" wailed the dragon, almost sobbing, gasping for breath. "Of course not, poor dear boy! But really, *he he*, the *idea* of it, *ha ha ha!* And that simply r*idiculous poem!*" Tears streamed from the dragon's eyes and he lay on his back perfectly helpless with laughter.

"It's a good poem," said the cobbler's youngest son loyally. "My father made it up." And growing angrier he shouted, "I want you to stop that laughing, or I'll— I'll—" But the dragon could not stop for the life of him. And suddenly, in a terrific rage, the cobbler's son began flopping the sword end over end in the direction of the dragon. Sweat ran off the youngest son's forehead, but he labored on, blistering mad, and at last, with one supreme heave, he had the sword standing on its handle a foot from the dragon's throat. Of its own weight the sword fell, slicing the dragon's head off.

"*He he ho huk*," went the dragon—and then he lay dead.

The two older brothers crawled out and thanked their younger brother for saving their lives. "We have learned our lesson," they said.

Then the three brothers gathered all the treasures from the dragon's cave and tied them to the back end of the youngest brother's horse, and tied the dragon's head on behind the treasures, and started home. "I'm glad I listened to my father," the youngest son thought. "Now I'll be the richest man in the kingdom."

There were hand-carved picture frames and silver spoons and boxes of jewels and chests of money and silver compasses and maps telling where there were more treasures buried when these ran out. There was also a curious old book with a picture of an owl on the cover, and inside, poems and odd sentences and recipes that seemed to make no sense.

When they reached the king's castle the people all leaped for joy to see that the dragon was dead, and the princess ran out and kissed the youngest brother on the forehead, for secretly she had hoped it would be him.

"Well," said the king, "which half of the kingdom do you want?"

"My wizard's book!" exclaimed the wizard. "He's found my wizard's book!" He opened the book and ran his finger under the words and then said in a loud voice, "Glmuzk, shkzmlp, blam!"

Instantly the queen stood before them in her natural shape, except she was soaking wet from being sprinkled too often. She glared at the king.

"Oh dear," said the king, hurrying toward the door.

❖

Responding to Literature

PERSONAL RESPONSE

- ◆ Do you find the story funny? What parts of the story are funniest?
- ◆ Is this dragon like any others you know about? Use ideas from the discussion for the **Focus Activity** on page 639.

Analyzing Literature

RECALL

1. What are some of the problems the people in the kingdom are having?
2. Why can't the wizard get rid of the dragon? What does the wizard do by accident?
3. What is the reward for getting rid of the dragon?
4. What are the cobbler's words of advice about defeating the dragon?

INTERPRET

5. Which problems in the kingdom are ones that you would expect to find in a fairy tale?
6. What ordinary human characteristics does the wizard possess?
7. Why doesn't the cobbler want the king's reward?
8. How were the cobbler's words of advice helpful in defeating the dragon? Why don't the cobbler's older sons take their father's advice?

EVALUATE AND CONNECT

9. Theme Connection Is this a real fairy tale? Why? How does Gardner use fairy tale elements to create humor?
10. Have you ever read—or watched on television—a spoofed fairy tale like this one? How was it like this tale?

LITERARY ELEMENTS

Irony

Readers might expect to find a scary dragon in this story, but the dragon turns out to be more of a prankster who gives people exploding cigars. The difference between what readers expect and what they find creates **irony.** In "Dragon, Dragon," Gardner counts on his readers to know what to expect in fairy tales so that they can smile to themselves when they see him twist the tale a bit.

1. How would you expect a princess to act as her suitors are defeated? How does this princess act?

2. Once a reader recognizes that "Dragon, Dragon" is a sort of fairy tale, which events in the story are predictable? Which are not predictable?

● See **Literary Terms Handbook,** p. R4.

Extending Your Response

Writing About Literature

Repetition   In "Dragon, Dragon" the repetition of a two-line poem helps tie together many events in the story. Review the events that lead up to and follow the saying of the poem each time. Then write a paragraph describing the pattern of actions.

Literature Groups

Modern and Traditional   "Take it or leave it," says the king. For humor, Gardner mixes modern expressions and ideas into a traditional story. Find and discuss modern elements in the story that don't quite fit in a kingdom long ago.

Learning for Life

Wanted: Dragon Slayer   In twisting the tale, Gardner might have had the king put a help-wanted ad in the local newspaper. Write the king's ad.

Describe the job, the qualifications needed to do the job, and the payment.

Creative Writing

Over-Watering the Queen   The queen became inactive rather early in the story. How do you think she will react to all the events that took place while she was under the wizard's spell? What will she have to say to the king? Write a paragraph from her point of view about what has occurred.

Reading Further

If you liked this story, you might enjoy these books by John Gardner:

Fairy Tales: *Gudgekin the Thistle Girl and Other Tales*

Poetry: *A Child's Bestiary*

📖 **Save your work for your portfolio.**

Skill Minilesson

VOCABULARY • ANTONYMS

When you learn a new word, it is worth thinking about what might be a good **antonym** for it. That helps you think about what the new word really means. Antonyms also help you when you are trying to say how two things are completely different.

Some words can be made antonyms, or opposites, just by attaching a prefix such as *in-. Inconvenient* is the exact opposite of *convenient,* and *indecent* is the exact opposite of *decent.*

PRACTICE   Choose the word that shows a contrast with the underlined word.

1. Why do dragons always <u>ravage</u> everything? Why don't they _____ things instead?
   a. plant   b. repair   c. crush
2. Most people who go out to fight a dragon would not speak <u>meekly</u> to it. They would speak quite _____ !
   a. quickly   b. fearfully   c. harshly
3. A dragon would not fear anyone who approached it <u>timidly</u>, but it might get nervous if someone approached _____ .
   a. loudly   b. confidently   c. cheerfully

Before You Read

The Enchanted Raisin

MEET JACQUELINE BALCELLS

Jacqueline Balcells (jak′ ə lēn bäl′ səlz), a journalist from Santiago, Chile, began writing stories to entertain her children while she was living in Paris, France. Some of these stories were published in French in 1984. The title story of the collection, "The Enchanted Raisin," was very popular in France. Balcells returned to Chile and published a Spanish version of the story in 1986. She went on to write science fiction novels and other books for young people. Her stories and books have won many awards in Europe and in South America.

Jacqueline Balcells was born in 1950.

FOCUS ACTIVITY

What stories have you read in which characters acted wildly and recklessly? What did the characters do? What were the consequences?

Discuss
What lessons might these stories have been trying to teach?

Setting a Purpose
Read "The Enchanted Raisin" to see what lesson the story might teach its readers.

BACKGROUND

Did You Know? Raisins don't grow on trees—at least not as raisins. They actually grow on vines as grapes. Only certain kinds of grapes are used for raisins. The grapes are picked in clusters, and the clusters are arranged on paper. The paper may lie on trays on the ground between the rows of grape vines. Over the course of two to three weeks, the grapes slowly dry in the sun and shrivel up into sweet raisins.

VOCABULARY PREVIEW

conceive (kən sēv′) *v.* to form a mental image or idea of; imagine; p. 651

invariably (in ver′ ē ə blē) *adv.* always; without exception; p. 653

lament (lə ment′) *v.* to express sorrow or regret; p. 654

anguish (an′ gwish) *n.* great mental or physical suffering; misery; p. 654

detest (di test′) *v.* to dislike greatly; hate; p. 654

oversight (ō′ vər sīt′) *n.* a careless mistake; p. 657

reconciled (rek′ ən sīld′) *adj.* once again friendly, as after an argument or disagreement; p. 657

remorse (ri môrs′) *n.* a deep, painful feeling of guilt or sorrow for wrongdoing; p. 658

The Enchanted Raisin

Jacqueline Balcells ∾
Translated by
Elizabeth Gamble Miller

Once upon a time there was a mother who had three absolutely incorrigible[1] children. They would get into all the mischief you could <u>conceive</u> of and even some you couldn't imagine. More than once they had come within an inch of burning the house down and numerous times they had flooded it. They broke up the furniture, shattered the dishes, fought and screamed as if they were crazy, spilled ink on the white sheets and swung on the curtains like monkeys in the jungle. And, needless to say, when they were forced to go outside, they terrorized the entire neighborhood.

---

1. *Incorrigible* (in kôr′ ə jə bəl) people are so firmly set in their bad ways that they can't be corrected or reformed.

Vocabulary

conceive (kən sēv′) *v.* to form a mental image or idea of; imagine

The Enchanted Raisin

Their father was almost never at home and their poor mother couldn't control the three little devils. She was exhausted by the end of each day from constantly running after them.

"Boys, boys," she would say to them, "Please stop this nonsense, at least for now. Look at the state you've put me in: with all your mischief and all your yelling I am getting more and more wrinkles in my face. I'm turning into an old woman."

And it was true. This lady who had been lovely and beautiful was becoming more and more wrinkled and every day she was shrinking smaller and smaller.

Her children didn't notice it at all. But one day when she went to get them at school, their friends saw her and, surprised, they asked them:

"Why is your grandmother picking you up today?"

At first the boys felt badly; to them it wasn't funny that their mother had been mistaken for their grandmother, but they didn't waste much time thinking about it, they had so much to do!

So the poor woman continued to get more and more wrinkles and to shrink at an incredible speed. The time came when she could scarcely walk: her legs had become so delicate, such tiny toothpicks they looked like two cherry stems, and her back was so hunched over she could scarcely see in front of her. But that didn't keep her three boys from dreaming up more and more frightful mischief.

"Let's shake the pillows till the feathers come out!"

"Let's pull out the dog's hair!"

"Let's cut off the cat's ears!"

"Let's dig a hole in the ground so the gardener will fall in!"

The mother, by now, was so very tiny that when she stood up she didn't reach as high as the kneecap of her youngest son. And she complained, sighing:

"Boys, boys, that's enough! Look at my size, look at my wrinkles . . . If this continues, I will shrink so much you won't even be able to see me."

But she never really thought that what she was saying was going to happen. One evening after dinner, she dragged herself up to her room. She put on her nightgown that was a hundred times too large for her now. She went to bed, and curling up into a little ball, she fell sound asleep.

On the following day, when the three boys awakened, they began their usual antics.

They jumped around on their beds like little devils and began yelling:

"Maaaaaaaaaaaama, bring us some breeeeeeakfast . . . !"

There was no answer.

They yelled louder, with no success. They began, then, to howl, once, twice, ten times, thirty times. At scream number fifty-one, their throats were aching and they decided to go to their mama's room.

They found her bed unmade, but she was nowhere to be seen.

The children realized that something strange was happening. Suddenly, the youngest boy leaned over the pillow and he cried out in alarm.

"What's wrong with you?" his brothers asked.

"Look . . . , look . . . , there . . . , there . . . !"

In the folds of their mother's nightgown was a dark little ball. It was a raisin.

The children became frightened. They yelled louder and louder: "Maaaama, Maaaama . . . !"

There was no more answer to this than to their other cries, but the eldest boy then realized that every time they yelled, the raisin on the pillow moved slightly. They looked at it silently: the raisin remained still. They yelled "Mama!": the raisin rocked a tiny bit.

Then they remembered their mama's words: "If this continues, I will shrink so much until finally you won't be able to see me. . . ."

And, horrified, they realized that that raisin moving around when they yelled "Mama!" was all that was left of their mother, and that she was trying to get them to recognize her.

How they cried and grieved!

"Poor us! What are we going to do now with Mama turned into a raisin? And what will Papa say when he comes home and sees her?"

Their father had left on a business trip for a few weeks, but he was supposed to return that very night. The boys, frightened and not knowing what to do, simply waited for him all day long in the bedroom. From time to time, just to reassure themselves, one or the other would go over to the raisin and would call to her: "Mama!" The raisin would invariably move.

At nightfall, the father arrived.

He opened the door, put down his briefcase, took off his hat, his coat, and from the entrance hall he called out to his wife:

"Oho! . . . Are you here? Aren't you coming to say hello? . . . to give me a kiss? . . . to bring me a glass of wine?"

Instead of his wife his three boys appeared, one after the other, each with his head hanging down. The eldest boy carried a little box in his hand.

"What does this mean? Why aren't you in bed? Where is Mama?"

"She is here, in this box," answered the boys in a dismal voice. "She's turned into a raisin . . ."

The father exploded in anger:

"You know very well I hate jokes! Go straight to bed, all of you!"

Then he searched the entire house for his wife. Needless to say, he didn't find her.

So he said to himself:

"She must have gone out for a walk!"

But an hour later, as she still didn't appear, he began to get really worried.

Vocabulary
invariably (in ver′ ē ə blē) *adv.* always; without exception

He put his hat on and went out. He walked through the neighborhood; he went to the neighbors' houses, to the relatives' houses, to their friends' houses. He asked everyone:

"Have you seen my wife?"

Next he went to the police. But they couldn't tell him anything either.

Another night passed, another day and another night.

And as time was passing and his wife was still gone, the father began to wonder if she could have died, and he was very sad.

"She must have taken a walk by the lake, fallen in, and surely drowned! And the worst of it is I will never know!" he <u>lamented</u> in <u>anguish</u>.

Months passed without any news. Finally this man felt so lonely, he decided to marry again.

"A new wife will help me care for these three savages . . ."

He then chose a woman who was not as pretty as the first—if not to say quite ugly—but who seemed sweet and submissive.[2] In fact, the ugliness of her face but matched the meanness of her heart: she made him believe she adored the boys; but the truth was she <u>detested</u> them.

The father realized nothing. But the three boys immediately understood that the stepmother was mean and they mistrusted her. Besides they were well aware that their real mother still lived in that small box they guarded so jealously. They were certain that one day she would no longer be a raisin and would again be as she was before.

Often, at night, the boys would gather around the little box, take off the lid and tenderly call to her:

"Mama . . . , Mama . . ."

And every time, the raisin would respond by swaying gently back and forth.

One day when their father was in a very good humor, they gathered up the courage to ask him again to come up to their room to show him what happened with the raisin. Perhaps he would understand!

But the father refused to listen. On the contrary, he became furious.

"How long are you going to continue playing that stupid joke! Darn it . . . , if you begin your stories again, you are going to get it . . . I refuse to hear another word about that raisin!"

The children, frightened, put the raisin away.

But, misfortune of all misfortunes, the stepmother, who was at that moment behind the door, had heard all the conversation. And she did believe them! She had suspected that little box for a long time now because the children always carried it with them and they took such extremely good care of it.

At first she said nothing. But a few days later, one afternoon when their father wasn't at home, she called the children to her and said to them:

---

2. A *submissive* person is humbly obedient, following the will and guidance of another.

Vocabulary

lament (lə ment´) *v.* to express sorrow or regret
anguish (an´ gwish) *n.* great mental or physical suffering; misery
detest (di test´) *v.* to dislike greatly; hate

"Boys . . . , I'm going to bake a raisin cake and I need just one more raisin. I think you have one. Go get it for me right now!"

The stepmother had a terrible face and she rolled her eyes around. The children dared not protest. They went to their room and there they asked each other:

"What can we do? We're not going to give her our mother so she can put her in the oven!"

The eldest one decided:

"Let's go to the attic. We will hide the little box and we will tell her we've lost it."

Unfortunately for them, the evil woman had followed them and, once again, hiding behind the door, she listened to their conversation. Like a whirlwind she burst into their room and screamed at them:

"Don't even dream of deceiving me! Give me the raisin this minute, I already have the oven hot . . . !"

The eldest boy had just enough time to grab the little box. He yelled to his brothers to follow him and he ran full speed upstairs. He pushed his stepmother as he passed her, and when she fell to the floor you could hear her bones creak as she was so skinny.

The boys reached the attic, shut the door and pushed a wardrobe against it.

The stepmother, meanwhile, got to her feet, rubbed her ailing bones and hurried up to the attic.

"Open up, you rascals! Open up, you monsters! You'll see what will happen when your father comes!"

But the boys, horror stricken, didn't move.

Then a chilling, evil, horrid fury possessed her.

"You won't open the door for me? Very well! You will stay locked up here as long as is necessary. And when you are dying of hunger . . . you will eat the raisin!" She took a key from her pocket and turned the lock three times. Next, she laughed three times: ha! ha! ha! with a strident, malevolent[3] cackle very unlike the musical laughter she offered to her husband's ear.

Later in the evening, he arrived home and asked:

"Where are the children?"

She answered, pretending to be surprised:

"Oh, don't you remember, they left to spend a few days with their grandmother in the country."

3. *Strident* means "loud and harsh," and *malevolent* (mə lev′ ə lənt) means "showing ill will or a desire to do harm to someone."

655

She lied so convincingly, that he said, distracted:

"Of course, I had forgotten."

Meanwhile, upstairs, in the attic, the three boys were savoring their victory in having escaped the cruel woman. But as the hours passed, tired of being prisoners, they began to think about a way to escape.

The only opening, apart from the sealed door, was a small skylight, very high and difficult to reach; it was at the top of the roof between the beams. But it was at least thirty feet down to the ground in the garden.

"We will never be able to jump," they said to each other. "We would need a parachute or a rope."

But there was nothing like that in the attic. Suddenly, in the middle of these considerations, the three boys realized, in

surprise, that they hadn't gotten into a fight for a long time, and they hadn't yelled, and they hadn't dreamed up any mischief. It was possible to behave! They were so happy with this discovery that they hugged each other and promised to continue that way or in any case to do everything possible. . . .

But now it was urgent to find a way of escape. It was getting dark and with nightfall they felt the first signs of cold and hunger. The eldest one sighed:

"If only I had my bed and a good blanket!"

"And a big glass of warm milk!" added the second.

"And Mama as pretty as before . . ." whispered the youngest.

And without knowing what to do, they stretched out in a corner on the floor, cuddling together, with the little box between them. Thus they remained until they fell asleep.

In the morning, they were awakened by their growling stomachs. They were so hungry they couldn't stand it.

"We absolutely have to have something to eat," they said to each other.

Then they looked at the little box.

"Oh, no!" spoke up the eldest. "We aren't going to eat the raisin . . . never that!"

And then, after considering it further, he continued in a serious voice:

"Brothers: remember the stories of the lost explorers and shipwrecked men who were left without food. They ended up eating anything or anyone . . . We can't let that happen to us!"

The youngest then said:

"Let's put Mama away from us so we are sure not to eat her."

"Yes!" said the second, "If we throw her out the window, she will land on the grass in the garden and, since she is light, nothing will happen to her."

The boys took a last look at the little raisin. Their eyes filled with tears. How terrible it was for them to be separated from their mama!

But, how could they get up high enough to reach the window to throw the raisin into the garden?

They could move the wardrobe that was against the door and climb up on it, but they would run the risk that the wicked woman would choose that moment to come to get them. No! The best thing was to try to climb up on one another until they reached the roof. The eldest would climb up on a chair, the second would climb up on the eldest one and the smallest one, on top of the two of them, would reach the skylight.

And that is what they did. Or is what they almost did, because the chair legs were uneven, which didn't help their project.

"Now, can you reach it? Are you touching the window?" the older ones asked the youngest as he tried to keep his balance on top of them and go up into the peak of the roof.

"Yes . . . , now I'm hitting it . . . pass me the box!"

"What? Don't you have it?"

"Well no! I left it on the floor . . ."

They had to start all over again!

There was a brief argument: each one blaming the other for this disastrous oversight.

But they quickly became reconciled.

"Courage!" said the eldest. "Let's begin again."

And once more they climbed up on each other: the eldest boy on the chair, the middle boy on the eldest, the smallest on top of the middle boy. A real acrobatic stunt! The small one now touched the window and was about to open it when suddenly: crack! the chair broke in two and the children fell to the floor with a deafening clamor.

At that moment the father was just coming into the house. He heard the noise and he said to his wife:

"Go upstairs and see what's happening!"

She disappeared and in a moment came back saying:

"It's nothing! It's just the rats running around the attic."

Meanwhile, in the attic the three brothers were crying. Great tears of distress were rolling down their cheeks—for they had hurt themselves in the fall—and they felt so helpless—how were they going to reach the window, now that the chair was broken? To console themselves, they opened the little box and looked at the raisin. But just seeing it made them even sadder and they began to cry over it heartily.

The boys' tears were flowing in torrents over the raisin, so much so that the little

---

Vocabulary

oversight (ō′ vər sīt′) *n.* a careless mistake
reconciled (rek′ ən sīld′) *adj.* once again friendly, as after an argument or disagreement

box was flooded and the raisin was left floating in a small tepid⁴ pool.

Suddenly, the youngest brother cried out: "Look it's getting bigger!"

It was true. The raisin, swollen by the tears of the brothers, began to get larger. The more they cried, the larger the raisin became. And the boys seeing it grow larger cried even more, but now from joy.

The raisin continued growing, getting longer, getting broader, growing larger and larger. Until . . . , right in front of their dumbfounded⁵ faces the three boys saw it change form and . . .

"Maaaaaama!" they screamed.

It was Mama! As tall and as beautiful as she was before she had gotten all wrinkled. The mother took the boys into her arms and laughing and crying at once, she hugged them against her body, very very tightly, for a long, long time.

Meanwhile, down on the first floor their father was still trying to figure out those really strange noises that were coming from the attic.

Finally, his curiosity got the best of him and he said to his wife:

"Those rats in the attic have a very strange way of squealing today. One could imagine that they were crying. Give me the keys . . . , I'm going to see what's going on."

The woman tried every possible way to stop him. But her efforts were in vain.⁶

He climbed up the stairs and tried to open the door with the key but, not succeeding, he pushed on it with all his strength. The wardrobe gave way and he was able to get inside. How surprised he was to find his three sons in the arms of his first, his very beautiful wife! And the four of them, hugging each other tightly, looked at him without saying a word.

Then the father, who was not as bad as he might have seemed, almost died of remorse and joy. He covered his children with kisses and then he knelt at the feet of his wife to ask her forgiveness for having forgotten her.

No sooner had he asked than he was forgiven. Father, mother and children went down together to supper, holding each others' hands and with their hearts full of joy.

The stepmother hadn't waited for them. Guessing what was happening, she had fled with her suitcases some time earlier.

The raisin cake in the oven was burnt.

So the mother threw it into the trash and quickly baked another, a delicious cake chock-full of candied fruits.

The entire family happily and heartily ate that new cake that had not a single raisin.

---

4. The tears flow in rushing streams *(torrents)*, forming a lukewarm *(tepid)* pool.
5. To be *dumbfounded* is to be speechless with amazement.

---

6. Here, the phrase *in vain* means "without success."

Vocabulary

remorse (ri môrs´) *n.* a deep, painful feeling of guilt or sorrow for wrongdoing

Responding to Literature

PERSONAL RESPONSE

- ◆ Do you think everything in the story turns out as it should?
- ◆ Does this story remind you of others you discussed in the **Focus Activity** on page 650? Explain.

Analyzing Literature

RECALL AND INTERPRET

1. What happens to the mother at the beginning of the story? Why don't the three boys do something to stop their mother from turning into a raisin?

2. What does the stepmother want to do with the raisin? Why?

3. How is the mother brought back to her normal size? What has happened to make this change possible?

EVALUATE AND CONNECT

4. What is the theme of "The Enchanted Raisin"? Give reasons for your answer.

5. Would you like to be one of the brothers in the mother's house before she shrinks? Why or why not?

6. **Theme Connection** Do you enjoy stories with a clear sense of right and wrong? Explain.

LITERARY ELEMENTS

Fairy Tales

In a **fairy tale** a giant can drop in, a toad can become a prince, or an animal can talk. Fairy tales take place "once upon a time," usually long ago. Such stories involve a struggle between good and evil (or right and wrong), and good almost always wins. Some characters are very good, and others are very evil.

1. Find two things that "The Enchanted Raisin" has in common with other fairy tales.

2. Many fairy tales teach a lesson. Does "The Enchanted Raisin" teach a lesson? Explain.

● See **Literary Terms Handbook,** pp. R3–R4.

Extending Your Response

Creative Writing

Point of View   Write a few paragraphs explaining what happened in "The Enchanted Raisin" from the stepmother's point of view. Tell how she met the father and how she felt when he asked her to marry him. Describe the boys' behavior toward her. Tell her story to the class.

Literature Groups

Humorous Approach   What in the story makes you smile? Find examples, and discuss whether the humor is in the characters' personalities, their situations, or their actions. What techniques—such as exaggeration or irony—help create this humor?

COMPARING SELECTIONS

Dragon, Dragon and The Enchanted Raisin

COMPARE OUTCOMES

In both stories, a parent offers guidance to his or her children.

- As a class, discuss what the parent in each story wants the children to do, and what the result is.
- Discuss why most of the young people in these stories do not follow their parents' suggestions. Are the ages of the characters important? How do the authors view their characters' actions?
- Write dialogue—the words the characters say—between two characters in one of these stories. Have the characters express what they have learned from the events.

COMPARE SETTINGS

Fairy tales usually take place a long time ago. Both "Dragon, Dragon" and "The Enchanted Raisin" are fairy tales, but their settings are unique.

1. In what ways are the settings of these two stories nontraditional for fairy tales?
2. Which story's setting do you like better? Why?
3. Tell a partner an event in one story using the setting of the other story. Discuss how or if changing the setting changes the story.

COMPARE EXPERIENCES

In many fairy tales, a character must accomplish a difficult task.

1. What is the difficult task for the three brothers in "Dragon, Dragon" and for the three brothers in "The Enchanted Raisin"?
2. Which task is the most difficult? Why?
3. Do the characters in either story change as a result of completing the task? If so, how?

Reading and Thinking Skills

Classifying

Why is "The Enchanted Raisin" called a fairy tale? After all, it takes place in a contemporary home and neighborhood, not in a castle or a kingdom. How can you decide? You can **classify** the elements of the tale. When you classify, you review information and organize the information into groups or categories.

First, review the characteristics of fairy tales. Then try to find these characteristics in the story. A chart can help you keep track of what you are looking for. Think about characteristics of fairy tales in these passages from "The Enchanted Raisin."

Story Passage

- Once upon a time there was a mother who had three absolutely incorrigible children.
- And, horrified, they realized that that raisin moving around when they yelled "Mama!" was all that was left of their mother. . . .
- The stepmother had a terrible face. . . . the evil woman had followed them and, once again, hiding behind the door, she listened to their conversation.
- . . . the three boys realized, in surprise, that they hadn't gotten into a fight for a long time. . . . It was possible to behave!
- No sooner had [the father] asked than he was forgiven. Father, mother, and children went down together to supper, holding each others' hands and with their hearts full of joy.

Fairy Tale Characteristics

- "Once upon a time" beginning; group of three brothers
- Magical events and characters

- Evil stepmother; conflict with a powerful evil force

- Moral lesson

- Happy ending

● For more about organizing information, see **Reading Handbook,** p. R92.

ACTIVITIES

1. Check for fairy tale features and classify the elements of "Dragon, Dragon." Complete a chart of these features for the story.

2. Choose two or three other stories you have read and classify them as other types of literature you have discussed—origin tales, myths, legends, and folktales.

DRAMA

Drama is an ancient form of entertainment. Long ago, people began to act out exciting stories of heroes and their deeds. Throughout the centuries, people have created all kinds of **plays**—stories that are written to be performed in front of an audience. In modern times, writers have produced plays to be performed on the radio or on television, as well.

● For more about drama, see **Literary Terms Handbook,** p. R3.

Rehearsal of a satyr play, before A.D. 79 (detail). Dioscurides of Samos. Mosaic from the House of the Tragic Poet, Pompeii. Museo Archeologico Nazionale, Naples, Italy.

ELEMENTS OF DRAMA

MODEL

SCRIPT A script is the written form of a play. It tells exactly what the characters say and gives suggestions for presenting the story. In the script, the **cast** is listed. The cast is the characters in the play. Each character is played by an actor.

> In a script, next to each character's name are the exact words for the actor to speak.

NARRATOR Many plays, especially radio plays, have a narrator. The narrator is the person who tells the story. The narrator may interact with the other characters, or may stand to the side, not participating and not noticed by the other characters. The comments of the narrator help the audience follow or interpret the events on the stage.

> In *Damon and Pythias,* the narrator is removed from the action. He or she can see what is happening and can relate information to the audience.

Examples from *Damon and Pythias* will show how the following elements of drama work together.

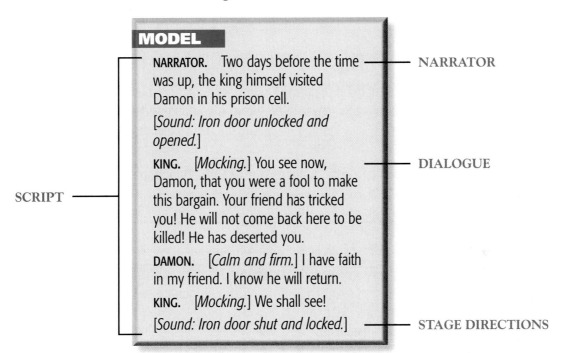

MODEL

NARRATOR. Two days before the time was up, the king himself visited Damon in his prison cell.

[*Sound: Iron door unlocked and opened.*]

KING. [*Mocking.*] You see now, Damon, that you were a fool to make this bargain. Your friend has tricked you! He will not come back here to be killed! He has deserted you.

DAMON. [*Calm and firm.*] I have faith in my friend. I know he will return.

KING. [*Mocking.*] We shall see!

[*Sound: Iron door shut and locked.*]

NARRATOR — (label)

DIALOGUE — (label)

STAGE DIRECTIONS — (label)

SCRIPT — (label)

DIALOGUE Dialogue is the words the characters say. A play is a story that is told almost entirely through dialogue. The audience learns about what is happening and how the characters think and feel through the dialogue. Dialogue reveals the characters' personalities, gives information to the audience, and moves the story forward.

In a few words, the king reveals that he is a cruel man and is enjoying Damon's misfortunes. Damon proves that he is a faithful friend who will never lose hope.

STAGE DIRECTIONS are instructions to guide how the play is presented. The **playwright,** the play's author, writes the stage directions as part of the script. Stage directions are often in brackets. They tell the actors what to do, such as when to enter and leave the stage, or how to stand, move, or speak. The stage directions can identify furniture and objects—**props**—to be placed on the stage. Stage directions can call for music, sounds, or lights during the play.

In *Damon and Pythias,* the playwright has included instructions for sound effects that suggest the opening and closing of a lock and an iron door. The sound effects suggest that the king is visiting a cold, unhappy jail cell.

Active Reading Strategies

Tips for Reading Drama

Plays are meant to be performed in front of audiences, but they can also be read. As a reader, check to be sure that you understand what is happening in the play. Take the time to picture the scenes that develop from the words of the play. These strategies can help you read drama selections.

● For more about reading strategies, see **Reading Handbook,** pp. R63–R94.

PREVIEW

As a form of literature, plays are not as familiar to most readers as short stories. Look over the play you want to read. Notice its features, such as the cast list and the way the dialogue is presented. Read the characters' names; look over the stage directions. Notice whatever words stand out to you on a page.

Ask Yourself . . .

● Am I familiar with any of the characters? Can I pronounce the names?

● Where does this play take place?

● What do I notice in the stage directions?

● What seems to be happening on this page in the play?

QUESTION

Remember that plays are written to be performed by actors. When you are reading a play, sometimes it is difficult to follow the action, especially when there are many characters speaking. From time to time, stop and reread sections to be sure that you understand what is happening.

Ask Yourself . . .

● Who is this character speaking to?

● Why is the character angry? frightened? happy?

● Where are these characters now?

● Did I miss something important? Should I reread a section?

VISUALIZE

Try to picture what is happening in the play. Imagine what the characters look like and where the action takes place. Try to "hear" the voices of characters and the music and other sounds you read about.

Ask Yourself . . .

- What do I think each character looks like? How is each one dressed?

- What does the setting look like?

- How would the characters talk? Would one's voice be high and childish? Would one talk with a low, powerful voice?

EVALUATE

As you read, pay close attention to what you learn about the characters. Then make some judgments about them. What do you learn about them from what they do and say? Why do they act as they do?

Ask Yourself . . .

- Are the character's actions logical given what I know so far?

- How would I describe this character's personality? Why?

- How do the other characters in the play feel about the character?

APPLYING THE STRATEGIES

Read the following play, *Damon and Pythias.* As you read, use the strategies in the margins to help you enjoy the play.

MEDIA Connection

Sound effects can be important in drama on radio, television, and film. Did you ever wonder how these effects are created?

Sounds Like Fun

by Jennifer A. Kirkpatrick
National Geographic World, February, 1996

On the screen a T-Rex crunches a small dinosaur. Most likely the bone-crunching sound you hear is the snap of crisp celery sticks, made by a Foley artist. A Foley artist, or sound effects artist, uses celery and hundreds of other objects—called props—to make many of the sounds in movies—from clangs and bangs to squeaks and creaks.

The term *Foley artist* comes from Jack Foley. He pioneered the art of making sound effects match the on-screen movie action.

"Sound mixers record the actors' voices when filming scenes. But noises like footsteps, raindrops, and crashes don't get recorded," says David Lee Fein, a Foley artist, who works at Paramount Studios in Hollywood, California. Ken Dufva is a Foley artist who works with Fein. He explains, "First we receive a film which we project on the screen in our studio. Then we figure out what sounds we need to make and the props we need to make them. We create the sounds in the studio and record them on audiotape to make them occur at *exactly* the same time as the actions on the screen." For example, at the moment a baseball breaks a window on a movie screen, Fein and Dufva drop some lightbulbs on the floor.

The most challenging sounds? "The weird and gushy sounds in science fiction movies—like eyeballs rolling off a plate," says Dufva.

Mix It Yourself!

Each action in the column on the left creates one of the sound effects in the column on the right. Match the number of the action to the letter of the correct sound effect.

1. Roll around a marble inside an inflated balloon.

2. Mash together wet newspapers.

3. Walk on cornstarch inside a dish towel.

4. Walk on magnetic recording tape (old audiocassette or videotape).

5. Pull apart two pieces of Velcro.®

6. Scrape two pinecones together.

7. Make a wooden chair wobble.

8. Wear a cotton glove with paper clips taped to each finger. Then tap on a hard surface.

A. CLICK CLICK

B. Crackling flames

C.

D. Walking in dry grass

E.

F. Walking on snow

G. SLURK

H. RIP

ART BY FRED SCHRIER

Respond

Think about a favorite television show or movie. What sound effects do you remember?

Before You Read
Damon and Pythias

MEET FAN KISSEN

Fan Kissen spent most of her writing career turning folktales and legends into plays for young people. The plays were first performed on radio in Kissen's series, *Tales from the Four Winds*. Later Kissen collected and published them in *The Bag of Fire and Other Plays*, *The Crowded House and Other Tales*, and *The Straw Ox and Other Plays*. Each play includes instructions for music and sound effects. Before writing radio plays, Kissen taught elementary school in New York City.

Fan Kissen was born in 1893 and died in 1978. Damon and Pythias was first published in 1964.

FOCUS ACTIVITY

How important is it for a friend to be loyal? Can a person be your friend if he or she is not loyal?

Journal
In your journal, write what loyalty means in a friendship. Explain how friends show loyalty or disloyalty.

Setting a Purpose
Read *Damon and Pythias* to find out about the importance of loyalty in a friendship.

BACKGROUND

Did You Know? The play is set in Syracuse, a city on the island of Sicily. At the time when Damon and Pythias lived, the fourth century B.C., Syracuse was a part of the Greek Empire. It was one of the most powerful cities in the ancient world and was ruled by a tyrant king, Dionysius the Elder. Although Dionysius was a tyrant, he appreciated and supported painting, music, and drama. Historians say that he even wrote plays himself.

VOCABULARY PREVIEW

proclaim (prə clām′) *v.* to declare publicly; announce; p. 669
champion (cham′ pē ən) *n.* one who fights or speaks for another person; one who defends a cause; hero; p. 670
traitor (trā′ tər) *n.* one who betrays one's country; p. 672

Damon and Pythias

Fan Kissen ∾

CAST

DAMON	SECOND ROBBER	THIRD VOICE
FIRST ROBBER	SECOND VOICE	SOLDIER
FIRST VOICE	KING	NARRATOR
PYTHIAS	MOTHER	

[*Sound: Iron door opens and shuts. Key in lock.*]

[*Music: Up full and out.*]

NARRATOR. Long, long ago there lived on the island of Sicily two young men named Damon and Pythias. They were known far and wide for the strong friendship each had for the other. Their names

have come down to our own times to mean true friendship. You may hear it said of two persons:

FIRST VOICE. Those two? Why, they're like Damon and Pythias!

NARRATOR. The king of that country was a cruel tyrant. He made cruel laws, and he showed no mercy toward anyone who broke his laws. Now, you might very well wonder:

SECOND VOICE. Why didn't the people rebel?

NARRATOR. Well, the people didn't dare rebel because they feared the king's great and powerful army. No one dared say a word against the king or his laws—except Damon and Pythias speaking against a new law the king had proclaimed.

SOLDIER. Ho, there! Who are you that dares to speak so about our king?

QUESTION

What do you think is the job of First Voice and Second Voice?

Vocabulary
proclaim (prə clām′) *v.* to declare publicly; announce

Damon and Pythias

ACTIVE READING MODEL

VISUALIZE

How do you picture Pythias before the king?

PYTHIAS. [*Unafraid.*] I am called Pythias.

SOLDIER. Don't you know it is a crime to speak against the king or his laws? You are under arrest! Come and tell this opinion of yours to the king's face!

[*Music: A few short bars in and out.*]

NARRATOR. When Pythias was brought before the king, he showed no fear. He stood straight and quiet before the throne.

KING. [*Hard, cruel.*] So, Pythias! They tell me you do not approve of the laws I make.

PYTHIAS. I am not alone, your Majesty, in thinking your laws are cruel. But you rule the people with such an iron hand that they dare not complain.

KING. [*Angry.*] But *you* have the daring to complain *for* them! Have they appointed you their champion?

PYTHIAS. No, your Majesty. I speak for myself alone. I have no wish to make trouble for anyone. But I am not afraid to tell you that the people are suffering under your rule. They want to have a voice in making the laws for themselves. You do not allow them to speak up for themselves.

Vocabulary

champion (cham′ pē ən) *n.* one who fights or speaks for another person; one who defends a cause; hero

Street Musicians, before A.D. 79 (detail). Dioscurides of Samos. Mosaic from the Villa of Cicero, Pompeii. Museo Archeologico Nazionale, Naples, Italy.

Viewing the mosaic: How do you imagine the crowd would respond to these street musicians? Why?

ACTIVE
READING
MODEL

KING. In other words, you are calling me a tyrant! Well, you shall learn for yourself how a tyrant treats a rebel! Soldier! Throw this man into prison!

SOLDIER. At once, your Majesty! Don't try to resist, Pythias!

PYTHIAS. I know better than to try to resist a soldier of the king! and for how long am I to remain in prison, your Majesty, merely for speaking out for the people?

KING. [*Cruel.*] Not for very long, Pythias. Two weeks from today at noon, you shall be put to death in the public square as an example to anyone else who may dare to question my laws or acts. Off to prison with him, soldier!

[*Music: In briefly and out.*]

NARRATOR. When Damon heard that his friend Pythias had been thrown into prison, and about the severe punishment that was to follow, he was heartbroken. He rushed to the prison and persuaded the guard to let him speak to his friend.

DAMON. Oh, Pythias! How terrible to find you here! I wish I could do something to save you!

PYTHIAS. Nothing can save me, Damon, my dear friend. I am prepared to die. But there is one thought that troubles me greatly.

DAMON. What is it? I will do anything to help you.

PYTHIAS. I'm worried about what will happen to my mother and my sister when I'm gone.

DAMON. I'll take care of them, Pythias, as if they were my own mother and sister.

PYTHIAS. Thank you, Damon. I have money to leave them. But there are other things I must arrange. If only I could go see them before I die! But they live two days' journey from here, you know.

DAMON. I'll go to the king and beg him to give you your freedom for a few days. You'll give your word to return at the end of that time. Everyone in Sicily knows you for a man who has never broken his word.

PYTHIAS. Do you believe for one moment that the king would let me leave this prison, no matter how good my word may have been all my life?

DAMON. I'll tell him that *I* shall take your place in the prison cell. I'll tell him that if you do not return by the appointed day, he may kill *me* in your place!

EVALUATE
Does Pythias seem like a criminal?

QUESTION
Why doesn't Pythias think that Damon can help him?

EVALUATE
Is the dialogue written the way people might actually speak?

Damon and Pythias

PYTHIAS. No, no, Damon! You must not do such a foolish thing! I cannot—I will not—let you do this! Damon! Damon! Don't go! [*To himself.*] Damon, my friend! You may find yourself in a cell beside me!

[*Music: In briefly and out.*]

DAMON. [*Begging.*] Your Majesty! I beg of you! Let Pythias go home for a few days to bid farewell to his mother and sister. He gives his word that he will return at your appointed time. Everyone knows that his word can be trusted.

KING. In ordinary business affairs—perhaps. But he is now a man under sentence of death. To free him even for a few days would strain his honesty—*any* man's honesty—too far. Pythias would never return here! I consider him a traitor, but I'm certain he's no fool.

DAMON. Your Majesty! I will take his place in the prison until he comes back. If he does not return, then you may take *my* life in his place.

KING. [*Astonished.*] What did you say, Damon?

DAMON. I'm so certain of Pythias that I am offering to die in his place if he fails to return on time.

KING. I can't believe you mean it!

DAMON. I do mean it, your Majesty.

KING. You make me very curious, Damon, so curious that I'm willing to put you and Pythias to the test. This exchange of prisoners will be made. But Pythias must be back two weeks from today, at noon.

DAMON. Thank you, your Majesty!

KING. The order with my official seal shall go by your own hand,[1] Damon. But I warn you, if your friend does not return on time, you shall surely die in his place! I shall show no mercy.

[*Music: In briefly and out.*]

NARRATOR. Pythias did not like the king's bargain with Damon. He did not like to leave his friend in prison with the chance that he might lose his life if something went wrong. But at last Damon persuaded him to leave and Pythias set out for his home. More than a

PREDICT

Do you think the king is likely to show mercy if Pythias fails? Why or why not?

---

1. In asking Damon to carry the order in his *own hand,* the king means that Damon should carry the order himself.

Vocabulary
traitor (trā′ tər) *n.* one who betrays one's country

week went by. The day set for the death sentence drew near. Pythias did not return. Everyone in the city knew of the condition on which the king had permitted Pythias to go home. Everywhere people met, the talk was sure to turn to the two friends.

FIRST VOICE. Do you suppose Pythias will come back?

SECOND VOICE. Why should he stick his head under the king's ax once he has escaped?

THIRD VOICE. Still would an honorable man like Pythias let such a good friend die for him?

FIRST VOICE. There's no telling what a man will do when it's a question of his own life against another's.

SECOND VOICE. But if Pythias doesn't come back before the time is up, he will be killing his friend.

THIRD VOICE. Well, there's still a few days' time. I, for one, am certain that Pythias *will* return in time.

SECOND VOICE. And *I am* just as certain that he will *not*. Friendship is friendship, but a man's own life is something stronger. *I* say!

NARRATOR. Two days before the time was up, the king himself visited Damon in his prison cell.

[*Sound: Iron door unlocked and opened.*]

KING. [*Mocking.*] You see now, Damon, that you were a fool to make this bargain. Your friend has tricked you! He will not come back here to be killed! He has deserted you.

DAMON. [*Calm and firm.*] I have faith in my friend. I know he will return.

KING. [*Mocking.*] We shall see!

[*Sound: Iron door shut and locked.*]

NARRATOR. Meanwhile, when Pythias reached the home of his family, he arranged his business affairs so that his mother and sister would be able to live comfortably for the rest of their years. Then he said a last farewell to them before starting back to the city.

MOTHER. [*In tears.*] Pythias, it will take you two days to get back. Stay another day, I beg you!

PYTHIAS. I dare not stay longer, Mother. Remember, Damon is locked up in my prison cell while I'm gone. Please don't weep for me. My death may help bring better days for all our people.

ACTIVE READING MODEL

PREDICT

Do you think Pythias will come back? Why or why not?

EVALUATE

What do the Voices help you think about?

Damon and Pythias

ACTIVE
READING
MODEL

NARRATOR. So Pythias began his journey in plenty of time. But bad luck struck him on the very first day. At twilight, as he walked along a lonely stretch of woodland, a rough voice called:

FIRST ROBBER. Not so fast there, young man! Stop!

PYTHIAS. [*Startled.*] Oh! What is it? What do you want?

SECOND ROBBER. Your money bags.

PYTHIAS. My money bags? I have only this small bag of coins. I shall need them for some favors, perhaps, before I die.

FIRST ROBBER. What do you mean, before you die? We don't mean to kill you, only take your money.

PYTHIAS. I'll give you my money, only don't delay me any longer. I am to die by the king's order three days from now. If I don't return on time, my friend must die in my place.

FIRST ROBBER. A likely story! What man would be fool enough to go back to prison ready to die.

SECOND ROBBER. And what man would be fool enough to die *for* you?

FIRST ROBBER. We'll take your money, all right. And we'll tie you up while we get away.

PYTHIAS. [*Begging.*] No! No! I must get back to free my friend! [*Fade.*] I must go back!

NARRATOR. But the two robbers took Pythias's money, tied him to a tree, and went off as fast as they could. Pythias struggled to free himself. He cried out for a long time. But no one traveled through that lonesome woodland after dark. The sun had been up for many hours before he finally managed to free himself from the ropes that had tied him to the tree. He lay on the ground, hardly able to breathe.

[*Music: In briefly and out.*]

NARRATOR. After a while Pythias got to his feet. Weak and dizzy from hunger and thirst and his struggle to free himself, he set off again. Day and night he traveled without stopping, desperately trying to reach the city in time to save Damon's life.

[*Music: Up and out.*]

NARRATOR. On the last day, half an hour before noon, Damon's hands were tied behind his back, and he was taken into the public square. The people muttered angrily as Damon was led in by the jailer. Then the king entered and seated himself on a high platform.

QUESTION

Do the robbers believe Pythias? Why do you think so?

VISUALIZE

How do you visualize the scene with the robbers?

[*Sound: Crowd voices in and hold under single voices.*]

SOLDIER. [*Loud.*] Long live the king!

FIRST VOICE. [*Low.*] The longer he lives, the more miserable our lives will be!

QUESTION

Why will their lives be miserable?

KING. [*Loud, mocking.*] Well, Damon, your lifetime is nearly up. Where is your good friend Pythias now?

DAMON. [*Firm.*] I have faith in my friend. If he has not returned, I'm certain it is through no fault of his own.

Did You Know?

The *noon mark* appears on a sundial, a device that indicates the time of day by the position and length of a shadow cast on a surface marked with numerals.

KING. [*Mocking.*] The sun is almost overhead. The shadow is almost at the noon mark. And still your friend has not returned to give back your life!

DAMON. [*Quiet.*] I am ready and happy to die in his place.

KING. [*Harsh.*] And you shall, Damon! Jailer, lead the prisoner to the—

[*Sound: Crowd voices up to a roar, then under.*]

FIRST VOICE. [*Over noise.*] Look! It's Pythias!

SECOND VOICE. [*Over noise.*] Pythias has come back!

PYTHIAS. [*Breathless.*] Let me through! Damon!

DAMON. Pythias!

PYTHIAS. Thank the gods I'm not too late!

DAMON. [*Quiet, sincere.*] I would have died for you gladly, my friend.

CROWD VOICES. [*Loud, demanding.*] Set them free! Set them both free!

EVALUATE

Is the king acting as you'd expect?

KING. [*Loud.*] People of the city! [*Crowd voices out.*] Never in all my life have I seen such faith and friendship, such loyalty between men. There are many among you who call me harsh and cruel. But I cannot kill *any* man who proves such strong and true friendship for another. Damon and Pythias, I set you both free. [*Roar of approval from crowd.*] I am king. I command a great army. I have stores of gold and precious jewels. But I would give all my money and power for one friend like Damon or Pythias.

EVALUATE

What is the message of the play?

[*Sound: Roar of approval from crowd up briefly and out.*]

[*Music: Up and out.*]

Responding to Literature

PERSONAL RESPONSE

- ◆ Do you think you could have done what Damon did for his friend?
- ◆ What do Damon and Pythias show about loyalty? Add to your journal notes from the **Focus Activity** on page 667.

Active Reading Response

- ◆ Could you visualize what was happening in the story? Which scenes were most vivid? Why?

Analyzing Literature

RECALL

1. How does Pythias act when the soldier arrests him and brings him before the king?
2. What crime did Pythias commit?
3. Why does Pythias want to leave the jail for several days?
4. What is the bargain Damon makes with the king?

INTERPRET

5. What is the king's attitude toward Pythias and toward his people? Explain.
6. Do you think what Pythias did was wrong? Explain.
7. What are some character traits of Pythias? Support your answer.
8. In your opinion, if Damon or Pythias were executed by the king, would either death help change the laws of the land? Explain.

EVALUATE AND CONNECT

9. What function does the **narrator** have in the play? Give examples.
10. How would you react if your best friend was about to be unjustly punished for a serious crime?

LITERARY ELEMENTS

Stage Directions

Stage directions suggest how to perform a play. They are commonly shown in brackets and in italics to make them stand out from the dialogue. Stage directions are notes rather than complete sentences. They include instructions for actors, directors, and stage crew (the people who help with scenery, costumes, lighting, and other elements of performance). Stage directions may suggest music, lighting and sound effects, and ways for actors to move and speak.

1. Write a line of dialogue and include a stage direction.

2. Notice the suggestions for music in the stage directions for *Damon and Pythias*. What music would you suggest? Why?

● See **Literary Terms Handbook,** p. R8.

Tragic and Comic Masks (details). Before A.D. 79. Mosaics from the House of the Faun, Pompeii. Museo Archeologico Nazionale, Naples, Italy.

Literature and Writing

Writing About Literature

Plot   Summarize the plot of *Damon and Pythias.* Remember to identify the conflict or problem with which the characters are faced, the climax or turning point of the action, and the resolution of the problem. Completing a **plot diagram,** as shown on pages 350–351, may help you think about the most important ideas to record in your summary.

Personal Writing

The Ties That Bind   *Damon and Pythias* is based on a legend. Two citizens of Syracuse were remembered for their faithful friendship. Think about other legends or stories from recent times that illustrate qualities people admire. Write a paragraph about one of these stories. Identify the characters, summarize the plot, and explain the theme of the story.

Extending Your Response

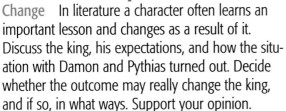

Literature Groups

Change   In literature a character often learns an important lesson and changes as a result of it. Discuss the king, his expectations, and how the situation with Damon and Pythias turned out. Decide whether the outcome may really change the king, and if so, in what ways. Support your opinion.

Interdisciplinary Activity

History   Suppose that you are staging *Damon and Pythias* and that you want the scenery, props, and costumes to re-create the world of ancient Sicily. Research the time and place. Based on your findings, what would the buildings, props, and clothing in your staging look like? Share your ideas with the class—in the form of sketches, if you like.

Performing

On with the Show!   With a small group, practice performing all or part of the play. Pay attention to the stage directions and to punctuation in the dialogue. Decide on music for the play. Have one or two group members handle the music and other sound effects. Then perform for the class.

📖 Save your work for your portfolio.

Skill Minilessons

GRAMMAR AND LANGUAGE • PUNCTUATION IN PLAYS

DAMON.   [*Begging.*] Your Majesty! I beg of you!

When Damon begs the king to let Pythias go home, his words are not set off in quotation marks, as they would be in a story. Since plays are written as dialogue, quotation marks are not used; such marks would make reading difficult. Actors, directors, and readers understand that the words in the play are the exact words the characters speak. Quotation marks may be needed, however, when quoting from a play. For example, you might write,

Then Damon was extremely upset and he pleaded, "Your Majesty! I beg of you."

PRACTICE With a partner, make up a situation in which two friends are helping each other or disagreeing with each other. Then write their conversation in the form of play dialogue.

● For more about quotation marks, see **Language Handbook,** p. R30.

READING AND THINKING • MAKING CRITICAL JUDGMENTS

Pythias asks the king how long he is to be kept in prison for speaking out against an unfair law, and the king says, "Two weeks from today at noon, you shall be put to death in the public square as an example to anyone else who may dare to question my laws or acts."

How do you respond to the king's decision? Is he justified? Is he acting in a way to uphold order in the community? Is he being unfair and tyrannical? When you form an opinion about a character's

actions based on information you read you are making a **critical judgment.**

PRACTICE Pythias makes a dangerous decision when he goes against the king. What dangerous decision does Damon then make? Do you think it was a wise or a foolish decision? Explain your critical judgment in a paragraph.

● For more about forming an opinion, see **Reading Handbook,** p. R83.

VOCABULARY • MULTIPLE-MEANING WORDS

The king asks if Pythias has been appointed to be the people's champion. At first, this question might not seem to make sense. Is the king asking if Pythias has been appointed the winner of a contest? No. By *champion* the king must mean something else: "one who fights for or defends another."

Most words have more than one meaning. These meanings are usually only slightly different, but they can be quite different. If one meaning is familiar to you and another is not, and it is the unfamiliar meaning that is being used, you may be confused.

PRACTICE Each pair of expressions below uses the same word. For each expression, write a synonym or short definition for the underlined word. Use a dictionary if necessary.

1. a. <u>draw</u> a picture
   b. <u>draw</u> a salary
2. a. score a <u>run</u>
   b. a <u>run</u> of bad luck
3. a. <u>dash</u> to the store
   b. <u>dash</u> a plate to the floor

Writing Skills

Finding Story Ideas

The world is full of story ideas—just ask Anansi. When you want to create a story, here are three ways to discover ideas of your own.

- Start with **setting**—the time and place of a story. To find a setting, try quickwriting. Begin describing places and times that interest you—places you've visited or read of and time periods that you know (or can imagine) something about. Any time and place that you can picture in detail can spark a story.

- Start with **characters**—the people (or other creatures) who will carry out the action. First, brainstorm a list of names: ones you like, ones you find funny, even ones you hate. Next, brainstorm a list of traits: *sly, bossy, nosy, generous,* and so on. Finally, try combining the names and traits in various ways.

- Start with **plot**—the basic story line. A plot usually involves a problem that characters must solve, or try to. The problem can be as mundane as a stalled car, or as fantastic as a monster in the sewers. You can use questions like those below to come up with a problem and solution for a story. Remember, it's your story—so give your imagination free rein.

FINDING PROBLEMS	FINDING SOLUTIONS
1. What problems might come from conflicts with nature?	1. What might have led up to the problem?
2. What problems might lead to conflicts with society?	2. What effects might the problem have?
3. What problems might pit one character against another?	3. What events might lead to a solution?
4. What problems might put a character into conflict with himself or herself?	4. What might the solution be?

ACTIVITIES

1. Use the suggestions above to come up with a story setting and characters. Then share your work with a small group of classmates. Compare your ideas.

2. Use the questions above to find a problem and solution that could form the plot of a story. Write a one-paragraph summary of your plot.

Writing WORKSHOP

Narrative Writing: Fable

A **fable** is a brief story that is told to teach a lesson. In most fables the characters are animals that act and speak like people. Many familiar fables are supposed to have been told by Aesop, an enslaved person in ancient Greece. Aesop's fables always end with a moral, or lesson about life. For example, "The Fox and the Goat" is about a fox who falls into a well. When a goat comes along, the fox tells him that the water in the well is the best he has ever tasted. The goat jumps in, and the fox climbs on his back and gets out of the well. The goat has no way to get out. The moral: "Look before you leap."

A story told, a lesson shared—that's the way a fable works. For this Workshop, you will reach into your imagination and write a fable. The characters you choose may be people or animals, or something else entirely. The setting may be as real as your own street or as fantastic as another universe. Your fable will demonstrate a lesson you've learned about human nature or about the world.

Assignment: Follow the process explained on these pages to develop your own fable.

● For more about narrative writing, see **Writing Handbook,** p. R47.

The Writing Process

PREWRITING

PREWRITING TIP
Try listing old sayings that you've heard. Which ones have you seen proven true?

● **Find the Moral**

The moral is the message or advice that is often stated at the end of a fable. To think of the moral you wish to write about, think about lessons you've learned that are important to you. Try these ideas:

● Ask yourself about lessons learned by characters in this theme. For example, what do the children learn in "The Enchanted Raisin"?

● Brainstorm for life lessons you've learned. Use headings such as "Learned by Experience," "Learned Through Advice," "Learned from Watching," "Learned from Reading," and so on.

● Explore Elements

Your fable needs characters, a setting, and a plot. Think about such elements in the tales in this theme and in other stories you know. What kind of characters, setting, and plot will best fit your own ideas? For example, might Anansi have an adventure that illustrates your moral?

● Remember Your Purpose and Audience

A fable has two purposes: to entertain and to teach. How you'll do those things depends on your audience. Will your readers be classmates, young children, or people your parents' age? Gear your fable toward your readers. Use details that your readers can identify with. Think about pacing, too: children might enjoy wild action, while older readers might enjoy a more gradual unfolding of events that allows characters and their relationships to be shown in greater depth.

● Lay Out Your Fable

Use a story map to pull the elements of your fable together.

Characters	Setting
Aunt Armadillo–insensitive, self-centered Virgil Vulture–offbeat eating habits, but old and wise Mr. and Mrs. Skunk–considerate and patient, but enough's enough Skunk Children–always hungry	Countryside between Austin and Dallas, Texas

Plot
Aunt Armadillo learns a lesson when she gets lost and no one will help her.

Moral
You should always be considerate of others, even if you're more powerful than they are.

DRAFTING

● Write Your Opener

Fables are brief stories that usually get to the point quickly. Opening sentences often state directly where the characters are and what their situation is. An example is, "A wolf and a dog were sitting by a stream." Action, dialogue, or an intriguing statement can also provide a "doorway" into your fable.

> **MODEL** · DRAFTING
>
> Aunt Armadillo never listened. She didn't have to. With her armor plates, she couldn't be hurt, no matter how mad she made anyone. When other animals complained that she had dug up their burrows or eaten their food, she just ignored them.

● Tell the Tale

Use your prewriting notes to guide you. Rather than explaining too much about your characters, let them show who they are through their actions and words. The action in your fable is important—it often illustrates or proves the moral. Tell your fable in chronological (time) order, using transitions such as *next, soon, meanwhile,* and *later*. End with your moral.

REVISING

● Fine-Tune Your Fable

Take a break, and then take a second look at your fable. Experiment with changes. You might ask a classmate for feedback and ideas. Use the **Questions for Revising** as guidelines.

QUESTIONS FOR REVISING

☑ What changes in my opening might make it more interesting?

☑ How do I keep the order of events clear? Where might transitions help?

☑ Where might I add action or dialogue?

☑ Is the moral clear? How could I improve the wording of the moral?

EDITING/PROOFREADING

Don't forget to check your revised draft for correct grammar, usage, and mechanics. Fix any errors that you spot. Pay special attention to correcting run-on sentences, following the tips in the **Grammar Link** on page 637.

Grammar Hint

If you use dialogue, your characters may speak in sentence fragments. Be sure the meaning of what they say is clear.

PROOFREADING CHECKLIST

☑ Sentences are complete; there are no fragments or run-ons.

☑ All subjects and verbs agree.

☑ Pronouns are in the correct forms and agree with their antecedents.

☑ Spelling, punctuation, and capitalization are correct.

MODEL · EDITING/PROOFREADING

Aunt Armadillo reached the outskirts of Dallas. then she lay down to rest. She would find her
                                                      but
sister's home tomorrow tonight she would have to sleep on the ground.

TECHNOLOGY TIP
If you and your classmates copy your fables onto the same disk, you can create an electronic anthology.

PUBLISHING/PRESENTING

Take turns sharing your fables in a small group. Then try creating riddles based on one another's fables. Challenge classmates to guess the answers to the riddles and to match them with the appropriate fables.

PRESENTING TIP
If you read your fable aloud, change your voice and posture to fit your characters.

Reflecting

Think about the following questions and then write responses.

- How did you come up with the moral for your fable?

- What challenged you in writing your fable? How did you deal with it?

📖 **Save your work for your portfolio.**

Theme Wrap-Up

Responding to the Theme

1. Which stories or other selections in this theme would you want to share by retelling in your own words? Explain your answer.

2. What new ideas do you have about the following as a result of your reading in this theme?
   - how stories are related to the cultures they come from
   - how traditional story elements can be used in modern stories

3. Present your theme project to the class.

Analyzing Literature

CHANGING GENRES

Think about the stories in this theme. How would each story be different if it was written as a play?
   - How are characters shown in the story? How would they be shown in a play?
   - How would the setting be shown in a play?
   - How would the theme be communicated?

Evaluate and Set Goals

1. Which of the following was most enjoyable to you? Which was most difficult?
   - reading and thinking about the selections
   - independent writing
   - analyzing the selections in discussions
   - making presentations
   - researching

2. How would you assess your work in this theme, using the following scale? Give at least two reasons for your assessment.

4 = outstanding	2 = fair
3 = good	1 = weak

3. Based on what you found difficult in this theme, choose a goal to work toward in the next theme.
   - Write your goal and three steps you will take to reach it.
   - Meet with your teacher to review your goal and your plan for achieving it.

Build Your Portfolio

SELECT

Choose two pieces of work you did in this theme to include in your portfolio. Use these questions to help you choose.

   - Which do you consider your best work?
   - Which challenged you the most?
   - Which did you learn the most from?
   - Which did you enjoy the most?

REFLECT

Write some notes to accompany the pieces you selected. Use these questions to guide you.

   - What do you like best about the piece?
   - What did you learn from creating it?
   - What might you do differently if you were beginning this piece again?

Reading on Your Own

If you have enjoyed the literature in this theme, you might be interested in the following books.

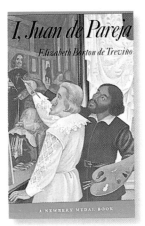

I, Juan de Pareja
by Elizabeth Borton de Trevino
This novel is based on the true story of the Spanish painter of the 1500s, Diego Rodriguez de Silva y Velazquez, and his servant and friend, Juan de Pareja.

The Firebringer and Other Great Stories: Fifty-five Legends That Live Forever
by Louis Untermeyer
This anthology includes retellings of tales from many cultures.

Plays Children Love, Volume II: A Treasury of Contemporary and Classic Plays for Children
edited by Coleman A. Jennings and Aurand Harris This anthology includes plays based on *The Wizard of Oz, Charlotte's Web,* and *The Wind in the Willows.*

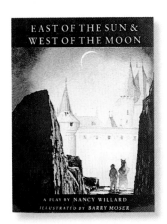

East of the Sun & West of the Moon
by Nancy Willard This poetic and amusing play tells the story of a woodcutter's daughter who travels to the ends of the earth to save her prince.

Standardized Test Practice

Read the following passage. Then read each question on page 687. Decide which is the best answer to each question. Mark the letter for that answer on your paper.

Kundalini Jeans

Rebecca's parents promised to buy her something special from the Designer Clothes Store if she received three As on her last report card for the year. When Rebecca's grades arrived, she had earned *four* As! Her father smiled and handed her the Designer Clothes Store catalog. It didn't take Rebecca long to find the exact article of clothing she had always wanted.

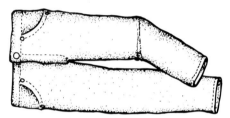

Kundalini Jeans

Feel the Power of Kundalini

Kundalini Jeans

are made in the U.S.A. with the finest Indian cotton denim. They'll keep you comfortable and stylish through every season.

Kundalini Jeans

perfectly complement any outfit. Wear them with a T-shirt for a classic American style or dress them with a tuxedo jacket for that rare touch of class. Women love them for their great fit, men love them for their comfort, and kids love them because they're cool. These jeans can be worn everywhere, and everyone's wearing them.

Kundalini Jeans

Let East Meet West

Available in fitted, tapered, boot-cut, and straight-leg styles. See your local Designer Clothes Store merchant for details, or use item number KJ302 on the catalog order form.

1   The ad for Kundalini Jeans tries to make you think that the product is very —

A   affordable

B   heavily lined

C   popular

D   traditional

2   According to the ad, men love Kundalini jeans because they —

F   are comfortable

G   come in a variety of colors

H   come from a foreign country

J   fit well

3   The advertiser changes the size and style of some letters in order to —

A   confuse their competitors

B   make the ad easier to read

C   show off a new style of lettering

D   make the ad look more interesting

4   Why does the author say "kids love them because they're cool"?

F   To convince young people to buy the jeans

G   To show that celebrities wear the jeans

H   To explain why the jeans cost so much

J   To explain why the company makes the jeans

5   In order to purchase the jeans, what should Rebecca do?

A   Go to Brennan's Department Store

B   Fill out the catalog order form with number KJ302

C   Call the manufacturer of Kundalini Jeans

D   Go to any mall

6   Which is a FACT expressed in the passage?

F   Kundalini Jeans are cool.

G   Kundalini Jeans are made entirely in India.

H   Kundalini Jeans are made of Indian cotton.

J   Kundalini Jeans perfectly complement any outfit.

To Strange Places

> **66** *Fantasy is a necessary ingredient in living; it's looking at life through the wrong end of a telescope . . . and that enables you to laugh at life's realities.* **99**
>
> —*Dr. Seuss (Theodor Seuss Geisel)*

People Flying. Peter Sickles. 11 x 14 in. Private collection.

THEME 8

THEME CONTENTS

Exploring the Theme

To Strange Places

How far can your imagination take you? When you were younger, you may have pretended that your bedroom floor was a lake or that your closet was a jungle. Perhaps now you close your eyes at night and pretend you're as far away as the moon. In this theme, you'll travel to strange places from the past, present, and future—and the only ticket you'll need is your imagination!

Starting Points

SPACE VEHICLES

Cartoon character Calvin can transport himself to outer space on his swing. For most people, it is more difficult to get in touch with their imaginations. What are some ways you use your imagination? To what places can it take you? Is there a special place you like to visit in your imagination? What is it like? Why do you like to go there? Share your answers with a small group.

Calvin and Hobbes

by Bill Watterson

Theme Projects

As you read the selections in this theme, try one of the projects below.
Work on your own, with a partner, or with a group.

INTERDISCIPLINARY ACTIVITY
Science

1. View photos of space and machines used for space exploration, such as the lunar rover and the Hubble Space Telescope. Check the library or Internet sites such as the *National Air and Space Museum.*

2. Make copies or printouts of the most interesting photos. Assemble the pictures into a book.

3. Write a caption for each picture. Identify what is shown. Tell what the space machines do.

4. Write a paragraph about each photo. Tell how you *imagine* such a place or such a machine could be used in an exciting fictional story.

5. Present your collection of images, captions, and writing ideas to the class.

*inter*NET
CONNECTION

Check out the Web for more project ideas or more books related to the theme. Type the keywords *outer space, travel,* or *science fiction* into a search engine. You can also check out the Glencoe Literature Web site for more about this theme: lit.glencoe.com

LEARNING FOR LIFE
Touring Your Community
Zoos create habitats, special places like animals' natural homes, for their animals. What places in your community—restaurants, stores, playgrounds, theme parks, libraries, or classrooms—create special or different worlds?

1. Find three places that create different worlds for visitors.

2. Make a display using note cards and photos or drawings. Describe the unique settings. Tell how and why each was created.

MULTIMEDIA PROJECT
Foreign Bodies
Use a computer software drawing program to draw alien beings.

1. Brainstorm details about the aliens' world. What is the name of their planet? What special abilities do the aliens possess?

2. Add captions to the images to create a computer slide show or a handbook.

Before You Read

The Pied Piper of Hamelin

MEET ROBERT BROWNING

Although Robert Browning was not honored as a great poet until late in his life, he is now known as one of the most important poets of his time. Browning wrote "The Pied Piper of Hamelin" for the young son of a friend, a boy named Willie Macready, who is mentioned in the last stanza of the poem. Browning wanted to entertain Willie while he was sick and give him a subject for illustrative drawings. Willie spent several weeks in bed making drawings that are now part of a collection of Browning material at Baylor University, in Texas.

Robert Browning was born in 1812 and died in 1889. "The Pied Piper of Hamelin" was written in 1842.

FOCUS ACTIVITY

What is your favorite kind of music? What kind of music would you recommend to a friend? Why? Do you think music can create a kind of spell?

Three-Step Interview
With a partner, interview another pair of students about their favorite kinds of music and what they like about the music.

Setting a Purpose
Find out how music is important in "The Pied Piper of Hamelin."

BACKGROUND

The Time and Place   The poem is based on a German legend about a piper who, in 1284, lured 130 children from the town of Hamelin (now Hameln) in the province of Hanover, Germany. Browning moved the town to the province of Brunswick and changed the year to 1376.

Some historians think that the legend may have been influenced by the Children's Crusade of 1212. Twenty thousand young people left Germany intending to walk across the Mediterranean Sea and recapture Jerusalem from the Muslims. Most of these children never returned home. Other historians have found evidence that in 1284, Hameln's young people were sent by their bishop as colonists to Moravia, now in the Czech Republic. It is also possible that young people from Hameln may have migrated to the Polish region of Pomerania.

The Pied Piper of Hamelin, 1842. Willie Macready. Drawing from Browning's *Pied Piper.* Armstrong Browning Library, Baylor University, Waco, TX.

The Pied Piper of Hamelin

Robert Browning

Hamelin Town's in Brunswick,
By famous Hanover city;
   The river Weser,° deep and wide,
   Washes its wall on the southern side;
5   A pleasanter spot you never spied;
But, when begins my ditty,
   Almost five hundred years ago,
   To see the townsfolk suffer so
     From vermin, was a pity.

10   Rats!
They fought the dogs, and killed the cats,
   And bit the babies in the cradles,
And ate the cheeses out of the vats,
   And licked the soup from the cooks' own ladles,
15 Split open the kegs of salted sprats,°
Made nests inside men's Sunday hats,
And even spoiled the women's chats,
     By drowning their speaking
     With shrieking and squeaking
20 In fifty different sharps and flats.

At last the people in a body
   To the Town Hall came flocking:
" 'Tis clear," cried they, "our Mayor's a noddy;°
   And as for our Corporation°—shocking
25 To think we buy gowns lined with ermine
For dolts that can't or won't determine
What's best to rid us of our vermin!
You hope, because you're old and obese,
To find in the furry civic robe ease?
30 Rouse up, Sirs!   Give your brains a racking
To find the remedy we're lacking,
Or, sure as fate, we'll send you packing!"
At this the Mayor and Corporation
Quaked with a mighty consternation.°

35 An hour they sate in council,
   At length the Mayor broke silence:

3 Weser (vā′ zər)

15 sprats: small, herring-like fish.

23 noddy: a fool.
24 Corporation: town council.

34 consternation: great shock or amazement mixed with confusion or fear.

"For a guilder° I'd my ermine gown sell;
   I wish I were a mile hence!
It's easy to bid one rack one's brain—
40 I'm sure my poor head aches again
I've scratched it so, and all in vain.
Oh for a trap, a trap, a trap!"
Just as he said this, what should hap
At the chamber door but a gentle tap?
45 "Bless us," cried the Mayor, "what's that?"
(With the Corporation as he sat,
Looking little though wondrous fat;
Nor brighter was his eye, nor moister
Than a too-long-opened oyster,
50 Save when at noon his paunch° grew mutinous°
For a plate of turtle green and glutinous°)
"Only a scraping of shoes on the mat?
Anything like the sound of a rat
Makes my heart go pit-a-pat!"

55 "Come in!"—the Mayor cried, looking bigger:
And in did come the strangest figure!
His queer long coat from heel to head
Was half of yellow and half of red;
And he himself was tall and thin,
60 With sharp blue eyes, each like a pin,
And light loose hair, yet swarthy° skin,
No tuft on cheek nor beard on chin,
But lips where smiles went out and in—
There was no guessing his kith and kin!
65 And nobody could enough admire
The tall man and his quaint attire:°
Quoth one: "It's as if my great-grandsire,
Starting up at the Trump of Doom's° tone,
Had walked this way from his painted tombstone!"°

70 He advanced to the council table:
And, "Please your honors," said he, "I'm able,
By means of a secret charm to draw
All creatures living beneath the sun,
That creep or swim or fly or run,

---

37 guilder (gil′ dər): the basic money of the Netherlands.

50 paunch: big belly. **mutinous** (mūt′ ən əs): rebellious.
51 glutinous (glōōt′ ən əs): sticky; gluey.

61 swarthy: dark or sunburned.

66 quaint attire: strange, old-fashioned clothes.

67–69 This speaker imagines that his dead great-grandfather might have been buried in clothes similar to the stranger's. Some Christians believe that the dead will rise from their graves when an angel's trumpet (**the Trump of Doom**) announces God's final judgment day.

Rats Lured by Pied Piper, late 18th century. O. Herrfurth. Illustration for book.

Viewing the art: What do the rats hear in the Piper's music? Find the words in the poem that explain the experience from their point of view.

75 After me so as you never saw!
And I chiefly use my charm
On creatures that do people harm,
The mole and toad and newt and viper;
And people call me the Pied° Piper."

79 **Pied**: having large spots or patterns of different colors. Lines 81–82 describe the striped scarf and checkered coat that give the piper his name.

80 (And here they noticed round his neck
A scarf of red and yellow stripe,
To match with his coat of the self-same check;
And at the scarf's end hung a pipe;
And his fingers, they noticed, were ever straying
85 As if impatient to be playing
Upon this pipe, as low it dangled
Over his vesture° so old-fangled.)
"Yet," said he, "poor piper as I am,
In Tartary° I freed the Cham,°
90 Last June, from his huge swarms of gnats;
I eased in Asia the Nizam°
Of a monstrous brood of vampire bats:
And as for what your brain bewilders,
If I can rid your town of rats
95 Will you give me a thousand guilders?"
"One? fifty thousand!"—was the exclamation
Of the astonished Mayor and Corporation.

87 **vesture**: clothing; garments.

89 **Tartary**: a region of Russia. **Cham**: a prince of Tartary.

91 **Nizam**: the ruler of a region of India.

Into the street the Piper stept,
    Smiling first a little smile,
100 As if he knew what magic slept
    In his quiet pipe the while;
Then, like a musical adept,°
To blow the pipe his lips he wrinkled,
And green and blue his sharp eyes twinkled
105 Like a candleflame where salt is sprinkled;
And ere three shrill notes the pipe uttered,
You heard as if an army muttered;
And the muttering grew to a grumbling;
And the grumbling grew to a mighty rumbling;
110 And out of the houses the rats came tumbling.
Great rats, small rats, lean rats, brawny rats,
Brown rats, black rats, grey rats, tawny rats,

102 **adept**: an expert.

Grave old plodders, gay young friskers,
   Fathers, mothers, uncles, cousins,
115 Cocking tails and pricking whiskers,
   Families by tens and dozens,
Brothers, sisters, husbands, wives—
Followed the Piper for their lives.
From street to street he piped advancing,
120 And step for step they followed dancing,
Until they came to the river Weser
Wherein all plunged and perished!
  —Save one who, stout° as Julius Caesar,°
Swam across and lived to carry
125 (As he, the manuscript he cherished)
To Rat-land home his commentary:
Which was, "At the first shrill notes of the pipe,
I heard a sound as of scraping tripe,
And putting apples, wondrous ripe,
130 Into a cider press's gripe:
And a moving away of pickle-tub boards,
And a leaving ajar of conserve cupboards,
And a drawing the corks of train-oil° flasks,
And a breaking the hoops of butter casks;°
135 And it seemed as if a voice
(Sweeter far than by harp or by psaltery°
Is breathed) called out, 'Oh rats, rejoice!
The world is grown to one vast drysaltery!°
So, munch on, crunch on, take your nuncheon,°
140 Breakfast, supper, dinner, luncheon!'
And just as a bulky sugar puncheon,
All ready staved, like a great sun shone
Glorious scarce an inch before me,
Just as methought it said, 'Come, bore me!'
145 —I found the Weser rolling o'er me."°

You should have heard the Hamelin people
Ringing the bells till they rocked the steeple;
"Go," cried the Mayor, "and get long poles!
Poke out the nests and block up the holes!
150 Consult with carpenters and builders,
And leave in our town not even a trace

123 stout: courageous. **Julius Caesar:** the general who disobeyed the Roman Senate's order to give up his command and marched his troops across the Rubicon (a stream) into Italy. He defeated his opponents and became the dictator of the Roman Empire.

126–134 The surviving rat reports that the piper's notes sounded like the noises of food being prepared and food containers being opened—sounds that would be "music" to the rats' ears.

133 train-oil: whale oil.

136 psaltery: an ancient musical instrument.

138 drysaltery: a store that sells dried foods.

139 nuncheon: a light snack eaten at midmorning or midafternoon.

141–145 The rat saw a barrel of sugar that had been broken open. The barrel seemed to say, "Help yourself!" Then the rat came to his senses and realized that he was in danger of drowning.

Of the rats!"—when suddenly, up the face
Of the Piper perked in the marketplace,
With a, "First, if you please, my thousand guilders!"

155   A thousand guilders!   The mayor looked blue;
So did the Corporation too.
For council dinners made rare havoc
With Claret, Moselle, Vin-de-Grave, Hock;
And half the money would replenish

160   Their cellar's biggest butt with Rhenish.°
To pay this sum to a wandering fellow
With a gipsy coat of red and yellow!
"Beside," quoth the Mayor with a knowing wink,
"Our business was done at the river's brink;

165   We saw with our eyes the vermin sink,
And what's dead can't come to life, I think.
So, friend, we're not the folks to shrink
From the duty of giving you something for drink,
And a matter of money to put in your poke;°

170   But as for the guilders, what we spoke
Of them, as you very well know, was in joke.
Beside, our losses have made us thrifty.
A thousand guilders!   Come, take fifty!"

The piper's face fell, and he cried,

175   "No trifling!   I can't wait, beside!
I've promised to visit by dinner time
Bagdat, and accept the prime
Of the Head Cook's pottage, all he's rich in,
For having left, in the Caliph's kitchen,

180   Of a nest of scorpions no survivor°—
With him I proved no bargain-driver,
With you, don't think I'll bate a stiver!°
And folks who put me in a passion
May find me pipe to another fashion."

185   "How?" cried the Mayor, "d'ye think I'll brook°
Being worse treated than a Cook?
Insulted by a lazy ribald°
With idle pipe and vesture piebald?°

156–160 The council members drink so much that they have used up their stock of wines. With five hundred guilders, they could resupply the wine cellar with a 130-gallon barrel of a good Dutch wine.

169 poke: wallet or purse.

176–180 The piper is going to Baghdad (in what is now Iraq). In return for killing poisonous scorpions, the ruler's cook will serve the piper his specialty, a tasty stew.

182 bate a stiver: lower (your bill) one tiny bit. The stiver is a Dutch coin of very low value, like a U.S. penny.

185 brook: stand for.

187 ribald: a good-for-nothing rascal.

188 piebald: covered with spots or patches of color; pied.

The Pied Piper of Hamelin

You threaten us, fellow?   Do your worst,
190   Blow your pipe there till you burst!"

Once more he stept into the street;
      And to his lips again
Laid his long pipe of smooth straight cane;
      And ere he blew three notes (such sweet
195   Soft notes as yet musician's cunning
            Never gave the enraptured air)
There was a rustling, that seemed like a bustling
Of merry crowds justling at pitching and hustling,
Small feet were pattering, wooden shoes clattering,
200   Little hands clapping and little tongues chattering,
And, like fowls in a farmyard when barley is scattering,
Out came the children running.
All the little boys and girls,
With rosy cheeks and flaxen curls,
205   And sparkling eyes and teeth like pearls,
Tripping and skipping, ran merrily after
The wonderful music with shouting and laughter.

The Mayor was dumb, and the Council stood
As if they were changed into blocks of wood,
210   Unable to move a step, or cry
To the children merrily skipping by—
And could only follow with the eye
That joyous crowd at the Piper's back.
But how the Mayor was on the rack,°
215   And the wretched Council's bosoms beat,
As the Piper turned from the High Street
To where the Weser rolled its waters
Right in the way of their sons and daughters!
However he turned from South to West,
220   And to Koppelberg Hill his steps addressed,
And after him the children pressed;
Great was the joy in every breast.
"He never can cross that mighty top!
He's forced to let the piping drop,
225   And we shall see our children stop!"
When, lo, as they reached the mountain's side,

214 on the rack: suffering great pain and worry. In the Middle Ages, the rack was an instrument of torture used to stretch or pull a victim's body in different directions.

Children of Hamelin Following the Piper, late 18th century. O. Herrfurth. Illustration for book.

Viewing the art: Do you think this illustration reflects the children's mood as described in the poem? Why or why not?

A wondrous portal opened wide,
As if a cavern was suddenly hollowed;
And the Piper advanced and the children followed,
230 And when all were in to the very last,
The door in the mountainside shut fast.
Did I say, all? No! One was lame,
And could not dance the whole of the way;
And in after years, if you would blame
235 His sadness, he was used to say,—
"It's dull in our town since my playmates left!
I can't forget that I'm bereft°

237 **bereft:** robbed; stripped.

Of all the pleasant sights they see,
Which the Piper also promised me.
240 For he led us, he said, to a joyous land,
Joining the town and just at hand,
Where waters gushed and fruit trees grew,
And flowers put forth a fairer hue,
And everything was strange and new;
245 The sparrows were brighter than peacocks here,
And their dogs outran our fallow deer,°

246 **fallow deer:** a small European deer, about three feet high at the shoulder.

And honeybees had lost their stings,
And horses were born with eagles' wings:
And just as I became assured
250 My lame foot would be speedily cured,
The music stopped and I stood still,
And found myself outside the Hill,
Left alone against my will,
To go now limping as before,
255 And never hear of that country more!"

Alas, alas for Hamelin!
    There came into many a burgher's pate°
    A text which says that Heaven's Gate
    Opes to the Rich at as easy rate

257 **burgher's pate:** citizen's head.

260 As the needle's eye takes a camel in!
The Mayor sent East, West, North and South,
To offer the Piper, by word of mouth,
    Wherever it was men's lot to find him,
Silver and gold to his heart's content,

265 If he'd only return the way he went,
  And bring the children behind him.
 But when they saw 'twas a lost endeavor,
 And Piper and dancers were gone for ever,
 They made a decree that lawyers never
270 Should think their records dated duly°
 If, after the day of the month and year,
 These words did not as well appear,
 "And so long after what happened here
  On the Twenty-second of July,
275 Thirteen hundred and seventy-six:"
 And the better in memory to fix
 The place of the children's last retreat,
 They called it, the Pied Piper's Street—
 Where any one playing on pipe or tabor°
280 Was sure for the future to lose his labor.
 Nor suffered° they hostelry° or tavern
  To shock with mirth a street so solemn;
 But opposite the place of the cavern
  They wrote the story on a column,
285 And on the great church window painted
 The same, to make the world acquainted
 How their children were stolen away,
 And there it stands to this very day.
 And I must not omit to say
290 That in Transylvania there's a tribe
 Of alien people that ascribe
 The outlandish ways and dress
 On which their neighbors lay such stress,
 To their fathers and mothers having risen
295 Out of some subterranean° prison,
 Into which they were trepann'd°
 Long time ago in a mighty band
 Out of Hamelin town in Brunswick land,
 But how or why, they don't understand.

300 So, Willy, let you and me be wipers
 Of scores out with all men—especially pipers;
 And, whether they pipe us free, from rats or mice,
 If we've promised them aught, let us keep our promise.

270 duly: properly.

279 tabor: a small, handheld drum.

281 suffered: permitted. **hostelry:** an inn or hotel.

295 subterranean: underground.

296 trepann'd (tri pand'): tricked; lured.

Responding to Literature

PERSONAL RESPONSE

◆ What do you think of the Pied Piper's action?
◆ Do you believe that music can have such power? Use your ideas from the **Focus Activity** on page 692 to respond in your journal.

Analyzing Literature

RECALL

1. What deal is made between the piper and the mayor?
2. What does the piper do to fulfill his half of the bargain? What does he do when he is not paid?

INTERPRET

3. Why doesn't the mayor fulfill his promise?
4. Why doesn't anyone stop the piper from taking his revenge on the town?

EVALUATE AND CONNECT

5. How do readers learn of the magic of the piper's music?
6. How does Browning remind the reader that the story is based on a legend?
7. What do you think the old expression, "You have to pay the piper" means? How does it apply to this selection?
8. By the end of the poem, who has your greatest sympathy? Why?
9. Would you have done what the piper did? Explain.
10. Theme Connection   What lesson do you take from the poem?

LITERARY ELEMENTS

Narrative Poetry

A **narrative poem** tells a story. It includes a setting, characters, action, and a conflict, just as a short story or novel does. To tell a story, narrative poetry can use all of the techniques of poetry, such as rhythm, rhyme, and repetition. Instead of being written in paragraphs as a story would be, a narrative poem is written in stanzas. Narrative poems are often fairly long.

1. Describe the setting, characters, and action in the story of the Pied Piper.

2. What effect do rhythm, rhyme, and repetition have on the story?

● See **Literary Terms Handbook,** p. R5.

Extending Your Response

Writing About Literature

Compare and Contrast How is the Pied Piper described as he first appears in the council chamber? In two paragraphs, contrast the piper's appearance with the descriptions given of the mayor and council members. Explain what the characters' appearances tell about them.

Creative Writing

News from Afar Imagine that you are traveling in Germany and you come across the column that tells the story of the Pied Piper and the church window that pictures what happened there. Write a letter to a friend at home to describe what you have seen and to share your reaction.

Interdisciplinary Activity

Music What haunting melodies might have the effect of the piper's song? Gather suggestions of songs that are powerful and could inspire or influence others. Tape-record a few of the strongest pieces to play for the class.

Literature Groups

Tracing the Plot Discuss the major elements of the plot in "The Pied Piper of Hamelin," including, the **exposition, rising action, climax, falling action,** and **resolution.** *Genre Focus: Short Stories* on pages 350–351 will help you identify these elements. Outline events on a plot diagram and share your conclusions with the class.

Reading Further

If you enjoyed this poem, you might enjoy these narrative poems:

"Paul Revere's Ride" by Henry Wadsworth Longfellow

"The Scroobious Pip" by Edward Lear, completed by Ogden Nash

A Visit to William Blake's Inn by Nancy Willard

If you would like to read another version of this story, try this historical novel:

What Happened in Hamelin by Gloria Skurzynski

📖 **Save your work for your portfolio.**

Skill Minilesson

VOCABULARY • ARCHAIC WORDS

When the mayor fears he will lose his job because of the rat problem, he says, "I wish I were a mile *hence!*" *Hence* means "from here." Words that are no longer commonly used are called **archaic.** Writers and poets may use archaic words to create the tone of old tales. Usually, readers can understand the meanings of archaic words by their **context**–the words and sentences that surround them.

PRACTICE Find the following archaic words in the selection. Then, based on their context, write a short definition for each word.

1. kith and kin (l. 64)
2. quoth (l. 67)
3. self-same (l. 82)
4. ere (l. 106)
5. methought (l. 144)

● For more on using context clues to unlock meaning, see **Reading Handbook,** p. R64.

Before You Read
The Walrus and the Carpenter

MEET LEWIS CARROLL

Lewis Carroll was the pen name of Charles Lutwidge Dodgson, a professor of mathematics at University of Oxford in England. Even before he became famous as a writer, Dodgson was well known as a photographer, especially of children. Although he was shy and sometimes stuttered with adults, he was comfortable with children and kept up friendships with many of them by writing letters. Some letters were written on paper no bigger than postage stamps and some were written in reverse so that they had to be read in a mirror.

Lewis Carroll was born in 1832 and died in 1898. Through the Looking-Glass *was published in 1872.*

FOCUS ACTIVITY

Has anyone ever played a trick on you? Was it fun? Did you laugh? Were you angry?

Think/Pair/Share
Think about tricks that characters on a favorite television show have played on each other. Were the tricks funny or clever? Why did one character trick another? How did the person who was tricked react? Share your ideas with another person in the class.

Setting a Purpose
Find out who is tricked in "The Walrus and the Carpenter."

BACKGROUND

While on a picnic, Lewis Carroll made up a story for three little girls—the daughters of the dean of his college. One of the girls was named Alice. In Carroll's story, a character named Alice falls down a rabbit hole and finds herself in a fabulous and strange wonderland.

Carroll later remembered how "in a desperate attempt to strike out some new line of fairy-lore, I had sent my heroine straight down a rabbit hole, to begin with, without the least idea what was to happen afterwards."

Young Alice made Carroll promise that he would write the story down. It became part of *Alice's Adventures in Wonderland.* The sequel to this book is *Through the Looking-Glass,* which contains the poem, "The Walrus and the Carpenter."

Alice, 1872. John Tenniel. Wood engraving from *Through the Looking Glass and What Alice Found There,* by Lewis Carroll. The Newberry Library, Chicago, IL.

The Walrus and the Carpenter

Lewis Carroll

The sun was shining on the sea,
　　Shining with all his might:
He did his very best to make
　　The billows° smooth and bright—
5　And this was odd, because it was
　　The middle of the night.

The moon was shining sulkily,
　　Because she thought the sun
Had got no business to be there
10　After the day was done—
"It's very rude of him," she said,
　　"To come and spoil the fun!"

---

4 *Billows* are big waves.

The Walrus and the Carpenter

The sea was wet as wet could be,
    The sands were dry as dry.
15 You could not see a cloud, because
    No cloud was in the sky:
No birds were flying overhead—
    There were no birds to fly.

The Walrus and the Carpenter
20   Were walking close at hand;
They wept like anything to see
    Such quantities of sand:
"If this were only cleared away,"
    They said, "it *would* be grand!"

25 "If seven maids with seven mops
    Swept it for half a year,
Do you suppose," the Walrus said,
    "That they could get it clear?"
"I doubt it," said the Carpenter,
30   And shed a bitter tear.

"O Oysters, come and walk with us!"
    The Walrus did beseech.°
"A pleasant walk, a pleasant talk,
    Along the briny° beach:
35 We cannot do with more than four,
    To give a hand to each."

The eldest Oyster looked at him,
    But never a word he said:

The eldest Oyster winked his eye,
40   And shook his heavy head—
Meaning to say he did not choose
    To leave the oyster-bed.

But four young Oysters hurried up,
    All eager for the treat:
45 Their coats were brushed, their faces
      washed,
    Their shoes were clean and neat—
And this was odd, because, you know,
    They hadn't any feet.

Four other Oysters followed them,
50   And yet another four;
And thick and fast they came at last,
    And more, and more, and more—
All hopping through the frothy° waves,
    And scrambling to the shore.

55 The Walrus and the Carpenter
    Walked on a mile or so,
And then they rested on a rock
    Conveniently low:
And all the little Oysters stood
60   And waited in a row.

"The time has come," the Walrus said,
    "To talk of many things:
Of shoes—and ships—and sealing-wax—
    Of cabbages—and kings—

---

32 *Beseech* means "to beg or ask earnestly."
34 Water that's salty, like ocean water, is *briny*.

53 Water that's bubbly, like the foam on root beer, is *frothy*.

65 And why the sea is boiling hot—
And whether pigs have wings."

"But wait a bit," the Oysters cried,
"Before we have our chat;
For some of us are out of breath,
70 And all of us are fat!"
"No hurry!" said the Carpenter.
They thanked him much for that.

"A loaf of bread," the Walrus said,
"Is what we chiefly need:

75 Pepper and vinegar besides
Are very good indeed—
Now if you're ready, Oysters dear,
We can begin to feed."

"But not on us!" the Oysters cried,
80 Turning a little blue.
"After such kindness, that would be
A dismal thing to do!"
"The night is fine," the Walrus said.
"Do you admire the view?

The Walrus and the Carpenter, 1872. John Tenniel. Wood engraving from *Through the Looking Glass and What Alice Found There,* by Lewis Carroll. The Newberry Library, Chicago, IL.

Viewing the engraving: How are your visualizations of Carroll's characters like and unlike those in Tenniel's engravings?

The Walrus and the Carpenter, 1872. John Tenniel. Wood engraving from *Through the Looking Glass and What Alice Found There,* by Lewis Carroll. The Newberry Library, Chicago, IL.

Viewing the engraving: Which lines in the poem are illustrated here?

85   "It was so kind of you to come!
          And you are very nice!"
      The Carpenter said nothing but
          "Cut us another slice:
      I wish you were not quite so deaf—
90   I've had to ask you twice!"

      "It seems a shame," the Walrus said,
          "To play them such a trick,
      After we've brought them out so far,
          And made them trot so quick!"
95   The Carpenter said nothing but
          "The butter's spread too thick!"

      "I weep for you," the Walrus said:
          "I deeply sympathize."
      With sobs and tears he sorted out
100   Those of the largest size,
      Holding his pocket-handkerchief
          Before his streaming eyes.

      "O Oysters," said the Carpenter,
          "You've had a pleasant run!
105   Shall we be trotting home again?"
          But answer came there none—
      And this was scarcely odd, because
          They'd eaten every one.

Responding to Literature

PERSONAL RESPONSE

- What do you imagine the walrus and the carpenter would say to each other as they walk back up the beach?
- Think back on the tricks you discussed in the **Focus Activity** on page 706. Do you think the young oysters would have any of the same thoughts you have about tricks?

Analyzing Literature

RECALL AND INTERPRET

1. According to the walrus and the carpenter, what is the problem with the beach? What solution is proposed?

2. How do the walrus and the carpenter get the young oysters to follow them? Why doesn't the old oyster go with the walrus and the carpenter?

3. What happens to the oysters? Whose fault is it, would you say? Do you think the walrus truly regrets what happens? Explain.

EVALUATE AND CONNECT

4. What makes this poem humorous? Give a few examples.

5. Based on this poem, would you like to read more by Lewis Carroll? Explain.

6. Does this poem remind you of any others you have read? If so, in what ways?

LITERARY ELEMENTS

Nonsense Verse

In the world created by Lewis Carroll, the shoes of the young oysters "were clean and neat– / And this was odd, because, you know, / They hadn't any feet." When a poem presents ridiculous, impossible, silly situations, the poetry is called **nonsense verse**. The general rules of life–such as that shoes go with feet–are over-ruled, and silly, nonsensical things happen. A strong rhythm and rhyme pattern add to the fun.

1. Give three examples of non-sense in this poem.

2. What is the poem's rhyme scheme? (See page 187 to review rhyme scheme.)

- For more about rhyme, see **Literary Terms Handbook**, p. R7.

Extending Your Response

Writing About Literature

Personification The poem contains **personification**–figures of speech that give human qualities to animals or things. For example, the moon shines "sulkily" because she is angry at the sun. Write a paragraph that explains other examples of personification in the poem.

Performing

Readers Theater Enjoy the rhythm and rhyme of this poem, as well as its story. With others in a group, take the parts of the characters and read the poem aloud. Practice until your group can say the poem together smoothly, and present it to the class.

COMPARING SELECTIONS

The Pied Piper of Hamelin **and** The Walrus and the Carpenter

COMPARE **CHARACTERS**

Both poems highlight unusual characters. Use these questions to compare the characters.

1. How would you describe the Pied Piper, the Walrus, and the Carpenter? Discuss the outstanding characteristics of each.

2. Discuss what the characters do. In what way is what the Walrus and the Carpenter do similar to what the Pied Piper does?

3. Discuss how the characters in each poem accomplish their purposes.

COMPARE **TECHNIQUES**

Both poems tell stories, but they tell them differently. Write a paragraph comparing the tone of the poems and explaining how each poet achieves the tone.

- Is the tone appropriate for the subject? Why or why not?
- What effect do rhyme, rhythm, word choice, and imagery have on each poem?

COMPARE **AUTHOR'S PURPOSE**

Think about the purpose for each of these poems and how well each poet accomplishes his purpose.

1. Which poem did you enjoy more? Explain.

2. Do you think either of these poems would have been more or less enjoyable if it had been written as a story instead of a poem? Explain.

3. Write a brief book review. Urge your readers to buy a book containing one of the poems, and give reasons for your recommendation.

Using Correct Capitalization

As a writer you will want to use capital letters correctly.

Problem 1 words referring to ethnic groups, nationalities, and languages

> *An english poet retold a legend familiar to german people.*

Solution Capitalize the names of ethnic groups, nationalities, and languages, and the adjectives formed from them.

> *An English poet retold a legend familiar to German people.*

Problem 2 the first word of a direct quotation

> *Our teacher said, "the town of Hamelin is now called Hameln."*
>
> *"The legend of the Pied Piper," he said, "May be based on fact."*

Solution Capitalize the first word of a direct quotation. If a quotation is interrupted by a speaker tag, do not begin the second part of the quotation with a capital letter.

> *Our teacher said, "The town of Hamelin is now called Hameln."*
>
> *"The legend of the Pied Piper," he said, "may be based on fact."*

Problem 3 an interrupted quotation made up of two sentences

> *"It is a mystery," he said, "no one knows what happened."*

Solution If the second part of a quotation is a complete sentence, put a period after the speaker tag. Begin the second part of the quotation with a capital letter.

> *"It is a mystery," he said. "No one knows what happened."*

● For more on capitalization, see **Language Handbook,** pp. R30–R32.

EXERCISE

If the sentence is capitalized correctly, write *Correct.* If it is not, rewrite the sentence.

1. Lewis Carroll taught Mathematics at the University of Oxford in england.
2. His books have been translated into French, german, Spanish, and many other languages, and are quoted almost as often as shakespeare.
3. In the 1800s, english children memorized long poems about proper behavior.

Before You Read
Aunt Millicent

MEET MARY STEELE

"I had my own small collection of books, which I read over and over again," Mary Steele recalls of her childhood, "and in them I could lose myself in another world." Steele lives in Australia. She has worked as a school librarian, university tutor, research assistant, and book reviewer. She says, "One need never be bored or lonely in the company of a good book—by the fire, in bed, up a tree, on the beach, in the bath, or on a train. Can the same be said of a television or a computer screen?"

Mary Steele was born in 1930. This story is from a book of Australian short stories called Dream Time, *published in 1991.*

FOCUS ACTIVITY

Think up an imaginary person with a very interesting life. How would you describe this person? What adventures has this person had?

Discuss
In a small group, decide on the age, gender, appearance, and past history of an imaginary person. Then "introduce" your imaginary person to the class, telling a bit about him or her.

Setting a Purpose
Read "Aunt Millicent" to find out about the interesting past of an unusual aunt.

BACKGROUND

Did You Know?
The *Cameroons* are areas of West Central Africa that were previously governed by France and Great Britain. These areas are now the nation of Cameroon and part of the nation of Nigeria.

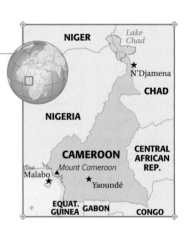

VOCABULARY PREVIEW

tedious (tē′ dē əs) *adj.* boring; tiresome; p. 716
scoff (skof) *v.* to speak with scorn; mock; p. 716
drab (drab) *adj.* lacking brightness; dull; cheerless; p. 718
spellbound (spel′ bound) *adj.* held, as if by magic; fascinated; charmed; p. 721
exotic (ig zot′ ik) *adj.* strangely beautiful or interesting; unusual; foreign; p. 722
encounter (en koun′ tər) *n.* a direct meeting, as between enemies in conflict or in battle; an unexpected meeting; p. 724
hoax (hōks) *n.* a trick, fraud, or practical joke; p. 727

Aunt Millicent

Mary Steele

"I," said Angelica Tonks, grandly, "have eight uncles and eleven aunts."

Angelica Tonks had more of most things than anyone else. She held the class record for pairs of fashion sneakers and Derwent pencil sets, and her pocket-money supply was endless. Now, it seemed, she also had the largest uncle-and-aunt collection in town. Her classmates squirmed and made faces at each other. *Awful* Angelica Tonks.

Mr. Wilfred Starling dusted the chalk from his bony hands and sighed. "Well, Angelica, aren't you a lucky one to have nineteen uncles and aunts. You'll just have to choose the most interesting one to write about, won't you?"

"But they're *all* interesting," objected Angelica. "The Tonks family is a wonderfully interesting family, you know. It will be terribly hard to choose just one."

Aunt Millicent

There were more squirms. The class was fed up with the wonderfully interesting Tonks family. In fact, Mr. Wilfred Starling nearly screamed. He just managed to swallow his exasperation, which sank down to form a hard bubble in his stomach. Straightening his thin shoulders, he said, "Right, everyone, copy down this week's homework assignment from the board. And remember, Angelica, a pen-portrait of just *one* aunt or uncle is all I want. Just *one*." *Please not a whole gallery of tedious and terrible Tonkses,* he thought to himself.

The class began to write. Jamie Nutbeam, sitting behind Angelica, leaned forward and hissed, "If the rest of your family is so *wonderfully interesting,* they must be a big improvement on you, Honky![1] And, anyway, I bet the aunt I write about will beat any of yours!"

"I bet she won't," Angelica hissed back. "She'll be so *boring.* What's her name, this boring aunt?"

Jamie finished copying and put down his pen. "Aunt Millicent, and she's pretty special."

"Millicent!" scoffed Angelica. "What a name! No one's called Millicent these days!"

"QUIET, you two!" barked Mr. Starling, massaging his stomach, "and start tidying up, everyone—it's time for the bell." *Oh bliss,* he thought.

As the classroom emptied, Jamie lingered behind.

"What is it, Jamie?" asked Mr. Starling wearily, piling his books and papers together and trying not to burp.

"Well, the trouble is I haven't any aunts or uncles to do a portrait of," said Jamie, turning rather red, "so is it all right if I make one up? An aunt?"

"Oh, I see! Well, in that case . . . yes, perfectly all right," replied Mr. Starling. He gazed rather sadly out the window. "The most interesting characters in the world are usually the made-up ones, you know, Jamie. Think of Sherlock Holmes and Alice and Dr. Who and Indiana Jones . . ."

Jamie interrupted. "Does anyone need to know I've made her up? This aunt?"

"Well, *I* won't say anything," promised Mr. Starling. "It's for you to make her seem real so we all believe in her. You go home and see what you can dream up."

"She has a name already," Jamie called back as he left the room. "She's Aunt Millicent."

Aunt Millicent Nutbeam! The hard bubble in Mr. Starling's stomach began to melt away.

That evening, Jamie Nutbeam said to his family at large, "Did you know that awful Angelica Tonks has eight uncles and eleven aunts?"

"Well, everybody knows that they're a big family," replied his mother.

"Prolific,[2] I'd call it," grunted Jamie's father from behind his newspaper.

---

1. Adding this nickname to Angelica's last name makes her *Honky Tonks,* and *honkytonks* just happens to be a term for cheap, noisy nightclubs.

2. Here, *prolific* means "producing many offspring."

Vocabulary

tedious (tē′ dē əs) *adj.* boring; tiresome
scoff (skof) *v.* to speak with scorn; mock

"Yes, dear—prolific. Now, Mrs. Tonks was a Miss Blizzard," continued Mrs. Nutbeam, "and there are lots of Blizzards around here as well as Tonkses, all related, no doubt. But fancy nineteen! Who told you there were nineteen, Jamie?"

"She did—old Honky Tonks herself. She told the whole class *and* Mr. Starling—boasting away as usual. She's a *pill*." Jamie was jotting things on paper as he talked. "We have to write a pen-portrait of an aunt or uncle for homework, and Honky can't decide which one to do because they're all so *wonderfully interesting*, she says. Urk!" He paused and then added, "I'm doing Aunt Millicent."

Jamie's father peered over the top of his newspaper. "Aunt who?"

"Who's Aunt Millicent?" demanded Jamie's sister, Nerissa.

"You haven't got an Aunt Millicent," said his mother. "You haven't any aunts at all, *or* uncles, for that matter."

"I *know* I haven't," Jamie snapped. "It's *hopeless* belonging to a nuclear family![3] It's unfair—I mean, awful Honky has nineteen aunts and uncles and Nerissa and I haven't got any, not one." Jamie ground the pencil between his teeth.

"You won't have any teeth either, if you munch pencils like that," remarked his father, who was a dentist.

Jamie glowered,[4] spitting out wet splinters.

"Anyway, he's right," announced Nerissa. "It would be great to have even one aunt or uncle. Then we might have some cousins, too. Everyone else has cousins. Angelica Tonks probably has about a hundred-and-twenty-seven."

"Well, I'm sorry," sighed Mrs. Nutbeam, "but your father and I are both 'onlys' and there's nothing we can do about that, is there? Not a thing! Now, what's all this about an Aunt Millicent?"

"Oh, it's okay," grumbled her son. "Mr. Starling said to write about *an* aunt or uncle, not exactly *my* aunt or uncle. He says I can invent one."

"Will you explain that she's not real?" asked Nerissa, doubtfully.

"Mr. Starling says I don't have to, and he's not going to tell. He says I have to make people believe that she *is* real. Anyway, I don't want Honky Tonks to know that she's made up, because Aunt Millicent is going to be amazing—much better than any of those boring Tonkses. It's time Honky was taken down a peg or two."[5]

Dr. Nutbeam quite understood how Jamie felt. From time to time Angelica Tonks visited his dentist's chair. She would brag about her "perfect" teeth if there was nothing to be fixed, but if she needed a filling her shrieks of "agony" would upset everyone in the waiting room and Mrs. Tonks would call Dr. Nutbeam a *brute*. He was often tempted to give Angelica a general anesthetic and post her home in a large jiffy bag.

Now he folded his newspaper; Jamie's project sounded rather fun. "Right, Jamie," he said, "tell us about Aunt Millicent and let us get some facts straight. Is she my

---

3. Parents and their children make up a *nuclear family*. Angelica has an *extended family*, which includes aunts, uncles, cousins, and other close relatives.
4. Jamie scowled (*glowered*).

5. The expression *taken down a peg or two* means "made less proud and more humble."

sister, or Mum's? We must get that settled to start with."

"I can't decide," frowned Jamie. "What do you think?"

"She'd better be your sister, dear," said Mrs. Nutbeam calmly to her husband. "I grew up here and everyone knows I was an only child, but you came from another town. You're more mysterious."

Dr. Nutbeam looked pleased. "Mm . . . mm. That's nice . . . having a sister, I mean. Is she younger than me?"

"No, older," said Jamie.

"Where does she live?" asked Nerissa. "Has she a family of her own? Lots of cousins for us?"

"No way—she hasn't time for all that sort of thing. And she doesn't live any-where in particular."

Mrs. Nutbeam looked puzzled. "What *do* you mean, dear? What does Auntie Millicent do, exactly?"

"She's an explorer," said Jamie, proudly. "She works for foreign governments, and she's terribly busy—flat out."

There was something of a pause. Then Dr. Nutbeam said, "Ah," and stroked his bald patch. "That explains why we haven't seen her for so long."

"What does she explore?" demanded Nerissa. "Is there anything left in the world to look for?"

Jamie was beginning to feel a bit rushed. "Well, I'm not sure yet, but foreign govern-ments need people like her to search for water in deserts and rich mineral deposits and endangered species and things . . . you know."

Nerissa lay on the floor with her eyes closed and began to imagine her new aunt slashing a path through tangled jungle vines, searching for a rare species of dark blue frog. The mosqui-toes were savage. The leeches were huge and bloated. Aunt Millicent's machete was razor sharp . . .

Did You Know?
A *machete* (mə shet′ ē) is a wide, heavy knife that can be used as a weapon and a tool.

"This is all very unexpected," murmured Mrs. Nutbeam, "to have a sister-in-law who is an explorer, I mean. I wonder how you get started in that sort of career?" Her own job as an assistant in an antique and curio shop[6] suddenly seemed rather drab.

Dr. Nutbeam was staring at the wall. In his mind's eye he clearly saw his sister on a swaying rope sus-pension bridge above a terrifying ravine. She was leading a band of native bearers to the other side. How much more adven-turous, he thought, than drilling little holes in people's

Did You Know?
A *suspension bridge* hangs from cables, chains, or ropes that are firmly attached to towers or posts at each end.

teeth. He wrenched his gaze back to Jamie and asked, "Do we know what Millie is actually exploring at present?"

---

6. A *curio shop* sells rare or unusual ornamental objects.

Vocabulary
drab (drab) *adj.* lacking brightness; dull; cheerless

Jamie munched his pencil for a moment and then said, "She's in Africa, somewhere near the middle, but I'm not sure where, exactly."

"In the middle of Africa, is she?" echoed Dr. Nutbeam. "Mm . . . then it wouldn't surprise me if she were in the Cameroons. There's a lot of dense forest in the Cameroons, you know."

"I thought Cameroons were things to eat," frowned Nerissa. "Sort of coconut biscuits."

"No, no, dear, those are macaroons," said her mother.

"*They're* bad for your teeth, too," remarked her father, absently, "like eating pencils."

Jamie fetched the atlas and found a map of Africa. His father stood behind him, peering at it. "There it is, in the middle on the left-hand side, just under the bump."

"It's called Cameroon here," Jamie said. "Just one of them."

"Well, there's East Cameroon and West Cameroon, see," pointed his father, "and sometimes you lump them together and call them Cameroons. Look—here's the equator just to the south, so it must be pretty hot and steamy at sea-level."

"Poor Millicent," sighed Mrs. Nutbeam. "I do hope her feet don't swell in the heat, with all that walking."

Jamie examined the map closely. "That's peculiar—the north border of the Cameroons seems to be floating in a big lake . . . um, Lake Chad[7] . . . it looks all swampy, with funny dotted lines and things. I bet that bit needs exploring. They've probably lost their border in the mud and Aunt Millicent could be on an expedition to find it."

"Is she all by herself?" asked Nerissa. "I'd be scared in a place like that."

"Of course she's not by herself," snorted Jamie. "She works for a foreign government, don't forget, and she'd have a whole support team of porters and cooks and scientists and things."

"She must be an expert at something herself, don't you think?" suggested Mrs. Nutbeam. "I would imagine that she's a surveyor."

"Yes, she'd use one of those instruments you look through, on legs," added Nerissa.

"You mean a theodolite, dim-wit," answered her brother.

"She'd certainly need one of those, if she's measuring angles and dis-

Did You Know?
The *theodolite* (thē od′ əl īt′) is used by land surveyors for measuring horizontal and vertical angles.

tances and drawing maps," agreed Dr. Nutbeam. "My word, what a clever old sister I have!"

"I wonder if she was good at geography at school?" said Nerissa.

"Well, you'll be able to ask Grandma tomorrow. She's coming for her winter visit, remember?"

"Oh help! What'll Grandma *say?*" gasped Jamie. "Do you think she'll mind? I mean—we've invented a daughter for her without asking!"

---

7. *Lake Chad,* in the nation of Chad, is on the northeastern border of Cameroon.

Aunt Millicent

"I shouldn't think she'd mind," said his mother. "We'll break the news to her carefully and see how she takes it."

Grandma Nutbeam, as it turned out, was delighted.

"How exciting!" she exclaimed. "I always wanted a daughter, and it's been very lonely since Grandpa died. Now I'll have a new interest! Just show me on the map where Millicent is at the moment, please dear."

Jamie pointed to the dotted lines in swampy Lake Chad near the top end of the Cameroons, and Grandma stared in astonishment.

"Gracious heaven! What an extraordinary place to go to, the silly girl! I hope she's remembered her quinine[8] tablets. Millicent was never very good at looking after herself, you know. Let me see—I think I'll get some wool tomorrow and knit her some good stout hiking socks."

Jamie blinked. "There's no need to do that, Grandma. She's not really real, you know."

"Well, she'll be more real to me if I make her some socks," Grandma declared.

"Wouldn't they be rather hot in the Cameroons?" objected Nerissa. "It's awfully near the equator, don't forget."

"Woollen socks are best in any climate," said Grandma firmly. "They breathe."

"Now, Mother," interrupted Dr. Nutbeam, "you can tell us what Millicent was like as a girl. I can't remember her very well, as she was so much older than me, but I have a feeling that she ran away from home a lot."

Grandma pondered a moment. "Now that you mention it, she did. She did indeed. I thought we'd have to chain her up sometimes! We lived near the edge of town, you'll remember, and Millie would look out towards the paddocks[9] and hills and say that she wanted to know what was over the horizon, or where the birds were flying to, or where the clouds came from behind the hills. We never knew where she'd be off to next—but she certainly ended up in the

---

9. *Paddocks* are small, fenced fields in which animals can graze and exercise.

---

8. *Quinine* (kwī′ nīn), a drug made from the bark of a tree, is used to treat malaria and other illnesses.

right job! I'm so glad she became an explorer. If I were a bit younger and had better feet, I might even go and join her. It would be most interesting to see the Cameroons. It's full of monkeys, I believe."

"Was Aunt Millicent good at geography at school?" Nerissa remembered to ask.

"Let me think—yes, she must have been because one year she won a prize for it, and the prize was a book called *Lives of the Great Explorers.*"

"Well, there you are," remarked Mrs. Nutbeam. "That's probably how it all started."

Next day, Grandma Nutbeam began to knit a pair of explorer's socks. She decided on khaki with dark blue stripes round the top.

Angelica Tonks had found it so difficult to select one of the nineteen aunts and uncles, that her pen-portrait was left until the very last minute and then scrawled out in a great hurry. She had finally chosen Aunt Daisy Blizzard, Mrs. Tonks's eldest sister.

Mr. Wilfred Starling asked Angelica to read her portrait to the class first, to get it over with. As he had expected and as Jamie Nutbeam had hoped, Angelica's aunt sounded anything but wonderfully interesting. She had always lived in the same street, her favorite color was deep purple and she grew African violets on the bathroom shelf, but that was about all.

Many of the other portraits weren't much better, although there was one uncle who had fallen into Lake Burley Griffin and been rescued by a passing Member of Parliament. Someone else's aunt had competed in a penny-farthing bicycle race in Northern Tasmania,[10] only to capsize and sprain both her knees; and there was a great-uncle who had been present at the opening of the Sydney Harbour Bridge in 1932, but couldn't remember it at all as he'd been asleep in his pram[11] at the time.

Mr. Starling saved Jamie's portrait until last, hoping for the best. Jamie cleared his throat nervously and began:

"I have never met Aunt Millicent and no one in my family knows her very well, as she hasn't been in Australia for a long time. This is because Aunt Millicent is an explorer . . ."

Mr. Wilfred Starling had been hoping for a bright spot in his day, and Aunt Millicent Nutbeam was it. He smiled happily when Jamie explained how Millicent had gained her early training as an explorer by regularly running away from home. He sighed with pleasure as Jamie described the swampy region of Lake Chad, where Millicent was searching through the mud and papyrus[12] for the northern border of the Cameroons. He positively beamed when he heard that Grandma Nutbeam was knitting explorer's socks for her daughter.

The rest of the class sat <u>spellbound</u> as Jamie read on, except for Angelica Tonks,

---

10. Lake Burley Griffith is a man-made lake near the *Parliament* buildings in Canberra, Australia's capital. The state of *Tasmania* is an island southeast of the mainland.
11. Australians call a baby carriage a *pram.*
12. Surrounded by swamps, Lake Chad is the sort of place where *papyrus*, a tall grassy plant, grows well.

Vocabulary
spellbound (spel′ bound) *adj.* held, as if by magic; fascinated; charmed

Aunt Millicent

whose scowl grew darker by the minute. Jamie had barely finished his portrait when her hand was waving furiously.

Mr. Starling's beam faded. "What *is* it, Angelica?"

"I don't believe it. Women don't go exploring! I think Jamie's made it all up! He's a cheat!"

Mr. Starling's stomach lurched, but before he had time to say anything the other girls in the class rose up in a passion and rounded on Angelica.

"Who *says* women don't go exploring?"

"Women can do anything they want to these days, Angelica Tonks! Don't you know that?"

"*I'd* really like to be an explorer or something—maybe a test-pilot."

"Well, *I'd* like to be a diver and explore the ocean floor and have a good look at the *Titanic*."[13]

"What does your aunt wear when she's at work?"

"What color are her new socks?"

The boys began to join in.

"Can your aunt really use a machete?"

"How many languages can she speak?"

"Does she always carry a gun? I bet she's a crack[14] shot!"

"How does a theodolite work?"

The clamor was so great that hardly anyone heard the bell. Angelica Tonks heard it and vanished in a sulk. Mr. Starling heard it and happily gathered up his books. He gave Jamie a secret wink as he left the room.

The end of the assignment was not the end of Aunt Millicent. At school, the careers teacher ran some special sessions on "Challenging Occupations for Women" after he had been stormed by the girls from Jamie's class for information about becoming test-pilots, mobile-crane drivers, buffalo hunters and ocean-floor mappers. The science teacher was asked to explain the workings of a theodolite to the class.

At home, Aunt Millicent settled happily into the Nutbeam family, who all followed her adventures with great interest. Dr. Nutbeam brought home library books about the Cameroons and Central Africa. Jamie roared his way through one called *The Bafut Beagles*. Mrs. Nutbeam rummaged through an old storeroom at the curio shop and began to collect exotic objects. She brought home a brace[15] of hunting spears from Kenya, which she hung on the family-room wall.

"Just the sort of souvenir Millicent could have sent us," she explained. "See—those marks on the blades are very probably dried bloodstains."

Another time she unwrapped a stuffed mongoose, announcing that

Did You Know?
The *mongoose* is a small animal native to parts of Asia, Africa, and Europe. It has a pointy face and shaggy fur and is about two to three feet long, including its tail.

---

13. The *Titanic* was an ocean liner that sank in the North Atlantic in 1912 after hitting an iceberg.
14. Here, *crack* means "excellent; first-rate."

15. A *brace* of things is a pair.

Vocabulary
exotic (ig zot′ ik) *adj.* strangely beautiful or interesting; unusual; foreign

Auntie had sent this from India on one of her earlier trips.

Jamie and Nerissa stroked it. "What a funny animal," said Nerissa. "Like a weasel."

Grandma was knitting her way down the second sock leg. "That funny animal is a very brave creature," she admonished,[16] tapping the mongoose with her knitting needle. "I'll always remember Kipling's story of Rikki-Tikki-Tavi and how he fought that dreadful king cobra. Brrr!"

"Who won?" asked Jamie.

"You could read it yourself and find out, young man," said Grandma, starting to knit a new row. "I expect Millicent has met a few cobras in her time."

Nerissa had splendid dreams nearly every night. Aunt Millicent strode through most of them, wielding her machete or shouldering her theodolite. Sometimes Nerissa found herself wading through swirling rivers or swinging on jungle vines like a gibbon. Jamie was often there, too, or some of her school friends, or Grandma followed by a mongoose on a lead.[17] Once, Mrs. Nutbeam speared a

Did You Know?
The *gibbon* is a type of small ape.

giant toad, which exploded and woke Nerissa up. In another dream, Nerissa's father was polishing the fangs of a grinning crocodile, which lay back in the dentist's chair with its long tail tucked neatly under the sterilizer. It looked slightly like Mrs. Tonks.

Mrs. Nutbeam brought home still more curios: a bamboo flute and a small tom-tom which Jamie and Nerissa soon learnt to play. Mysterious drumbeats and thin flutey tunes drifted along the street from the Nutbeams' house. School friends came to beat the tom-tom and to stroke the mongoose and to see how the explorer's socks were growing.

"Will you be sending them off soon, to the Cameroons?" they asked Grandma, who was turning the heel of the second sock.

"I think I'll make another pair, perhaps even three pairs," replied Grandma. "I might just as well send a large parcel as a small one."

"Yes, and then Aunt Millie will have spare pairs of socks she can wash," said Nerissa. "Socks must get very smelly near the equator."

Word of Millicent Nutbeam, intrepid[18] explorer, began to spread through the town. Children told their families about the spears, the tom-tom, the mongoose and the khaki socks. Not every small town could claim to be connected to a famous international explorer—it was exciting news.

Angelica Tonks, however, told her mother that she didn't believe Jamie's aunt was an explorer at all. "I bet he just invented that to make his aunt seem more interesting than all the rest," she scoffed.

Mrs. Tonks sniffed a good deal and then decided it was time to have a dental check-up. "I'll get to the bottom of that Millicent Nutbeam, you mark my words,"

---

16. Grandma scolded mildly (*admonished*).
17. The mongoose is on a leash (*lead*).

18. Someone who is *intrepid* is very brave.

Aunt Millicent

she told Angelica, as she telephoned Dr. Nutbeam's surgery[19] for an appointment.

Well, well—good morning Mrs. Tonks," said Dr. Nutbeam, a few days later. "We haven't seen you for a while! Just lie right back in the chair please, and relax!"

Mrs. Tonks lay back, but she didn't relax one bit. Her eyes were sharp and suspicious. "Good morning, Dr. Nutbeam. How is the family?" she enquired. "And how is your sister?"

Dr. Nutbeam pulled on his rubber gloves. "My sister? Which one? . . . Er, probe, please nurse."

Before he could say "Open wide," Mrs. Tonks snapped, "Your sister the so-called explorer. Huh! The one in the Cameroons."

"Ah, *that* sister. You mean Millicent . . . now, just open wider and turn this way a little. Yes, our Millie, she does work so hard . . . oops, there's a beaut cavity! A real crater!" He crammed six plugs of cotton wool around Mrs. Tonks's gums. "My word, what a lot of saliva! We'll have some suction please nurse, and just wipe that dribble from the patient's chin." He continued to poke and scrape Mrs. Tonks's molars, none too gently. "Ah, here's another trouble spot. Mm . . . have you ever been to the Cameroons, Mrs. Tonks?"

Mrs. Tonks's eyes glared. She tried to shake her head, but could only gurgle, "Arggg . . ."

"No, I didn't think you had. Such a fascinating place!" Dr. Nutbeam turned on the squealing high-speed drill and bored into her decaying tooth, spraying water all over her chin.

When he had told his family about this encounter with Mrs. Tonks, his wife complained, "It's all very well for you. *You* can just cram people's mouths full of wadding and metal contraptions and suction tubes if they start asking awkward questions, but what am I supposed to do?"

The truth was that increasing numbers of townsfolk were calling at the antique shop where Mrs. Nutbeam worked. They were eager to know more about Millicent Nutbeam and her adventurous life. They felt proud of her.

"It's getting quite tricky," Mrs. Nutbeam explained. "People are asking to see photos of Millicent and wanting us to talk at the elderly citizens' club about her. This aunt is becoming an embarrassment. I wish people weren't so curious. Sometimes I don't know what to say!"

Grandma found herself on slippery ground, too, when she met the postman at the gate.

"Morning," he said, sorting through his mailbag. "You must be Jamie's grandmother, then."

"Yes, I am," Grandma replied, rather surprised.

"Mother of the explorer, eh?"

"Gracious!" exclaimed Grandma. "Fancy you knowing about that!"

---

19. In Australia, a doctor's or dentist's office is called a *surgery*.

Vocabulary

encounter (en koun′ tər) *n.* a direct meeting, as between enemies in conflict or in battle; an unexpected meeting

Dear Jamie

I was in
and then s
very active

"Oh, my girl Julie has told us all about it. She's in Jamie's class at school. Funny thing—Julie's gone round the twist since she heard about all that exploring business. Says she wants to buy a camel and ride it round Australia, and one of her friends is going to apply for a job on an oil rig. I ask you!"

"Well, that's nice," said Grandma, soothingly. "Girls are so enterprising[20] these days."

"Huh! Mad, I call it." The postman held out a bundle of letters. "Here you are. Now, that's *another* funny thing—the Nutbeams don't get much foreign mail, come to think of it. You'd think the

explorer would write to them more often, her being in the traveling line."

Grandma breathed deeply. "Oh, it's not easy, you know, writing letters when you're exploring. For one thing, there's never a decent light in the tent at night—and besides, there's hardly ever a post office to hand when you need it. She glanced through the letters. "Goodness! There's one from South America . . . Peru."

"That's what made me wonder. Is it from her?" asked the postman, eagerly.

"Her? Ah . . . Millicent. I don't know. It's for Dr. Nutbeam, my son, and it's typed. Anyway, as far as we know, Millicent is still in the Cameroons, although we've not had word for some time."

"She could have moved on, couldn't she?" suggested the postman, "Peru, eh?

---

20. Someone who is *enterprising* is ready and willing to undertake new projects.

Aunt Millicent

Oh well, I'd better move on, too. G'day to you!"

At school, Julie the postman's daughter said to Jamie, "Why has your auntie gone to South America? What's she exploring now?"

"Who said she's gone to South America?" demanded Jamie. He felt he was losing control of Aunt Millicent.

"My dad said there was a letter from her in Peru," replied Julie.

"Well, no one told *me*," growled Jamie.

At home he announced, "Julie is telling everybody that our Aunt Millicent is in Peru! What's she talking about? What's happening?"

Grandma stopped knitting. "Julie. Is that the name of the postman's girl?"

"Yes—her dad said there was a letter for us from Auntie in Peru, or somewhere mad."

"Oh, I remember—he asked me about it," said Grandma.

"Well . . . what did you *say?*" wailed Jamie.

"I just said I didn't know who the letter was from and that I thought Millicent was still in the Cameroons, but that we hadn't heard for a while where she was. That's all."

"The letter from Peru," chuckled Dr. Nutbeam, "is about the World Dental Conference on plaque, which is being held next year in Lima.[21] It has nothing to do with Millicent."

"Well of *course* it hasn't," spluttered Jamie. "She doesn't exist!"

"But Jamie, in a funny sort of way she *does* exist," said Mrs. Nutbeam.

His father grinned. "My sister is quite a girl! She's begun to live a life of her own!"

"That's the trouble," said Jamie. "She seems to be doing things we don't know about."

While they were talking, the telephone rang. Dr. Nutbeam was no longer grinning when he came back from answering it. "That was Frank Figgis from the local paper."

"Frank, the editor?" asked Mrs. Nutbeam. "What did he want?"

"He wants to do a full-page feature on our Millicent," groaned her husband. "He's heard that she's about to set out on a climbing expedition in the Andes! Up some peak that has never yet been conquered!"

"What nonsense!" snapped Grandma. "She's too old for that sort of thing."

"It's just a rumor!" shouted Jamie. "Who said she's going to the Andes? *I* didn't say she was going there. She's still in the Cameroons!"

"Calm down, dear," said his mother, "and let's hear what Dad said to Frank Figgis."

Dr. Nutbeam was rubbing his head. "I stalled for time—I said we'd not heard she was in the Andes, but that we'd make enquiries and let him know. Whatever happens, Millicent mustn't get into print. We'll all be up on a charge of false pretenses[22] or something!"

Jamie snorted. "Well, if she's climbing an Ande, it might be best if she fell off and was never seen again."

Nerissa shrieked, "*No!* She mustn't— she's our only aunt and we've only just got her!"

---

21. This kind of *plaque* (plak) is film that forms on teeth and will harden to form tartar if it is not removed by regular cleaning. The conference is in *Lima* (lē′ mə), Peru.

22. The legal term *false pretenses* refers to lying or misleading.

Mrs. Nutbeam sighed. "Listen, Jamie, perhaps the time has come to own up[23] that Aunt Millicent is not real."

"We can't do that!" wailed Jamie. "Everyone would think we're loony . . . and that Grandma's absolutely bonkers, knitting socks for an aunt who isn't there. And what about the mongoose? Anyway, I *can't* let Honky Tonks find out now—she'd never stop crowing and she'd be more awful than ever."

Jamie decided to lay the whole problem of Aunt Millicent Nutbeam before Mr. Starling, right up to her unexpected expedition to the Andes and Mr. Figgis's plan to write a full-page feature about her for the local paper. He finished by saying, "I think I might have to kill her off."

"That'd be a shame," sighed Mr. Starling. "She's quite a lady, your aunt!"

"It would be pretty easy to get rid of her," Jamie went on. "In her sort of job she could sink into a quicksand, or be trampled by a herd of elephants, or something."

Mr. Starling shook his head violently. "No, no—it would only make things worse if she died a bloodcurdling death like that. No one would be likely to forget her if she was squashed flat by a stampeding elephant. She'd become more interesting than ever!"

"Well, she could die of something boring, like pneumonia," said Jamie. "Or . . . will I have to own up that she isn't real?"

"Do you want to own up?"

"Not really. I'd feel stupid, and I specially don't want Angelica Tonks to know I invented an aunt."

Mr. Starling quite understood. "I see! Anyway, a lot of people would be sad to discover that Millicent Nutbeam was a hoax. The girls in your class, for example—she means a lot to them."

"What'll I do then?"

"If you want people to lose interest in her, you'll just have to make her less interesting. I think she should retire from exploring, for a start."

"Aw, gee!" Jamie felt very disappointed. "I suppose so. I'll see what they think at home."

"What he means," said Dr. Nutbeam, when Jamie had repeated Mr. Starling's advice, "is that it's time my dear sister Millicent settled down."

"I quite agree with that," remarked Grandma, who was up to the sixth sock foot. "She's not as young as she was, and it's high time she had some normal home life. I think she should get married, even though she's getting on a bit. Perhaps to a widower."

"That sounds terribly boring," yawned Nerissa.

"Well, that's what we need," said Jamie, "something terribly boring to make people lose interest."

Grandma sniffed. "In my day it would have been called a happy ending."

"Well, I suppose it's a happier ending than being squashed by an elephant," conceded Jamie.

---

23. The expression *own up* means "confess fully."

Vocabulary
hoax (hōks) *n.* a trick, fraud, or practical joke

Aunt Millicent

"How about marrying her to a retired accountant who used to work for a cardboard box company?" suggested his father. "That sounds pretty dull."

"Good heavens, it's all rather sudden!" said Mrs. Nutbeam. "Last time we heard of her she was climbing the Andes!"

"No, she *wasn't*." At last Jamie felt he had hold of Aunt Millicent again. "That South American stuff was just a rumor. The postman started it because of the letter from Peru, and then the story just grew!"

Dr. Nutbeam nodded. "Stories seem to have a habit of doing that, and so do rumors! But we can easily squash this one about the Andes. I'll just explain about the World Dental Conference on plaque. I even have the letter to prove it."

Dr. Nutbeam called Frank Figgis on the phone. He explained about the letter from Peru and about the ridiculous rumor which the postman had started. "In your profession, Frank," he added sternly, "you should be much more careful than to listen to baseless[24] rumor. It could get you into all sorts of trouble! In any case, Millicent is giving up exploring to marry a retired accountant. She's had enough."

Frank Figgis was fast losing interest. "I see—well, sometime when she's in Australia, we could do an interview about her former life . . . maybe."

"Maybe, although she has no immediate plans to return here. I believe she and her husband are going to settle down in England—somewhere on the seafront, like Bognor."

Jamie passed on the same information to his classmates. The girls were shocked.

"She's what?"

"Getting married to an *accountant?*"

"She can't be!"

"How boring for her!"

"Where in the world is Bognor? Is there really such a place?"

Angelica Tonks smiled like a smug pussycat. "See! Your Aunt Millicent is just like any other old aunt, after all!"

Jamie caught Mr. Starling's eye. It winked.

Aunt Millicent Nutbeam retired, not to Bognor but to live quietly with her family. Nerissa still had wonderful dreams. Dr. Nutbeam still brought home books about far-off places. The blood-stained spears remained on the wall and the mongoose on the shelf. Jamie and Nerissa still played the tom-tom and the bamboo flute.

Grandma Nutbeam's holiday came to an end and she packed up to return home. She left a parcel for Jamie. When he opened it, he found three pairs of khaki socks with dark blue stripes, and a card which said:

Dear Jamie,
Aunt Millicent won't have any use for these now that she has settled down, so you might as well have them for school camps. Isn't it lucky that they are just your size!

> With love from Grandma

---

24. A *baseless* rumor is not supported by facts.

Responding to Literature

PERSONAL RESPONSE

◆ Would you like to have a relative like Aunt Millicent? Why?

◆ Is Aunt Millicent anything like the character you invented in the **Focus Activity** on page 714? If so, in what ways?

Analyzing Literature

RECALL

1. What is Mr. Starling's assignment for the class?

2. How does Jamie feel about Angelica Tonks? Why? Support your answer.

3. What is Aunt Millicent's occupation? Where is she believed to be and what is she doing there?

4. What problems result from inventing Aunt Millicent? What does Jamie do about them?

INTERPRET

5. Why does Jamie make up an aunt? How does Mr. Starling feel about it?

6. Why does Jamie's father decide to help him? Who else helps invent Aunt Millicent?

7. Does Grandma react to the idea of Aunt Millicent in the way you would expect? Explain.

8. How are the lives of Jamie's family and classmates changed as a result of hearing about Aunt Millicent?

EVALUATE AND CONNECT

9. Do you think it's right that Jamie, his family, and his teacher never reveal the truth about Aunt Millicent? Explain.

10. How do Nerissa and her father picture Aunt Millicent? How do you visualize her?

LITERARY ELEMENTS

Characterization

Mr. Starling tells Jamie to make his imaginary aunt real and believable, and Jamie does so. Writers bring characters to life

• through the character's own words or actions

• by revealing the character's thoughts and feelings

• by revealing what others think about a character

• by stating directly what a character is like

1. What makes Jamie's aunt an interesting character? When does she become less interesting?

2. How does the author let readers get to know Angelica Tonks's personality? Find examples, and identify which of the above ways are used to reveal her personality.

● See **Literary Terms Handbook,** p. R2.

Literature and Writing

Writing About Literature

Brainstorming   When each member of a group contributes ideas and makes connections with other people's ideas, the group is **brainstorming**. How does Jamie's family brainstorm? Write a paragraph describing how family members work together to "create" an aunt.

Creative Writing

Imagining a Relative   Imagine that you are in Mr. Starling's class and you, like Jamie, don't have an aunt or uncle to describe. Write a "portrait" of a made-up aunt or uncle. Follow Mr. Starling's advice: make the aunt or uncle "seem real so we all believe in her [or him]."

Extending Your Response

Literature Groups

Questioning Jamie   How would you react to hearing about Aunt Millicent if you were in Jamie's class? Make up two lists of questions. On one list, write questions you would ask if you were suspicious of Aunt Millicent, as Angelica is. On the other list, write questions you would ask if you believed Jamie and wanted to know more.

*inter*NET CONNECTION

Learn about explorers in Australia or Africa or around the world. When were different parts of the world explored and by whom? Where are explorers exploring now? Use a search engine and browse under *History–Exploration*.

Interdisciplinary Activity

Mathematics   Trace Aunt Millicent's journey from Australia to Cameroon on a map or globe. Approximately how many miles did she travel? How many additional miles would she have traveled if she had gone to Peru?

Performing

Dialogue   Enjoy the excitement of Aunt Millicent's creation by taking the parts of members of Jamie's family and reading the dialogue from the selection.

Reading Further

If you'd like to read more by Mary Steele, you might enjoy these books:
A Bit of a Hitch
Arkwright
Citizen Arkwright
Featherbys

Save your work for your portfolio.

Skill Minilessons

GRAMMAR AND LANGUAGE • LEVELS OF USAGE

Language used in dialogue is often informal and may include **idioms,** expressions that cannot easily be understood from the meanings of the individual words in them. For example, Jamie uses the idiom "taken down a peg or two" when he is talking about Angelica. It is probably clear that the expression means "to make someone less boastful or proud of himself or herself."

PRACTICE Write the meaning of each underlined expression.

1. In his mind's eye Dr. Nutbeam clearly saw his sister on a swaying rope suspension bridge.
2. Grandma found herself on slippery ground, too, when she met the postman at the gate.
3. Perhaps the time has come to own up that Aunt Millicent is not real.
4. Aunt Millicent should get married, even though she's getting on a bit.

READING AND THINKING • PROBLEM AND SOLUTION

As you read, think about how the writer has organized the text. For example, sometimes the plot of a story revolves around one or more problems and their solutions. The problems may be caused by the characters, or the problems may simply be a part of the situation in the story. By using a problem/solution structure, the writer can often get readers more deeply involved in the story.

PRACTICE Complete a problem-solution chart for "Aunt Millicent." Then write a few paragraphs explaining what new problems are created by

Jamie's "solution," inventing an aunt. How do the characters deal with the new problems?

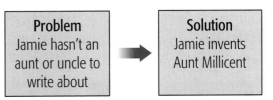

- For more on problem and solution, see **Reading Handbook,** p. R78.

VOCABULARY • THE PREFIXES *ex-* AND *exo-*

A **prefix** is a word part that is added to the beginning of a whole word or a root and changes its meaning in some way. The prefix *ex-* has several meanings, but it usually has to do with "out." An *exit* is where you go out; when you breathe out, you *exhale.*

The prefix *exo-* means "outside." The meaning of *exotic* comes from this idea of "outside." Something that is "outside" of our regular experience seems *exotic* to us. This is why foreign countries or customs are often described as *exotic.*

PRACTICE Use what you know about familiar words and the prefixes *ex-* and *exo-* to answer the following questions.

1. You know what *include* means, so what does it mean to *exclude* someone from a club?
2. You know that a *tractor* is a machine for pulling, so what does a dentist do to a tooth by *extracting* it?
3. You know what a *skeleton* is, so which animal has an *exoskeleton*—a dog, a clam, or a bird?

- For more on prefixes, see **Language Handbook,** pp. R40–R41.

Vo·cab·u·lar·y *Skills*

Using Base Words

A **base word** is a whole word to which an affix, that is, a suffix or prefix, or both can be attached to make a new word. For example, the words *comfortable, discomfort, comforting,* and *uncomfortable* all contain the base word *comfort.* The meaning of a word changes when an affix is added. If you come across an unfamiliar word, you should look at it carefully to see if it contains a base word you know. A familiar base word can be a big help in figuring out what a new word means.

If a base word ends with a vowel, the spelling often changes when a suffix is added to the end of the word. The *e* in *nature* disappears when *natural* is formed. The *y* in *happy* changes to an *i* to make *happiness.*

Here are some examples of base words and words formed from them:

Base Words	Words Formed from Base Words
child	children, childish, childhood, unchildlike, childless
appear	appearance, reappear, appearing, disappear
nature	naturally, unnatural, naturalize, supernatural

● For more on spelling words with affixes, see **Language Handbook,** pp. R40–R41.

EXERCISES

1. Write the base word from which each of the following words is formed.
   (Remember, a base word is a *whole* English word without a prefix or suffix.)
   a. cashier **d.** heroism **g.** celebratory **j.** unmindful
   b. concave **e.** solidify **h.** secretively
   c. disjoin **f.** abnormality **i.** disagreeable

2. Use your knowledge of the base words in the underlined words to answer the questions.
   a. If Jamie was emboldened to invent an aunt, did he become clever, sneaky, or brave?
   b. When Angelica belittled Jamie, did she act like he was odd, unimportant, or lying?
   c. If Jamie was momentarily nervous, was he worried for a few minutes, for a few hours, or all day?
   d. When Angelica thought that Jamie's report was falsified, did she think it was untrue, boring, or too long?
   e. If Jamie needed inventiveness, did he need to be accurate, neat, or creative?

MEDIA Connection

WEB SITE

Ordering books on-line is very convenient. Some on-line book sites also provide a place to share ideas about a book or to read others' reactions. Readers of Roald Dahl's *Charlie and the Chocolate Factory* share their reactions to it.

Readers' Comments

Address: ▼ www.amazon.com

Synopsis

Four nasty, repulsive children and one honest, loyal, and starving boy win a tour of the world's most fantastic chocolate factory from the world's most eccentric chocolatier.

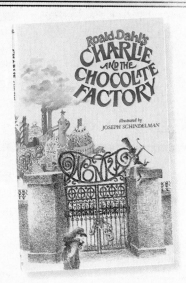

Customer Comments

A reader from Spain: I liked this book. This book was pretty cool because a lot of stupid, stubborn kids got what they deserved at the factory. Mr. Willy Wonka was pretty cool because he was always calm even though the kids' parents were getting mad at him. I also liked the neat candy he made. I hope he makes another book with more stubborn kids and candy.

From Anonymous: Charlie shouldn't have gotten the golden ticket. All of the other kids didn't deserve to be sent home. Charlie also shouldn't have gotten complete control of the factory. The Oompa-Loompas are very annoying and are way too hairy. The drawings are very badly drawn and I don't recommend this book.

A reader from Kingston, Jamaica, West Indies: This book is one of my favorite books, and I like it because it is about chocolate and I love chocolate and I like it also because it is very creative and exciting.

A reader from North Carolina: The movie and book are both good, but the movie is better. It is a great horror movie.

A reader from the US: This book paints a very negative picture of children. Are most children fundamentally bad and deserving terrible punishment at the moment they least expect it? I recommend this book to adults who do not like children.

Respond

1. Discuss these opinions with classmates who are familiar with the book. Which of these opinions do they share?

2. What differences do you think there might be between the book, the movie, and the play?

Before You Read

Charlie and the Chocolate Factory

MEET ROALD DAHL

At seventeen Roald Dahl was hired by an oil company to work in Africa. When World War II broke out, he became a fighter pilot in the Royal Air Force. Eventually he married and had five children. He once said, "Had I not had children of my own, I would never have written books for children, nor would I have been capable of doing so."

Richard R. George adapted Dahl's popular book into a play for his sixth-grade class.

Roald Dahl was born in 1916 and died in 1990. The novel Charlie and the Chocolate Factory *was published in 1964. The play was published in 1976.*

FOCUS ACTIVITY

Have you ever imagined yourself in a chocolate factory? What might it be like?

Journal

Write in your journal what you would hope to see in a chocolate factory. Share your ideas.

Setting a Purpose

Read *Charlie and the Chocolate Factory* to find out what happens in one chocolate factory.

BACKGROUND

Did You Know?   Roald Dahl once told the *New York Times Book Review* that writing for young people is a great discipline "because they are highly critical. . . . You have to keep things ticking along." Much criticized for the violence in his books, Dahl pointed out that the young people who wrote to him "invariably pick out the most gruesome events as the favorite parts of the books. . . . They don't relate it to life. They enjoy the fantasy. And my nastiness is never gratuitous [without good reason]. It's retribution [just punishment]. Beastly people must be punished."

VOCABULARY PREVIEW

repulsive (ri puls′ iv) *adj.* causing dislike; disgusting; p. 739
morsel (môr′ səl) *n.* a small portion or quantity; p. 742
infest (in fest′) *v.* to occur in large numbers so as to be harmful or troublesome; overrun; p. 746
colossal (kə los′ əl) *adj.* extraordinarily large; huge; p. 748
alter (ôl′ tər) *v.* to make or become different; change; p. 748
culprit (kul′ prit) *n.* one who is guilty of some crime or misdeed; offender; p. 758
tamper (tam′ pər) *v.* to interfere or meddle in a way that causes harm; p. 759

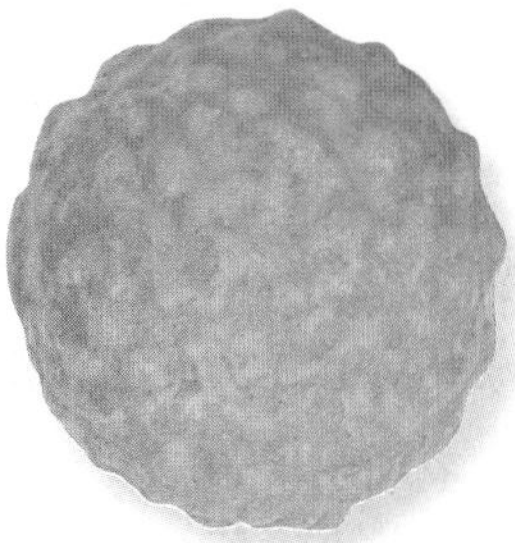

Charlie and the Chocolate Factory

Roald Dahl :~
Adapted by Richard R. George

CHARACTERS *(in order of appearance)*

NARRATOR
AUGUSTUS[1] GLOOP
VIOLET BEAUREGARDE[2]
VERUCA[3] SALT
MIKE TEAVEE
MR. BUCKET
GRANDMA JOSEPHINE

GRANDPA GEORGE
GRANDMA GEORGINA
MRS. BUCKET
GRANDPA JOE
CHARLIE BUCKET
MRS. GLOOP
WILLY WONKA

MRS. TEAVEE
MR. SALT
MRS. SALT
MRS. BEAUREGARDE
MR. TEAVEE
OOMPA-LOOMPAS
(offstage, if necessary)

⊱ SCENE 1 ⊰

[*NARRATOR enters in front of curtain.*]

NARRATOR. Welcome to the tale of a delicious adventure in a wonderful land. You can tell it will be delicious—can't you smell it already? [*Sniffs.*] Oh, how I love that gorgeous smell! You've all heard of Kraft, Neilson, Hershey, Nestlés, Wonka—what's that? You say, what's Wonka? You mean you *don't* know what Wonka is? Why . . . Wonka Chocolate . . . of course! I admit that Willy Wonka's Chocolate is fairly new but it's also the greatest chocolate ever invented. Why, Willy Wonka himself is the most amazing, the most fantastic, the most extraordinary chocolate maker the world has ever seen.

---

1. *Augustus* (ô gus′ təs)
2. *Beauregarde* (bō′ rə gärd′)
3. *Veruca* (və rōō′ kə)

He's invented things like . . . say . . . why . . . I'm not going to *tell* you what he's invented. You came to see for yourself! So I'll let you do just that. But before I do, I should perhaps fill you in on what's been happening around here lately. Because Mr. Willy Wonka makes the best chocolate in the whole wide world, three other great chocolate makers known as Mr. Fickelgruber, Mr. Prodnose, and Mr. Slugworth sent spies to work for Mr. Wonka in order to discover his secrets. Well, they must have been good spies because soon afterward, these three chocolate makers began making such delicious Wonka favorites as ice cream that never melts, chewing gum that never loses its flavor, and candy balloons that you could blow up to huge sizes before you popped them with a pin and gobbled them up. Mr. Wonka didn't know what to do. He didn't know who the spies were, and if he continued to operate his factory *all* his secrets might be stolen. So he did the only thing he could; he sent all the workers home and closed the factory. You might think that that would be the end of Mr. Willy Wonka but no sireeee—not him. After months and months went by, the factory suddenly began operating again. But nobody knew who was running the place. Nobody *ever* went *in* and nobody *ever* came *out.* The only thing anyone could see were shadows dancing around in front of the lighted windows . . . mighty strange. . . . Well anyway, to get back to the story, soon there was a big article in the town paper saying that Mr. Willy Wonka, in order to sell a lot of candy once again, was running a contest. Yes sir, that's right . . . a contest! He had secretly wrapped a Golden Ticket under ordinary wrapping paper in five ordinary candy bars. The candy bars were said to be found anywhere . . . in any shop . . . in any street . . . in any town . . . in any country in the world, upon any counter where Wonka's candies are sold. The five winners will tour Mr. Wonka's new factory and take home enough chocolate for the rest of their lives. Now *that,* my friends, is where our story begins. Four of the tickets have already been found. Oh, by the way, would you like to meet the four lucky people? All right, listen and watch carefully! I think they're here somewhere. [*Looks out over audience.*] Let's see . . . *Augustus Gloop!* Where are you, Augustus Gloop?

AUGUSTUS GLOOP. [*From somewhere in audience.*] Chocolate . . . chocolate . . . *chocolate* . . . CHOCOLATE!!! I . . . LOVE . . . CHOCOLATE! Ummmmmmm-mmmmmmmmmmmmmmmmmmm . . . food . . . FOOD! [*Smacks lips repeatedly.*] *Ummmmmmmmmmmmmmmmmmmmmmmmm-mmmm* . . . I MUST EAT ALL THE TIME . . . *Ummmmmmmmmmmmm* . . . CHOCOLATE! This Golden Ticket is my meal ticket to . . . uh . . . eat . . . and eat . . . and *eat* . . . and EAT!!! Ummmmmmm-mmmmm . . . CHOCOLATE . . . *chocolate* . . . chocolate. . . .

NARRATOR. Well, uh, friends, that was our first Golden Ticket finder—Augustus Gloop. Let's see now if the lucky girl who found our second Golden Ticket is here. Oh Violet . . . *Violet Beauregarde?*

VIOLET BEAUREGARDE. [*Chewing ferociously on gum, waving arms excitedly, talking in a rapid and loud manner, from somewhere in audience.*] I'm a gum-chewer normally, but when I heard about these ticket things of

Mr. Wonka's, I laid off the gum and switched to candy bars in the hope of striking it lucky. *Now,* of course, I'm right back on gum. I just *adore* gum. I can't do without it. I munch it all day long except for a few minutes at mealtimes when I take it out and stick it behind my ear for safe-keeping. To tell you the honest truth, I simply wouldn't feel *comfort-able* if I didn't have that little wedge of gum to chew on every moment

Viewing the photograph: What do you think is happening in this scene from the movie *Willy Wonka and the Chocolate Factory*?

of the day, I really wouldn't. My mother says it's not ladylike and it looks ugly to see a girl's jaws going up and down like mine do all the time, but I don't agree. And who's she to criticize, anyway, because if you ask me, I'd say that *her* jaws are going up and down almost as much as mine are just from *yelling* at me every minute of the day. And now, it may interest you to know that this piece of gum I'm chewing right at this moment is one I've been working on for over *three months solid.* That's a record, that is. It's beaten the record held by my best friend, Miss Cornelia Prinzmetel. And was she ever mad! It's my most treasured posses-sion now, this piece of gum is. At nights, I just stick it on the end of the bedpost, and it's as good as ever in the mornings . . . a . . . bit . . . hard . . . at . . . first . . . maybe . . .

NARRATOR. Such a, uh, lucky, uh, girl. Isn't she, uh, uh, wonderful? The third Golden Ticket was found by another lucky girl. Her name is Veruca Salt. Is *Veruca here now?*

VERUCA SALT. [*From somewhere in audience.*] Where's my Golden Ticket? I want my Golden Ticket! Oh yes . . . *here* it is! As soon as I told my father that I simply *had* to have one of those Golden Tickets, he went out into the town and started buying up all the Wonka candy bars he could lay his hands on. *Thousands* of them, he must have bought. *Hundreds* of thousands! Then he had them loaded onto trucks and sent directly to his own factory. He's in the peanut business, you see, and he's got about a hundred women working for him over at his joint, shelling peanuts for roasting and salting. That's what they do all day long, those women . . . they just sit there shelling peanuts. So he says to them, "Okay, girls," he says, "from now on, you can stop shelling peanuts and start shelling the wrappers off these crazy candy bars instead!" And they did. He had every worker in the place yanking the paper off those bars of chocolate, full speed ahead, from morning 'til night. But three days went by, and we had no luck. Oh . . . it was terrible! I got more and more upset each day, and every time he came home I would scream at him, "Where's my Golden Ticket! I want my Golden Ticket!" And I would lie for hours on the floor, kicking and yelling in the most disturbing way. Then suddenly, on the evening of the fourth day, one of his women workers yelled, "I've got it! A Golden Ticket!" And my father said, "Give it to me, quick!" And she did. And he rushed it home and gave it to me, and now . . . I'm all smiles . . . and we have a happy home . . . once again.

NARRATOR. Thank you, Veruca. Isn't she a lovely girl? Now the fourth and last ticket was found by a boy named Mike Teavee. I wonder if Mike's got his ticket with him? *Where are you, Mike?*

MIKE TEAVEE. [*From somewhere in audience.*] Of course I've got a Golden Ticket, but why can't everyone leave me alone? I want to watch television!!! [*He pulls out his guns and fires into the air.*] I watch all of the shows every day, even the crummy ones where there's no shooting. I like the gangsters best. They're terrific, those gangsters! Especially when they start pumping each other full of lead . . . or flashing the old stilettos . . . or giving each other the one-two-three, with their knuckledusters![4] Oh boy, what wouldn't I give to be doing that myself! It's the *life*, I tell you. It's terrific!

---

4. *Stilettos* (stə let′ ōz) are daggers with very narrow blades. *Knuckledusters*, or "brass knuckles," are a set of metal rings that fit over the knuckles and are used in rough fighting.

NARRATOR. And that folks is, uh, Mike Teavee. Sorry for, uh, bothering you, Mike.

[*End of Scene 1.*]

 SCENE 2

[*NARRATOR enters in front of curtain.*]

NARRATOR. Now we're going to take a look at the hero of our story, Charlie Bucket, and his family. Let me introduce them to you. [*Curtain opens on Bucket home, a bare room with one chair and a bed. Characters are frozen in place: the four GRANDPARENTS in the bed; MR. BUCKET in chair, reading a newspaper, CHARLIE, and MRS. BUCKET on other side of room.*] This is the home of Charlie Bucket. Seven people live here. There are only two rooms and only one bed, so you can see that life is extremely uncomfortable. [*Walks over to the bed.*] These two very old people are the father and mother of Mr. Bucket. Their names are Grandpa Joe and Grandma Josephine. And these two very old people are the father and mother of Mrs. Bucket. Their names are Grandpa George and Grandma Georgina. The bed was given to the four old grandparents because they were so old and tired—and of course they're all over ninety years old. [*Goes to MR. BUCKET.*] This is Mr. Bucket. This is Mrs. Bucket. They and little Charlie Bucket sleep in the other room, upon mattresses on the floor. As you know, this can be very cold in the wintertime. They can't buy a better house because they don't have any money and there aren't any better jobs. Mr. Bucket is the only one that can work and, well, he lost his job a few weeks ago. Yes, it's very sad, but you see, the toothpaste factory *had* to close down. Without Mr. Willy Wonka's

Chocolate Factory open, nobody ever got cavities anymore and they didn't buy any toothpaste and . . . well, you know how it goes. Oh wait . . . gee, I almost forgot . . . this is our hero—Charlie Bucket. Charlie's a nice boy. Of course he's been starving lately. In fact the whole family has. I'm worried about Charlie, though. Why, did you know that Charlie is so weak from not eating that he walks slowly instead of running like the other kids, so he can save his energy? Well, I've said far too much already. Let's find out what's happening at the Bucket house now . . . uhh, I'll see you later.

[*NARRATOR exits. BUCKET FAMILY comes to life.*]

MR. BUCKET.   Well, I see that four children have found Golden Tickets. I wonder who the fifth lucky person will be?

GRANDMA JOSEPHINE.   I hope it's no one like that <u>repulsive</u> Gloop boy!

GRANDPA GEORGE.   Or as spoiled as that Veruca Salt girl!

GRANDMA GEORGINA.   Or as beastly as that bubble-popping Violet Beauregarde!

MRS. BUCKET.   Or living such a useless life as that Teavee boy!

Viewing the photograph: Will Charlie be lucky with his candy bar? What do you think Grandpa Joe wishes for?

Vocabulary
repulsive (ri puls′ iv) *adj.* causing dislike; disgusting

MR. BUCKET. [*Looking up from his paper.*] It makes you wonder if all children behave like this nowadays . . . like these brats we've been hearing about.

GRANDPA JOE. Of course not! Some do, of course. In fact, quite a lot of them do. But not all.

MRS. BUCKET. And now there's only one ticket left.

GRANDMA JOSEPHINE. Quite so . . . and just as sure as I'll be having cabbage soup for supper tomorrow, that ticket'll go to some nasty little beast who doesn't deserve it!

GRANDPA JOE. I bet I know somebody who'd like to find that Golden Ticket. How about it, Charlie? You love chocolate more than anyone I ever saw!

CHARLIE. Yes, I sure would, Grandpa Joe! You know . . . it just about makes me faint when I have to pass Mr. Wonka's Chocolate Factory every day as I go to school. The smell of that wonderful chocolate makes me so dreamy that I often fall asleep and bump into Mr. Wonka's fence. But I guess I should realize that dreams don't come true. Just imagine! Me imagining that I could win the fifth Golden Ticket. Why, it's . . . it's . . . it's pure imagination.

GRANDPA JOE. Well my boy, it may be pure imagination, but I've heard tell that what you imagine sometimes comes true.

CHARLIE. Gee, you really think so, Grandpa Joe? Gee . . . I wonder. . . .

[*End of Scene 2.*]

SCENE 3

[*Bucket home, several days later.* GRANDPARENTS, MR. *and* MRS. BUCKET, *as before.*]

MR. BUCKET. You know, it sure would have been nice if Charlie had won that fifth Golden Ticket.

MRS. BUCKET. You mean with that dime we gave him for his birthday present yesterday?

MR. BUCKET. Yes, the one we gave him to buy the one piece of candy he gets every year.

GRANDMA GEORGINA. And just think how long it took you two to save that dime.

GRANDPA GEORGE. Yes, now that was really a shame.

GRANDMA JOSEPHINE. But think of how Charlie enjoyed the candy. He just loves Willy Wonka chocolate.

MRS. BUCKET. He didn't really *act* that disappointed.

MR. BUCKET. No, he didn't—

Viewing the photograph: Which words in the play go with this picture?

GRANDPA JOE. Well, he might not have acted disappointed, but that's because he's a fine boy and wouldn't want any of us to feel sorry for him. Why—what boy wouldn't be disappointed? I sure wish he'd won. I'd do anything for that boy. Why, I'd even—

CHARLIE. [*Running in excitedly.*] Mom! Dad! Grandpa Joe! Grandfolks! You'll never believe it! You'll never believe what happened!

MRS. BUCKET. Good gracious, Charlie— what happened?

CHARLIE. Well . . . I was walking home . . . and the wind was so cold . . . and the snow was blowing so hard . . . and I couldn't see where I was going . . . and I was looking down to protect my face . . . and . . . and—

MR. BUCKET. [*Excitedly.*] Go on, Charlie . . . go on, Charlie . . . what is it?

CHARLIE. And there it was . . . just lying there in the snow . . . kind of buried . . . and I looked around . . . and no one seemed to look as if they had lost anything . . . and . . . and . . . and so I picked it up and wiped it off . . . and I couldn't believe my eyes—

ALL. [*Except CHARLIE. Shouting and screaming.*] You found the Golden Ticket! Charlie found the Golden Ticket! Hurray! Hurray! He did it! He did it!

CHARLIE. No . . . no . . . I . . . I found a dollar bill. [*Everybody looks let down and sad.*] But, but, but . . . then I thought it wouldn't hurt if I bought a Wonka Whipple-Scrumptious Fudgemallow Delight since it was . . . my dollar . . . and I was just *sooo* hungry for one.

ALL. [*Getting excited again.*] Yes . . . yes . . . go on . . . go on.

CHARLIE. Well . . . I took off the wrapper slowly . . . and—

ALL. [*Shouting and screaming.*] YOU FOUND THE GOLDEN TICKET! Charlie found the Golden Ticket! Hurray! Hurray! He did it! He did it!

CHARLIE. No . . . no . . . no . . . I ate the candy. There wasn't any Golden Ticket. [*Everybody groans and sighs, acting very sad again.*] But then . . . I still had ninety cents left and . . . well . . . you know how I love chocolate—

MRS. BUCKET. Oh Charlie, you're not sick are you? You didn't spend all of the money on—

CHARLIE. Well no, as a matter of fact . . . I bought another Whipple-Scrumptious Fudgemallow Delight . . . and . . . and . . . and I FOUND THE FIFTH GOLDEN TICKET!!!

ALL. You *what?*

CHARLIE. I did! I did! I really did! I found the fifth Golden Ticket!!

ALL. [*Everyone yelling and dancing around.*] Hurray! Hurray! Hurray! Yippppppeeeeeeeeeee! It's off to the chocolate factory!!!

[*End of Scene 3.*]

 SCENE 4

[*In front of the Chocolate Factory. CHARLIE and GRANDPA JOE enter together as scene opens.*]

CHARLIE. Boy, Grandpa Joe, I sure am glad that Dad let you take me today.

GRANDPA JOE. Well, Charlie, I guess he just feels that we understand each other.

CHARLIE. Plus, you seem to know all about Willy Wonka and what's happened to him.

GRANDPA JOE. Well, he's been an important man in this town for a good long time. A lot of people said some unkind things about him after he closed down the factory, but I always felt that he had his reasons. Actually I'm quite excited about this "Golden Ticket" thing. It's a good excuse to see what *is* going on in that factory and how he's running it.

CHARLIE. Speaking of the Golden Ticket, Grandpa Joe, could I read it one more time? I know it sounds silly, but the whole thing seems so magical.

GRANDPA JOE. [*Searching his pockets.*] Sure, Charlie . . . let me see if I can find it . . . ah, here it is.

[*He pulls out a small ticket.*]

CHARLIE. Let's see now . . . it says, "Greetings to you, the lucky finder of this Golden Ticket, from Mr. Willy Wonka! I shake you warmly by the hand! Tremendous things are in store for you! Many wonderful surprises await you! For now, I do invite you to come to my factory and be my guest for one whole day—you and all others who are lucky enough to find my Golden Tickets. I, Willy Wonka, will conduct you around the factory myself, showing you everything that there is to see, and afterwards, when it is time to leave, you will be escorted home by a procession of large trucks. These trucks, I can promise you, will be loaded with enough delicious eatables to last you and your entire household for many years. If, at any time thereafter, you should run out of supplies, you have only to come back to the factory and show this Golden Ticket, and I shall be happy to refill your cupboard with whatever you want. In this way, you will be able to keep yourself supplied with tasty morsels for the rest of your life. But this is by no means the most exciting thing that will happen on the day of your visit. I am preparing other surprises that are even more marvelous and more fantastic for you and for all my beloved Golden Ticket holders—mystic and marvelous surprises that will entrance, delight, intrigue, astonish, and perplex[5] you beyond measure. In your wildest dreams you could not imagine that such things could happen to you! Just wait and see! And now, here are your instructions: the day I have chosen for the visit is the first day in the month of February. On this day, and on no other, you must come to the factory gates at ten o'clock sharp in the morning. Don't be late! And you are allowed to bring with you either one or two members of your own family to look after you and to ensure that you don't get into mischief. One more thing—be certain to have this ticket with you, otherwise you will not be admitted. Signed, Willy Wonka."

GRANDPA JOE. And today is the first of February, and say, Charlie—look, we're here already . . . and I guess everyone else is arriving together.

---

5. Here, *mystic* means "secret or mysterious." Things that *entrance* (en trans´) people fill them with joy or wonder, whereas things that *perplex* them cause doubt or uncertainty.

Vocabulary
morsel (môr´ səl) *n.* a small portion or quantity

Viewing the photograph: In what ways does the movie character, Willy Wonka, look as you expected him to? Would you change him in any way if you were making the movie? Explain.

[*AUGUSTUS GLOOP, VIOLET BEAURE-GARDE, VERUCA SALT, MIKE TEAVEE, MRS. GLOOP, MR. and MRS. TEAVEE, MR. and MRS. SALT, MRS. BEAUREGARDE enter. WILLY WONKA enters from opposite side.*]

MRS. GLOOP. There he is! That's him! It's Willy Wonka!

WILLY WONKA. Welcome! Welcome! Welcome! Hello, everyone! Let's see now. I wonder if I can recognize all of you by the pictures of you in the newspaper. Let's see. [*Pause.*] You're Augustus Gloop.

AUGUSTUS GLOOP. Uhhhhh . . . y-e-a-hhhhh and this is . . . uhh . . . my mother.

WILLY WONKA. Delighted to meet you both! Delighted! Delighted! [*Turns to VIOLET.*] You're Violet Beauregarde.

VIOLET BEAUREGARDE. So what if I am— let's just get on with the whole thing, huh?

WILLY WONKA. And you must be Mrs. Beauregarde. Very happy to meet you! Very happy! [*Turns to VERUCA.*] I think you are . . . yes . . . you're Veruca Salt. And you must be Mr. and Mrs. Salt.

VERUCA SALT. Don't shake his hand, Daddy—it's probably all sticky and choco-latey from working in the factory. After all, he *does* only run a silly little factory. He's not important enough for you to bother shaking hands with, anyway!

WILLY WONKA. You're Mike Teavee. Enchanted to meet you! Yes . . . enchanted.

MIKE TEAVEE. [*Blasting his guns.*] Come on! I'm missing all my favorite TV shows!

MR. AND MRS. TEAVEE. And we're the Teavees. Pleased to meet you.

WILLY WONKA. Overjoyed! Overjoyed! [*Turns to CHARLIE.*] And you must be the boy who just found the ticket yesterday. Congratulations! You're . . . Charlie Bucket—aren't you?

CHARLIE. Yes sir, thank you. And this, sir, is my Grandpa Joe.

GRANDPA JOE. Howdy, Mr. Wonka. I'm real pleased to meet you!

WILLY WONKA. How do you do, Mr. Grandpa Joe. How *do* you do! Well now, is that everybody? Hmmmmmm . . . why . . . I guess it is! Good! Now will you please follow me! Our tour is about to begin! But *do* keep together! Please don't wander off by yourselves! I shouldn't like to lose any of you at this stage of the proceedings! Oh, dear me, no! Here we are! Through this big red door, please. That's right! It's nice and warm inside! I have to keep it warm inside the factory because of the workers! My workers are used to an extremely hot climate! They can't stand the cold! They'd perish if they went outdoors in this weather! Why, they'd freeze to death!

AUGUSTUS GLOOP. But . . . who . . . are these . . . uhh . . . workers?

WILLY WONKA. All in good time, my dear boy! Be patient! You shall see everything as we go along! [*All exit with WILLY WONKA remaining alone.*] Are all of you inside? Good! Would you mind closing the door? Thank you!

[*Exit.*]

[*End of Scene 4.*]

 **SCENE 5**

[*The Chocolate Room. The Chocolate River runs across the stage, surrounded by trees and pipes. All enter as scene opens.*]

AUGUSTUS GLOOP. I'm tired! It seems like we've been turning left, turning right,

Viewing the photograph: Do these look like good, reliable workers? How are they using teamwork to get their work done?

turning left, and turning right again for a whole hour or so. When are we going to eat? I'm hungry! I want to eat right now! Do you all hear me? *Now!!*

CHARLIE. Did you notice that we've been going downward for the longest time, Grandpa Joe?

GRANDPA JOE. Yes, Charlie, I think I heard Mr. Wonka say that we were going underground and that all the most important rooms in his factory are deep down below the surface.

CHARLIE. I wonder why?

GRANDPA JOE. Well, I think he said that there wouldn't be nearly enough space for them up on top. He said that the rooms we are going to see are enormous. *Some* are supposed to be larger than football fields!

WILLY WONKA. Here we are everybody! This is the Chocolate Room. This room is the nerve center of the whole factory. It's the heart of my whole operation!

AUGUSTUS GLOOP. Uhh . . . I don't see anything but that old river over there. Where's the food? I'm hungry!

MRS. GLOOP. And just look at those enormous pipes over there. There must be ten or eleven of them. I wonder what they're for?

CHARLIE. Gee, Mr. Wonka, what's wrong with your river? It's all brown and muddy-looking.

WILLY WONKA. *Nothing* wrong with it, my boy! *Nothing!* Nothing at all! It's all chocolate! Every drop of that river is hot melted chocolate of the finest quality. The *very finest* quality. There's enough chocolate in there to fill every bathtub in the entire country! *And* all the swimming pools as well! Isn't it *terrific?* And just look at my pipes! They suck up the chocolate and carry it away to all the other rooms in the factory where it is needed! Thousands of gallons an hour, my dear children! Thousands and thousands of gallons!

VERUCA SALT. [*Screaming as she looks over the edge of the river.*] Look! Look over there! What is it? He's moving! He's walking! Why, it's a little person! It's a little man! Down there behind one of the pipes!

[*Everyone rushes to the edge of the river to get a better look.*]

CHARLIE. She's right, Grandpa! It *is* a little man! Can you see him?

GRANDPA JOE. I see him, Charlie!

[*All now shout in turn.*]

MRS. GLOOP. There's two of them!

MR. SALT. My gosh, so there is!

MRS. BEAUREGARDE. There's more than two! There's four or five!

MR. TEAVEE. What are they doing?

MRS. GLOOP. Where do they come from?

VIOLET BEAUREGARDE. Who are they?

CHARLIE. Aren't they fantastic?

GRANDPA JOE. No higher than my knee!

CHARLIE. Look at their funny long hair! They can't be *real* people!

WILLY WONKA. Nonsense! Of course they are real people! They are some of my workers!

MIKE TEAVEE. That's impossible! There are no people in the world as small as that!

WILLY WONKA. No people in the world as small as that? Then let me tell you something. There are more than three thousand of them in my factory! They are Oompa-Loompas!

CHARLIE. Oompa-Loompas! What do you mean?

WILLY WONKA. Imported direct from Loompaland. And oh, what a terrible country it is! Nothing but thick jungles infested by the most dangerous beasts in the world—hornswogglers and snozzwangers and those terrible wicked whangdoodles. A whangdoodle would eat ten Oompa-Loompas for breakfast and come galloping back for a second helping. When I went out there, I found the little Oompa-Loompas living in tree-houses. They *had* to live in tree-houses to escape from the whangdoodles and the hornswogglers and the snozzwangers. When I found them they were practically starving to death. They were living on green caterpillars, red beetles, eucalyptus leaves, and the bark of the bong-bong tree. They loved cacao beans too, but only found about one or two a year. They used to dream about cacao beans all night and talk about them all day. It just so happens that the cacao bean is the thing from which all chocolate is made. I myself use billions of cacao beans every week in this factory. So I talked to the leader of the tribe in

Did You Know?
Cocoa and chocolate are the two main products made from *cacao* (kə ka′ ō) *beans.*

Oompa-Loompish and told him that his people could have all the cacao beans they wanted if they would just come and work for me and live in my factory. Well, the leader was so happy that he leaped up in the air and threw his bowl of mashed caterpillars right out of his tree-house window. So, here they are! They're wonderful workers. They all speak English now. They love dancing and music. They are always making up songs. I expect you will hear a good deal of singing today from time to time.

VERUCA SALT. Mummy! Daddy! I want an Oompa-Loompa! I want you to get me an Oompa-Loompa! I want an Oompa-Loompa right away! I want to take it home with me! Go on, Daddy! Get . . . me . . . an . . . Oompa-Loompa!

MRS. SALT. [*Mildly.*] Now, now, my pet. We mustn't interrupt Mr. Wonka.

VERUCA SALT. [*Screaming.*] But I want an Oompa-Loompa!!!

MR. SALT. All right, Veruca, all right. But I can't get it for you this second, sweetie. Please be patient. I'll see that you have one before the day is out.

[*AUGUSTUS GLOOP leans over river.*]

MRS. GLOOP. Augustus! Augustus, sweetheart! I don't think you had better do that.

WILLY WONKA. Oh, no! Please, Augustus, p-l-e-a-s-e! I beg of you not to do that. My chocolate must be untouched by human hands!

MRS. GLOOP. Augustus! Didn't you hear what the man said? Come away from that river at once!

Vocabulary
infest (in fest′) *v.* to occur in large numbers so as to be harmful or troublesome; overrun

Viewing the photograph: How did Augustus get himself into this situation?

AUGUSTUS GLOOP. [*Leaning over further.*] This stuff is *teee-rrific!* Oh boy, I need a bucket to drink it properly!

WILLY WONKA. Augustus . . . you *must* come away! *You are dirtying my chocolate!*

MRS. GLOOP. Augustus! You'll be giving that nasty cold of yours to about a million people all over the country! Be careful Augustus! You're leaning *too far out!!!*

[*AUGUSTUS shrieks as he falls in.*]

MRS. GLOOP. Save him! He'll drown! He can't swim a yard! Save him! Save him!

AUGUSTUS GLOOP. Help! Help! Fish me out!

MRS. GLOOP. [*To everybody.*] Don't just stand there! *Do* something!

VERUCA SALT. Look! He's being sucked closer to one of the pipes!

MIKE TEAVEE. There he goes!

MRS. GLOOP. Oh, help! Murder! Police! Augustus! Come back at once! Where are you going? [*Pause.*] He's disappeared. He's *disappeared!* Where does that pipe go to? Quick! Call the fire brigade!

WILLY WONKA. Keep calm. He'll come out of it just fine, you wait and see.

MRS. GLOOP. But he'll be turned into marshmallows!

WILLY WONKA.   Impossible!

MRS. GLOOP.   And why *not*, may I ask?

WILLY WONKA.   Because that pipe doesn't go anywhere near the Marshmallow Room. It leads to the room where I make a most delicious kind of strawberry-flavored chocolate-coated fudge.

MRS. GLOOP.   Oh, my poor Augustus! They'll be selling him by the pound all over the country tomorrow morning! [*WILLY WONKA is laughing and MRS. GLOOP begins to chase him, trying to hit him with her purse.*] How *dare* you laugh like that when my boy's just gone up the pipe! You monster! You think it's a joke, do you? You think that sucking my boy up into your Fudge Room like that is just one great colossal joke?

WILLY WONKA.   He'll be perfectly safe.

MRS. GLOOP.   He'll be chocolate fudge!

WILLY WONKA.   Never! I wouldn't allow it!

MRS. GLOOP.   And why not?

WILLY WONKA.   Because the taste would be *terrible!* Just imagine it! Augustus-flavored chocolate-coated Gloop! No one would buy it.

MRS. GLOOP.   I don't want to *think* about it!

WILLY WONKA.   Nor do I, and I do promise you, madam, that your darling boy *is* perfectly safe.

MRS. GLOOP.   If he's safe, then where is he? Lead me to him this instant!

WILLY WONKA.   Go over to one of the Oompa-Loompas and ask him to show you to the Fudge Room. When you get there, take a long stick and start poking around inside the big chocolate-mixing barrel. He should be there. Don't leave him in there too long though, or he's liable to get poured out into the fudge boiler, and that really would be a disaster, wouldn't it? My fudge would become *quite* uneatable!

MRS. GLOOP.   [*Shrieking.*] What . . . what . . . *what* did you say?

WILLY WONKA.   I'm joking—forgive me. Good-bye, Mrs. Gloop . . . see you later.

[*MRS. GLOOP exits. All others exit in opposite direction.*]

OOMPA-LOOMPAS.   Augustus Gloop!
   Augustus Gloop!
The great big greedy nincompoop!
How long could we allow this beast
To gorge and guzzle,[6] feed and feast
On everything he wanted to?
Great Scott! It simply wouldn't do!
So what we do in cases such
As this, we use the gentle touch,
"Come on!" we cried. "The time is ripe
To send him shooting up the pipe!"
But don't, dear children, be alarmed;
Augustus Gloop will not be harmed,
Although, of course, we must admit
He will be altered quite a bit.
He'll be quite changed from what he's been,
When he goes through the fudge machine:
Slowly, the wheels go round and round,

---

6. To *gorge* and *guzzle* is to eat and drink greedily.

Vocabulary
colossal (kə los′ əl) *adj.* extraordinarily large; huge
alter (ôl′ tər) *v.* to make or become different; change

The cogs[7] begin to grind and pound;
A hundred knives go slice, slice, slice;
We add some sugar, cream, and spice;
Then out he comes! And now! By
   grace!
A miracle has taken place!
This boy, who only just before
Was loathed by men from shore to
   shore,
This greedy brute, this louse's ear,
Is loved by people everywhere!
For who could hate or bear a grudge
Against a luscious bit of fudge?

[*End of Scene 5.*]

⊰◈⊱ SCENE 6 ⊰◈⊱

[*NARRATOR enters in front of curtain.*]

NARRATOR. Poor Augustus . . . well, I bet we've seen the last of him for a while. Now you folks are really in for a treat! Did you know that Willy Wonka had his very own yacht? That's right! His very own! And boy, is it sharp! It's bright pink and has about ten Oompa-Loompas inside, pulling all of the oars! Well there's no point telling you all about the boat, because in just a second . . . you should . . . be able to see it coming . . . up the tunnel . . . yes . . . yes . . . *here it comes now!*

[*NARRATOR exits. Curtain opens to Chocolate River, now stage front. There are three doors behind the river which say "Cream Room," "Whip Room," and "Bean Room." Boat with visitors enters as scene opens.*]

---

7. In a machine, *cogs* are the teeth on the edge of a wheel that lock into the teeth on another wheel. When an engine turns the first wheel, the cogs make the second wheel turn too.

VIOLET BEAUREGARDE. It sure is dark in here! How can these dumb Oompa-Loompas see where they're going?

WILLY WONKA. [*Hooting with laughter.*]
There's no knowing where they're
   going!
There's no earthly way of knowing
Which direction they are going!
There's no knowing where they're
   rowing,
Or which way the river's flowing!
Not a speck of light is showing,
So the danger must be growing,
For the rowers keep on rowing,
And they're certainly not showing
Any signs that they are slowing . . .

MRS. SALT. He's gone off his rocker!

ALL. He's crazy!

MIKE TEAVEE. He's balmy!

VERUCA SALT. He's nutty!

VIOLET BEAUREGARDE. He's screwy!

MRS. BEAUREGARDE. He's batty!

MRS. TEAVEE. He's dippy!

MR. SALT. He's dotty!

MIKE TEAVEE. He's daffy!

VERUCA SALT. He's goofy!

VIOLET BEAUREGARDE. He's buggy!

MRS. BEAUREGARDE. He's wacky!

MR. TEAVEE. He's loony!

GRANDPA JOE. Oh, no he's not!

WILLY WONKA. Switch on the lights! Row faster! Faster!

[*The boat moves along.*]

CHARLIE. Look, Grandpa! There's a door in the wall! It says . . . Cream Room—

Viewing the photograph: Where may Willy Wonka's yacht be headed?

dairy cream, whipped cream, violet cream, coffee cream, pineapple cream, vanilla cream, and . . . hair cream?

MIKE TEAVEE. Hair cream? You don't eat *hair cream!*

WILLY WONKA. Row on! There's no time to answer silly questions!

[*The boat moves along.*]

CHARLIE. Look . . . another door! Whip Room!

VERUCA SALT. Whips? What on earth do you use whips for?

WILLY WONKA. For whipping cream, of course! How can you whip cream without whips? Whipped cream isn't whipped cream at all, unless it's been whipped with whips—just as a poached egg[8] isn't

a poached egg unless it's been stolen from the woods in the dead of night! Row on, please!

[*The boat moves along.*]

CHARLIE. Bean Room! Cacao beans, coffee beans, jelly beans, and Has Beans.[9]

VIOLET BEAUREGARDE. Has Beans?

WILLY WONKA. You're one yourself! No time for arguing! Press on! Press on! [*Pause.*] Stop the boat! We're *there!*

MIKE TEAVEE. We're where?

WILLY WONKA. Up there!

MIKE TEAVEE. What's up there?

WILLY WONKA. You'll see.

[*End of Scene 6.*]

---

8. A *poached egg* is one that has either been stolen or cooked without its shell in water.

9. *Has Beans* is a play on words; the term "has-beens" refers to people who are no longer popular.

Responding to Literature

PERSONAL RESPONSE

- ◆ Would you have liked to have won one of the Golden Tickets? Why or why not?
- ◆ Were you surprised by what happens to Augustus Gloop?

Analyzing Literature

RECALL AND INTERPRET

1. Why does Willy Wonka close his factory? In what special way does he reopen it?
2. Who are the winners of the Golden Tickets? How would you characterize each one?
3. Who are the Oompa-Loompas? Where are they from? What are they known for?

EVALUATE AND CONNECT

4. How does Augustus Gloop's accident fit his personality? What do you think will happen to Augustus?
5. Authors often use **exaggeration,** or making something seem bigger than it really is, to create humor. Do you think Dahl uses too much exaggeration to describe the first four winners? Explain why or why not.
6. Based on what happens to Augustus Gloop, what do you think might happen to the other winners?

LITERARY ELEMENTS

Props

Props are the objects and furniture used on the stage during a play. Sometimes the objects are actual things people could use, such as a brush for brushing hair. Often they are specially made objects. Willy Wonka's yacht will not sail in a real river, but it gives the impression of a boat for the audience. The audience uses imagination when viewing props such as these, accepting the props for what they are supposed to be.

1. List three props that have been used so far in the play.
2. What does Willy Wonka's yacht look like? How would you create the prop of Willy Wonka's yacht? What materials would you use?

● See **Literary Terms Handbook,** p. R7.

A machine in Willy Wonka's factory. Describe to a partner how you imagine this machine works.

Charlie and the Chocolate Factory

continued

 SCENE 7

[*The Invention Room. It is filled with stoves and pipes, pots and kettles, and many strange machines. All enter as scene opens.*]

WILLY WONKA. This is the most important room in the entire factory! All my most secret new inventions are cooking and simmering in here! Old Fickelgruber would give his front teeth to be allowed inside, just for three minutes! So would Prodnose and Slugworth and all the other rotten chocolate makers! But now, listen to me! I want no messing about when you go in! No touching! No meddling! And *no tasting!* Is that agreed?

ALL CHILDREN. Yes, yes! We won't touch a thing!

[*Everyone looks around in amazement. WILLY WONKA runs around and jumps in excitement from place to place. He approaches and gazes into a machine.*]

WILLY WONKA. Everlasting Gobstoppers! They're completely new! I am inventing them for children who are given very little pocket money. You can put an Everlasting Gobstopper in your mouth and you can suck it and suck it and suck it and suck it and suck it and . . . it will never get any smaller!

VIOLET BEAUREGARDE. It's like gum!

WILLY WONKA. It is *not* like gum! Gum is for chewing, and if you tried chewing one of these Gobstoppers here, you'd break your teeth off. But they *taste* terrific! And they change color once a week! Now that machine over there makes hair toffee, but it's not quite perfected yet. But I'll get the mixture right soon! And when I do, then

Viewing the photograph: What kind of candy is being made here?

there'll be no excuse any more for little boys and girls going about with bald heads!

MIKE TEAVEE. But Mr. Wonka, little boys and girls never go about with—

WILLY WONKA. Don't argue, my dear child . . . *please* don't argue! Now over here, if you will all step this way, I will show you something I am *terrifically* proud of. Oh, do be careful! Stand back!

[*He stops at center stage in front of the Great Gum Machine.*]

WILLY WONKA. Here we go!

[*He begins pushing buttons, and all kinds of noises and lights occur. Finally a small strip of gray cardboard appears from side of machine.*]

MIKE TEAVEE. You mean that's *all*?

WILLY WONKA. [*Proudly.*] That's all! Don't you know what it is?

VIOLET BEAUREGARDE. [*Yelling.*] By gum, it's *gum!!!* It's a stick of chewing gum!

WILLY WONKA. Right you are! [*Slapping VIOLET hard on the back.*] It's a stick of the most amazing and fabulous and sensational gum in the world! This gum is a fantastic gum—in that it's a chewing-gum meal! It's a whole three-course dinner all by itself! When I start selling this gum in the shops, it will change everything. It will be the *end* of cooking, marketing, forks, plates, washing up, and garbage! This piece of gum I've just made happens to be tomato soup, roast beef, *and* blueberry pie! But you can have almost anything you want!

VIOLET BEAUREGARDE. What do you mean by that?

WILLY WONKA. If you were to start chewing it, you would actually taste *all* of those things. *And* it fills you up! It satisfies you! It's terrific!

VERUCA SALT. It's utterly impossible!

VIOLET BEAUREGARDE. Just so long as it's gum, and I can chew it . . . then that's for me! [*She takes her own piece of gum out of her mouth and sticks it behind her left ear.*] Come on, Mr. Wonka, hand over this magic gum of yours . . . and we'll see if the thing works!

MRS. BEAUREGARDE. Now, Violet . . . let's not do anything silly.

VIOLET BEAUREGARDE. I want the gum! What's so silly?

WILLY WONKA. I would rather you didn't take it. You see, I haven't got it quite right yet. There are still one or two things—

VIOLET BEAUREGARDE. [*Interrupting.*] Oh, to heck with that!

[*She grabs the gum and pops it into her mouth.*]

WILLY WONKA. Don't!

VIOLET BEAUREGARDE. Fabulous! It's great!

WILLY WONKA. Spit it out!

MRS. BEAUREGARDE. Keep chewing, kiddo! Keep right on chewing, baby! This is a great day for the Beauregardes! Our little girl is the first person in the world to have a chewing-gum meal!

WILLY WONKA. [*Wringing his hands.*] No—no—no—no—no! It isn't ready for eating! It isn't right! You mustn't do it!

MRS. BEAUREGARDE. Good heavens, girl! What's happening to your nose? It's turning *blue*!

VIOLET BEAUREGARDE. Oh, be quiet, mother, and let me finish!

MRS. BEAUREGARDE. Your cheeks! Your chin! Your whole face is turning *blue!* Mercy save us! The girl's going blue and purple all over! Violet, you're turning violet, Violet! What *is* happening to you? You're glowing all over! The whole room is glowing!

[*Blue lights on only.*]

WILLY WONKA. [*Sighing and shaking head sadly.*] I *told* you I hadn't got it quite right. It always goes wrong when we come to the dessert. It's the blueberry pie that does it. But I'll get it right one day, you wait and see!

MRS. BEAUREGARDE. Violet . . . you're swelling up!

[*VIOLET begins backing off stage.*]

VIOLET BEAUREGARDE. I feel most peculiar!

[*VIOLET now disappears offstage.*]

MRS. BEAUREGARDE. You're swelling up! You're *blowing up like a balloon!*

WILLY WONKA. Like a *blueberry!*

MRS. BEAUREGARDE. Call a doctor!

MR. SALT. Prick her with a pin!

MRS. BEAUREGARDE. [*Wringing her hands helplessly.*] Save her!

WILLY WONKA. It always happens like this. All the Oompa-Loompas that tried it finished up as blueberries. It's *most* annoying. I just *can't* understand it.

MRS. BEAUREGARDE. But I don't *want* a blueberry for a daughter! Put her back this instant!

WILLY WONKA. Tell the Oompa-Loompas over there to roll Miss Beauregarde into the Juicing Room at once!

MRS. BEAUREGARDE. The *Juicing Room?* What for?

WILLY WONKA. To *squeeze* her! We've got to squeeze the juice out of her immediately. After that, we'll just have to see how she comes out. But *don't* worry. We'll get her repaired if it's the *last thing we do.* I *am* sorry about it all . . . I really am . . .

[*MRS. BEAUREGARDE walks off following VIOLET.*]

CHARLIE. Mr. Wonka? Will Violet ever be all right again?

WILLY WONKA. She'll come out of the de-juicing machine just as thin as a whistle—and she'll be purple. Purple from head to toe! But there you are! That's what comes from chewing disgusting gum all day long!

MIKE TEAVEE. If it's so *disgusting*, then why do you make it in your factory?

WILLY WONKA. I can't hear a word you're saying. Come on! Off we go! Follow me!

[*All exit.*]

OOMPA-LOOMPAS. Dear friends, we surely
    all agree
There's almost nothing worse to see
Than some repulsive little bum
Who's always chewing chewing gum.
This sticky habit's bound to send
The chewer to a sticky end.
Did any of you ever know
A person called Miss Bigelow?
This dreadful woman saw no wrong
In chewing, chewing all day long.
And when she couldn't find her gum,
She'd chew up the linoleum,

Viewing the photograph: How did Violet swell up? What are the Oompa-Loompas going to do about it?

Or anything that happened near—
A pair of boots, the postman's ear,
Or other people's underclothes,
And once she chewed her boyfriend's
    nose.
For years and years she chewed away,
Consuming fifty packs a day,
Until one summer's eve, alas,
A horrid business came to pass.
Miss Bigelow went late to bed,
For half an hour she lay and read,
At last, she put her gum away
Upon a special little tray,
And settled back and went to sleep—
(She managed this by counting sheep).
But now, how strange! Although she
    slept,
Those massive jaws of hers still kept
On chewing, chewing through the
    night,
Even with nothing there to bite.

This sleeping woman's great big trap
Opening and shutting, snap-snap-snap!
Faster and faster, chop-chop-chop,
The noise went on, it wouldn't stop.
Until at last her jaws decide
To pause and open extra wide,
And with the most tremendous chew
They bit the lady's tongue in two.
And that is why we'll try so hard
To save Miss Violet Beauregarde
From suffering an equal fate.
She's still quite young. It's not too late,
Provided she survives the cure.
We hope she does. We can't be sure.

[*End of Scene 7.*]

✧◆✧ SCENE 8 ✧◆✧

[*In front of the Nut Room. At center stage, facing stage left, is a door with a glass panel; behind it, a pile of nuts and a garbage chute (inside the room). All enter as scene opens.*]

WILLY WONKA. All right, stop here for a moment and catch your breath. And take a peek through the glass panel of this door. But don't go in! Whatever you do, don't go into . . . The Nut Room! If you go in, you'll disturb the miniature squirrels!

CHARLIE. [*Peeking through the panel.*] Oh *look*, Grandpa! Look!

VERUCA SALT. Miniature squirrels!

MIKE TEAVEE. Jeepers! There must be a hundred of them around that pile of walnuts over there.

WILLY WONKA. These squirrels are specially trained for getting the nuts out of walnuts.

MIKE TEAVEE. Why use squirrels? Why not use Oompa-Loompas?

WILLY WONKA. Nobody can get walnuts out of walnut shells in one piece, except squirrels. I *insist* on using only *whole* walnuts in my factory—so I use squirrels to do the job. And see how they first tap each walnut with their knuckles—to be sure it's not a bad one! If it's bad, it makes a hollow sound, and they don't bother to open it. They simply throw it down the garbage chute.

VERUCA SALT. Hey Daddy! I've decided I want a squirrel! Get me one of those squirrels!

MR. SALT. Don't be silly, sweetheart. These all belong to Mr. Wonka.

VERUCA SALT. I don't care about that! I want one! All I've *got* at home is two dogs, and four cats, and six bunny rabbits, and two parakeets, and three canaries, and a green parrot, and a turtle, and a bowl of goldfish, and a cage of white mice, and a silly old hamster! I . . . want . . . a . . . *squirrel!!!*

MR. SALT. All right, my pet, Daddy'll get you a squirrel just as soon as he possibly can.

VERUCA SALT. But I don't want any . . . old . . . squirrel! I want a *trained* squirrel.

MR. SALT. Very well. [*Taking out a wallet full of money.*] Wonka? How much d'you want for one of these crazy squirrels? Name your price!

WILLY WONKA. They're not for sale. She can't have one.

VERUCA SALT. [*Furious.*] Who says I can't?! I'm going in to grab me a squirrel this very minute!

WILLY WONKA. Don't!

[*VERUCA goes through the door and approaches the squirrel she wants.*]

VERUCA SALT. All right, I'll have *you!*

[*As she reaches out, she acts as if all the squirrels are leaping onto her. She struggles and wriggles and screams.*]

WILLY WONKA. No—no—no! They've all jumped on her! All of them! Twenty-five of them have her right arm pinned down. Twenty-five have her left arm pinned down. Twenty-five have her right leg anchored to the ground. Twenty-four have her left leg. And the last squirrel . . . it's . . . it's climbed up on her shoulders and started tap-tap-tapping on Veruca's head with its knuckles!

MRS. SALT. Save her! Veruca! Come back! What are they doing to her?

WILLY WONKA. They're testing her to see if she's a bad nut—watch! [*VERUCA now acts as if she's being dragged across the floor toward the garbage chute.*] My *goodness!* She is a bad nut after all. Her head must have sounded quite hollow!

[VERUCA *kicks and screams but to no avail.*]

MRS. SALT. Where are they taking her?

WILLY WONKA. She's going where all the other bad nuts go—down the garbage chute!

MR. SALT. By golly . . . she *is* going down the chute!

[VERUCA *wriggles herself into chute and out of sight.*]

WILLY WONKA. She's gone!

MRS. SALT. Where do you suppose she's gone to?

WILLY WONKA. That particular chute runs directly into the great big main garbage pipe which carries away all the rubbish from every part of the factory—all the floor sweepings and potato peelings and rotten cabbages and fish heads and stuff like that.

Viewing the photograph: What do you imagine the Oompa-Loompas will have to say about Veruca?

MIKE TEAVEE. Who eats fish and cabbage and potatoes in this factory, I'd like to know?

WILLY WONKA. I do, of course. You don't think I live on cacao beans, do you? And of course, the pipe goes to the furnace in the end.

MR. SALT. Now see here, Wonka . . . I think you've gone just a shade too far this time, I do indeed. My daughter may be a bit of a frump[10]—I don't mind admitting it—but that doesn't mean you can roast her to a crisp. I'll have you know I'm extremely cross about this—I really am.

WILLY WONKA. Oh, don't be cross, my dear sir! I expect she'll turn up again sooner or later. She may not even have gone down the pipe at all. She may be stuck in the chute, just below the entrance hole. And if that's the case, all you'll have to do is go in and pull her up again.

[MRS. SALT *runs into the Nut Room and looks into the hole, bending over.*]

MRS. SALT. Veruca! Are you down there?

[*She leans over further and falls into the chute, as if pushed by the squirrels.*]

WILLY WONKA. Oh no! The squirrels have pushed her, too!

MR. SALT. Good gracious me! What a lot of garbage there's going to be today! [*He leans over the hole and peers in.*] What's it like down there, Angina? [*Acts as if being pushed by the squirrels too.*] Help!

[*He also falls into the chute.*]

---

10. Usually, *frump* refers to a woman who is neither neat nor stylish; here, however, its older meaning is used: "a bad-tempered woman."

CHARLIE. Oh dear! What on earth's going to happen to them now?

WILLY WONKA. I expect someone will catch them at the bottom of the chute.

CHARLIE. But what about the great fiery incinerator?

WILLY WONKA. Oh *that!* They only light it every other day. Perhaps this is one of the days when they let it go out. You never know—they might be lucky. I've never seen anything like it! The children are disappearing like rabbits! Oh well, shall we move on?

CHARLIE AND GRANDPA JOE. Oh, yes!

MIKE TEAVEE. My feet are getting tired! I want to watch television!

WILLY WONKA. If you're tired then we'd better take the elevator. It's just down the hall. Come on!

[*All exit.*]

OOMPA-LOOMPAS. Veruca Salt, the little brute,
Has just gone down the garbage chute,
(And as we very rightly thought
That in a case like this we ought
To see the thing completely through,
We've polished off her parents, too.)
Down goes Veruca! Down the drain!
And here, perhaps, we should explain
That she will meet, as she descends,
A rather different set of friends
Some liverwurst so old and gray
One smelled it from a mile away,
A rotten nut, a reeky[11] pear,

A thing the cat left on the stair,
And lots of other things as well,
Each with a rather horrid smell.
These are Veruca's new found friends
That she will meet as she descends,
And this is the price she has to pay
For going so very far astray.
But now, my dears, we think you might
Be wondering—is it really right
That every single bit of blame
And all the scolding and the shame
Should fall upon Veruca Salt?
Is she the only one at fault?
For though she's spoiled, and dread-
      fully so,
A girl can't spoil herself, you know.
Who turned her into such a brat?
Who are the culprits? Who did that?
Alas! You needn't look so far
To find out who these sinners are.
They are (and this is very sad)
Her loving parents, Mum and Dad.
And that is why we're glad they fell
Into the garbage chute as well.

[*End of Scene 8.*]

 SCENE 9

[*By the Great Glass Elevator. Elevator is at center stage, and all enter and gather around it as scene opens.*]

CHARLIE. Wow! Look at that! It's a Great Glass Elevator! And look at all the buttons all over.

WILLY WONKA. This isn't just an ordinary up-and-down elevator! This elevator can go sideways and longways and slantways and any other way you can think of! It can

---

11. Veruca's new "friends" will include sausage *(liverwurst)* that is rotting and a bad-smelling *(reeky)* pear.

Vocabulary
culprit (kul′ prit) *n.* one who is guilty of some crime or misdeed; offender

visit any single room in the whole factory, no matter where it is! You simply press the button and *zing!* You're off!

GRANDPA JOE. Fantastic!

CHARLIE. *Look!* Each button is labeled!

WILLY WONKA. And each button stands for a room!

MIKE TEAVEE. Yeah . . . let's see. It says, Strawberry-juice Water Pistols, Exploding Candies for your enemies, Stickjaw for talkative parents, Invisible Chocolate Bars for eating in class, Rainbow Drops—suck them and you can spit in six different colors—

WILLY WONKA. Come on! Enough! Enough! We can't wait all day!

[*They enter the elevator.*]

MIKE TEAVEE. Isn't there a *Television* Room in all this lot?

WILLY WONKA. Certainly! Right here!

[*He points to a button.*]

MIKE TEAVEE. Whoopee! That's for me!

[*He presses a button and the elevator shakes.*]

WILLY WONKA. [*Laughing.*] Hang on, everybody!

MR. TEAVEE. I'm going to be *sick!*

WILLY WONKA. Please don't be sick.

MR. TEAVEE. Try and stop me!

WILLY WONKA. [*Holding his hat in front of* MR. TEAVEE.] Then you'd better take this!

MR. TEAVEE. Make this awful thing stop!

WILLY WONKA. Can't do that! It won't stop 'til we get there. I only hope no one is using the other elevator at this moment.

MIKE TEAVEE. What . . . other . . . elevator?

WILLY WONKA. The one that goes the opposite way on the same track as this one!

MR. TEAVEE. Holy mackerel! You mean we might have a collision?

WILLY WONKA. I've always been lucky so far.

MR. TEAVEE. Now I *am* going to be sick!

WILLY WONKA. No! No! Not now! We're nearly there! Don't spoil my hat!

[*Elevator stops shaking.*]

MIKE TEAVEE. Some . . . ride!

MR. TEAVEE. Never again!

WILLY WONKA. Just a minute now! Listen to me! Before we go into this Television-Chocolate Room, I want to warn you. There is dangerous stuff around in here and you *must not* <u>tamper</u> with it! [*Pause.*] Okay, everybody out!

[*All leave elevator and exit.*]

[*End of Scene 9.*]

◈◯◈ SCENE 10 ◈◯◈

[*The Television-Chocolate Testing Room. It is completely bare except for a large television camera at one end, a large television screen at the other, and several bright floodlights. All enter as scene opens.*]

WILLY WONKA. [*Hopping up and down with excitement.*] Here we go! This is the Testing Room for my very latest and greatest invention—*Television Chocolate!*

Vocabulary

tamper (tam′ pər) *v.* to interfere or meddle in a way that causes harm

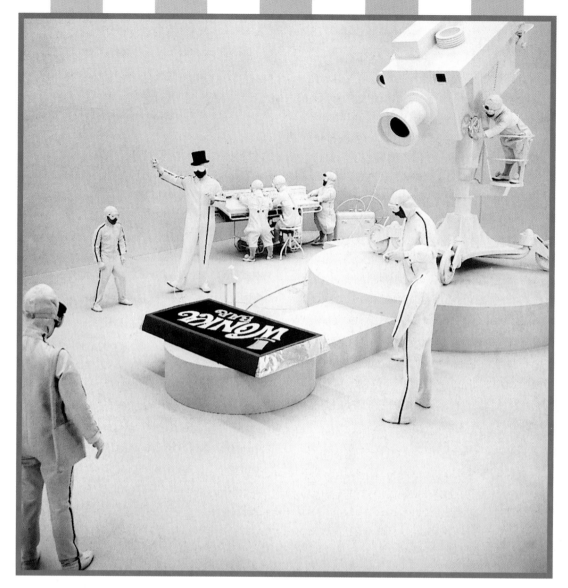

Viewing the photograph: What is happening here? How does Mike Teavee react?

MIKE TEAVEE. But *what* is Television Chocolate?

WILLY WONKA. Good heavens, child, stop interrupting me! It works by television. I don't like television myself. I suppose it's all right in small doses, but children never seem to be able to take it in small doses. They want to sit there all day long . . . staring and staring at the screen—

MIKE TEAVEE. That's me!

MR. TEAVEE. Shut up!

WILLY WONKA. Thank you. Now then! The very first time I saw ordinary television working, I was struck by a tremendous idea. If a photograph could be broken up into millions of pieces, and the pieces sent whizzing through the air until they hit an antenna, and then put together again on a screen—why couldn't I send a *real* bar of chocolate whizzing through the air in tiny pieces, and then put the pieces together at the other end, all ready to be eaten?

MIKE TEAVEE. Impossible!

WILLY WONKA. Think so? Watch me send a bar of chocolate from one end of this room to the other—by television. Bring me that chocolate bar, please. [CHARLIE *brings over an enormous bar of chocolate from offstage.*] It has to be big, because whenever you send something by television, it always comes out much smaller than it was when it went in. Here we go then! Get ready! [MIKE *wanders curiously toward the camera.*] No! No! Stop! You there! Mike Teavee! Stand back! You're too close! There are dangerous rays coming out of that thing! They could break you up into a million tiny pieces in one second! [MIKE *backs away.*] That's better! Now then . . . switch on!

[*Lights flash and bar disappears through slit in curtain.*]

GRANDPA JOE. [*Waving his arms and shouting.*] The chocolate's gone!

WILLY WONKA. It's on its way! It's now rushing through the air above our heads in a million tiny pieces. *Quick!* Come over here! [*All dash over to the other side of the stage, to TV screen.*] Watch the screen! [*Small bar of chocolate appears through slit in curtain and lighted screen.*] Take it!

MIKE TEAVEE. [*Laughing.*] How *can* you take it? It's just a picture on a television screen!

[CHARLIE *reaches out and the chocolate miraculously goes into his hands.*]

GRANDPA JOE. It's absolutely fantastic! It's . . . it's . . . it's a *miracle!*

WILLY WONKA. Just *imagine*—when I start using this across the country, a commercial will flash onto the screen and a voice will say, "Eat Wonka's Chocolates! They're the best in the world! If you don't believe us, try one for yourself . . . now!!!!"

GRANDPA JOE. Terrific!

MIKE TEAVEE. [*Shouting.*] But Mr. Wonka, can you send other things through the air in the same way? Like people? Could you send a real live person from one place to another in the same way?

WILLY WONKA. A person? Are you off your rocker?

MIKE TEAVEE. But *could* it be done?

WILLY WONKA. Good heavens, child. I really don't know . . . I suppose it could . . . yes, I'm pretty sure it could . . . of course it could. I wouldn't like to risk it though—it might have some very nasty results.

[MIKE *is off and moving when he hears* WILLY WONKA *say "I'm pretty sure."*]

MIKE TEAVEE. Look at me! I'm going to be the first person in the world to be sent by television!

WILLY WONKA. No! No! No! *No!*

MR. TEAVEE. Mike! Stop! Come back! You'll be turned into a million tiny pieces!

MIKE TEAVEE. See you later, alligator!

[*He jumps into the glare of the light and then disappears through folds in curtain.*]

MR. TEAVEE. [*Running to spot where* MIKE *disappeared.*] He's gone!

WILLY WONKA. [*Placing a hand on* MR. TEAVEE's *shoulder.*] We shall have to hope for the best. We must pray that your little boy will come out unharmed at the other end. We must watch the television screen. He may come through at any moment.

[*Everyone stares at the screen.*]

MR. TEAVEE. [*Wiping his brow nervously.*] He's taking a heck of a long time to come across.

WILLY WONKA. Hold everything! Watch the screen! Something's happening!

MR. TEAVEE. Here he comes! Yes, that's him all right! [*Pause.*] But he's a *midget!* Isn't he going to get any bigger?

WILLY WONKA. Grab him! *Quick!* [MR. *TEAVEE acts as if he grabs something.*] He's *completely* okay!

MR. TEAVEE. [*Acting as if something is in his hand.*] You call that okay? He's *shrunk!*

WILLY WONKA. Of course he's shrunk. What did you expect?

MR. TEAVEE. This is terrible! I can't send him back to school like this! He'll get squashed! He won't be able to do *anything!* [*He acts as if he is listening to* MIKE, *in his hand.*] What did you say, Mike? [*Pause.*] Never! No, you will *not* be able to watch television! I'm throwing the television set right out the window the moment we get home. I've had *enough* of television! What, Mike? [*Pause.*] I don't care what you want . . . or how much you jump and scream! [*He puts him in his pocket, acting as if he is secure there, slapping his pocket.*] There!

CHARLIE. Gee, how will Mike ever grow again?

WILLY WONKA. [*Stroking his beard thoughtfully.*] Well . . . small boys *are* extremely springy and elastic, so maybe he'll stretch if we put him on a special machine I have for testing the tough stretchiness of chewing gum!

MR. TEAVEE. How far do you think he'll stretch?

WILLY WONKA. Maybe *miles!* Anyway, he'll be awfully thin! But we'll fatten him up with all my super vitamin candy. It contains all the vitamins from A to Z! [*Writing instructions on a sheet of paper.*] Mr. Teavee, just hand these orders to the Oompa-Loompas over there . . . and don't look so worried! They all come out in the wash you know—every one of them.

[*All exit.*]

OOMPA-LOOMPAS.   The most important
   thing we've learned,
So far as children are concerned,
Is never, never, never let
Them near your television set—
They loll[12] and slop and lounge about,
And stare until their eyes pop out.
Oh yes, we know it keeps them still,
They don't climb out the window sill,
They never fight or kick or punch,
They leave you free to cook the lunch
And wash the dishes in the sink—
But did you ever stop to think,
To wonder just exactly what
This does to your beloved tot?
It rots the senses in the head!
It kills imagination dead!
His brain becomes as soft as cheese!
His powers of thinking rust and freeze!
He cannot think—he only sees!
"All right!" you'll cry. "All right!"
   you'll say,
"But if we take the set away,
What shall we do to entertain

---

12. To *loll* is to lean or lie down in a lazy, relaxed way.

Our darling children? Please explain!"
We'll answer this by asking you,
What used the darling ones to do?
They . . . used . . . to . . . read! They'd
    read and read,
And read and read, and then proceed
To read some more. Great Scott!
    Gadzooks!
One half their lives was reading books!
Such wondrous, fine, fantastic tales
Of dragons, gypsies, queens, and whales
And pirates wearing purple pants,
And sailing ships and elephants,
And cannibals[13] crouching 'round
    the pot,
Stirring away at something hot.
Oh, books, what books they used to
    know,
Those children living long ago!
So please, oh please, we beg, we pray,
Go throw your TV set away,
Fear not, because we promise you
That, in about a week or two
Of having nothing else to do,
They'll now begin to feel the need
Of having something good to read.
P.S. regarding Mike Teavee,
We very much regret that we
Shall simply have to wait and see
If we can get him back his height.
But if we can't—it serves him right.

[*End of Scene 10.*]

 SCENE 11

[*Somewhere in the Chocolate Factory. WILLY WONKA, CHARLIE, and GRANDPA JOE enter as scene opens.*]

WILLY WONKA. Which room shall it be next? Hurry up! We must be going! And how many children are left now? [*Looks around.*] Hmmmmmmmmmmmmmmmmmm!

GRANDPA JOE. I guess there's only Charlie left now, Mr. Wonka.

WILLY WONKA. [*Pretending to be surprised.*] You mean . . . you're the only one left?

CHARLIE. Why . . . yes.

WILLY WONKA. [*Suddenly exploding with excitement.*] But my dear boy, *that means you've won!* [*He shakes CHARLIE'S hand furiously.*] Oh, I do congratulate you! I really do! I'm absolutely delighted! It couldn't be better! How wonderful this is! I had a hunch, you know—right from the beginning—that it was going to be you! Well done, Charlie . . . well done! But we mustn't dilly! We mustn't dally![14] We have an *enormous* number of things to do before the day is out! Just think of the *arrangements* that have to be made!

CHARLIE. Wait, Mr. Wonka . . . I'm afraid I don't understand all of this! What are you talking about?

WILLY WONKA. Oh . . . *do* forgive me! I get carried away at times. I forgot that you didn't know—

CHARLIE. Know *what?*

WILLY WONKA. [*Becoming quiet and serious.*] You know, Charlie, I love my chocolate factory. [*Pause.*] Tell me, Charlie, do you love my chocolate factory? Think carefully, because it's very important—how you feel.

CHARLIE. [*Very thoughtfully.*] Well, Mr. Wonka, all that I can say is that I've *never*

---

13. *Cannibals* are people who eat people.

14. To *dilly-dally* is to waste time.

Viewing the photograph: Do you think Charlie is "the type of person that will appreciate this factory," as Willy Wonka says? Why?

CHARLIE. What job?

WILLY WONKA. Well you see, I'm tired, Charlie. I'm not getting any younger, and it isn't as easy to carry out my ideas as . . . as . . . it once was. I need some help. That means . . . *you!*

CHARLIE. Me?

WILLY WONKA. Yes! I would like you and Grandpa Joe and, of course, all the rest of your family, to move here—and live here—*permanently!* I would like to have someone who will take over . . . after I've gone. I have no family, and I can think of *no one* I would like to run the factory more than *you.* This would be after I've trained you and taught you everything I know, of course! I've watched you all day, and *you* are the type of person that will appreciate this factory . . . and care for it as I have, all these years. Will you accept my offer? If you do, *everything* that I have is yours.

spent a more fantastic day *anywhere* . . . in my *whole life.* I've been *very, very* happy. Do I love this factory? [*Pause.*] Yes . . . yes, I think I do! It means . . . a great deal to me.

GRANDPA JOE. Why do you ask, Mr. Wonka?

WILLY WONKA. Well . . . of course Charlie and all of the others will receive all of the candy I promised, but I want *Charlie* to receive *much more!* You see, this whole day has been a *contest.* It's been a contest to find out who would be the best person for the job.

CHARLIE. Will I? *Wow!* This is more than I could have ever imagined! *Will* I? Of course I will, Mr. Wonka! Thank you! *Thank you!* Just think of it, Grandpa Joe! Wait until we tell Dad and Mom and the grandfolks! It's going to be *our* chocolate factory! And we're never *ever* going to starve again! Just think of all that chocolate! Oh, just you wait and see!

[*Curtain.*]

Responding to Literature

PERSONAL RESPONSE

- ◆ Were you surprised by the fates of Augustus, Violet, Veruca, Mike, or Charlie? Explain.
- ◆ Is Willy Wonka's Chocolate Factory like the factory you imagined in the **Focus Activity** on page 734? Explain.

Analyzing Literature

RECALL

1. What happens to Violet, Veruca Salt and her parents, and Mike Teavee?
2. What do the Oompa-Loompas have to say about gum chewers, spoiled children, and television addicts?
3. What is Willy Wonka's response to the accidents that occur to the first four winners?
4. What is Charlie's reward at the end of the tour?

INTERPRET

5. How does each winner's accident fit his or her personality? What do you think will happen to each of them?
6. Do you agree or disagree with the Oompa-Loompas' views on gum chewing, spoiled children, and television? Why or why not?
7. How does Willy Wonka change his behavior at the end of the tour? Do you think he has been completely sincere and honest throughout the tour? Explain your answer.
8. What is Willy's attitude toward Charlie at the end of the tour? What do you think will happen to Charlie and his family?

EVALUATE AND CONNECT

9. What do you think were Dahl's **purposes** for writing this story? Explain your answer.
10. Theme Connection   Would you have enjoyed the tour of the chocolate factory? Why or why not?

LITERARY ELEMENTS

Dialogue

". . . I'd say that *her* jaws are going up and down almost as much as mine are just from *yelling* at me. . . ." says Violet of her mother. From this little bit of **dialogue**—the words characters say—the audience learns that Violet is a rude person. Her personality comes across not only through her words but in how she says them—in a mocking way. Playwrights write dialogue with an awareness of how the words should be spoken. They italicize or capitalize words that are to be emphasized and use ellipses (three dots) to indicate pauses.

1. What do you learn about Augustus Gloop, Veruca Salt, and Mike Teavee from their dialogue? Find examples to support your ideas.

2. Find examples of dialogue spoken by Willy Wonka and Charlie that reveal their personalities.

● See **Literary Terms Handbook,** p. R2.

Literature and Writing

Writing About Literature

Teasing the Reader At the outset of the play, the audience expects Charlie to get a Golden Ticket. Why doesn't the playwright tell the audience immediately and directly how Charlie gets the ticket? Write a paragraph explaining how Charlie gets the ticket. Tell which "false starts" are included in this scene and why.

Creative Writing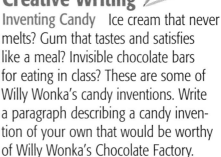

Inventing Candy Ice cream that never melts? Gum that tastes and satisfies like a meal? Invisible chocolate bars for eating in class? These are some of Willy Wonka's candy inventions. Write a paragraph describing a candy invention of your own that would be worthy of Willy Wonka's Chocolate Factory.

Extending Your Response

Literature Groups

Hero The narrator introduces Charlie Bucket as "the hero of our story." A hero is the main character of a story and can also sometimes be described as someone who is much admired and respected. How is Charlie a hero in this play? Support your ideas with information in the selection.

Learning for Life

Reading the Small Print Just how lucky was Charlie to win a Golden Ticket? Check magazines, newspapers, and coupon displays in stores. With a partner, collect information about chances of winning from different contest entry forms, and share your findings with the class.

*inter*NET CONNECTION

Charlie and the Chocolate Factory was made into a movie called *Willy Wonka and the Chocolate Factory.* Search the Internet using the two titles as keywords to find out more interesting facts about the book, the movie, and the author.

Listening and Speaking

Oompa-Loompas The Oompa-Loompas have their own way of explaining what happens. With a small group, practice reading aloud their songs, and share your reading with the class.

Reading Further

If you enjoyed this selection by Roald Dahl, you might enjoy these books:
Danny: The Champion of the World
James and the Giant Peach
Matilda

📑 **Save your work for your portfolio.**

Skill Minilessons

GRAMMAR AND LANGUAGE • PUNCTUATION IN VERSE

Augustus Gloop! Augustus Gloop!
The great big greedy nincompoop!

The Oompa-Loompas make up verses about the characters in the play and what happens to them. As you say the lines above aloud, you pause after each exclamation mark.

Punctuation and capitalization in verse show not only where sentences begin and end, but also how to read the lines—when to pause and when to continue without pausing. Notice that most of the

Oompa-Loompas' lines begin with capital letters. The lines, however, should be read as parts of continuing sentences. Readers should pause only at commas, dashes, or end punctuation marks.

PRACTICE Find five complete sentences in the Oompa-Loompas' verses. Write the lines as sentences with beginning capital letters and final punctuation marks.

● For more on punctuation, see **Language Handbook,** pp. R33–R37.

READING AND THINKING • COMPARING AND CONTRASTING

Comparing and contrasting is a way to analyze what you have read or heard. When you compare people or things, you look for ways that they are the same, or similar. When you contrast, you look for ways they are different. How Charlie behaves when he meets Willy Wonka is very different from how the other characters act.

PRACTICE Write two or three paragraphs comparing and contrasting the behavior of the Golden Ticket winners during the tour.

● For more on comparing and contrasting, see **Reading Handbook,** p. R78.

Augustus Gloop	introduces his mother, but seems reluctant to do so
Violet Beauregarde	hurries Wonka, saying, "Let's just get on with the whole thing"
Veruca Salt	doesn't want her father to touch Willy Wonka's hand
Mike Teavee	shoots his guns off and says, "Come on! I'm missing all my favorite TV shows!"
Charlie Bucket	calls Wonka "Sir," says "Thank you," and introduces his grandfather

VOCABULARY • SYNONYMS AND ANTONYMS

Willy Wonka promises he will "entrance, delight, intrigue, astonish, and perplex" the Golden Ticket holders. For emphasis, he uses several **synonyms,** words that mean nearly the same thing. **Antonyms** are words that have opposite meanings. A synonym for *happy* is *glad,* and an antonym for *happy* is *sad.* Some words don't have synonyms or antonyms, but many words have several of each. Language skills exercises often ask you to come up with synonyms

or antonyms because doing so makes you think about the meanings of words.

PRACTICE If the two words in each pair are synonyms, write *S.* If they are antonyms, write *A.*
1. *culprit* and *victim*
2. *colossal* and *gigantic*
3. *alter* and *vary*
4. *morsel* and *bit*
5. *repulsive* and *attractive*

SCIENCE FICTION

Made-up stories set in the real world are *realistic fiction*. Stories set in worlds where magic rules—or at least works—are *fantasy*. Stories set in the universe as we may come to know it are **science fiction.** Often it's difficult to draw the line between fantasy and science fiction. Good examples of true science fiction can be found in the popular TV series *Star Trek*.

MODEL: *Star Trek*

SETTING Some science fiction is set on other planets or in future eras on Earth. Other stories have a familiar setting with unfamiliar details.

> *Star Trek* is set several centuries in the future. Its episodes take place on starships, space stations, and other planets. The characters include aliens, such as the Vulcan officer, Mr. Spock.

SCIENTIFIC BASIS All the details in a strange setting should be explainable, preferably according to science as we understand it today. If a writer invents a new world, all its parts must follow consistent rules.

> The speed with which the starship *Enterprise* travels is explained by the use of an imaginary fuel, dilithium crystals.

PLOT In effective science fiction, the central problem in the plot grows out of the special conditions of the strange setting.

> The problems that the *Star Trek* crew face—such as dealing with aliens or dangers in space—could never happen in an everyday, normal setting.

THEME Most science fiction tries to teach as well as entertain. A writer may use an unfamiliar setting to make readers see everyday problems in a new way.

> When two alien groups war because their skin is colored in opposite patterns, *Star Trek* deals with a universal theme—the senselessness of racial prejudice.

Active Reading Strategies

Tips for Reading Science Fiction

Science fiction is a blend of reality and imagination, of fun and serious thinking. To fully appreciate this type of writing, you need to see both the details and the big picture. Here are some strategies that will help.

● For more on reading strategies, see **Reading Handbook,** pp. R63–R94.

EVALUATE

For science fiction, probably more than for any other kind of literature, readers willingly "go along" with the author and accept the world the author creates. However, the rules of the new world have to follow a certain logic. The "laws" of science, whether real or invented, should make sense in the context of the setting.

Ask Yourself . . . Do the explanations for unusual characters, setting, and events in the plot make sense? Are the laws, rules, or ideas from science used consistently here? Do plot events arise from the special setting? Why does the author tell this story—as a warning, or for fun and thrills?

APPLYING THE STRATEGIES

Read the following selection, "Future Tense." Use the Active Reading Model notes in the margins as you read.

CONNECT

Decide whether the events of the story shed light on real-life situations. Is there a useful lesson in the tale?

Ask Yourself . . . What special characteristics of the setting remind me of life on Earth? What scientific ideas do I wish I understood better? How can we keep from creating such a danger on Earth? Who would I recommend this story to and why?

Before You Read
Future Tense

MEET ROBERT LIPSYTE

Writing to meet a deadline "is often exhilarating," says Robert Lipsyte (lip′ sīt), "and if you're lucky . . . , a rhythm develops and the story just flows." Lipsyte was about to enter graduate school when he took a summer job as a copy boy—a person who delivers writers' articles to different departments—at the *New York Times*. He worked at the *Times* for the next fourteen years, becoming a sports reporter and sports columnist. He has written several books for young people, most of them on sports-related subjects.

Robert Lipsyte was born in 1938. This story was first published in the anthology Sixteen *in 1984.*

FOCUS ACTIVITY

Do you like to make up stories about monsters or space creatures?

Brainstorm
As a class, brainstorm ideas for a story about monsters or space creatures.

Setting a Purpose
Read to find out what the title "Future Tense" means.

BACKGROUND

Did You Know? Is there such a thing as a flying saucer? Is it possible that life exists in some other corner of the universe? In *Unidentified Flying Objects and ExtraTerrestrial Life*,  Carole Marsh writes, "With the discovery of information of new planets and the aid of ever more sophisticated space telescopes and probes, the answer to the question 'Are we alone?' may be just around the . . . corner."

VOCABULARY PREVIEW

expand (iks pand′) *v.* to develop (something) in greater detail; make larger or more complete; p. 773

conspiracy (kən spir′ ə sē) *n.* the act of secretly planning together, especially for an illegal purpose; p. 773

twinge (twinj) *n.* a sudden, sharp feeling of pain, grief, shame, and so on; p. 776

vivid (viv′ id) *adj.* forming clear or lifelike pictures in the mind; lively; p. 776

impulse (im′ puls) *n.* an internal force that causes one to act without thinking; p. 777

manipulative (mə nip′ yə lā′ tiv) *adj.* able to influence or control in a clever, often unfair way; p. 778

quaver (kwā′ vər) *n.* a trembling or shaking; p. 779

FUTURE TENSE

Robert Lipsyte ∾

GARY COULDN'T WAIT FOR TENTH GRADE TO START
so he could strut his sentences, parade his paragraphs, renew his reputation as the top creative writer in school. At the opening assembly,
he felt on edge, psyched,[1] like a boxer before the first-round bell. He
leaned forward as Dr. Proctor, the principal, introduced two new staff
members. He wasn't particularly interested in the new vice-principal,
Ms. Jones; Gary never had discipline problems, he'd never even had to
stay after school. But his head cocked alertly as Dr. Proctor introduced
the new Honors English[2] teacher, Mr. Smith. Here was the person he'd
have to impress.

QUESTION

What is Gary's spe-
cialty? Whom does
he want to impress?

---

1. By *psyched,* Gary means that he's in the right mental state.
2. *Honors English* is an advanced class for above-average students.

FUTURE TENSE

He studied Mr. Smith. The man was hard to describe. He looked as though he'd been manufactured to fit his name. Average height, brownish hair, pale white skin, medium build. Middle age. He was the sort of person you began to forget the minute you met him. Even his clothes had no particular style. They merely covered his body.

Mr. Smith was . . . just there.

Gary was studying Mr. Smith so intently that he didn't hear Dr. Proctor call him up to the stage to receive an award from last term. Jim Baggs jabbed an elbow into his ribs and said, "Let's get up there, Dude."

Dr. Proctor shook Gary's hand and gave him the County Medal for Best Composition. While Dr. Proctor was giving Jim Baggs the County Trophy for Best All-Round Athlete, Gary glanced over his shoulder to see if Mr. Smith looked impressed. But he couldn't find the new teacher. Gary wondered if Mr. Smith was so ordinary he was invisible when no one was talking about him.

On the way home, Dani Belzer, the prettiest poet in school, asked Gary, "What did you think of our new Mr. Wordsmith?"[3]

How do you picture Mr. Smith so far? Which words help you picture him?

"If he was a color he'd be beige," said Gary. "If he was a taste he'd be water. If he was a sound he'd be a low hum."

"Fancy, empty words," sneered Mike Chung, ace[4] reporter on the school paper. "All you've told me is you've got nothing to tell me."

Dani quickly stepped between them. "What did you think of the first assignment?"

"Describe a Typical Day at School," said Gary, trying unsuccessfully to mimic Mr. Smith's bland voice. "That's about as exciting as tofu."

"A real artist," said Dani, "accepts the commonplace as a challenge."

That night, hunched over his humming electric typewriter, Gary wrote a description of a typical day at school from the viewpoint of a new

Did You Know?
Tofu (tō′ fōō) is a protein-rich food made from soybeans.

teacher who was seeing everything for the very first time, who took nothing for granted. He described the shredded edges of the limp flag outside the dented front door, the worn flooring where generations of kids had nervously paced outside the principal's office, the nauseatingly[5] sweet pipe-smoke seeping out of the teachers' lounge.

---

3. A *wordsmith* is someone who works with words.

4. Here, *ace* means "top-ranked; best."

5. In Gary's story, the teacher *took nothing for granted*—he notices and thinks about all he sees. For example, he observes that the pipe smoke that comes from the teachers' lounge smells sickeningly (*nauseatingly*) sweet.

And then, in the last line, he gave the composition that extra twist, the little kicker on which his reputation rested. He wrote:

> *The new teacher's beady little eyes missed nothing, for they were the optical recorders[6] of an alien creature who had come to earth to gather information.*

RESPOND

How do you respond to reading this sudden twist in Gary's composition?

The next morning, when Mr. Smith asked for a volunteer to read aloud, Gary was on his feet and moving toward the front of the class-room before Mike Chung got his hand out of his pocket.

The class loved Gary's composition. They laughed and stamped their feet. Chung shrugged, which meant he couldn't think of any criticism, and Dani flashed thumbs up. Best of all, Jim Baggs shouldered Gary against the blackboard after class and said, "Awesome tale, Dude."

Gary felt good until he got the composition back. Along one margin, in a perfect script, Mr. Smith had written:

EVALUATE

Do Gary's friends sound like everyday kind of people?

> *You can do better.*

"How would he know?" Gary complained on the way home.

"You should be grateful," said Dani. "He's pushing you to the farthest limits of your talent."

"Which may be nearer than you think," snickered Mike.

Gary rewrote his composition, <u>expanded</u> it, complicated it, thickened it. Not only was this new teacher an alien, he was part of an extraterrestrial[7] <u>conspiracy</u> to take over Earth. Gary's final sentence was:

> *Every iota of information, fragment of fact, morsel of minutiae[8] sucked up by those vacuuming eyes was beamed directly into a computer circling the planet. The data would eventually become a program that would control the mind of every school kid on earth.*

VISUALIZE

How do you picture the scene that Gary describes in his composition?

---

6. *Optical* has to do with vision, so the *optical recorders* are like cameras.
7. Anything that is *extraterrestrial* comes from beyond the earth.
8. Both *iota* (ī ō′ tə) and *morsel* mean "a small amount," and *minutiae* (mi nōō′ shē ī′) are very small or unimportant details.

Vocabulary

expand (iks pand′) *v.* to develop (something) in greater detail; make larger or more complete

conspiracy (kən spir′ ə sē) *n.* the act of secretly planning together, especially for an illegal purpose

FUTURE TENSE

Do you agree with
Dani about Gary's
composition?

Gary showed the new draft to Dani before class. He stood on tiptoes so he could read over her shoulder. Sometimes he wished she were shorter, but mostly he wished he were taller.

"What do you think?"

"The assignment was to describe a typical day," said Dani. "This is off the wall."[9]

He snatched the papers back. "Creative writing means creating." He walked away, hurt and angry. He thought: *If she doesn't like my compositions, how can I ever get her to like me?*

That morning, Mike Chung read his own composition aloud to the class. He described a typical day through the eyes of a student in a wheelchair. Everything most students take for granted was an obstacle: the bathroom door too heavy to open, the gym steps too steep to climb, the light switch too high on the wall. The class applauded and Mr. Smith nodded approvingly. Even Gary had to admit it was really good— if you considered plain-fact journalism as creative writing, that is.

---

9. The expression *off the wall* describes something that is considered unusual, weird, or crazy.

Viewing the image: In what ways might these flying saucers be similar to the ones Gary writes about?

ACTIVE
READING
MODEL

Gary's rewrite came back the next day marked:

Improving. Try again.

Saturday he locked himself in his room after breakfast and rewrote the rewrite. He carefully selected his nouns and verbs and adjectives. He polished and arranged them in sentences like a jeweler strings pearls. He felt good as he wrote, as the electric typewriter hummed and buzzed and sometimes coughed. He thought: *Every champion knows that as hard as it is to get to the top, it's even harder to stay up there.*

His mother knocked on his door around noon. When he let her in, she said, "It's a beautiful day."

"Big project," he mumbled. He wanted to avoid a distracting conversation.

She smiled. "If you spend too much time in your room, you'll turn into a mushroom."

He wasn't listening. "Thanks. Anything's okay. Don't forget the mayonnaise."

Gary wrote:

> **The alien's probes[10] trembled as he read the student's composition. Could that skinny, bespectacled[11] earthling really suspect its extraterrestrial identity? Or was his composition merely the result of a creative thunderstorm in a brilliant young mind?**

Before Gary turned in his composition on Monday morning, he showed it to Mike Chung. He should have known better.

"You're trying too hard," chortled Chung. "Truth is stronger than fiction."

Gary flinched at that. It hurt. It might be true. But he couldn't let his competition know he had scored. "You journalists are stuck in the present and the past," growled Gary. "Imagination prepares us for what's going to happen."

Dani read her composition aloud to the class. It described a typical day from the perspective of a louse choosing a head of hair to nest in.

CONNECT

Have you ever felt this way when you were working on something you cared about?

QUESTION

Whom is Gary really talking about in his composition?

---

10. Like an insect, the alien has feelers, or *probes,* that are used to gather certain kinds of information from the world around it.

11. Someone who is *bespectacled* wears eyeglasses, which are sometimes called *spectacles.*

FUTURE TENSE

ACTIVE
READING
MODEL

The louse moved from the thicket of a varsity crew-cut to the matted jungle of a sagging perm to a straight, sleek blond cascade.

The class cheered and Mr. Smith smiled. Gary felt a <u>twinge</u> of jealousy. Dani and Mike were coming on. There wasn't room for more than one at the top.

In the hallway, he said to Dani, "And you called my composition off the wall?"

Mike jumped in. "There's a big difference between poetical metaphor and hack[12] science fiction."

Gary felt choked by a lump in his throat. He hurried away.

Mr. Smith handed back Gary's composition the next day marked:

See me after school.

Gary was nervous all day. What was there to talk about? Maybe Mr. Smith hated science fiction. One of those traditional English teachers. Didn't understand that science fiction could be literature. *Maybe I can educate him,* thought Gary.

When Gary arrived at the English office, Mr. Smith seemed nervous too. He kept folding and unfolding Gary's composition. "Where do you get such ideas?" he asked in his monotone voice.

Gary shrugged. "They just come to me."

"Alien teachers. Taking over the minds of schoolchildren." Mr. Smith's empty eyes were blinking. "What made you think of that?"

"I've always had this <u>vivid</u> imagination."

"If you're sure it's just your imagination." Mr. Smith looked relieved. "I guess everything will work out." He handed back Gary's composition. "No more fantasy, Gary. Reality. That's your assignment. Write only about what you know."

Outside school, Gary ran into Jim Baggs, who looked surprised to see him. "Don't tell me you had to stay after, Dude."

"I had to see Mr. Smith about my composition. He didn't like it. Told me to stick to reality."

PREDICT

Why do you think Mr. Smith wants to see Gary?

RESPOND

What do you think of Gary's teacher?

---

12. The louse could be a *metaphor*—a comparison in which one thing is said to be another—for a human who makes many bad choices before settling on the right one. In *hack* writing, the characters, situations, and ideas are uninteresting because the reader has seen them in many other stories.

Vocabulary

twinge (twinj) *n.* a sudden, sharp feeling of pain, grief, shame, and so on
vivid (viv' id) *adj.* forming clear or lifelike pictures in the mind; lively

"Don't listen." Jim Baggs body checked Gary into the schoolyard fence. "Dude, you got to be yourself."

Gary ran all the way home and locked himself into his room. He felt feverish with creativity. Dude, you got to be yourself, Dude. It doesn't matter what your so-called friends say, or your English teacher. You've got to play your own kind of game, write your own kind of stories.

The words flowed out of Gary's mind and through his fingers and out of the machine and onto sheets of paper. He wrote and rewrote until he felt the words were exactly right:

> **With great effort, the alien shut down the electrical panic _impulses_ coursing through its system and turned on Logical Overdrive.[13] There were two possibilities:**
>
> **1. This high school boy was exactly what he seemed to be, a brilliant, imaginative, apprentice[14] best-selling author and screen-writer, or,**
>
> **2. He had somehow stumbled onto the secret plan and he would have to be either enlisted into the conspiracy or erased off the face of the planet.**

First thing in the morning, Gary turned in his new rewrite to Mr. Smith. A half hour later, Mr. Smith called Gary out of Spanish. There was no expression on his regular features. He said, "I'm going to need some help with you."

Cold sweat covered Gary's body as Mr. Smith grabbed his arm and led him to the new vice-principal. She read the composition while they waited. Gary got a good look at her for the first time. Ms. Jones was . . . just there. She looked as though she'd been manufactured to fit her name. Average. Standard. Typical. The cold sweat turned into goose pimples.

How could he have missed the clues? Smith and Jones were aliens! He had stumbled on their secret and now they'd have to deal with him.

He blurted, "Are you going to enlist me or erase me?"

Ms. Jones ignored him. "In my opinion, Mr. Smith, you are over-reacting. This sort of nonsense"—she waved Gary's composition—"is

13. *Logical Overdrive* appears to be an additional system that allows the alien to use reasoning, or logic, without interference by the *panic impulses*.
14. An *apprentice* is a beginner who learns a skill from an experienced professional.

Vocabulary
impulse (im′ puls) *n.* an internal force that causes one to act without thinking

FUTURE TENSE

ACTIVE READING MODEL

EVALUATE

Does Ms. Jones's explanation of Gary's essay make sense? Does it sound like what a teacher or vice principal might say?

the typical response of an overstimulated[15] adolescent to the mixture of reality and fantasy in an environment dominated by <u>manipulative</u> music, television, and films. Nothing for us to worry about."

"If you're sure, Ms. Jones," said Mr. Smith. He didn't sound sure.

The vice-principal looked at Gary for the first time. There was no expression in her eyes. Her voice was flat. "You'd better get off this science fiction kick," she said. "If you know what's good for you."

"I'll never tell another human being, I swear," he babbled.

"What are you talking about?" asked Ms. Jones.

"Your secret is safe with me," he lied. He thought, *If I can just get away from them. Alert the authorities. Save the planet.*

"You see," said Ms. Jones, "you're writing yourself into a crazed state."

"You're beginning to believe your own fantasies," said Mr. Smith.

"I'm not going to do anything this time," said Ms. Jones, "but you must promise to write only about what you know."

"Or I'll have to fail you," said Mr. Smith.

"For your own good," said Ms. Jones. "Writing can be very dangerous."

"Especially for writers," said Mr. Smith, "who write about things they shouldn't."

"Absolutely," said Gary, "positively, no question about it. Only what I know." He backed out the door, nodding his head, thinking, *Just a few more steps and I'm okay. I hope these aliens can't read minds.*

QUESTION

Why might Ms. Jones think of writing as dangerous?

Jim Baggs was practicing head fakes in the hallway. He slammed Gary into the wall with a hip block. "How it's going, Dude?" he asked, helping Gary up.

"Aliens," gasped Gary. "Told me no more science fiction."

"They can't treat a star writer like that," said Jim. "See what the head honcho's[16] got to say." He grabbed Gary's wrist and dragged him to the principal's office.

"What can I do for you, boys?" boomed Dr. Proctor.

"They're messing with his moves, Doc," said Jim Baggs. "You got to let the aces run their races."

---

15. Ms. Jones says that Gary is a teenager *(adolescent)* who has been excessively affected or excited *(overstimulated)* by ideas he has taken from music and other places.

16. The *head honcho* is the leader, boss, or top manager; here, it is the principal. *Honcho* comes from Japanese words meaning "squad leader."

Vocabulary

manipulative (mə nip′ yə lā′ tiv) *adj.* able to influence or control in a clever, often unfair way

Viewing the image: Which would you prefer—an alien who looks like this or one who looks like Mr. Smith? Explain your choice.

"Thank you, James." Dr. Proctor popped his forefinger at the door. "I'll handle this."

"You're home free, Dude," said Jim, whacking Gary across the shoulder blades as he left.

"From the beginning," ordered Dr. Proctor. He nodded sympathetically as Gary told the entire story, from the opening assembly to the meeting with Mr. Smith and Ms. Jones. When Gary was finished, Dr. Proctor took the papers from Gary's hand. He shook his head as he read Gary's latest rewrite.

"You really have a way with words, Gary. I should have sensed you were on to something."

Gary's stomach flipped. "You really think there could be aliens trying to take over Earth?"

"Certainly," said Dr. Proctor, matter-of-factly.[17] "Earth is the ripest plum in the universe."

Gary wasn't sure if he should feel relieved that he wasn't crazy or be scared out of his mind. He took a deep breath to control the quaver in his voice, and said: "I spotted Smith and Jones right away. They look

RESPOND

Is Dr. Proctor joking? How do you react to his comment? Why?

---

17. Dr. Proctor speaks unemotionally, or *matter-of-factly.*

Vocabulary
quaver (kwā′ vər) *n.* a trembling or shaking

ACTIVE READING MODEL

PREDICT

Will the story end with Gary's ideas brought back to reality?

like they were manufactured to fit their names. Obviously humanoids.[18] Panicked as soon as they knew I was on to them."

Dr. Proctor chuckled and shook his head. "No self-respecting civilization would send those two stiffs to Earth."

"They're not aliens?" He felt relieved and disappointed at the same time.

"I checked them out myself," said Dr. Proctor. "Just two average, standard, typical human beings, with no imagination, no creativity."

"So why'd you hire them?"

Dr. Proctor laughed. "Because they'd never spot an alien. No creative imagination. That's why I got rid of the last vice-principal and the last Honors English teacher. They were giving me odd little glances when they thought I wasn't looking. After ten years on your planet, I've learned to smell trouble."

Gary's spine turned to ice and dripped down the backs of his legs. "You're an alien!"

"Great composition," said Dr. Proctor, waving Gary's papers. "Grammatical,[19] vividly written, and totally accurate."

"It's just a composition," babbled Gary, "made the whole thing up, imagination, you know."

VISUALIZE

How do you picture Dr. Proctor using his wristwatch?

Dr. Proctor removed the face of his wristwatch and began tapping tiny buttons. "Always liked writers. I majored in your planet's literature. Writers are the keepers of the past and the hope of the future. Too bad they cause so much trouble in the present."

"I won't tell anyone," cried Gary. "Your secret's safe with me." He began to back slowly toward the door.

Dr. Proctor shook his head. "How can writers keep secrets, Gary? It's their natures to share their creations with the world." He tapped three times and froze Gary in place, one foot raised to step out the door.

"But it was only a composition," screamed Gary as his body disappeared before his eyes.

"And I can't wait to hear what the folks back home say when you read it to them," said Dr. Proctor.

RESPOND

What do you think of the ending of the story?

"I made it all up." Gary had the sensation of rocketing upward. "I made up the whole . . ."

---

18. Since the suffix *-oid* means "having the form or appearance of," *humanoids* refers to nonhumans who look like humans.

19. A *grammatical* composition uses correct grammar.

Responding to Literature

PERSONAL RESPONSE

Which ideas, if any, from the **Focus Activity** on page 770 appear in the selection?

Active Reading Response
Which strategy described on page 769 was most helpful as you read this story?

Analyzing Literature

RECALL

1. What is Gary's writing assignment?
2. Describe Mr. Smith, the new English teacher, and Ms. Jones, the new vice-principal.
3. Why did the principal hire Mr. Smith and Ms. Jones?
4. What happens to Gary at the end of the story?

INTERPRET

5. Why do you think Gary writes about aliens?
6. Why does Gary think Mr. Smith and Ms. Jones are aliens?
7. Why do you think the principal tells, or seems to tell, Gary the truth about himself?
8. Why does Dr. Proctor feel that Gary can't be trusted?

EVALUATE AND CONNECT

9. Using what you know about Gary, what logical explanation could there be for the events at the end of the story?

10. Theme Connection Do you think there could be any truth to reports about UFOs and extraterrestrial life? Give reasons for your answer.

Literature and Writing

Writing About Literature

Inferences   As a former newspaper reporter, Lipsyte is experienced at getting a lot of information into his opening sentence. Write a paragraph telling what you learn about Gary from the first sentence. Include information you learn directly (what the writer tells you) and indirectly (what you infer from "reading between the lines").

Personal Writing

Descriptively Yours   In your journal, describe someone you know by using the kinds of metaphors that Gary uses to describe Mr. Smith.

If _____ were a color, he/she would be (a color).
If _____ were a taste, he/she would be (a food or drink).
If _____ were a sound, he/she would be (a sound).

Extending Your Response

Literature Groups

Earthling Analysis   Science fiction often relies on using ordinary characters, events, and setting with the addition of something that is out of sync or strange. Make a chart of the normal, everyday things in the selection and the unusual or bizarre events or ideas.

Learning for Life

Take a Survey   Find out what percentage of people in a group believe that aliens exist or that there is life on other planets. Devise a list of questions to ask of at least twenty people. Count your results, and compute the percentages of people who answer in different ways. Share your research with the class.

*inter*NET
CONNECTION

When we are millions of miles away, how do we use our senses to explore space? How do we listen, see, or touch? Check *PBS Online, NOVA,* to find out more about space probes, telescopes, and other ways scientists are reaching out to outer space.

Reading Further

If you'd like to read other science fiction stories about aliens, try these books:
Escape to Witch Mountain by Alexander Key
Interstellar Pig by William Sleator

📙 **Save your work for your portfolio.**

Skill Minilessons

GRAMMAR AND LANGUAGE • PAST TENSES

Gary's classmates "laughed and stamped their feet" after hearing his story. The *-ed* ending on the verbs *laugh* and *stamp* lets readers know that these actions took place in the past. Using a **past participle** with a form of the word *have* also shows that an action took place in the past. For example, Gary believed he *had stumbled* on the secret that his teachers were aliens. Often, as with *stumbled,* the past tense form and the past participle form of a verb are the same. However, some past participles are irregular.

	Past Tense	**Form of *have* with Past Participle**
Regular	Gary laughed.	Gary had laughed.
Irregular	Gary fell.	Gary had fallen.

PRACTICE Correct each sentence below by using the correct past participle form of the underlined verb.

1. Gary <u>rewrited</u> his paper to satisfy the new teacher.
2. The principal said, "I <u>lived</u> on your planet ten years now."
3. The principal had fired the teachers because they <u>given</u> him trouble.
4. Gary <u>had flew</u> up in space.
5. Gary realized that he <u>had finded</u> the real alien at last.

● For more on verbs, see **Language Handbook,** pp. R28–R29.

READING AND THINKING • EVALUATING

When Gary suspects that Mr. Smith is an alien, he wonders "how could he have missed the clues?" Gary is scolding himself for not using his knowledge about aliens to evaluate whether Mr. Smith is an alien.

Evaluating is making an assessment or judgment about something. The judgment is based on a set of standards or criteria. Use your knowledge of science fiction elements to evaluate "Future Tense."

PRACTICE Reread "Future Tense." Evaluate how well the author uses scientific laws and ideas to create the setting. Give examples from the story.

● For more on reading strategies, see **Reading Handbook,** pp. R63–R94.

VOCABULARY • ETYMOLOGY

The history of a word is its **etymology.** The word *vivid* comes from a Latin word that means "live." A *vivid* painting makes a scene seem lifelike. *Conspiracy* comes from the Latin prefix *con-,* which means "together," and *spirare,* which means "to breathe." Imagine people making a secret plan, so close together in this *conspiracy* that they are breathing the same air. *Manipulative* comes from a

Latin word that means "hand." To *manipulate* is to move something by hand.

PRACTICE Answer the following questions.

1. Is a *vivacious* person grumpy, shy, or lively?
2. Does a *spirometer* measure the power of your lungs, your heart, or your brain?
3. If an arrested person was put in *manacles,* what did the police put on that person?

Writing Skills

Bringing Descriptions to Life

Gary, the star creative writer of Robert Lipsyte's "Future Tense," carefully selects his nouns, verbs, and adjectives. "He polished and arranged them in sentences like a jeweler strings pearls." So do the writers of effective stories. Instead of saying, "Gary typed," Lipsyte tells us that Gary's electric typewriter "hummed and buzzed and sometimes coughed." In the story you will read next, Alma Luz Villanueva's "The Sand Castle," Masha and her grandchildren do not just walk toward the sea on the sand. Villanueva tells us that they "trudged on the thick, dense sand toward the hiss of pale blue." The words used in these descriptions are **precise**—they let you picture exactly what the authors mean.

General words are less interesting and less precise than specific words. For example, it is more interesting to read *Cocker spaniels have long, droopy ears* than to read *Some dogs have long ears.* Read over sentences you have written to find places where you have used general words. Then see if you can substitute more precise, interesting words that will help your reader see what you see.

The chart below lists some vague verbs, nouns, and modifiers. When you find these words in your writing, look for ways to replace them with more precise words or phrases.

VAGUE VERBS	VAGUE NOUNS	VAGUE MODIFIERS
go (went)	thing	nice, great
make (made)	person	fun, awesome
say (said)	place	awful, boring

Vague
He went away.

More Precise
The dog ran away.

Still More Precise
The copper-colored setter loped down the alley.

EXERCISES

1. Write two sentences describing a place. Use precise nouns, verbs, and modifiers.

2. Replace the following vague sentence with a paragraph using precise words to describe one of your friends: *This person is fun.*

Reading and Thinking Skills

Evaluating Media

Everyday you view visual presentations, such as movies, photos, art, television programs, ads, plays, and images on the computer screen. When you watch a movie, play, or television show, do you ask the same kinds of questions that you ask when you read a book? When you watch an episode of a science fiction series, how do you analyze and evaluate it? How do you "read" things that aren't even written? The guidelines below can help you get the most out of your viewing.

Tips for Critical Viewing

Identify Purpose

- What is the goal of the presentation you're viewing? Is it intended to entertain, to inform, or to persuade—or a little of each? To evaluate what you see, you need to understand its purpose.

Analyze Strengths

- What is most effective about the presentation? If it is intended to entertain, which parts are most creative or memorable? If it is intended to inform, which parts seem most complete and accurate? If it is intended to persuade or to sell something, is it "honest" persuasion, free of propaganda and sensationalism?

Analyze Weaknesses

- If it is a drama, do the characters seem believable? Does the theme come across clearly? What changes in staging might improve it? If it is a factual presentation, are the sources named? Are they reliable? If it is a persuasive presentation, does it show bias?

Notice Your Responses

- What questions does the presentation leave you with? Which parts appeal to you most and least—and why? How would you compare this presentation with other materials that explore the same topic or theme?

● For more on evaluating, see **Reading Handbook,** pp. R86–R94.

ACTIVITIES

1. View a drama, such as a play, a video, or an episode of a television series. Use the tips above to evaluate it. Share your evaluation with the class.

2. View a travel documentary on television, or find travel information on the Internet. Evaluate the presentation by using the **Tips for Critical Viewing.**

Before You Read
The Sand Castle

MEET ALMA LUZ VILLANUEVA

Known for her poetry, Alma Luz Villanueva says that one of the most important influences on her writing has been the stories and poems that her grandmother shared with her when she was a young girl. Her goal in life, she says in one of her poems, is "to stand in the center of magic; to see the impossible, to hear what cannot be heard."

Alma Luz Villanueva was born in 1944. "The Sand Castle" was published in 1994.

FOCUS ACTIVITY

Do you enjoy being outside on a warm, bright day?

Make a Web
Make a web around the word *sun.* Connect your thoughts and feelings about the sun and being outdoors.

Setting a Purpose
Find out how important the sun is in "The Sand Castle."

BACKGROUND

The Time and Place   This story takes place in the future.

Did You Know?   Ultraviolet rays help our bodies produce vitamin D, and they kill harmful bacteria and viruses. Too much ultraviolet light can cause sunburn and even skin cancer. Ozone is a thin layer of gas in the atmosphere that absorbs most harmful ultraviolet rays from the sun and prevents heat from leaving Earth. Environmentalists warn that the ozone layer could be damaged by chemicals used on Earth.

VOCABULARY PREVIEW

ban (ban) *v.* to forbid; outlaw; prohibit; p. 788
intensely (in tens' lē) *adv.* very strongly; p. 790
cumbersome (kum' bər səm) *adj.* not easily handled or carried; clumsy; awkward; p. 790
listlessly (list' lis lē) *adv.* in a way that shows little energy, interest, or concern; p. 790

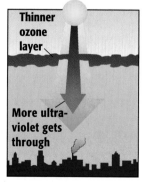

THE SAND CASTLE

Alma Luz Villanueva ~

"HAVE YOU DRESSED YET?"
their grandmother called. "Once a
month in the sun and they must almost
be forced," she muttered. "Well, poor
things, they've forgotten the
warmth of the sun on their
little bodies, what it is to
play in the sea, yes. . . ."
Mrs. Pavloff reached
for her protective sun
goggles that covered
most of her face.

THE SAND CASTLE

It screened all ultraviolet light[1] from the once life-giving sun; now, it, the sun, scorched the Earth, killing whatever it touched. The sea, the continents, had changed. The weather, as they'd called it in the last century, was entirely predictable now: warming.

Mrs. Pavloff slipped on the thick, metallic gloves, listening to her grandchildren squabble and she heard her mother's voice calling her, "Masha, put your bathing suit under your clothes. It's so much easier that way without having to go to the bathhouse first. Hurry! Father's waiting!" She remembered the ride to the sea, the silence when the first shimmers of water became visible. Her father had always been first into the chilly water. "Good for the health!" he'd yell as he dove into it, swimming as far as he could, then back. Then he'd lie exhausted on the sand, stretched to the sun. Such happiness to be warmed by the sun.

Then the picnic. She could hear her mother's voice, "Stay to your knees, Masha! Only to your knees!" To herself: "She'd be a mermaid if I didn't watch," and she'd laugh. Masha would lie belly down, facing the sea and let the last of the waves roll over her. She hadn't even been aware of the sun, only that she'd been warm or, if a cloud covered it, cold. It was always there, the sun: its light, its warmth. But the sea— they traveled to it. So, she'd given all of her attention to the beautiful sea.

She saw her father kneeling next to her, building the sand castle they always built when they went to the sea. Her job was to find seashells, bird feathers, and strips of seaweed to decorate it. How proud she'd felt as she placed her seashells where she chose, where they seemed most beautiful. Only then was the sand castle complete. She heard her father's voice, "The Princess's castle is ready, now, for her Prince! Come and look, Anna! What do you think?" She saw herself beaming with pride, and she heard her mother's laugh. "Fit for a queen, I'd say! Can I live in your castle, too, Masha? Please, Princess Masha?" "Of course, Mother! You can live with me always. . . ." She remembered her mother's laughing face, her auburn hair lit up by the sun, making her look bright and beautiful.

The sun, the sun, the sun. The scientists were saying that with the remedies they were employing now and the remedies begun twenty years ago—they'd stopped all nuclear testing and all manufacturing of ozone-depleting[2] chemicals was <u>banned</u> worldwide—the scientists were saying that the sun, the global problem, would begin to get better. Perhaps for her grandchildren's children. Perhaps they would feel the sun on their unprotected bodies. Perhaps they would feel the delicious warmth of the sun.

All vehicles were solar powered. The populations took buses when they needed transportation and people emerged mainly at night. So, most human activity was

---

1. Life on Earth depends on heat and "visible light" from the sun. The sun's *ultraviolet light* is invisible, and it can be harmful.

2. It is believed that chemical reactions reduce (*deplete*) the ozone layer.

Vocabulary
ban (ban) *v.* to forbid; outlaw; prohibit

At the Beach (detail). Edward Henry Potthast (1857–1927). Oil on canvas, 24 x 30 in. Private collection.

Viewing the painting: How does the subject of this painting compare to Mrs. Pavloff's memories? to her present-day experiences?

THE SAND CASTLE

conducted after the sun was gone from the sky. Those who emerged during the day wore protective clothing. Everything was built to screen the sun's light. Sometimes she missed the natural light of her childhood streaming through the windows so intensely the urge to just run outside would overtake her. She missed the birds, the wild birds.

But today they were going out, outside in the daytime, when the sun was still in the sky. Masha knew they were squabbling because they hated to dress up to go outside. The clothing, the gloves, the goggles, were uncomfortable and cumbersome. She sighed, tears coming to her eyes. Well, they're coming, Masha decided. They can remove their goggles and gloves on the bus.

The sea was closer now and the bus ride was comfortable within the temperature controlled interior. Those with memories of the sea signed up, bringing grandchildren, children, friends, or just went alone. Masha had taken her grandchildren before, but they'd sat on the sand, listlessly, sifting it through their gloved hands with bored little faces. She'd tried to interest them in the sea with stories of her father swimming in it as far as he could. But they couldn't touch it, so it, the sea, didn't seem real to them. What was it: a mass of undrinkable, hostile water. Hostile like the sun. They'd taken no delight, no pleasure, in their journey to the sea.

But today, yes, today we will build a sand castle. Masha smiled at her secret.

She'd packed everything late last night to surprise them at the sea.

Why haven't I thought of it before? Masha asked herself, and then she remembered the dream, months ago, of building a sand castle with her father at the sea. It made her want to weep because she'd forgotten. She'd actually forgotten one of the most joyful times of her girlhood. When the sea was still alive with life.

Today we will build a sand castle.

They trudged on the thick, dense sand toward the hiss of pale blue. Only the older people picked up their step, excited by the smell of salt in the air. Masha's grandchildren knew they'd be here for two hours and then trudge all the way back to the bus. The darkened goggles made the sunlight bearable. They hated this forlorn place where the sun had obviously drained the life out of everything. They were too young to express it, but they felt it as they walked, with bored effort, beside their grandmother.

"We're going to build a sand castle today—what do you think of that?" Masha beamed, squinting to see their faces.

"What's a sand castle?" the boy mumbled.

"You'll see, I'll show you. . . ."

"Is it fun, Grandmama?" the girl smiled, taking her grandmother's hand.

"Yes, it's so much fun. I've brought different sized containers to mold the sand, and, oh, you'll see!"

Vocabulary

intensely (in tens′ lē) *adv.* very strongly
cumbersome (kum′ bər səm) *adj.* not easily handled or carried; clumsy; awkward
listlessly (list′ lis lē) *adv.* in a way that shows little energy, interest, or concern

The boy gave an awkward skip and nearly shouted, "Show us, Grandmama, show us what you mean!"

Masha laughed, sounding almost like a girl. "We're almost there, yes, we're almost there!"

The first circle of sandy shapes was complete, and the children were so excited by what they were building they forgot about their protective gloves.

"Now, we'll put a pile of wet sand in the middle and build it up with our hands and then we'll do another circle, yes, children?"

The children rushed back and forth from the tide line carrying the dark, wet sand. They only had an hour left. Their eyes, beneath the goggles, darted with excitement.

"Just don't get your gloves in the water, a little wet sand won't hurt, don't worry, children. When I was a girl there were so many birds at the sea we'd scare them off because they'd try to steal our food. Seagulls, they were, big white birds that liked to scream at the sea, they sounded like eagles to me. . . ."

"You used to eat at the sea, Grandmama?" the girl asked incredulously.[3]

"We used to call them picnics. . . ."

"What are eagles, Grandmama?" the boy wanted to know, shaping the dark sand with his gloved hands.

"They used to be one of the largest, most beautiful wild birds in the world. My grandfather pointed them out to me once. . . ." Until that moment, she'd forgotten that memory of nearly sixty years ago. They'd gone on a train, then a bus, to the village where he'd been born. She remembered her grandfather looking up toward a shrill, piercing cry that seemed to come from the sky. She'd seen the tears in her grandfather's eyes and on his cheeks. He'd pointed up to a large, dark flying-thing in the summer blue sky: "That's an eagle, my girl, the spirit of the people."

Sadness overtook Masha, but she refused to acknowledge its presence. The sand castle, Masha told herself sternly—the sand castle is what is important now. "I've brought a wonderful surprise, something to decorate the sand castle with when we're through building it."

"Show us, Grandmama, please?"

"Yes, please, please show us now!"

Masha sighed with a terrible, sudden happiness as she brought out the plastic bag. Quickly, she removed each precious shell from its protective cotton: eight perfect shells from all over the world.

"But Grandmama, theses are your *special* shells! You said the sea doesn't make them anymore. . . ."

"It will, Anna, it will." Masha hugged her granddaughter and made her voice brighten with laughter. "Today we will decorate our sand castle with the most beautiful shells in the world, yes!"

---

3. The girl is unwilling or unable to believe Grandmama's statement; she is *incredulous*.

Responding to Literature

PERSONAL RESPONSE

- ◆ What would you say to the grandmother if you could speak to her?
- ◆ Does the sun in the story seem like the sun you described in the **Focus Activity** on page 786? Discuss how they are alike and different.

Analyzing Literature

RECALL

1. Where are the children and their grandmother going? How are they preparing to go?
2. Summarize the memories of Mrs. Pavloff about her day with her father and mother.
3. What is daily life on Earth like at the time of the story?
4. What is Mrs. Pavloff's secret surprise? Is her surprise a success?

INTERPRET

5. Why must people follow so many rules to go out during the day?
6. Why do Mrs. Pavloff's memories make her want to weep?
7. Does Mrs. Pavloff accept the changes in the world around her? Justify your answer with examples from the story.
8. Do you think the children's attitudes change about the type of outing described in the story? Why or why not?

EVALUATE AND CONNECT

9. What scientific ideas does the author use in telling this story?
10. Theme Connection   If you lived in the time of the story, what would you miss the most about the world you live in now? Explain your answer.

LITERARY ELEMENTS

Theme in Science Fiction

The **theme** of a story is the story's main idea, or the message the author wants to communicate to the readers. Science fiction themes often show the outcome, for a person or for humankind, of right or wrong decisions. For example, a story might show a world without fresh water and tell about a time when governments wouldn't pass laws to protect the rivers. Seeing the author's view of the future sometimes causes readers to take a different look at today's world.

1. What is the message of "The Sand Castle"?

2. What makes the author's message especially chilling?

● See **Literary Terms Handbook**, p. R9.

Literature and Writing

Writing About Literature

Point of View   An author often tells a story from the **point of view** of a character. Readers see what happens in the story through that character's eyes. Write a paragraph explaining why it is important that this story be told from the grandmother's point of view.

Creative Writing

Boxed In   Villanueva doesn't tell much about the children's lives, other than that they can never go out during the day without wearing protective clothing. Use your imagination and describe in a few paragraphs what life must be like for the children.

Extending Your Response

Literature Groups

New Worlds   Because this story is about a world that doesn't exist, the author uses **specific details** so that readers can visualize it. Skim through the story and find examples of specific, descriptive details of the grandmother's existing world. Contrast them with the details of the world she remembers.

interNET CONNECTION

What are scientists saying about the hole in the ozone layer? What are politicians saying? Find information about the *ozone layer, global warming,* and the *greenhouse effect.* Also check out ecology games on a search engine under the heading *Science and Oddities.*

Art Activity

Sand Architecture   Have a sand castle building contest with another group of students. Consult books and magazine and Internet articles on sand castle designs. Begin with a supply of wet sand. Use cups, jars, pans, and funnels to shape castle towers. Use shovels and spoons to form walls and walkways.

Reading Further

If you liked this story, you might enjoy these science fiction stories about the future:
Below the Root by Zilpha Keatly Snyder
The Green Book by Jill Paton Walsh
Virtual War by Gloria Skurzynski

 **Save your work for your portfolio.**

Skill Minilessons

GRAMMAR AND LANGUAGE • ADVERBS

Adverbs modify verbs and tell how, when, or where things are done. Many adverbs end in *-ly*. What is described in these sentences?

The sun shone *intensely*.

"Is it true?" she asked *incredulously*.

The adverbs in italics describe **how** the sun shown and **how** she spoke.

PRACTICE Look through the story and list adverbs ending in *-ly*. Next to each adverb, write another adverb that would make sense in the sentence.

● For more on adverbs, see **Language Handbook,** p. R24.

READING AND THINKING • SEQUENCE

To understand a story, you need to understand the **sequence,** or order of events. A **flashback** interrupts the sequence or chronological order of a story to move the action back in time. For example, showing an event from a character's childhood can help explain why she acts a certain way in the present. Mrs. Pavloff remembers her own childhood excursions to the beach and contrasts them with her grandchildren's experience.

PRACTICE Reread the story. List the places where the time order changes. The first flashback occurs on page 788 when Mrs. Pavloff remembers her mother's voice. Where does the action flash forward again? What other episodes does Mrs. Pavloff describe from her childhood? What purpose do these flashbacks serve?

● For more on sequence, see **Reading Handbook,** p. R80.

VOCABULARY • OLD WORDS

The suffix *-less* usually means "without." If someone is *listless,* is that person "without a list," perhaps a shopping list? No. This particular *list* is a very old word that means "to wish, like, or choose." If you are *listless,* you have no wishes; you have no likes (or dislikes); you make no choices. You just don't care one way or the other. Sometimes a word such as *list* goes out of use, but another word that was made from it remains in use. Another example is *ruthless.* A *ruthless* person has no pity. Although *ruthless* remains in use today, the word *ruth,* which means "pity," is hardly ever used.

PRACTICE Look at the following old words and their meanings. Then write a sentence using as many of the old words as possible.

1. *snirtle:* to snicker or giggle
2. *glop:* to swallow greedily
3. *cosh:* a small hut or cottage
4. *turngiddy:* dizzy
5. *fopdoodle:* a fool

The Ozone Layer

The sun is our source of life. However, along with heat and light, the sun gives off some rays that can damage living things. These harmful rays, called ultraviolet or UV radiation, can cause sunburn and even skin cancer. They weaken the immune systems of people and animals, increasing the chances that they will become sick. They cause plants to stop making new seeds.

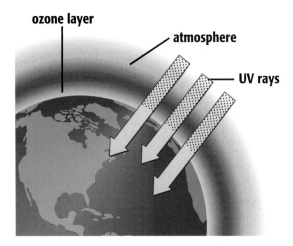

ozone layer

atmosphere

UV rays

Ozone is a thin layer of gas in Earth's atmosphere that shields us from most of the harmful rays of the sun. Scientists have known since the 1970s that there was sometimes a hole in the layer of ozone that covers the earth. The hole in the ozone layer appeared over Antarctica for a short time each year and then closed up. By the mid-1980s scientists learned that the hole was growing. Through tests and experiments, they showed that chemical compounds called chlorofluorocarbons (CFCs) were causing the problem in the ozone layer. CFCs rise up to the stratosphere. There, the strong UV rays cause the CFCs to release chlorine atoms, which in turn destroy ozone molecules.

In the 1980s, CFCs were used to cool the air in air conditioners and refrigerators. They were used in plastic foam boxes for food products. CFCs were also used in aerosol cans containing these products:

- hairsprays
- cleaning liquids
- deodorants
- shaving creams

In 1990 officials from ninety-three countries met in Canada and agreed to stop making and using many of these damaging chemicals. Some people started using pump sprays rather than aerosols and refused to buy foam packaging made with CFCs. Scientists continue to search for substitute chemicals that can do the jobs that CFCs have done in the past. For example, aerosol cans in the United States now use other chemicals, not CFCs, to cause products to spray from the can. Many countries have made laws about making or using CFCs. By working together, scientists, governments, manufacturers, and consumers can protect the ozone layer.

ACTIVITY

Learn more on the Web or at the library about the ozone layer. Then make a poster showing how people can protect the ozone layer.

Writing WORKSHOP

Descriptive Writing: Travel Brochure

By now you know that literature is an adventure. You can't always predict the kinds of travels you'll take in your reading. For this workshop, you'll create a travel brochure, introducing your readers to a place you've visited—either in reality or in your imagination. Your brochure may help your readers to make plans for travels of their own.

Assignment: Use the writing process to develop an interesting, exciting travel brochure to a real or an imaginary place.

● For more on descriptive writing, see **Writing Handbook,** pp. R43–R47.

The Writing Process

PREWRITING

PREWRITING TIP
Close your eyes and picture the place you have chosen. Form mental images of things you might see, hear, smell, taste, and touch there.

● **Choose a Place**

Your brochure might describe a local area that you know well, a more distant place that you've visited, or a place—real or imaginary—that you know through reading or viewing. (You might focus on an exotic place mentioned in "Aunt Millicent," or on Dr. Proctor's otherworldly home in "Future Tense.") Brainstorm a list of possible places. Choose one that you can recall—or imagine—in detail.

● **Gather Information**

For your brochure, you'll need geographic facts about the place you've chosen, such as location, climate, and local landforms (mountains, rivers, and so on). You'll also need interesting historical facts, such as who early explorers in the area were. Include facts about current attractions, such as art fairs, carnivals, parks, zoos, and museums. For imaginary places, sketch or freewrite to find "facts." For places in the real world, try the following sources. The tips on page 785 can help you evaluate media sources.

travel films or videos	encyclopedias
museums	atlases
knowledgeable people	the Internet
travel magazines	Chambers of Commerce

● Consider Your Audience and Purpose

Your main audience will be your classmates and teacher. Your purpose is not only to inform them, but also to make the place you have selected interesting to them. As you plan your brochure, choose facts that will appeal to their interests, and present your information in a way that will catch their attention.

● Find Your Form

Decide on the format of your brochure. It might be a single sheet of paper folded into three columns, or it might be a longer pamphlet. It will probably include visuals, such as a map and an illustration, as well as written information, such as geographic, historical, and current facts. Plan where to put each piece of information.

Place Name:
Hameln, Germany

Geographic Facts:
- On the Weser River
- Current population 58,000

Historical Facts:
1284: events on which "Pied Piper" is based (overpopulation; young people sent away)
1426–1572: member of Hanseatic trading league
1866: scene of big battle between Hanoverians & Prussians

Current Attractions:
- Pied Piper drama staged weekly, May–Sept.
- Medieval and Renaissance houses and churches
- Historical Museum; 11,000 tin soldiers showing 1866 battle

DRAFTING

DRAFTING TIP

If you get stuck, try telling a friend about the place your brochure will describe. Your words, or your friend's responses and questions, can help you start writing again.

● Pull Your Readers In

A brochure has to catch readers' interest right away. You might start with a mind-teasing question, a tantalizing detail, or a surprising statement. Be sure the place name and location appear near the beginning of your brochure.

> **MODEL** · DRAFTING
>
> Be like the Pied Piper—visit Hameln! This centuries-old German town is full of surprises, both ancient and modern. Hameln, or Hamelin, lies southwest of Hanover, in western Germany, on the Weser River.

● Keep the Facts Flowing

Go on to present your other facts and details. Follow your prewriting plan, but if new ideas come to you as you draft, feel free to try them out. The main thing is to put your information into sentence and paragraph form. You can make any needed changes when you revise.

REVISING

REVISING TIP

Using scissors, cut your draft into separate paragraphs. Rearrange the paragraphs in various ways until you find the order that works best.

● Play with Changes

After a break, read your first draft and plan improvements. Use the **Questions for Revising** to help you find ways to make your brochure better. The **Writing Skill** on page 784 can help you make your descriptions more effective. Ask one or more classmates for feedback.

QUESTIONS FOR REVISING

☑ How might I reword my first lines to make them more eye-catching?

☑ What other geographic facts might make my brochure clearer?

☑ How might I change the order of my information to make my brochure easier to follow?

☑ Where might I add more historical or current information?

☑ How does my brochure make the place seem inviting to readers?

EDITING/PROOFREADING

Before putting your travel brochure into its final form, check for errors in grammar, usage, punctuation, and spelling. The **Grammar Link** on page 713 can help you with capitalization.

Grammar Hint

Capitalize proper nouns and the first word of direct quotations.

"Yosemite isn't just another national park," he said. "There's no place like it on Earth."

PROOFREADING CHECKLIST

☑ Punctuation and capitalization are correct.

☑ Sentences are complete; there are no fragments or run-ons.

☑ Verbs are in the correct forms and agree with their subjects.

☑ Pronouns agree with their antecedents.

☑ Spelling and capitalization are correct.

MODEL · EDITING/PROOFREADING

In Hameln, germany, your host will greet you with a friendly "good morning."

TECHNOLOGY TIP
Some software programs will let you create maps and other graphics, and then insert them into your draft.

PUBLISHING/PRESENTING

Put your brochure into its final form, including maps and illustrations. As a class, pool your brochures. Then spend time browsing through the brochures, deciding which of the featured places you'd especially like to visit. Take turns explaining to the class which destinations you chose, and why.

PRESENTING TIP
Photos clipped from magazines can enliven your brochure. Write captions for your photos.

Reflecting

Think about the following questions, and then write responses.

- What techniques did you use to interest readers in the place featured in your brochure?

- Which would you rather write: a travel brochure or a magazine article about the same place? Why?

📗 **Save your work for your portfolio.**

Theme Wrap-Up

Responding to the Theme

1. Which selections in this theme helped you think about fantasy and reality? Explain.

2. What new ideas do you have about the following as a result of your reading in this theme?
   - how writers create imaginary worlds
   - how fantasy can be used to convey ideas about reality

3. Present your theme project to the class.

Analyzing Literature

CONSIDER AUTHOR'S PURPOSE

Choose a piece from this theme to evaluate in terms of how well the work achieves the author's purpose. Consider these questions:
- What was the author's purpose for this piece?
- What was the theme, or main idea, of this piece?
- How well did the piece achieve the author's purpose or convey the main idea? Explain.

Evaluate and Set Goals

1. Which of the following was most enjoyable to you? Which was most difficult?
   - reading and thinking about the selections
   - independent writing
   - analyzing the selections in discussions
   - making presentations
   - researching

2. How would you assess your work in this theme, using the following scale? Give at least two reasons for your assessment.

   4 = outstanding   2 = fair

   3 = good   1 = weak

3. Based on what you found difficult in this year's work, choose a goal to work toward in your understanding of literature or your writing for the future.
   - Write down your goal and three steps you will take to help you reach it.
   - Meet with your teacher to review your goal and your plan for achieving it.

Build Your Portfolio

SELECT

Choose two pieces of work from this theme to include in your portfolio. Write some notes to accompany each piece. Use these questions to guide you.

- ✦ What do you like best about the piece?
- ✦ What did you learn from creating it?

REFLECT

Take some time to review all of the work in your portfolio. Organize the pieces by theme, by genre, or by order of preference. Then prepare a table of contents and an introductory note for your completed portfolio.

Reading on Your Own

If you have enjoyed the literature in this theme, you might be interested in the following books.

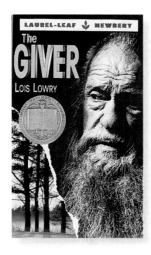

Tuck Everlasting
by Natalie Babbitt The Tuck family is willing to share the secret of immortality with young Winnie Foster. Problems arise, however, when a stranger wants the secret.

The Giver
by Lois Lowry In the seemingly perfect world of the future, a boy is chosen to receive memories of the past.

The Lion, the Witch, and the Wardrobe
by C. S. Lewis Four children find a secret passage into a magical world.

The Hobbit
by J. R. R. Tolkien The hobbit Bilbo Baggins, a wizard, and thirteen dwarves set off to kill a dragon and find a treasure.

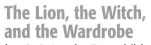

Standardized Test Practice

Read the passage and choose the word or group of words that belongs in each space. Mark the letter for that answer on your paper.

One summer night, thirteen-year-old Mark and his dad set out on __(1)__ first camping trip. After setting up camp, they __(2)__ a fire and shared scary stories. Mark went first, and told his dad a story about __(3)__ transported to another place—a strange world. While in this __(4)__ world, he encountered wild creatures, primitive plants, and an advanced group of "super-humans." Mark explained how he learned to survive in this dangerous jungle, calling on reserves of __(5)__ strength he hadn't known __(6)__. Mark and his dad had a good laugh at Mark's imagination.

---

1 A its
   B they
   C their
   D them

2 F have built
   G build
   H built
   J builds

3 A being
   B has been
   C is
   D had been

4 F amazingly
   G amazed
   H amazing
   J amazement

5 A greater
   B great
   C greatest
   D greatly

6 F he did not have
   G he hardly had
   H he never had
   J he had

Read the passage. Some sections are underlined. The underlined sections may be one of the following:

- Incomplete sentences
- Run-on sentences
- Correctly written sentences that should be combined
- Correctly written sentences that do not need to be rewritten

Choose the best way to write each underlined section. Mark the letter for your answer on your paper. If the underlined section needs no change, mark the choice "Correct as is."

Over the years our family has taken many great vacations. The most memo-
(1)
rable vacation was the trip to the Ozark Mountains in Arkansas. On our way we

stopped at a restaurant that was half in Texas and half in Arkansas. Bull Shoals
(2)

Lake is a huge lake high in the Ozarks, it was created by the Army Corps of

Engineers to control flooding in the plains. If our family goes on another vaca-

tion soon, we will definitely go back to the Ozarks.

---

1 A Over the years our family has taken many great vacations, since the most memorable vacation was the trip to the Ozark Mountains in Arkansas.

B Before the most memorable vacation was the trip to the Ozark Mountains in Arkansas, our family has taken many great vacations.

C Over the years our family has taken many great vacations, the most memorable vacation was the trip to the Ozark Mountains in Arkansas.

D Over the years our family has taken many great vacations, but the trip to the Ozark Mountains in Arkansas was the most memorable one.

2 F Bull Shoals Lake is a huge lake high in the Ozarks. Created by the Army Corps of Engineers to control flooding in the plains.

G Located high in the Ozarks, Bull Shoals Lake is a huge lake created by the Army Corps of Engineers to control flooding in the plains.

H Bull Shoals Lake was created by the Army Corps of Engineers to control flooding in the plains, being a huge lake high in the Ozarks.

J Correct as is

Reference Section

Literary Terms Handbook

A

Act A major division of a play. A play may be subdivided into several acts. Most modern plays have one, two, or three acts. A short play, such as *Damon and Pythias,* by Fan Kissen, can be composed of one or more scenes but only one act.

   See also SCENE.

Alliteration The repetition of consonant sounds, most often at the beginnings of words and syllables. The following lines from E. E. Cummings's poem "in Just-" contain an example of alliteration:

In Just- / spring when the world is mud- / luscious the little / lame balloonman / whistles. . . .

   See page 176.

Allusion A reference in a work of literature to a well-known character, place, or situation from another work of literature, music, or art, or from history. Richard Peck's "Priscilla and the Wimps" contains an allusion to the biblical story of the Garden of Eden.

The school was old Monk's Garden of Eden. Unfortunately for him, there was a serpent in it.

Anthropomorphism Attributing human characteristics to an animal or object. For example, in Rudyard Kipling's story, "Mowgli's Brothers," the Pack follows laws just as people do. According to the Law of the Jungle, two members of the Pack must speak to accept Mowgli into the Pack.

   See page 555.

Author's purpose The intention of the writer—for example, to explain, to tell a story, to persuade, to amuse, or to inform. An author may have more than one purpose. In "The Sand Castle," author Alma Luz Villanueva may have wished not only to entertain readers, but also to persuade them to take care of the environment.

   See page 536.

Autobiography The story of a person's life written by that person. In the excerpt from Jean Little's autobiography *Little by Little,* the author describes a difficult time as she began attending a new school.

   See pages 60–61.
   See also BIOGRAPHY.

B

Ballad A short narrative song or poem. Folk ballads, which usually tell of an exciting or dramatic episode, were passed on by word of mouth for generations before being written down. Literary ballads, which usually have known authors, are written in imitation of folk ballads.

Biography The account of a person's life written by someone other than the subject. Biographies can be short or book-length. "Satchel Paige," by Bill Littlefield, is an example of a short biographical sketch.

   See page 266.
   See also AUTOBIOGRAPHY.

C

Character A person or other creature in a literary work. A **dynamic character** is one who changes during the story, as does the boy's uncle in "The Boy Who Lived with the Bears," by Joseph Bruchac. A **static character** remains the same throughout the story. The Emperor in Ray Bradbury's "The Flying Machine" is a static character.

> See page 73.
> See also CHARACTERIZATION.

Characterization The methods a writer uses to develop the personality of a character. In **direct characterization**, the story's narrator makes statements about a character's personality. In **indirect characterization**, a character's personality is revealed through his or her words and actions and through what others think and say about him or her. These techniques are often combined, as in the characterization of Walt Masters in Jack London's "The King of Mazy May."

> See pages 173, 262, and 729.
> See also CHARACTER.

Climax The point of greatest interest or suspense in a narrative. Usually the climax comes at the turning point in a story or drama. In "Priscilla and the Wimps," by Richard Peck, the climax occurs as Priscilla faces Monk, the leader of Klutter's Kobras.

> See page 526.
> See also PLOT.

Comedy A type of drama that is humorous and has a happy ending.

> See also TRAGEDY.

Conflict The central struggle between opposing forces in a story or play. An **external conflict** is the struggle of a character against an outside force, such as another person, nature, society, or fate. An example is the conflict between Shere Khan and Mowgli in Rudyard Kipling's "Mowgli's Brothers." An **internal conflict** exists within the mind of a character, such as the narrator's conflict in not admitting that her mother is working, in Gish Jen's "The White Umbrella."

> See pages 146 and 633.
> See also PLOT.

D

Description Writing that creates an impression of a setting, a person, an animal, an object, or an event by appealing to one or more of the five senses. The following example of description comes from Laurence Yep's *The Lost Garden:*

At one end of the studio apartment was a tiny shower and toilet; and at the other end was a kitchenette into which my grandmother could barely squeeze. Every inch of space in the studio was accounted for. Between the door and the bathroom sat her phonograph player and Chinese records as well as her radio within reach of the bed.

> See pages 58 and 542.
> See also IMAGERY.

Dialect A variation of language spoken by a particular group, or by many people within a geographic region. Dialects differ from standard language. They may contain different vocabulary, pronunciation, or grammar. An example of dialect appears in "The King of Mazy May" by Jack London.

"An' sure, can't ye keep warm by jumpin' off the sleds an' runnin' after the dogs?" cried an Irishman. . . . "An' if ye don't run, it's mebbe you'll not get the money at all, at all."

> See page 468.

Dialogue Conversation between characters in a literary work. These lines from "The Flying Machine," by Ray Bradbury, are an example of dialogue in a work of fiction.

"Oh, Emperor, Emperor, a miracle!"

"Yes," said the Emperor, "the air *is* sweet this morning."

"No, no, a miracle!" said the servant, bowing quickly.

See page 765.

Drama A work of literature intended to be performed for an audience. *Charlie and the Chocolate Factory,* a play by Richard R. George based on the novel by Roald Dahl, is an example of drama.

See pages 662–663.
See also STAGE DIRECTIONS.

E

Essay A short piece of nonfiction writing on a single topic. The purpose of the essay is to communicate an idea or opinion. The **formal essay** is serious and impersonal. The **informal essay** may be written in a more conversational style. "Koko: Smart Signing Gorilla," by Jean Craighead George, is an example of an essay.

Exposition The author's introduction to the characters, setting, and situation of a story. In the opening paragraphs of "The Stone," Lloyd Alexander introduces the characters—Maibon and his wife, who live in a cottage in the country—and Maibon's worry about growing old.

See also PLOT.

F

Fable A short, usually simple tale that teaches a moral and often uses animal characters. Morals are often stated directly at the end of the fable. Aesop's tale "The Hare and the Tortoise" is an example of a fable.

See page 680.
See also THEME.

Fiction Literature in which situations and characters are invented by the writer, such as "La Bamba" by Gary Soto. Two types of fiction are short stories and novels.

See page 12.
See also NONFICTION, NOVEL, SHORT STORY.

Figurative language Language that communicates ideas beyond the literal meanings of words. Figurative language includes elaborate expressions or figures of speech, as opposed to literal language. Although it appears in all kinds of writing, figurative language is especially common in poetry.

See also METAPHOR, PERSONIFICATION, SIMILE, SYMBOL.

Figure of speech Language that compares one thing to something that is familiar or that carries a familiar connotation. Simile, metaphor, and personification are examples of figures of speech. In "Baker's Bluejay Yarn," by Mark Twain, Jim Baker uses the following figure of speech to describe how well a bluejay uses language:

[Words] just boil out of him!

See also FIGURATIVE LANGUAGE.

Flashback An interruption in a chronological narrative. A flashback presents readers with scenes from events that occurred earlier than those in the story. Alma Luz Villanueva uses a flashback in "The Sand Castle."

See page 794.

Folklore The traditional beliefs, customs, stories, songs, and dances of a culture. Folklore is an oral tradition and is based on the lives and values of the people who create it.

See also FOLKTALE, LEGEND, MYTH, ORAL TRADITION.

Folktale An anonymous, traditional story passed down orally long before being written down. The author of a folktale is generally anonymous. Folktales include animal stories, trickster tales, fairy tales, myths, legends, and tall tales. "All Stories Are Anansi's," retold by Harold Courlander, is an example of a folktale.

> See pages 442–443.
> See also LEGEND, MYTH, ORAL TRADITION, TALL TALE.

Foreshadowing The use of clues by the author to prepare readers for events that will happen in a narrative as in "The Gold Cadillac" by Mildred D. Taylor.

My uncles argued with him and tried to talk him out of driving the car south. . . . They said it was a dangerous thing, a mighty dangerous thing, for a black man to drive an expensive car into the rural South.

> See page 339.
> See also PLOT, RISING ACTION, SUSPENSE.

Free verse Poetry that has no fixed pattern of meter, rhyme, line length, or stanza arrangement. "Daydreamers" by Eloise Greenfield is an example of free verse.

> See page 177.
> See also METER, RHYME, RHYTHM.

G

Genre An artistic or literary category. Fiction, nonfiction, poetry, and drama are the main literary genres.

H

Haiku A Japanese form of poetry that has three lines and seventeen syllables. The first and third lines have five syllables each; the middle line has seven syllables.

Hero The main character of a literary work, usually a person with admirable qualities. Pecos Bill is the hero of the tall tale "Pecos Bill," told by Mary Pope Osborne.

Historical fiction Fiction that sets characters, who are sometimes historical figures, in historical periods and contains accurate details about those periods. "The Dog of Pompeii," by Louis Untermeyer, is an example of historical fiction.

> See page 555.

I

Imagery Language that emphasizes sense impressions that help the reader see, hear, feel, smell, and taste things described in the work. In "How soft a Caterpillar steps–," Emily Dickinson uses imagery to describe the world of a caterpillar.

From such a velvet world it comes / Such plushes at command.

> See page 177.
> See also FIGURATIVE LANGUAGE.

Irony A contrast between what is and what is expected. **Situational irony** exists when the outcome of a situation is the opposite of what readers might expect. For example, in John Gardner's "Dragon, Dragon," an unheroic person almost effortlessly kills a dragon. **Verbal irony** exists when a person says one thing and means another–for example, saying "Nice guy!" about someone you dislike.

> See page 648.

J

Journal An account of day-to-day events or a record of experiences, ideas, or thoughts. A journal may also be called a diary.

L

Legend A traditional story handed down orally and believed to be based on actual people and events. The drama *Damon and Pythias* is based on a legend.

> See pages 338 and 611.
> See also FABLE, FOLKLORE, FOLKTALE, MYTH, ORAL TRADITION, TALL TALE.

Limerick A short, usually humorous poem with a regular rhythm pattern and a rhyme scheme of *aabba*.

Lyric A verse or poem that can be sung.

Lyric poetry Poems that express thoughts or emotions about a subject. Many of Robert Frost's poems, such as "A Minor Bird," are lyric poems.

> See page 195.
> See also POETRY.

M

Metaphor A figure of speech that compares seemingly unlike things. In contrast to a **simile,** a metaphor implies the comparison instead of stating it directly; so there are no connecting words such as *like* or *as.* "To Young Readers," by Gwendolyn Brooks, contains examples of metaphors.

Good books are / bandages / and voyages / and linkages to Light.

> See pages 36 and 250.
> See also FIGURE OF SPEECH, IMAGERY, SIMILE.

Meter A regular pattern of stressed (ˊ) and unstressed (˘) syllables that gives a line of poetry a predictable rhythm. For example, the meter is marked in the following lines from Lewis Carroll's poem "The Walrus and the Carpenter":

"Ŏ Oýstĕrs, cŏmé ănd wálk wĭth ús!"
Thĕ Wálrŭs dĭd bĕseéch.
"Ă pleásănt wálk, ă pleásănt tálk,
Ălóng thĕ briný beách."

> See page 183.
> See also RHYTHM.

Mood The emotional quality or atmosphere of a story. For example, Sandra Cisneros establishes a mood of unhappiness and distress in "Eleven."

> See page 201.
> See also SETTING.

Myth A traditional story of anonymous origin that explains the beliefs and practices of a people. Myths may tell of extraordinary events from earliest times and may deal with gods, heroes, and supernatural events. Jane Yolen's "Wings" is based on an ancient Greek myth.

> See pages 338 and 611.
> See also FOLKLORE, FOLKTALE, HERO, LEGEND, ORAL TRADITION, TALL TALE.

N

Narration The telling of a sequence of events. "Zlateh the Goat," by Isaac Bashevis Singer, relies on narration to develop the plot.

> See page 83.
> See also NARRATIVE POETRY, NARRATOR.

Narrative poetry Verse that tells a story. "The Pied Piper of Hamelin," by Robert Browning, is a narrative poem.

> See page 704.
> See also NARRATION.

Narrator The person who tells a story. In fiction, the narrator may be a character in the story. Panchito is the narrator in "The Circuit" by Francisco Jimenez.

> See page 378.
> See also NARRATION, POINT OF VIEW.

Nonfiction Writing based mainly on fact, not on imagination. Among the categories of nonfiction are biographies, autobiographies, and essays. "Volcano," by Patricia Lauber, is nonfiction.

> See pages 560–561.
> See also AUTOBIOGRAPHY, BIOGRAPHY, ESSAY, FICTION, JOURNAL.

Novel A book-length fictional narrative. The novel has more space than a short story to develop its plot, characters, setting, and theme.

> See also FICTION, SHORT STORY.

O

Onomatopoeia The use of a word or phrase that actually imitates or suggests the sound of what it describes. The opening line of "Ankylosaurus," by Jack Prelutsky, is an example of onomatopoeia.

Clankity Clankity Clankity Clank!

> See page 176.

Oral tradition Literature that passes by word of mouth from one generation to the next. "The End of the World," by Jenny Leading Cloud, retold by Richard Erdoes and Alfonso Ortiz, is an example of a story from the oral tradition.

> See also FOLKLORE, FOLKTALE, LEGEND, MYTH.

P

Personification A figure of speech in which a human quality is given to an animal, object, or idea. The following lines from "Leyenda," by Pat Mora, contain examples of personification:

Plants danced out of the ground.
By dawn, green leaves swayed.

> See page 327.
> See also ANTHROPOMORPHISM, FIGURATIVE LANGUAGE, FIGURE OF SPEECH.

Plot The sequence of events in a story, novel, or play. The plot begins with **exposition,** which introduces the story's characters, setting, and situation. The **rising action** adds complications to the story's conflicts, or problems, leading to the **climax,** or point of greatest interest or suspense. The **falling action** is the logical result of the climax, and the **resolution** presents the final outcome.

> See pages 350–351, and 393.
> See also CONFLICT, EXPOSITION, RISING ACTION.

Poetry A type of literature in which language, images, sound, and rhythm are combined to create an emotional effect. Poetry is a compact form of writing that often, but not always, uses rhyme, meter, and figurative language. Other characteristics of some, but not all, poems are a use of metaphor and simile and the division of the work into stanzas.

> See pages 176–177.
> See also FIGURATIVE LANGUAGE, METAPHOR, METER, RHYME, SIMILE.

Point of view The relationship of the narrator to the story. A story using **first-person point of view** is told by one of the characters, as in "The All-American Slurp" by Lensey Namioka. The reader sees everything through the narrator's eyes. In a story with a **limited third-person point of view,** the narrator is outside the story and reveals the thoughts of only one character, but refers to that character as *he* or *she,* as in "The Stone" by Lloyd Alexander. In a story with an **omniscient point of view,** like Rudyard Kipling's "Mowgli's Brothers," the narrator is also outside the story, but can reveal any or all events, thoughts, and actions of the characters, as well as background information important to the story.

> See page 49.
> See also AUTHOR'S PURPOSE.

Props Theater slang (a shortened form of *properties*) for objects and elements of the scenery of a stage play or movie set.

> See page 751.

R

Refrain A line or lines repeated regularly, usually in a poem or song. Maya Angelou repeats a refrain similar to the title of her poem "Life Doesn't Frighten Me."

> See page 498.
> See also REPETITION.

Repetition The recurrence of sounds, words, phrases, lines, or stanzas in a speech or piece of writing. When a line or stanza is repeated in a poem, it is called a refrain. Langston Hughes uses repetition in "April Rain Song."

The rain makes still pools on the sidewalk.
The rain makes running pools in the gutter.
The rain plays a little sleep-song on our roof
    at night—

> See pages 183 and 243.
> See also REFRAIN.

Rhyme The repetition of identical or similar sounds at the ends of words used close to one another. **End rhyme** occurs at the ends of lines, as in "Ankylosaurus" by Jack Prelutsky. **Slant rhyme** occurs when words include sounds that are similar but not identical. An example of slant rhyme are the words *over* and *discover* in these lines from T. S. Eliot's "The Naming of Cats":

But above and beyond there's still one name
    left over,
And that is the name that you never will guess;
The name that no human research can
    discover—

> See page 176.
> See also REPETITION, RHYME SCHEME.

Rhyme scheme The pattern formed by the end rhyme in a poem. The rhyme scheme is shown by the use of a different letter of the alphabet to name each new rhyme. The first two stanzas of Theodore Roethke's poem, "The Bat," has a rhyme scheme of *aabb*.

By day the bat is cousin to the mouse.	*a*
He likes the attic of an aging house.	*a*
His fingers make a hat about his head.	*b*
His pulse beat is so slow we think him dead.	*b*

> See page 187.
> See also RHYME.

Rhythm The pattern created by the arrangement of stressed syllables, especially in poetry. Rhythm gives poetry a musical quality. Rhythm can be regular, with a predictable pattern or meter, or irregular.

> See also METER.

Rising action The part of a plot that adds complications to the problems in the story and increases reader interest. In "The Horse Snake," by Huynh Quang Nhuong, the tension in the story increases when the horse that neighed during the night is found dead.

> See also PLOT.

S

Scene A subdivision of an act in a play. Each scene presents action in one place or one situation.

> See also ACT.

Science fiction Fiction dealing with the impact of science on societies of the past, present, or future. "Future Tense," by Robert Lipsyte, is science fiction.

> See page 768.
> See also FICTION.

Screenplay The script of a film, which, in addition to dialogue and stage directions, usually contains detailed instructions about camera shots and angles.

> See pages 784–785.
> See also DRAMA, STAGE DIRECTIONS.

Setting The time and place in which the events of a short story, novel, or drama occur. The setting often helps create an atmosphere, or mood.

> See pages 100 and 346.
> See also DESCRIPTION, PLOT.

Short story A brief fictional narrative in prose. Elements of the short story include plot, character, setting, point of view, and theme.

> See pages 350–351.
> See also CHARACTER, PLOT, POINT OF VIEW, SETTING, THEME.

Simile A figure of speech using *like* or *as* to compare seemingly unlike things. Jack Prelutsky gives this example of a simile in "Ankylosaurus":

Anyklosaurus was built like a tank.

> See page 225.
> See also FIGURES OF SPEECH.

Speaker The voice in a poem, like the narrator in a work of fiction. The speaker's tone may communicate an attitude toward the subject of the poem. For example, the speaker of John Ciardi's "The Shark" adopts the tone of an older person warning about the dangers of a shark.

Be careful where you swim, my sweet.

> See page 498.
> See also TONE.

Stage directions In a drama, instructions that describe the appearance and actions of characters, as well as sets, costumes, and lighting. Examples of stage directions can be found in *Charlie and the Chocolate Factory,* by Roald Dahl, adapted by Richard R. George.

[*Chewing ferociously on gum, waving arms excitedly, talking in a rapid and loud manner, from somewhere in the audience.*]

> See page 676.

Stanza A group of lines forming a unit in a poem. Stanzas are, in effect, the paragraphs of a poem.

Stereotype A character who is not developed as an individual, but who shows traits and mannerisms supposedly shared by all members of a group. The character of the stepmother in Jacqueline Balcells's "The Enchanted Raisin" is a stereotype.

> See page 635.

Style The author's choice and arrangement of words and sentences in a literary work. Style can reveal an author's purpose in writing and attitude toward his or her subject and audience. Judith Viorst uses an unusual style in telling a story through exchanged notes in "The Southpaw."

> See also AUTHOR'S PURPOSE, GENRE.

Suspense A feeling of curiosity, uncertainty, or even dread about what is going to happen next. Writers increase the level of suspense in a story by giving readers clues to what might happen. In "The King of Mazy May," Jack London builds suspense by giving details of the claim-jumpers' chase of Walt Masters along the frozen creek.

> See page 432.
> See also PLOT, RISING ACTION.

Symbol Any object, person, place, or experience that stands for something else because of a resemblance or association. The sand castle in Alma Luz Villanueva's story, "The Sand Castle," is a symbol of an environment that is safe for living things, one that Mrs. Pavloff remembers from her childhood.

> See page 365.

T

Tall tale An imaginative tale of adventures or amazing feats of folk heroes. Descriptions of people and events are exaggerated, but settings are realistic. "Pecos Bill," by Mary Pope Osborne, is an example of a tall tale.

> See page 456.
> See also FOLKLORE, FOLKTALE, HERO,
>   LEGEND, MYTH, ORAL TRADITION.

Theme The main idea of a story, poem, novel, or play. Some works have a stated theme. More frequently, works have a theme that is not stated but is revealed gradually through other elements such as plot, character, setting, point of view, symbol, and irony. In "Why Dogs Are Tame," Julius Lester states the theme in the last sentence.

What I do know is that Brer Dog has been living in people's houses ever since.

> See pages 27, 236, and 319.
> See also AUTHOR'S PURPOSE.

Title The name of a literary work.

Tone An author's attitude toward a subject. The tone may be eerie, threatening, serious, or light, for example. The tone is serious in "Abd al-Rahman Ibrahima" by Walter Dean Myers.

> See page 123.
> See also MOOD, STYLE, VOICE.

Tragedy A play in which a main character suffers a downfall. The tone of a tragedy is serious, and the ending is usually an unhappy one.

> See also DRAMA, HERO.

V

Voice An author's distinctive style, or the particular speech patterns of a character in a story. In "Priscilla and the Wimps," Richard Peck uses the voice of a teenaged student.

> See also AUTHOR'S PURPOSE, STYLE, TONE.

Language Handbook

Troubleshooter

The Troubleshooter will help you recognize and correct common writing errors.

Sentence Fragment

A sentence fragment does not express a complete thought. It might lack a subject or verb or both.

Problem: Fragment that lacks a subject

Vera looked out the window. Watched the snow falling. *frag*

Solution: Add a subject to the fragment to make a complete sentence.

Vera looked out the window. She watched the snow falling.

Problem: Fragment that lacks a predicate

Tony slammed the door. Everybody in the room. *frag*

Solution: Add a predicate to make the sentence complete.

Tony slammed the door. Everybody in the room gasped.

Problem: Fragment that lacks both a subject and a predicate

I dropped my sandwich. On the sidewalk. *frag*

Solution: Combine the fragment with another sentence.

I dropped my sandwich on the sidewalk.

Rule of Thumb

You can use fragments when talking with friends or writing personal letters. Some writers use fragments to produce a special effect. Use complete sentences, however, for school or business writing.

Run-on Sentence

A run-on sentence is two or more sentences written incorrectly as one sentence.

Problem: Two main clauses separated only by a comma

Kim saw one movie yesterday, she saw another one today. *run-on*

Solution A: Replace the comma with a period or other end mark. Start the second sentence with a capital letter.

Kim saw one movie yesterday. She saw another one today.

Solution B: Replace the comma with a semicolon.

Kim saw one movie yesterday; she saw another one today.

Solution C: Add a coordinating conjunction after the comma.

Kim saw one movie yesterday, and she saw another one today.

Problem: Two main clauses with no punctuation between them

Vernon studied hard for the spelling test he passed it. *run-on*

Solution A: Separate the clauses with a period or other end mark.

Vernon studied hard for the spelling test. He passed it.

Solution B: Place a semicolon between the main clauses.

Vernon studied hard for the spelling test; he passed it.

Solution C: Add a comma and a coordinating conjunction between the main clauses.

Vernon studied hard for the spelling test, and he passed it.

Problem: Two main clauses with no comma before the coordinating conjunction

I took a deep breath and I jumped into the water. *run-on*

Solution: Add a comma before the coordinating conjunction.

I took a deep breath, and I jumped into the water.

Lack of Subject-Verb Agreement

A singular subject calls for a singular verb. A plural subject calls for a plural verb.

Problem: A subject that is separated from the verb by an intervening prepositional phrase

The eggs in the carton (was) broken. *agr*

Solution: Make sure that the verb agrees with the subject of the sentence, not with the object of the preposition. The object of a preposition is never the subject.

The eggs in the carton were broken.

Rule of Thumb

When subject and verb are separated by a prepositional phrase, check for agreement by reading the sentence without the prepositional phrase.

Problem: A sentence that begins with *here* or *there*

Here (come) that noisy motorcycle again. *agr*

There (is) the neighbors with the noisy dog. *agr*

Solution: The subject is never *here* or *there.* In sentences that begin with *here* or *there,* look for the subject after the verb. The verb must agree with the subject.

Here comes that noisy motorcycle again.

There are the neighbors with the noisy dog.

Problem: A compound subject that is joined by *and*

Soccer and basketball (is) her favorite sports. *agr*

Bacon and eggs (are) my favorite breakfast. *agr*

Solution A: If the parts of the compound subjects do not belong to one unit or if they refer to different people or things, use a plural verb.

Soccer and basketball are her favorite sports.

Solution B: If the parts of the compound subject belong to one unit or if both parts refer to the same person or thing, use a singular verb.

Bacon and eggs is my favorite breakfast.

Problem: A compound subject that is joined by *or* or *nor*

Either magazines or a book ⟨make⟩ a thoughtful get-well gift. *agr*

Neither Ann nor her brothers ⟨knows⟩ how to swim. *agr*

Solution: Make the verb agree with the subject that is closest to it.

Either magazines or a book makes a thoughtful get-well gift.

Neither Ann nor her brothers know how to swim.

Incorrect Verb Tense or Form

Verbs have different tenses to show when the action takes place.

Problem: An incorrect or missing verb ending

Ronnie ⟨collect⟩ the club dues yesterday. *tense*

Darnela and her family ⟨have visit⟩ Cape Cod before. *tense*

Solution: To form the past tense and the past participle, add *-ed* to a regular verb.

Ronnie collected the club dues yesterday.

Darnela and her family have visited Cape Cod before.

Problem: An improperly formed irregular verb

Alice ⟨throwed⟩ all the soda cans into the recycling bin. *tense*

I ⟨drinked⟩ a whole pitcher of lemonade. *tense*

Solution: Irregular verbs vary in their past and past participle forms. Look up the ones you are not sure of.

Alice threw all the soda cans into the recycling bin.

I drank a whole pitcher of lemonade.

Problem: Confusion between the past form and the past participle

I have ⟨rang⟩ this doorbell five times, but no one answers. *tense*

Our class already ⟨seen⟩ both of these videos. *tense*

Solution A: Use the past participle form of an irregular verb, not the past form, when you use the auxiliary verb *have.*

I have rung this doorbell five times, but no one answers.

Solution B: When you do not use the auxiliary verb *have,* use the past form, not the past participle.

Our class already saw both of these videos.

Rule of Thumb

Because irregular verbs vary, it is useful to memorize the verbs that you use most often.

Incorrect Use of Pronouns

The noun that a pronoun refers to is called its antecedent. A pronoun must refer to its antecedent clearly. Subject pronouns refer to subjects in a sentence. Object pronouns refer to objects in a sentence.

Problem: A pronoun that can refer to more than one antecedent

When my father spoke to the principal, ⟨he⟩ was very angry. *ant*

Solution A: Substitute a noun for the pronoun to make your sentence clearer.

When my father spoke to the principal, my father was very angry.

Solution B: Reword the sentence to make the antecedent clear.

My father was very angry when he spoke to the principal.

Problem: Object pronouns as subjects

(Him) and Tony could not stop laughing. *pro*

Otchan and (me) got the last tickets to the show. *pro*

Solution: Use a subject pronoun as the subject part of a sentence.

He and Tony could not stop laughing.

Otchan and I got the last tickets to the show.

Problem: Subject pronouns as objects

Ms. Lee reminded Sonja and (I) to return our library books. *pro*

I have to stay home tonight with (he) and Sara. *pro*

Solution: Use an object pronoun as the object of a verb or a preposition.

Ms. Lee reminded Sonja and me to return our library books.

I have to stay home tonight with him and Sara.

Rule of Thumb

When a pronoun is part of a compound subject or object, try saying the sentence with only the pronoun as the subject or object. That often makes the correct choice clear. For example, change *Ms. Jones let Dave and I sit in the front row* to *Ms. Jones let I sit in the front row.* The pronoun *I* sounds wrong and should be changed to *me*.

Incorrect Use of Adjectives

Some adjectives have irregular forms: comparative forms for comparing two things and superlative forms for comparing more than two things.

Problem: Incorrect use of *good, better, best*

Ashley felt (more better) after we called her up. *adj*

My mother's tacos are the (most good) I've ever tasted. *adj*

Solution: The comparative and superlative forms of *good* are *better* and *best.* Do not use *more* or *most* before irregular forms of comparative and superlative adjectives.

Ashley felt better after we called her.

My mother's tacos are the best I've ever tasted.

Problem: Incorrect use of *bad, worse, worst*

That was the (baddest) pitching of the game. *adj*

His sprained ankle hurts (worser) than his broken leg. *adj*

Solution: The comparative and superlative forms of *bad* are *worse* and *worst.* Do not use *more* or *most* or the endings *-er* or *-est* with *bad.*

That was the worst pitching of the game.

His sprained ankle hurts worse than his broken leg.

Problem: Incorrect use of comparative and superlative adjectives

My mother is (more older) than my father. *adj*

This mountain is (most steepest) near the top. *adj*

Solution: Do not use both *-er* and *more* or both *-est* and *most* at the same time.

My mother is older than my father.

This mountain is steepest near the top.

Incorrect Use of Commas

Commas signal a pause between parts of a sentence and help to clarify meaning.

Problem: Missing commas in a series of three or more items

I saw books clothes papers and toys on the floor of his room. *com*

Marcelle went to the mall watched a movie and ate pizza. *com*

Solution: If there are three or more items in a series, use a comma after each one, including the item preceding the conjunction.

I saw books, clothes, papers, and toys on the floor of his room.

Marcelle went to the mall, watched a movie, and ate pizza.

Problem: Missing commas with direct quotations

"Your hamster" my brother exclaimed "just bit me!" *con*

Solution: The first part of an interrupted quotation ends with a comma followed by quotation marks. The interrupting words are also followed by a comma.

"Your hamster," my brother exclaimed, "just bit me!"

Incorrect Use of Apostrophes

An apostrophe shows possession. It can also indicate missing letters in a contraction.

Problem: Singular possessive nouns

The turtles cage was bigger than Carlos backyard. *poss*

Solution: Use an apostrophe and an *-s* to form the possessive of a singular noun, even one that ends in *-s.*

The turtle's cage was bigger than Carlos's backyard.

Problem: Plural possessive nouns ending in *-s*

The chimpanzees games delighted their visitors at the zoo. *poss*

The dancers costumes shimmered under the spotlights. *poss*

Solution: Use an apostrophe alone to form the possessive of a plural noun that ends in *-s.*

The chimpanzees' games delighted their visitors at the zoo.

The dancers' costumes shimmered under the spotlights.

Problem: Plural possessive nouns not ending in *-s*

The womens group raised thousands of dollars. *poss*

Solution: Use an apostrophe and *-s* to form the possessive of a plural noun that does not end in *-s.*

The women's group raised thousands of dollars.

Problem: Possessive personal pronouns

The woolen cap is (her's,) but the scarves are (their's.) *poss*

Solution: Do not use apostrophes with possessive personal pronouns.

The woolen cap is hers, but the scarves are theirs.

Incorrect Capitalization

Proper nouns, proper adjectives, and the first words of sentences always begin with a capital letter.

Problem: Words referring to ethnic groups, nationalities, and languages

Luisa studied (spanish) before visiting her (mexican) friend. *cap*

Solution: Capitalize proper nouns and adjectives that refer to ethnic groups, nationalities, and languages.

Luisa studied Spanish before visiting her Mexican friend.

Problem: The first word of a direct quotation

Mary whispered, ("my) baby brother is asleep." *cap*

Solution: Capitalize the first word in a direct quotation.

Mary whispered, "My baby brother is asleep."

Rule of Thumb

If you have difficulty with a rule of usage, try rewriting the rule in your own words. Check with your teacher to be sure you understand the rule.

Troublesome Words

This section will help you choose between words that are often confusing or misused.

---

accept, except

Accept means "to receive." *Except* means "other than."

That store **accepts** cash, checks, and credit cards.

I ate everything on my plate **except** the Brussels sprouts.

---

affect, effect

Affect is a verb meaning "to cause a change in" or "to influence." *Effect* as a verb means "to bring about or accomplish." As a noun, *effect* means a "result."

This snowstorm will **affect** our travel plans.

Math tutoring **effected** higher test scores for most students.

The dust storm was one **effect** of the drought.

---

ain't

Ain't is never used in formal speaking or writing unless you are quoting the exact words of a character or a real person. Instead of using *ain't,* say or write *I am not, she is not,* etc., or use contractions: *I'm not, she's not.*

That furniture **is not** going to fit in our van.

That furniture **isn't** going to fit in our van.

---

a lot

The expression *a lot* means "very much." It should always be written as two words. Some authorities discourage its use in formal writing.

A lot of students will attend the game.

Many students will attend the game.

---

all ready, already

All ready means "completely prepared." *Already* is an adverb that means "before" or "by this time."

If I wait until you are **all ready** to go, the party will **already** be over.

---

all right, alright

The expression *all right* should be written as two words. Some dictionaries do list the single word *alright* but usually not as a preferred spelling.

After taking a nap, I'm feeling **all right** again.

all together, altogether

All together means "in a group." *Altogether* means "completely."

Our class sat **all together** on the bleachers.

I'm not **altogether** sure how to get to your house.

among, between

Use *among* for three or more people, things, or groups. Use *between* for two people, things, or groups.

I wandered **among** the crowd of people at the beach.

The shark swam slowly **between** me and the boat.

amount, number

Use *amount* with nouns that cannot be counted. Use *number* with nouns that can be counted.

I added the wrong **amount** of salt to the brownies.

Cary invited a large **number** of girls to her sleepover.

bad, badly

Bad is an adjective and modifies a noun. *Badly* is an adverb and modifies a verb, an adjective, or another adverb.

Her **bad** mood didn't last long.

The team played so **badly** that Jamie felt **bad.**

beside, besides

Beside means "next to." *Besides* means "in addition to."

The goldfish tank is **beside** Ms. Vasquez's desk.

Besides Olivia, only David plays an instrument.

bring, take

Bring means "to carry from a distant place to a closer one." *Take* means "to carry from a nearby place to a more distant one."

Please **bring** that poster here so I can see it better.

Take your dishes over to the kitchen counter.

can, may

Can implies the ability to do something. *May* implies permission to do something or the possibility of doing it.

You **may** watch that movie if you **can** figure out how to fix the VCR.

Rule of Thumb

Although *can* is sometimes used in place of *may* in informal speech, a distinction should be made when speaking and writing formally.

choose, chose

Choose means "to select." *Chose,* the past tense of *choose,* means "selected."

You **choose** which one to take with us.

Yesterday the soccer coach **chose** the new team members.

doesn't, don't

The subject of the contraction *doesn't (does not)* is the third-person singular (*he* or *she*). The subject of the contraction *don't (do not)* is *I, you, we,* or *they.*

She **doesn't** get sick very often.

I **don't** want to get a cold.

farther, further

Farther refers to physical distance. *Further* refers to time or degree.

How much **farther** do we have to walk?

We have to discuss this a little **further.**

fewer, less

Fewer is used to refer to things or qualities that can be counted. *Less* is used to refer to things or qualities that cannot be counted. In addition, *less* is used with figures that are regarded as single amounts.

Fewer songbirds returned to the orchard this year.

This breakfast cereal contains **less** fiber.

I have **less** than five dollars in my wallet. [Money is treated as a single sum, not as individual dollars.]

good, well

Good is often used as an adjective. *Well* may be used as an adverb of manner, telling how ably something is done, or as an adjective meaning "in good health."

The whole team had a **good** season.

The team played **well.**

Lynn was sick last week, but now she is **well** again.

in, into

In means "inside." *Into* indicates a movement from outside toward the inside.

If it rains, we'll have the party **in** the house.

A caterpillar crawled **into** my lunchbox.

it's, its

Use an apostrophe to form the contraction of *it is.* The possessive of the personal pronoun *it* does not take an apostrophe.

It's important to start the day with a good breakfast.

Our class had **its** picture taken today.

lay, lie

Lay means "to place." *Lie* means "to recline."

Frank, please **lay** the softball glove under your chair.

I like to **lie** in the hammock on hot summer days.

learn, teach

Learn means "to gain knowledge." *Teach* means "to give knowledge."

My younger brother is trying to **learn** how to read.

I'm trying to **teach** my younger brother to read.

leave, let

Leave means "to go away." *Let* means "to allow."

The bus will **leave** at noon.

The driver will **let** us board at eleven.

like, as

Use *like,* a preposition, to introduce a prepositional phrase. Use *as,* a subordinating conjunction, to introduce a subordinate clause. Many authorities believe that *like* should not be used before a clause in formal English.

My bedroom looks **like** a disaster area.

As I just said, there will be no bus service tomorrow.

Rule of Thumb

As can be a preposition in some cases, as in *He donated all the dance decorations as a favor to our class.*

loose, lose

Loose means "not firmly attached." *Lose* means "to misplace" or "to fail to win."

When the line got **loose,** the boat drifted away.

Did you **lose** a pair of gloves?

If we **lose** this game, we won't make the finals.

raise, rise

Raise means to "cause to move up." *Rise* means "to move upward."

If you know the answer, **raise** your hand.

Marco will **rise** to sing the national anthem at the beginning of the ceremony.

set, sit

Set means "to place" or "to put." *Sit* means "to place oneself in a seated position."

Please **set** the groceries on the kitchen table.

There is no place in the cafeteria to **sit** down.

than, then

Than introduces the second part of a comparison. *Then* means "at that time" or "after that."

My older brother is taller **than** my father.

First we ate our picnic, and **then** we went fishing.

their, they're

They're is the contraction of *they are*. *Their* is the possessive form of *they*.

They're saving **their** money to buy a computer.

to, too, two

To means "in the direction of." *Too* means "also" or "to an excessive degree." *Two* is the number after one.

We took our cat **to** the vet. Our dog should go, **too.**

I'm **too** full to eat more. I had **two** pieces of chocolate cake.

who, whom

Who is a subject pronoun. *Whom* is an object pronoun.

Who ate the rest of the popcorn?

To **whom** should I give these papers?

whose, who's

Whose is the possessive form of *who*. *Who's* is the contraction of *who is*.

Whose drawing is this?

Who's going to clean up this mess?

Grammar Glossary

This glossary will help you quickly locate information on parts of speech and sentence structure.

A

Action verb. *See* Verb.

Adjective A word that describes a noun or a pronoun. An adjective answers one of these questions: *What kind? How many? Which one?* (My mother bought some *Italian* pastries. I ate *two* pastries. I prefer *this* pastry.)

Many adjectives have different forms to indicate degree of comparison. *(bright, brighter, brightest)*

The comparative degree compares two persons, places, things, or ideas. *(better, happier)*

The superlative degree compares more than two person, places, things, or ideas. *(best, happiest)*

Demonstrative adjectives are pronouns that answer the questions *Which one? How many?* and *How much?* (*That* butterfly drinks flower nectar.)

Possessive adjectives are possessive pronouns that answer the question *Which one? (my, your, her, his, its, our, their)*

A predicate adjective always follows a linking verb. It modifies the subject of the sentence by telling what it is like. (These pastries are *delicious.*)

A proper adjective is formed from a proper noun. It always begins with a capital letter. Most proper adjectives are formed by using the following endings: *-an, -ian, -ese, -ish.* (Italian)

Sometimes pronouns are used as adjectives.

Adverb A word that describes a verb, an adjective, or another adverb by making its meaning more specific. Adverbs answer the questions *How? When?* and *Where?* When modifying a verb, an adverb may appear in various positions in a sentence. (I *usually* do my homework after supper. *Usually,* I do my homework after supper.) When modifying an adjective or another adverb, an adverb appears directly before the modified word. (Last Saturday's storm was *totally* unexpected. The wind blew *extremely* hard.) The negatives *no, not,* and the contraction *-n't* are adverbs. (I ate until I could eat *no* more.) Other negative words, such as *nowhere, hardly,* and *never,* can function as adverbs of place, degree, and time. (She has *never* visited us.) Some adverbs have different forms to indicate degree of comparison. *(close, closer, closest; gentle, more gently, most gently)* Many adverbs are formed by adding *-ly* to adjectives. *(quickly)* However, not all words that end in *-ly* are adverbs. *(lonely)*

Antecedent. *See* Pronoun.

Article The adjective *a, an,* or *the.*

A and *an* are indefinite articles. They refer to any one item of a group. (I've never had a big role in *a* play before.)

The is a definite article. It indicates that the noun is a specific person, place, or thing. (I auditioned for *the* role of the Wicked Witch in *The Wizard of Oz.*)

B

Base form. *See* Verb tense.

C

Collective noun. *See* Noun.

Common noun. *See* Noun.

Comparative degree. *See* Adjective; Adverb.

Complete predicate. *See* Predicate.

Complete subject. *See* Subject.

Compound predicate. *See* Predicate.

Compound sentence. *See* Sentence.

Compound subject. *See* Subject.

Conjunction A word that joins single words or groups of words.

A coordinating conjunction *(and, but, or, nor, for, yet)* joins words or groups of words that are equal in grammatical importance. (You can walk to the fourth floor *or* take the elevator.)

Correlative conjunctions *(both . . . and, just as . . . so, not only . . . but also, either . . . or, neither . . . nor)* are pairs of words used to connect words or phrases in a sentence. (I'll *either* take a bus to the amusement park *or* someone will give me a ride.)

Coordinating conjunction. *See* Conjunction.

Correlative conjunction. *See* Conjunction.

Declarative sentence. *See* Sentence.

Definite article. *See* Article.

Demonstrative adjective. *See* Adjective.

Demonstrative pronoun. *See* Pronoun.

Direct object A direct object answers the question *What?* or *Whom?* after an action verb. (I drank a *glass* of milk. Then I read the *newspaper.*)

Exclamatory sentence. *See* Sentence.

Future tense. *See* Verb tense.

Helping verb. *See* Verb.

Imperative sentence. *See* Sentence.

Indefinite article. *See* Article.

Indefinite pronoun. *See* Pronoun.

Indirect object An indirect object answers the question *To whom? For whom? To what?* or *For what?* after an action verb. An indirect object may be a noun or a pronoun. (My aunt gave *our family* tickets to the circus. Tell *me* a story.)

Interjection A word or phrase that expresses strong feeling. An interjection has no grammatical connection to other words in the sentence. Commas follow mild ones; exclamation points follow stronger ones. (*Oh,* thank you. *Quick!* Answer the phone!)

Interrogative sentence. *See* Sentence.

Intransitive verb. *See* Verb.

Inverted order In a sentence written in inverted order, the predicate comes before the subject. Some sentences are written in inverted order for variety or special emphasis. (Right in the middle of my path stood the biggest dog I had ever seen.) The subject generally follows the predicate in a sentence that begins with *there* or *here.* (Here is the script for the play. There are parts in the play for the whole class.) Questions, or interrogative sentences, are generally written in inverted order. Questions that begin with *who* or *what* follow normal word order.

Irregular verb. *See* Verb.

Linking verb. *See* Verb.

Noun A word that names a person, a place, a thing, or an idea. The chart on this page shows the main kinds of nouns.

Number A noun, pronoun, or verb is singular in number if it refers to one; plural if it refers to more than one.

Object pronoun. *See* Pronoun.

P

Past tense. *See* Verb.

Perfect tenses. *See* Verb tense.

Personal pronoun. *See* Pronoun.

Phrase A group of words that acts in a sentence as a single part of speech.

A **prepositional phrase** begins with a preposition and ends with a noun or a pronoun called the object of the preposition. A prepositional phrase can function as an adjective, modifying a noun or a pronoun.

(A dragonfly *with glittering wings* flew by.) A prepositional phrase can also function as an adverb when it modifies a verb, an adverb, or an adjective. (The earth moves *around the sun.*)

A **verb phrase** consists of one or more helping verbs followed by a main verb. (I *have been swimming* laps.)

Plural. *See* Number.

Possessive noun. *See* Noun.

Possessive pronoun. *See* Pronoun.

Predicate The verbs or verb phrases and any modifiers that tell what the subject of a sentence does, has, is, or is like.

A **simple predicate** is a verb or verb phrase that tells something about the subject. (The ice cream *disappeared.*)

A **complete predicate** includes the simple predicate and any words that modify it. (The ice cream *disappeared into our mouths.*)

A **compound predicate** has two or more verbs or verb phrases that are joined by a conjunction and share the same subject. (The children *ate* popcorn *and waited* for the movie to begin.)

Predicate adjective A predicate adjective follows a linking verb and describes the subject. (The cake tasted *delicious.*)

Predicate noun A predicate noun is a noun or pronoun that follows a linking verb and gives more information about the subject. (The backpack was my favorite *gift.*)

Preposition A word that shows the relationship of a noun or pronoun to some other word in the sentence. Prepositions include *about, above, across, among, as, behind, below, beyond, but, by, down, during, except, for, from, into, like, near, of, on, outside, over, since, through, to, under, until, with.* (We moved our chairs *into* a circle.)

Nouns		
Kind	**Function**	**Examples**
collective	Names a group of people or things	council, crew
common	Names a general—not a particular—person, place, or thing	city, athlete
compound	Made up of two or more words	homework, sidewalk
possessive	Shows possession, ownership, or the relationship between two nouns	**Mark's** homework
predicate	Follows a linking verb and renames the subject	Adele is a **nurse.**
proper	Names a particular person, place, thing, or idea	Ellen, Newark, White House

A compound preposition is made up of more than one word: *according to, across from, ahead of, as to, because of, by means of, far from, in front of, in addition to, in spite of, on account of.* (*In spite of* my head start, I ended up just one place ahead of Sheryl.)

Prepositional phrase. *See* Phrase.

Present tense. *See* Verb.

Progressive forms. *See* Verb tense.

Pronoun A word that takes the place of a noun, a group of words acting as a noun, or another pronoun. (When the judge spoke to the jury, *he* sounded angry.)

An antecedent is the word or group of words that a pronoun refers to. (When the *judge* spoke to the jury, he sounded angry.)

A personal pronoun refers to a specific person or thing by indicating the person speaking, the person being spoken to, or any other person or thing being spoken about. The first chart below shows the subject and object personal pronouns.

A subject pronoun functions as the subject or follows a linking verb. (*I, you, he, she, it, we, you, they*)

An object pronoun functions as the object of a verb or of a preposition. (*me, you, her, him, it, us, them*)

A possessive pronoun takes the place of the possessive form of a noun. Some forms of possessive pronouns can be used before a noun, playing the role of modifiers. See the chart of possessive pronouns on this page. (*His* apartment is at the end of this street.) Others can be used alone. (The tickets are *theirs.*)

A demonstrative pronoun points out specific persons, places, things, or ideas. (*this, that, these, those*)

An indefinite pronoun refers to persons, places, or things in a more general way than a noun does. (*all, another, any, both, each, either, enough, everything, few, many, most, much, neither, nobody, none, one, other, others, plenty, several, some*)

Proper adjective. *See* Adjective.

Proper noun. *See* Noun.

Regular verb. *See* Verb.

Sentence A group of words expressing a complete thought. Every sentence has a subject and a predicate. The chart on page R28 shows the kinds of sentences according to use. *See also* Predicate, Subject.

Personal Pronouns		
	Singular	**Plural**
Used as subject	I, you, he, she, it	we, you, they
Used as object	me, you, him, her, it	us, you, them

Possessive Pronouns		
	Singular	**Plural**
Before a noun	my, your, her, his, its	our, your, their
Alone	mine, yours, hers, his, its	ours, yours, theirs

Sentences According to Use			
Kind	**Function**	**End Punctuation**	**Example**
Declarative	Makes a statement	Period	This book has sixty pages.
Interrogative	Asks a question	Question mark Often begins with a verb or a helping verb	Where did I leave my soccer ball? Have you seen it?
Imperative	Gives a command or makes a request	Period or exclamation point	Open it now! Please read this book.
Exclamatory	Expresses strong feelings	Exclamation point	What a surprise this is!

A simple sentence has only one subject and one predicate. A simple sentence may contain a compound subject or a compound predicate or both. The subject and the predicate can be expanded with adjectives, adverbs, or prepositional phrases. (*Our dance troupe will perform. Our dance troupe will perform in a citywide festival next July. A dance troupe from our neighborhood will practice all spring and perform in a citywide festival next July.*)

A compound sentence has two or more simple sentences joined by *and, but,* or *or.* Each simple sentence in a compound sentence has its own subject and predicate. (*Kai will perform in a dance at the Chinese festival, and she hopes we can come to see her.*) Semicolons may also be used between the two simple sentences in a compound sentence. (*Kai will perform in a dance at the*

Chinese festival; she hopes we can come to see her.*)

Simple predicate. *See* Predicate.

Simple sentence. *See* Sentence.

Simple subject. *See* Subject.

Singular. *See* Number.

Subject The key noun or pronoun that tells what the sentence is about.

A simple subject is the main noun or pronoun. (*The Wright brothers designed the first successful aircraft.*)

A complete subject includes the simple subject and any words that modify it. (*Orville Wright's first plane flight lasted twelve seconds.*)

A compound subject has two or more simple subjects that are joined by a conjunction. The subjects share the same verb. (*The science museum and the children's museum need volunteers.*)

Superlative degree. *See* Adjective; Adverb.

Tense. *See* Verb tense.

Transitive verb. *See* Verb.

Verb A word that expresses action or a state of being and is necessary to make a statement. (*has, run, was*)

An action verb names an action and tells what a subject does. Action verbs can express either physical or mental action. (*Gavin threw the Frisbee. Anna estimated an answer for the math exercise.*)

A linking verb links, or connects, the subject of a sentence with a noun or adjective that identifies or describes the subject. (My uncle *became* a carpenter. My uncle *is* clever.) A linking verb does not show action. *To be* in all its forms is the most common linking verb. *(am, is, are, was, were, will be, been, being)* Other linking verbs are *appear, become, feel, grow, look, remain, seem, sound, smell, stay, taste.*

Some verbs can be used as action verbs or linking verbs. (Sunflowers *grow* quickly. That plant *grew* very tall.)

A **regular verb** forms its simple past and past participle by adding *-ed* to the base form. The present participle is formed by adding *-ing* to the base form. Verbs that do not form their past and past participle by adding the ending *-ed* are called **irregular verbs.** *(swim, swam, swum; do/does, did, done)*

A **transitive verb** is an action verb that is followed by a direct object that answers the question *What?* or *Whom?* (Marco *ate* three bagels.)

An **intransitive verb** is an action verb that is not followed by a direct object. (Marco *smiled.*) A dictionary will indicate how a verb should be used.

Helping verbs help the main verb tell about an action or make a statement. (Terry, Gwen, and I *had been* painting a mural in the cafeteria.) The forms of *be* and *have* are the most common helping verbs. *(am, is, are, was, were, being, been; has, have, had, having.)* Other helping verbs are *can, could; do, does, did; may, might; must; shall, should; will, would.*

Verb phrase. *See* Phrase.

Verb tense A verb can express time—present, past, and future—by means of **tense.** All the verb tenses are formed from the four principal parts of a verb—a **base form** (*drive* for **present tense** and with *will or shall* for **future tense**), a **present participle** *(driving),* a simple **past form** *(drove),* and a **past participle** *(driven).*

The **present perfect tense** expresses an action or condition that occurred at some indefinite time in the past. This tense also shows an action or condition that began in the past and continues into the present. (Michelle *has babysat* for her cousin every day this week.)

The **past perfect tense** indicates that one past action or condition began and ended before another past action started. (Before you invited me, I *had accepted* another invitation.)

The **future perfect tense** indicates that one future action or condition will begin and end before another future event starts. Use *will have* or *shall have* with the past participle of a verb. (By the time Jake turns thirteen, he probably *will have grown* another inch.)

Each of the six tenses has a **progressive form** that expresses a continuing action. To make the progressive form, use the appropriate tense of the verb *be* with the present participle of the main verb. (Luke *is sleeping.*)

Mechanics

This section will help you use correct capitalization, punctuation, and abbreviations in your writing.

Capitalization

Capitalizing Sentences, Quotations, and Salutations	
Rule	**Example**
A capital letter appears at the beginning of a sentence.	**W**orld leaders held an economic conference this week.
A capital letter marks the beginning of a direct quotation that is a complete sentence.	Sabrina said, "**B**uy some milk after you rent the video."
When a quoted sentence is interrupted by explanatory words, such as *she said*, do not begin the second part of the sentence with a capital letter.	"Buy some milk," said Sabrina, "**a**fter you get the video."
When the second part of a quotation is a new sentence, put a period after the explanatory words, and begin the new part with a capital letter.	"Please get some milk," she said. "**G**et some cereal, too."
Do not capitalize an indirect quotation.	Sabrina asked me to **b**uy a half gallon of milk.
Capitalize the first word in the salutation and closing of a letter. Capitalize the title and name of the person addressed.	**D**ear **D**r. **B**arnett, **D**ear **J**oanie, **S**incerely,

Capitalizing Names and Titles of People	
Rule	**Example**
Capitalize the names of people and the initials that stand for their names.	**W**oodrow **W**ilson **H**arriet **T**ubman **M**arlene **J**oanas **J. P. M**organ
Capitalize a title or an abbreviation of a title when it comes before a person's name or when it is used in direct address.	**S**enator George Sanchez "The jury, **Y**our **H**onor, has reached a verdict."

Rule	Example
Do not capitalize a title that follows or is a substitute for a person's name.	Grover Cleveland was elected **p**resident twice. I think you should see a **d**octor about that cough of yours.
Capitalize the names and abbreviations of academic degrees that follow a person's name. Capitalize *Jr.* and *Sr.*	Sandra Anderson, **Ph.D.** Charles Bridge **J**r.
Capitalize words that show family relationships when used as titles or as substitutes for a person's name.	This cartoon shows a picture of **U**ncle Sam. Ask **M**other if you can come.
Do not capitalize words that show family relationships when they follow a possessive noun or pronoun.	I'm staying at my **g**randmother's house.
Always capitalize the pronoun *I*.	When **I** finish my homework, **I**'ll practice the piano.

Capitalizing Names of Places	
Rule	Example
Rule of Thumb Do not capitalize articles and prepositions in proper nouns. (**t**he Rock **of** Gibraltar, **t**he Cape **of** Good Hope)	
Capitalize the names of cities, counties, states, countries, and continents	**S**uffolk **C**ounty **C**oncord, **M**assachusetts **A**sia
Capitalize the names of bodies of water and other geographic features.	**P**acific **O**cean the **O**lympic **P**eninsula **M**ississippi **R**iver
Capitalize the names of sections of a country and regions of the world.	**N**ew **E**ngland **L**atin **A**merica
Capitalize compass points when they refer to a specific section of a country.	the **N**ortheast the **W**est

Rule	Example
Do not capitalize compass points when they indicate direction.	Florida is **s**outh of Georgia.
Do not capitalize adjectives made from words indicating direction.	**s**outhern Illinois
Capitalize the names of streets and highways.	**S**outheast **E**xpressway **A**ppleton **S**treet
Capitalize the names of buildings, bridges, monuments, and other structures.	**E**iffel **T**ower **A**rlington **N**ational **C**emetery **P**elham **P**arkway

Capitalizing Other Proper Nouns and Adjectives	
Rule	**Example**
Capitalize the names of clubs, organizations, businesses, institutions, and political parties.	**B**etter **B**usiness **B**ureau **YMCA** the **D**emocratic **P**arty **B**oys **S**couts of **A**merica
Capitalize brand names but not the nouns following them.	**M**unchy brand granola
Capitalize the names of days of the week, months, and holidays.	**S**unday **J**uly **V**alentine's **D**ay
Do not capitalize the names of seasons.	**w**inter, **s**pring, **s**ummer, **f**all
Capitalize the first word, the last word, and all important words in the title of a book, play, short story, poem, essay, article, film, television series, song, magazine, newspaper, and chapter of a book.	*The **D**iary of **A**nne **F**rank* **W**orld **B**ook **E**ncyclopedia *Highlights for **C**hildren* *Porgy and **B**ess* **C**hapter 6 "**T**he **G**ift of the **M**agi"
Capitalize the names of ethnic groups, nationalities, and languages.	**H**ispanic **P**olish **A**sian
Capitalize proper adjectives that are formed from the names of ethnic groups and nationalities.	**I**ndonesian dances **M**exican food **A**frican **A**merican history

Punctuation

Using the Period and Other End Marks

Rule	Example
Use a period at the end of a declarative sentence.	The Civil War lasted for four years.
Use a period at the end of an imperative sentence that does not express strong feeling.	Write your name at the top of the page.
Use a question mark at the end of an interrogative sentence.	Will we study the Civil War this year?
Use an exclamation point at the end of an exclamatory sentence or a strong imperative.	What a great game! Stop, thief!
Use an exclamation point at the end of an interjection that expresses strong emotion.	Ouch! Watch where you're going!

Using Commas

Rule	Example
Use commas to separate three or more items in a series.	My grandmother studied Latin, reading, arithmetic, cooking, and sewing when she went to school.
Use commas to show a pause after an introductory word and to set off names used in direct address.	Yes, she also had homework to do. Please, Marty, take your feet off the table.
Use a comma after two or more introductory prepositional phrases or when the comma is needed to make the meaning clear. A comma is not needed after a single, short prepositional phrase, but it is acceptable to use one.	In American schools of the last century, students memorized long lists of facts. After a few minutes the lions seemed to ignore us. (no comma needed)
Use commas to set off words that interrupt the flow of thought in a sentence.	My teacher, unlike my parents, thinks that memorization is often helpful.

Rule	Example
Use a comma before *and, or,* or *but* when it joins simple sentences.	The bus driver asked the passenger to move to the back of the bus, but Rosa Parks refused.
Use commas before and after the year when it is used with both the month and the day. If only the month and the year are given, do not use a comma.	On December 1, 1955, Rosa Parks boarded the Cleveland Avenue bus to go home. I was born in May 1955.
Use commas before and after the name of a state or a country when it is used with the name of a city. Do not use a comma after the state if it is used with a ZIP code.	After growing up in Pine Level, Alabama, Rosa Parks moved to Montgomery, Alabama. Send the package to 401 Western Ave., Apt. 3, Rockville, MD 20851.
Use a comma or commas to set off *too* when *too* means "also."	Ants are hardworking insects, and they are valuable recyclers, too.
Use a comma or commas to set off a direct quotation.	Dave announced, "I want to start an ant farm." "I want to start an ant farm," said Dave, "but I'm going to need some help."
Use a comma after the salutation of a friendly letter and after the closing of both a friendly letter and a business letter.	Dear Meg, Fondly, Yours sincerely,
Use a comma when necessary to prevent misreading of a sentence.	During the trial, lawyers argued endlessly over points of procedure.

Using Semicolons and Colons

Rule	Example
Use a semicolon to join the parts of a compound sentence when a coordinating conjunction, such as *and, or, nor,* or *but,* is not used.	I'm sorry to be late this morning; I missed the bus.
Use a colon to introduce a list of items that ends a sentence. Use a phrase such as *these, the following,* or *as follows* to signal that a list is coming.	Stir together the following ingredients: 1 egg, 1/2 cup milk, 1/2 cup orange juice, and 1 tsp. vanilla.

Rule	Example
Do not use a colon to introduce a list preceded by a verb or preposition.	Nathan ate three cookies, two pieces of pie, and a dish of ice cream. (No colon is used after *ate*.)
Use a colon to separate the hour and the minutes when you write the time of day.	Our practice ends at 3:15.
Use a colon after the salutation of a business letter.	Dear Dr. Chin: To the School Committee:

Using Quotation Marks and Italics

Rule	Example
Use quotation marks before and after a direct quotation.	"Elementary, my dear Watson," said Sherlock Holmes.
Use quotation marks with both parts of a divided quotation.	"If Professor Holmes can't help me," sobbed the young woman, "then I will lose my entire fortune!"
Use a comma or commas to separate a phrase such as *she said* from the quotation itself. Place the comma that precedes the phrase inside the closing quotation marks.	"Those footprints are mine," said the housekeeper.
Place a period that ends a quotation inside the closing quotation marks.	The policeman said, "There are strange footprints in the garden."
Place a question mark or an exclamation point inside the quotation marks when it is part of the quotation.	"What crime are you talking about?" asked Watson.
Place a question mark or an exclamation point outside the quotation marks when it is part of the entire sentence.	Didn't you hear me shout "Stop thief"?
Use quotation marks for the title of a short story, essay, poem, song, magazine or newspaper article, or book chapter.	"Piper at the Gates of Dawn" is my favorite chapter in the book *Wind in the Willows.* Poem: "The Naming of Cats" Article: "How to Train Your Dog"

Rule	Example
Use italics or underlining for the names of ships, trains, airplanes, and spacecraft.	Ship: *Mayflower* Spacecraft: *Apollo 13*
Use italics or underlining for the title of a book, play, film, television series, magazine, cartoon, newspaper, or work of art.	Book: *Roll of Thunder, Hear My Cry* Cartoon: *Garfield* Newspaper: *Los Angeles Times* Television series: *Nova*

Using Apostrophes

Rule	Example
Use an apostrophe and an -s ('s) to form the possessive of a singular noun.	our school**'s** soccer field Sally**'s** room
Use an apostrophe and an -s ('s) to form the possessive of a plural noun that does not end in -s.	the mice**'s** hiding place the children**'s** gifts

Rule of Thumb

> If a thing is jointly owned by two or more individuals, only the last name needs an apostrophe: *Karen and Keith's group project.* If the ownership is not joint, each name needs an apostrophe: *Karen's and Keith's grades improved this term.*

Rule	Example
Use an apostrophe alone to form the possessive of a plural noun that ends in -s.	the elephant**s'** water hole the citie**s'** population
Use an apostrophe and an -s ('s) to form the possessive of an indefinite pronoun.	anyone**'s** guess someone**'s** responsibility
Do not use an apostrophe in a possessive pronoun.	The leopard paced in **its** cage. **Yours** is the best blueberry pie. **His** solo was the last number in the concert.
Use an apostrophe to replace letters that have been omitted in a contraction.	it + is = it**'s** do + not = do**n't** is + not = is**n't**

Rule	Example
Use an apostrophe to form the plural of letters, figures, and words when they are used as themselves.	Write three *7*'s. The word is spelled with two *l*'s. The sentence contains two *and*'s.
Use an apostrophe to show missing numbers in a year.	the class of '01

Using Hyphens, Dashes, and Parentheses

Rule	Example
Use a hyphen to show the division of a word at the end of a line. Always divide the word between its syllables.	Last term, my grade was a disappoint-ment.

Rule of Thumb

One-letter divisions are not permissible. Proper nouns should not be divided if possible.

Rule	Example
Use a hyphen in compound numbers.	My bus ticket cost twenty-five dollars.
Use a hyphen in a fraction that is used as a modifier. Do not use a hyphen in a fraction used as a noun.	I added one-third cup of flour. One quarter of our class is sick with the flu.
Use a hyphen or hyphens in certain compound nouns.	brother-in-law bull's-eye jack-o'-lantern

Abbreviations

Rule	Example
Abbreviate the titles *Mr., Mrs., Ms.,* and *Dr.* before a person's name. Also abbreviate any professional or academic degree that follows a name, along with the titles *Jr.* and *Sr.*	**Dr.** Henry Higgins (doctor) Carlos Obligatto, **Ph.D.** (Doctor of Philosophy)
With exact times use *A.M.* (ante meridiem, "before noon") and *P.M.* (post meridiem, "after noon"). For years use *B.C.* (before Christ) and, sometimes, *A.D.* (anno Domini, "in the year of the lord," after Christ).	4:15 **A.M.** 3:30 **P.M.** 2000 **B.C.** **A.D.** 635
Abbreviate days and months only in charts and lists.	Play rehearsals will be held on the following dates: **Oct.** 28 **Nov.** 5
In scientific writing abbreviate units of measure. Use periods with English units but not with metric units.	yard(s) **yd.** meter(s) **m** milliliter(s) **ml**
On envelopes only, abbreviate street names and state names. In general text, spell out street names and state names.	Ms. Wendy Robbins 21 Puffin **Dr.** Cambridge, **MA** 02138 Wendy lives on Puffin **Drive** in Cambridge, **Massachusetts.**
Use Postal Service abbreviations for the names of states in written addresses with zip codes. A Postal Service abbreviation is written with two capital letters and no periods. Spell out state names within text.	Indiana **IN** Massachusetts **MA** Maine **ME** Connecticut **CT** California **CA**
Use capital letters and no periods with abbreviations that are pronounced letter by letter or as words. Exceptions are U.S. and Washington, D.C., which do use periods.	**YMCA** Young Men's Christian Association **VIP** very important person **CEO** chief executive officer

Writing Numbers

Rule	Example
In charts and tables, always write numbers as numerals. Other rules apply to numbers not in charts or tables.	**Student Test Scores** Student Test **1** Test **2** Test **3** Foster, W. **72** **79** **84** Gutierrez, M. **91** **90** **83**
Spell out numbers that you can write in one or two words.	I've told you **three** times to turn off the TV.
Use numerals for numbers of more than two words.	Between the years 1870 and 1916, **12,412,144** immigrants came to the United States from southern and eastern Europe.
Spell out any number that begins a sentence, or reword the sentence so that it does not begin with a number.	**One hundred seventy-one** steps are in the spiral staircase of the Statue of Liberty. The spiral staircase in the Statue of Liberty has **171** steps.
Write very large numbers as a numeral followed by the word *million* or *billion*.	More than **12 million** immigrants came to the United States from southern and eastern Europe.
If related numbers appear in the same sentence, use all numerals.	The Statue of Liberty stands **151** feet high and the right arm is **42** feet long.
Spell out ordinal numbers (*first, second,* and so forth).	The Statue of Liberty was the **first** structure immigrants saw after crossing the Atlantic.
Use words to express the time of day unless you are writing the exact time or using the abbreviation *A.M.* or *P.M.*	School gets out at **two-thirty.** It begins at **8:00 A.M.**
Use numerals to express dates, house and street numbers, apartment and room numbers, telephone numbers, page numbers, amounts of money of more than two words, and percentages. Write out the word *percent*.	June **25, 1897** **54** College Rd. Apartment **4D** **2** percent

Spelling

The following rules, examples, and exceptions can help you with the spellings of many words.

Spelling Words Containing *ie* and *ei*

Rhyming Rule	Examples
Put *i* before *e* except after *c* or when sounded like *a,* as in *neighbor* and *weigh.*	believe, thief receive, ceiling weight, veil

Exceptions include the following words: *species, science, weird, either, seize, leisure, protein.*

Suffixes and the silent e

For most words with silent *e,* keep the *e* when adding a suffix. When you add the suffix *-ly* to a word that ends in *l* plus silent *e,* drop the *le.* Also drop the silent *e* when you add a suffix beginning with a vowel or a *y.*

sure + ly = surely
make + ing = making

careful + ly = carefully
gentle + ly = gently

Exceptions The exceptions to the rule include the following words:

awe + ful = awful
true + ly = truly
dye + ing = dyeing

judge + ment = judgment
mile + age = mileage

Suffixes and the final y

When you add a suffix to words ending with a vowel + *y,* keep the *y.* For words ending with a consonant + *y,* change the *y* to *i,* unless the suffix begins with *i.* To avoid having two *i*'s together, keep the *y.*

joy + ful = joyful
try + ing = trying
try + ed = tried

messy + ness = messiness
city + es = cities

Adding prefixes

When you add a prefix to a word, do not change the spelling of the word.

re + peat = repeat
un + clear = unclear

il + legal = illegal

Doubling the final consonant

Double the final consonant when a word ends with a single consonant following one vowel and the word is one syllable, or when the last syllable of the word is accented both before and after adding the suffix.

fit + ing = fitting   cut + ing = cutting

Do not double the final consonant if the suffix begins with a consonant, if the accent is not on the last syllable, or if the accent moves when the suffix is added.

travel + ing = traveling   confer + ence = conference

Do not double the final consonant if the word ends in two consonants or if the suffix begins with a consonant.

howl + ing = howling   depart + ment = department

When adding -ly to a word that ends in ll, drop one l.

dull + ly = dully   full + ly = fully

Forming Plurals

General Rules for Plurals		
If a word ends in	**Rule**	**Example**
ss, ch, sh, x, or z	add -es	toss, tosses beach, beaches
a consonant + y	change y to i and add -es	cherry, cherries
a vowel + y or o	add -s	essay, essays video, videos
a consonant + o	usually add -s	burro, burros

Special Rules for Plurals	
Rule	**Example**
To form the plural of hyphenated compound nouns, make the most important word plural.	merry-go-round, merry-go-rounds brother-in-law, brothers-in-law
Some nouns have irregular plural forms and do not follow any rules.	goose, geese tooth, teeth crisis, crises
Some nouns have the same singular and plural forms.	moose species sheep

Forming compound words

When forming compound words, keep the original spelling of both words.

some + time = sometime
child + like = childlike
base + ball = baseball

Editing/Proofreading Checklist

Use this proofreading checklist to help you check for errors in your writing, and use the proofreading symbols in the chart below to mark places that need corrections.

☑ Have I avoided run-on sentences and sentence fragments and punctuated sentences correctly?

☑ Have I used every word correctly, including plurals, possessives, and frequently confused words?

☑ Do verbs and subjects agree? Are verb tenses correct?

☑ Do pronouns refer clearly to their antecedents and agree with them in person, number, and gender?

☑ Have I used adverb and adjective forms and modifying phrases correctly?

☑ Have I spelled every word correctly, and checked the unfamiliar ones in a dictionary?

	Proofreading Symbols	
⊙	Lieut Brown	Insert a period.
∧	No one came the party.	Insert a letter or a word.
≡	I enjoyed paris.	Capitalize a letter.
/	The Class ran a bake sale.	Make a capital letter lowercase.
⌒	The campers are home sick.	Close up a space.
ⓢⓟ	They visited N.Y. ⓢⓟ	Spell out.
∧ ⸴	Sue please come I need your help.	Insert a comma or a semicolon.
∩	He enjoyed feild day.	Transpose the position of letters or words.
#	alltogether	Insert a space.
୭	We went to to Boston.	Delete letters or words.
∨ ∨ ∨	She asked Who's coming?	Insert quotation marks or an apostrophe.
/ = /	mid January	Insert a hyphen.
¶	"Where?" asked Karl. "Over there," said Ray.	Begin a new paragraph.

Writing Handbook

The Writing Process

Writing is a process with five stages: *prewriting, drafting, revising, editing/proofreading,* and *publishing/presenting.* By following each stage, you can turn your ideas into polished pieces of writing. Most writers take their writing through all five stages and repeat stages when they need to.

The Writing Process

Prewriting ➡ Drafting ➡ Revising ➡ Editing/Proofreading ➡ Publishing/Presenting

Prewriting

Prewriting is the process of gathering and organizing your ideas. It begins the moment you start to think about what might interest you and your readers. Prewriting techniques include listing, questioning, and clustering.

Listing	Questioning	Clustering
Try making a list of whatever comes into your head on a particular subject. This is called brainstorming. Then go back over the list and circle the ideas you like best. These ideas might become part of your paper.	If your audience is your classmates, ask yourself the following questions: • What do my friends like to learn about? • What do my friends like to read about? • What have I done that my friends might like to hear about?	As you gather ideas, you may find that some of them fit together. You can organize your ideas in a cluster diagram, which is a series of circles, with lines showing how they are related. A cluster diagram is a way of taking notes on your topic.

Referring to notes in your journal and logs, or records, of your daily activities can also help you generate ideas for writing. When you have selected your topic, ask yourself questions about it. Then write a plan for what you want to say. The plan might be an organized list or a cluster diagram. It does not have to include complete sentences.

Drafting

Drafting is the stage that turns your list into sentences and paragraphs.

Tips for drafting

- Use your prewriting notes.
- Write an introduction that catches the reader's attention.
- Add details to support your ideas.
- Let your words flow. You can correct mistakes in spelling and grammar later.
- Make sure each paragraph relates to the main idea.

If you get stuck, try one of the strategies below:

- Freewrite your thoughts and images. You can organize them later.
- Talk about your writing with a friend.
- Ask more questions about your topic.
- Read what you have written aloud to yourself.
- Take a walk or listen to music. Return to your writing later.

Revising

The goal of revising is to make your writing clearer and more interesting. When you revise, you add or delete information. You might decide to organize your writing in a different way. Some writers make several revisions before they are satisfied. Feedback from a peer is also important.

Using peer review

Ask someone to read your paper. Direct their responses in these ways:

- Ask the reader to tell you what they have read in their own words. If you do not hear your ideas restated, revise your writing for clarity.
- Repeat what the reader has told you in your own words. Ask the reader if you have understood his or her suggestions.
- Discuss your writing with your readers. Listen to their suggestions carefully.

Tips for revising

Ask yourself the following questions:

- Have I said what I intended to say clearly and correctly?
- Is my writing appropriate for my intended audience?
- Do all the details work together to support the main idea? Have I included any unnecessary or distracting details?
- Is the order of information clear and logical?

- Have I accomplished my purpose in writing?
- How does my paper sound when I read it aloud?

If you have time, put your draft away for a day or two. When you look at it again, you might see it from a new point of view. Use your own insights and the comments of your peer reviewer to revise your writing.

Editing/Proofreading

The editing stage is the time to correct errors in spelling, grammar, capitalization, and punctuation. Use the following checklist as you edit for style. Then use the proofreading checklist on page R42 and on the inside back cover of this book.

> ☑ Have I varied the length and structure of my sentences?
> ☑ Have I made clear connections between ideas?
> ☑ Do my sentences and paragraphs flow smoothly?

Publishing/Presenting

Prepare your writing for an audience. Check that the paper has a title. Hand it in to your teacher, or share it in one of the ways described below. When the paper is returned, keep it in your writing portfolio.

Ideas for Presenting	
Illustrations	A photograph, diagram, or drawing can convey useful information.
Oral presentation	Almost any writing can be shared aloud. Try including music, slides, or a group oral reading.
Class book	A collection of class writing is a nice contribution to the school library.
Newspaper	Some schools have their own newspaper, and local newspapers often publish writing.
Bulletin board	Illustrations and photographs add interest.
Literary magazine	Magazines such as *Cricket* and *Stone Soup* publish student writing. Some schools have a literary magazine that publishes student writing.

Some writing, such as journal writing, is private and not intended for an audience. However, even if you don't share your paper, don't throw it away. It might contain ideas that you can use later.

Writing Modes

Writing can be classified under four different headings: expository, narrative, descriptive, and persuasive. Each of these types has a specific purpose or purposes.

Expository Writing

Expository writing communicates knowledge and covers a wide range of styles. It might be an essay, an explanation, directions, or instructions.

Kinds of Expository Writing	Examples
A general explanation of how to do something.	Explain how to hit a baseball or how to clean up a messy room.
Compare-and-contrast essay	Compare two sports, two characters, two books, or two cartoons.
Step-by-step directions	Give directions for building a tree house or operating a lawnmower.
Information and explanation	Explain why oil burns, how polar bears stay warm, or why birds migrate.
A written report	Write a report on the past basketball season.

Guidelines for expository writing

When you have selected your subject, decide what details to include and how to organize them.

Use the checklist before submitting your final draft.

☑ Is the opening paragraph interesting?

☑ Are explanations accurate, complete, and clear?

☑ Is information presented in a logical order?

☑ Does each paragraph have a main idea? Does all the information support the main idea?

☑ Does my essay have an introduction, a body, and a conclusion?

☑ Have I defined any unfamiliar terms?

Descriptive Writing

Descriptive writing paints a picture with words. It brings the reader into the scene of the action, whether an icebound landscape in the Arctic or a back porch in the Midwest. Effective descriptions use details that appeal to the reader's senses.

☑ Are the details I selected vivid? Have I appealed to all of the reader's senses?

☑ Does each paragraph contain a main idea?

☑ Are transitions between ideas and paragraphs clear?

☑ Do the paragraphs follow a logical order?

Narrative Writing

Narrative writing tells a story, either about real events or about made-up events. It answers the question What happened? A well-written narrative holds the reader's attention by presenting interesting characters in a carefully ordered series of events.

☑ Does my first sentence attract the reader's attention?

☑ Have I included all the important information about characters, setting, and story line?

☑ Are the events presented in a logical order?

☑ Are there places where dialogue would make my narrative more interesting?

☑ Does my narrative have a satisfying conclusion?

Persuasive Writing

Persuasive writing presents an opinion. Its goal is to make readers feel or think a certain way about a situation or an idea. Another purpose is to make readers take action. Sometimes persuasive writing does both. In persuasive writing, you use both facts and opinions.

☑ Is my main idea expressed in a clear statement?

☑ Have I supported my point of view?

☑ Have I presented my arguments in a logical order?

☑ Have I addressed the interests of my audience?

☑ Is the tone of my writing convincing?

☑ Have I ended with a strong argument or with a call to action?

Research Report Writing

When you write a research report, you explore a topic by gathering factual information from several sources. Through your research you develop a point of view or draw a conclusion, which becomes the main idea, or thesis, of your report.

Select a Topic

To choose a topic for your research report, follow these guidelines:

- Brainstorm a list of questions about a subject. Choose one that is neither too narrow nor too broad for the length of your paper.
- Be sure your topic genuinely interests you.
- Be sure information from several different sources is available.

Do Research

First, find general information about your topic in an encyclopedia. Then use the computerized or card catalog in the library to locate books. Search for up-to-date information in periodicals (magazines) or newspapers and from CD-ROMs or the Internet. Ask the librarian if you need help.

As you gather information, make sure each source you use relates closely to your topic. Also be sure that your source is reliable. Be extra careful if you are using information from the Internet. If you are not sure about the reliability of a source, consult the librarian or your teacher.

Make Source Cards

Document the source of your information. Write the author, title, publication information, and location of each source on a separate card. Give each card a number, and write it in the upper right-hand corner. Use these cards to prepare a bibliography or a list of works cited.

Sample Source Card

Source number — 7

Author(s) — Cerullo, Mary M. and Jeffrey L. Rotman. *Sharks: Challengers of the Deep*. Freeport, ME: Cobblehill, 1993. — Title

City of publication/ Publisher/Date of publication

Location of source — Wentworth Public Library — 930 B285 — Library call number

Take Notes on Note Cards

As you read, take notes to help you keep track of information.

- Use a new card for each important piece of information.
- At the top of each card, identify the reference you used.
- Write only details and ideas that relate to your topic.
- Summarize information in your own words.
- Write down a phrase or a quote only when the words are especially interesting or come from an important source. Enclose all quotes in quotation marks.

Write a keyword or phrase that tells you what the information is about.

Sample Note Card

Exaggerated dangers of sharks

"You are about fifty times more likely to be killed by a bee sting than a shark." pp. 11–13

7 — Write the source number from your source card.

Write the number of the page or pages on which you found the information.

Develop Your Thesis

As you begin researching and learning about your topic, think about the point you want to make. Write a thesis statement to help you determine what information is important.

Write an Outline

When you finish taking notes, organize the information in an outline. Follow an outline form like the one below.

Sample Outline

Sharks are not as dangerous as most people think.

I. Misinformation about sharks

   A. Movies about man-eating sharks

   B. Ancient myths

II. True facts about sharks

   A. Eating habits

   B. Mating and reproduction

The thesis statement identifies your topic and the overall point you will make.

If you have subtopics under a main topic, there must be at least two. They must relate directly to your main topic.

Document Your Information

You must document, or show the source of, information you use in your paper. Only information that can be found in several widely available sources does not need to be documented. To document information, use parentheses to enclose the name of the author of your source followed by the page on which you found the information.

Bibliography or Works Cited

At the end of your paper, list all the sources that you documented in your paper. Arrange them alphabetically by the author's last name or, if no author is given, by the title, as shown below.

Indent all but the first line of each entry. If your sources are all print media (books, magazines, newspapers), label your list "Bibliography." If you used other media, such as on-line articles, videotapes, or interviews, label your list "Works Cited."

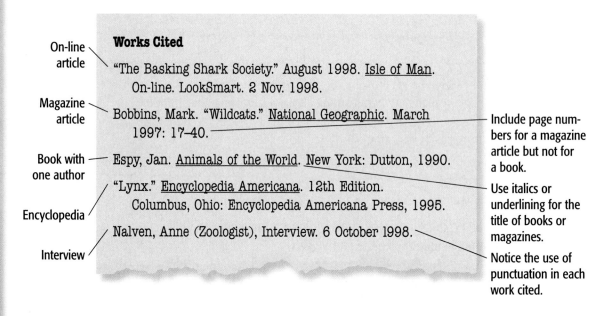

On-line article

Works Cited

"The Basking Shark Society." August 1998. Isle of Man. On-line. LookSmart. 2 Nov. 1998.

Magazine article

Bobbins, Mark. "Wildcats." National Geographic. March 1997: 17–40.

Include page numbers for a magazine article but not for a book.

Book with one author

Espy, Jan. Animals of the World. New York: Dutton, 1990.

Encyclopedia

"Lynx." Encyclopedia Americana. 12th Edition. Columbus, Ohio: Encyclopedia Americana Press, 1995.

Use italics or underlining for the title of books or magazines.

Interview

Nalven, Anne (Zoologist), Interview. 6 October 1998.

Notice the use of punctuation in each work cited.

Business Writing

Writing a Business Letter

An effective business letter can serve many purposes. The following are a few of them.

Purpose	Example
To request information	Write to the Woods Hole Marine Biological Laboratory in Massachusetts, requesting information about sharks.
To request an interview	Request an interview with the founder of the Ready Riders Bike Safety Club.
To make a complaint or a suggestion	After witnessing a bicycle accident, write a letter to your local newspaper complaining that many cyclists do not follow traffic regulations.

General guidelines

Follow these guidelines when writing a business letter.

- Use correct business-letter form, as shown on page R52.
- Use 8½-by-11-inch white or off-white paper.
- Use Standard English. Check your spelling carefully.
- Be polite, even if you are making a complaint.
- Be brief and to the point.
- Include all necessary information.

Structure, form, and style

Like an essay, a business letter should have an introduction, a body, and a conclusion.

Introduction: Explain who you are and why you are writing.

Body: Support your purpose for writing with details, developing each main point in a separate paragraph.

Conclusion: If you are writing to express an opinion or complaint, conclude your letter with a polite but strong statement that wraps up what you have said. If you are making a request, thank the reader for his or her help. You might also want to restate the purpose of your letter.

Two standard formats for business letters are block style and modified block style.

The letter on the next page is in modified block style.

124 Cleveland Circle
Tempe, AZ 85282
November 16, 1999

In the heading, write your address and the date on separate lines.

Ms. Doreen Ampudia
Editor-in-Chief
Tempe News Chronicle
567 West Cactus Dr.
Tempe, AZ 85282

In the inside address, write the name and address of the person to whom you are sending the letter.

Dear Ms. Ampudia:

I am a student at South Tempe Middle School. Last Wednesday my friends and I saw a bad bicycle accident at the corner of Cactus Drive and Main Street. The bike rider had not obeyed the traffic light at that intersection.

Bike riders in the city should be required to pass a riding test. Police officers should enforce traffic rules for bikers, just as they do for drivers.

I hope you will share my concern with your readers. Thank you.

Use a colon after the greeting.

In Lisa's introduction, she lets Ms. Ampudia know who she is and why she is writing.

In the body of her letter, Lisa provides details about her suggestion.

Sincerely,
Lisa Wilder
Lisa Wilder

In the closing, use *Sincerely, Sincerely yours,* or *Yours truly* followed by a comma. Include both your signature and your printed or typed name.

Writing a Memo

A memorandum, or memo, is an efficient way of communicating. A header provides basic information.

TO: Middle School clean-up volunteers
FROM: Sarah Hardy
SUBJECT: Town field clean-up
DATE: Oct. 20, 1999

Our school's volunteer crew has been assigned to clean the town field on October 26. We need the following supplies: garbage bags, paper recycling bags, rakes. Please let Sarah know what you can bring.

Using a Computer for Writing

A computer offers advantages throughout the writing process.

Prewriting

A computer can help you gather and organize ideas and information.

Brainstorming

While brainstorming for topics or details, write freely, or dim the computer screen and do "invisible writing."

Researching

If your computer has a CD-ROM player, you can use a CD-ROM encyclopedia to find not only text and pictures but also sound, animated cartoons or graphics, and live-action video clips.

You can also use the Internet to find information from universities, news organizations, government organizations, and experts in their fields. The global system that uses the Internet is called the World Wide Web.

Outlining

Some word-processing programs offer an outlining feature that automatically indents headings and uses different type styles for main headings and subheadings.

Drafting/Revising

Word processing lets you make changes quickly. You can

- *insert* new text at any point in your document
- *delete* text
- *move* text from one position to another
- *copy* text
- *undo* a change you just made
- *save* each draft or revision of your document in case you want to return to an earlier idea
- *print* copies of your work-in-progress for others to read

Editing/Proofreading

You can edit and proofread directly on the computer, or you can mark your changes on a printout, or hard copy, of your document and then input the changes on screen. Either way, the following word-processing features are helpful:

- **Grammar checker** The computer finds possible errors in grammar and suggests revisions.
- **Spelling checker** The computer finds misspellings and suggests corrections.
- **Thesaurus** If you want to replace an inappropriate or overused word, you can highlight the word and the computer will suggest synonyms.
- **Search and replace** If you want to change or correct something that occurs several times in your document, the computer can instantly make the change throughout the document.

Rule of Thumb: The grammar checker, spelling checker, and thesaurus cannot replace your own careful reading and judgment.

Presenting

The computer allows you to enhance the readability, attractiveness, and visual interest of your document in many ways.

Formatting your text

The computer gives you a variety of options for the layout and appearance of your text. You can easily add or change the following elements:

- margin width
- number of columns
- type size
- type style
- page numbering
- header or footer (information such as a title that appears at the top or bottom of every page)
- borders or shading to highlight sections of text

The manual that is supplied with the software program will tell you what options are available and how to access them.

Visual aids

Some word-processing programs have graphic functions that allow you to create graphs, charts, and diagrams. Collections of clip art, pictures you can copy and paste into your document, are also available.

Study and Test-Taking Skills

Study Skills

Good study skills grow out of good habits. Here are some useful studying guidelines:

- Keep an assignment notebook. Be sure it is up-to-date.
- Keep your notes for each course together in one place.
- Find a good place to study. Choose a place that has as few distractions as possible. Try to study in the same place each day.
- Schedule enough time for studying. Try to study at the same time each day.
- For each assignment, set a study goal. Decide how long it will take you to meet each goal. Be realistic.
- Take notes on your reading, and keep them in one place.

Taking Tests

How well you perform on a test is not a matter of chance. Some specific strategies can help you answer test questions. This section of the handbook will show how to improve your test-taking skills.

Tips for preparing for tests

Here are some useful guidelines:

- Gather information about the test. When will it be given? How long will it take? Exactly what material will it cover?
- Review material from your textbook, class notes, homework, quizzes, and handouts.
- Gather all your study materials in one folder. Review the study questions at the end of each section of a textbook. Try to define terms in boldface type.
- Make up some sample questions and answer them. As you skim selections, try to predict what may be asked. Remember what your teacher stressed when the material was presented in class.
- Draw charts and cluster or Venn diagrams to help you remember information and to picture how one piece of information relates to another.
- Give yourself plenty of time to study. Avoid staying up late cramming before a test. Several short review sessions are more effective than one long one.
- In addition to studying alone, study with a partner or small group. Quiz one another on topics you think the test will cover.

Tips for using test time

Try following these steps:

- Read all directions carefully. Understanding the directions can prevent mistakes. Ask for help if you have a question.
- Answer the easier items first. By skipping the hard items, you will have time to answer all the easy ones.
- In the time that is left, return to the items you skipped. Answer them as best you can. If you won't be penalized for doing so, guess at an answer.
- If possible, save some time at the end to check your answers.

Taking objective tests

An objective test is a test of factual information. The questions are generally either right or wrong; there is no difference of opinion. On an objective test, you are asked to recall information, not to present your ideas. Objective test questions include true or false items, multiple-choice items, fill-in-the-blanks statements, short-answer items, and matching items. At the beginning of an objective test, scan the number of items. Then budget your time.

Multiple-choice items Multiple-choice questions ask you to answer a question or complete a sentence. They are the kind of question you will encounter most often on objective tests. Read all the choices before answering. Pick the best response.

What is a lever?
  (a) a pulley
  (b) a simple machine used to move something
  (c) a credit card
  (d) none of the above

Correct answer: (b)

- Read the first question carefully. Be sure that you understand it.
- Read all the answers before selecting one. Reading all of the responses is especially important when one of the choices is "all of the above," or "none of the above."
- Eliminate responses that are clearly incorrect. Focus on the responses that might be correct.
- Look for absolute words, such as *never, always, all, none.* Most generalizations have exceptions. Absolute statements are often incorrect. (Note: This tip applies to true/false items also.)

Answering essay questions

Essay questions ask you to think about what you have learned and write about it in one or more paragraphs. Some tests present a choice of essay questions. If a test has both an objective part and an essay part, answer the objective questions first. Then leave yourself enough time to work on the essay.

Read the essay question carefully. What does it ask you to do? discuss? explain? define? summarize? compare and contrast? These key words tell what kind of information you must give in your answer.

Tips for answering essay questions

Keep these steps in mind:

- Read the question or questions carefully. Determine the kind of information required by the question.
- Plan your time. Do not spend too much time on one part of the essay.
- Make a list of what you want to cover.
- If you have time, make revisions and proofreading corrections.

Taking standardized tests

Standardized tests are taken by students all over the country. Your performance on the test is compared with the performance of other students at your grade level. There are many different kinds of standardized tests. Some measure your progress in such subjects as English, math, and science, while others measure how well you think. Standardized tests can show how you learn and what you do best.

Preparing for standardized tests

There is no way to know exactly what information will be on a standardized test, or even what topics will be covered. Therefore, the best preparation is to do the best you can in your daily schoolwork. However, you can learn the kinds of questions that will appear on a standardized test. Some general tips will also help.

Tips for taking standardized tests

You might find the following suggestions helpful:

- Get enough sleep the night before the test. Eat a healthful breakfast.
- Arrive early for the test. Try to relax.
- Listen carefully to all test directions. Ask questions if you don't understand the directions.
- Complete easy questions first. Leave harder items for the end.

- On standardized tests, you will mark your answers on a separate answer sheet. Be sure your answers are in the right place. Use the right kind of pencil.
- If you can, find out whether points will be subtracted for the wrong answers. If they are not, you should guess at questions that you aren't sure of.

Analogies Analogy items test your understanding of the relationships between things or ideas. On standardized tests, analogies are written in an abbreviated format, as shown below.

man : woman :: buck : doe

The symbol : means "is to"; the symbol :: means "as."

The following chart shows some word relationships you might find in analogy tests:

Relationship	Definition	Example
Synonyms	Two words have a similar meaning.	huge : gigantic :: scared : afraid
Antonyms	Two words have opposite meanings.	bright : dull :: far : near
Use	Words name a user and something used.	farmer : tractor :: writer : computer
Cause-effect	Words name a cause and its effect.	tickle : laugh :: polish :: shine
Category	Words name a category and an item in it.	fish : tuna :: building : house
Description	Words name an item and a characteristic of it.	knife : sharp :: joke : funny

Listening, Speaking, and Viewing Skills

Listening Effectively

A large part of the school day is spent either listening or speaking to others. By becoming a better listener and speaker, you will know more about what is expected of you, and understand more about your audience.

Listening to instructions in class

Some of the most important listening in the school day involves listening to instructions.

Use the following checklist to help you:

- First, make sure you understand what you are listening for. Are you receiving instructions for homework or for a test? What you listen for depends upon the type of instructions being given.
- Think about what you are hearing, and keep your eyes on the speaker. This will help you stay focused on the important points.
- Listen for key words or word clues. Examples of word clues are phrases, such as *above all, most important,* or *the three basic parts.* These clues help you identify important points that you should remember.
- Take notes on what you hear. Write down only the most important parts of the instructions.
- If you don't understand something, ask questions. Then, if you're still unsure about the instructions, repeat them aloud to your teacher to receive correction on any key points that you may have missed.

Interpreting nonverbal clues

Understanding nonverbal clues is part of effective listening. Nonverbal clues are everything except what a speaker says. Notice where and how a speaker is standing. Notice whether some words are spoken more loudly than others. Pay attention to gestures and facial expression. Does the speaker make eye contact? Does he or she smile or look angry?

Speaking Effectively

- Speak slowly, clearly, and in a normal tone of voice. Raise your voice a bit or use gestures to stress important points.
- Pause a few seconds after making an important point to let your audience think about what you've said.
- Use words that help your audience picture what you're talking about. Visual aids such as pictures, graphs, charts, and maps can also help make your information clear.
- Stay in contact with your audience. Make sure your eyes move from person to person in the group you're addressing.

Speaking informally

Most conversations are informal. When you speak casually with your friends, family, and neighbors, you use informal speech. Human relationships depend on this routine but effective form of communication.

- Be courteous. Listen until the other person has finished speaking. Do not interrupt.
- Speak in a relaxed and spontaneous manner.
- Make eye contact with your listeners.
- Do not monopolize a conversation. Let others have a chance to speak.
- When telling a story, show enthusiasm. Act out the parts and draw in your audience.
- When giving an announcement or directions, speak clearly and slowly. Check that your listeners understand the information.

Presenting an oral report

The key to presenting a successful oral report is preparation. The steps in preparing an oral report are similar to the steps in the writing process. Complete each step carefully.

Steps in Preparing an Oral Report	
Prewriting	Determine your purpose and audience. Decide on a topic and narrow it.
Drafting	Make an outline. Fill in the supporting details. Write the report.
Revising and editing	Review your draft. Check the organization of ideas and details. Reword unclear statements.
Practicing	Practice the report out loud. Time the report. Then practice the report in front of a family member. Ask for and accept advice.
Presenting	Relax in front of your audience. Make eye contact with your audience. Speak slowly and clearly.

Viewing Effectively

Critical viewing means thinking about what you see while watching a TV program, news broadcast, film, or video. It requires paying attention to what you hear and see, and deciding whether information is true, false, or exaggerated. If the information seems true, try to determine whether it is based on a fact or an opinion.

Fact versus opinion

A fact is something that can be proved. An opinion is what someone believes is true. Opinions are based on feelings and experiences, but they cannot be proved.

Television commercials, political speeches, and even the evening news contain both facts and opinions. They use emotional words and actions to persuade the viewer to agree with a particular point of view. They may also use faulty reasoning, such as linking the wrong cause and effect. Think through what is being said. Even when the speaker seems sincere, his or her reasons may not make sense. Many arguments are based on unfair generalizations. Others are based on facts that have been rearranged and distorted.

Commercials contain both obvious and hidden messages. The obvious message is the spoken words of the commercial. The hidden message comes across in how the message is presented. Look carefully at commercials to see whether a product is really worth buying.

Working in Groups

Working in a group is an opportunity to learn from others. Whether you are planning a group project, such as a class trip, or solving a math problem, each person in a group brings particular strengths and interests to the task. When a task is large, such as planting a garden, a group provides the necessary energy and talent to get the job done.

Small groups vary in size according to the nature of the task. Three to five students is a good size for most small-group tasks. Your teacher may assign you to a group, or you may be asked to form your own group. Don't work with your best friend if you are likely to chat too much. Successful groups often have a mix of student abilities and interests.

Individual role assignments give everyone in a group something to do. One student, the group recorder, might take notes. Another might lead the discussion, and another might report the results to the rest of the class.

Roles for a Small Group	
Reviewer	Reads or reviews the assignment to make sure that everyone understands it
Recorder 1	Takes notes on the discussion
Recorder 2	Takes notes on the final results
Reporter	Reports results to the rest of the class
Discussion leader	Asks questions to get the discussion going; keeps the group focused on the topic
Facilitator	Helps the group resolve disagreements and reach a compromise

For a small group of three or four students, some of these roles can be combined. For a larger group, two or more people may be assigned the same role. Your teacher may assign a role to each student in your group. Or you may be asked to choose your own role.

Tips for working in groups

- Review the group assignment and goal. Be sure that everyone in the group understands the assignment.
- Review the amount of time allotted for the task. Decide how your group will organize its time.
- Check that all participants understand their roles in the group.
- When a question arises, try to solve it as a group before asking a teacher for help.
- Listen to every group member's point of view.
- When it is your turn to talk, address the subject and help move the discussion forward.

Reading Handbook

The Reading Process

As reading materials get more difficult, you'll need to use a variety of active reading strategies to help you understand texts. This handbook is designed to help you find and use the tools you'll need before, during, and after reading.

Word Identification

Word identification skills are building blocks for understanding what you read. They prepare you to deal with unknown words you'll encounter as you read.

Look before, at, and after an unfamiliar word. Use the other words and sentences around an unknown word to help you make an educated guess about what that word might be. Think about the following questions as you try to read new words:

- Can I sound out this new word?
- What other words or word parts do I know that might provide clues to this new word?
- Can I figure out its meaning from its place in the sentence?
- What other word would make sense in this sentence?

Using letter-sound cues

Here are some tips for sounding out new words.

- Look at the beginning of the word. What letter or group of letters makes up the beginning sound or syllable?

  Example: In the word *seasoning, sea* is a familiar word.

- Look at the end of the word. What letter or group of letters makes up the ending sound or syllable?

  Example: *Seasoning* ends with *-ing,* a familiar syllable.

- Look at the middle of the word. Is there a word you already know inside the new word? What vowel or vowel pattern is represented in each syllable?

  Example: In the word *seasoning, son* is a word you know.

Now try pronouncing the whole word: *sea son ing.*

Using language structure cues

Word order, or **syntax,** helps you make sense of a sentence, so looking at the position of a new word in a sentence can help you identify a word. Look at the following nonsense sentence:

Several blazzy urfs were stingling hard.

Your experience with English sentence patterns and parts of speech tells you that the action word, or verb, in this sentence is *were stingling.* Who were *stingling?*—the *urfs.* What kind of *urfs* were they?—*blazzy.* How did they *stingle?*—hard. Even though you still do not know word meanings in the nonsense sentence, you can make some sense of the entire sentence by using syntax.

Use the order of words in a sentence to help you figure out parts of speech. Use that knowledge to identify new words and their meanings.

Using context clues

When you read on your own, you can often figure out the meaning of a new word by looking at its **context,** the other words and sentences that surround it. For instance, look at the following example:

My three-year-old cousin fought my attempt to dress her warmly, but she was *pacified* when I let her wear her pink T-shirt under a woolly sweater.

You can guess from the first sentence that *pacified* is a word that means something different than fighting. If you guessed that it means *made to quit fighting* or *made to behave peacefully,* you successfully used context to determine meaning.

Tips for Using Context

- Look before, at, and after the unknown word for
  —a synonym or definition of the unknown word in a sentence.
    *The **luge,** a **small, fast sled,** moved with incredible speed.*
  —a clue to what the word is like or not like.
    Unlike** his **morose** friend, Andrew is very **cheerful.
  —a general topic associated with the word.
    *The **photographer** demonstrated how to use a **zoom lens.***
  —a description or action associated with the word.
    *She uses an old **loom** to **weave** those beautiful blankets.*
- Connect what you know with what the author has written.
- Predict a possible meaning.
- Apply the meaning in the sentence.
- Try again if your guess does not make sense.

Using word parts to read new words

Noticing word parts can help you sound out and understand unknown words. Look at some of the following word parts:

- **Roots** The base part of a word is called its **root.** If you know a root within a new word, start from there to figure out the rest of the word. *(inter**national**)*
- **Plurals** Most nouns are changed from singular to plural by adding *-s, -es,* or *-ies.* Some nouns have irregular plurals *(child, children).*
- **Comparative endings** The endings *-er* or *–est,* used for many adjectives and adverbs, make comparisons *(kind, kinder, kindest).*
- **Inflectional endings** Other endings, such as *-ing* or *–ed,* can be important parts of both the meaning and pronunciation of a word *(walk, walked, walking).*
- **Prefixes** These syllables, added to the beginning of a word, change the meaning of the words. For example, *semi-* means "half," so *semicircle* means "half circle."
- **Suffixes** These syllables are added to the ends of words. For example, *-ful* means "full of," so *fearful* means "full of fear."

Using reference materials

When looking at or around an unknown word does not help you identify the word, dictionaries, glossaries, and other reference sources can be useful tools. References provide derivations and spellings as well as pronunciations.

A **dictionary** provides the pronunciation and literal meaning or meanings of a word. It also gives other forms of the word, its part of speech, alternate spellings, examples, synonyms, origins, and other useful information. Look at the dictionary entry below to see what valuable information it provides.

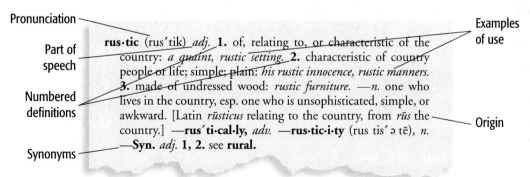

Pronunciation

Part of speech

Numbered definitions

Synonyms

Examples of use

Origin

rus·tic (rus′tik) *adj.* **1.** of, relating to, or characteristic of the country: *a quaint, rustic setting.* **2.** characteristic of country people or life; simple; plain: *his rustic innocence, rustic manners.* **3.** made of undressed wood: *rustic furniture.* —*n.* one who lives in the country, esp. one who is unsophisticated, simple, or awkward. [Latin *rūsticus* relating to the country, from *rūs* the country.] —**rus′ti·cal·ly,** *adv.* —**rus·tic·i·ty** (rus tis′ ə tē), *n.* —**Syn.** *adj.* **1, 2.** see **rural.**

A **glossary** is a condensed dictionary within a specific text. It provides an alphabetical listing of words used within that text, together with their definitions and other information necessary to understand the word as it appears in the text. Look at the example below.

revelation [rev′ ə lā′ shən] *n.* the recognition of new information.
reverence [rev′ər ens, rev′rəns] *n.* a feeling of deep respect.
revision [ri vizh′ ən] *n.* a change made in order to improve.
revive [ri vīv′] *v.* to come to life or consciousness.
revoke [ri vōk′] *v.* to take back; withdraw.
ridicule [rid′ ə kūl′] *n.* words or actions intended to make someone or something feel or seem foolish.
ritual [rich′ o͞o əl] *n.* a routine faithfully followed.
rogue [rōg] *n.* a dishonest person; villain.
rout [rout] *v.* to drive out.
ruthless [ro͞oth′ lis] *adj.* without mercy or pity.

A **thesaurus** is a dictionary of synonyms and antonyms, and can be especially useful for choosing precise, descriptive language. Picture dictionaries, special-subject dictionaries, foreign-language dictionaries, and other references can also help you identify new words and their meanings. Some of these are available on CD-ROM and on the Internet.

Reading Fluency

Becoming an accomplished reader is like becoming a good athlete or musician: the more you practice, the better you get. The more you read, the less attention you need to pay to sounding out words, and the more attention you can give to understanding the meaning of a selection.

Tips for Becoming a Fluent Reader

- Develop a good sight vocabulary.
- Practice reading out loud on independent level materials.
- Begin with a short, interesting passage.
- Reread the same passage out loud at least three times. As your reading sounds smoother, move on to a longer or slightly more difficult passage.

Reading in appropriate level materials

How do you decide if something is too easy, too hard, or just right for you to read? If you want to develop into a smooth, fluent reader, it is important to read regularly in materials that are easy for you. It is also important to grow as a strategic reader, and to do that, you will want to read materials that are challenging but manageable.

To decide what level of reading material is right for each reading task, look at the following chart:

Reading level	Definition/Criteria	When to use
Independent level	No more than 5 difficult words per 100 words read	On your own, anytime To practice smooth reading
Instructional level	No more than 10 difficult words per 100 words read	With support from teacher, parent, or other more experienced reader To challenge yourself
Beyond instructional level	More than 10 difficult words per 100 words read	As material read to you by someone else To develop new vocabulary through listening

Adjusting reading rate—skimming, scanning, and careful reading

It is important to adjust your reading speed to suit your purposes and the task you face. When you read for enjoyment, you might read quickly. If you want to refresh your memory of a passage or get a quick impression of new material, skim the selection. **Skimming** is reading quickly over a piece of writing to find its main idea or to get a general overview of it. When you need to find a particular piece or type of information, scan the selection. In **scanning,** you run your eyes quickly over the material, looking only for key words or phrases that have to do with the information you seek.

When you read a chapter of a textbook filled with new concepts, when you follow complex written directions, or when you study for a test, read slowly, take notes, make a graphic organizer, and even reread passages in order to remember them later.

Look at the following models.

The blacktop road cut across the land in a perfectly straight line. Clifford could see the blurry horizon where the sky met the prairie. There were no flowers, no trees, no hills, and, except for the gas station where Mom had stopped the car, no buildings anywhere. Across the road stood a metal framework that Grandfather said was a windmill. At its base were six cows twitching their tails.

A volcanic eruption in the Rocky Mountains about ten million years ago and an unusually heavy rainfall in northern Nebraska in 1971 combined to create one of the most unusual and interesting museums in the United States. The rain opened a gully in a cornfield, exposing the skull of a baby rhinoceros. Scientists soon found other animal skeletons, most still intact. They have been uncovered, but left in place. Visitors can watch as paleontologists continue their work, carefully brushing away the ash from more fossils of prehistoric animals.

Which paragraph could you read more quickly? Why? What would you do to be sure you remembered the information in each paragraph?

Reading aloud

Reading aloud, alone or with others, can make a writer's work come to life and can be an enjoyable way of sharing a memorable selection. Reading a complicated paragraph aloud can also be a powerful aid to understanding. Here are some suggestions for reading aloud:

- First, read the selection silently a number of times. Then think about how to make the main ideas understandable to listeners.
- Use pauses to separate complete thoughts, and be sure you observe all punctuation marks.
- Read carefully and clearly. Vary your speed and volume to reflect the important ideas in a passage.
- Use a lively voice. Emphasize important words and phrases to make the meaning clear.
- Practice difficult words and phrases until you've mastered them.
- Practice in front of another person if possible, or use a tape recorder to hear how you sound.

Reading silently

When do you do silent reading? What environments do you find best for different kinds of silent reading? When you are reading for personal enjoyment, you may prefer silence or you may like background music. When you are using silent reading to help you learn or study, however, you should try to organize your surroundings in order to avoid distractions and interruptions.

Tips for Silent Reading and Study

- Be sure you're comfortable, but not too comfortable.
- Check your concentration regularly by asking yourself **questions** about the selection.
- **Summarize** what you've read from time to time.
- Use a **study guide** or **story map** to help you keep focused through difficult passages. Your teacher may provide a guide for you, or you might use questions provided at the beginning or end of selections in your text.
- Make a **graphic organizer,** if necessary, to understand and remember important concepts or a sequence of events.
- Take regular breaks when you need them, and vary your reading rate with the demands of the text.

Reading a Variety of Texts

Reading is one of the most enjoyable habits you'll develop in your lifetime. Throughout this textbook, you've found examples of writing from ancient myths to a play based on *Charlie and the Chocolate Factory* by Roald Dahl. This wide variety of selections can broaden your knowledge and deepen your appreciation of people and cultures. Learn to read a wide range of materials for a variety of purposes.

Reading varied sources

Strategic readers take advantage of a variety of sources for information and for entertainment. For example, to create a detailed portrait of a famous person, you might refer to sources like those listed below:

- **Textbooks** provide a basic foundation of information.
- **Letters, memos, speeches, newspapers,** and **magazines** add perspectives not available in other sources.
- **Databases, library indexes,** and **Internet sites** often supply information unavailable in other sources.
- **Novels, poems, plays,** and **anthologies,** or collections of literature, provide excellent opportunities to read for pleasure and to explore the ideas of a writer in a particular time.

Reading for various purposes

Active reading begins with thinking about a reason for reading. You may find that you have more than one purpose, or that your purposes overlap. For instance, you might read an intense and thrilling mystery, and also discover how police detectives work. The reading strategies you use to guide you through a text will depend on your purposes.

When your purpose for reading is

- **to be informed,** read slowly, take notes, construct a graphic organizer, reread, and review difficult sections.
- **to be entertained,** read at any rate that adds to your enjoyment.
- **to appreciate a writer's craft,** take time to appreciate how well others write.
- **to discover models for your own writing,** look at other writers' works to help stimulate your own ideas.
- **to take action,** be sure you understand all facts, directions, and instructions.

TRY THE STRATEGIES

Choose a topic that interests you, and read about it in at least three different sources. Decide on some sort of action to take as a result of your reading. You may write a short report, give a speech, demonstrate how something works, or try to persuade your classmates to believe or do something. Make a short presentation to your class, explaining your purpose for reading and the value of each of your sources.

Vocabulary Development

Having a good vocabulary means more than just knowing the meanings of isolated words. It means knowing the larger concepts that surround those words. The very best way to build a good vocabulary is to read widely, listen carefully, and participate actively in discussions where new words and concepts are used.

Listening

Books that may be just a little too hard for you to read on your own are often excellent choices as selections to be read aloud to you. They provide a good way to learn new vocabulary. Hearing selections read aloud also gives you a model for your own oral reading. As you hear new words, pay attention to their **context**—the words and ideas surrounding the unknown words. Guess at meanings that make sense for new words. Many times you will guess accurately if you pay careful attention.

Using experience and prior knowledge

Because of your life experiences, you know certain facts and ideas. Your experiences, called **prior knowledge,** also help you determine word meanings. For instance, if you have had experience using computers, you'll understand the following questions:

Why wasn't the diary icon still on the desktop? Had his sister the hacker invaded his files?

You may need to look beyond the dictionary meaning of a word. Here are some ways writers extend the meaning of words:

- Idioms An expression that has a meaning apart from the literal meaning of the words is called an idiom. If you are *up the creek without a paddle,* you are in a bad position with no way out. If you are told to *set the pace* for your younger brother or sister, you are being asked to set an example for that child. In each case, combine the words with prior knowledge to interpret what the expression really means.
- Multiple meanings Words can have more than one meaning, so check the context to be sure the meaning you have chosen makes sense.
  *Did I **point** out that the **point** on that stick is dangerous?*
  *Ms. Casey works at the **bank** on the **bank** of the river.*
- Figurative language Writers sometimes make comparisons by using figurative language, such as similes and metaphors.
  A **simile** uses *like* or *as* to compare two unlike things: *His laughter exploded **like** soda from a can that has been shaken.*
  A **metaphor** compares two unlike things without using *like* or *as:* *Her words of praise were sunshine on a cold, dark day.*
- Analogies A comparison based on the relationship between two things or ideas is called an **analogy.** Analogies sometimes are written like this: *fox : kit :: sheep : lamb.* To understand the analogy, try turning it into short, identical sentences. For instance, *A young fox is a kit. A young sheep is a lamb.*

Clarifying meanings with reference aids

Sometimes meanings of words and phrases can remain unclear even after using context, drawing on your personal background, and listening carefully. In that case, look to other reference aids to help clarify the meanings and usage of difficult terms.

- **Thesauruses** and books of synonyms can clarify a word by listing other words that have similar meanings. Be sure to notice what part of speech a word is, so you can determine how to use it in a sentence.

- **Dictionaries** will often be able to clear up word meanings because they provide a variety of definitions for a word and examples of each definition in a sentence. You can often find the meaning of idioms by looking in a dictionary under the main word in the phrase. Look at the following example.

> **pace** (pās) *n.* **1.** single movement made by the leg in walking; step. **2.** distance covered in a step, often used as a variable measure of length averaging from 2½ to 3½ feet. **3.a.** rate of speed in walking or running: *to quicken one's pace.* **b.** rate of speed in any movement, activity, or progression: *They worked at a hectic pace to meet the deadline.* **4.** manner of stepping, as in walking or running; gait. **5.** gait, esp. of a horse, in which both feet on the same side are lifted and put down together. **6. to keep pace with. a.** to maintain the same speed of movement as: *The child ran along, trying to keep pace with the adults.* **b.** to maintain the same rate of progress as. **7. to put (someone) through his paces.** to test or exhibit the talents or abilities of: *The animals were put through their paces for the judges.* **8. to set the pace. a.** to set the speed for others to maintain or go beyond. **b.** to be an example for others to follow: *Our store set the pace in book sales.* —*v.t.,* **paced, pac·ing. 1.** to walk back and forth across, esp. with a slow, steady gait: *He paced the room while he waited.* **2.** to measure by paces (often with *off*): *They paced off twenty feet.* **3.** to set the rate of speed for. **4.** to train (a horse) to move at a certain gait, esp. the pace. —*v.i.* **1.** to walk with slow, steady steps. **2.** (of a horse) to move with the gait of the pace. [Old French *pas* step, rate, from Latin *passus* step.]

- **Software** for a computer will often include reference materials that clarify meanings and usage for difficult words.

Using word parts and origins to determine meaning

Another way to determine the meaning of a word is to take the word apart. If you understand the meaning of the **base,** or **root,** part of a word and also know the meanings of syllables added either to the beginning or end of the base, you can usually figure out what a word means.

Word Part	Definition	Example
Root or base	The main part of a word	*urbs* means "city" in Latin
Prefix	a syllable used before a root or base word to add to or change its meaning	*Inter-* means "between" *Interurban* means "between cities"
Suffix	a syllable used after a root word to add to or change its meaning	*-ize* means "make" or "make into" *urbanize* means "make city-like"

Word origins English contains many words based on roots from ancient languages like Greek and Latin. Having some knowledge of word derivations in either of these languages can help you determine meanings, pronunciations, and spellings in English. Look at the following examples.

Root	Meaning	Example
sphere (Greek)	ball	atmosphere, hemisphere
ject (Latin)	throw	projection, eject
duct (Latin)	lead	viaduct, deduction
auto (Greek)	self	automatic, automobile

Affixes These syllables are added either to the beginning or end of the word. For example, the word *ejected* is made up of the root *ject* and the affixes *e-* and *-ed.* The prefix *e-* means "out." The suffix *-ed* indicates past tense. If you put them together, *ejected* means "threw out" or "thrown out."

Using word meanings across subjects

Have you ever learned a new word and then noticed it in different places or in different classes? The word may not mean exactly the same thing each time, but you can often use what you know about a word's meaning to help you interpret its meaning in a different context. Look at the following example from two different situations:

Literature class: *What do you think is the **theme** of that fable?*

Conversation: *This music is the **theme** for my favorite TV show.*

A theme in literature is the main idea focused on by the writer. A theme is also a melody or phrase focused on repeatedly until it becomes identified with a person or performance.

Listening to news stories and current events is a good way to increase your vocabulary. Discuss ideas and new vocabulary that you hear in news reports. Friends, teachers, and parents will have their own ideas about the many meanings that words can have, so careful listening will add to your vocabulary. Look at the model on the next page. Can you figure out the meaning of the italicized word in the first sentence of the news report?

School-board members were *unanimous* in their decision to keep the school gym and pool open throughout the summer for the use of students and their families. The fact that no member voted against the plan was a surprise to some teachers.

What strategies did you use to determine that *unanimous* means "in complete agreement"? How could you use the word in another context?

TRY THE STRATEGIES

Find a science or social studies textbook that includes a list of vocabulary words at the beginning of a chapter. Use prior knowledge or your understanding of word parts and origins to predict what the words might mean. Then read the passages where the words are located and use syntax or context to check or further refine your predictions.

Determining connotation and denotation

Determining special meanings of words is an important aid to understanding. Look at these two examples of ways to distinguish between word meanings:

- Denotation A **denotation** expresses the literal, or dictionary, meaning of a word. A word may have more than one denotation.
- Connotation When a word has an underlying value that accompanies its dictionary meaning, it has a **connotation.** If you make an intelligent comment, you sound *smart.* If you make a sassy, out-of-line comment, you may be told not to be so *smart.* In the second case, *smart* has a negative connotation.

Understanding historical influences of words

A dictionary also gives the historical background of a word. For example, in the ancient language from which many modern languages come, the root word referring to a kind of tree was *bhago.* Symbols were carved on staffs (canes or walking sticks) from the tree. Soon the root *bhago* referred to the carved surface, and then to any surface with symbols or letters. Over time spelling, meaning, and pronunciation of *bhago* changed. Today we have the word *book.*

Comprehension

The main concern you should have as you read is to understand the material. Using the best strategies at the right times will help you improve your understanding and will make reading interesting and fun.

Previewing

Before you begin to read, it's helpful to **preview** a selection.

- **Look** at the title and the illustrations that are included.
- **Read** the headings, subheadings, and anything that might be in bold letters.
- **Skim** the passage; that is, take a quick look at the whole thing.
- **Decide** what the author's purpose might be for writing.
- **Predict** what the selection will be about.
- **Set a purpose** for your own reading.

Using knowledge and experience to understand

Reading is an interactive process between you and a writer. When you combine your knowledge and experience with the words on a page, you create meaning in a selection. Drawing on this personal background is **activating prior knowledge.** To expand and extend your prior knowledge, share it in classroom discussions. Ask yourself questions like these as you read:

- What do I know about the **topic?**
- Have I seen or read about places similar to the **setting** described by the writer?
- What **experiences** have I had that compare with what I am reading?
- What **characters** from life or literature remind me of the characters or narrator in the selection?

Establishing and adjusting purposes for reading

Think about these possible purposes that you might have for reading:

- to discover something new
- to understand a process or an idea
- to interpret a writer's work and create meaning in a passage
- to enjoy a selection or be entertained by a story
- to solve problems or to perform a task

Each purpose allows for different active reading strategies. To **find information** for a report, you might skim an entire passage until you find the section you're looking for and then read more slowly. To **understand new information,** you might read slowly from beginning to end, or even reread passages that are unclear. To simply **enjoy** a piece of good writing, you may allow yourself to read quickly or slow yourself down to appreciate something beautifully written.

Whatever your reasons are for reading, it's important to be able to adjust your purposes and strategies to get the most from a selection.

Making and verifying predictions

As you read, make educated guesses about story events and outcomes. **Make predictions** before and during your reading. Using your prior knowledge and the information you have gathered in your preview, predict what you will learn or what might happen. As you read, **adjust** your prediction. Finally, **verify** your prediction. Whether your original prediction is accurate does not always matter, but careful predictions and later verifications or adjustments, based on your reading, can increase your understanding of a selection.

Monitoring and modifying reading strategies

No matter what your purposes for reading, your most important task is to understand what you have read. Ask yourself questions as you read. Monitor or check your understanding using the following strategies:

- **Summarize** what you read by answering *who, what, where, why,* and *when.*
- **Clarify** what you don't understand by careful rereading.
- **Question** important ideas and story elements.
- **Predict** what will happen next.
- **Evaluate** what you have read so far.

Tips for Monitoring Understanding

- **Reread.** If silently rereading a passage several times does not help to clear it up, try reading it aloud. Take it a sentence at a time.
- **Map out the main thoughts or ideas.** A graphic organizer can help get your thoughts on track.
- **Look for context clues.** Often a writer will include an example or a definition of a difficult word or idea somewhere in the surrounding sentence or sentences.
- **Ask questions.** Teachers, parents, and other classmates can shed light on difficult written passages if you let them.
- **Write comments** as well as questions on another piece of paper for later review or discussion.
- **Use reference aids.** Dictionaries, glossaries, thesauruses, and encyclopedias–electronic or print–provide easy access to most information.

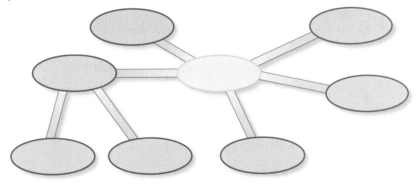

Visualizing

For many readers, creating mental pictures is a help to understanding and enjoyment. Do you use your imagination and the text to visualize characters or settings? Can you picture the steps in a process when you read nonfiction? If you can visualize what you read, selections may be more vivid, and you'll recall them better later on. Be sure, though, that what you picture is accurately based on information from the text.

TRY THE STRATEGIES

During a time when your teacher is reading aloud to you, sketch what you're hearing. If the selection is fiction, draw a character, setting, or action, based on text description. If the selection is nonfiction, draw the steps in a process or make a small diagram of a place or thing described. Later, compare your sketch with that of a partner. Use the text to adjust or verify information.

Constructing graphic organizers

Graphic organizers help you draw a picture of what you're reading, so you can sort ideas out, clear up difficult passages, and remember important ideas in a selection. Look at the following examples of good graphic organizers and notice how they are used.

Web You can show a main idea and supporting details by using a web. Put the main idea in the middle circle and the supporting details in the surrounding circles. Notice how you might include other circles branching off from the detail circles. Use those for further information about your details.

Flow chart When you want to keep track of events in time order or show a cause-and-effect relationship between events, use a flow chart. Arrange your ideas or events in the boxes, putting them in their logical order. Then draw arrows between the boxes to show how one idea or event flows into another.

Venn diagram To look at the similarities and differences between two ideas, characters, or events, use a Venn diagram. The outer portions of each circle will show how two items contrast or are different. Use the overlapping portion of the circles to show how they are the same.

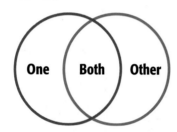

Using text structures

Writers organize ideas in a variety of ways, depending on the topic and the purpose for writing. When you find a pattern of organization or **text structure** within a selection, it's easier to identify and recall the writer's ideas. Here are four ways that writers structure or organize text, with signal words that give clues to the text structures.

Kind of Organization	Purpose	Clues
Comparison and contrast	To determine similarities and differences	Words and phrases such as *similarly, on the other hand, in contrast to, but, however*
Cause and effect	To explore the reasons for something and to examine the results of events or actions	Words and phrases such as *so, because, as a result*
Chronological order	To present events in time order	Words and phrases such as *first, next, then, later, finally*
Problem/Solution	To examine how conflicts or obstacles are overcome	Words and phrases such as *need, attempt, help, obstruction*

To find the text structure of a passage, look for **signal words and phrases** that contain clues about how the writer has arranged main ideas. Read the following models.

If Latitia wanted a party the Saturday after next, she had to get busy. **First,** she needed to make a guest list. **Then** she should make out a menu and ask someone to help her shop. The **next** steps would be making decorations, cleaning the basement and the back yard, and arranging indoor and outdoor furniture. **Finally,** Latitia wanted to choose terrific music. If she had her way, this would be a party her friends would talk about for weeks.

Signal words and phrases

On Saturday Latitia noticed that the weather had turned sultry, and that the sky was filling with dark, brooding clouds. **Because** the humidity was so high, the crepe paper decorations around the patio area drooped sadly. If it rained hard, Latitia thought, the party would be doomed. **So** she decided to quickly vacuum and dust the family room and put up the decorations there. **Because** she was working inside now, she had more available space to hang balloons and posters. Using both the family room and the basement would give her friends plenty of space to eat and dance. **As a result** of Latitia's careful planning, her party was a great success. No one seemed to hear the thunderstorm outside.

What is the basic text structure of the first model? of the second? Explain how you determined your answers.

Determining main ideas and supporting details

The most important idea in a paragraph or passage is called the **main idea.** The examples or ideas that further explain the main idea are called **supporting details.** Some main ideas are clearly stated in sentences within a passage. Other times, without directly stating a main idea, an author will suggest it by providing a variety of clues.

Many times the main idea will be the first sentence of a paragraph, but not always. A main idea might be anywhere, even in the last sentence in a passage.

A selection can have a number of main ideas in it. Each paragraph might contain a main idea, as in most nonfiction, or entire passages can have a main idea, as in both fiction and nonfiction.

When you need to find the main idea, ask yourself these questions:

- What is each sentence about?
- Is there one sentence that tells about the whole passage or that is more important than the others?
- If the main idea is not directly stated, what main idea do the supporting details point out?

Finding the main ideas will help you understand a selection. Look at the following model.

Main idea —— **The achievements of Maria Mitchell, a nineteenth-century scientist, are many.** She was the first person to discover a comet with the use of a telescope. She was the first woman admitted to the American Academy of Arts and Sciences and to the American Philosophical Society. Mitchell led the 1875 Women's Congress. She became a professor of astronomy at Vassar College, although she had been mostly self-educated. A crater on the moon has been named for Maria Mitchell to honor the achievements of this remarkable woman.

Supporting details ——

Sequencing

The order in which thoughts are arranged is called **sequence.** A good sequence is one that is logical, given the ideas in a selection. Here are three common forms of sequencing:

- **Chronological order**–time order
- **Spatial order**–the order in which things would be arranged within a certain space
- **Order of importance**–going from most important to least important or the other way around

Recognizing the sequence of something is very important when you have to follow **directions.** If you fail to follow steps in a certain order, you may not be able to accomplish your task.

Paraphrasing

When you retell something using your own words you are **paraphrasing.** You might paraphrase just the main ideas of a selection or you might retell an entire story in your own words. Paraphrasing is a useful strategy for reviewing and for checking comprehension.

Original text: *The quick snapshots of someone who is unaware that you and your camera are near are often the photos you value for years. Catch your subjects in moments that show something important about their personalities—in poses that are thoughtful, funny, or unusual.*

Paraphrase: *Take surprise snapshots of people in moments that reveal their personalities. You will value these for a long time.*

Summarizing

When you **summarize,** you relate the main ideas of a selection in a logical sequence and in your own words. You are combining three skills in one. To create a good summary, include all the main ideas and only essential supporting details.

A good summary can be easily understood by someone who has not read the whole text. Look at the following model and summary.

The Great Lakes–St. Lawrence Waterway is a major link in North America's transportation network. Users of the waterway have access to the world, since the waterway connects the heartland of the North American continent to the Atlantic Ocean. The route has been popular with many shippers because of its convenience and because travel by water is considered to be the most environmentally responsible and the safest method of transportation today.

Summary: Shipping on the Great Lakes–St. Lawrence Waterway is convenient, safe, and does little harm to the environment.

TRY THE STRATEGIES

Read "The Pied Piper of Hamelin" on page 693 of this book. On separate paper, list the main ideas in the narrative poem. Under each main idea, list the details that explain it. Use this information to write a summary of what you have read.

Drawing and supporting inferences

Writers don't always directly state what they want you to understand in a selection. By providing clues and interesting details, they suggest certain information. Whenever you combine those clues with your own background and knowledge, you are drawing an inference. An **inference** involves using your reason and experience to come up with an idea based on what an author implies or suggests. The following active reading behaviors are examples of drawing an inference.

- Inferring You infer when you use context clues plus your own knowledge to figure out what an author is suggesting.
- Predicting When you guess what a story will be about or what will happen next, you are drawing an inference.
- Drawing conclusions A conclusion is a general statement you can make and explain with reasoning, or with supporting details from a selection.
- Generalizing When you draw an inference that can apply to more than one item or group, you are making a generalization.
- Classifying When you recognize something as fitting into a category, you classify it.

Finding similarities and differences across texts

As your reading takes you across a variety of sources, **compare and contrast** the things you've read. When you look for similarities and differences in your reading selections, you'll gain a better understanding of all the material you've read. Ask yourself in what ways sources might be alike or different? What is included in one selection that might be left out of another? Why might that be?

Here are some of the ways you can compare and contrast writers' works:

- Scope Take a broad look at each entire selection. How would you compare the time periods covered? How much information is given in each nonfiction selection? How many characters and settings are involved in fiction pieces?
- Treatment Look at how each writer presents important ideas. Who tells the story? Is the narrator's attitude serious or funny? How would you compare the writers' purposes? styles?
- Organization Compare selections in terms of how writers arrange their thoughts. Is a writer following a **chronological order? a cause-and-effect order? a problem-and-solution order?** Or is the writer **comparing and contrasting?**

When you look for similarities and differences in what you've read, you'll learn to read more critically and get more out of each selection.

Distinguishing fact from opinion

When deciding whether to believe what a writer has written, you need to distinguish between fact and opinion. A **fact** is a statement that can be proved or disproved with supporting information. An **opinion,** on the other hand, is what a writer believes, based on his or her personal viewpoint. Writers can support their opinions with facts, but an opinion is something that cannot be proved. Look at the following examples of fact and opinion.

Fact: *Six Internet service providers are based in this city.*

Opinion: *The provider I use is the best one.*

When interpreting anything you read, be sure that you distinguish between statements of fact and opinion.

Answering questions

How do you decide where to look for answers to questions about selections you've read? Look at the chart below to help you decide.

Type of question	What is it?	Example	How to find the answer
Literal	Has a definite answer	What kind of animal is Anansi?	Look for direct statement in text.
Interpretive	Answer based on text and prior knowledge	What quality makes Anansi an important folktale character?	Use text information and/or prior knowledge.
Open-ended	No right or wrong answer	Does Anansi have meaning to today's readers?	Use personal background and opinions.

You may find a different type of question on a test.

Tips for Answering Test Questions

- **True or false questions** If any part of a true or false question is false, the correct answer is "false."
- **Short answer** Use complete sentences so your responses will be clear. Try to put your thoughts in a logical order.
- **Multiple choice** First read all the responses. Eliminate the answers you know are incorrect. Choose the best answer from the remaining responses.

Representing text information

After you've read in various sources, you may need to reproduce what you learned in a visual way, perhaps to present it to your class or to show the teacher that you have understood it.

- Outlines An **outline** is helpful if you are organizing information to present a report. Roman numerals, together with upper- and lower-case letters show the basic structure of the report. Look at this sample of a topic outline.

Each main topic is one of the big ideas of your subject. Suppose that your subject is surfing. The first main topic could be the history of surfing.

If you have subtopics under a main topic, there must be at least two. They must relate directly to the main topic.

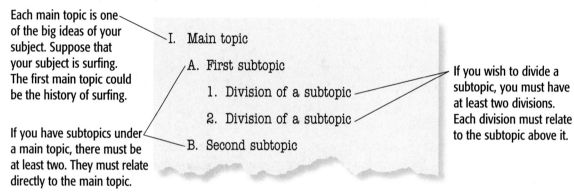

I. Main topic

A. First subtopic

   1. Division of a subtopic

   2. Division of a subtopic

B. Second subtopic

If you wish to divide a subtopic, you must have at least two divisions. Each division must relate to the subtopic above it.

- Time lines A **time line** shows the chronological order of events over a period of time. Look at the example below.

The title shows the subject of the time line. It also may include the dates covered.

Space between events shows the amount of time that passed between them. Which two events came closest together?

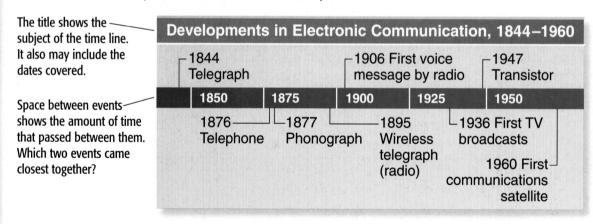

Developments in Electronic Communication, 1844–1960

1844 Telegraph		1906 First voice message by radio		1947 Transistor
1850	1875	1900	1925	1950

1876 Telephone — 1877 Phonograph — 1895 Wireless telegraph (radio) — 1936 First TV broadcasts — 1960 First communications satellite

- Graphic organizers Word webs, flow charts, Venn diagrams, and other kinds of graphic organizers can help you present information in a visual way.

Using study strategies

If you're preparing for a quiz or test, or getting ready for a class presentation, you'll want to use a study strategy that helps you organize and remember the material you've read. Here are some useful strategies.

- **Using story maps** A **story map** can help you sort out important literary elements in works of fiction. Look at the model below to see how a story map works as a tool for review.

STORY MAP

Characters	Setting
Plot Conflict (problem)	**Plot** Resolution (solution)

- **Using KWL** A KWL chart is a good way to keep track of what you are learning when you read informational text. Make three columns on a page. Label the first column *What I Know,* the second column *What I Want to Know,* and the third column *What I Learned.* Before you begin reading, list the things you already know about a topic in the first column. Preview the material and list your questions about it in the second column. When you're done reading, record what you've learned in the third column. You can add more columns to record places where you found information and places to look for more.

KWL

What I Know	What I Want to Know	What I Learned	Where I Got Information
			Where I Can Get More

- **Using SQ3R** A useful study strategy for studying subject areas like science or social studies is **SQ3R**. It stands for **s**urvey, **q**uestion, **r**ead, **r**ecord, and **r**eview. Here's how it works:
  1. **Survey** Take a quick look over the entire selection you need to study. Notice anything boldfaced. Look at any headings, sub-headings, or pictures.
  2. **Question** Think of a number of questions you'll want to answer as you read.
  3. **Read** Read the selection carefully, varying your reading rate. Try to summarize information as you read.
  4. **Record** Take notes about important ideas. Record your comments and any additional questions that come up as you read.
  5. **Review** When you've finished reading, go back over the text once again to be sure you've understood important ideas.
- **Creating and using study guides** Your teacher may provide you with a guide to focus your attention as you study. You can create your own guide by using end-of-chapter questions to focus your reading.

TRY THE STRATEGIES

Select a chapter from your social studies or science text. Use SQ3R as you read the material. Have a classmate quiz you by using end-of-chapter questions to see how well you remember what you studied.

Literary Response

Whenever you share your thoughts and feelings about something you've read, you are responding to text. You have your own learning style, so you will want to respond in ways that are comfortable for you. Some students learn best when speaking and writing, while others enjoy moving around or creating something artistic.

Tips for Responding to and Interpreting Literature

- **Discuss** what you have read, and share your views in active classroom discussions or at home.
- **Keep a journal** about what you read. Record your thoughts and feelings as well as what you've learned.
- **Take part in dramatizations, oral interpretations,** and **readers theater.** These activities allow you to present characters through actions and dialogue and give you the opportunity to use your voice, facial expressions, and body language to convey meaning.
- **Tape record** or **videotape** your oral readings or dramatizations.

Supporting responses and interpretations

Whether you respond with your mind or with your emotions, you need to support your responses by going back to the text itself. Make sure you provide details from the author's work to back up your thoughts and feelings. It is not enough to say, "I really liked the main character." You must show what you liked about him or her. Look for specific descriptions and information. Ask yourself questions like these:

- What is interesting about this story's setting?
- What do I like or dislike about this character?
- How is the overall theme or idea expressed?
- What specific details account for my views about this selection?
- How have my own experiences and prior knowledge influenced my feelings in this selection?

Identifying the purpose of a text

Authors have a variety of reasons for writing. They may simply want to **entertain** you. They may want to **inform** you about a topic. They may feel the need to **express** thoughts and emotions through a narrative or biographical essay. They also may want to **influence** your thinking so that you believe something or are motivated to act in a certain way. Knowing the author's purpose can help you understand what you read.

How can you tell what a writer's purpose is? To identify the purposes of different types of texts, use the following tips:

Tips for Identifying the Purpose of a Text

- **Look at word choices.** Authors select words according to their connotations, which carry emotional or implied meanings, as well as their denotations, or dictionary meanings.
- **Consider the intended audience.** Most selections are written with an audience in mind. A speech at a pep rally might have a different purpose than one given before the local school board.
- **Look at the structure of the text.** Writers use patterns of organization to clearly present their messages. By figuring out if a writer has used chronological order, comparison-and-contrast structure, or perhaps cause-and-effect structure, you can help determine his or her purpose.

Comparing elements across genres and across cultures

Have you ever seen a movie or a television program based on a book you read? How were they similar or different? For example, scenes may have been left out of the movie to make the plot move faster. As you look to see how the same story may vary across cultures or genres, look at similarities and differences in the following story elements.

- Characters Are all characters represented? Are some characters combined?
- Settings Is the setting presented similarly in each work? What differences affect the story as a whole?
- Themes or ideas Are important ideas well developed?
- Author's point of view Does the author's attitude affect how the story is told?
- Author's purpose Why is the author telling this story?
- Author's style How do the format and word choices influence each selection?

Analyzing inductive and deductive reasoning

As you think about works you've read, ask yourself whether the reasoning behind an author's ideas are logical. Here are two kinds of logical reasoning writers use.

Inductive reasoning When you consider a certain number of examples a writer gives you, or if you can see a particular number of cases to illustrate a point or an idea, you may be able to arrive at a **generalization**—a conclusion or general statement—by using **inductive reasoning.** If the tulips your class planted on the shady side of your school building did not grow, there is never any grass on that side of the building, and a bush planted there last year still has no leaves, you can inductively reason that the shady side of buildings may not be the best place to plant things. This logic moves from the **specific** to the **general.**

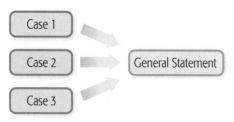

Deductive reasoning When you take a general statement and apply it to a number of specific situations, you are using **deductive reasoning.** For example, you know that most plants do not grow well in shady places. Therefore, you can deductively reason that it might not be wise to plant tulips or to expect grass to grow well on the shady side of a building. This logic moves from the **general** to the **specific.**

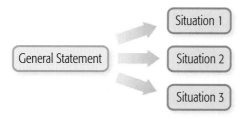

Inquiry and Research

Asking and answering questions is at the heart of being an active reader. As you read material in a variety of sources, you will think of new questions or revise the ones you started with to take new information into account. When you ask important questions and research answers, you will draw conclusions about your topic. This process should lead you to other interesting questions and areas for further study.

Forming and revising questions

Finding an interesting and relevant question or topic is an important first step in research. It deserves careful attention.

Tips for Asking Research Questions
• Think of a question or topic that interests you.
• Choose a question that helps you focus your investigation on one main idea.
• Be sure the question is not too broad or too narrow. **Too broad:** *What kinds of weather changes do other planets have?* **Better:** *Does it ever storm on Jupiter?*

Using text organizers

Once you've found an interesting question to investigate, the next step is to locate and organize information you find. Textbooks, references, magazines, and other sources use a variety of ways to help you find what you need quickly and efficiently.

- **Tables of contents** Look at a table of contents first to see whether a resource offers information you need.
- **Indexes** An index is an alphabetical listing in the back of a book of people, places, and significant topics covered in a book.
- **Headings and subheadings** Headings often identify the information that follows.
- **Graphic features** Photos, diagrams, maps, charts, graphs, captions, and other graphic features provide information at a glance.

Using multiple sources for research

Any research you do will be more interesting and balanced when you include different types of sources. Each source will provide a different slant to your topic. To find the most recent information, it may be necessary to use sources other than books. The following are some helpful resources for conducting research:

- **Print resources:** textbooks, magazines, reference books, and other specialized references
- **Nonprint information:** films, videos, and recorded interviews
- **Electronic texts:** CD-ROM encyclopedias and the Internet
- **Experts:** people who are specialists on the topic you've chosen

Interpreting graphic aids

When you're researching a topic, be sure to read and interpret the graphic aids included. **Graphic aids** let you see information at a glance. Maps, graphs, charts, and tables show you how pieces of information relate to each other.

Reading a map Most maps use a **compass rose** to show the four directions. A **legend** explains the map's symbols, and a **scale** shows you how the size of the map relates to the actual distances covered. Look at the map below.

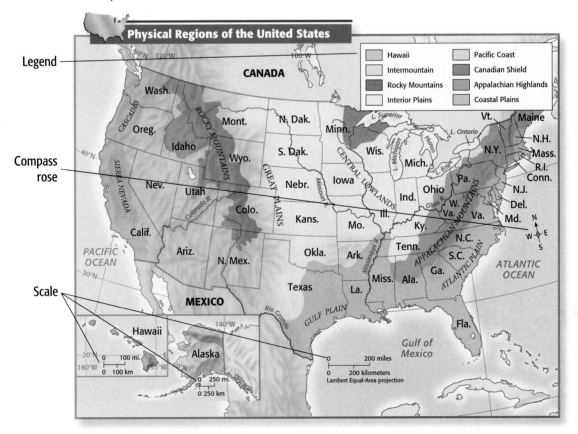

Legend

Compass rose

Scale

Physical Regions of the United States

Legend:
- Hawaii
- Intermountain
- Rocky Mountains
- Interior Plains
- Pacific Coast
- Canadian Shield
- Appalachian Highlands
- Coastal Plains

Reading a graph You can see how two or more things relate in a graph. Graphs use circles, dots, bars, or lines. Look at the graph below. Each bar represents an age group. The numbers along the side tell you the amount of time in hours. Can you interpret the information?

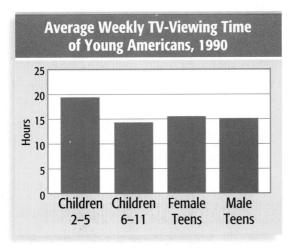

Average Weekly TV-Viewing Time of Young Americans, 1990

Reading a table A table allows you to group numbers or facts together and put them into categories so you can compare what is in each category. Look at the table below. Read the title first. You are looking at numbers of endangered species throughout the world. Now read the labels at the top of each column. The information in Column 1 identifies groups of animals on the endangered species list. Columns 2 and 3 show you the number of species in each group in the United States and in the rest of the world. What other information can you gather from this table?

Numbers of Endangered Species in the United States and the Rest of the World		
Group	U.S.	Rest of World
Mammals	36	249
Birds	57	153
Reptiles	8	58
Amphibians	6	8
Fishes	51	11
Insects	12	1

Source: Fish and Wildlife Service, U.S. Department of Interior, 1991

TRY THE STRATEGIES

Look in a current newspaper or newsmagazine to find an example of a chart, graph, or table. Explain the graphic aid briefly to the class, and analyze the information presented.

Organizing information

Now that you've read about your research topic in a variety of sources, how will you put it all together? Here are some suggestions:

- **Record** information on note cards. Use a new card for each main idea or important piece of information so you can organize and rearrange them later.
- **Summarize** information before you write it on a card. That way you'll have the main ideas in your own words.
- **Outline ideas** by putting your note cards in order and creating a written outline so you can see how subtopics and supporting information will fit under the main ideas.
- **Make a table or graph** to compare items or categories of information.

Tips for Charting Information

- Decide what information you want your audience to see at a glance.
- Decide what kind of table or graph will best show the information.
- Choose a title for your graphic aid, and label the categories horizontally and vertically.
- Check the accuracy of your information, and then plot it out carefully.
- Use different colors, if possible, to distinguish between items.

Producing projects and reports

How should you present the information you've gathered? Before you decide, think about these questions:

- How can I briefly and clearly convey important information?
- What would best capture the attention of my audience?
- What graphic aids can I use to illustrate my main ideas?
- What pattern of organization would suit this information— chronological order? comparison and contrast? cause and effect?
- Would an illustration or cartoon help to make a point?

When considering a format for your report, consider a **written** or **oral report,** a **debate,** an **interview,** or a **dramatic** or **video presentation.** Ask yourself which format would most creatively and completely present your ideas.

Drawing conclusions and asking further questions

You will certainly form opinions about your topic by the time you've finished your research. A **conclusion** is a general statement that you'll make about what you have learned. Remember that you started your research with an important question, so your answer to that question may help to form your conclusion. Pay attention to those conclusions. They may lead you to other interesting questions and areas for further reading.

Read the excerpt and the conclusion that follows. Then look at the question for further research.

StarDate: January 20, 1999

Two Storms in One

Three planets highlight the evening sky right now. Each one looks like a dazzling star.

Venus is the brightest of the three, and the lowest in the sky; it sets about an hour and a half after sunset. Well above Venus is Jupiter, which is still brighter than any of the true stars in the night sky. And higher still is Saturn, the faintest member of the trio.

All three planets are completely enshrouded by clouds, and that's one reason they all appear so bright—clouds reflect a lot of sunlight. But Jupiter's clouds are by far the most interesting to watch. They show bands of color, big swirls, and oval-shaped storms thousands of miles across.

Last year, two of those big storms merged to form a single storm as wide as Earth. The storms had raged for half a century before they joined.

There were actually three of these "white ovals," as scientists call them. The one in the middle was a little warmer than the surrounding atmosphere, while the other two were cooler. The warmer system may have acted as a buffer between the cool ones. But last year, the warm system cooled off a bit. Scientists who study the system say that it may have lost some of its punch.

When it cooled, it could no longer keep the other storms apart. They drifted toward each other, and finally merged. Scientists don't know how long this big storm will last. But Jupiter's biggest storm, the Great Red Spot, has been spinning along for at least 300 years.

Conclusion: Storms on the planet Jupiter are far more violent and long-lasting than anything we have seen on Earth.

Question for further research: Venus and Mercury are between Earth and the Sun. Are there storms on these inner planets too?

Tips for Drawing Conclusions

- Don't try to twist the facts to support your ideas.
- Don't make statements that go beyond the facts you've gathered.
- Recognize that your conclusions might be different than you originally thought.
- Be sure to record accurately where you got your information.
- Never present other people's ideas as if they were your own.

Glossary

This glossary lists the vocabulary words found in the selections in this book. The definition given is for the word as it is used in the selection; you may wish to consult a dictionary for other meanings of these words. The key below is a guide to the pronunciation symbols used in each entry.

a	at	**ō**	hope	**ng**	sing
ā	ape	**ô**	fork, all	**th**	thin
ä	father	**oo**	wood, put	**th**	this
e	end	**ōo**	fool	**zh**	treasure
ē	me	**oi**	oil	**ə**	ago, taken, pencil,
i	it	**ou**	out		lemon, circus
ī	ice	**u**	up	**'**	indicates primary stress
o	hot	**ū**	use	**'**	indicates secondary stress

A

absurdity (ab sur' də tē) *n.* something ridiculous; nonsense; p. 467

acquire (ə kwīr') *v.* to get or have as one's own; p. 8

acute (ə kūt') *adj.* sharp and strong or intense; p. 80

adaptable (ə dap' tə bəl) *adj.* able to change to meet the needs of a certain situation; p. 581

adjoining (ə joi' ning) *adj.* located next to; p. 425

agony (ag' ə nē) *n.* great pain and suffering of the mind or body; p. 504

alight (ə līt') *v.* to come down after flight; land; p. 631

allot (ə lot') *v.* to distribute or give out; p. 384

alter (ôl' tər) *v.* to make or become different; change; p. 748

amass (ə mas') *v.* to pile up; collect or gather (a great quantity); p. 255

anguish (an' gwish) *n.* great mental or physical suffering; misery; p. 654

antic (an' tik) *n.* an odd, silly, or comical action; p. 431

anticipate (an tis' ə pāt') *v.* to look forward to; expect; p. 55

apparatus (ap' ə rat' əs) *n.* something created or invented for a particular purpose; p. 343

aptitude (ap' tə tood') *n.* a natural ability; talent; p. 293

astray (ə strā') *adv.* off the right path; p. 168

audible (ô' də bəl) *adj.* capable of being heard; loud enough to be heard; p. 356

avalanche (av' ə lanch') *n.* the swift, sudden fall of a mass of snow, ice, earth, or rocks down a mountain slope; p. 569

B

badlands (bad' landz') *n.* a dry region that has numerous ridges and peaks cut by erosion, but little plant life; the Badlands is a region of South Dakota; p. 619

ban (ban) *v.* to forbid; outlaw; prohibit; p. 788

barren (bar′ ən) *adj.* having little or no plant life; empty; p. 454

bazaar (bə zär′) *n.* a place for the sale of a variety of goods; marketplace; p. 548

bearing (bār′ ing) *n.* way of carrying oneself and behaving; manner; p. 503

bemoan (bi mōn′) *v.* to express grief; cry out; p. 335

bewildering (bi wil′ dər ing) *adj.* very confusing; p. 57

blissfully (blis′ fə lē) *adv.* in an extremely happy way; joyfully; p. 391

bolt (bōlt) *v.* to dash away suddenly; p. 270

bondage (bon′ dij) *n.* slavery; p. 507

burrow (bur′ ō) *n.* a hole dug in the ground, as by a rabbit, for shelter; p. 151

C

calamity (kə lam′ ə tē) *n.* great misfortune; disaster; p. 580

camouflaged (kam′ ə fläzhd′) *adj.* concealed by a disguise that blends in with the surroundings; p. 256

capsize (kap′ sīz) *v.* to overturn; p. 429

caravan (kar′ ə van′) *n.* a number of people or vehicles traveling together, especially for safety through dangerous regions; p. 518

catastrophe (kə tas′ trə fē′) *n.* a great and sudden disaster; p. 454

cavity (kav′ ə tē) *n.* a hollow space in a tooth, caused by decay; any hollow place or hole; p. 259

chagrin (shə grin′) *n.* a feeling of annoyance or distress arising from disappointment, failure, or embarrassment; p. 540

champion (cham′ pē ən) *n.* one who fights or speaks for another person; one who defends a cause; hero; p. 670

chaos (kā′ os) *n.* complete confusion and disorder; p. 66

characterize (kar′ ik tə rīz′) *v.* to be a quality of; p. 413

clamor (klam′ ər) *n.* a loud, noisy outcry; p. 135

classic (klas′ ik) *adj.* serving as a standard, model, or guide, because of excellence or lasting appeal; p. 222

colossal (kə los′ əl) *adj.* extraordinarily large; huge; p. 748

commiserate (kə miz′ ə rāt) *v.* to express sympathy; p. 120

commonplace (kom′ ən plās′) *adj.* ordinary; not original or interesting; p. 464

compassion (kəm pash′ ən) *n.* sympathy for another's suffering combined with a desire to help; p. 390

conceive (kən sēv′) *v.* to form a mental image or idea of; imagine; p. 651

confirm (kən furm′) *v.* to uphold the truth of something; remove all doubts or suspicion; p. 364

confiscate (kon′ fis kāt′) *v.* to take away from a person or persons as a result of greater power or authority; p. 630

confrontation (kon′ frun tā′ shən) *n.* a face-to-face meeting; p. 413

conquest (kon′ kwest) *n.* the act of taking control over people or territory; p. 269

consequence (kon′ sə kwens′) *n.* the result of an earlier action or condition; effect; p. 332

console (kən sōl′) *v.* to comfort or cheer someone who is sad or disappointed; p. 386

conspiracy (kən spir′ ə sē) *n.* the act of secretly planning together, especially for an illegal purpose; p. 773

consumption (kən sump′ shən) *n.* the act of eating, drinking, or using up; p. 46

contempt (kən tempt′) *n.* a feeling toward something or someone considered to be low or worthless; scorn; p. 273

contrary (kon′ trer ē) *adj.* opposite, entirely different; p. 540

convenient (kən vēn′ yənt) *adj.* favorable to one's needs or purposes; providing advantage; p. 643

coordinator (kō ôr′ də nā′ tər) *n.* one who brings people or events into proper order; p. 219

cope (kōp) *v.* to deal with something successfully; p. 48

corrupt (kə rupt′) v. to change from good to bad; make spoiled, evil, dishonest; p. 549

credibility (kred′ ə bil′ ə tē) n. the power to encourage or inspire belief; believability; p. 357

culprit (kul′ prit) n. one who is guilty of some crime or misdeed; offender; p. 758

cumbersome (kum′ bər səm) adj. not easily handled or carried; clumsy; awkward; p. 790

cunning (kun′ ing) n. craftiness; intelligence; p. 134

D

debut (dā bū′) n. a beginning, as of a career or course of action; first public appearance; p. 219

decent (dē′ sənt) adj. courteous, proper; p. 645

decline (di klīn′) v. to become less; fall into a worse condition; p. 294

defiance (di fī′ əns) n. bold resistance to authority; p. 66

dejection (di jek′ shən) n. sadness; low spirits; p. 391

dense (dens) adj. thick; difficult to get through; p. 168

desolate (des′ ə lit) adj. deserted or uninhabited; p. 449

destined (des′ tind) adj. fixed or decided beforehand; p. 502

detest (di test′) v. to dislike greatly; hate; p. 654

devastate (dev′ əs tāt′) v. to cause great pain, damage, or destruction; overwhelm; p. 583

devise (di vīz′) v. to think out; invent; plan; p. 333

devour (di vour′) v. to eat up greedily; p. 334

discredit (dis kred′ it) v. to reject as untrue; cause to be doubted or disbelieved; p. 587

discreet (dis krēt′) adj. showing care and good judgment; cautious; p. 356

dislodge (dis loj′) v. to move or force out of a place or position; p. 552

dismal (diz′ məl) adj. gloomy; miserable; cheerless; p. 389

dispute (dis pūt′) n. a difference of opinion; argument or quarrel; p. 616

divert (di vurt′) v. to draw the attention away; distract; p. 364

dominant (dom′ ə nənt) adj. having the greatest power or force; controlling; p. 390

dominate (dom′ ə nāt) v. to rule or control; p. 502

dominion (də min′ yən) n. the territory or country under the authority of a particular ruler or government; p. 341

drab (drab) adj. lacking brightness; dull; cheerless; p. 718

drone (drōn) n. a steady, low, humming sound; p. 9

E

eddy (ed′ ē) n. small whirlwind or whirlpool; p. 168

embrace (em brās′) v. to hug; p. 626

emerge (i murj′) v. to come out; p. 66

emphatically (em fat′ i kəl ē) adv. forcefully; p. 24

encounter (en koun′ tər) n. a direct meeting, as between enemies in conflict or in battle; an unexpected meeting; p. 724

endearing (en dēr′ ing) adj. arousing affection or warm feelings; lovable; p. 161

endure (en door′) v. to hold up under (pain or other hardship); put up with; p. 424

ensue (en sōō′) v. to come afterward or as a result; p. 631

envious (en′ vē əs) adj. jealous; p. 627

evidently (ev′ ə dent′ lē) adv. clearly; p. 426

exasperated (ig zas′ pə rā′ tid) adj. angered or greatly annoyed; irritated; p. 631

exile (eg′ zīl) n. one who is forced to leave his or her home, community, or country; p. 332

exotic (ig zot′ ik) adj. strangely beautiful or interesting; unusual; foreign; p. 722

expand (iks pand′) v. to develop (something) in greater detail; make larger or more complete; p. 773

exploit (eks′ ploit) n. a heroic deed; p. 415

extravagantly (iks trav′ ə gənt lē) adv. going beyond reasonable limits; p. 81

F

fate (fāt) *n.* a power that determines events before they happen; p. 438

feature (fē′ chər) *n.* a part or quality that makes a thing outstanding or different from similar things; p. 516

feeble (fē′ bəl) *adj.* lacking physical strength; weak; p. 620

fell (fel) *v.* to cut down; chop; p. 566

flail (flāl) *v.* to wave or swing, especially swiftly or violently; p. 219

flounder (floun′ dər) *v.* to move in an awkward way; p. 430

fluent (fl‌oo′ ənt) *adj.* spoken or written smoothly and effortlessly; p. 464

flustered (flus′ tərd) *adj.* embarrassed, nervous, or confused; p. 91

forlorn (fôr lôrn′) *adj.* sad because of being abandoned; p. 287

frail (frāl) *adj.* lacking in strength; weak; p. 311

frustrating (frus′ trāt ing) *adj.* disappointing or irritating; p. 159

fulfill (fool fil′) *v.* to carry out or bring to completion; cause to happen; p. 161

futile (fū′ til) *adj.* useless or hopeless; not effective; p. 583

G

gait (gāt) *n.* a particular manner of moving on foot; p. 119

gape (gāp) *v.* to stare in wonder or surprise, often with the mouth open; p. 312

glazed (glāzd) *adj.* covered with a smooth, shiny coating; p. 168

gratification (grat′ ə fi kā′ shən) *n.* the condition of being pleased or satisfied; p. 465

gravely (grāv′ lē) *adv.* very seriously; p. 97

H

heed (hēd) *n.* careful attention; notice; p. 315

heedful (hēd′ fəl) *adj.* giving careful attention (to); mindful; p. 521

hesitantly (hez′ ət ənt lē) *adv.* in a way that shows one is undecided or fearful; p. 11

hoax (hōks) *n.* a trick, fraud, or practical joke; p. 727

horde (hôrd) *n.* a large group; crowd; p. 342

hostile (host′ əl) *adj.* feeling or showing strong dislike; p. 20

hover (huv′ ər) *v.* to remain as if suspended in the air over a particular spot; p. 274

hygiene (hī′ jēn) *n.* practices that support good health; p. 219

I

immense (i mens′) *adj.* of great size; huge; p. 438

imply (im plī′) *v.* to suggest without directly stating; p. 587

impudence (im′ pyə dəns) *n.* speech or behavior that is offensively forward or rude; p. 270

impulse (im′ puls) *n.* an internal force that causes one to act without thinking; p. 777

incompetent (in kom′ pət ənt) *adj.* not having enough ability; not capable; p. 79

indifference (in dif′ ər əns) *n.* a lack of feeling or concern; p. 67

industrious (in dus′ trē əs) *adj.* steady, hard-working; p. 424

infest (in fest′) *v.* to occur in large numbers so as to be harmful or troublesome; overrun; p. 746

inscription (in skrip′ shən) *n.* something that is written, carved, or marked on a surface; p. 235

insistence (in sis′ təns) *n.* the act of taking a stand and sticking strongly to it; determination; p. 632

insolent (in′ sə lənt) *adj.* boldly disrespectful; p. 632

inspire (in spīr′) *v.* to be the cause or source of something; p. 162

instinctively (in stingk′ tiv lē) *adv.* in a way that comes naturally; p. 9

intellectual (int′ əl ek′ ch‌oo əl) *n.* one who tries to know and understand things mainly through thinking; p. 290

intensely (in tens′ lē) *adv.* very strongly; p. 790

intently (in tent′ lē) *adv.* in a focused way; with attention; p. 222

intrigue (in trēg′) *v.* to arouse the curiosity or interest of; fascinate; p. 294

invariably (in vār′ ē ə blē) *adv.* always; without exception; p. 653

irony (ī′ rə nē) *n.* an event or result that is the opposite of what was expected; p. 82

J

jargon (jär′ gən) *n.* terms used in certain art, science, or other fields that may not be understood by outsiders; p. 224

jaunty (jôn′ tē) *adj.* lively and carefree; p. 94

K

keen (kēn) *adj.* highly sensitive; sharp; p. 551

L

laden (lād′ ən) *adj.* loaded; weighed down; burdened; p. 318

lair (lār) *n.* a home or resting place, especially of a wild animal; p. 133

lament (lə ment′) *v.* to express sorrow or regret; p. 654

laughingstock (laf′ ing stok′) *n.* a person or thing that is made fun of; p. 260

lavishly (lav′ ish lē) *adv.* abundantly; generously; p. 42

limelight (līm′ līt) *n.* the center of interest or attention; p. 218

listlessly (list′ lis lē) *adv.* in a way that shows little energy, interest, or concern; p. 790

literally (lit′ ər ə lē) *adv.* without exaggeration; actually; p. 541

lofty (lôf′ tē) *adj.* high in rank, character, or quality; elevated; p. 278

luminous (lōō′ mə nəs) *adj.* shining; bright; p. 288

lunge (lunj) *v.* to make a sudden forward movement; charge; p. 644

lurch (lurch) *v.* to move suddenly in an uneven manner; plunge forward or to the side; p. 552

lure (loor) *n.* a powerful attraction that is hard to resist; temptation; p. 337

lurk (lurk) *v.* to stay hidden, ready to attack; p. 122

M

maim (mām) *v.* to injure so that a part of the body is lost or unusable; p. 142

majestic (mə jes′ tik) *adj.* impressive; grand; p. 632

makeshift (māk′ shift′) *adj.* suitable as a temporary substitute for the proper or desired thing; p. 411

maneuver (mə nōō′ vər) *v.* to move or handle skillfully; p. 79

manipulative (mə nip′ yə lā′ tiv) *adj.* able to influence or control in a clever, often unfair way; p. 778

meager (mē′ gər) *adj.* not enough in amount or quantity; p. 292

meander (mē an′ dər) *v.* to wander aimlessly; p. 119

meekly (mēk′ lē) *adv.* in a patient and mild manner; gently; p. 643

menacing (men′ əs ing) *adj.* threatening; dangerous; p. 22

merely (mēr′ lē) *adv.* no more than; only; p. 618

mimicry (mim′ ik rē) *n.* the act of copying closely; imitation; p. 71

mingle (ming′ gəl) *v.* to join together; mix; p. 224

mishap (mis′ hap′) *n.* an unfortunate accident; p. 24

morsel (môr′ səl) *n.* a small portion or quantity; p. 742

mortified (môr′ tə fīd′) *adj.* greatly embarrassed; p. 43

N

nocturnal (nok turn′ əl) *adj.* active at night; p. 532

O

obsessed (əb sest´) *adj.* concentrating too much on a single emotion or idea; p. 389

overseer (ō´ vər sē´ ər) *n.* one who watches over and directs the work of laborers; p. 373

oversight (ō´ vər sīt´) *n.* a careless mistake; p. 657

P

pang (pang) *n.* a sudden sharp feeling of pain or distress; p. 21

parched (pärcht) *adj.* severely in need of rain; very dry; p. 452

pelt (pelt) *v.* to strike repeatedly by throwing something; p. 256

penetrate (pen´ ə trāt´) *v.* to pass into or through; p. 168

perilously (per´ ə ləs lē) *adv.* dangerously; riskily; p. 428

periodically (pēr´ ē od´ i kəl ē) *adv.* once in a while; p. 79

perish (per´ ish) *v.* to die, especially in a violent way or unexpectedly; p. 535

persist (pər sist´) *v.* to continue firmly and steadily, especially in the face of difficulty; p. 541

perspective (pər spek´ tiv) *n.* the ability to see things in relationship to one another; point of view; p. 413

petrify (pet´ rə fī´) *v.* to paralyze with astonishment, fear, or horror; p. 535

plight (plīt) *n.* an unfortunate, distressing, or dangerous situation; difficulty; p. 312

pondering (pon´ dər ing) *n.* the act of thinking over carefully; serious thought; p. 551

potential (pə ten´ shəl) *adj.* capable of being; p. 411

practical (prak´ ti kəl) *adj.* sensible about everyday activities, work, and so on; p. 516

prejudice (prej´ ə dis) *n.* an unfavorable opinion or a judgment formed unfairly; p. 413

principle (prin´ sə pəl) *n.* a basic law, truth, or belief; rule of personal conduct; p. 465

procession (prə sesh´ ən) *n.* a steady forward movement, especially in a grand, formal manner; p. 277

proclaim (prə clām´) *v.* to declare publicly; announce; p. 669

proposition (prop´ ə zish´ ən) *n.* something offered for consideration; suggestion; p. 120

prosper (pros´ pər) *v.* to grow, especially in wealth; to succeed; p. 508

Q

quarry (kwôr´ ē) *n.* anything that is hunted or pursued, especially an animal; p. 132

quaver (kwā´ vər) *n.* a trembling or shaking; p. 779

quest (kwest) *n.* a search; pursuit; p. 643

R

ravage (rav´ ij) *v.* to destroy violently; ruin; p. 640

realm (relm) *n.* a kingdom; any area of knowledge, power, or control; p. 337

reconciled (rek´ ən sīld´) *adj.* once again friendly, as after an argument or disagreement; p. 657

reflective (ri flek´ tiv) *adj.* showing serious and careful thinking; thoughtful; p. 289

register (rej´ is tər) *v.* to show or record, as on a scale; indicate; p. 569

relentless (ri lent´ ləs) *adj.* unyielding; endless; p. 589

relieve (ri lēv´) *v.* to remove or make easier to bear; lessen; reduce; p. 569

relish (rel´ ish) *v.* to take pleasure in; enjoy; p. 71

remorse (ri môrs´) *n.* a deep, painful feeling of guilt or sorrow for wrongdoing; p. 658

rendition (ren dish´ ən) *n.* a performance; p. 357

replenish (ri plen´ ish) *v.* to provide a new supply for; restock; p. 79

reprove (ri proov´) *v.* to scold; p. 56

repulsive (ri puls′ iv) *adj.* causing dislike; disgusting; p. 739

resent (ri zent′) *v.* to feel anger toward a person or thing; p. 56

resigned (ri zīnd′) *adj.* accepting or giving in unhappily but without resistance or complaint; p. 234

resort (ri zôrt′) *v.* to make use of something for support or relief; p. 161

retort (ri tôrt′) *v.* to reply, especially in a sharp, witty, or clever manner; p. 315

retreat (ri trēt′) *v.* to withdraw, as from battle; pull back; p. 257

revelation (rev′ ə lā′ shən) *n.* information that had been unknown or secret and is now revealed; p. 363

reverently (rev′ ər ənt lē) *adv.* in a way that shows deep honor; respectfully; p. 24

revert (ri vurt′) *v.* to return to an earlier condition, behavior, or belief; p. 454

S

saunter (sôn′ tər) *v.* to walk in a leisurely way; stroll; p. 99

savor (sā′ vər) *v.* to take great delight in; p. 10

scoff (skof) *v.* to speak with scorn; mock; p. 716

scour (skour) *v.* to make a thorough search of; p. 130

scruffy (skruf′ ē) *adj.* worn or dirty; shabby; p. 374

serene (sə rēn′) *adj.* calm; peaceful; undisturbed; p. 344

sham (sham) *adj.* pretended or staged; fake; imitation; p. 547

sharecropper (shār′ krop′ ər) *n.* a farmer who farms land owned by someone else and shares the crop or the proceeds from its sale with the landowner; p. 5

shuffle (shuf′ əl) *v.* to walk by dragging the feet; p. 151

sideline (sīd′ līn′) *n.* the side boundary line of a playing field; p. 89

signify (sig′ nə fī′) *v.* to represent; mean; p. 465

singe (sinj) *n.* a burning or scorching, especially at the tip or edge; p. 337

skirmish (skur′ mish) *n.* a brief or minor conflict; p. 385

slither (slith′ ər) *v.* to move along with a sliding or gliding motion, as a snake; p. 436

smugly (smug′ lē) *adv.* in a self-satisfied way; p. 43

snowball (snō′ bôl) *v.* to grow rapidly larger in size or importance; p. 540

solace (sol′ is) *n.* relief from sorrow; comfort; p. 345

solemn (sol′ əm) *adj.* serious; p. 93

spellbound (spel′ bound) *adj.* held, as if by magic; fascinated; charmed; p. 721

spitefully (spīt′ fəl lē) *adv.* in a way that shows bad feelings toward another; hatefully; p. 130

splendor (splen′ dər) *n.* a great display, as of riches or beautiful objects; p. 171

splurge (splurj) *v.* to spend money without worrying; p. 386

stodgy (stoj′ ē) *adj.* heavy and slow in movement; dull and lacking interest; p. 547

straggler (strag′ lər) *n.* one who lags behind the main group; p. 438

straightaway (strāt′ ə wā′) *adv.* at once; immediately; p. 375

stupendous (stoo pen′ dəs) *adj.* causing surprise or amazement; p. 357

succumb (sə kum′) *v.* to yield to a wound or disease; die; p. 533

sulking (sulk′ ing) *adj.* silent and unfriendly; bad-tempered; p. 233

sullenly (sul′ ən lē) *adv.* in a sulky or gloomy way due to feeling angry or hurt; p. 140

superb (soo purb′) *adj.* of superior quality; fine; first-rate; p. 275

swagger (swag′ ər) *v.* to walk or behave in a bold, rude, or proud way; p. 437

systematic (sis′ tə mat′ ik) *adj.* well-organized; following a certain way of doing things; p. 45

T

tamper (tam′ pər) *v.* to interfere or meddle in a way that causes harm; p. 759

taunt (tônt) *n.* an insulting remark; p. 21

tedious (tē′ dē əs) *adj.* boring; tiresome; p. 716

threadbare (thred′ bār′) *adj.* shabby; worn-out; p. 312

timidly (tim′ id lē) *adv.* lacking courage; shyly; p. 643

tolerate (tol′ ə rāt′) *v.* to endure; put up with; p. 582

touching (tuch′ ing) *adj.* affecting or appealing to the emotions; heartwarming; p. 161

traitor (trā′ tər) *n.* one who betrays one's country; p. 672

treacherous (trech′ ər əs) *adj.* dangerous; p. 256

trek (trek) *n.* a journey, especially one that is slow and difficult; p. 505

trifling (trī′ fling) *n.* the act of treating or handling something as if it had little value or importance; p. 56

troublesome (trub′ əl səm) *adj.* causing trouble, p. 150

twinge (twinj) *n.* a sudden, sharp feeling of pain, grief, shame, and so on; p. 776

U

unique (ū nēk′) *adj.* having no like or equal; p. 70

unmindful (un mīnd′ fəl) *adj.* not aware; p. 71

unsanitary (un san′ ə ter′ ē) *adj.* dirty in a way that could cause disease; unclean; p. 92

V

vainly (vān′ lē) *adv.* without success; p. 317

veranda (və ran′ də) *n.* a long porch, usually with a roof, along one or more sides of a house; p. 372

verge (vurj) *n.* the point just before something occurs or begins; the edge; p. 56

virtually (vur′ choo ə lē) *adv.* for all practical purposes; truthfully; p. 539

vivid (viv′ id) *adj.* forming clear or lifelike pictures in the mind; lively; p. 776

vulnerable (vul′ nər ə bəl) *adj.* capable of being damaged or wounded; easily hurt; p. 588

W

warily (wār′ ə lē) *adv.* in a cautious manner; p. 502

wedge (wej) *v.* to push or crowd into a narrow space; p. 438

well (wel) *v.* to flow up or out; gush; rise; p. 540

writhe (rīth) *v.* to move with a twisting motion; p. 342

Y

yearning (yur′ ning) *n.* a strong feeling of longing; p. 68

yield (yēld) *v.* to give forth; produce; p. 568

Spanish Glossary

A

absurdity/absurdo *s.* algo ridículo; algo que no tiene sentido; p. 467

acquire/adquirir *v.* obtener, comprar o conseguir algo; p. 8

acute/agudo *adj.* fuerte o intenso; p. 80

adaptable/adaptable *adj.* que cambia o se ajusta a las necesidades de cierta situación; p. 581

adjoining/adyacente *adj.* ubicado al lado; p. 425

agony/agonía *s.* gran dolor y sufrimiento mental o físico; p. 504

alight/aterrizar *v.* tocar tierra después de un vuelo; p. 631

allot/asignar *v.* distribuir o repartir; p. 384

alter/alterar *v.* cambiar o hacer que algo cambie; modificar; p. 748

amass/amontonar *v.* acumular; reunir en gran cantidad; p. 255

anguish/angustia *s.* gran sufrimiento físico o mental; miseria; p. 654

antic/bufonada *s.* acción extraña, tonta o cómica; p. 431

anticipate/anticipar *v.* esperar que algo ocurra; aguardar; p. 55

apparatus/aparato *s.* algo creado o inventado con un fin particular; p. 343

aptitude/aptitud *s.* habilidad natural; talento; p. 293

astray/descarriado *adv.* fuera del camino; por mal camino; extraviado; p. 168

audible/audible *adj.* que se puede oír; con el suficiente volumen para escucharse; p. 356

avalanche/avalancha *s.* caída rápida y repentina de una masa de nieve, hielo, tierra o rocas por una pendiente; p. 569

B

badlands/tierras baldías *s.* región seca con muchas rocas y escasa vegetación debido a la erosión; los Badlands son una región de Dakota del Sur; p. 619

ban/prohibir *v.* censurar; p. 788

barren/yermo *adj.* que tiene poca o ninguna vegetación; desértico; p. 454

bazaar/bazar *s.* lugar donde se venden diversos artículos; mercado; p. 548

bearing/porte *s.* apariencia y actitud; p. 503

bemoan/lamentar *v.* expresar dolor; gemir; p. 335

bewildering/desconcertante *adj.* que causa confusión; p. 57

blissfully/jubilosamente *adv.* de un modo muy feliz; alegremente; p. 391

bolt/arrancar *v.* salir a toda prisa y de repente; p. 270

bondage/cautiverio *s.* esclavitud; servidumbre; p. 507

burrow/madriguera *s.* agujero donde viven los conejos y otros animales; p. 151

C

calamity/calamidad *s.* gran desdicha; desastre; p. 580

camouflaged/camuflado *adj.* oculto o encubierto de forma que se confunde con el medio ambiente; p. 256

capsize/volcar *v.* derribar; voltear; p. 429

caravan/caravana *s.* grupo de personas o vehículos que viajan juntos, especialmente por motivos de seguridad, a través de regiones peligrosas; p. 518

catastrophe/catástrofe *s.* desastre repentino de grandes dimensiones; p. 454

cavity/caries *s.* picadura o hueco en un diente causada por descomposición; p. 259

chagrin/mortificación *s.* sensación de molestia o angustia debida a un disgusto, fracaso o vergüenza; p. 540

champion/paladín *s.* el que lucha o habla por otra persona; el que defiende una causa; héroe; p. 670

chaos/caos *s.* total confusión y desorden; p. 66

characterize/caracterizar *v.* determinar los atributos de una persona o cosa; p. 413

clamor/algarabía *s.* ruido fuerte y continuo; p. 135

classic/clásico *adj.* que sirve como norma, modelo o guía debido a cualidades duraderas o excelencia; p. 222

colossal/colosal *adj.* extraordinariamente grande; inmenso; p. 748

commiserate/compadecer *v.* expresar lástima; p. 120

commonplace/común *adj.* ordinario; que no es original ni interesante; p. 464

compassion/compasión *s.* expresión de lástima por el sufrimiento ajeno, junto con el deseo de ayudar; p. 390

conceive/concebir *v.* formarse una imagen o idea mental; imaginar; p. 651

confirm/confirmar *v.* sostener la verdad de algo; descartar toda duda o sospecha; p. 364

confiscate/confiscar *v.* quitarle algo a una persona o grupo de personas por medio del poder o la autoridad; p. 630

confrontation/confrontación *s.* enfrentamiento entre dos o más personas; p. 413

conquest/conquista *s.* acto de tomar control sobre un pueblo o territorio; p. 269

consequence/consecuencia *s.* resultado de una acción o condición anterior; efecto; p. 332

console/consolar *v.* animar o alentar a alguien que sufre o tiene un problema; p. 386

conspiracy/conspiración *s.* acto de planear secretamente en conjunto, especialmente con fines ilegales; p. 773

consumption/consumo *s.* acto de comer, beber o usar; p. 46

contempt/desdén *s.* desprecio hacia alguien o algo; p. 273

contrary/contrario *adj.* opuesto; totalmente diferente; p. 540

convenient/conveniente *adj.* que se ajusta a las necesidades o propósitos; favorable; p. 643

coordinator/coordinador *s.* el que organiza a un grupo o coordina un suceso; p. 219

cope/salir adelante *v.* enfrentar algo con éxito; p. 48

corrupt/corromper *v.* cambiar de bueno a malo; pervertir; dañar o volver deshonesto; p. 549

credibility/credibilidad *s.* confianza; p. 357

culprit/acusado *s.* culpado de un crimen o delito; ofensor; p. 758

cumbersome/engorroso *adj.* que no es fácil de agarrar o llevar; complicado; difícil; p. 790

cunning/astuto *adj.* pícaro; socarrón; p. 134

D

debut/debut *s.* estreno; comienzo de una carrera o actividad; primera aparición en público; p. 219

decent/decente *adj.* cortés, decoroso; p. 645

decline/declinar *v.* decaer; deteriorarse; p. 294

defiance/desafío *s.* resistencia a la autoridad; p. 66

dejection/aflicción *s.* tristeza; desaliento; p. 391

dense/denso *adj.* espeso o compacto; difícil de atravesar; p. 168

desolate/desolado *adj.* desértico o inhabitado; p. 449

destined/destinado *adj.* determinado o dispuesto de antemano; p. 502

detest/detestar *v.* despreciar; odiar; p. 654

devastate/devastar *v.* causar gran dolor, daño o destrucción; arruinar; p. 583

devise/ingeniar *v.* idear; inventar; trazar un plan; p. 333

devour/devorar *v.* comer con gran apetito; tragar rápidamente; p. 334

discredit/desacreditar *v.* desprestigiar; hacer que algo o alguien parezca dudoso o falso; p. 587

discreet/discreto *adj.* que demuestra sensatez y cuidado al actuar; cauto; p. 356

dislodge/desalojar *v.* sacar a la fuerza de un lugar o de una posición; p. 552

dismal/desconsolador *adj.* sombrío; miserable; triste; p. 389

dispute/disputa *s.* diferencia de opinión; discusión; altercado; p. 616

divert/distraer *v.* apartar la atención de algo; p. 364

dominant/dominante *adj.* que tiene poder para controlar; p. 390

dominate/dominar *v.* mandar o controlar; p. 502

dominion/dominio *s.* territorio o país bajo la autoridad de un gobernante o gobierno; p. 341

drab/opaco *adj.* que carece de brillo; apagado; triste; p. 718

drone/zumbido *s.* sonido constante, bajo y monótono; p. 9

E

eddy/remolino *s.* pequeño torbellino o corriente en círculos; p. 168

embrace/abrazar *v.* estrechar entre los brazos p. 626

emerge/emerger *v.* salir; surgir; p. 66

emphatically/enfáticamente *adv.* de modo enérgico; p. 24

encounter/encuentro *s.* acto de coincidir en un punto dos o más personas, como dos enemigos que se enfrentan en un conflicto o batalla; reunión inesperada; p. 724

endearing/encantador *adj.* que despierta afecto o sentimientos cálidos; adorable; p. 161

endure/soportar *v.* aguantar un dolor u otra circunstancia difícil; p. 424

ensue/sobrevenir *v.* que ocurre o surge como resultado de algo; p. 631

envious/envidioso *adj.* celoso; p. 627

evidently/evidentemente *adv.* claramente; p. 426

exasperated/exasperado *adj.* enfurecido o muy molesto; irritado; p. 631

exile/exilado *s.* el que ha tenido que dejar su hogar, comunidad o país; p. 332

exotic/exótico *adj.* con una belleza o atractivo extraño; raro; foráneo; p. 722

expand/expandir *v.* ampliar o completar algo; ensanchar; p. 773

exploit/proeza *s.* hazaña o acto heroico; p. 415

extravagantly/extravagantemente *adv.* que se sale de lo adecuado o normal; p. 81

F

fate/hado *s.* poder que determina los sucesos antes de que ocurran; destino; p. 438

feature/característica *s.* componente o cualidad que hace que algo sobresalga o sea diferente de cosas similares; p. 516

feeble/endeble *adj.* sin fortaleza física; débil; p. 620

fell/talar *v.* cortar; podar; p. 566

flail/agitar *v.* sacudir o hacer un ademán rápido y brusco; p. 219

flounder/moverse torpemente *v.* forcejear o caminar con dificultad; p. 430

fluent/fluente *adj.* que se habla o escribe de modo natural y sin esfuerzo; p. 464

flustered/turbado *adj.* avergonzado, nervioso o confundido; p. 91

forlorn/solitario *adj.* triste por haber sido abandonado; p. 287

frail/frágil *adj.* que no tiene fuerza; débil; p. 311

frustrating/frustrante *adj.* que causa decepción o irritación; p. 159

fulfill/cumplir *v.* efectuar a cabalidad; llevar a cabo o hacer realidad; p. 161

futile/fútil *adj.* inútil o insignificante; que no es efectivo; p. 583

G

gait/andadura *s.* modo particular de caminar; p. 119

gape/boquear *v.* mirar con asombro o sorpresa, a menudo con la boca abierta; p. 312

glazed/glaseado *adj.* cubierto con una capa suave y brillante; p. 168

gratification/satisfacción *s.* placer; agrado; p. 465

gravely/gravemente *adv.* muy seriamente; p. 97

H

heed/atención *s.* mucho cuidado o interés; p. 315

heedful/atento *adj.* que hace caso o presta atención; p. 521

hesitantly/vacilantemente *adv.* con dudas o inseguridad; p. 11

hoax/engaño *s.* truco, fraude o broma; p. 727

horde/horda *s.* grupo grande; multitud; p. 342

hostile/hostil *adj.* que siente o demuestra gran desagrado; p. 20

hover/revolotear *v.* permanecer suspendido en el aire o en un mismo lugar; p. 274

hygiene/higiene *s.* hábitos que promueven una buena salud; p. 219

I

immense/inmenso *adj.* de gran tamaño; enorme; p. 438

imply/implicar *v.* sugerir sin decirlo directamente; p. 587

impudence/impudencia *s.* comportamiento atrevido o descarado; p. 270

impulse/impulso *s.* fuerza interna que hace actuar sin pensar; p. 777

incompetent/incompetente *adj.* que no tiene suficiente habilidad; incapaz; p. 79

indifference/indiferencia *s.* falta de interés o preocupación; p. 67

industrious/industrioso *adj.* aplicado; trabajador; hacendoso; p. 424

infest/infestar *v.* ocurrir en grandes cantidades, de modo que causa daño o dificultades; plagar; p. 746

inscription/inscripción *s.* algo que está escrito, tallado o marcado en una superficie; p. 235

insistence/insistencia *s.* acto de tomar una posición y no echarse para atrás; determinación; p. 632

insolent/insolente *adj.* que falta el respeto abiertamente; p. 632

inspire/inspirar *v.* ser la causa o fuente de algo; p. 162

instinctively/instintivamente *adv.* de modo natural; p. 9

intellectual/intelectual *s.* quien trata de captar y entender las cosas a través de la inteligencia; p. 290

intensely/intensamente *adv.* muy fuertemente; p. 790

intently/atentamente *adv.* con mucha atención o cuidado; p. 222

intrigue/intrigar *v.* despertar la curiosidad o el interés; fascinar; p. 294

invariably/invariablemente *adv.* siempre; sin excepción; p. 653

irony/ironía *s.* suceso o resultado opuesto a lo que se esperaba; p. 82

J

jargon/jerga *s.* palabras usadas en cierto arte, ciencia o campo, que quizá otros no entiendan; p. 224

jaunty/garboso *adj.* vivaz y despreocupado; p. 94

K

keen/agudo *adj.* muy sensible; despierto; p. 551

L

laden/cargado *adj.* repleto; atiborrado; p. 318

lair/guarida *s.* vivienda o lugar de descanso, especialmente de un animal salvaje; p. 133

lament/lamentar *v.* expresar pena o arrepentimiento; p. 654

laughingstock/hazmerreír *s.* persona o cosa de la que otros se burlan; p. 260

lavishly/pródigamente *adv.* abundantemente; generosamente; p. 42

limelight/punto focal *s.* punto de interés o atención; p. 218

listlessly/desganadamente *adv.* de un modo que muestra poca energía, interés o preocupación; p. 790

literally/literalmente *adv.* sin exagerar; exactamente; p. 541

lofty/encumbrado *adj.* que tiene un rango, posición o cualidad elevada; poderoso; p. 278

luminous/luminoso *adj.* resplandeciente; brillante; p. 288

lunge/arremeter *v.* moverse hacia adelante de manera repentina; atacar; p. 644

lurch/dar tumbos *v.* moverse de repente meciéndose hacia adelante o hacia los lados; p. 552

lure/tentación *s.* atracción poderosa a la cual es difícil resistirse; p. 337

lurk/acechar *v.* estar escondido y listo para atacar; p. 122

M

maim/lisiar *v.* herir de tal forma que una parte del cuerpo se pierde o queda inservible; p. 142

majestic/majestuoso *adj.* impresionante; grandioso; p. 632

makeshift/improvisado *adj.* substituto de algo apropiado o deseado; p. 411

maneuver/maniobrar *v.* mover o manejar con habilidad; p. 79

manipulative/manipulador *adj.* capaz de influenciar o controlar de un modo astuto y a menudo injusto; p. 778

meager/exiguo *adj.* que no es suficiente en cantidad o volumen; p. 292

meander/vagar *v.* caminar sin rumbo; divagar; serpentear (río); p. 119

meekly/dócilmente *adv.* de un modo paciente y suave; gentilmente; p. 643

menacing/amenazante *adj.* peligroso; arriesgado; p. 22

merely/meramente *adv.* tan sólo; simplemente; p. 618

mimicry/mímica *s.* acto de copiar o imitar; remedo; p. 71

mingle/entremezclar *v.* mezclar; unir; p. 224

mishap/percance *s.* contratiempo; accidente; p. 24

morsel/bocado *s.* pequeña porción o cantidad; p. 742

mortified/mortificado *adj.* muy humillado; p. 43

N

nocturnal/nocturno *adj.* activo durante la noche; p. 532

O

obsessed/obsesionado *adj.* concentrado en una sola emoción o idea; p. 389

overseer/supervisor *s.* quien vigila y dirige el trabajo de los empleados; p. 373

oversight/descuido *s.* error; falla; p. 657

P

pang/punzada *s.* sensación repentina y aguda de dolor o molestia; p. 21

parched/reseco *adj.* que necesita urgentemente de lluvia; muy seco; p. 452

pelt/tirar *v.* golpear repetidamente lanzando algo; p. 256

penetrate/penetrar *v.* atravesar o pasar; p. 168

perilously/peligrosamente *adv.* de modo azaroso; arriesgadamente; p. 428

periodically/periódicamente *adv.* de vez en cuando; p. 79

perish/perecer *v.* morir, especialmente de modo violento o inesperado; p. 535

persist/persistir *v.* continuar de modo firme y constante, a pesar de las dificultades; p. 541

perspective/perspectiva *s.* habilidad de ver las cosas en su debida relación con otras; punto de vista; p. 413

petrify/petrificar *v.* paralizar de asombro, miedo o terror; p. 535

plight/aprieto *s.* situación difícil o peligrosa; p. 312

pondering/ponderación *s.* acto de pensar cuidadosamente; consideración; p. 551

potential/potencial *adj.* que puede llegar a ser; p. 411

practical/práctico *adj.* que se ajusta a las necesidades y actividades diarias; p. 516

prejudice/prejuicio *s.* opinión o juicio desfavorable sin bases justas; p. 413

principle/principio *s.* ley, verdad o creencia básica; norma de conducta; p. 465

procession/procesión *s.* grupo que avanza en un desfile o ceremonia; p. 277

proclaim/proclamar *v.* declarar públicamente; anunciar; p. 669

proposition/proposición *s.* algo que se ofrece a consideración; sugerencia; p. 120

prosper/prosperar *v.* tener éxito; enriquecerse; p. 508

Q

quarry/presa *s.* cualquier cosa que se quiere cazar o atrapar, especialmente un animal; p. 132

quaver/estremecerse *v.* temblar o agitarse; p. 779

quest/búsqueda *s.* busca; exploración; rastreo; p. 643

R

ravage/asolar *v.* destruir violentamente; arruinar; p. 640

realm/reino *s.* dominio; cualquier área de conocimiento, poder o control; p. 337

reconciled/reconciliado *adj.* que vuelve a ser amigo después de una pelea o desacuerdo; p. 657

reflective/reflexivo *adj.* que piensa seria y cuidadosamente; p. 289

register/registrar *v.* mostrar o anotar, como en una escala; indicar; p. 569

relentless/inexorable *adj.* inflexible; severo; p. 589

relieve/aliviar *v.* quitar una carga o hacerla menos difícil; reducir; p. 569

relish/deleitarse *v.* disfrutar; gozar; p. 71

remorse/remordimiento *s.* sentimiento de culpa o arrepentimiento por una mala acción; p. 658

rendition/representación *s.* interpretación; actuación; p. 357

replenish/aprovisionar *v.* llenar de nuevo; suministrar; p. 79

reprove/reprender *v.* regañar; p. 56

repulsive/repulsivo *adj.* que causa desagrado; muy molesto; p. 739

resent/resentir *v.* sentir rabia hacia alguien o algo; p. 56

resigned/resignado *adj.* que acepta o cede de mala gana pero sin resistirse ni quejarse; p. 234

resort/recurrir *v.* usar algo como apoyo o alivio; p. 161

retort/replicar *v.* responder de modo sagaz o ingenioso; p. 315

retreat/retroceder *v.* retirarse o huir, como en una batalla; p. 257

revelation/revelación *s.* información que ha estado oculta o secreta y que se da a conocer; p. 363

reverently/reverentemente *adv.* de un modo que muestra profundo respeto; respetuosamente; p. 24

revert/revertir *v.* volver al estado original; p. 454

S

saunter/deambular *v.* caminar tranquilamente; pasearse; p. 99

savor/saborear *v.* gozar; percibir o comer con gran deleite; p. 10

scoff/escarnecer *v.* hablar de modo ofensivo; humillar; mofarse; p. 716

scour/registrar *v.* hacer una inspección detallada; examinar; p. 130

scruffy/zarrapastroso *adj.* desaliñado; harapiento; p. 374

serene/sereno *adj.* calmado; pacífico; imperturbable; p. 344

sham/fingido *adj.* falso; adulterado; ficticio; p. 547

sharecropper/aparcero *s.* granjero que cultiva tierras de otra persona y comparte las cosechas y las ganancias con el propietario; p. 5

shuffle/chancletear *v.* caminar arrastrando los pies; p. 151

sideline/línea lateral *s.* barrera del campo de juego donde se colocan los jugadores; p. 89

signify/significar *v.* representar; querer decir; p. 465

singe/chamuscar *s.* quemar las puntas o esquinas de algo; p. 337

skirmish/escaramuza *s.* conflicto de poca importancia o duración; p. 385

slither/culebrear *v.* deslizarse o escurrirse por el suelo como una culebra; p. 436

smugly/presumidamente *adv.* de un modo engreído o vanidoso; p. 43

snowball/acrecentar *v.* aumentar rápidamente en tamaño o importancia; p. 540

solace/solaz *s.* alivio de una pena; consuelo; p. 345

solemn/solemne *adj.* serio; p. 93

spellbound/hechizado *adj.* encantado, como si estuviera bajo un hechizo o magia; fascinado; p. 721

spitefully/rencorosamente *adv.* de un modo que muestra malos sentimientos hacia otra persona; con odio; p. 130

splendor/esplendor *s.* gran despliegue de riquezas o bellos objetos; p. 171

splurge/gastar a manos llenas *v.* gastar dinero sin preocupación; p. 386

stodgy/soso *adj.* pesado y lento al moverse; simple y aburridor; p. 547

straggler/rezagado *s.* el que se queda atrás del grupo; retrasado; p. 438

straightaway/directamente *adv.* de una vez; inmediatamente; p. 375

stupendous/estupendo *adj.* que causa sorpresa o asombro; p. 357

succumb/sucumbir *v.* rendirse a una herida o enfermedad; morir; p. 533

sulking/enfurruñado *adj.* silencioso y malhumorado; p. 233

sullenly/malhumoradamente *adv.* de modo enfadado o sombrío; p. 140

superb/magnífico *adj.* de primera calidad; excelente; p. 275

swagger/contonearse *v.* caminar o comportarse de modo altanero, brusco o demasiado orgulloso; p. 437

systematic/sistemático *adj.* bien organizado; que sigue ciertos pasos en orden; p. 45

T

tamper/alterar *v.* interferir o afectar de un modo que causa daño; p. 759

taunt/mofa *s.* comentario insultante; p. 21

tedious/tedioso *adj.* aburridor; desagradable; p. 716

threadbare/gastado *adj.* raído; en malas condiciones; p. 312

timidly/tímidamente *adv.* sin suficiente valor; débilmente; p. 643

tolerate/tolerar *v.* soportar; aceptar; p. 582

touching/conmovedor *adj.* que causa emoción; enternecedor; p. 161

traitor/traidor *s.* el que traiciona a su país; p. 672

treacherous/traicionero *adj.* peligroso; p. 256

trek/travesía *s.* viaje largo o difícil; p. 505

trifling/insignificancia *s.* algo considerado de poco o ningún valor; p. 56

troublesome/problemático *adj.* que causa problemas; p. 150

twinge/punzada *s.* sensación repentina y aguda de dolor, pena o vergüenza; p. 776

U

unique/único *adj.* que no hay otro igual; p. 70

unmindful/distraído *adj.* que no presta atención; p. 71

unsanitary/antihigiénico *adj.* algo que por estar sucio puede causar enfermedades; insalubre; p. 92

V

vainly/en vano *adv.* sin éxito; p. 317

veranda/barandal *s.* balcón largo, por lo general con techo, a lo largo del costado de una casa; p. 372

verge/borde *s.* punto preciso donde algo ocurre o comienza; vera; p. 56

virtually/virtualmente *adv.* desde todo punto de vista; claramente; p. 539

vivid/vívido *adj.* que muestra una imagen mental clara; auténtico; p. 776

vulnerable/vulnerable *adj.* que se puede dañar o lastimar; frágil; p. 588

W

warily/cautelosamente *adv.* de modo cuidadoso; p. 502

wedge/encajar *v.* meter en un espacio estrecho; p. 438

well/manar *v.* brotar; salir a borbotones; p. 540

writhe/retorcerse *v.* arquearse; torcerse; p. 342

Y

yearning/anhelo *s.* deseo intenso; aspiración; p. 68

yield/dar *v.* producir; dar ganancias; p. 568

Index of Skills

Boldface page references indicate an extensive treatment of the topic.

References beginning with R refer to handbook pages.

Literary Concepts

Reading and Thinking

Vocabulary

Writing

Index of Authors and Titles

Index of Art and Artists

Acknowledgments

(Continued from page iv)

Literature

Theme 1

"The Circuit" by Francisco Jimenez, from *The Arizona Quarterly,* Autumn 1973. Reprinted by permission of the author.

From "American Album" by Mike Clary. Copyright © 1997, Los Angeles Times. Reprinted by permission.

Excerpt from *Little by Little: A Writer's Education* by Jean Little. Copyright © Jean Little, 1987. Reprinted by permission of Penguin Books Canada Limited.

"To Young Readers" from *Very Young Poets* (Third World Press, Chicago). Copyright © 1991 by Gwendolyn Brooks Blakely. Reprinted by permission of the author.

"Arithmetic" from *The Complete Poems of Carl Sandburg,* copyright 1950 by Carl Sandburg and renewed 1978 by Margaret Sandburg, Helga Sandburg Crile and Janet Sandburg, reprinted by permission of Harcourt Brace & Company.

"Chopsticks" from www.cuisinet.com. Copyright © 1997 CyberPalate LLC. Reprinted by permission.

"The All-American Slurp" by Lensey Namioka, copyright © 1987, from *Visions,* edited by Donald R. Gallo. Reprinted by permission of Lensey Namioka. All rights are reserved by the author.

"Primary Lessons" by Judith Ortiz Cofer is reprinted with permission from the publisher of *Silent Dancing* (Houston: Arte Publico Press— University of Houston, 1990).

Reprinted with the permission of Simon & Schuster Books for Young Readers, an imprint of Simon & Schuster Children's Publishing Division. From *The Lost Garden* by Laurence Yep. Copyright © 1991 by Laurence Yep.

Excerpt from *Homesick: My Own Story* by Jean Fritz, text copyright © 1982 by Jean Fritz. Reprinted by permission of G. P. Putnam's Sons.

Theme 2

Excerpts from *Brother Wolf.* Copyright © 1993 by Jim Brandenburg. Reprinted by permission of Judy Brandenburg.

"Why Dogs Are Tame" from *The Last Tales of Uncle Remus* by Julius Lester. Copyright © 1994 by Julius Lester. Used by permission of Dial Books for Young Readers, a division of Penguin Books USA, Inc.

"Gorilla Saves Tot in Brookfield Zoo Ape Pit" by Jeffrey Bils and Stacey Singer. Copyright © 1996 Chicago Tribune Company. All rights reserved. Used with permission.

"The Boy Who Lived with Bears" Copyright © 1995 by Joseph Bruchac. Reprinted by permission of Barbara S. Kouts.

"Koko: Smart Signing Gorilla" from *Animals Who Have Won Our Hearts,* copyright © 1994 by Jean Craighead George. Used by permission of HarperCollins Publishers.

"Zlateh the Goat" from *Zlateh the Goat and Other Stories* by Isaac Bashevis Singer. Text copyright © 1966 by Isaac Bashevis Singer. Reprinted by permission of HarperCollins Publishers.

"The Naming of Cats" from *Old Possum's Book of Practical Cats,* copyright 1939 by T. S. Eliot and renewed 1967 by Esme Valerie Eliot, reprinted by permission of Harcourt Brace & Company.

"Ankylosaurus" from *Tyrannosaurus Was A Beast* by Jack Prelutsky. Copyright © 1988 by Jack Prelutsky. Reprinted by permission of Greenwillow Books, a division of William Morrow & Company, Inc.

"The Shark" from *Fast and Slow.* Copyright © 1975 by John Ciardi. Reprinted by permission of Houghton Mifflin Co. All rights reserved.

"Dinner Together," copyright © 1996 by Diana Rivera. Reprinted by permission of the author.

Poem #1448 reprinted by permission of the publishers and the Trustees of Amherst College from *The Poems of Emily Dickinson,* Thomas H. Johnson, ed., Cambridge, Mass.: The Belknap Press of Harvard University Press, Copyright © 1951, 1955, 1979, 1983 by the President and Fellows of Harvard College.

"The Bat," copyright © 1938 by Theodore Roethke, from *The Collected Poems of Theodore Roethke,* by Theodore Roethke. Used by permission of Doubleday, a division of Bantam Doubleday Dell Publishing Group, Inc.

"A Minor Bird" from *The Poetry of Robert Frost,* edited by Edward Connery Lathem. © 1956 by Robert Frost, copyright 1928, © 1969 by Henry Holt & Co., Inc. Reprinted by permission of Henry Holt & Co., Inc.

Theme 3

"La Bamba" from *Baseball in April and Other Stories,* copyright © 1990 by Gary Soto, reprinted by permission of Harcourt Brace & Company.

"Blue Suede Shoes" by Carl Perkins. Copyright © 1956 Hi-Lo Music, Inc. Controlled in the U.S.A. by Unichappell, Inc. International copyright secured. All rights reserved.

"Shoes for Hector" from *El Bronx Remembered: A Novella and Stories* by Nicholasa Mohr. Copyright © 1975 by Nicholasa Mohr. Used by permission of HarperCollins Publishers.

"Eleven" from *Woman Hollering Creek.* Copyright © 1991 by Sandra Cisneros. Published by Vintage Books, a division of Random House, Inc., and originally in hardcover by Random House, Inc.

"The Sidewalk Racer or On the Skateboard" from *The Sidewalk Racer and Other Poems of Sports and Motion* by Lillian Morrison. Copyright © 1965, 1967, 1968, 1977 by Lillian Morrison. © renewed Lillian Morrison. Reprinted by permission.

From *Daydreamers* by Eloise Greenfield. Copyright © 1981 by Eloise Greenfield. Used by permission of Dial Books for Young Readers, a division of Penguin Putnam, Inc.

"Concha" by Mary Helen Ponce. First appeared in *Women for All Seasons: Prose and Poetry About the Transitions in Women's Lives.* Reprinted by permission of the author.

"The Southpaw" Copyright © 1974 by Judith Viorst. From *Free to Be . . . You and Me*. This usage granted by permission.

"Blowing the Whistle on Inequality for Girls" by Kymberli Hagelberg and Cristine Marn, reprinted courtesy of Sun Newspapers, Cleveland, Ohio.

Excerpt from *The Golden Days of Greece,* reprinted by permission of Russell & Volkening as agents for the author. Copyright © 1968 by Olivia Coolidge, copyright renewed 1996 by Olivia Coolidge.

"A Backwoods Boy" from *Lincoln: A Photobiography.* Copyright © 1987 by Russell Freedman. Reprinted by permission of Clarion Books/Houghton Mifflin Company. All rights reserved.

Theme 4

"The Stone" from *The Foundling and Other Tales of Prydain* by Lloyd Alexander, © 1973 by Lloyd Alexander. Reprinted by permission of Henry Holt and Company, Inc.

"April Rain Song" from *Collected Poems* by Langston Hughes. Copyright © 1994 by the Estate of Langston Hughes. Reprinted by permission of Alfred A. Knopf, Inc.

"in Just—", copyright 1923, 1951, © 1991 by the Trustees for the E. E. Cummings Trust. Copyright © 1976 by George James Firmage, from *Complete Poems 1904–1962* by E. E. Cummings. Edited by George J. Firmage. Reprinted by permission of Liveright Publishing Corporation.

Excerpt from "Leonardo's Inventions" *Kids Discover,* February 1997. Reprinted by permission.

Wings, copyright © 1991 by Jane Yolen, reprinted by permission of Harcourt Brace & Company.

"The Flying Machine" by Ray Bradbury. Reprinted by permission of Don Congdon Associates. Copyright © 1953, renewed 1981 by Ray Bradbury.

"The White Umbrella," copyright © 1984 by Gish Jen. First published in *The Yale Review.* Reprinted by permission of the author.

"Becky and the Wheels-and-Brake Boys" from *A Thief In the Village and Other Stories* by James Berry. Copyright © 1987 by James Berry. Reprinted by permission of the publisher, Orchard Books, New York.

"Brother Can You Spare a Dime?" by E. Y. Harburg and Jay Gornay. Copyright ©1932 by Harms Inc. Administered by Warner Bros. Publications. All rights reserved.

"President Cleveland, Where Are You?" from *Eight Plus One: Stories by Robert Cormier* by Robert Cormier. Copyright © 1965 and renewed 1993 by Robert Cormier. Reprinted by permission of Pantheon Books, a division of Random House, Inc.

Theme 5

"Satchel Paige" from *Champions* by Bill Littlefield. Text copyright © 1993 by Bill Littlefield; illustrations copyright © 1993 by Bernie Fuchs. By permission of Little, Brown and Company.

"Junior Itadarod" copyright © 1997 Iditarod Trail Committee, Inc.

"Priscilla and the Wimps" by Richard Peck, copyright © 1984 by Richard Peck, from *Sixteen: Short Stories* by Donald R. Gallo, ed. Used by permission of Dell Books, a division of Bantam Doubleday Dell Publishing Group, Inc.

"Pecos Bill" from *American Tall Tales* by Mary Pope Osborne. Text copyright © 1991 by Mary Pope Osborne. Reprinted by permission of Alfred A. Knopf, Inc.

"Doc Rabbit, Bruh Fox and Tar Baby" from *The People Could Fly* by Virginia Hamilton. Text copyright © 1985 by Virginia Hamilton. Reprinted by permission of Alfred A. Knopf, Inc.

Theme 6

"Whatif" from *A Light in the Attic* by Shel Silverstein. Copyright © 1981 by Evil Eye Music, Inc. Used by permission of HarperCollins Publishers.

"Life Doesn't Frighten Me" from *And Still I Rise* by Maya Angelou. Copyright © 1978 by Maya Angelou. Reprinted by permission of Random House, Inc.

"Abd Al-Rahman Ibrahima" from *Now Is Your Time: The African-American Struggle for Freedom,* Copyright © 1991 by Walter Dean Myers. Used by permission of HarperCollins Publishers.

From *The Gold Cadillac* by Mildred D. Taylor. Copyright © 1987 by Mildred D. Taylor. Used by permission of Dial Books for Young Readers, a division of Penguin Books USA, Inc.

"The Horse Snake" from *The Land I Lost* by Huynh Quang Nhuong. Copyright © 1982 by Huynh Quang Nhuong. Reprinted by permission of HarperCollins.

Reprinted with the permission of Simon & Schuster Books for Young Readers, an imprint of Simon & Schuster Children's Publishing Division from *Woodsong* by Gary Paulsen. Text copyright © 1990 by Gary Paulsen.

Excerpt from "Violent Vesuvius" *Kids Discover* August/September 1995. Reprinted by permission.

"The Dog of Pompeii" by Louis Untermeyer is reprinted with the permission of Simon & Schuster from *The Fireside Book of Dog Stories,* edited by Jack Goodman. Copyright © 1943, 1971 by Simon & Schuster, Inc.

Reprinted with the permission of Simon & Schuster Books for Young Readers, an imprint of Simon & Schuster Children's Publishing Division from *Volcano* by Patricia Lauber. Copyright © 1986 by Patricia Lauber.

Excerpt from *When Plague Strikes: The Black Death, Smallpox, AIDS.* Text copyright © 1995 by James Cross Giblin. Illustrations copyright © 1995 by David Frampton. Used by permission of HarperCollins Publishers.

Theme 7

"Creation" from *Navajo: Visions and Voices Across the Mesa* by Shonto Begay. Copyright © 1995 by Shonto Begay. Reprinted by permission of Scholastic, Inc.

"Leyenda" by Pat Mora is reprinted with permission from the publisher of *Chants* (Houston: Arte Publico Press—University of Houston, 1985).

"All Stories Are Anansi's" from *The Hat Shaking Dance and Other Ashanti Tales from Ghana* by Harold Courlander (with Albert Kofi Prempeh). Copyright © 1985 by Harold Courlander. Reprinted with permission of The Emma Courlander Trust.

"The End of the World" from *The Sound of Flutes* by Richard Erdoes. Copyright © 1976 by Richard Erdoes. Reprinted by permission of Pantheon Books, a division of Random House, Inc.

"Porcupine and Sky Mirrors" by Katherine Davison, from *Moon Magic: Stories from Asia.* Text copyright © 1994 by Katherine Davison and illustrations copyright © 1994 by Thomas A. Rosborough. Used by permission of the publisher, Carolrhoda Books, Inc. All rights reserved.

"The Fly" from *The Toad Is the Emperor's Uncle* by Mai Vo-Dinh. Copyright © 1970 by Mai Vo-Dinh. Reprinted by permission of the author.

"Dragon, Dragon" from *Dragon, Dragon and Other Tales* © 1975 by Boskydell Artists Ltd. Reprinted by permission of Georges Borchardt, Inc. on behalf of the Estate of John Gardner.

"The Enchanted Raisin" reprinted from *The Enchanted Raisin* by Jacqueline Balcells by permission of the publisher, Latin American Literary Review Press, Pittsburgh, Pennsylvania.

"Sounds Like Fun" by Jennifer A. Kirkpatrick. *National Geographic World,* February 1996. Reprinted by permission of the National Geographic Society.

"The Legend of Damon and Pythias" from *The Bag of Fire and Other Plays* by Fan Kissen. Copyright © 1964 by Houghton Mifflin Company, renewed © 1993 by John Kissen Heaslip. Reprinted by permission of Houghton Mifflin Company. All rights reserved.

Theme 8

"Aunt Millicent" by Mary Steele, from *Dream Time,* edited by Toss Gascoigne, Jo Goodman and Margot Tyrrell. Copyright © 1989 by Mary Steele. Collection copyright © 1989 by Children's Book Council of Australia. Reprinted by permission of Houghton Mifflin Co. All rights reserved. "Aunt Millicent" appears in *A Bit of a Hitch and Other Stories* by Mary Steele, published by Hyland House.

Roald Dahl's Charlie & the Chocolate Factory, adapted by Richard R. George. Copyright © 1976 by Roald Dahl and Richard R. George. Reprinted by permission of David Higham Associates.

"Future Tense" by Robert Lipsyte, copyright © 1984 by Robert Lipsyte, from *Sixteen: Short Stories* by Donald R. Gallo, ed. Used by permission of Dell Books, a division of Bantam Doubleday Dell Publishing Group, Inc.

"The Sand Castle" from *Weeping Woman* by Alma Luz Villanueva. Copyright © 1994 by Alma Luz Villanueva. Reprinted by permission of the author.

"Two Storms in One" written by Damond Benningfield. Script © 1998 Damond Benningfield.

StarDate © 1998 The University of Texas McDonald Observatory.

Maps

Ortelius Design, Inc.

Photography

Abbreviation key: **AH**=Aaron Haupt; **AR**=Art Resource, New York; **BAL**=Bridgeman Art Library, London/New York; **CB**=Corbis-Bettmann; **CI**=Christie's Images; **LPBC/AH**=book provided by Little Professor Book Company. Photo by Aaron Haupt; **LOC**=Library of Congress;

NWPA=North Wind Picture Archives; **PR**=Photo Researchers; **SIS**=Stock Illustration Source; **SS**=SuperStock; **TSI**=Tony Stone Images; **TSM**=The Stock Market.

Cover Dallas & John Heaton/Stock Boston, (painting) CI; **vii** (t to b) CI, Michio Hoshino/Minden Pictures, SS, SS, NWPA, CB, The Cummer Museum of Art and Gardens, Jacksonville/SS, Ben Verkaaik; **vii** KS Studio/Bob Mullenix; **ix** (t)Jim Brandenburg/Minden Pictures, (b)Catherine Gehm Photography; **x** James E. Stahl; **xi** (t)KS Studio/Bob Mullenix, (b)Mark Burnett; **xii** Richard Laird/FPG; **xiii** John Henley/TSM; **xiv** Ruben de Anda/Stockworks; **xv** (t)Mark Steinmetz, (b)National Baseball Hall of Fame Library, Cooperstown NY, photo by Milo Stewart Jr.; **xvi** Warren Faidley/Digital Stock Corp.; **xvii** The Grand Design, Leeds, England/SS; **xviii** Peter Sickles/SS; **xix** Matt Meadows; **xx** CI/SS; **xxi** (l)courtesy Faren Okray, (r)courtesy Center For Western Studies, Augustana College, Sioux Falls SD; **xxii** Thaine Manske/TSM; **xxiii** Illustration by Margot Tomes, by permission of Putnam Publishing; **xxviii–1** KS Studio/Bob Mullenix; **2** Courtesy P.C. Vey; **3** (tl)George C. Anderson, (tr)file photo, (bl)Latent Image, (br)Doug Martin; **4** *San Jose Mercury News,* photographer Eugene Louie; **5** National Archives/FPG, (bkgd)Ed and Chris Kumler; **7, 10** CI; **12** AH; **14** Pat Sullivan/AP/Wide World Photos; **15** (t)©1969 Time, Inc. reprinted by permission, (b)Mark E. Gibson/International Stock Photo, (bkgd)Doug Martin; **16** (l)courtesy Penguin Books, Toronto, (r)Doug Martin; **17** Courtesy Jean Little; **17, 21, 22, 26** (frame)KS Studio/Bob Mullenix; **18** National Museum of American Art, Smithsonian Institution, Washington DC/AR; **21** Courtesy Penguin Putnam, Inc; **24** AH; **25** Kactus Foto, Santiago, Chile/SS; **27, 28** AH; **32** (t)Nancy Crampton, (bl)UPI/CB, (br)Peter Pearson/TSI; **33** National Museum of American Art, Washington DC/AR; **35** ©Jasper Johns/Licensed by VAGA, New York, NY/Tate Gallery, London/AR; **36, 37** AH; **38** (t)Michael Newler/TSM, (b)Doug Martin; **39** Don Perkins; **40, 42** KS Studio/Bob Mullenix; **44** Doug Martin; **47** Arthur Beck/TSM; **48** (t)Doug Martin, (b)AH; **49** Mary Kate Denny/TSI; **50** AH; **54** (l)Dakota Indian Foundation, (r)Mark E. Gibson; **55, 57** PA State Archives; **58** David McGlynn/FPG; **60** Courtesy Center For Western Studies, Augustana College, Sioux Falls SD; **63** Geoff Butler; **64** Miriam Berkley; **65** The Butler Institute of American Art, Youngstown OH; **67** UPI/CB; **70** Courtesy Judith Ortiz Cofer; **72** Alan Schein/TSM; **73, 74** AH; **76** (l)Joanne Ryder/Harper Collins, (r)Mark E. Gibson; **77** AH; **78** Phil Palmer/FPG; **80** Brian Brake/PR; **81** AH; **82** Phil Palmer/FPG; **84** AH; **86** Jill Krementz; **87** Mark Burnett; **88** SS; **90** Bruce Dale/National Geographic Society Image Collection; **92** Peter A. Davis/FPG; **94** Haroldo Castro/FPG; **95** Hubertus Kanus/SS; **97** AKG Berlin/SS; **100** Geoff Butler; **103** Illustration by Margot Tomes, by permission of Putnam; **105** AH; **109** (br)Geoff Butler; (others)LPBC/AH; **112–113** Jim Brandenburg/Minden Pictures; **115** (tl)Workman Publishing Company/Animals Animals, (tr)Latent Image, (cr)Quad Cities—CVB, IA; (b)StudioOhio; **116** (t)Anthony Brandenburg/Minden Pictures, (bl)AP/Wide World Photos, (br)StudioOhio; **117** Jim Brandenburg/Minden Pictures; **121** Christian Pierre/SS; **123** AH; **124** Jim Brandenburg/Minden Pictures; **126** *People Weekly* ©1996/John Zich; **127** Bassano/Camera Press/Globe Photos; **128** Daniel Cox/TSI; **132** SS; **133** Jagdeep Rajput/ENP Images; **134** (t)Bill Brooks/Masterfile; **134–135** (border)Hubertus Kanus/SS; **136** Paul Crum/PR; **137** Bruce Dale/National Geographic Society Image Collection; **138** Art Wolfe/TSI; **139** Bill Brooks/Masterfile; **141** Shin Yoshino/Minden Pictures; **142–143** (border)Hubertus Kanus/SS; **144** Tom Tietz/TSI; **146** Art Wolfe/TSI; **148** (l)John Pflug, (r)Lawrence Migdale; **149** Michio Hoshino/Minden Pictures; **150** (t)Catherine Gehm Photography, (b)Marilyn "Angel" Wynn/Sun Valley Video and Photography; **151** Marilyn "Angel" Wynn/Sun Valley Video and Photography; **153** Catherine Gehm Photography; **155** (t)Jeff Lepore/PR, (b)Tom Tietz/TSI; **158** (l)Ellan Young, (r)Dr. Ronald Cohn/Gorilla Foundation; **159 through 163** Dr. Ronald Cohn/Gorilla Foundation; **164** AH/courtesy WBNS 10-TV; **165** (t)Larry Hamill, (b)Robert M. Campbell, National Geographic Society Image Collection, (bkgd)William

Waterfall/Pacific Stock; **166** (l)Susan Greenwood/Gamma-Liaison, (r)Doug Martin; **167, 168** Orion Press/Natural Selection; **169, 171, 172** (l)reprinted from Harper-Collins, illustration by Maurice Sendak, (r)Doug Martin; **173** Frederick McKinney/FPG; **175** CI; **176** Zefa Germany/TSM; **177** John Dyes/FPG; **179** Goeff Butler; **180** (l)Ida Kar/Globe Photos, (r)photo by Martha Swope/Graphics designed by DeWinters Ltd, London. ©1981 The Really Useful Company Ltd. All rights reserved; **181** Christian Pierre/SS; **184** (tl)Evergreen Studios, (tr)National Museum of Natural History, (b)Archive Photos; **185** SS; **186** Amos Nachoum/TSM; **187** Jesse Cancelmo; **188** ©1999 Universal City Studios, Inc. Courtesy Universal Studios Publishing Rights, a division of Universal Studios Licensing, Inc. All rights reserved; **190** Timothy Fuller; **192** (tl)courtesy Diana Rivera, (tr)Premium Stock Photography/Natural Selection, (b)J. Sommer Collection/Archive Photos; **193** SS; **194** Buddy Mays/International Stock Photo; **195** James E. Stahl; **196** Lynn M. Stone; **198** (tl)Archive Photos, (tr)Lynn M. Stone, (b)Ken Hayman/Woodfin Camp & Assoc.; **199** SS; **200** Scott Wm. Hanrahan/International Stock Photo; **201** Merlin D. Tuttle/PR; **203** SIS/Larry Moore; **205** Jeri Gleiter/FPG; **209** (br)Geoff Butler, (others)LPBC/AH; **212–213** KS Studio/Bob Mullenix; **214** Photofest; **216** (l)Carolyn Soto, (r)Archive Photos/Griggs; **217** AH; **218** Gilbert Mayers/SS; **219** AH; **220** Richard Laird/FPG; **221** Mark Burnett; **223** Gilbert Mayers/SS; **224** (t)Mark Burnett, (b)AH; **225** AH; **226** Harry Fredman; **228** (t)AH, (b)Fred Maroon/PR, (bkgd)Bert Sagara/TSI; **229** Retna Ltd. USA; **230** (l)Phil Cantor, (r)AH; **233** The Cleveland Museum of Art, purchased with a grant from the National Endowment of Arts and matched by gifts from members of the Cleveland Society for Contemporary Art 1974.53; **237** AH; **238** (l)M. Toussant/Gamma-Liaison, (r)Ken Frick; **239** AH; **240** Columbus Museum of Art OH, bequest of Frederick W. Schumacher, Cat.#17 accession; **242, 244** AH; **246** (tl)Isidro Rodriguez, (tr)Ken Frick, (b)courtesy Penguin Putnam; **247** (t)S. Legrand/Vandystadt/PR, (b)Aaron Chang/TSM; **248–249** Mark E. Gibson; **250, 251** AH; **254** (tl)courtesy the author, (tr)John Dawson ©National Geographic Society Image Collection, (b)AP/Wide World Photos; **256** Diana Ong/SS; **257** AH; **255 through 258** (title & border)Larry West/FPG; **259 through 262** Mark Burnett; **263** DUOMO/Darren Carroll; **264** Nike, Inc.; **267** Geoff Butler; **268** Michelle Smith/Media Vision Creative Group; **269** National Museum, Naples, Italy/Canali PhotoBank, Milan/SS; **271** Staatliche Glypothek, Munich, Germany/E.T. Archive, London/SS; **272** Scala/AR; **274** (l)Mary Evans Picture Library, (r)Frank & Helen Schreider/National Geographic Society Image Collection; **275** SS; **279** Nimatallah/AR; **280** Frank & Helen Schreider/National Geographic Society Image Collection; **284** Charles Osgood ©1988 The Chicago Tribune Company; **285** David M. Dennis, (inset)NWPA; **286** SS; **286–287** (bkgd)David M. Dennis; **288** The Abraham Lincoln Museum; **288–289** (bkdg)David M. Dennis; **289** (t)Hulton Getty/TSI; **291** LOC; **292** Illinois State Historical Library; **292–293, 294** (bkgd)David M. Dennis; **295** US Naval Academy, Annapolis/Jack Novak/SS; **299** AH; **303** (bl)Geoff Butler, (others)LPBC/AH; **306** (l)John Henley/TSM, (r)Comstock; **306–307** (b)Telegraph Colour Library/FPG; **307** Comstock; **309** Doug Martin; **310** (l)AP/Wide World Photos, (r)Geoff Butler; **311** Mark Burnett; **313** Musée de Laval, Canada/Explorer, Paris/SS; **314** AH; **316** SS; **317** Geoff Butler; **319, 320** Mark Burnett; **324** (tl)Archive Photos, (tr)Peter French/Pacific Stock, (b)National Portrait Gallery, Smithsonian Institution/AR; **325** BAL; **326** Mark Steinmetz; **327** Peter Harholdt/SS; **329** (bl)AR, (others)Scala/AR; **330** Jason Stemple; **331** SS; **332** Jason Hawkes/TSI; **332–337** (border)Richard Martin; **336** CI; **338** Pal Hermansen/TSI; **340** (l)Ralph Merlino/Shooting Star, (r)SS; **341** The Metropolitan Museum of Art, New York; **343** Daryl Benson/Masterfile; **344** Peter Harholdt/SS; **347** (t)Robin Smith/FPG, (b)Peter Harholdt/SS; **349** (t)Knossos, Crete/Kurt Scholz/SS, (bkgd)Carl Shaneff/Pacific Stock; **350** L.D. Franga; **353** Geoff Butler; **354** AP/Wide World Photos; **355** AH; **356** William D. Popejoy; **359** SS; **362** Jacqueline Osborn/Stockworks; **365** AH; **366** C. Lewis Harrington/FPG; **368** Mak-1; **370** Camera Press/Globe Photos; **371** Brent Turner/BLT Productions;

372 (t)AH, (b)Leonard Lee Rue III/Stock Boston; **373** Stephen J. Krasemann/DRK Photo; **374** Diana Ong/SS; **375** Richard Shiell; **376** Collection of the artist; **377** SS; **378** Brent Turner/BLT Productions; **380** SIS/Larry Moore; **381** CB; **382** (l)Beth Bergman, (r b)from the collection of David J. and Janice L. Frent; **383** (t)from the collection of David J. and Janice L. Frent, (b)AH; **384** AH; **385** (t)UPI/CB, (b)AH; **386** FPG; **388** MN Historical Society/CB; **391** (l)David L. Frazier, (r)Elaine Shay; **393** from collection of David J. and Janice L. Frent; **394** Mark Burnett; **397** Scala/AR; **401** (bl)Geoff Butler, (others) LPBC/AH; **404–405** Ruben DeAnda/Stockworks; **407** (tl, tr)SS, (bl)Dimaggio/Kalish/TSM, (br)Audrey Gibson; **408** L. Barry Hetherington; **409 through 416** National Baseball Hall of Fame Library, Cooperstown NY; **417** Doug Martin; **418** Baseball Hall of Fame Library, Cooperstown NY/photo by Milos Stewart Jr.; **419** K. Cavanagh/Photo Researchers, (bkgd)AH; **420** (l)courtesy of Faren Okray, (r)courtesy Daniel Seavey; **421** Archive Photos; **422–423** Paul Souders/TSI; **425, 427, 430** NWPA; **432** William Johnson/Stock Boston; **434** Courtesy Penguin Putnam; **435** Mark Burnett; **437** Ron Chapple/FPG; **438** David Madison; **440** Geoff Butler; **440** NWPA; **442** AH; **443** Musée de Laval, Canada/Explorer, Paris/SS; **445** Geoff Butler; **446** (l)Paul Coughlin, (r)AH; **447** Donald A. Daily; **447, 448, 453, 455** (frames)Mark Steinmetz; **448** Donald A. Daily; **451** Mary Clay-TCL/Masterfile; **453** Donald A. Daily; **454** (t)CB, (b)Susan Martin; **455** Donald A. Daily; **456** AH; **457** Randall L. Scheiber; **459** SIS/Larry Moore; **460–461** Matt Meadows; **462** (l)National Portrait Gallery, Smithsonian Institution/AR, (r)Jeanne White/PR; **463** ©1977 Hubert Shuptrine; **463–467** (bkgd)Mark Steinmetz; **464** ©Carl Brenders. By arrangement with Mill Pond Press, Inc. For information on the limited edition prints by Carl Brenders, contact Mill Pond Press, Inc., Venice FL 34292. 1-800-535-0331; **468** Courtesy Wells Fargo Bank; **472** (t)courtesy Virginia Hamilton/Scholastic, Inc., (bl)©1998 Bill Gaskins, (br)Pougeoise/Explorer/PR; **473, 475** Stock Montage; **477** Edward Pierce; **478** Larry West/FPG; **479** Rosemary Calvert/TSI; **480** John Foster/Masterfile; **482** Geoff Butler; **487** (bl)Lawrence Migdale, (others)LPBC/AH; **490–491** Warren Faidley/Digital Stock Corp.; **492** CB; **493** SS; **494** (t)AP/Wide World Photos, (bl)Gregory Pace/Sygma, (br)AH; **497** Diana Ong/SS; **498** Geoff Butler; **499** Diane Graham-Henry & Kathleen Culbert-Aguilar; **500** Courtesy Scholastic, Inc.; **501** National Maritime Museum; **503** Stock Montage; **504** file photo; **506** LOC, LC-US262-39606; **510** The Charleston Museum; **511** AH; **513** Gaslight Advertising Archives, Inc; **514** (l)Jack Ackerman, (r)LOC/PR; **515, 516** Mark Burnett; **517** Collection of Georgia A. Hardrick Rhea; **518** Mark Burnett; **520** Private collection; **521, 522** Mark Burnett; **524** SS; **525** Mark Burnett; **526** SS; **527** AH; **530** Courtesy the *Columbia Missourian* Newspaper Library; **531, 532–533** David M. Dennis; **534** (t)David M. Dennis, (b)AKG, Berlin/SS; **534–535** (t)David M. Dennis, (b)M. Krishnan/Animals Animals; **536** Keren Su/TSI; **538** Ruth Wright Paulsen; **539** SS; **540–541** (t)J. Robert Stottlemeyer/International Stock Photo, (b)William D. Popejoy; **543** J. Robert Stottlemeyer/International Stock Photo; **544** Rob Wood/Wood Ronsaville Harlin, Inc; **545** CB; **546** Raymond V. Schoder/CB; **549** Adrian "Ace" Williams/Archive Photos, (inset)Alinari/AR; **550** Tim Courlas; **551** Stock Montage; **552** Mary Evans Picture Library; **554** Holton Collection/SS; **555** Museo Archeologico Nazionale, Naples, Italy/Erich Lessing/AR; **560** Pat and Tom Leeson/PR; **563** Geoff Butler; **564** Courtesy Scholastic, Inc.; **565** Krafft-Explorer/Science Source/PR; **567** Harald Sund/The Image Bank; **571** Vanessa Vick/PR; **573** Gary Braasch/TSI; **577** SIS/Larry Moore; **578** (l)Sarah Hoe Sterling, (r)AH; **579** Mercury Archives/The Image Bank; **580** CB; **584** Correr Civic Museum, Venice, Italy/ET Archive/SS; **586** Stock Montage; **587** Jeff Hunter/The Image Bank; **591** Mercury Archives/The Image Bank; **593** Barry Dowsett/Science Photo Library/PR, (bkgd)TSI; **594** Geoff Butler; **599** (br)Geoff Butler, (others)LPBC/AH; **602–603** The Grand Design, Leeds, England/SS; **605** (t)Reprinted by permission of Houghton Mifflin Co. All rights reserved, (b)The Walt Disney Company/Movie Still Archives; **606** (t)George Marsden, (bl)Pat Mora, Arte Publico Press, (br)Clive

Ruggles; **607, 609** from *Navajo: Visions and Voices Across the Mesa* by Shonto Begay. ©1995 by Shonto Begay. Reprinted by permission of Scholastic, Inc.; **610** Edward Dawson; **611** Dennis and Janis Lyon/ Jerry Jacka Photography; **612** Sylvain Randadam/TSI; **613** (t)Thaine Manske/TSM, (b)David L. Frazier Photolibrary; **614** (t)Michael Courlander, (bl)Richard Erdoes, (br)Harn Museum of Art Collection, University of FL, gift of Rod McGalliard, 1990.14.93; **615** Photo by Claude Postel/C.A.A.C. The Pigozzi Collection; **616** Ian Murphy/TSI; **617** The Field Museum, Chicago IL, Neg #109098c/photograph by Fleur Hales; **618** Harn Museum of Art Collection, University of FL, gift of Rod McGalliard, 1990.14.103; **619, 620** (bkgd)courtesy Colter Bay Indian Arts Museum, Grand Teton National Park WY/Jerry Jacka Photography; **621** Wesley Hitt/Picturesque; **622** FPG; **624** file photo; **625** Private collection, Milan/E.T. Archive, London/SS; **626** Doug Martin; **628** The Grand Design/SS; **633** C.J. Newbauer/FPG; **639** (l)CB, (r)SS; **640–641** AR; **645** Galleria Dell' Academia, Venice/Giraudon, Paris/SS; **646** Giraudon/AR; **650** (l)courtesy Latin American Literary Review Press, (r)Doug Martin; **652** Telegraph Colour Library/FPG; **655** H. Armstrong Roberts; **656** B. Taylor/H. Armstrong Roberts; **660** (t)Mjeda/AR, (b)Telegraph Colour Library/FPG; **662** Alinari/AR; **665** Lawrence Migdale; **666** Fred Schrier/National Geographic Society Images; **668–669** Mattes/Explorer/PR; **670** Leonard von Matt/PR; **675** SS; **676** (l)Museo Archeologico Nazionale, Naples, Italy/photo by Erich Lessing/AR, (r)The Cummer Museum of Art and Gardens, Jacksonville/SS; **677** AH; **681** (t)Larry Hamill, (b)file photo; **685** (br)Geoff Butler, (others)LPBC/AH; **688–689** Peter Sickles/SS; **691** (l, r)SS, (b)NASA; **692** Armstrong Browning Library, Baylor University, Waco TX; **693** Mansell/Time, Inc., (bkgd)CB; **694–695** Mansell/Time, Inc.; **696** CB; **698–699** Mansell/Time, Inc.; **701** CB; **702–703** Mansell/Time, Inc; **704** SS; **706** (t)CB, (b)Stock Montage/ The Newberry Library; **707, 709, 710** Stock Montage/The Newberry Library; **712** (t)Luc Hautecoeur/TSI, (b)Alvin E. Staffan; **714** Courtesy Mary Steele; **715** Steve Bloom/Masterfile; **718** (t)Doug Martin, (b)Georg Gerster/PR; **719** Matt Meadows; **720** Ric Ergenbright Photography; **722** Stan Osolinski/FPG; **723** Tom McHugh/PR; **724** David L. Perry; **725** AH; **729** Doug Martin; **733** AH; **734** (l)Nancy Crampton, (r)Movie Still Archives; **735** Matt Meadows; **737, 739, 740** Movie Still Archives; **743** Photofest; **744** Movie Still Archives; **746** SS; **747, 750, 751** Movie Still Archives; **752** Shooting Star; **755** Photofest; **757** Shooting Star; **760** Movie Still Archives; **764** Photofest; **766** AH; **769** Geoff Butler; **770** (l)John Chiasson/ Gamma-Liaison, (r)SS; **771** Ben Verkaaik; **772** KS Studio/Bob Mullenix; **774** Dennis Meyler/TSM; **779** Joe McBride/TSI; **781** Matt Meadows; **786** Courtesy of Alma Villanueva; **787** Steve Lissau; **789** CI/SS; **792** Garry Gay/The Image Bank; **793** Steve Lissau; **795** Richard Hutchings/PR, (bkgd)David M. Dennis; **797** (t)Doug Martin, (b)Lowell D. Franga; **801** (br)Lawrence Migdale, (others)LPBC/AH.